AF541230

Selected Speeches of
Maharaja Ganga Singhji
of Bikaner

# Selected Speeches of Maharaja Ganga Singh Ji of Bikaner

(1880–1943 A.D.)

*Edited by :*

**Prof. Tej Kumar Mathur**

**Head, Department of History,**

**Maharshi Dayanand Saraswati University,**

**Ajmer**

Maharaja Ganga Singhji Trust

Bikaner

Dev Publishers & Distributors

New Delhi

Selected Speeches of
Maharaja Ganga Singh Ji
of Bikaner
(1880-1943 AD)
*Edited by* Prof Tej Kumar Mathur

*Cover photo*: Portrait of Maharaja Ganga Singhji taken at Geneva in 1930 at the Assembly of the League of Nations.
*Back photo*: Maharaja Ganga Singhji in full military uniform photographed during his visit to London for the coronation of King George VI, May 1937.
*End papers:* A Painting by Sir James Guthrie titled "Some Statesmen of the Great War". The painting was presented to the National Portrait Gallery by Sir Bailey.

Published *for*
Maharaja Ganga Singhji Trust
Lallgarh Palace
Bikaner – 334 001
Rajasthan, India
Tel: +91-151- 252 2464
Fax: +91-151-254 1388
Email: bikanertrusts@yahoo.com
Web: www.maharajagangasinghjitrust.org.in

*by*
Dev Publishers & Distributors
Second Floor, Prakashdeep,
22, Delhi Medical Association Road,
Darya Ganj, New Delhi – 110 002
India
Tel No: +91-11-43572647
E-mail: devbooks@hotmail.com
Web: www.devbooks.co.in

ISBN (10): 93-81406-28-6, ISBN (13): 978-93-81406-28-1

First Published 2014

# *Contents*

L.S. RATHORE
Former Vice-Chancellor

PHONE, Res. 0291-720640
0291-726446

# Foreword

MAHARAJA GANGA SINGH (AD 1880-1943) succeeded to the throne of Bikaner State at the age of seven and ruled for a fairly long period extending to nearly fifty five years. He was an illustrious ruler, the chief architect and the builder of modern Bikaner, for he played a vigorous part in the revival and regeneration of the State. Tall, robust, magnanimous, perfectly dressed, having soldierly moustaches, he was perhaps the best looking and the best dressed among all the rulers in India. He was in many ways the ideal figure for the contemporary television age. He spoke with clarity and sincerity in the language of an ordinary man. He was no phrase maker or a jargon constructor. There were no echoes of looking back in his utterances, for he had the phenomenal vision of always looking forward. He possessed many of the clements of a genius, and that he was a most innovative administrator and a thinker, ever to preside over the House of Bikaner. He was determined to live up to the ideals of a benevolent monarch, combining with it a tinge of Plato's philosopher king. He could radiate so many different utility oriented ideas, at a time when the theory of the welfare state was still in its intra-uterine stage. His habit of ordering the bureaucracy and ministers was replete with a seriousness of purpose, a toughness of mind, and a devotion of duty, which were quite alien to the feverish frivolity of the other princes in India. He was not averse to getting rid of colleagues doing a bad job. If Henry Fairlie is to be believed that, "ruthlessness is necessary in politics," then Maharaja Ganga Singh certainly had one of the necessary qualities. He was a highly cultured and civilized figure, keenly interested in literature and arts, and his choice of paintings and sculptors, fondness to construct magnificent buildings and public utility institutions, reflected his excellent taste.

Maharaja Ganga Singh was perhaps at his best in propounding the salient norms and principles regarding the conduct of the rulers, their obligations and duties towards the people, and the seminal guidelines regarding the art of statecraft. He fully realized that a ruler must ceaselessly strive for the welfare, prosperity and the happiness of the ruled. He recognized that through the individual development and progress, the stability and legitimacy of the State could be fully assured. His concept of the state, to a great extent, reflected the principles of a welfare state, not altogether unmixed with Bentham's utilitarianism.

The administration, for him, was more an art than a science. It was more a craft based on certain philosophical ideals and postulates, and that its objective was quick, efficient and effective service to the community. He once said, "If administration were like mathematics" or physics governed by definite laws, it would have been comparatively easy to save some of the worst political blunders in the world. But being a highly practical art it eludes regulation and definition for all circumstances and for all times. A course of action that may be wise one set of circumstances may be positively pernicious in another.

He knew it well that a ruler ought to be vigilant, prompt and discreet. A ruler ought to 'think big' and the administration ought to be in harmony with local traditions and requirements. A ruler ought to look with sympathy the legitimate grievances of the people and ought to live up to their expectations and aspirations. A ruler ought to follow a code of conduct, which he expressed in the following words: "A clean and honourable life, a strict adherence to accepted moral codes, polished manners and dignified deportment, a desire at all times to serve others to the best of one's ability, to be courteous and polite in one's dealings with all kinds and conditions of men, and above all a sense of honour, loyalty and chivalry—these alone will earn the respect of one's fellow beings." He often said, "to govern men there is but one way and it is eternal truth. Get into their skins. Try to realize their feelings. That is the true secret of government.

His capacity for mastering the flow of information was phenomenal. He was able to establish a congenial method of administration, based on an equilibrium of inputs and outputs. As a first servant of the State, he had the audacity and the initiative to expound and implement with precision, the manifold socio-economic welfare programmes and the administrative innovations in a rather neat style. His administrative acumen and vision was superb.

Maharaja Ganga Singh had a profound understanding of the Indian freedom struggle and had the clarity of vision that ultimately the monarchical order was bound to collapse, giving place to responsible government in one form or the other. As such, he established a Representative Assembly (with limited powers) in the State as early as AD 1913. He was deeply interested in the constitutional reforms in India and his famous Rome note (May, 1917), written prior to Montague-Chemlsford Report, was indicative of his erudite political thinking. His speeches and role in the Round Table Conferences received a great applause from his contemporaries. In the Round Table Conferences, he upheld the idea of a federal constitution for India contrary to the expectations of the British statesmen. D.R. Mankekar, a journalist-writer has duly acknowledged his role by saying: "he (Maharaja Ganga Singh) hit the headlines when, on behalf of the Indian Princes, he supported Sir Tej Bahadur Sapru's proposal for a federal constitution for India and created a flutter in British dovecotes by backing British Indian leaders demand for responsible government in India. In fact, Maharaja Ganga Singh had a perceptive analysis of the Indian political situation prior to AD 1943.

Maharaja Ganga Singh's administration was a landmark in the field of development administration, for it led to a phenomenal expansion in the parameters of State activity and functions. He had initiated the multifarious projects of economic. social and political development in the State. Renovation and expansion of the administrative apparatus, the modernization of the State army, the far-reaching reforms in the judiciary, the re-vitalisation of revenue administration, establishment of a net-work of educational institutions, social homes, Gang canal, hospitals, railways, public libraries, and other public utility projects amply testify that Maharaja Ganga Singh was wide awake to the needs and requirements of the people.

To evaluate Maharaja Ganga Singh's role and achievements is not easy; on the contrary it is difficult and onerous. The historian Professor (Dr.) T.K. Mathur has edited and compiled in a book form 'Selected speeches of Maharaja Ganga Singhji of Bikaner' from AD 1898 to 1941. The speeches selected by Professor T.K. Mathur relate to some vital themes; namely, the views and performance of Maharaja Ganga Singh relating to Representative Assembly, Chamber of Princes, Judicial reforms, relations with nobility, Round Table Conferences and Federal structure, League of Nations, and general reforms. These speeches delivered by Maharaja Ganga Singh on various occasions reflect a part of his qualities; they do not portray the whole of his personality. I am happy to record. that Professor T.K. Mathur is aware of it.

Professor T.K. Mathur has shown a good skill and ability while preparing this edited work. If objectivity is the hallmark of a historian; that is clearly reflected in the edited notes written by Professor T.K. Mathur. The painstaking and laborious exercise undertaken by Professor T.K. Mathur is, indeed, praiseworthy. For understanding and assessing the reign of Maharaja Ganga Singh, who was the most outstanding and unequalled ruler of the former State of Bikaner and his period had been unforgettable in the annals of the State; Professor T .K. Mathur's edited work, in my opinion, is highly useful. It is beyond doubt a welcome addition towards assessing the role and contributions of Maharaja Ganga Singh. To the teachers and researchers engaged in the field, this edited book is of great utility. The book has enough qualities of being useful to general readers too.

The beauty of Prof. T.K. Mathur's edited work lies in its brevity. The sentences are short and heavily content-oriented. He has been able to highlight the substance, or the essential meaning and interpretation of Maharaja Ganga. Singh's speeches. He has shown an excellent ability to understand clearly the tenor and tone of Maharaja Ganga Singh's speeches. That is an achievement for which Professor T.K. Mathur deserves admiration.

Professor T.K. Mathur!s edited work is worthy of praise. I have no hesitation in saying that it is a highly commendable exercise; wherein neither the scholarship has been diluted, nor the objectivity or the accuracy of judgement has been sacrificed. I would, therefore, like to convey my congratulations to Professor T.K. Mathur.

Professor (Dr.) L.B. RATHORE
M.A., LL.B., Ph.D., D.Litt., D.P.A.(The Hague)
Vice-Chancellor
Jai Narain Vyas University
JODHPUR (Rajasthan -INDIA)

# Preface

The history of mankind has been replete with examples of how from time to time there has emerged on the world stage a person who, by sheer dint of his many faceted genius, has single handed guided the destinies of millions and shaped the future of nations and States in such a manner that it has left a lasting impact on the sands of time. The passage of time enhanced the memory of legacy of such persons and raises it to cult status. Their innovations, responses to challanges, commitment to human values and abiding faith in traditional principles of sound governance placed them on a pedestal where mere mortals simply gazed in awe and sought inspiration to better their daily existence.

One such star who shone very brightly on the firmament was Maharaja Ganga Singh Ji of Bikaner who dominated and played a very crucial role in shaping the destinies of India in the closing decade of the nineteenth century and the first half of the twentieth century. During this eventful era he also represented India with rare distinction on many an international fora and his role in these won him universal respect. On the domestic front at the same time he transformed a backward desert state of western Rajasthan into a progressive state which became a role model for other princely states in India.

This enlightened ruler was born on the auspicious day of Vijaydashmi (13th October) in 1880. He was the son of Maharaja Lal Singhji and ascended the throne of Bikaner as its 21st ruler at the tender age of 7 years when Maharaja Dunger Singh Ji passed away on the 9th August, 1887. For the next fifty six years till his death on 2nd February, 1943, he strode like a colossus on the Indian political stage and his impact was felt in many institutions with which he had been associated or had been created by him. Maharaja Ganga Singh Ji was cast in the ideal mould of a far-sighted Statesman whose political acumen and astuteness were widely respected and his advice was invariably sought on weighty national and international issues. His vision and broad-mindedness contrasted starkly with the narrow-mindedness of the age. At the international level he enjoyed the rare distinction of representing India and for being a signatory to the historic Treaty of Versailles (1919). He subsequently represented the Ruling Princes of India at the Assembly of League of Nations. He served as the leader of the Indian Delegation. His growing stature made him an automatic choice for representing the Ruling Princes of India at the Imperial Conference (October 1930). At the same time he had the distinction of attending the 1st and 2nd Indian Round Table Conferences in London (1930-31). The role of 'Ganga Risala' during the Second World War and the active part the Maharaja and the Risala played in the war won warm appreciation from all quarters. On the home front the Maharaja was equally busy and his achievements in transforming the desert state of Bikaner into a highly progressive State speaks volumes of his visionary approach and administrative abilities which were marked by a flair for innovation. Whether it was the expansion of the Railway network, or the legislative and judicial reforms, the stamp of Maharaja Ganga Singh Ji's competence was clearly manifest. Self-governing institutions, medical health care and education also received due care and patronage of the Maharaja. The great centre of learning at Varanasi, the Benaras Hindu University, was as much a contribution of Ganga Singh Ji as that of another great visionary of the age, Pandit Madan Mohan Malviya. Though a monarch and a person committed to the Chamber of Princes, Maharaja Ganga Singh Ji had the inborn instincts of a democrat. His patriotism was unmatched and unrivalled as was his bond with nationalism as evident from the fact that he was the first among the princes to realize the spirit of nationalism that was sweeping the nation during the first World War. His public pronouncements in England and his desire for a firm commitment from the British on the ultimate goal of self-government in India bear ample testimony to the Maharaja's abiding faith in the success and growth of nationalistic fervour in India.

**Background—The Ruling Rathore Dynasty of Bikaner**

Maharaja Ganga Singh Ji, as mentioned earlier, was the 21st ruler of Bikaner which was founded by Rao Bika of the Rathore clan around 1488 AD. The Rathores were an illustrious clan whose days of glory began in 470 AD when they established themselves as rulers in the wealthy and powerful state of Kanauj. The Rathore power in Kanauj was terminated in the early 13th century by the Muslim armies and the clan moved towards the desert of Rajasthan where one Siha Rathore carved out a small principality of his own in and around Pali. Herein lay the seeds of what later emerged as the powerful kingdom of Marwar with its capital at Jodhpur. In the latter half of the 15th century Rao Bika, the fifth son of Jodha, the ruler of Marwar, ventured into the region which became famous as Bikaner in later years. Rao Bika conquered extensive territories in the region with active help from his uncle Kandhal and brother Bida. The various tribes, heriditary possessors of land in this area, were soon subdued and Bika also added areas like Chandasar, Kodamdesar and Jangala to his new possessions. In a rare show of military brilliance, Bika led a highly successful campaign towards the southern limits of the Punjab which included the areas of Sirsa, Ladnu, Bhatner, Bhatinda, Singhana, Rini, Nohar and Pugal. Bika culminated his triumphant march in this area with the founding of the city of Bikaner in 1488. By the close of the 15th century the newly established kingdom of Bikaner covered an extensive area of about 40,000 Sq. miles of land comprising of some 3000 villages.

The sixteenth century witnessed far reaching changes in the political senario of northern India when the Moghal Emperor Akbar (1556-1605) initiated a policy of friendship and co-operation with the Rajput rulers. He brought them into the ambit of his famous Mansabdari system. The Bikaner ruler Kalyan Mal also submitted to Akbar's game plan and after attending the famous imperial durbar of Akbar at Nagore in 1570 AD Kalyan Mal was admitted to the administrative folds of the Moghuls. The next century saw successive rulers of Bikaner performing creditably in imperial service and it was during this period that Bikaner had the good fortune of producing an outstanding ruler Anup Singh (1669-98) who was by far the most eminent and scholarly ruler of his dynasty. Captain Powlett describes his rule as "the golden time of Bikaner's valour and fame" in his Gazetter of The Bikaner State of 1874. This scholar—monarch was the first ruler of his line to be conferred upon the title of Maharaja and his administrative acumen got him the governorships of Bijapur and Aurangabad in the Deccan.

The alliance forged with the Moghuls provided an umbrella of security for the desert state of Bikaner which prospered under a series of able rulers. Being geographically located on the caravan route to various Indian ports, Bikaner was able to exchange items of manufacture from far off countries like China, Africa, Persia and Arabia. A modern scholar of Bikaner, Naveen Patnaik in his book "A Desert Kingdom, New York, 1990" informs us that trade in Bikaner consisted of dried fruits from Isphan, furs from Kabul, scimitars from Damascus, porcelain from Peking, carpets from Herat, slaves from Abyssinia, Arab stallions were exchanged for India's elephant tusks, cottons, wools, spices, gems, indigo, silks and opium. This newly found prosperity led to architectural marvels in the shape of stately mansions built in red sandstone and embellished in exquisite carvings. The goldsmiths, silversmiths, carpet weavers and other craftsmen also benefitted from this economic upsurge and Bikaner soon became a great cultural centre.

The decline of the Moghul empire also signalled the decline in the power and prestiage of Bikaner. Contumatious thakurs and lawless Pindaris on the borders forced the rulers of Bikaner to turn to the British for succour and this resulted in the negotiation of a treaty between Bikaner and the East India Company in 1818. The Treaty was to be based on 'perpetual friendship, alliance and a unity of interests'. Though Bikaner was secure from external and internal threats, no progress was discernable on the economic front nor did the administration inspire any confidence among the masses. The British on the other hand reaped the benefits of the Bikaner armed forces and used them effectively in the threatres of war in Punjab, Kabul and other hot spots. A ray of hope came with the accession of Maharaja Dungar Singh on the throne of Bikaner in 1872 AD. He initiated wide ranging reforms in the fields of land revenue,judiciary, police, medical and education. His death in 1887 AD. brought to the throne of Bikaner its most illustrous son and outstanding statesman, Maharaja Ganga Singh Ji at the tender age of 7 years.

Maharaja Ganga Singh Ji ascended the throne at a time when reforms were the need of the hour and the masses sought re-assurance from the Royal family of continuity of the age of reconstruction as initiated by Maharaja Dungar Singh. Maharaja Ganga Singh did not disappoint his subjects and during his long reign which spanned over more than five decades he elevated Bikaner to the ranks of the leading and progressive states in the country and at the same time his role in various international fora not only enhanced his stature as the outstanding statesman of the age but won him the admiration of the Viceroy, national leaders like Mahatma Gandhi, Pandit Madan Mohan Malviya etc., his contemporary rulers and captains of the industry.

Ganga Singh Ji had an uneasy accession to the throne as the State was placed at the mercy of the Regency Council because of the young age of the new Maharaja. Regency always evoked bitter and in some cases not so bitter memories in most of the Princely states. K.M. Panikkar, who compiled and authored a highly authoritative Biography of Ganga Singh Ji titled HIS HIGHNESS THE MAHARAJA OF BIKANER (London 1937) quoted Ganga Singh Ji extensively about the uncertainty of the time during the Regency years thus:

"There are certain aspects of a Regency administration which States like Bikaner with their bitter experience of the past naturally find it impossible to forget, even though they may appreciate some of the advantages which were accrued during such periods in Bikaner As in the past, so in the future, we cannot exclude the possibility of local traditions, sentiments and feelings being arbitrarily ignored or overridden by them, or what is even worse, of individuals in their anxiety to gain or retain power or influence or for other undesirable motives involving the State in a network of intrigue and leaving to the young ruler when he comes of age a legency of hate and other evils which it would take a great many years to combat and overcome."

The personality of Maharaja Ganga Singh shone through his copious correspondence and speeches delivered. They reveal his grasp of the finer points of administration especially in the fields of land revenue, judicial reforms, legislative issues, self-governing institutions, education and railways. His assessment of diplomats, rulers, ministers bureaucrats and Heads of State clearly highlight his understanding of human beings and human values. His concern for the well being of his subjects and fierce nationalism are also amply reflected in his speeches and letters. Thanks to the metaculous researches conducted by Thakur Duleep Singh Ji of the Maharaja Ganga Singh Trust a collection of around 110 major speeches delivered by the Maharaja during his lifetime, especially between 1898 to 1943, has been compiled and preserved for posterity. It is a difficult task to divide and periodize these speeches into compartments but it should suffice to state that in the initial phase (1898-1914) the young Maharaja appeared to come to grips—with the administration of the State and the myraid problems it faced. The issues which the Maharaja tried to solve related to the coming to grips with the post,—Regency phase in Bikaner—the miseries heaped upon Bikaner because on account of the Great Famine or 'Chhapno-Akal' (1899-1900) and attempts to ammoleriote the condition of the masses, expansion of railways, police reforms, administrative reforms and educational reforms. The second phase (1915-31) witnessed the consolidation of gains of the initial phase coupled with a more dominant role in national and international affairs. The role played by Maharaja Ganga Singh in the First World War and in the succeeding conclusions of the treaty of Peace of Paris (1919) was highly laudable. His able representation in the League of Nations and participation in the Round Table

Conferences also ensured him a secure place in the history of the nation. The final phase (1932-43) saw the blossoming of the Maharaja into the elder statesman whose vision transcended the boundaries of the state and the nation. The golden jubilee celebrations of the rule of Ganga Singh Ji in 1937 was a time for gaiety and introspection when a grateful state and its people rose up to gracefully acknoweledge the contributions of Ganga Singh Ji to the development of Bikaner into a modern State.

**Brief Life Sketch and Major Landmarks in the Life of Maharaja Ganga Singh**

A brief life sketch of the Maharaja and major landmarks in his life are in order before an analysis of his speeches can be undertaken. As mentioned earlier the Maharaja was born on the auspicious day of Vijay Dashmi in 1880 and soon ascended the throne in 1887 AD upon the death of his elder brother Maharaja Dungar Singh. As Ganga Singh was a minor a Regency Council was setup under the Presidentship of Colonel Thorton, the then Resident Political Agent in Bikaner. As per tradition the early education of the Maharaja took place at home under the guidance and tutelage of Pandit Chandra Dubey of Ajmer. Besides installing in Ganga Singh a flair for languages and Indian history, Pandit Dubey made the young ruler imbibe all the finer points of Indian culture, tradition and ethos and concern for the well being of the masses was made the cardinal point of the thought process of the Prince. For five years (1889-94) the Maharaja was sent to the Eton of the east, Mayo College of Ajmer, where he was coached in the essentials of what constituted as a must for the scoins of the ruling families of India. The Maharaja performed as per expectations and excelled in many sports and subjects including English and History. His knowledge of languages stood him in good stead in later years when his proficiency in the English languag[illegible] compared to that of an Oxford don!

The return to Bikaner of the young prince was marked with an effort to initiate him into the intricicies of administration and for this purpose the Government of India appointed an Englishman, Brian Egerton, as his tutor. His military training also took place simultaneously under Lt. Col. Bell of Deoli Regiment at Deoli. Ganga Singh Ji assumed full powers to rule the State of Bikaner on 16th December, 1898 in an impressive ceremony at the 400 years old Junagarh fort—the symbol of royal power of the Rathores in Bikaner. But the throne was no bed of roses for the prince as Bikaner still reeled under the shadow of backwardness despite the good intentioned rule of Maharaja Dungar Singh in the late nineteenth century. Immediate problems that needed redressal were combating harsh geographical conditions, meeting the aspirations of a restless populance and dealing with an untamed aristocracy. Furthermore the vast mineral wealth of the State remained untapped and the lack of adequate rainfall hampered the irrigation facilities of the land. On top of all this, network of roads and railways was virtually non-existant. As if these handicaps were not daunting enough for the new ruler, Bikaner and the whole of Northern India were in the grip of a severe draught in the closing years of the ninteenth century. The Regency was not prepared for the draught and the grain stores were empty. The Maharaja set about providing succour to the improvished in a determined manner which belied his youth and he toured the whole of the State distributing loans and setting up medical camps to prevent the spread of epidemics. The Prince's efforts won the appreciation of even Lord Curzon, the then Viceroy of India who felt that the desert ruler had set precedents and standards for others to follow and emulate. In 1900 the Queen-Empress, Victoria conferred upon Ganga Singh Ji the Kaiser-i-Hind, Gold Medal for humanitarian work done during the Great Famine.

In the same year the Maharaja was called upon to lead his troops against the Dowager Empress of China during the Boxer Rebellion. This was the Maharaja's first military campaign overseas in the service of the British Empire and was the forerunner of more successful campaigns in other continents in the years to follow. Military honours were soon to follow in the shape of Knight Commander of the Indian Empire (1901) and award of Coronation Medal and China War Medals (1902). In the same year the Bikaner Camel Corps—the Ganga Risala—left Bikaner to participate in the Somaliland campaign where it performed with valour and distinction. Affairs at home also kept the Maharaja fully occupied and during the course of time railways received a boost with the commissioning of the Bikaner—Dulmera and the Suratgarh—Bhatinda Railway Sections. As a part of administrative reforms Ganga Singh Ji took the unprecedented step in 1902 of separating the Privy Purse from the General Budget of the State. The Power Sector also received its due share of reforms during the first decade of the twentieth century. Around the same time an effort was initiated to deal with refactory nobles of the State. By 1910 AD the Maharaja was sufficiently emboldened when the post of the Political Agent in the State was abolished. In the process of judicial reforms he established the Chief Court. By 1910 the Medical Services came under the State administration from the Chief Medical officer of Rajputana.

In 1912 was inaugurated the silver jubilee of the reign of Maharaja Ganga Singh Ji. The Jubilee co-incided with the thrust towards more efficient and modern administration. Some of the measures introduced were:

i. Appointment of separate secretaries for various departments.
ii. The complete reorganization of the Revenue Department under the able guidance of Mr. G.D. Rudkin, I.C.S. whose services were borrowed from the Punjab Government.
iii. Replacement of Urdu by Hindi in all official works.
iv. Creation of the post of the Director of Education.

A major highlight of the reform programme was the inauguration of the Representative Assembly on the 10th November, 1913.

While the State of Bikaner was/moving towards modernization, war clouds were menacing Europe and in August 1914 the British Empire formally declared war against Germany. The war was to last till 1918 and soon engulfed virtually all the countries of the civilized world.

The start of the war was a landmark year in the reign of Ganga Singh Ji and capitulated him into the international arena where he successfully essayed the role of a seasoned diplomat and statesman for the next quarter of the century or so. The war saw the Maharaja serving in Flanders and Egypt. His growing stature ensured his representing his fellow rulers at the meetings of the Imperial War Cabinet held in England in 1917, 1918 and 1919. He was accorded the signal honour of being one of the signatories to the Treaty of Versailles which was concluded between the victorious Allied Forces and the defeated German Nation. But the terms of the treaty disturbed the Maharaja who was constrained to observe publically that such imposed crippling and ruineous treaties could not lead to lasting peace. These thoughts were indeed prophetic as a resurgent Germany plunged the world into another war in just twenty years. The Paris Conference brought Ganga Singh Ji in close contact with President Clemenceau of France, President Wilson of U.S.A. and Prime Minister Llyod George of England. With Clemenceau, the Maharaja formed an abiding bond of friendship which the former responded by accepting the latter's invitation to visit Bikaner for a shoot.

It was during the Paris Conference that the Maharaja, along with the other Indian representative, made forceful pleas that India should be included in the newly formed League of Nations in the teeth of opposition from England. Ganga Singh had his way and India found a place in the League of Nations. But preoccupation with world affairs did not prevent Maharaja Ganga Singh Ji from his relentless pursuit of administrative reforms at home. Railways continued to rate high on his agenda and in 1916 the Ratangarh-Sardarshahr Branch Railway was inaugurated. It is to the lasting credit of Ganga Singh Ji that the Railway mileage during his reign multiplied ten times and at the time of his death stood at 884 miles. He was the guiding spirit behind the Chamber of Princes which was setup in 1916 and was elected as its First Honorary General Secretary—an office he held for successive years till 1920. 1916 continued to be a major year of achievements in more areas than one. He attended the foundation ceremony of the famous Benaras Hindu University in his capacity as one of the founding members. The Hindu University ownes as much to Maharaja Ganga Singh Ji as it does to Pandit Madan Mohan Malviya.

The ever expanding railway network and improved roads, coupled with ambitious water-works and electrical schemes led to the rapid industrialization of the State of Bikaner. Coal mining flourished and new cotton ginning mills came up along with new wool, glass and soap factories. The prosperity of the masses increased and the revenue of the State multiplied. Perhaps the most lasting and enduring achievement of Ganga Singh Ji was the building of the 89 miles long Ganga Canal. The tragedy of the famine years of 1899-1900 left a deep imprint on the mind of the Maharaja who toiled ceaselessly for more than a quarter of a century to bring the waters of the river Sutlej to the northern region of the State in the heart of the Thar desert, through the Gang Canal. The British initially seemed reluctant on the idea of the Canal but the perseverence of the Maharaja paid dividents which resulted in the signing of the momentous agreement on the Sutlez Valley Irrigation Scheme among Punjab, Bahawalpur and Bikaner on the 4th September, 1920. This concrete-lined canal reclaimed nearly 1000 square miles of land from the grips of the desert and transformed the area into the grainary of Rajasthan. This achievement was more laudable in the sense that it was accomplished with very meagre resources at the disposal of the State and no fresh taxes were levied for the project. It was therefore, only in the fitness of things that the canal was inaugurated by Vicroy Lord Irvin on the 26th October, 1927.

Maharaja Ganga Singh was a pragmetic and far sighted ruler who thought of the future while formulating plans for the present. Early in his life he was convinced that the old feudalestic character of the State based on the concept of absolute monarchy was a great inhibator of the growth and development of the masses. Like minded statesmen had convinced him of the benefits of a constitutional monarchy. The establishment in 1913 of the Representative Assembly comprising of elected members was a natural culmination of this thought process. In 1917 the Representative Assembly was renamed as the Legislative Assembly and vested with more powers. Judicial reforms also continued at par as the Maharaja was convinced that the law courts should be independent of external influence and interference. The establishment of a High Court of judicature on the 3rd May, 1922 was a step in this direction. At the same time a number of lower courts were also set up. Ganga Singh Ji also granted a full charter of powers to the State's High Court.

The Maharaja was also a firm advocate of education for the masses. He always felt that reforms in any field were meaningless unless the masses were literate enough to appreciate them. He formulated a new Educational Scheme for the State in 1918 with the aim of spreading education to even distant villages. The opening of the Walter Nobles' High School (1893) and the upgrading of the Dungar College were steps in this direction. He had enduring ties with the Benaras Hindu University of which he was a founder member. He served it in various capacities—first as its Pro-Chancellor (1922-29) and subsequently as its Chancellor from 1929 till his death in 1943.

Maharaja Ganga Singh was always conscious of the role the ruling princes were to play in the years to come and the future course of action the nation would pursue in the decades to come. As mentioned earlier he had clear cut notions of what constituted as rights and duties of the ruling princes in India - what they were expected to do in their States and what should be the nature of their relationship with the rest of India. His able guidance to the Conference of Princes which was the forerunner of the Chamber of Princes (established on February 8, 1921) clearly set the tone for the future course of action the ruling princes were to adopt. While acknowledging the rights and previleges of the rulers, Ganga Singh Ji was of ten at pains to demonstrate that the survival of States depended on administrative reforms based on the needs of modernization. The British armed might or the local armies were no guarantee for the continued well being of the monarchies. The Maharaja also advocated that reforms should go hand in hand with the support and co-operation of the masses. Alienation of the affection of the masses simply eroded the State from within, was the oft-repeated refrain of the Maharaja to his co-rulers. The issue of internal reforms became not only an obsession but an article of faith with Maharaja Ganga Singh in the twenties. He moved a resolution in the Chamber of Princes in 1928 in which he exhorted the other members of the Chamber to see the writing on the wall and to liberalize and humanise their autocratic rule because history had been extremely unkind to despotic rulers. Such rulers, the refrain continued, menaced the very institution of monarchy.

Good governence was synonymous with the rule of the law. According to Maharaja Ganga Singh the issues enumerated in the concept of good government would include a well defined Privy Purse, efficient and honest police force, uniform application of just laws, an independent judiciary and an efficient bureaucracy. Towards the close of his reign the Maharaja also enjoined on the administration the security of the rights and individual liberty of the masses.

The Maharaja's views on nationalism and national movements were liberal in approach and in confirmity with the spirit of the times. Even during the First World War and in his meetings with various diplomats, statesmen and leaders of Europe, he was at pains to emphasize that a fresh wind was sweeping the nation and no one could afford to go against it. In 1917 he had boldly asserted that Great Britain "will not forget the just claims and aspirations of India to enable her to workout her destiny under Britain's guiding hand and protection." The Maharaja was thus echoing the ideas and demands of the leaders of the Home Rule Movement. It is a lesser known fact of history that Maharaja Ganga Singh was one of those who inspired the new policy of the British Government which was initiated by the proclamation of August 20, 1917. The proclamation reflected in a major way the minute Ganga Singh had enclosed in his famous Rome Note to Austen Chamberlain, Secretary of State for India in which he laid down and implored Chamberlain thus "I would beg leave once again to urge and implore you to do something on a really liberal, sympathetic and generous scale and in such a manner as will strike the imagination and sentiments of the East and bind India and England closer together."

Ganga Singh's Ji's presence in the First and Second Round Table Conference as a representative of Princely India in 1930 and 1931 A.D. was forcefully felt and it was here that his previously held beliefs that there should be an All India Federation of both, Indian States and British India, was finally accorded the attention it merited.

The closing years of the reign of Maharaja Ganga Singh saw the total transformation of the ruler into the senior statesman of the nation. The confidential letter of the Maharaja to Sir Donald Field, Chief Minister of the Jodhpur State of 21st February, 1937 revealed the functioning of a very mature and thoughtful statesman and showed a very astute grasp of national affairs. He was one of the few who accurately predicted the course of the winds of change blowing accross the country.

The year 1937 AD saw the celebrations of the Golden Jubilee, of the reign of Maharaja Ganga Singh. This was also the occasion for a grateful nation to warmly acknowledge the contribution of a genius in transforming a desert state, reeling in the thores of backwardness, into a modern industrialised state run on efficient lines. The Golden Jubilee was also marked by a visit of the Viceroy Marquis of Lintigthgow and Lady Linlithgow to Bikaner in November 1937.

Though age was catching up with the Maharaja, the outbreak of the Second World War in 1939 AD saw the Bikaner ruler volunteering his services for defence of the Empire. The Ganga Risala left for the Middle-East by mid-1940. Soon other contingents from Bikaner also left for the front. At home the pace of reforms continued unabated. On the 23rd October, 1941 the Maharaja issued a historic proclamation in which he promised to uphold and maintain the progressive character of the administration and the rights and liberties of his subjects. This pledge was given on behalf of his successors as well. But time and toil were taking their toll and Maharaja Ganga Singh passed away on the 2nd February, 1943 in Bombay.

For a ruler so singularly gifted, the Maharaja surprisingly had little time for the appreciation of fine arts. Thus he had little time for persuing the literary traditions of the Bikaner family. His reading was confined to subjects that were of immediate interest to him. While he appreciated good music he was not a devotee of it. His interest in painting was restricted to the subject of the painting rather than the art itself. Wild game was a favourite theme of painting of his age. Sculptures of animals dotted the Lallgarh Palace and could be safely housed in a separate museum. It was in the field of architecture that Ganga Singh took great delight in following the tradition of great rulers being great builders. His lack of humanistic interest gave him a mainly utalitarian outlook on life and made him inelastic in his general ideas. The Maharaja often surprised many of his guests by his abhorrance for and lack of profligate ostentation. While even his lesser placed brethren were not averse to extravagence in order to uphold and maintain their dignity, the Maharaja exercised great moderation. He thus tried to draw a fine line between necessary pomp in the life of a ruler and vulger and unwarranted display. He was always a true connoisseur. Tradition also had a treasured place in the life of the Maharaja. He often asserted that ceremonies and prestiege of the dynasty on especial festivals (the Grand Durbar on Dusserah for one) demanded pomp to mark the occasion much he detested ostentation personally. This formality and etiquette was necessary, it was argued, as it adhered to tradition which had knit the society together over the ages.

To his qualities of initiative and driving capacity, the Maharaja added the virtue of persistence. It was this last quality that saw the achievements of goals which lesser and impatient rulers would have abondoned on the wayside.

He was a completely organisation man—committed to scrutiny of the minutest detail. He appreciated those ministers and officials who displayed the flair to take decisions at their own level rather than passing on the responsibility to others.

He was an excellent host. His 'Shikar' parties were legendary. It was an invitation from the Maharaja that the high and mighty from all over craved for. The Maharaja also formed lasting friendships in which there was no room for distrust or misunderstanding. His was a very sophisticated and urbane personality. He was charming, witty and ambitious in his beliefs.

PROF. T.K. MATHUR
Ajmer

# *Introduction*

RAO BIKA, A YOUNG Rathore Rajput prince, son of Rao Jodha, Maharaja of Jodhpur dared to penetrate the desert, the endless stretches of sand dunes, where the sun blazed down mercilessly with temperatures often exceeding forty-five degrees Celsius, and where there was an acute shortage of water. The absence of trees provided no shelter from the harsh, and frequent, dust storms. It was here in the middle of the Thar Desert that a new kingdom was formed in AD 1465 – Bikaner – named after its founder, Rao Bika, the first ruler. The erstwhile state of Bikaner was the sixth largest princely state in India, having an area of 23,317 square miles.

During the course of 300 years of their patriotism the Rajas and Maharajas of Bikaner had demonstrated their worth in the history of India. Their patriotism, valour, sacrifice, secular outlook and benevolence were of a high order. In addition to this, they were great patrons of art, architecture, music, literature and culture. Looked at from every aspect the history of the Bikaner state is fabulously rich.

A focal point of Bikaner is the village of Deshnoke. Here in this small, quiet and peaceful town twenty miles from the city of Bikaner, is situated a marble temple in the memory of a Charan lady, Karniji. She is the deity of the Bikaner family and after whom my father was named. When Rao Bika came to carve out a kingdom for himself some five centuries ago, he stopped at the village of Deshnoke. It is said that Karniji provided the inspiration to Rao Bika in his quest for a kingdom.

Maharaja Ganga Singh succeeded to the gaddi of his ancestors after the demise of Maharaja Dungar Singh, who was Maharaja Ganga Singh's elder brother and had no son; in 1887 he adopted his younger brother as his heir, Maharaja Dungar Singh died on 19 August 1887 and on 21 August 1887 Maharaja Ganga Singh was proclaimed the 21st Maharaja of Bikaner. However, according to the customs of the state he was formally installed on 31 August 1887 – after the twelve-day ceremonies. The young Maharaja Ganga Singh was only seven years old at the time when the Herculean task of ruling the state fell upon his young shoulders.

The Maharaja assumed full powers of government on 16 December 1898. The state of Bikaner with its arid 23,000 square miles, complex interests, conditions and problems, isolated position, scanty and precarious rainfall, restless populace, and proud and untamed aristocracy, required constant vigilance and increasing activity. In comparison to the other great states in Rajputana, its peers in rank, Bikaner's income was inconsiderable.

Maharaja Ganga Singh was a very prominent Maharaja in the history of the Bikaner state – of that there is no doubt. The period of five decades – from 1887 when he came to the throne of his ancestors as the twenty-first Maharaja till his demise in 1943 – he was to see major changes that took place in the Indian subcontinent leading up to the Independence movement.

Maharaja Ganga Singh impressed all who met him. Friends and guests, Indian and European alike, were struck by his handsome soldierly bearing and by his routine life of hard work, dedication and devotion to the state. The city of Bikaner had advanced beyond comprehension – from a small desert town it had turned into a thriving, modern, well-laid-out city, Maharaja Ganga Singh had modernised the machinery in every department and had transformed his capital with parks, monuments and public buildings, electric lighting, telephones and water supply, excellent medical facilities, busy magistrates courts, well-laid-out roads, and schools for both girls and boys.

Maharaja Ganga Singh was an intrepid and colourful personality, and had earned a high place in the gallery of great Indian rulers of the era. Apart from being a visionary administrator, he was also an eminent statesman who was held in the highest esteem in New Delhi and in London.

Though he knew what was expected of Indian princes on formal occasions, he personally led the life of a country gentleman, permitting himself only a few luxuries. Widely acknowledged for his prowess as a warrior, he had fought for the crown in three continents commanding his troops in China during the Boxer Rebellion and in France and Egypt during the Great Wars.

He was also regarded as an able statesman and visionary, both nationally and at international forums, many of which he attended as Indian's representative. He represented the princes of India in the Imperial War Cabinet, at the Peace Conference, at the League of Nations and as a signatory of the Treaty of Versailles. Apart from being an Architect-builder, warrior, trusted and benevolent ruler, able diplomat, he was an eloquent orator.

He spoke perfect English, had understanding of the mood of times and accordingly aired his views. His personality and command over English was outstanding and impressed one and all. After his visit to England in 1910 to attend the Coronation of King George V, a royal Private Secretary wrote to him *"His Majesty is much struck by your command of the English language, and your letter, written without a mistake in spelling or phraseology, reaches high standard of English scholarship"*.

His ability to create an impression while delivering a speech was described by Wickham Steed, the famous publicist and former editor of the Times, who was present at Geneva as a witness to the proceedings of the Assembly.

*"The President, Mr. Motta, announces: 'The Maharaja of Bikaner, delegate of India, will address the Assembly . . . its resignation quickly gives place to attention, and attention to admiration. Clear, brief, to the point, matter-of-fact yet elevated, the Maharaja soon convinces his hearers that he knows what he is saying, means what he says, says what means. Ten minutes later he descends from the tribune – amid rousing applause and markedly different in quality from the initial greeting. He had made the best of all the English speeches at the Assembly."*

The present book represents the overall scenario of his selected speeches delivered during his regime. The topics of his speeches cover the vast field of international and national issues. These selected speeches of Maharaja Ganga Singhji have been systematically edited by Prof. Tej Kumar Mathur for this book and are being published on the repeated public demand and vast interest shown on the subject.

In the nutshell, the present book is a fine collection of the selected speeches delivered by a visionary administrator, an eminent statesman and an eloquent orator who was held in the highest esteem all over the world. I hope it will prove interesting reading and also a great reference material for young history scholars' and persons who wish to master the art of compiling a speech.

RAJYASHREE KUMARI BIKANER

# 1

## *Maharaja Ganga Singh and Relations With His Nobility*

THE LONG AND EVENTFUL reign of Maharaja Ganga Singh was spread over nearly fifty years. During this period he was the chief architect of a modern and resurgent Bikaner. As an administrator he was innovative in his approach and he brought a fresh whiff of revolutionary thought process in his dealing with day to day problems and long range issues. The cardinal point of his administrative thrust was the welfare of the masses. Towards this end he was even accused of ruthlessness and autocratic behaviour—a charge he ignored where the interests of the state were concerned. His early education at Mayo College, Ajmer, served him in good stead and exposed his receptive mind to the enlightenment of the west. Thus he freely imbibed the minetenth century liberalism as was propounded by the western philosphers of that age.

The Maharaja was catholic in his ideas as was evident by his contact with a wide range of leaders of different streams which ranged from national leaders like Mahatma Gandhi, Pt. Madan Mohan Malviya, Sir Pheroz Shah Mehta, G.K. Gokhale, Sir Tej Bahadur Sapru to foreign lumanaries and statesman like, King George V, Llyod George, Viceroys in India including Lord Curzon and Lord Linlinthgow, Cleamenshu and others. Their ideas helped shape his administrative acemen and helped in the infusion of fresh ideas in a hitherto antiquited administrative system. His experience was enhanced with his participation in Imperial War Conferences, Paris Peace Conference, Round Table Conferences, Chamber of Princes Conferences, League of Nations and other related international gatherings and meeting. All these exposed him to new ideas which he was willing to implement in his state. It was this trait in him that attracted some of the finest brains and ablest administrators to the service of the state of Bikaner. This list included such talent as Manu

Bhai Mehta, K.M. Pannikar, R.G. Fagon, G.D. Rudkin I.C.S., R. Douglas I.C.S. and J.N. Atal. Above all he had abiding faith in secularism. All these factors contributed to an administration sensitive to the aspirations of the masses.

The varied achievements of Maharaja Ganga Singh have been left for posterity in the shape of well-documented, and thought provoking brilliant speeches which he delivered on various occasions from different platforms. The range of these speeches was enormous—they covered a wide spectrum of topics and issues. The major speeches relate to:

(i) The Bikaner Legislative Assembly or Repreentative Assembly.
(ii) The formulation and role of the Chamber of Princes.
(iii) Judicial Reforms and Accountability
(iv) Relations with the Nobility
(v) Round Table Conferences and Federal Structure.
(vi) Participation in the proceedings of League of Nations.
(viii) General reforms not covered in above areas.

The speeches delivered on visits of dignatories, state banquets, farewells, birthday celebrations, inaugration of Assembly etc. were all occasions for important pronouncements on administration and policy pronouncements. It is proposed to deal with these speeches subject and issue wise. With each passing year the tenor and text of the speeches showed the growing confidence and maturity in the thought process of the Maharaja. The speeches delivered cover a period of 45 years (1898-1943 AD) and have been used mainly as annexures at the end of chapters.

One of the earliest speeches Ganga Singhji delivered was the one he delivered on being invested with ruling powers on 16th December, 1898. (No. 1). For an inaugural speech it augured well for Bikaner as it reflected a wise head on young shoulders while expressing commitment to accepting the rules which the Government of India laid down for his guidance, he also pledged that he would do his duty towards the subjects whom he loved immensely and was duty bound to serve.

Dinner speeches were ceremonial (No. 2) but more often than not were a means to make important pronouncements or to review important steps undertaken sometime back. The State banquet in honour of Viceroy and Lady Curzon during their visit to Bikaner on 25th November, 1902 was one such Banquet speech (No. 3). The young Maharaja used the occasion to assess four years of his reign.

The famine of 1899-1900 AD came in for special mention and while the speech dwelt with the courage and fortitute of the people in trying times it also stressed that one good that emerged was that it brought the people and the ruler closer to each other. The Maharaja also pondered upon the possibility of bringing in waters from Sutlej through a good canal. Satisfaction was also expressed at the openning of the Bikaner—Bhatinda Railway route. The Maharaja also expressed his thanks to the Viceroy for permitting him to serve outside India in China in a military capacity

**Relations with Nobles**

One of the issues that engaged the attention of the young Maharaja on the assumptions of full powers was the future shape of the relations with the nobility of the State. There was hardly any State in Rajasthan in which the ruler did not have serious points of dispute and discord with his nobles. Nearly a century back Col. James Tod, the celebrated historian of Rajasthan, in his Annals and Antiquities of Rajputana had tried to study the problem in the broader context of what was termed as 'Feudalism'. When Ganga Singh Ji came of age one of the problems he faced was the ruineous effect the two factors of the nobility (the faction led by Sodhi Hukum Singh and the one opposed to it) were having on the State of Bikaner. In a hard hitting speech, the young Maharaja was at pains to stress that this party system with its schisms was ruining Bikaner and how he wished that the Sirdars would close ranks and behave in a mature manner. The Maharaja was also at pains to state that he strongly disapproved the policy of the wives of the nobles involving the royal Harem in the politics of the State. Maharaja Ganga Singh was apprehensive from the start that reforms in administration would be misconstrued by the nobility as an infringement on their rights. In a birthday speech in 1904 the Maharaja tried to convince the nobles that the future of Bikaner lay in the Chiefs paying attention to the administration of their jagirs and the welfare of the subjects residing in them. Furthermore he reminded the nobles that the State had no intention of depriving them of their previleges or concessions provided their loyalty to the State remained uninstinted. The speech ended with the ruler tackling the two bones of contention viz. (a) the realisation of marriage 'Neota' and (b) the question of quarring stones. (No. 4).

But the vieled warnings of the Maharaja went unheaded by an influential section of the nobility which included Thakur Bahadur Singh—considered to be most astute of the nobles. Attempts were also made to win over petty, non-tazami sardars and Bhogtas. By

November 1904 AD. Maharaja Ganga Singh was forced to appoint a commission comprising of some 'Rajvis', sardars and officials, to look into matters of sedetion and conspiracy against Hukum Singh of Bidasar, Bhairon Singh of Ajitpura and Ram Singh of Gopalpura. The Commission in its findings declared that the three Thakurs were not only guilty of holding seditious meetings at their houses but also inciting other nobles and even the urban populance to join them in their designs against the Maharaja and the State. The centres of unrest were Bidasar and Ajitpura. The dissatisfied nobles even petitioned the A.G.G. against the Maharaja's autocratic ways.

The Commission in its capacity as a judicial body imposed a heavy punishment of ten years of simple imprisionment and a fine of Rs. 10,000 each on Thakur Hukum Singh of Bidasar and Bhairon Singh of Ajitpura. The punishment awarded to Thakur Ram Singh of Gopalpura was slightly less severe. But the Maharaja had his eye on the future with the aim of preventing similar action on part of other chiefs and insuring that the three chiefs were not driven against the wall completly leading to further action on their part. As a consequence, the Maharaja decreed that Bidasar be made Khalsa for three years and the village of Momasar be confiscated permanently. The Jagir of Bhairon Singh was confiscated and the status of Bhairon Singh was degraded among the ranks of tazims. Ram Singh of Gopalpura again got offlightly. The message to the nobles was clear-firmess would be tempered with clemency provided the nobles behaved in future and co-operated with the State.

But the nobles did not respond favourably to the Maharaja's decision and on the contrary appealed to the Government of India against the alleged arbitrary behaviour of the Maharaja which was not in confirmity with either the offence committed or past practice. The Foreign Department concurred with the stand of the nobles and suggested certain modifications in the punishments awarded. It was advocated to the Maharaja that in the case of Thakur Bhairon Singh of Ajitpura half of his estate be resumed if his future behavior confirmed to nonns. In the case of Thakur Hukam Singh of Bidasar it was suggested that the village of Momasar be remitted at the expiry of the stipulated three years. Thakur Ram Singh of Gopalpura got off very lightly once more. The petitioners even approached members of the British Parliament.

The preceedings placed Ganga Singh Ji in a dilemma as in case the advice of the Government of India was upheld his prestiege at home among his subjects would suffer and his grip over administration would slaken automatically. The situation was not remedied by the fact that despite the best of efforts the village of Momasar in Bidasar jagir could not be taken over by the State. The issue was further complicated for Ganga Singh Ji with the death of Thakur Hukam Singh in jail in 1906 and, resorting to diplomacy, he tried to placate Bahadur Singh, father of the late Hukam Singh. Meanwhile the hostility of the nobles continued and other chiefs like Moti Singh of Sandawa, Raghunath Singh of Harasar and Bagh Singh of Loha defied the authority of the Maharaja. Further defiance to the Maharaja's authority came when Bhairon Singh's successor at Ajitpura, Balwant Singh, even refused to accept the saropas from the Maharaja on his accession. Matters reached a head when the chiefs even tried to rope in the loyal state troops in their agitation. By 1907 the ranks of the rebels and discontented multiplied with leading men of the houses of Parawa, Khera, Johara, Dhingaria, Ghanital, Baleran, Sarangsar and Takhmisar also siding with the cause of the original rebels.

The Maharaja retaliated by appealing directly to Lord Curzon and strongly urging the Viceroy to disregard the advice of the Foreign Department which was based on misinformation. The former also informed the Viceroy that in extreme case, the Maharaja might seriously contemplate abdication. Fortunately for the Bikaner ruler the Viceroy appreciated the former's stand and overruled the advice of the Foreign Department. Thus emboldened Ganga Singhji struck at the very bases and citidels of the rebels and convinced the Government of India that exile of Thakur Bahadur Singh of Bidasar from Bikaner would break the back of the rebels. Bahadur Singh was secretly escorted out of Bikaner and sent to Jaipur where he stayed in comfort till 1910 when he was permitted to return to Bikaner to spent his remaining days in peace.

Though the backs of the rebels were broken, many of them continued to conspire against the State through the active connivence of the Political Agent. But the determination and diplomacy of the Maharaja resolved the issue in favour of the latter. The relations with the chiefs also brought the role of the Political Agent into focus. Maharaja Ganga Singh had observed that during the course of conversation with a Political Agent he had been informed that intervention in internal affairs of a state was not official policy but the personal prerogative of the Political Agent. The Agent had further informed the Maharaja that during minority rule the former sided with the ruler against the nobles but reversed the policy once the ruler assumed full powers!

The Silver Jubilee of the reign of the Maharaja in 1912 was another occasion for the ruler to address the 'Sardars' with the aim of normalisation of 'feudalties' between the ruler and the feudatories. In a forceful speech on the occasion of the Jubilee Darbar, the Maharaja was forthright in his assertion that justificable boons and privileges could be granted to the nobles if the nobles continued to support measures of reconstruction and reform. (No. 5 ). But nearly nine years were to pass before the Maharaja addressed the Sardars in a meeting at Lallgarh Palace on 20th March, 1921. Using the platform Ganga Singh Ji was at pains to explain that since his coming of age he was always desireous of doing the needful and just for his Sardars. A promise he had since reintreated in his Silver Jubilee Darbar Speech. It was to the regret of the Maharaja that circumstances conspired otherwise and rewards towards the Sardar were not forthcoming. A committee meeting of Representative Sardars could be convened at the earliest, was also used as a sounding board for the sentiment that the 'izzat' (dignity) and prestiege of the 'Sardars' was the 'izzat' and prestiege of the state. Concessions could be negotiated in a free and frank atmosphere of give and take. The Maharaja also said broader interests of the nobles and the state could only be kept in view during discussions.

The Maharaja also used the occasion to announce the creation of an 'Sardars Advisory Committee' which would not only regulate the relations between the ruler and his chiefs, but also advise the ruler on feudal matters of non-political nature. The ruler would not impose restrictions on the committee but its final shape would be arrived at only after consultations with senior Sardars, it was also announced. At the same time the Sardars were also cautioned that proper decorum and customs were to be adhered to while conducting relations with the ruler. In the closing part of his address the ruler held out to the chiefs that they should not lose touch with ground realities by alienating the masses. They were reminded that in Princely India, unlike as in British India, there were close ties of human bonds between the ruler and the ruled.

In a subsequent Banquet speech to the sardars on 30th September, 1925(Draft given as No. 6), the issue of ' 'izzat' of the chiefs was once again discussed. The Maharaja had been toying with the idea that the birth of the 'Bhanwar Sahib' was the occasion for conferring on the ladies of the families of all Tazimi Sardars the right to wear gold ornaments on their feet. The Sardars themselves already enjoyed that privilege. But it was brought to the royal notice that such a right already existed. A scrutiny of the records proved that conferring of any such privilege was the right of the Maharaja alone. Hence a new order was issued in which all Thukranies, daughters, tikai kumaris and wives of tikai grandsons of all Tazimi Sardars would be entitled to wear gold ornaments on their feet. On the question of jewelled ornaments on the feet, it was laid down that they were permitted only on special cases.

On the issue of pensions it was also announced that all Sardars who entered permanent state service were entitled to pension and gratuity from the state Treasury upon their attaining the age of superannuation. In the same vien it was also announced that the 'Advisory Committee' which was to be constituted, was in its final stages of commissioning. It was to compromise of six members—three to be elected by the Sardars and the other three to be nominated by the Maharaja. The committee was to be presided over by a President who was to be nominated by the Maharaja.

The matter of realisation of demands from Chhut-Bhais and agriculturists was referred to a committee of eight Sardars and Mr. Rudkin. Another point touched upon by the Maharaja in his speech was one which caused him great pain and anxiety viz.—the placing of the affairs of the Sardars, Bhogtas and Chhutbhais under the Foreign and Political Minister. This was in supersession of the previous order of 1917 when the affairs of the sardars were placed under the Political Department. The Maharaja attempted to explain that the Department of Foreign and Political was arguably the most important administrative unit in the state and was not expected to deal with trifles. The Maharaja ended his speech with an appeal to give the experiment some time to succeed.

In 1928 the Maharaja made another address to the Tazimi Sardars and attempted to resolve the vexatous problem of the gradation of the Sardars. He traced the system of gradation of chiefs to the Regency period during which the chiefs were placed into four grades. This step was taken for the sole purpose of regulating the grant of 'Parwarish' to Tazimi Sardars on occassions of births, marriages and deaths in their families. This proposal had been earlier shot down by the late Maharaja Dungar Singh on the plea that it was the sole prerogative of the ruler to decide on the 'Parvarish' to be granted on different occasions. But the Regency council could not calculate 'parvarish' without some sort of gradation which, at the sametime, did not strictly conform to the different kinds of Tazim which they actually enjoyed at that time. Maharaja Ganga Singh conceeded that the Sardars were justified in having apprehensions that those grades represented gradation of rank and privileges. He concurred with the views of the Sardars and advocated immediate abolishing of gradation. He also felt that scale of 'parvarish' was to be decided solely by the

Maharaja of Bikaner. Furthermore the kind of Tazim enjoyed would be the sole criteria for judging the status of the chief. Ganga Singh Ji decided to abide by the old system of Tazim which was as follows:

1. Dolri (or double) Tazim or those who enjoy the honour of HAT RO QURD.
2. Ikolri (or single) Tazim or those who enjoy the honour of BANU PASAV.
3. Other Tazims.

Among those who enjoyed the highest class of Tazim i.e., Dolri Tazim were the Raja of Mahajan, The Rawat of Bidasar, the Rawat of Rawatsar and the Rao of Bhukarka. The Maharaja could promote some Ikolri Tazims to Dolri Tazim category.

Ganga Singh Ji agreed to lend his good offices in case of dispute between Tazimi Sardars as regards rank and precedence. But, it was added, that unsubstantiated or unfounded claims were no excuse for non-attendence at the Darbar on special occasions as demanded by past practice. The Maharaja appreciated the fact that some chiefs had resolved their differences over seniority amicably amongst themselves. A suggestion was also mooted by the Maharaja that seniority and issue of precedence amongst chiefs of equal rank could be decided (a) according to the date of their succeeding to the 'Gaddis' of their thikanas or (b) settle the issue of preceedence according to seniority of age. Such agreements were applicable only during the lifetimes of the nobles in question. (No. 7).

## References


1. 'Maharaja Ganga Singh Ji and The Nobles (1898-1919 AD)' by (Late) Tolaram Agarwal in Maharaja Ganga Singh Ji Centenary Volume Ed. G.S.L. Deora, Delhi, 1980.
2. Pannikar, K.M., His Highness, the Maharaja of Bikaner, Oxford, 1937.
3. Private Secretary Files, Lalgarh, Bikaner.
4. Mahakma Khas Records, Lalgarh, Bikaner.
5. Speech in Jublee Darbar, 1912.
6. Banquet Speech to Sardars of Bikaner, 1925.
7. Speech to Tazimi Sardars, 1928.

# Annexure 1

## Speech given by His Highness the Maharajah of Bikaner on the occasion of his being invested with ruling powers on the 16th December, 1898

*Mr. Martindale and gentlemen,*

I must first express my feeling of gratitude to His Excellency the Viceroy for the kind and cordial letter which has just been read. I wish to assure you that I will faithfully observe His Excellency's wishes, and accept the rules which the Government of India have laid down for my guidance. I hope that I do, and I believe that I do, thoroughly appreciate the responsibility and the magnitude of the work which from tomorrow will devolve upon me. It is more than 11 years since I succeeded my brother, and during these years, though at first but dimly, I have always been looking forward to this time with the resolution that when the Government of India should be pleased to entrust the ruling of this State to me, I would make every endeavour to do my duty well, that I would not look upon the people and the land as merely the sources of obtaining revenue, and that I would not devote that revenue entirely to my own gratification. I have a great love for my people and my country and, please God, I will do my duty by them. I would now like to express my gratitude to those who have befriended and helped me in the past. My thanks are chiefly due to Mr. C.S. Bayley and Colonel Vincent. I had hoped to have the pleasure of seeing Mr. Bayley here today, and I am very sorry he could not come, as he has always been the best of friends to me. To Colonel Vincent I owe all my happiness in every way. I shall never forget the deep affection and kindly interest which he has always felt for me, and it is most satisfactory to think that I shall be fortunate enough to have the pleasure and benefit of his advice for a long time to come. I must thank you most warmly, Mr. Martindale, for what you have said about Rajputs and their loyalty. I do appreciate so much what you have said about loyalty being two sided. I can assure you that whenever called upon I and my people will be ready, aye, more than ready, we shall be proud and happy, to fight side by side with England for the defence of the Indian Empire or wherever Her Majesty may want us. From this day to the end of my life it shall be my aim, all my heart shall be in it, to justifY the confidence in me which you have expressed.

# Annexure 2

## Speech delivered by His Highness the Maharajah on 30th November, 1901 at a dinner in honour of Sir Arthur Power Palmer, Commander-in-Chief

*Your Excellency, Lady Palmer, Ladies and Gentlemen,*

I do not wish to detain you by making a long speech but before proposing the health of my distinguished guests Sir Palmer and Lady Palmer I should like to thank them for the honour they have done me and my State by accepting my invitation to visit Bikaner.

The days have flown so quickly since their arrival that I feel as if it had only occurred yesterday.

It has been a great pleasure and a holiday to me and I only wish that they could have stayed here longer.

It was due greatly to your kind help Sir Power that I and my Regiment were allowed to go on active service to China and words cannot express how grateful we are to Your Excellency for the same. It was a terrible disappointment to us that we had no fighting and I hope that should occasion arise Your Excellency will not forget that we are always ready and keen to go to fight the enemies of Our Sovereign H.M. the King Emperor, to die in whose service—as we Rajputs say—would be envied by every one.

On this occasion I must by no means omit to gratefully acknowledge the friendly help and advice I have always received and the benefits derived by my Regiment from Col. Sir H. Melliss and Col. Stuart Beatson, the past and present Inspector General of the Imperial Service Troops and the various Inspecting officers and it is a great pleasure to us all to see my old friend Major Coran back again among us as our I.O.

I am very glad to welcome so many of my old friends to Bikaner on this occasion my only regret is that more of them could not come. I thank you all Ladies and Gentlemen for giving me the pleasure of your company here and will now ask you to join me in drinking the health of His excellency and Lady Palmer and in wishing them health, wealth and prosperity. I hope I may someday have the pleasure of again entertaining them in Bikaner.

# Annexure 3

**Speech given by Major H.H. the Maharajah of Bikaner, K.C.I.E. A.D.C. at the State Banquet given to Their Excellencies the Viceroy and Lady Curzon, the occasion of Their Excellencies' visit to Bikaner on Tuesday the 25th November, 1902**

*Your Excellencies, Ladies and Gentlemen,*

I cannot describe what real pleasure it gives me to-night in rising to propose the health of my distinguished guests, Their Excellencies the Viceroy and Lady Curzon, and to offer them a most hearty welcome to Bikaner, as having had the privilege of Their Excellencies acquintance since May 1899, and also the pleasure of enjoying their hospitality before now, it was my greatest desire that I should some day have the honour of entertaining them in my own Capital.

My hopes, which seemed likely to be realised during Your Excellency's proposed visit in 1899, were doomed to disappointment owing to the terrible Famine then prevailing, and we were afraid that on account of the Delhi Durbar Your Excellency might have to again postpone your tour through Rajputana this year. We are, therefore, more than pleased that, Your Excellency's long-looked for visit has come of f at last, and come off under happier circumstances than in 1899.

"Although my kind friend Lord Elgin, when he came here in 1896, to quote his own words, 'established a record by being the first Viceroy to visit Bikaner", Your Excellency is the first Viceroy to be received in Bikaner by its Maharaja with full ruling powers.

"It was when toasting Lord and Lady Elgin at the State Banquet here that I, with a full sense of the responsibility of my position, expressed a resolution to do my duty by my people and my country when I came of age, and I can conscientiously state that in the last four years, I have done my very best to fulfil that promise by carrying on the Bikaner administration in an honest and straight-forward manner, and in the best interests of my State and subjects.

"The encouragement which I have received at your Excellency's hands and the kindly interest you have been pleased to take in me and my State, prompt me, with Your Excellency's permission, to take this opportunity of briefly reviewing my administration since I assumed charge of the State on December 16, 1898.

"Barely six months after that, and before I had hardly time to gain much actual experience, I found myself confronted with one of the most severe famines that ever visited India, when measures were promptly taken to cope with it. But Bikaner and its people are more accustomed to scarcities than to bumper harvests which unfortunately are rare, and that is where, at such times, we are at an advantage compared to some other States, because the people here have a greater vitality in resisting such hardships, and one really good year enables them to pull through, perhaps, a couple of successive bad years. All the same, it cannot, of course, be said that the Famine did not leave its ill effects behind it, but I do think that the liberal treatment extended to the ryots in the way of revenue collections and the help given them by means of taccavi advances and otherwise is steadily improving their condition and although in the last, Census the total population of the State was found to have fallen from 8,32,000 to 5,84,627, it by no means indicates that so many people have perished, it being due to the majority of them having emigrated to and taken employment in more fertile lands. Emigration being considered an ordinary thing here in bad years, the people always returning to their villages after a few good seasons.

"It is an ill wind that blows no-body any good, and one good thing was that the famine brought me and my people in closer contact.

"To disgress for a moment, it was most pleasant for me to be the recipient of such hearty congratulations and sentiments of good, wishes and rejoicings, expressed by my people, not only in Bikaner, but throughout the districts, on the recent birth of my Son and Heir.

"Just as the famine was over I had the lively satisfaction of hearing that my offer to take my Regiment to China was accepted and I am extremely indebted to Your Excellency for allowing me to go in command of it.

"Bikaner is so situated that it is unhappily not possible to do much in the way of irrigation. There are two small canals in the State, but I regret, they have not proved successful so far, and the matter is being taken up. There is, also I believe, a possibility of bringing a good canal in, but this question I have no doubt will be taken fully into consideration by the Rajputana Irrigation Commission.

Your Excellency is forming this Commission has put as under a deep obligation.

"I had lately the great good fortune, through Your Excellency's kind of fices, to attend the Coronation of our Sovereign in England, when His Royal Highness the Prince of Wales did me the great honour of appointing me his AD.C., a privilege I value very much. My trip there has been a most interesting and enjoyable one and of great benefit to me in the future.

"Since my return, the Bikaner-Bhatinda Section of my Railway has been opened, thus directly connecting us with the Punjab. This has been followed by the usual advantages of opening up the country, and bringing down the prices of grain, &c. and as soon as possible we intend taking up another project now under consideration.

"The Palana Colliery, though, owing to the somewhat inferior quality of the coal, it has not yet found much outside market, is of great benefit to us locally for our electric light and for the railway and pumping engines, and it is hoped that gradually, now with the Bhatinda Section open, the coal will have a large sale.

"The financial condition of the State can fairly be said to be satisfactory, and we are, I am glad to say, free from debts other than the 12 lakhs kindly lent us by the Government of India for completing our Railway, and it was only the extra Famine expenditure which necessitated our borrowing.

"I have lately received permission to introduce, tentatively, a revised scheme of administration, which I hope will have the desired effect of bringing me in closer touch with the working of the State, and in the work being done in a prompt and more efficient manner.

"In concluding my remarks here on the administration, I should like to acknowledge, with hearty thanks, the support, and kind and friendly advice, I have always received from Your Excellency's Agent in Rajputana, the Honourable Mr. Martindale, who has happily been Agent to the Governor-General here, with only a short break since my attaining my majority.

"I have here, also to mention the name of Major Manners Smith, coupled with that of Major Minchin, whom I have found good friends and sympathetic advisers.

"I should further indeed be lacking in gratitude, if I forgot, at this moment, my best friend and late guardian, Mr. Brian Egerton, to whose attention and careful training I owe so much.

"It may not be out of place for me to bring to Your Excellency's notice here, that in commemoration of His Most Gracious Majesty the King-Emperor's Coronation, I am remitting a considerable amount of arrears of land revenue in the State.

"I need hardly assure Your Excellency of my loyalty to His Majesty, and that the services of myself and those of my Camel Corps are always at His Majesty's disposal, and I would earnestly beg that our services should be utilized in Somaliland.

"Your Excellency has given us a greater opening in accepting our offers of Imperial Service troops for active service outside India. In this and in the formation of the Imperial Cadet Corps., Your Excellency will have earned the undying gratitude, both of the present and the future generations of Rajputs.

"I am afraid that my speech has been a long one, but before resuming my seat, I should like to thank Your Excellencies for the honour you have done me by coming to Bikaner and to say how much Lady Curzon's presence here adds to the pleasure of welcoming you. I only wish Your Excellencies would have stayed on longer.

"It is now my pleasing duty to ask you, ladies and gentlemen, to raise your glasses to Lord and Lady Curzon of Kedleston, and to join me in drinking to Their Excellencies' long life, health and every success."

# Annexure 4

**Speech delivered by Major His Highness the Maharajah of Bikaner, K.C.S.I.-K. C.I.E.-A.D.C., at the Birthday Banquet at the Ganga Niwas Durbar Hall on Sunday, the 23rd October, 1904 :**

*Members of Council, Sirdars and Gentlemen,*

I rise to thank you heartily for the loyal manner in which you have just drunk my health and that of the Maharaj Kumar.

I am speaking at length on many important matters of State at the Durbar to be held shortly, but as the audience present here to-day is almost exclusively composed of Sirdars, I feel this would be a suitable occasion to speak on certain matters which closely concern the State and them.

In the last few years, I have had special opportunities of meeting you here on my Birthday and of again seeing many of you and your villages, & c., while out of tours, specially in the last cold weather, and I should like to express any gratification at the loyalty shown by the Sirdars, and at the manner in which they are discharging their duty to their Ruler and to their State.

But gentlemen, I regret extremely to have to notice that these harmonious relations are not without a discordant note. On an occasion like the present (Birthday rejoicings), I feel very loath to touch on a topic like this, but I am of opinion that it would be unwise were no notice taken of a matter which has been going on for the last 3 or 4 years, and I think the time has now come when this state of affairs should be exposed.

I have observed that each year when the Sirdars come in from the Districts for my Birthday celebrations, a strong attempt is made by a few of them (who shall be nameless) to instigate a large number of other Sirdars to start an opposition to the State. I am glad to see that these attempts have not been successful, but I mention this as a warning, lest such Sirdars may, through their ignorance, be drawn into the clique and thus cast a stain on the time-honoured loyalty of their families, while they would do absolutely no good to themselves, for I challenge anyone here to prove, to the satisfaction of all present, that they could in the end gain anything by going against the State.

Moreover, the Sirdars would be well advised if they carefully went into the alleged grievances of the people, who try to instigate them, when they will find that not only have they not got any real grievances, but that their actions are the out-come of mischievous intentions towards the State.

It is, I feel sure, not necessary for me to here speak to the Sirdars about their loyalty to the State and their Ruler and of the duty they owe to the State, to their Pattas, and to the people living in the latter, which none know better than the Sirdars themselves. The Council, in their excellent short speech when proposing my health, have admirably touched on the former.

The State, on the other hand, has also its duties to perform towards the Sirdars. It is keenly interested in their welfare and that of the people living in their Jagirs.

While the State cannot allow any of its rights to be encroached upon, it has not the slightest desire to deprive the Sirdars of any concessions or privileges, that have been granted to them by the State from time to time, so long as they are loyal to the State, and the conditions on which those grants were made are fully and faithfully carried out, or unless the Sirdars are bound, under an obligation, to give them up for any State purposes, works of public utility, or the like.

Only recently, the State gave a further concession to the Sirdars in the shape of grants on the occasions of marriages and deaths of some members of their families, which had not been allowed by the Council of Regency when the question of Rijh Bakhshish was originally settled. The State is providing the very best education for the young Nobles and thus giving the younger generation a splendid opportunity of taking part in the administration of their country at some future date, which is my earnest desire. The Court of Wards Department admirably manages the Jagirs of minor Sirdars, or of those who are incapable of managing them themselves and obtains the most favourable terms for clearing off heavy debts, which they would not obtain elsewhere, and hands back the Jagirs either free of debt, or, at any rate, with the burden greatly lightened.

It should be remembered that the State is responsible to the Government of India not only for the Khalsa or State land, but for the whole of the State, including Jagir villages, and the State, therefore, cannot allow, or shut its eyes to, any acts of oppression on the Ryots or such as would tend to ruin the Jagirs, and the Jagirdars must, in turn, be held responsible to the State. If any Sirdar or Sirdars consider that he or they have any grievances, let him or them come to the State and make their representations in due form and they may rest assured of a sympathetic hearing, but do not, let there be any underhand or disloyal dealings, agitations, and intrignes—as much out of keeping with the position of the Sirdars as with the dignity of the State to which they have the honour to belong.

I believe the alleged grievances of the Sirdars are mainly:

1. The realisation of Marriage Neota, and
2. The question of quarrying stone.

I cannot admit the validity of the first. The Neota cess is nothing unusual, having been levied from time immemorial. Indeed I should have imagined that, the Sirdars would have been grateful for the special leniency shown in the matter. For, although levied by the Council of Regency in November 1898, and temporarily postponed owing to a bad year, this had, till last year been deferred by me ever since my getting full powers in December 1898 for the same reasons. Considering the above, if a cess due full 7 years ago, the collection of which was generously delayed, is now being realised, I fail to see where the grounds for grievences, or highhanded action on the part of the State, come in.

The question of stone quarries is under consideration and I am looking into the matter very carefully and hope to be able to announce the decision of the State before long.

I have also heard of certain other points but it would be absurd to even talk of them as grievances considering they were settled some 20 years ago or so by the authorities concerned.

In conclusion, I would like to remind the Sirdars that the State has helped the Ryot greatly by the recent Revenue Remissions and I hope very much the Sirdars will also be able to see their way to giving similar concessions to the great benefit of all concerned.

# Annexure 5

## His Highness's Draft Speech at the Banquet to the Sardars on the 30th September, 1925

..............................

I do not ordinarily make a speech at this annual function which affords a special opportunity, to which I always look forward, of close personal intercourse with so many of my Chiefs and Nobles, whose well-being I always have so much at heart.

2. But tonight it is my pleasure to make two announcements which concern the Tazimi Sardars of the State.

3. You, the Tazimi Sardars of the State, are already in the enjoyment of high izzat and dignity and of the various privileges and rights which have from time to time been granted by the Rulers of this State as marks of their Royal favour or as rewards for gallantry displayed on the battle-fields, or in recognition of loyal and valuable services rendered at other times during the long and glorious history of our State.

4. It will be recalled that on the occasion of my Silver Jubilee over a decade ago, took the. opportunity vouchsafed to me by Providence of granting to you further privileges and boons; and at the Conference held in March 1921 I again summoned several Sardars with a view to ascertaining in what practical manner it was possible further to enhance your dignity or to remove any difficulties that you may still be experiencing as a result of which final decisions have already been arrived at on certain points and further action is being taken in regard to those still pending.

When it pleased the Almighty to bless me with a grandson about a year and a half ago, I desired to signalize the happy event by the grant to the Sardar of some further token of my favour, and I also consulted some of the more prominent Sardars who happened to be here at the time. But difficulties were experienced, since any other suitable means of enhancing their izzat were found hardly possible, and in fact that no new suggestions of any importance in other directions were made to me, is not really a matter for regret; for surely it testifies to the fact that not only is the State anxious as it has all along been to do everything reasonable—whether on its own initiative or on the suggestions of other responsible persons—to enhance the izzat and to add to the personal convenience of its Chiefs and Nobles but that everything possible, within the knowledge of the State, has already been done to this end.

6. There was, however, one question which I took up on that occasion relating to the honour, granted from time to time by the Ruler of the State, of the wearing of gold ornaments on the feet by the ladies of the families of certain Tazimi Sardars. It is unnecessary here to go into the circumstances and reasons for the wearing of gold being confined exclusively to those on whom such an honour was expressely conferred. But with a view to marking my appreciation of the loyalty and devotion to my Throne and Person of the Sardars as a body I came to the conclusion that the birth of the Bhanwar Sahib was a suitable occasion on which to confer this general honour on all ladies of the families of all the Tazimi Sardars in the same manner as I had previously conferred upon all Tazimi Sardars themselves and some of their male issue the honour of the wearing of gold on their feet.

7. But when I discussed the question further it appeared that some of the Sardars were under the impression that the wearing of gold on their feet by the ladies of the families of the Tazimi Sardars was a right already enjoyed by the whole Order of Tazimi Sardars. It will be apparent that it would have been absurd to grant as a new honour that which was already enjoyed as a right. On the other hand, since the Ruler of the State is universally held to be the fountainhead of all honour, and as it is his right and his prerogative to grant honour to all classes and creeds of his subjects, it would have been wrong for the State and its Ruler to renounce the right and prerogative of the Sovereign Ruler of the State or to detract from the value of such an honour or privilege by conceding a right which, on verification, might reveal not really to exist. The obvious need in the circumstances of further examination of this question therefore rendered it impossible for anything to be done in the matter at the time when some other announcements were made on the 1st May 1924, and I directed that the matter should be put up to me for final orders on my Birthday, some five months later. I had however, in the meanwhile proceeded to Europe on an Imperial Mission when I represented India, and particularly the Princes of India, at the Assembly of the League of Nations, and thus no Honours' Gazette was issued last year.

8. When I recently took up this question again, all doubts were laid finally at rest and it was conclusively proved without the least

room for any doubt or uncertainty that the wearing of gold ornaments on the feet by the ladies of the family of ant Tazimi Sardar is entirely dependent on the express grant of such an honour by the Ruler of the State.

9. It therefore, affords me pleasure in now commanding that henceforth in addition to the Thakuranis of all the Chiefs and Nobles upon whose ancestors, or upon whom themselves, this honour has already been conferred, all the Thakuranies, and Daughters, Takai Kumranis, and the wives of the Tikai grandsons of all Tazimi Sardars, shall be entitled to the honour of wearing gold ornaments on their feet; and also the wives of the younger sons, so long as and until their husbands live with the Tazimi Sardar. As regards however the wearing of jewelled ornaments on the feet, the matter is different and, in accordance with the advice tendered to me by all concerned who have been consulted in the matter, it has been decided that the present procedure should be maintained and that jewelled ornaments can only be worn on the feet when such an honour has been expressly granted by the Ruler of the State.

10. I trust that the grant of this general honour to the entire order of Tazimi Sardars will be a further source of gratification to the Chiefs and Nobles and their families.

11. The other announcement that I wish to make tonight relates to the question of pensions and gratuities for such Chiefs and Nobles as are in the permanent service of the State. I have had a search made, but so far no papers bearing definitely on this particular point have been forthcoming. In accordance, however, along with the practice which has grown up of calling their emoluments honorarium, I understand that the service of such Tazimi Sardars have been so far deemed to be ineligible for purposes of pension or gratuity. Anyhow I have directed that all Chiefs and Nobles as well as any other Non-Tazimi Jagir village holders who enter the permanent Service of the State, shall be entitled to the benefits of pension and gratuity to which the other State servants are ordinarily entitled according to the rules in force for the time being.

12. We want as many of you, Sardars of the State, as are qualified to come forward and enter the State Service out of patriotism for your country, loyalty for your Ruler and the desire to serve your country and your fellow-subjects and country-men. Nobody can have a greater interest or stake in the State and there is plenty of room in the State in the various branches of the State administration and in the various grades of the State Service. The interests of the State and of yourselves are really identical and will be more and more so in the difficult

times ahead. In the State and its Ruler on the one hand and the Chiefs and Nobles and the Thikana on the other being strongly united instead of divided in their closest cooperation and mutual trust and confidence, as also in their united strength lies the strength of the State and the well-being of all classes and communities including the Chiefs and Nobles. Times have changed and are changing, and many of the States as well as their feudatories will at no very distant date have to face a situation which will very closely concern them both. I am not a pessimist, but anyone who looks ahead or who studies what is happening in British India and what is being said about the future of the States by certain schools of political thought in British India will have no difficulty in appraising the future situation which is bound to arise one day. Enough harm has been done in many States through dissension and suspicion. We have no aggressions or hostile designs on people outside our State, but we are entitled to take every reasonable precaution and measure which lies within our power for the preservation under God's providence of our State and heritage which our ancestors have built and handed down to us at no small sacrifice of blood and treasure. The relations of my Government with my feudatories have, I am happy to feel, never been more cordial than they are now, see to it, Sardars of the State, that such relations are not only maintained but daily strengthened and even improved where possible. Wake up Sardars and unite with the State in the preservation of our rights and holdings, so that we may, please God, have the satisfaction not only of handing them unimpaired to our successors, but that we may also be able to feel that by our own efforts and acts we have been able, under divine assistance and guidance, to render secure all that we hold for our children's children.

13. I will take this opportunity of speaking on one or two other subjects which are of interest to the Tazimi Sardars.

14. I referred in the earlier portion of my speech to some matters which were discussed at the Sardars' Conference in 1921, regarding which final decisions have already been arrived at, and about some of which further action is still being taken.

15. First and foremost, I will mention the Sardars Advisory Committee which I had in my speech on that occasion announced my intention of establishing. This has now received my final sanction and the rules and regulations relating to its being brought into being and its functions and powers, which will . . . of a purely advisory and consultative nature, will be made known to you in due course.

16. The Tazimi Sardars' Advisory Committee will consist of six Members, three elected by the Sardars and three to be nominated by

me, and there will also be a President of this Committee who will be nominated by me either from amongst its six Members or in addition to them. For the present, at any rate, I have decided that the same three members who are returned by you to the Legislative Assembly shall be the elected Members of the Advisory Committee, since those whom you elect for membership of the Legislative Assembly must be Sardars who possess your confidence and are best qualified to represent your interests. In regard to the nominated Members of the Advisory Committee, there will be a bigger scope for me to select from, in that some of the Sardars who sit in the Legislative Assembly as Members of my Government will also be eligible to give us the benefit of their experience and advice.

17. I hope things will be sufficiently advanced to enable a meeting of this Advisory Committee to be convened by my, Government about the time of the next session of the Legislative Assembly, which has been fixed for the 18th December, 1925.

18. There is, I am sorry to find, one matter which, for one reason or other, has unavoidably been delayed now for a considerable period, and that is in regard to the request preferred by the Sardars regarding help from the State in the realization of demands from Chhut-bhais and agriculturiests. The file relating to this matter was specially entrusted, at the request of the Sardars, to Mr. Rudkin; but there are certain details in this connection which require further consideration and decision. In order to place these points clearly and frankly before you, the Revenue Minister proposes to convene a meeting tomorrow after-noon at 3-00 P.M. which, besides Mr. Rudkin, will consist of :

1. The Raja of Mahajan.
2. The Thakur of Jassana.
3. The Thakur of Sandwa.
4. The Thakur of Sattasar.
5. The Thakur of Bagseu.
6. The Thakur of Sinjguru.
   and two other Sardars, who should be selected and deputed by you.
7. Lala Raj Kanwar.

I will not detain you by dealing at length with each of the other remaining points. I wish it had been possible for the necessary details connected with such questions, which are still pending, to have been disposed of earlier. They had received the considered attention of my Ministers and of the Council and had also been dealt with in an active and sympathetic manner by the Maharaj Kumar as Chief Minister. But the further delay in the issue of final orders on the subject is ascribable to two reasons. One of these is my pre-occupations on more urgent matters which have in recent years demanded my attention as well as to my prolonged indisposition shortly after the last Sardar's Conference, as also to my absences from India on Imperial Missions, &c. Another contributory cause has been that until recently the practice in force did not permit of the energies and attention of any single whole time Minister being devoted to such important affairs connected with the Sardars of the State, in regard to which I have some further observations to make. Had it been so these matters would have been dealt with more expeditiously and with greater thoroughness.

I will, however, first add that every one of these points was again fully gone into by me today with the Members of my Government and I have returned such pending files to the Council for completing at an early date all that remains to be done before final orders can be issued.

21. And this brings me to a matter of no small importance to the State as well as to the Sardars, on which I desire expressly to touch tonight. Just before I had to proceed to Europe last year a redistribution of the business of the Government of our State amongst the different Departments and under the various portfolios was effected and the business relating to the Tazimi Sardars, Bhogtas and Chhutbhais etc. of the State was placed under the Foreign and Political Minister. This was entirely in the best interests of the Sardars themselves and I had hoped that the advantages accruing from such an arrangement would be at once appreciated and gratefully recognised by all of you. But it was with no small surprise and concern that I heard a few weeks ago from an influential and important Member of your Order that some anxiety was entertained by some of the Sardars in regard to this arrangement.

22. It would, therefore, perhaps be as well in attempt tonight briefly to make the situation quite clear to you all, in the hopes that all anxiety and suspicions for which there is of course, not the slightest ground, will be definitely laid at rest. The deep and sympathetic interest which I take in all matters relating to my Chiefs and Nobles and my great personal solicitude in their welfare and in the well-being of their Thikanas is, I trust, sufficiently known, and it is because of these reasons and because of the importance which I and my Government attach to everything relating to the Sardars being dealt with in as sympathetic and satisfactory a manner as possible that after my

assuming the administration of the State I myself for some time retained direct charge of such work. It is, however, difficult for the Ruler of the State to find the necessary time and attention for such work, and when the next redistribution of business took place in 1910 this work was placed under the then senior Member of Council, my Cousin, Maharaj Sir Bhairun Singhji Bahadur. In 1917 the business of the Sardars was placed under the portfolio of the Political Department and the same and nothing new was therefore, done when it was again placed under the portfolio of the Foreign & Political Department last year.

23. There is much work which is not strictly connected with the terms—"Foreign and Political" which, according to the present distribution, is also under the portfolio of the Foreign & Political Minister, amongst which I might cite as examples all work relating to local self-government, Municipalities and Panchayats, the Legislative Department including enactments and all work connected with the Legislative Assembly, the preparation and publication of annual administration reports, and so on.

24. I trust therefore, that every Tazimi Sardar of the State, and indeed all concerned, will rest fully assured that the arrangement of placing of the affairs relating to the Sardars under the portfolio of the Foreign & Political Department was made entirely in the interests of the Sardars themselves. In the first place, it should be understood that the arrangement of portfolios and the distribution of work to the various Ministers of the State is a matter of pure administrative convenience and one with which only the Government are concerned. But in this particular instance I felt that some improvement was necessary in the former system under which the important work relating to the Sardars—important both to the State and to the Sardars—important both to the State and to the Sardars—was dealt with, specially in the last 15 years or so. It was never intended that the Minister concerned to whom the work of theSardars was entrusted should merely dealt with comparatively trifling matters such as applications for leave or summoning them to Bikaner on the occasion of the Dasehra and of my Birthday etc. or with such other purely ceremonial or formal matters. The Minister and Department responsible for seeing to the work connected with the Tazimi Sardars was, of course, intended to deal with far more important matters relating to the izzat, and privileges of the Sardars, to disputes between the various Sardars and to the other important matters relating to their successions, etc. But as it happened, practically all such work was recall dealt with my Departments other than that under whose

portfolio the work relating to the Sardars was actually shown in the distribution of business. As I considered that this was unsatisfactory and as whenever the Sardars came here to my Birthday or when I was on tour, they were frequently preferring various requests relating to the affairs of their Thikanas in which they wanted my help, but in regard to which there was no one officer to whom they could go for assistance and advice in such matters I felt that it was best to entrust all these duties to one whole time Minister, viz., the Foreign & Political Minister, and I am convinced that, when the system has been given full and fair trial under the capable charge of Lala Rajkanwar, it will prove satisfactory not only to myself and the State but also to all of you Sardars.

25. In the meanwhile I and my Government have not lost sight of the fact that a certain amount of administrative inconvenience to the Government and doubtless some inconvenience to yourselves has been caused during the period of transition between the issue of such orders and the settling of certain necessary details in regard to what work will still continue to be dealt with by the Revenue Department which it was found most convenient to all concerned to have dealt with in the past by that Department. The matter is engaging the attention of my Government, and I hope that further orders in regard to all such outstanding details will be issued before long, which will tend to the greater facility of all concerned.

# Annexure 6

**Speech delivered to the Tazimi Sardars of the State by His Highness the Maharajah on the 30th October, 1928, at Lallgarh.**

*Sardars,*

The following was the speech which I intended delivering at the Banquet given to you on the 28th October but which I was unable to deliver on account of downpour of rain.

2. After my speech at the Banquet given by you on the night of the 27th I will allude tonight only to one particular matter.

3. It concerns the Izzat and dignity of the Chiefs and Nobles of the States, which, as I have said before, I always regard as my own Izzat and dignity, and which I am ever solicitous of safeguarding as far as lies in my power, and which no Ruler who aspires to a reputation for greatness or being just could in honour or equity disregard. For the rest, the maintenance of your position and Izzat lies largely in your own hands.

4. When I look around me today and see, alas! so many young faces, I wonder how many of the Sardars present here tonight really know the history of the so-called grades into which the Tazimi Sardars of the State were divided during the period of my minority by the Council of Regency by a Circular order dated the 15th May, 1889 and how many understand the significance of the departure thus made by the Council of Regency or realize some of the anomalies that have crept into such gradation; and, above all, I wonder how many are aware of the fact that this gradation does not correctly represent the rank proper of the various Chiefs and Nobles of the State. Along with other important States in Rajputana there never existed in Bikaner, till 1889 any such grades into which the Sardars were divided:

1st Grade
2nd Grade
3rd Grade
and 4th Grade

nor was there really any necessity for doing so. Such a gradation was made by the Council of Regency for the sole purpose of regulating the grant of Parwarish to Tazimi Sardar on occasion of births, marriages, and deaths in their families.

5. From a perusal of the file I find that on the 30th August, 1886, the State Executive Council made a submission to His Highness the Late Maharajah stating that they experienced difficulties in dealing with applications for the grant of Parwarish to the various Tazimi Sardars and making recommendations that grades, together with amounts to be granted in Parwarish to such Sardars of the proposed different grades should be fixed. As was to be expected from a wise Ruler whose Reign will be memorable for the attention he paid to such matters as the prerogative of the State and its Ruler and the rank and dignity of the Sardars, His Late Highness declined to accept the recommendation of the State Council; and in the orders passed on the file by His Late Highness it was recorded that to grant, or not to grant, or to make any increase or decrease in, such Parwarish to the Sardars depended solely on the pleasure of His Highness the Maharajah and that as such grants could not be claimed or demanded as a right by any of the Sardars, it was unnecessary to frame any Rules or scale of Parwarish and that the old procedure should remain in force intact.

6. But the question was again taken up at a later date by the Council of Regency, for whom in justification it can be said that they did undoubted experience difficulty in sanctioning such Parwarish grants during the period of my minority. Although the Recenty Administration apparently tried to acquaint themselves with the different kinds of Tazim Conferred upon the Sardars, it is obvious that they did not succeed in making such gradation—made, as I have already said, only for purposes of the grant of Parwarish on a strict consideration of the Dolri or higher grade of Tazim, and the Ikolri and the other kinds of Tazim, enjoyed by the Sardars. And thus it came to pass that, whilst the placing of the four Sirayats alone in the 1st grade of Tazimi Sardars coincided with actual facts and past procedure, the placing of the various Sardars in the 2nd, 3rd and 4th grades did not conform strictly to the different kinds of Tazim, which they actually enjoyed at that time.

7. Now, after the lapse of nearly 40 years since this new system of gradation was made, it is not surprising that many persons even of this State and including several of the Sardars themselves, should, erroneously, look upon the different grades as actually representing the difference in the rank and dignity of the various Sardars, or that

the fact is often lost sight of that the Council of Regency, as I have said more than once tonight, had made this gradation merely for purposes of regulating grants for Parwarish. I have, therefore, for some years past been anxious that we should revert to the procedure in force up to the time of, and even a little after, the demise of His late Highness, so that by the kind of Tazimi enjoyed by the various Sardars of the State, their respective rank and dignity could at once be known to every one—and known correctly. I however could not, to my regret, find the time for going into this important matter till a few months ago; and after carefully persuing the old records and after an exhaustive examination of the details, I have come to the following decisions, which I have commanded shall come into force at once and which shall govern the future practice and procedure in our State:

1. that all the four grades into which the Tazimi Sardars were divided by the Council of Regency for purpose of Parwarish shall be abolished forth with;
2. that the scale of Parwarish shall remain as now in force, it being noted that Parwarish cannot be claimed as a right by any one and that the grant of Parwarish is entirely dependent on the pleasure and prerogative of the Sovereign Ruler of the State;
3. that henceforth, as in the past, the name of the Sardars will be entered according to the kind of Tazim which they may have had the honour of having conferred, or which may hereafter be conferred, upon them by the Ruler of the State in the exercise of his sovereign powers and pleasure;
4. that the following are, have been and shall remain, the various kinds of Tazim enjoyed by the various Chiefs and Nobles of the Bikaner State:

   i. Dolri (or double) Tazim or those who enjoy the honour of HAT RO QURB
   ii. Ikolri (or single) Tazim or those who enjoy the honour of BANV PASAV.
   iii. Other Tazims.

8. Amongst those who enjoy the highest class of Tazim, i.e., HAT RO QURB or the Dolri Tazim, stand today, as they have done throughout the past centuries, the 4 Sirayats of the State:

The Raja of Mahajan, the Premier Chief of the State; and then

come next in rank and precedence:
The Thakur of Bidasar, and The Rawat of Rawatsar who are of equal rank and have one and the same seat in Durbars.
and The Rao of Bhukarka, the second Bikha Chief amongst the Sirayats.

9. Amongst those next in rank also enjoying the Dolri Tazim or the HAT RO QURB, it is my pleasure to promote some Sardars who have till now been included in the Ikolri Tazim; and when the list is read out today after my speech of the Sardars enjoying various kinds of Tazmins, the names will also be announced of those whom I have honoured by promotion to the Dolri Tazim.

10. I hope you will bear in mind that the time at our disposal so far has not permitted to all the names being entered in the list in strict order of precedence and I hope that no Sardar will feel, if his name is not in the correct place, that he is in any way being degraded, or put below those who are admittedly his juniors in rank.

11. Then though there are happily some very few cases of their disputes between Tazimi Sardars as regards rank and precedence; and it is my hope and desire that, as far as possible, such disputes should be settled in a manner which will prove honourable to the disputants on both sides; and in this connection, I should very much like to help you, Sardars, who have such disputes by landing you my good offices if I can enable you to come to any settlement or compromise which whilst, as I have said, being honourable to all concerned, would at the same time put an end, in I hope the grant majority of the cases, to the various difficulties which the disputants experience at present. It will be obvious to you all that in the ordinary course the attendance of Sardars at Durbars as feudatories of the State—GADI-RA-TABEDAR is obligatory, and that the State cannot allow any Sadar to raise unfounded or false claims of dispute about rank and thus to stay away from the Karan Mahal. For it follows that the splendour of the Durbar depends on the attendance thereat of as large a number of its Sardars and Feudatories as possible. Thus, when a Noble is so ill-advised to aspire by false pretensions to a rank higher than he really and actually enjoys, the State is compelled to intervene and to adjudicate on the point and to give a decision and to insist on the attendance at Durbars and other functions of any such admittedly junior Sardar and on his sitting or standing below a Sardar unquestionably his senior. A case in point was the false, foolish and astounding claim made by the Ex—Rawat of Rawatsar who claimed at least equality with, and even hinted at seniority over, the

Chiefs of Mahajan who, for all these centuries and for 19 generations, have enjoyed undisputed honour and dignity as Premier Nobles of our State.

12. At the same time, there are a few—happily a very few-cases, where it may be really difficult if not impossible correctly to gauge any difference in rank between two disputants, and where, after a strict and imperial consideration of the merits and claims of the case, the Ruler of the State may not be able to gauge who exactly is the senior. Where the two disputants are undoubtedly equal in rank, it has never been the policy of my Ancestors in the State, nor is it the policy of myself or my Government to coerce them to attend the Durbar or to make one sit below the other, or to make an unjust and indivious distinction of seniority and juniority where no such seniority or juniority can really be said to exist. Some of the disputant Sardars have in the past made amicable settlements between themselves which the State has recognized, of attending Durbars in turns, whilst some cases still remain unsettled and uncompromised. In regard to such Sardars, who are admittedly of an equal rank, and who have one and the same seat, I would like you Sardars to consider a suggestion and I wish to make it clear that it is only a suggestion and not in any way my order and that I am putting forward this suggestion with the sole object of helping you to arrive at a decision satisfactory to you both.

13. There are one or two ways of setting such disputes:

1. that, where such Sardars are of an indisputably equal rank, they should agree voluntarily amongst themselves to take precedence, for the time being, one below the other according to the date of their succeeding to the Gadies of their Thinkanas;
2. the other alternative would be again by a mutual compromise, to settle one Sardar taking precedence over the other according to seniority or age.

14. I wish to make it clear that there will be no compulsion used by the State in any such matters of equal rank; but I would also like to make it clear that by the two suggestions have made, no one Sardar of equal rank would, for all time, become senior or junior to the other; and that thus both such Sardars would still continue to enjoy the same rank and still to maintain, and to have, the same sent in Durbar. For, it follows that no one can live for ever in this world. There will thus be periods during which the two disputants according to the ate of their succession—which is, perhaps a better solution of the two—or according to age, will, during their life-time, by a

compromise, be sitting one above the other; but as I have said, they would still be of the same rank; and they would still have the same sent in Durbar and the Sardar of the other Thikana will, some time or other, also his turnof seniority.

15. If I can, during my life-time, help you in solving these difficulties and arriving at such compromises, it will be a matter of great satisfaction to me.

# 2

## *Initiation of Early Administrative Reforms—The Establishment of Board of Revenue and Related Reforms*

THE EARLY YEARS OF the reign of Maharaja Ganga Singh had been significant enough as they contained promise of the genius that was to flourish in the later years. Honours from the crown were also not lacking with the appointment of Maharaja Ganga Singh as Gazetted Honorary Major (Youngest Major at that time in British Army) and the award of Kaiser-i-Hind Gold Medal (1900). In 1901, he was honoured with Knight Commander of the Indian Empire and shortly afterwards appointed as Honorary A.D.C. to the Prince of Wales in 1907. It was upon his return from the coronation of King Edward VII in England that Ganga Singh Ji came to grips with administrative problems and initiated reforms from within. The young Maharaja was convinced that the Regency administration would have to go or be altered drastically if a modern state of Bikaner was to emerge. After 1898 the Regency Council had been converted into State Council and continued to exercise the powers it had enjoyed earlier on—a situation that caused great administrative confusion. The Maharaja was also quick to grasp the fact that individual Members of Council of the Dewan functioned arbitrarily in many matters as their powers were not suitably defined. Responsibility could not be fixed for administrative failures or short comings. He was not keen to act as a mere figure head while the Dewan exercised the actual power. It was with this in view that Ganga Singh Ji embarked on an ambitious programme of Secretariat reforms and reorganisation. He desired the following changes:

i. libration of the Maharaja from departmental administration to enable him to concentrate on policy implementation.
ii. definite powers to Secretaries working directly under the Maharaja.

iii. the transformation of the Secretariat into an efficient instrument for the initiation and execution of the durbar's policy.

As the process of administrative reforms continued, the Mahkma Khas was constituted as the Central Secretariat. The post of Dewan or Prime Minister was abolished. The Maharaja was convinced that more often than not the loyalty of the Dewan was suspect as he tended to look to appease and favour the Political Agent more. As expected the Political Agent did not view these proposed changes with favour as they tended to erode his authority and influence, but concurred reluctantly and with poor grace. The first cabinet consisted of the following:

Maharaja Bhairon Singh Ji (Secretary, Foreign and Political Department)
Raja Hari Singh Ji (Secretary, Public Works and Railway Department)
Mr. Rustomji Cooper (Secretary, Medical and Jail Department)
Kanwar Prithwi Raj Singh (Secretary, Military Department)

The Police and Education Departments were placed under a Home Secretary.

It was also felt that a complete overhaul of the administrative system was not possible until Judical and Revenue Departments were not reorganized to meet the needs of the changing times.

**The Establishment of The Board of Revenue**

Matters pertaining to Revenue Affairs had always been a high priority zone for Ganga Singh Ji. Relentless pursuit of reforms in this area led to the creation of the Board of Revenue in 1910 the year of other major administrative reforms and innovations as well. The Maharaja attached great importance to the establishment of the Board of Revenue and he went to the extent that he addressed senior functionaries in the Council Chamber on August 1, 1910 explaining the full impact of the purported changes (No. 1). The Maharaja was hopeful that the benefits of the new dispension would be viable within six months of its announcement. The Board of Revenue, it was envisaged, would also lead to administrative changes in Revenue administrative machinery below the Mahakma Khas.

The Board of Revenue had to have under it crucial departments like Land Revenue, Customs and Excise, Court of Wards, Stamp and

Registration, Municipalities, Cattle Pounds and Settlement Operations. It was also felt that the creation of the Board would lessen the burden on the Revenue Member and the Maharaja himself. The Maharaja proposed that the Revenue Member of the Council was to function as the President of the Revenue Board who would have under his control three very important ministries led by senior and seasoned administrators. Thakur Sadul Singh was made the Head of the Revenue Department and was to function as one of the three ministers, the other two being Babu Sheo Ghulam and Mr. Lajorie who were respectively the Inspector General of Customs and Excise and President of the Bikaner Municipal Board. The fifth member was to be appointed at a later date though for the time being Mr. K. Rustomji, the Maharaja's Private Secretary was made a Honarary Member of the Board. Babu Chowharji Prasad was to act as Secretary of the Board of Revenue. The Maharaja was at pains to impress that the creation of the Board of Revenue was in no means an attempt to detract from the individual duties, authority and responsibilities of the Revenue Member of Council who would continue and remain the Chief and Central Revenue Authority of the State. Thus it would seem that the Maharaja, while establishing the Board of Revenue, was committed to harmoneous relations at various level of revenue administration.

The latter part of The Maharaja's speech was devoted to the conduct of Business Rules and Powers and Duties of the Board of Revenue. One of the most important duties of the Board, which was specially cited in the speech, was the selection and recommendations for various posts of Nazims, Tehsildars and Naib-Tehsildars on whose talent and capabilities the well being of the State and subjects largely rested.

In the same year 1910, the Maharaja delivered another major speech on 29th September, 1910 at a Durbar held at the Lallgarh Palace, highlighting the sucess of reforms already undertaken since 1898 and those projected to be undertaken or initiated from 1st October, 1910. (No. 2). The Maharaja expressed satisfaction that despite deep-rooted conservatism and opposition to any change, the State had made progress in the field of administrative reforms. The results were eloquent testimony to the efficasy of the changing times. Those who oposed changes did so on basis of dishonest motives, it was pointed out. The Maharaja also declared on that occasion that certain measures, if carried out in the interests of the subjects and the State, could also overrule public sentiment as it was based more on sentiment and less on logic. By 1910 the ruler was able to report progress in various fields enumerated below:

(a) In the Revenue Department large number of Kutcha and Pucca wells were dug for facilitating irrigation and Taccari advances or loans without interest were made to those who wanted to start cultivation in hitherto barren fields. Thus between 1898 and 1910 the area under Rabi cultivation had gone up from 1,12,398 bighas to 9,87,764 bighas. Remission of arrears totalling Rs. 7,57,414 was also recorded. At the sametime the settlement of the State was also keeping pace with other similar reforms.

(b) Under guidence of an expert in Customs and Excise matters, Mr. J.H. Cox, a new amalgamated department of Customs and Excise under the charge of a Gazetted Inspector General was created and the appointment was filled by Babu Sheo Ghulam. The issue of privileges enjoyed by Rajvis and Pattedars in these matters was also resolved to the general satisfaction of all parties.

(c) The Municipal Act was revised and updated and new District Municipalities were set up. Colonel Wake, the tutor of the elder Maharaj Kumar, was asked to take up charge as President of the Municipal Board.

(d) In the field of irrigation the Government of India had assured of supply of more water to the Ghaggar Canals. The assistance from Government of India was assured for the construction of a large canal from river Sutlez.

(e) The financial report card of the State made interesting reading. At the death of Maharaja Dungar Singh Ji in 1887 the income of StatewasaroundRs.16,15,319. During the first twelve years of the reign of Gariga Singh Ji the annual income of the State rose to Rs 40 lakhs by 1910 thanks to sound administrative initiatives. The Maharaja also explained that the rise in income was also attributed to ethical Principles and methods adopted rather than recourse to questionable means.

(f) The famine years' memory was slowly receding and thanks to a humanitarian administration and adequate monsoon in the following years, the prosperity level of the people and State was returning. According to the census of 1901 the population of the State during the hard times had come down to 5,84,627 from 8,31,955 of pre-famine years. The trend fortunately had been reserved and people who had emigrated from the State were returning in adequate numbers.

(g) The Public Works Department was one of the most active department. The following buildings and offices were constructed by the Department which was an indication of an vibrant economy recovering from stagnation.

| | Construction Work | Cost (in Rupees) |
|---|---|---|
| (i) | Mahakma Khas office | 52,331 |
| (ii) | Walter Nobles' School Building | 35,728 |
| (iii) | Prince of Wales Hall | 69,726 |
| (iv) | Victoria Memorial Club (partly raised by subscription) | 1,50,508 |
| (v) | Renovation & repair of old forts and Palaces | 50,508 |
| (vi) | Central Electric Station | 85,822 |

Also in various stages of construction and completion were the Dungar Memorial College Building (Rs. 125,000), Customs office (Rs. 25,000), Pucca Barracks for Ganga Risala(Rs. 167,698) and the magnificient temples of Raj Ratan Biharji and Rasik Siromaniji.

Pucca roads were also constructed and their network extended to cover 60 miles. An attempt was also made to link the city with important religious centres and centres of business and commerce.

(h) An initial amount of Rupees one and a half lakhs was sanctioned for introduction of new water supply scheme-boon for the subjects of a desert State. A large and updated Electric Installation helped to light up the roads and this benefit was soon to be extended in the shape of City Lighting Scheme. Telephone links were established between all major offices and residences which greatly enhanced the working of the State administration. The above works were carried out at the cost of Rs. 4,89,713.

(i) The Maharaja was fully alive to the importance of the growth of the Railway net work within the State and outside. At the time of his assumption of full powers, the total milage was around 86 and by 1910 it had gone upto 307. The completion of the Railway link upto Hissar would increase the Railway mileage by another 82 miles, it was announced.

(j) The achievements of the Ganga Risala in China were already legendary and a new Infantry Regiment called Sadul Light Infantry came into being. The army morale, after successes abroad, was rated very high. Around the sametime the entire Police Department was reorganised and under MunshiSadiq Ali, the Inspector General of Police, and serious crime became virtually non-existant.

Education and Judiciary were also mentioned in the speech but will be subject of discussion elsewhere.

Towards the conclusion of his marathan speech, the Maharaja declared that since 1902, Members of Council were also Secretances on the Executive side of the administration and henceforth from October 1910 they would be styled as Members only in charge of their respective portfolios. Thus the major departments were headed by Foreign Member, Revenue Member, Public Works Member and Home Member respectively. It was not deemed necessary to have a Military Member and Kamdar Prithviraj Singh continued to be styled Secretary for the Military Department in the Mahakma Khas. Around the sametime the work and duties of these Members were redistributed to make the administration more effective.

## References

1. Pannikar, K.M. : His Hghness THE MAHARAJA OF BIKANER, Oxford, 1935.
2. "Four Decades of Progress in Bikaner", A State publication, Bikaner,1937.
3. Report on the Administration of Bikaner for 1926—1927.
4. Karni Singh, The Relations of the House of Bikaner with Central Powers, Delhi, 1974.
5. Maharaja Ganga Singh: Speeches on the occasion of the Coming of age of the Heir-apparant.
6. Speech on the Inauguration of the Board of Revenue, 6th September, 1910.

# Annexture 1

## The Bikaner State Rajpatra

*Published by Authority*

**Bikaner, Tuesday, 6th September, 1910**

**Speech delivered by Colonel H.H. the Maharajah of Bikaner, G.C.I.E., K.C.S.I., A.D.C., on the Occasion of the Inaugration of the Board of Revenue, Bikaner State, on the 1st of August, 1910.**

*Members of Council, and Gentlemen,*

I have summoned you all to the Council Chamber to-day to announce an important—and what I earnestly hope and pray will also be a most beneficial reform. I refer to the creation of the "Board of Revenue" to control and deal with matters connected with the Revenue Administration of the State.

2. First of all, however, I should like to briefly touch upon certain important questions which have been occupying my earnest attention for some time past and then I propose to go into some details regarding the Board of Revenue which I shall have the pleasure of inaugurating to-day.

3. Ordinarily it would have sufficed to have published the orders and the Rules of the Revenue Board and to have notified its constitution in the State Rajpatra; but for one thing I was anxious to take you all into my confidence at the earliest possible opportunity and to give you some idea, as far as I can at this early stage—specially in view of the wild rumours and unfounded gossip which on all such occasions unfortunately run riot in the City—of the big Changes that are imminent and which I hope will before long be introduced to further reorganize the Administration of the State, and I am in hopes that through you these facts will become known to a much wider audience and particularly to the officials of all the State Departments both at the Capital and in the Districts as well as to the people of the State. In the second place I am desirous of expounding the policy of

the Durbar to the Members whom I wish to personally instal on the Board and who will from this day onward assume their onerous and very responsible duties.

4. I have considered the institution of the Board of Revenue such a very important and urgent matter that I decided that it should not be postponed a day longer than is necessary. My Council and I have of late been busily occupies with settling all the necessary details in connection therewith, which will shortly be read out to you and about which—as I said a little while ago—I shall have something more to say later on. The Board will be passing through a more or less experimental stage for the first few months. That is bound to succeed and that both the State and my subjects will derive manifold and greater advantages than they do now, I have not the least doubt about. But at the same time it is only to be expected that after the Board has had some practical experience of its work and duties, some changes will be found to be necessary. These we should be able to deal with before the end of the present official year or within some 6 months or so at the outside. Till then the Rules we have drafted must obviously be more or less provisional.

5. It is not difficult to foresee that as a sequel to the creation of the Board of Revenue there will be some significant changes in the Revenue administrative machinery below the Mahkma Khas. These are being duly considered and will in all probability come into force from the first October next.

6. I hope to be able about that time to also provide the public with an improved Judicial administration which will be done by the establishment of an independent Chief Court. I will reserve fuller details for another occasion but I might perhaps mention here that the proposal is to have three judges including a Chief Judge and to make the Chief Court the highest Judicial Tribunal in the State under its Ruler.

7. This while not revolutionizing the present judicial system of the State will of course entail some alterations in the existing courts. The Council to whom I am grateful for having so far exercised the functions of the Chief Court when they were so busy with other administative work, will then be able to still more closely associate themselves with the administration of the State-their legitimate sphere of work. This has for long been my desire for I felt that hitherto the Members of Council owing to the dual nature of their task have not been able to give me all the assistance and co-operation which I require from them.

8. In consequence of this, and as often happens when any scheme

has worked for some time—as the present Mahkma Khas administration scheme has done for some 8 years—some further reforms have become necessary though no radical or very great changies are anticipated in this connection.

9. Some improvements in, and reorganisation of , the Customs and Excise Departments and in the Municipalities of the State and specially at the Capital are also under my consideration about which orders will, I hope, be issued before long. I intend to convene a big Durbar at the end of the present official year when I propose announcing all these important reforms and changes. By that time all the details will have been worked out and sanctioned by me when they will also be made public.

10. To return to the business of the day. The Board of Revenue is being constituted with the objects of providing better and more efficient supervision and control of , and the quicker despatch of work connected with, the Revenue administration of the State and will have under it the important departments of Land Revenue, Customs and Excise, Court of Wards, Stamp and Registration, Municipalities and Cattle Pounds and also Settlement whenever Settlement operations will be in progress. It should also prove to be of the greatest adminiatrative convenience as the creation of the Board will lead to more decentalization of work whereby I myself and the Revenue Member will be relieved of a considerable amount of unnecessary references and work. For instance it is estimated that out of 73 classes of references and cases which hitherto were submitted to me by the Revenue Member, only 11 in future will come to me and the rest will be disposed of by the Board presided over by the Revenue Member. The Revenue Member in his turn, by the arrangements already made and by those now being made will find similar relief I need not enumerate the decided advantages of such a relief to us from such routine matters, and the advantages to the State and to the people of our having more time to spare to consider and formulate more important measures and schemes cannot be over-rated. At the same time it need not be apprehended that already hard worked Heads of departments will have their labours unnecessarily extended. The mere fact of their being able to deliberate and confer at such meetings and discussing important proposals and schemes connected with the various departments and of thinking out and deciding upon new measures and proposals will not only save a great deal of the time of all concerned and lengthy correspondence and unnecessary references to and fro but will also result in great improvements in their departments. Whilst I quite appreciate the truth of the proverb,

"too many cooks spoil the broth" we have to remember that the area of the State is very large and it is really almost impossible for the Head of each Department to satisfactorily or thoroughly inspect and supervise in the districts the work of his subordinates. Given co-operation and good will on the part of the Members of the Board and a perfect friendly understanding, I am convinced that there will be great advantages accruing from the inspection on tours of the work of all the departments under the Board by its Members. And finally, gentlemen, I entertain great hopes that by the institution of this Board, the Members will get more in touch with not only the different departments but what is most essential and still more desirable, they will get in touch with the officials and the people in the districts which I am afraid has not been the case in the past to the extent which I should like to see.

11. When you hear the rules read out, you will notice that the Revenue Member of the Council is to be the President of the Board and under him are the three of the most important officers whose departments of the Board will control. They are the Head of the Revenue Department under the Revenue Member—I have nominated Thakur Sadul Singh for this purpose—Babu Sheo Ghulam who is the Custom officer but who under the new scheme of reorganisation will be Inspector General of Customs and Excise, and the President of the Municipal Board, Bikaner,—the duties of which office Babu Sheo Ghulam and Mr. Lajoie have, in the absence at the time of a suitable incumbent, been so creditably performing in spite of their time being fully occupied with their own respective departments and whom also I hope to a ford relief' in a short time. Including the President we have thus got 4 officers or Heads of Departments permanently on the Board. But the Board will consist of 5 Members and it is not yet finally decided as to who the 5th Member should be. In the meanwhile I have nominated Mr. K. Rustomji, my hard-working Private Secretary to sit on the Board as a temporary Member. And Babu Chowharja Prasad is appointed Secretary to the Board as a temporary measure also.

12. The question as to whether the Members of the Board should be these Heads of Departments or whether at least the greater majority of such Members should be appointed solely and expressly on the Board with no other duties has received my most careful consideration and the conclusion has been arrived at that considering that the greater portion of the duties, which the Board will have to discharge is only a re-distribution and decentralization of work, the arrangements now decided upon will be quite sufficient for some

time to come. At the same time it is only fair to the Durbar as well as to the officers who will be Members of the Board to say that we realize that in years to come and under altered circumstances the other alternative just referred to may become necessary and have to be resorted to.

13. I should like to lay the greatest stress on one point and to impress it very clearly on all concerned and that is that although the Board has been constituted with the objects mentioned above, its constitution and collective duties and powers and responsibilities shall however in no way detract, as has been clearly laid down in the rules, from the individual duties, authority and responsibilities of the Revenue Member of Council and of the Secretary for the Revenue Department as also of the Heads of Departments sitting on the Board.

14. At the same time I want it to be distinctly understood that although the Board will be responsible to the Durbar and me for the efficient and steady progress in the departments under its control, the Revenue Member will, as in the past, still remain the chief and central Revenue authority of the State and is principally responsible for the work of all the departments under his charge and for directing the approved revenue policy of the State. In this connection, Members of the Board, I am sure there is no necessity for me to exhort you to see, that whilst the reasonable independence of the Members of the Board is not sacrificed in any way and that your candid views are freely yet politely given, you will all combine to work in a spirit of disinterested friendship and good will and strive only for the zealous discharge of your responsible duties and for the well being of the departments under your charge and of the people of the State who will be brought in contact with such departments. I am confident that with such members the meetings of the Board will be conducted in perfect harmony and that no personal feelings or selfish motive will be allowed to come in between and that the common aim and object will throughout be kept in view. Loyal to your Ruler and the State and to your "chief"—the Head of the Revenue Department—and the sacred trust that is entrusted to you—the happiness and welfare of my subjects whom you are called upon to look after—you may always be absolutely assured of my hearty and strong support in all your well considered proposals and legitimate aspirations.

15. It is very desirable that you should meet punctually and regularly on fixed dates and at fixed hours without which you can never hope to carry on your work in a responsible or business-like manner. Your decisions and proposals should be well considered and carefully thought out from all points of view and whilst you should not be

hasty you must on no account allow unnecessary delays or procrastination to occur in the transection of your business and, above all, you must strive not only to show that the confidence placed in you has not been to vain but you must give a tangible proof of the success of your labours and unfailingly keep in view the amelioration of the condition of the riot and see that they are not oppressed or in any way ill-treated by the subordinates of your department and I hope that both at the Head-quarters and on tour in the Districts you will not consider it as a waste of your time to personally listen to the grievances and trouble of the people and that you will earnestly strive to redress them. If you do all this you will be doing really good and useful work thereby given me very great satisfaction indeed.

16. Whilst you will find the Durbar sympathetically responsive to all your proposals for attaining these rules, I would invite your attention to and co-operation in checking reckless or unnecessary waste of public money, as, without the exercise of due economy, and the prudent husbanding of one's resources, nothing but the road to bankruptcy is open.

17. One of the most important of your duties will be the selection and recommendation for the various posts of Nazims, Tehsildars and Naib- Tehsildars, on whose efficiency and zeal and character and capabilities the well being of the State and subjects so largely depends, and I am confident that you will exercise your power of doing good in this connection as in all other matters without favouritism or fear and without any regard for the feelings of the incompetent, dishonest and otherwise unsuitable officials. To suffer such officials to stay on in the State service is an altogether mistaken and false notion of kindness and you would be sadly failing in your responsible duties towards the State and its people were you to allow yourself to be guided by such unworthy impulses. Although I have the satisfaction of knowing that a great deal has been done in the interests of the people during my 12 years' administration, ably assisted as I have been by the different members and other officers serving in the State, I feel that there is yet a great deal of scope for ceaseless activity in this direction and that, without the active co-operation of many other officers besides the Council we cannot do. This co-operation I have every hope of receiving from the RevenueBoard and of their insisting on the same from the District officers under them.

18. Members of the Board of Revenue, I need not go into further details about your powers and duties which have all been laid down and will now be read out to you. You know already that in the light of experience which you will gain, they will where necessary, be altered

and it will be for you to carefully go into this question and to submit your recommendations and proposals, but I might specially invite your attention to a very few points. You will observe that no details have been worked out in connection with the Settlement work. This has partly been due to want of time and partly because the most of the details of the present Settlement have already been decided upon and it is hoped that a great deal of the Settlement work in the Suratgarh, Reni and Sujangarh, Nizamats will be finished before very long. For such work as may yet remain and for your dealing with matters in connection with the present Settlement I shall await your proposals as soon as you have had time to go through them. For the next Settlement which will come many years hence there will be plenty of time.

19. There are some matters in connection with the administration of the Courts of Wards which have lately been taken up and are under consideration. Some of these will doubtless go to you in due course; but it should be noted that the rules drafted in so far as they apply to the Court of Wards have been based on the existing conditions. You will no doubt be able, in the light of the changes that may be made, to obtain sanction for altering your rules, etc., accordingly.

20. One of the most troublesome questions that you will have to go into and submit your proposals about with as little as possible is the present extraordinary and quite unusual procedure that has only in the last few years come into practice about objections and revisions in regard to municipal disputes and matters coming first in their administrative capacity, before the State and then very of ten going to the Judicial courts. This obviously is wrong and not only duplicates work but is not warranted or authorized by any State Rules on the subject so far as we cansee. I consider the work in connection with the Municipalities of the city as one of the most important of your duties.

21. I regret that the Revenue Member and President of your Board is unavoidably absent to-day but as he was engaged on most urgent and important work in the Districts in connection with the settlement operations I have excused his attendance on this occasion.

22. It now only remains for me to formally declare the constitution of the Board of Revenue and the appointment of the Members already alluded to and to offer you my congratulations and at the same time my good wishes for the future and I pray that the Almighty will crown your labours with success and that they will result in substantial good to the State and its people.

## RULES

## BOARD OF REVENUE, BIKANER STATE.

Where it is expedient to constitute a Board for the control of all matters connected with the Revenue Administration of the Bikaner State, it is hereby ordered as follows:

2. The Board of Revenue shall exercise control and supervision over the Revenue Department and other Departments closely connected to it, viz., Customs and Excise, Court of Wards and Municipalities, Stamp and Registration and Cattle Pounds and, also Settlement (when operations are in progress). It shall under the Presidentship of the Revenue Member of Council of the State, be responsible to His Highness the Maharajah for the efficiency and steady progress in the Departments under its control.

3. His Highness the Maharajah shall have the power to appoint the Members of the Board. The Revenue Member of Council shall be the President of the Board. The appointment of President and Secretary to the Board shall rest with His Highness who shall also have the power to remove any Member or to direct any change in the personnel, constitution, powers and functions of the Board.

4. Although the Board of Revenue is constituted for purpose of affording better facilities for the more prompt and efficient control and despatch of work and on grounds of administrative convenience, its constitution and collective duties, powers and responsibilities shall however in no way detract from the individual duties, authority and responsibilities of the Revenue Member of Council and of the Secretary for the Revenue Department as also of the Heads of Departments sitting on the Board. The Revenue Member shall as hithertofore still remain the Chief and Central Revenue authority of the State under the Durbar and as such shall be responsible for the work of all the Departments under his charge and he shall further more continue to be principally responsible for formulating, guiding and directing the approved Revenue policy of the State. The Revenue Board being composed mostly of Heads of Departments subordinate to Revenue Member shall in addition to the duties prescribed and specifically laid down hereafter be a kind of Council to assist its President—the Revenue Member—in the Revenue Administation of the State.

5. The following officers shall be Members of the Board—

| | |
|---|---|
| 1. Revenue Member | President |
| 2. Thakur Sadul Singh | Member |
| 3. Inspector-General of Customs & Excise | Member |
| 4. President, Municipal Board, Bikaner | Member |
| 5. Mr. K. Rustomji | Member |

6. Babu Chowharja Prasad, to be Secretary.

The Settlement officer shall be an ex-officio Member of the Board when Settlement is on.

## CONDUCT OF BUSINESS

6. (1) The Board shall ordinarily meet at least twice a week and oftener if necessary at the Mahkma Khas office for the regular transaction of business on such days and at such time as may be fixed by the President of the Revenue Board. The hours and day to be however permanently fixed.

(2) In case of emergent business however the President shall have power to convene special meetings of which the Secretary shall give a due notice to the Members or to circulate any file or files, should there not be sufficient cases of convene a meeting.

(3) In the absence on State duty or leave of the Revenue Member, another Member of Council or the Revenue Secretary will be appointed by His Highness to temporarily preside over the sittings and deliberations of the Board.

(4) The quorum necessary for the transaction of business shall be of 3 Members. In the event of more than 2 Members being on tour, His Highness the Maharajah may nominate any other officer or officers to temporarily sit on the Board as a Member or Members so that work may not be suspended or suffer.

(5) All questions which may come before the Board shall be decided by a majority of votes.

Cases may however, occur in which the President may be against the majority of the votes and where he-being primarily responsible for all revenue matters to His Highness and for the carrying out of the Revenue Policy of the State—may consider that such orders of the Board would be highly inadvisible. In such cases the President of the Revenue Board shall have the right and power, as Member of Council for the Revenue Department and President of the Revenue Board, to direct that final orders be not issued or that the orders of the Board be not given effect to, until he can obtain the orders of His Highness the Maharajah on the question under discussion. Thus the Revenue Member shall accordingly do with as little delay as possible and within a week at the latest from the date of such meeting and in submitting the case to His Highness he shall give his full reasons for recommending the orders of the Board to be cancelled.

(6) Every resolution or order passed by the Board at its meeting shall be recorded in a Minute Book which will be sent by the Board to the Revenue Member for record in the Mahkma Khas office.

All important resolution and orders or those which are of special interest or worth being brought to His Highness's notice will be marked by the Revenue Member in the Minute Book which will be laid before High Highness for information.

## POWERS AND DUTIES OF THE BOARD OF REVENUE

I. POWERS

7. (1) All cases intended for orders of the Mahkma Khas relating to Departments under the control of the Board which are above the powers of the Revenue Member shall be sent to the Board.

(2) The Board shall itself dispose of such cases as are within its powers. The others will be fully discussed, put to votes, and then submitted to His Highness with its opinions and recommendations for orders.

(3) The Board shall have power to appoint, degrade, fine, dismiss, and grant leave to all officials in the Departments under its control (Officer, Court of Wards and Naib-Tehsildars excepted), holding appointments on salaries ranging from Rs. 51 to 100 per mensem. Above that the Board shall obtain sanction of His Highness to its recommendations.

Khalsa villages to be struck off the accounts which are found to be irrecoverable to the entire satisfaction of the Board, after the expiry of the period prescribed in the State rules.

(16) The Board shall have power to sanction writing off, of bad debts, and irrecoverable arrears, dues and advances upto Rs. 200.

(17) The Board shall have power to assume the superintendence of and to release from such superintendence the person and property of all disqualified and minor Pattedars and Bhogtas except the Tazimi ones. The assumption of the superintendence and control of the person and property of the Tazimi Pattedars and their release should be sanctioned by His Highness.

(18) The Board shall have power to sanction attachment and sale

of moveable property of Pattedars (Tazimis excepted) and Bhogtas and the attachment of their immoveable propertys (villages) for arrears of rakam due from them. The attachment and sale of moveable property and the attachment of their (Tazimi Pattedars) immoveable property within their Pattas shall only be allowed under sanction of His Highness.

The Board shall have power to order release of the villages of all Pattedars and Bhogtas which have been attached for arrears of rakam after all demands have been satisfied.

The Board shall have power to sanction attachment and sale of immoveable property of Pattedars and Bhogtas outside their Patta villages. But in the case of the Tazimi Pattedars sanction of His Highness shall be necessary.

(19) The Board shall have power to sanction the attachment and sale of immoveable property of tenants-at-will for arrears of rakam.

(20) The Board shall have power to sanction sale of proprietary rights in Tibi Pargana for arrears of rakam.

(21) The Board shall have power to sanction the transfer of holdings for arrears of rakam.

(22) The Board shall have power to sanction succession of Bhogtas. In cases of successions of Tazimi Pattedars the Board shall forward the files for His Highness's approval with its recommendations.

(23) The Board shall have power to sanction the succession to a deceased Chaudhri out of his family. The grant of Chaudhar to outsiders shall resı with His Highness.

(24) The Board shall have power to sanction the appointment of headmen (Mukhias) in Sagan and Huzuri villages.

(25) The Board shall have power to impose an executive fine not exceeding Rs. 50 on any Chaudhri who may be found guilty or any neglect of duty, misdemeanour or disobedience to roders promulgated by the State.

(26) The Board shall have power to sanction sale of "SAFED" lands for a sum not exceeding Rs. 5000.

(27) The Board shall have power to sanction the widening of roads and pathways and of grant of compensation for habitable lands taken for such extension provided the budgetted allotment is not exceeded.

(28) The Board shall have power to grant land not exceeding 500 bighas (Chaks escepted) for tenancy.

(29) The Board shall have power to sanction the renewal and resumption of rent free holdings granted in lieu of menial village service. Mafis granted in lieu of service rendered to the State shall be liable to resumption only under orders of His Highness.

(30) The Board shall hear appeals or revisions against the decision of the Customs, Excise, Court of Wards, Municipal and Settlement officers, and dispose of them after hearing and examining the grounds of their decision. The orders of the Board shall in all such cases be final.

(31) The Board shall have power to dispose of all cases relating to irrigation.

(32) The Board shall have power to sanction the sale of trees in the Nali area.

The Board shall see that the orders relating to the preservation and growth of trees and their cutting are duly-observed. The Board, while on tour, will see that the Nazims and Tehsildars have duly followed the instructions under which such cuttings are to be allowed and that they and the village chaudhris have not abused their powers. They will also see that the growth and preservation of young trees have been encouraged by the grant of rewards.

(33) The Board shall have power to examine the Criminal Tribes and see that the Nazims, Tehsildars and Naib-Tehsildars have been alert to their duties connected with the reclamation and settlement of the Tribes as prescribed in the State rules, and that no unnecessary delay has occured in the grant of land and Takavi etc., for cultivation.

(34) The Board shall have power to arrange for the supply of fodder and provisions for the Ganga Risala. The Board shall see that no undue influence or coercion is exercised on the State Ryots in collecting such supplies.

(35) The Board shall exercise any other powers which His Highness, may, by a special order, be pleased to grant to it.

## II DUTIES

8. The Board may from time to time make rules subject to the sanction of His Highness the Maharajah:

(1) prescribing the duties of Nazims, Teḥsildars and Naib-Tehsildars,

(2) regulating within their power, and above power of officer or Head of Department and recomending the same to His Highness above their powers, the appointment of officers and officials (Heads of Departments excepted) in the Customs, Excise, Court of Wards and Municipal Departments, to their salaries, qualifications and duties, removal, punishment, suspension and dismissal,

(3) regulating the appointment of Qanungos and Patwaris, their salaries, qualifications, duties, removal, punishment, suspension or dismisal,

(4) regulating the appointment, duties, and dismissal of Lumberdars, Chaudharis and Mukhias,

(5) regulating the imposition of fines for failure to notify successions and transfers,

(6) prescribing the manner in which the Settlement officer shall report proposals of assessment for any area,

(7) regulating the distribution of assessment,

(8) directing with regard to what matter the Settlement officer is to ascertain and record the village custom and what matters are to be determined and recorded,

(9) fiaming rules for the guidance of Nazims and Settlement officer in fixing rent rates,

(10) framing rules for the grant of Mafis and their resumption etc.,

(11) regulating the assessment of resumed Mafis or the reduction of the assessment or the suspension of revenue of a village,

(12) prescribing rules for partition of villages or of Haq-Chaudhar and regulating the costs of such partition,

(13) providing for the payment of revenue through Chaudhris and Lumberdars and for payment of Pachotra,

(14) regulating the instalments in which and the persons, places and times to whom and at which the revenue shall be paid,

(15) regulating the issue of writs of demand and citations to appear and the exercise of power of arrest and detention in custody and directing by what officer or class of officers such powers shall be exercised or such process shall be issued and fixing the costs to be recovered from defaulters,

(16) regulating the method or attachment and sale of moveable and immoveable property,

(17) regulating the recovery of rent due from under proprietors,

(18) regulating the recovery of arrears due to Lumberdars and Chaudhris,

(19) regulating the grant of Chaks,

(20) regulating transfer of holdings for arrears of rakam,

(21) regulating the sale of waste (Safed) lands in Municipalities and places where such sales have been allowed and the treatment of Nazul and State property,

(22) framing rules for the assumption of Superintendence of

persons and property of disqualified and minor Pattedars and Bhogtas, ascertainment of debts, their guardianship and management, institution and defence of suit by and against them and the release of their person and property from such superintendence,

(23) framing rules for the disposal of Gaiwal property,

(24) prescribing fees for adoption and inheritance,

(25) framing rules for the grant and regulating the distribution of Takavi advances,

(26) framing rules for the commutation of kind rents into cash and vice versa in the Nali and other canal irrigated areas,

(27) framing rules for the construction of works of public utility,

(28) framing rules regulating the succession and grant of Chitthis etc., to Pattedars and Bhogtas,

(29) framing rules for the collection of Peshkashi and Mohar Lazma from Pattedars,

(30) framing rules for fixing extra rates for Bhonga collections,

(31) framing rules for the better control and supervision of the Members of the Criminal Tribes and for the grant of Pattas to such Members at favourable rates,

(32) prescribing rules for the ejectment, relinguishment and exchange of holdings,

(33) framing rules for the enhancement of rent in Tibi Pargana,

(34) framing rules for rent deposits,

(35) framing rules for the repayment of deposits and the procedure to be followed in the treatment of deposits,

(36) framing rules for the attachment of livestock,

(37) framing rules for suspension and remission of revenue and rent in case of calamity,

(38) framing rules under the Registration, Excise, Customs and Stamp, Municipal and Court of Wards and the Cattle Pound Laws,

(39) prescribing rules for the better keeping and checking of Revenue, Customs, Excise, Court of Wards and Municipal Board, and Cattle Pounds Records and Accounts,

(40) prescribing rules for keeping the accounts of canal revenue its collections and charges,

(41) prescribing the forms, contents, method of preparation, attestation and maintenance of village records, maps field books, registers and lists,

(42) framing rules for the safe custody of Settlement records and their being kept up-to-date in future,

(43) framing rules for:

(i) classification of records in the current department and the Record Room,
(ii) destruction of useless records,
(iii) Patwaris' records,
(iv) transmission of records from Tehsils and Nazamats,
(v) transmission to courts of records of rent and revenue court.

(44) framing rules for the touring of district officers i.e., Nazims, Tehsildars and Naib-Tehsildars and of the Heads of Departments under control of the Board and the mode of inspecting offices and testing village records,

(45) regulating the procedure to be followed by any officer or other person who is required or empowered to take action, in any matter,

(46) prescribing rules for the preparation, regular entry and safe custody of character and service books and rolls, and

(47) framing rules generally for the guidance of all persons in all proceedings connected with the Revenue Administration of the State in the several branches.

# Annexure 2

## Abstract from Speech of 29 September, 1910 with regard to Board of Revenue

In my speech whilst inaugurating the Board of Revenue I had foreshadowed some important changes in the Revenue Department. It has now been found that the Revenue officer and his establishment are no longer required, and from the 1st of October, the post of the Revenue officer will be abolished and his office amalgamated with the Mahkma Khas—the work so far performed by the Revenue office being distributed between the Revenue Secretary and the Board of Revenue under the orders and control of the Revenue Member.

As to the Board of Revenue I feel that there is nothing special for me to allude to, at this Durbar. My speech on the occasion of its inauguration was, I think, comprehensive and covered the necessary points and I can only add that during the two months of its existence, it has given me satisfaction and fully strengthens my belief and conviction that it will be a valuable and most useful institution in the State, under the able direction and guidance of Babu Harbishen Dayal, our new Revenue Member.

Before turning to other topics, I have the pleasant duty to perform of thanking all the State officers for their faithfull services and their loyal co-operation and able assistance which has so largely contributed to the success of the Administration.

My sincere thanks are specially due to all the Members of Council and the Secretaries and Staff of the Mahkma Khas who have slured with me all the toil and the stress of work, as well as elation at the success achieved and anxiety at the difficulties and setbacks we have at different times experienced.

The good work done by my dear cousin Maharaj Bhairon Singh, his absolute integrity and honesty of purpose, his devotion to duty and loyalty to the State and myself, and the laudable example he has set, by strictly keeping himself aloof from intrigues of all kinds and all party politics, have been so widely known and so fully appreciated as to reader superfluous any further remarks from me here; whilst the well deserved distinction of a C.S.I. conferred upon him by His majesty the Kind—Emperor some 2 years ago and his popularity in the State speak for themselves. The satisfactory and efficient manner too in which Maharaj Bhairun Singh, as President of the Council-ably assisted as he was, by his other colleagues—conducted the administration of the State during my five months' absence in England in 1907, reflects great credit on him.

In Thakur Hari Singh of Mahajan I have one of my ablest Assistants and Members of Council who is making himself more and more useful as each day goes by. It is a happy augury indeed to see our Sirdars like our premier noble the Thakur of Mahajan so patriotically and public-spiritedly serving the State and his master; whilst in Thakur Jeoraj Singh of Reri the State possesses an experienced Sirdar and valuable adviser.

I am sure, the valuable services, rendered in many ways by Thakur Raghuvar Singh, are widely appreciated whilst the exceptionally good record of his able work in this State must be very gratifying to him personally also. It is sad to think that owing to family reasons he will soon be severing his long connection with this State and I wish him all happiness after his retirement. I am glad that in the meanwhile he is going to stay on a little longer as Member of Council in special charge of Settlement operations to complete the Settlement work in the Suratgarh Nizamat and possibly also the Reni and Sujangarh Nizamats.

Although he has been only a short time amongst us, Babu Harbishen Dayal, our new Revenue Member, has come to us with the best of recommendations and a record of which anyone would be proud. The little we have so far seen of him, encourages us to hope that we have been fortunate in finding in Babu Harbishen Dayal a suitable successor to Thakur Raghuvar Singh, from whose administration of the Revenue Department great expectations are entertained.

The thoroughly well-earned and admittedly rapid promotion of Babu Kamta Prasad is in itself a testimony of his good work and of the value of his services and he has cheerfully borne with me the brunt of many a hard day's work—at times, I am afraid, to the prejudice of his health which not infrequently finds some difficulty in standing the strain.

I regret that Mr. R.D. Cooper—who during his long official career here was my Private Secretary for 10- 1/2 years and had done a great deal of good work—shou ld have have had to retire from the State service before this, but I have been happy in finding in his successor Mr. K. Rustomji a very hardworking and energetic Private Secretary who came here with a very successful record from our Educational Department and who had also worked as Assistant to Mr. Cooper for some time prior to his present elevation. The duties of a Private Secretary are multifarious and often of a difficult and delicate nature and I specially wish to take this opportunity of publicly thanking Mr. Rustamji.

And last but not least I must, on no account, leave out the name of Thakur Sadul Singh of Bagseu from the praise which he, by his untiring and unostentatious hard work and upright and honourable character, has no thoroughly gained and which was the reason for his recent promotion at such a comperatively early age. I wish there were more of our Bikaner Sirdars and young men who would follow Thakur Sadul Singh's good example.

In my speech in 1902 after explaining the System of Administration which has since been in force, I dealt briefly with certain matters connected with the various Departments of the State and attempted to show what room there was for activity and improvement in those directions.

The standard of our Administration at the present time is happily greatly improved and as we have for many years past been working on a carefully considered programme, it is unnecessary for me to say anything in that connection here but I feel that there are a few points of a general nature about which I could, with advantage, say a few words.

I think it can be said to the credit of all concerned, that there is not that unnecessary amount of day in dealing with and disposing of matters but at the same time, there is still considerable room for improvement in this direction. The same remarks apply to officers taking more individual responsibility, and I would like to impress upon you all that so long as there is a tendency to shirk responsibility, you can never achieve success to the fullest extent.

One of the worst practices, that can creep into any Administration and which is responsible for a considerable amount of harm, is the fact that people, through carelessness, want of leisure or indifference and lack of interest, are very apt to forget or disregard the orders and instructions that are issued from time to time, and I hope that henceforth not only will all the officers in their respective posts see that such instructions are scrupulously obeyed when issued from the higher authorities, but that they will also see that their own orders are similarly attended to, by the Departments below them.

There are moreover several points which I dealt with in my speech when inaugurating the Board of Revenue relating to the need of perfect harmony amongst the various officials, of no personal feelings or selfish motives being allowed to come in, about scrupulous regard for the happiness and welfare of the subjects of the State, about decisions and proposals being clear, well considered and carefully thought out from all points of view, about not working in a hasty manner nor allowing at the same time unnecessary delays and procrastination to occur in the transaction of your business, of giving tangible proofs of the success of your labours, and unfailingly keeping in view the amelioration of the condition of the ryot and to use your best endeavours to prevent them from being oppressed or in any way ill treated by the subordinates of your departments and of your making thorough inspections on tours in the Districts and of personally going into and earnestly attempting to redress the grievances and troubles of the people, of your exercising due economy in the State expenditure and checking and preventing reckless and unnecessary waste of public money and last but not least, of your exercising your power for doing good in every way and faithfully discharging your duty to the State without fear or favouritism and without any regard for private feelings seeing that incompetent, dishonest, oil otherwise unsuitable officials and subordinates under you are replaced by better and more suitable ones—these are all matters on which the instructions which I gave to the Revenue Board apply, with equal force, to all the various Departments of the State.

On the subject of the suitability or otherwise of the different officials of the State it is a fact that at the present day the Durbar have, on the whole, a better and more efficient class of servants.

# 3

## *The Bikaner Legislative (Representative) Assembly: Innovation of Far Reaching Consequence*

As discussed earlier the first two decades of the reign of Maharaja Ganga Singh Ji were devoted to administrative reorganisation with an attempt to transform the desert State of Bikaner into a modern State. Power equations changed and old institutions were replaced by new daring ones.

In the Jubilee Durbar held on 24th September, 1912, the Maharaja had announced the undertaking of a series of measures which he termed as 'boons' to the people of Bikaner. A major boon was the setting up of a People's Representative Assembly, the setting up of which was termed by the eminent political scientist, Prof. L.S. Rathore as an 'structural innovation of immense political prudence'. While mooting the idea of an Representative Assembly the Maharaja had expressed his conviction that 'the rulers and the ruled have an equal interest in the well being of the State and that, therefore, as they prove themselves fit, the ruled have a right to have a progressive voice and share in the Government' In the same vien the Maharaja had also observed that 'the end and aim of all Governments is, and ought to be, good of the people and that Government justifies itself best which secures the greatest possible good of the greatest possible number of people entrusted to its case. It is my firm conviction that the possibilities of achieving such a result are vastly greater under a system of Government which is carried on in consonance with the wishes and opinions of the people, are where possible with the advice and consent of its subjects, or their chosen subjects'. (Extracts from Jubilee Durbar speech of 1912).

Striking a sombre tone the Maharaja had gone on to state that had the general level of education among the masses been high or public training been higher than he would have welcomed the assistance the administration of a Legislative Assembly or Legislative Council in the true sense of the term. But being a pragmatist, Ganga Singh Ji felt that in those existing circumstances, a truly Representative Assembly would make the Bikaner State the laughing stock of the world. The aim of the Representative Assembly at that stage was to initiate the masses in a system under which they would be trained to become efficient members of a truly Representative Assembly with considerable enhanced powers. He was of the opinion that members of the Assembly would range between 20 to 30 in numbers composed of ex-officio and nominated as well as elected members. He further expounded that there would be no restrictions as to caste and creed and that he would attempt to have all communities represented in the Assembly. No special privileges, in the way of nomination or election on the grounds of religion would be entertained as it was rightly felt that 'special privileges to one class are synonymous with corresponding disabilities to others'.

The Maharaja desired to give the proposed Assembly the same powers as the Imperial Legislative Council of His Excellency the Viceroy enjoyed. These were in regard to right of interpellation of moving resolutions, as well as of submitting private Bills. The only projected difference was that in the case of the Legislative Assembly the sanctioned budget would be laid on the table of the Assembly and any suggestions offered by it would be duly considered by the Durbar later on. Furthermore, private members would have the right to move Bills and discussing them would be dealt with the Maharaja in Council. It was also felt by the Maharaja that the future salvation of the Assembly and that of the ruler of the State, the State itself and the subjects of the State could only be attained by a system of peaceful evolution to the advantage of all concerned. At another place the Maharaja had observed—"I can only pray and hope that the confidence which I am reposing in my people in thus spontaneously conferring upon them, this substantial privilege, will be as warmly reciprocated by a loyal and patriotic effort on their part to make this experiment a complete success by the sacrifice of selfish interests and by their determination to serve me and my successors and my State with loyalty, faithfulness and devotion".

The Bikaner Representative Assembly was formally inaugurated on 10th November 1919.(No. 1). Maharaja Ganga Singh delivered a historic speech to mark the occasion. He described the hardships witnessed by the State during the 450 years of its existence. The growth of Bikaner into a strong State was made possible due to the strongly felt presence of a strongly central government. He also talked of the era of reforms inituated by his predecessor, his late brother, Maharaja

Dungar Singh. Expressing the belief that the time was ripe for the inauguration of a Representative Assembly, Ganga Singh stated that "It is also becoming more and more obvious to you all as time goes on and you are better able to appreciate things that the interests of the State and of the general community are quite inseparable and that we must all stand or fall together. My people who were children have now grown up and I can deal with them as men". The Maharaja also used the occasion to propound the theme that the laws of the State should be framed by those who are to be affected by them the most. Quoting Lord Curzon's speech on the occasion of the Viceroy's visit to Bikaner in 1902, Ganga Singh Ji reechoed his sentiments thus "A good Indian Prince must live for his people. He must know them, go in and out among them, typify all that is best in their national character and traditions". It was in this spirit that the Representative Assembly was conceived.

The constitution, powers and duties of the Assembly had already been discussed at length in the Jubilee Durbar speech cited earlier. The Assembly was to. consist of 35 members of whom 10 were elected (3 representing the Tazimi Sardars and 7 the larger Municipalities), 19 nominated, and six were members of His Highness' Executive Council. At the outset all elected members were to be nominated but after three years the members were to be elected to the Assembly by their different electorates as laid down in the Constitution.

In September 1917, a further advance was made when the elective element in the constitution of the Assembly was increased by grant of the right of election to all the principal towns of the State with a population of over 2,500 resulting in a increase of 5 elected members representing the smaller municipalities. The total strength was raised to 45 (No. 2) To make the Assembly more broad-based and representative another change was introduced in 1925 when three seats were allotted to the Zamidars' Board (established in 1921) and two seats in the Assembly were reserved for agriculturists. In 1929 AD, another Zamindari Board was formed and thus both Boards elected one representative each. A Local District Board constituted in Ganganagar district was also empowered to elect three representatives. The powers of the Bikaner Legislative Assembly were curtailed and limited in nature.

In the legislative field, with certain restrictions, the Assembly was authorised to make laws for all purposes within the State of Bikaner. The validity of the law was subject to consent of the Maharaja who could even refer the law back to the Assembly for further consideration. The Maharaja's prerogative, rights,powers, duties etc.

were outside the pale of the Assembly so were the relations of the Maharaja with the Government of India or other Princes. Former Treaties negotiated and Military matters were outside the scope of the Assembly. Matters pertaining to public revenue or any tax, duty or cess could not also be legislated without the prior permission of the Maharaja.

The annual budget had to be laid before the Assembly in the month of October every year and it could be subject to discussion but no resolution could be passed with regard to it. The budget could also not be voted in the Assembly. All quiries regarding the budget were to be replied to by either the Finance Member of the Council or the Finance Secretary.

A perusal of the rules of the Legislative Assembly made it abundantly clear that the Maharaja had vested within himself over riding powers. He could make rules regarding the appointment, nomination or election of the members and at the same time decide the manner in which the business of the Assembly was to be conducted. He had the right to summon or prorogue the Assembly at his desire and convenience. The Maharaja was also empowererd to enact laws within the State without reference to the Assembly.

Upon sombre reflection it was evident that the Representative Assembly created in 1913 was never truly representative in the modern sence of the term. Nor were its functions, especially in relation to legislation, resolutions and Budget making, given the free rein they merited. Thus it was evident from the outset that a truly responsible government was never on the agenda in Bikaner in 1913. Thus, at best, what we had was the establishment of an institution which went against the norms of the monarchical system.

Its composition was mainly aristocratic; the franchise was extremely limited; and in its deliberations one could hardly hear a note of dissent. In it there was neither the dominance of the Chief Minister, nor the functioning of a party system as in modern times. The Assembly could not and did not deliberate matters nor was the theory of collective responsibility in evidence. The paraphernalia of 'a voting machine' was also willfully absent. The two fold functions of Parliament : 'action and criticism', as enunciated by Walter Bagehot, a British Constitutional authority, were absent in the operational framework of the Bikaner Assembly. Whatever might have been the inherent weaknesses and contradictions within the Assembly it was a lauditory step in more ways than one. It was a serious attempt to re-structure the decision making process and institutions with the aim of trying to establish more harmoneous relations between the ruler and the ruled.

For the Maharaja it was evident that he had seen the writing on the wall and had been able to gauge the emerging and surging currents in British India could not could be at bay for long in the Indian States. The Legislative Assembly was also viewed as an instrument that stood to strike at the roots of 'feudalism' and challenge the structural formation of the feudal society that had for long resisted change. The Assembly also stood to confound the critics of Indian Princess that the latter were not at the behest of the British Government, but, as in the case of Bikaner, were committed towards the welfare of the subjects.

During his long reign Maharaja Ganga Singh continued to nuture the Legislative Assembly with loving care and devotion. The importance he granted to the Assembly could be vouchsafed by the fact that the Inaugurations and Proroguing of the Assembly were occasions not only for assessing the progress in the State but for spelling out the shape of things to come. Momentous issues were discussed or laid out which gave the impression that there was no platform more suited than that of the Assembly to make crucial announcements. These speeches were at par in importance and content with those delivered in the meetings of the Council of Ministers, Administrative Conferences, Chamber of Princes, etc (No. 3). It was in this context his speech is delivered on the occasions of the Proroguing of the Assembly in 1928 (No. 4) and 1929 (No. 5) assumed great significance. In the 1928 speech the Maharaja started off by complementing the masses on the completion of the Engineering marvel- the Gang Canal- which brought the waters of Sutlej flowing from the peaks of Himalayas to the desert. More important still the Maharaja dwelt on the formation of the Indian States Committee under the Chairmanship of Sir Harcourt Butler to report on the relations between the British Government and the States with particular reference to the rights and obligations arising from the Treaties, Engagements and Sanads. The Committee was further expected to enquire and report into the financial and economic relations between British India and the Indian States. At a personal level, Sir Harcourt Butler was looked upon as an eminent statesman and sagacious administrator and by mutual consent one of the greatest Governors of British Provinces. But it was regretted, the Commission lacked the presence of some Princes and Ministers in its composition. The Maharaja enjoined upon the members of Assembly not to get carried away by demands in certain sections of the Press to boycott the Commission as it was at the request of the Princes that the Committee was constituted.

The Assembly was further taken in confidence that the irresponsible arguments being voiced in certain quarters that the Princes were conspiring with the British Government in blocking constitutional reforms in British India was baseless and lacked total verification. He once more reiterated that the Indian States Commission was not created to be hostile or to conspire against British India, but was there to 'safeguard the rights of the States, their Governments and their people, and their internal autonomy and independence'. Elaborating further on the theme Maharaja Ganga Singh felt a deep sense of regret that many in .British India were advocating the scrapping of existing Treaties between the Indian States and the British Government. Replying to such statements the Maharaja was at pains to furnish that the Treaties were not the outcome of any process of conquest but through a desire for alliance for mutual benefit. The British guaranteed certain rights which the rulers had long held or possessed. Those Treaties had also been accepted by the British Parliament as binding on the Crown. The British monarch had proclaimed at the inauguration of the Chamber of Princes in February 1921 that it was the royal determination ever to 'maintain' unimpaired the privileges, rights and dignities of the Princes of India. The Princes may rest assured that this pledge remains inviolate and inviolable'.

Continuing in the same vein, the Maharaja said that when States talked of internal autonomy they were not asking for anything for themselves to the exclusion of their people but their demands expressly included their subjects. Elaborating further he stated that "The term 'State' includes not the ruler alone, but the Ruler, his Government and his subjects, which are all component parts of and all go to comprise the State." Independence of a State went with the integrity and individuality of the subjects. Towards the end Maharaja Ganga Singh felt that what the Assembly should ensure and work for were the general principles of god governance listed below.

I. For the Ruler of a State to have a fixed and well defined Privy Purse and a clear dividing line between his personal expenditure and that of the State.

II. Security of life and property by the employment of as efficient and uncorrupt a Police as possible for the maintenance of Law and Order.

III. Independent Judiciary.

IV. The Reign of Law, including certainty of Law, its uniformity and approximation where possible with the laws of British

India with such additions and alterations as local conditions may render necessary.

V. Stability of Public Services.

VI. Efficiency and continuity of administration.

VII. Beneficient rule in the interests of general well-being and contentment of the subjects.

## References


1. Rathore, L.S., (i) 'The Bikaner Legislative Assembly: A Structural Innovation of Immense Political Prudence' in Maharaja Ganga Singh Ji Centenary Volume, Delhi, 1980. (ii) Political Ideas of Maharaja Ganga Singh Ji: Its Relevance in Nation Building, Bikaner, 1934.
2. Capt. P.W. Powlett, Gazetteer of the Bikaner State, Bikaner, 1935.
3. K.M. Pannikar, His Highness the Maharaja of Bikaner, Oxford, 1937.
4. Speech delivered by His Highness the Maharaja at the Inauguration of the Bikaner Representative Assembly, Nov. 1913.
5. Speech of Ganga Singh Ji to Members of Municipalities, June 1917.
6. Speech of Maharaja Ganga Singh at opening of Legislative Assembly October, 1921.
7. Proroguing of the Legislative Assembly speech of Maharaja Ganga Singh, January, 1928.
8. Proroguing of Legislative Assembly speech of Maharaja Singh, December 1929.

# Annexure 1

## Speech Delivered by His Highness the Maharajah at the Inauguration of the Bikaner Representative Assembly, on Monday the 10th November, 1913

*Gentlemen,*

All the necessary formalities having now been observed, I have much pleasure in hereby declaring open the Representative Assembly of the Bikaner State.

Gentlemen of the Representative Assembly, I offer you one and all a most cordial welcome, and at the outset of our proceedings and as our first corporate set, I ask you, my first Representative Assembly, to join me in formally tendering through the Government of India to His Imperial and Most Gracious Majesty the King-Emperor a respectful message of our unflinching loyalty and deep devotion to His Imperial Majesty, and of our devout wishes for the health and long life of the King-Emperor and Queen Empress and the Royal Family.

The gracious interest which our King-Emperor is pleased to take in the Rulers and States of India and the unmistakable sympathy which His Imperial Majesty evinces for India and the millions of his subjects out here is well-known throughout the length and breadth of India and I consider it a most auspicious omen that my Representative Assembly should have its permanent home in the building associated with the name of our King-Emperor and built to commemorate the visit of Their Imperial Majesties to Bikaner with which they honoured us in 1903.

I am sure I am echoing the sentiments of my people when I say with what pleasure we see present here to-day in the galleries of this hall, the British Resident who has officially come here on this great occasion in response to my formal invitation, and also with what pleasure we welcome His Highness the Maharao Sahib of Kotah, and the Nawabzada Sahib of Palanpur, who are here as my honoured guests.

Gentlemen, the State of Bikaner has now been in existence for near 450 years. At first, and for a very long time after, it had to fight for its very life and all its energies were practically devoted to this end. It was not till the advent of the England and the peace which they brought with them that our forefathers were able to turn their uninterrupted attention to other things and begin undisturbed to set in order the house that they had won.

Now, no house could be successfully managed or be comfortable for those who lived in it if everyone were trying to do the same thing at the same time, if jurisdictions overlapped, and if the children were allowed to quarrel among themselves or to be disrespectful to their father. There must be one supreme authority to whom all would look for everything they had.

The first thing that had to be done therefore, after the period of fighting was over, was to organize a strong central government that could afford protection to life and property within the State and give us an opportunity for growth. You all know how my ancestors and I have worked and struggled and studied to make our Government efficient for these objects and suitable for the welfare and happiness of all sections of the community and no one is in a better position gratefully to appreciate than you all who are assembled in this chamber to-day, how much the State and the people of Bikaner owe to the sagacious and statesman like policy pursued during the Reign of His late Highness Maharajah Dungar Singhji Saheb Bahadur, prior to whose lamentable and untimely demise in 1887 almost all the important departments of the State had been re-organised, proper judicial tribunals created, a responsible and efficient system of government established and the foundations of a sound system of education laid by the institution of schools at the capital and in the districts, the fruits of which we are now reaping. I can only leave it to you and to posterity to judge how far we have succeeded.

But this was not enough. We had set our house in order, but we had also to live, to make our lives more interesting and comfortable. The bare desert that was our patrimony, as it was, afforded a poor sustenance and so the next step that we had to look to was to make at least a portion of the desert blossom, if not as the rose, at any rate as the comfield. Here again I can only mention that when His late Highness ascended the gaddi in 1872, the revenues of the State were but seven and a half lakhs of rupees. His late Highness was able to leave the State in a prosperous condition, considering the circumstances then existing, for in the all too short a space of the fifteen years of his Reign, not only were the heavy State debts cleared off but the income of the State was more than doubled, the figures standing at Rs. 16,15,319 in the years of his demise. During the 11 years' regime of the Council of Regency the State revenues were on an average enhanced by another 3 lakhs approximately, whilst the total figures for the official financial year ending the 30th September, 1913 were Rs. 53,61,047 as against the ordinary receipts of 20 lakhs in the year 1897-98, when I assumed the reins of Government, which represent a net increase of Rs. 7¾ lakhs in the financial year just over as compared with the year preceding and of 33 lakhs since my coming of age nearly 15 years ago. The income of a State can sometimes be easily and temporarily raised by methods of a questionable nature with immediate serious and unfair results so far as the ryot and the inhabitants of the State are concerned and which methods in the long run prove equally injurious to the true interests of the State and Government also; but it is a source of the highest gratification to myself and the members of my Administration to know that no such aspersions can be cast in our case. The burdens of taxation on the people have side by side been very considerably lightened in past years: you will remember that a most undesirable tax, i.e., the import and export duty on grain, averaging over one lakh of rupees per annum and which has in the past yielded to the State as much as over 2-1/4 lakhs under both heads, was remitted only last year on the occasion of my Jubilee; while the State has in addition given the most liberal advances and aid to the people for taccavi and for the construction of and repairs to wells, tanks, etc., and remissions of land revenue. The income of the State in such circumstances can, I think, be fairly taken to be the best measure of the prosperity of the people for it is formed of a percentage of what the latter have. We have done all we could to develop our heritage. We have already a splendid asset in our State railways and we are, I hope, with the sanction of the Government of India, for which we have applied, about to embark on the construction of a very important section forming a valuable addition to our railway system; and we further hope we shall ere long be enabled, with the kind assistance of and the sympathetic consideration which happily our States now receive from His Excellency the Viceroy and the Government of India, to have some very important canal irrigation in the northern portions of our State, which question at present forms the subject of communications between the Punjab Government and the Government of India and about which I am sure we may also count on the sympathy, good will and sense of justice of His Honour Sir, Michael O'Dwyer, the Lieutenant Governor of the Punjab. We have done and are doing all that is possible in the way of education to fit our people for the competition of life both inside and outside the State but every year new developoments and new problems constantly arise and the burden of government, to which I have devoted all my energies and the best years of my youth, is ever becoming heavier and more difficult to carry. It is also becoming more and more obvious to you all as time goes on and you are better able to appreciate things that the interests of the State and of the general community are quite inseparable and that we must all stand or fall together. My people who were children have now grown up and I can deal with them as men. They have ever been noted for their loyalty to the King-Emperor, their Maharajah and his House. They have become more prosperous and they have also now a greater stake in their country and a greater interest in its prosperity.

I feel, therefore, for all these reasons that a further stage has now been reached in the evolution of our State and it is to mark this that we are gathered here this day. I think the time has come when I have a right to look to you and to all sections of the community for a greater measure of assistance in the government of the State than has, hitherto been possible. I, as the father and the Ruler and leader of my people, desire to take them into my confidence now that they are daily proving themselves more worthy of it and to seek their regular and formal help in the heavy responsibilities that weigh me down. I desire to have your advice and counsel on the many difficult problems of administration that now constantly arise, and I wish also as a mark of my trust and affection for my people that the laws by which their lives are governed shall, so far as possible, be framed by them themselves. But it would, of course, not be feasible to call together all the citizens even of one town to advise and deliberate on any point of public interest and it becomes necessary, therefore, to introduce the principle of representation, that is, that only a practicable number of individuals who have your confidence and mine should be summoned for this purpose. The principle referred to, although generally accounted to be of western origin, is nothing new among you and has been applied in various ways since time immemorial.

It has, therefore, given me great pleasure, of my own free will and accord and with the sole view to our common welfare and benefit to have issued an Edict to-day for the constitution of a Representative-Assembly in our State.

I have done this after much earnest deliberation and with a full sense of my responsibility to those who have gone before and to those who follow after, and with the greatest anxiety that the continuance of my line, by the favour of Providence, shall ever be a blessing to this little part of India. Those who have to steer the ship of State must not look behind to the mere memories of an illustrations past, but must peep out into the distance to descry what lies ahead and in doing so I am satisfied that this milestone placed to-day lies on the line of happiness and progress.

Let not any one go away with the idea that in bringing this new feature into the organisation of the State I am acting on a hasty impulse or that I am slavishly adopting a thing of western growth. I spoke at some length on the subject in the speech which I delivered at the Jubilee Durbar in September, 1912. I need not re-iterate here what I then said, but I hope enough has been said to make it apparent that the creation of this Assembly is a natural development and you know as well as I that there is no Ruler in India who elings more closely than I do to all that is best in our old traditions, our faiths and our ancient civilisation and methods, things that have grown for many thousand years from the very dawn of history. We will not alter them or give them up. We will construct but we will not destroy and in adapting ourselves and our arrangements to meet new needs evolved by time, we give up nothing but only add something.

I say that this development would have come to us whether it was suited to, or had occurred about the same time, in other parts of India or not. I have had it in contemplating now for several years. It has for long been my ambition. As Lord Curzon said during his visit to Bikaner in 1902, a good Indian Prince must live for his people. He must know them, go in and out among them, typify all that is best in their national character and traditions. But I do not say that we are not affected by what goes on around us. We owe a great deal to the discipline and methods and experience associated with the British system. We are constantly guided by the great political and administrative experience of those who rule over the Imperial Territories. They have splendid traditions at their back and a genius for government and I confess that I have been greatly encouraged by the success of their experiments in the same direction and am proud to think that my State, in the oldest and most traditional part of India, should be independently endeavouring to reach the same stage along the line of progress and reform, not lagging very far behind.

The Edict and the rules published to-day in connection with the Representative Assembly are, I hope, clear. So only a few remarks are called for from are to the actual constitution of the Assembly, its powers and duties. On a comparision you will find that none of the important principles have been curtailed which were mentioned in my speech at the Jubliee Durbar on the 24th September, 1912, when I announcd my intention of establishing a Representative Assembly. In accordance with the rule which I have made, never to promise or announce anything which even, with the best of intentions I may not afterwards be able to carry out, I could then only speak in a general way as to the proposed powers and constitution of the Assembly, as the various details had yet to be carefully worked out. I had indicated in that speech that the Assembly would consist of some twenty to thirty members and that in regard to legislative measures the Assembly would be empowered only to discus Bills and that after being considered in the Assembly they would be dealt with by me in Council in the same way as had hitherto been done.

As you will have gathered from the appointment rules, the Assembly is to consist of 35 members including the six members of my Executive Council, ten members to be elected and nineteen to be nominated by me. The preparations and considerations of all the rules connected with the Assembly and the working out of all the details naturally took some time and as I did not wish further to delay the inauguration of the Assembly, I have on this occassion, nominated all the members to represent the various communities; but at the expiry of the term of 3 years of the present Assembly, the members who have to be elected shall be sent to the Assembly by their different electorates as shown in the rules, Some day, no doubt, when the State and the people have acquired more practical experience in such matters, the number of elected members may be increased, but in the meantime the deficiency must be met by the greater breadth of view and the knowledge of individuals which my position as head of the State gives me.

While on the subject of elections, I might add that it is my intention to pass a Municipal Act and I have all or a certain proportion of Municipal Commissioners elected by electorates of residents in the Municipality when the Municipal Act comes into operation; and I am at present also considering a scheme for organising and improving the District Municipalities and the Municipal system throughout the State.

As regards legislation, when the details came to be examined it was with great pleasure that I found it possible to grant to the Representative Assembly enhanced powers and to remove the restrictions which I had foreshadowed in my speech last year, for it will be apparent from the rules that the Representative Assembly, subject to certain safeguards and stipulations, will now finaly deal with legislative measures in the State.

So far I have considered this new move from the point of view of our own advantage and benefit and so far as it concerns our State and ourselves but there is another and a greater standpoint.

By the grace of Her late Majesty Queen Victoria of blessed and revered memory we were offered privileges greater than any held by Indian States before—the privileges of admission to the citizenship of a world-wide Empire, a growth of hearts not hands, which by the statesmanship and sympathy of our first Queen Empress and of Her Majesty's Illustrious Successors, has become the most powerful influence for the good of huminity that mankind has known. We, that is the Rulers and States of Rajasthan, were at first connected with the British Government only by treaties of alliance and friendship, acting in subordinate co-operation with the paramount power—mere detached appendages with a purely formal bond. But we now have become, and that right gladly, welded into, so to speak, the confederation of the Empire, its participators and instruments yielding tono one in the world in loyalty and respectful affection for His Imperial Majesty the King-Emperor and retaining at the same time what we prize dearer than life and what was more than guaranteed to us by virtue of the now historic Proclamation of the late Queen Victoria in Council of 1858, where Her Majesty was most graciously pleased to announce that "we shall respect the Right, Dignity, and Honour of Native Princess as our own". There have also been no prouder moments in my life than when I paid, by personal service, my homage to our beloved King—Emperor or when Viceroys have hailed Ruling Princes as "colleagues and partners" and as "Pillars of the Empire. " But my pride was for our States as well as for my brother Princes and myself.

If we are part of a great and world-wide Empire, we must prove that we are worthy of the privilege and do not leg behind the rest. If the Empire is a living thing we must be alive ourselves and our Emperor must know that we are always at his service no less in the cause of general progress and humanity than on the field of war.

I believe that the Representative Assembly which I launch into existence to-day will help us to this end.

We are all proud of our independence, of our liberty and freedom. We dearly love our desert land which has never yet been conquered, save by sympathy and friendship, and I am happy in the loyalty and goodwill of my subjects. But we all of us together have a stronger feeling still of allegiance and devotion for the Sovereign under whose protection I reign over the State of Bikaner and to whose service both in peace and war all over blood is consecrated.

It is also to enable us to express this feeling if necessity arises, to increase our capacity for usefulness in the service of His Imperial Majesty the King-Emperor that I have now strengthened our internal organisation by a closer union of its elements.

Gentlemen of the Representative Assembly, I look for great assistance from your deliberations and I anticipate from your advice and your shaping of the laws, great benefit and advantages to the State over which by the grace of God I am called upon to rule and which I personify and represent. I equally confidently hope that the Assembly will be a vital factor in the lives of the people of the State, my subjects, and destined to shed its influence on their very existence and to bring them increased happiness and still further to ameliorate their condition which has always been my constant aim and earnest desire. I would offer you only a few words of advice on this occasion. You must, as the old saying goes, jestina lente 'hasten slowly'. Nobody at the beginning can be expected to do very much and you are like a person learning a new game and it will be some time, even with the constant efforts of the Ruler of the State and his Government, before you can become thoroughly proficient at it. You must never forget the old fable about the different members of the body but remember always that the successful exercise of your new functions depends entirely on the maintenance of cordial relations with the other parts of the body, of which, you form a limb. An arm, however strong, that is severed from the head and the heart can do nothing and I shall expect you to keep the closest touch with me and my Government on the one hand and the people whom you present on the other. Then all will go well and you will prove yourselves really useful and be able to work for the benefit and nourishment of the whole body.

You will, I have every hope, never abuse the confidence I have reposed in you and I can only exhort you most earnestly never to wander from the purpose of the origin of the Assembly and never to offer advice or propose a new law, except after the most careful consideration of the matter to be dealt with and with a due sense of your duty and responsibility to the Emperor and the Empire, to your Ruler, to your State and to your constituents. The Assembly is for the benefit of the State and the people and not of any community or individual. The interests of the State and the people are identical. The Assembly must be disinterested and independent and the members must co-operate spontaneously and without pressure for the interests and purposes that are common to the whole community, for the greatest good of the greatest number. When you once enter the Assembly Hall, you must endeavour to leave self-interest and self-glorification outside and I feel it my duty to say that there is nothing that will be visited with my displeasure so severely as any appearance of self-seeking or pesoul motive or any undignified conduct or unbecoming demeanour.

Subject to these remarks, however, and to your constant remembrance of the inherent suppremacy of the Ruler of the State in all matters and causes with which you deal, I invite from you the most full and free discussion of all the business that I have authorised to come within your sphere. It is the honest and candid opinion of every one that I desire to have in the future as I have also always asked for in the past. Let no one be deterred from speaking his own mind by fear that his views will not be acceptable to me or to my Government. Your deliberations will be privileged and no one shall suffer in any way for the opinions he expresses, subject of course to the provision already referred to, and that freedom of debate is always combined with loyalty to the State and its Ruler and to his House and subject further to your discussions being couched in respectful and courteous language to all concerned. There must be one spirit and one purpose to make the State in all its activities and all its parts a more efficient and more effective instrument for the furtherance of our corporate welfare and for the strength and unity and growth of the State itself.

Gentlemen of the Representative Assembly, not only do I welcome you but no one will rejoice more heartily than myself should this important experiment, on which we are today embarking, ultimately will prove the unqualified success which, in common with all well-wishers of the State and the people, I desire it to be. So long as you work on the right line and are guided by indispensable principles of loyalty, public spirit, patriotism for your country and devotion to duty, combined with a full sense of justice and equity, you cannot go wrong and you have a grand field and unexceptional opportunities before you for rendering yeoman service to your Maharajah, your State and banquet here last year testified to the great advantage it had been to the Government of India to hear questions affecting the moral and material interests of the people frankly discussed in the Imperial Legislative Council and he added that in his judgement the enlarged Councils had done nothing but good and had been of great assistance in legislation and after expressing his pleasure at hearing of the proposal to create a Representative Assembly in this State, His Excellency expressed the hope that we should have the same experience as the Government of India. I feel sure that such words of encouragement from such a broad-minded Viceroy and such a true friend of India and the Indians as also of the Indian States and their Rulers will be of great encouragement to you when entering upon your new duties and that at the same time they will bring home to you a full sense of your very heavy responsibilities and that you will endeavour throughout to fulfil the expectations that are formed of you. I would like to remind you also that your success or failure is of importance not only to the Bikaner State but that the failure of this experiment, which is a novel one for this part of India, might ultimately retard similar development and progress in other States, whilst speaking in all modesty, the failures of such institutions in Oriental countries and States, large and small, can but have a prejudicial effect on the development of Governments on such progressive and liberal lines, a fonn of government in which I am a great believer, subject to certain safeguards and alterations, wherever required to meet peculiar and local circumstances, and further a form of government, which is my personal opinion will be the one prevailing in most countries in the not very distant future.

With these remarks I must leave the future in your hands with a devout prayer to the Almighty to guide your labours so that they may always be directed towards the safety, honour, and welfare of the State and people of Bikaner.

# Annexure 2

## Speech delivered by Colonel His Highness the Maharaja of Bikaner, G.C.S.I., G.C.I.E., A.D.C., LL. D., On the 29th June, 1917 in Reply to the Address Presented by the Members of the Thirteen Municipalities of the State

I thank you sincerely, Gentlemen of the Bikaner and District Municipalities of the State, for your loyal address and the words of welcome and congratulations with which you have greeted me on my return to Bikaner from a mission which to me will be an ever memorable one.

It is always sweet to return to one's native land. To be the receipient of the loyal welcome and affectionate greetings from his Nobles, officials and other subjects, must always be a source of real gratification to the Ruler of the State. But for me the pleasure is further enhanced in that today for the first time I meet you, the Members and Representatives of the various Municipalities of the State, since you were granted greater autonomy and enhanced powers in the management of your affairs and finances—to which you, Gentlemen, have yourselves referred tin graceful and appreciative terms in your address.

It is hardly necessary for me to say how glad I was to be able, just before my departure for England some five months ago, to sanction these further reforms in the direction of local self-government. For the policy pursued by myself and my government is, I hope already well-known throughout the State. Obviously every Indian State must be free to decide for itself how best to promote the welfare of its people and to conduct its internal affairs in ways most suited to local circumstances, peculiarities, traditions, and sentiments, and according to the different ideals and standards of administrative efficiency existing in each State. But the ideals and policy which I and my Government have consistently set before us are based on the conviction which I have more than once expressed in Public already, that the possibilites of securing the greatest possible good of the greatest possible number of my people are vastly greater under a system of Government which is carried on in consonance with the wishes and opinions of the people themselves and, where possible, with the advice and consent of my subjects or their chosen representatives. We further realize that the Rulers and the ruled have an equal interest in the well-being of the State and that, therefore, the ruled, as they prove themselves fit, should have a progressive voice and share in the government and affairs of the State. Although I look forward to much greater progress and further all-round advance on the part of my people—and it behaves us all always to keep this steadily in view—the loyalty and devotion of my subjects, their good sense and the strides which, under God's Providence, they are making in education and other directions, have, happily, rendered it possible for us to take some important steps in the past few years.

It was in pursuance of this settled policy that I had the pleasure, in November 1913, of inaugurating our representative Assembly. At the end of the first triennial term the elections have, as you are aware, already taken place and we shall welcome the newly-elected and nominated Members to our next session in September or October. I might add that we are also revising the Rules of business in the direction of greater liberality and of removing, what experience had shown us to be unnecessary restrictions. Side by side with these steps taken in the direction of representative government, it was, of course, equally necessary that a further advance should be made in the direction also of local self-government, and the recent municipal reforms ought really to have taken place earlier than they did. I regret, however, that the very unusual times and unsettled period of the past few years as well as the necessary consideration and solution of some difficult points should unfortunately have prevented us from taking any final action prior to February last.

Gentlemen, under the new system you have not only been granted greater autonomy and powers, but the number of our non-official Members who form the preponderating majority has been still further increased in each Municipality on a systematic basis according to the size of the towns so as to give each important community a reasonable chance of representation on the Municipal Boards. You have been given practically independent control over your finances and been authorised to raise the necessary funds by such taxation as will, we believe, be considered fair and suitable for your requirements. And it is gratifying to feel that the District Municipalities will be self-supporting and that, so far as can be seen, the Bikaner Municipality will also not be in need of any further State Grants in ordinary circumstances after next couple of years. The status of Municipal Commissioners has been raised by the grant of honours and privileges and you are doubtless aware that it is proposed to build a suitable

Municipal Hall in the Capital at the expense of the State.

I hope we shall very soon be able to substitute—at least in Bikaner Municipality—an elective system for returning non-official Members to the Municipal Boards in place of the present system of nomination by Government. I may add that this question has already been ordered to be looked into and worked out in the meanwhile so that a begining can, if possible, be made from the next year. When more experience has been gained and the various Municipalities have, as we hope, shown that they have made good use of the opportunities now offerred to them, the question of still greater powers and privileges for all District Municipal Boards will also be promptly and sympathetically taken up by my Government.

I am glad to note that none of the Municipalities, which you represent, have any requests to lay before me on this occasion and I am further pleased to receive an expression of our gratitude for the privilege which the bigger Municipalities enjoy in electing Representatives to our Assembly.

In your determination, Gentlemen, to do your best to carry out the responsible duties which have now develoved upon you and in all your labours in the interests of your Towns and fellow citizens you know that you can always safely rest assured of the sympathetic attitude of myself and of my Government. Although much was accomplished under the late system both in the capital and in the Districts, a great deal of heavy and responsible work will fall on your shoulders and I offer you my best wishes for your future success and prosperity. During the course of my tours I shall look forward with personal interest to seeing the many further improvements which, I hope, you will be able to effect in your respective cities.

Let me also thank you warmly, Gentlemen, for the remarks which you were good enough to make in regard to my recent mission to England. I take them as the expression of your personal loyalty and devotion to myself and I only wish I could feel that I had really deserved them. I can but respect however that I consider it a very high honour to have gone as one of the three Representatives from India to the Imperial War Cabinet and the Imperial War Conference, and that I consistently and conscientiously strove to the utmost of my poor ability and power to discharge what I felt was my bare duty to our beloved Emperor and the British Empire no less than to India and our Indian States.

Much of our labours were of a confidential nature to which it is obviously impossible for me to refer, but if some day all the details come to be known, India will realise what a very real and heavy debt of gratitude it owes to His Honour Sir James Meston and the Hon'ble Sir Satyendra Sinha—than whom no man can desire better colleagues or, what is more important, more loyal and staunch champions of Indian interests. That Sir Satyendra Sinha, as a wise and patriotic Indian, endeavoured at all times to serve his Motherland and his brethren in this vast Continent, of course, goes without saying, but it cannot be too of ten gratefully emphasized that no Indian could have been more loyal to India than Sir James Meston. We were all in constant and intimate contact for nearly four months and our relations throughout were of the happiest and frankest description and we never had a moment's disagreement or difference of opinion on any important point.

To us, the two Indian Representatives, it is, I know a source of unalloyed pleasure to find that the Indian public are gradually beginning to realise the true nature and merit of Sir James Meston's services to India while on this mission. On landing at Bombay I met some Indian friends who occupy prominent public positions and in the course of our conversation on current public topics I had occasion to emphasize the value of the work done in the service of India by Sir James Meston and Sir Satyendra Sinha and I pointed out how wrong it appeared that instead of expressing well deserved gratitude and appreciation, a few people should still have persisted in unfair criticisms about Sir James Meston's work. Some days later, I got a letter from one of these friends which in regard to Sir James Meston's signal services to India speaks for itself and I will quote an extract from that letter. My friend wrote:

> "The publishing in the Times of India of Saturday of Your Highness' and Sir James Meston's speech has created the right kind of feeling towards Sir James Meston. A cultured friend of mine told me that for sometime he thought that there might be some mistake in giving the names of the speakers and that probably Sir S.P Sinha must be the speaker and not Sir James Meston."

From a telegram which has been published and which we sent to His Excellency the Viceroy immediately after our landing in Bombay, you will have learnt with pride and joy of the gracious interest with which Their Imperial Majesties were pleased to honour India and the Indians and with pleasure of the gratifying and cordial receiption which was extended to us by His Imperial Majesty's Government and the Ministers of the Overseas Dominions, of the spirit of friendliness and sympathy exhibited by them towards our Indian people, as well as of the courtesy and consideration shown us by the Secretary of State for India.

In my speech at the Banquet in Bombay on the 7th February on the eve of my departure for England, I had ventured to point out that a great step had already been taken in securing the representation of Indian views at the Conference and to express my honest and firm conviction that this and many other signs were good omens full of bright promise for the future of India. Well, Gentlemen, I have returned from England more firmly convinced than ever of the real change in the angle of vision in favour of India, of the sympathetic attitude of the British people and of the desire of Great Britain to deal with India in a fair and sympathetic manner. The future may not always be plain sailing and there may even, at times, be disappointments, but personally I shall be very surprised if, with the help and sympathetic support of Ris Majesty's Governments both in England and in India, the bright promise for the future is not maintained, and speaking generally I am positive that we in India can count on the hand of fellowship and of sympathy of both the Government and the people of Great Britain. The official announcement, which we have just seen, in regard to the appointment of Indian Members to the Council of the Secretary of State for India, is an instance in point which can, I think fairly be cited and the fact, that there will now be three instead of two Indian Members on that Council as well as the selection of two such loyal, talented and patriotic Indians as Mr. Bhupendra Nath Basu and Dir Prabha Shankera Pattani, will doubtless be hailed with satisfaction in India.

Anyhow certain it is that India has never been better understood or appreciated by the people of England as it is at the present moment and, as I also stated in my speech at the Guildhall early last month it is unquestionable that 'out of the crucible of common danger and of mutual sacrifice . . . we will emerge with a closer and better comprehension of one another, linking us in stronger bonds of understanding, brotherhood, and affection than were ever dreamt of by our ancestors on either side! 'What we the Indian Representatives—ventured to say on behalf of India to the English people when we were in England is already known in India, so today I would only take the liberty of saying that it behaves us, Indians—whether in the States or in British India—to see to it that this friendly feeling and sympathy, so strongly evinced in England at the present moment in no unmistakeable manner is not estranged through any hasty or ill-considered action or any unfounded suspicions of unfriendly attitude on the part of any important class or community in India.

Although I have nothing new to add to what you already know you will doubtless expect me to say a few words in regard to the War in which our Empire is engaged in combating an unscrupulos foe, whose disregard of all treaty rights, international rules and obligations of all humane considerations towards mankind have forfeited his claim to be classed amongst the Civilised Nations of the World, and whose barbarous and in human crimes, even against innocent women and children, and wanton deeds of destruction and devastation have horrified and enraged the whole world-atrocities of which I speak from personal knowledge or observation both when I was on Active Service in France in the early stages of the War and again during my recent brief stay there. But the day of retribution for the enemy, thank God, is surely and steadily approaching. We in Bikaner, indeed together with people practically everywhere else, have always shared the conviction that the arms of our King-Emperor and his gallant Allies will ultimately be crowned with victory, and what I saw and heard during my recent visit to Europe fully and firmly strengthens me in that belief. The might of England has always been proverbial and at no time has England been mightier than at the present moment. He is a bold man who could venture to prophesy when the War will be over but there is little doubt that had the revolution there not unfortunately temporarily disorganized the forces and Government of Russia, the War would have been over in the automn of 1917, This incident however is unfortunately likely to prolong the War into the next year, but that the ultimate triumph will be our is by the grade of God beyond question.

On my way to England I had the pleasure of spending about a week at the Front with our gallant Camel Corps and I am happy to be able to give you excellent accounts of them. They are in good spirits and fine form and General Sir Archibald Murray, the Commander-in-Chief in Egypt, spoke to me in the highest terms of appreciation of the splendid services rendered by our gallent soldiers of whom we have every reason to be justly proud.

I am also glad to announce that there is a prospect of Bikaner being honoured with a Viceregal Visit in November next and I am sure all classes and communities of my subjects will join me tin offering a warm and hearty welcome to Their Excellencies The Viceroy and Lady Chelmsford. I have to proceed to Simla in a coupld of days' time to attend a committee meeting there, and on my return we shall, I hope, know more definitely the various details in connection with the visit.

I would also like to express the lively gratification which I feel at the success of the War Loan subscriptions in our State, and I think we may safely assume that the Bikaner State has the proud privilege of heading the list of subscriptions in Rajputana. The sum of 24 lakhs of Rupees actually subscribed within my territories does not, of course, include the substantial sums which doubtless have been subscribed also in British India by my subjects who have such important business dealings all over India. This is a matter of congratulation both for my Government and people, and we may further mutually congratulate ourselves that, in this respect too Bikaner has maintained its past reputation of loyalty and service to our Emperor.

Gentlemen, once more I thank you for your address and for the beautiful Casket in which you have presented it. I wish you all Godspeed!

# Annexure 3

**Speech by His Highness The Maharajah when opening the Session of the Bikaner Legislative Assembly on 26th October, 1921.**

*Gentlemen of the Legislative Assembly,*

I am very glad to have this opportunity of personally opening this Session of the Assembly and of welcoming the new Members, who were returned in December last, whom I was unable to see during the previous session owing to my absence at Delhi on important public business while ill-health prevented my meeting you during the autumn session last year.

2. It is, however, a matter of satisfaction to me, as I hope and trust it is in you, that in my absence the Heir—Apparent is able to represent me in your midst during your deliberations and I should like to take this opportunity of expressing both my gratification and my gratitude for the loyal and dutiful manner in which the Maharaj Kumar is endeavouring to relieve me to his utmost of the heavy burden of work and responsibility that rests on my shoulders. I feel sure that you will join me in the devout prayer that he may by Dine Grace, be spared to a ripe old age and that many years of useful and devoted service to his Country and people may be in store for him.

3. At the present moment, when we are all looking forward with eager anticipations to the visit with which His Royal Highness, Prince of Wales is to honour us, in a short time, it is but fitting that a Resolution of loyal and enthusiastic welcome to His Royal Highness to our Capital should be moved by such a distinguished Member of the Assembly as the Rawatji of Ravatsar, which I am confident, echoes the sentiments of all classes and communities of my faithful subjects.

4. On this occasion it also gives me very great pleasure in announcing that soon after wards, viz., at Christmas, Bikaner is to be further honored by the Visit of His Excellency the Viceroy, who I rejoice to feel, will be accompanied by Her Excellency the Countess of Reading. I feel sure that the Chiefs and Nobles and the general public of the State will all join me in tendering a respectful and warn welcome to Their Excellencies when we shall have in our midst not only the illustrations Representative of our beloved King-Emperor

but one of the greatest statesmen whom England has ever sent out to India to hold the highest office under the Crown.

5. I shall not attempt to anticipate the speech of the Finance Member which he will shortly make in laying before the Assembly the Budget for the new financial year, but I would like to take this opportunity of expressing through you, the representatives of the people, to all classes of my subjects my sincere sympathy and deep concern at the fact that in spite, in each case, of a promising earlier rainfall, we should for the second year be faced with conditions of scarcity and hardship, resulting in unprecedented high prices and increased cost of living, combined with unusually slack trade conditions and dislocation of business on a large scale, due to causes beyond the control of man. I need hardly add that I and my Government are fully alive to the seriousness of the situation and that everything that lies in our power will be done to alleviate the distress and suffering of my beloved subjects. The Finance Member will describe some of the measures already sanctioned by me and it goes without saying, other steps will be taken as circumsatances demand. This has not only affected the budget estimates for the new financial year but will, it is feared, also be found to have a prejudicial affect on the current year's budget estimates. I am, however, happy to feel that the financial condition of the State, nevertheless, continues to remain satisfactory, which I trust will be some consolation to you in these hard and anxious times. This is borne out by the record revenue of Rs. 80,35,961 for the year 1919-20 which Rs. 78,12,766 comprised the ordinary receipt of Rs. 2,23,195 Further gratifying evidence of a similar character will be furnished by the fast that in spite of the considerable expenditure incurred up till now, and the still heavier expenditure which we shall have to meet during the ensuing financial year, for railway extensions and other remunerative schemes, the State has not only had no necessity to resort to a public loan but that on the other hand there will, at the end of the ensuing financial year, still be a substantial cash balance available at our disposal to meet further calls for the development of the State and of its resources.

6. Let me conclude by making two further highly gratifying announcements, which I hope will enable you to go back to your homes in a happy state of mind. The sanction of His Majesty's Secretary of State for India has been received to the carrying out of our far-reaching railway projects, viz., an extensions to Delhi from the vicinity of Rajgarh, with a branch line running through Loharu to Rewari, and the Bikaner—Gujner-Kolayat—Sindh extension which,

it is a matter of special gratification to me, will pass through the Jaisalmer State and its Capital. Construction work has already been commenced from Bikaner towards Kolayat and my sanction was recently accorded to the earth work being started on the Hanumangarh—N ohar—Bhadra Sirala line.

7. In my speech during the festivities connected with the Coming of Age of the Hair-Apparent last year, I announced that an agreement had been signed in regard to the Sutlej Canals and I am now very happy to be able to State that the sanction of the Secretary of State to the Project has also since been received and that it is hoped that the work of constructing the Canal will be taken in hand at an early date.

8. It is my earnest prayer that the recent unsettled conditions and the projudicial effects on business and trade as the aftermath of the War and of the recent bad years, may be followed at an early date by an era of general contentment and happiness and that my State and people may also be blessed with a full share of all such peace and prosperity, which they so thoroughly deserve, and with all good fortune.

# Annexure 4

## Speech Delivered by His Highness the Maharajah on the 20th January, 1928, Proroguing The Bikaner Legislative Assembly

*Members of the Legislative Assembly,*

I desire at the outset to express the pleasure which I derieve in seeing you all here again before this Session is prorogued. It had been my intention to convene a meeting of the Assembly in October last for the special purpose of ascertaining your views and securing your advice regarding the State Budget for the Financial Year 1927-28, which commenced with the 1st November last; but the great historic Assemblage at Ganga Nagar, where His Excellency the Viceroy performed the Opening Ceremony of the Gang Canal on the 26th October last, kept us all busily engaged and the final consideration of the Budget had perforce to be postponed for some months. It has already been placed before you during the present Session of the Assembly and I look forward to perusing useful suggestions and constructive proposals on the Receipts and Expenditure of the State at your hands which I need hardly add will receive my earnest consideration.

2. Two non-official Resolutions were admitted for this meeting for the purpose of of fering felicitations on the occasion of an epoch-making event in the annals of Bikaner—the Opening of the Gang Canal, which now brings down waters of the Sutlej to our beloved country and will lead to the conversion of our sandy desert into a fertile garden, smiling with waving corn. "It was a great victory" both for Engineering Science as well as, I think I may fairly say, for our Government—of man over nature-and I am gratified to find that you share my joy at the happy realisation of this my life's dream. As I hope you are all aware the one sacred ideal that has ever inspired my thoughts, shaped my actions, and moulded my policy has been the advancement of the prosperity of my beloved people, and I fervently pray to God that the prosperity and plenty that are sure to follow in the wake of the Sutlej waters flowing from the snowy peaks of the Himachala, may only be the early harbingers of further favours from

the Almighty, so as to bless the land over which Providence has called upon me to reign.

3. In the interval since we last met some very important things have happened, and are still happening. Besides the advent of the Sutlej waters, which promise to affect materially the internal aspects of the State, other events are influencing its external relations as well. As you are aware, His Excellency the Viceroy announced a little while ago the appointment of an Indian States Committee which is to report upon the relationship between the British Government and the States with particular reference to the rights and obligations arising from our Treaties, Engagements and Sanads and from political usage, etc.; and the Committee is secondly to enquire into the fmancial and economic relations between British India and the Indian States and to make any recommendations that it may consider desirable and necessary for the more satisfactory adjustment of such relations. The Princes of india had for long been desirous of seeing their political relations with the British Government widely understood and appreciated in their correct constitutional and historical aspects, and of having their fiscal relations with British India carefully examined and adjusted in a manner equitable and just both to British India and the Indian States.

4. The request for a proper enquiry into these matters of such momentous importance to the Rulers, Governments and people of the Indian States was put forward on behalf of the States at a Round Table Conference held at Simla last May, which was presided over by His Excellency the Viceroy and was attended by some High officers of the British Government and some Princes and Ministers representing the States. I had put forward the proposal for the urgent necessity of convening such an informal Conference nearly 8 years ago when I was Chancellor of the Chamber of Princes; and it has been consistently and strongly urged ever since. I should, therefore, not only be failing in my duty but would also be erring against the well-known qualities of our Race-grateful response to sympathy manifested and gratitude for good done—if, fore the appointment of the Indian States Committee as well as for convening the Round Table Conference, I did not take this opportunity of publicly giving expression to the feeling of deep indebtedness of the Princes and States to His Excellency Lord Irwin, our popular and noble Victory, who—notwithstanding some ill-informed and ill-advised criticism appearing in a section of the Press, which I honestly consider to be as injustifiable as it is unfair to His Excellency—has, in the comparatively short time that he has been Viceroy of India, already given various

practical proofs of his generous feelings, sympathy and friendship for the Princes and States of India.

5. It is impossible to over-estimate the importance of the work which will be undertaken by the Indian States Committee, or of the most far-reaching consequences to the States which are likely to result from its labours and recommendations. Indeed, in certain aspects, it is no exaggeration to add that the very existence of our States in the future may be both directly and indirectly affected thereby.

6. As is the case in all such matters, much depends on the terms of reference, the scope of the enquiry and the personnel of the Committee, as well as on the manner, spirit and atmosphere in which its work will be undertaken. And, taking the various circumstances into consideration, it will, I think, be generally agreed that so far as the atmosphere and personnel of the Committee are concerned the States have much to encourage them; and I for one rejoice—and I feel sure that I am voicing the sentiments of the Princes and States generally when I say this—that it is a matter of congratulation and gratification and in the Imperial interests, as well as in the interests of the States, that such an important investigation is to be carried out in Lord Irwin's Viceroyalty, with, at his side as his Political Secretary and chief expert adviser—a sympathetic Political officer like Mr. C.C. Watson; whilst the whole of Indian India will be highly gratified at the appointment as Chairman of the Committee of such an eminent Statesman and sagacious Administrator as my old and valued friend, Sir Harcourt Butler. Sir Harcourt has inspired general respect and confidence and made a great name for himself both as one of the greatest Governor of modern times of more than one British Province, and as, by universal consent, the most popular and sympathetic Foreign Secretary at least in our life time, when he proved himself to be such a genuine and true friend of the Princes and States, and gained their undying friendship and gratitude by being instrumental in bringing about a generous and liberal policy of greater sympathy and trust for the Indian States, and thereby rendered the States considerably happier than he found them.

7. It is true that the scope of the enquiry is not as complete or wide as we should have wished, in that the future position of the Indian States in a self-governing India in days to come is not covered by the present terms of reference. But with an equitable and just appreciation and recognition of the constitutional relations. of the States with the British Government, and a fair adjustment of our financial and economic relations with British India, the path it is to be hooped will be paved, and the task rendered easier, of ensuring that the Indian

States shall fmd and take their rightful place in the future polity of India; and the corollary to the present investigations must, in my opinion, be that in days to come and I think in the near, rather than in the distant future—a further investigation will have to be made with a view to safeguarding the just rights of the Princes and people of the States as a politically separate and constitutionally independent unit of the great Indian Empire.

8. As regards the personnel, I will straight away concede that the States would have preferred some Princes and Ministers appointed on the Committee. But with no Indians appointed on the Parliamentary Commission in regard to British Indian Constitutional Reforms that was not to be expected. Here I would disgress for a moment to refer to the slogan of certain newspapers and politicians in British India that the Indian States are a hindrance to political progress in British India. I will for the moment not make any comments on the correctness or otherwise of such a statement, but will merely content myself by pointing out that there is also a reverse side of the shield, and that the Indian States themselves suffer on account of the political situation in British India, which often has an adverse effect on the march of the Indian States towards their legitimate goal. Component members of one integral body have to suffer as much disability as they derive advantage from their mutual juxtaposition.

9. Be that as it may, with the appointment specially of Sir Harcourt Butler as Chairman and another sympathetic and popular Political officer as Secretary, the Indian States have in my opinion no reason to doubt that the questions coming up before the Committee will received fair, generous and sympathetic treatment. It is a fact that the other two distinguished Members of the Committee have hitherto not come into personal touch with the problems concerning the Indian States; but I am not sure that in an investigation of this kind it is not an advantage to have some Members on the Committee who will approach their task with absolutely open minds, free from all preconceptions or prejudices.

10. As for the manner and spirit in which their task will be undertaken, it is inconceivable to my mind that the Committee, with so much of the winter already gone, will attempt to rush through its work merely to finish it by a certain date. Nor is there any reason to anticipate that the Princes and States, and specially the Chamber of Princes and its Standing Committee, will not be kept in close touch with, and taken into the confidence of, the Committee at all stages. What is desirable—and what I confidently anticipate—is that the

Committee and the States should work together in a spirit of mutual trust, confidence and goodwill-without any recriminations or raking up the past.

11. Some so-called friends have, in the press and on the platform, been good enough to urge the States to boycott this Committee. Considering that this Committee is appointed at our request, such a course would, in my judgement, be the height of folly, and the very negation of all that counts for statesmanship, which demands that we should seize every opportunity offered to us with a view to securing our rightful dues by friendly and whole-hearted co-operation and persuasion, and by putting forward our claims in a just and clear manner. I will not attempt to controvert the fact that the States too have had to face various vicissitudes and have had their ups and downs, which have at times caused them anxiety and concern during the last century and more since they came into political relationship with the British Government, through Treaties of Alliance and Friendship as in the case for instance of the Rajputana States, or through other causes.

12. But I feel sure you will agree with me that it is all important that we should at no time fail to retain our sense of proportion or to keep the right perspective in view. In spite of the suspicion and misgivings which certain so-called friends are striving to create in our minds as to be possible difficulties and dangers to which the Princes would be exposing themselves, and in spite of the apprehensions which, in all loyalty to the Crown and in perfect good faith, may be entertained by a few people in the States through extreme caution and conservatism—and such extreme caution and conservatism are also unfortunately not altogether unknown in the case of some officers of the British Government as well-regarding the possible consequences of our inviting such an enquiry, I am convinced—and I am sure you will agree with me—that the only right course for the Princes and States is to look forward to the deliberations of this most important Committee with faith and hope, and with a robust confidence not only in the righteousness and justness of their cause, but also in the good faith, goodwill and sympathy of Great Britain and the British Government and their High officers both in England and in India.

13. I would add that, during the meetings of the Standing Committee at Delhi, I conveyed an invitation to the Indian States Committee to visit Bikaner and I hope that we shall have the pleasure of welcoming them here before long, when I look forward to showing them our various institutions and the internal working of our Administration as well as the condition of my State and subjects.

14. Before turning to other subjects there are one or two more points in this connection to which I feel constrained to refer. Extraordinaty statements have been made on the platform and in the press of British India alleging a deep-laid conspiracy on the part of the Princes of India, and an unholy alliance with the 'foreign' Rulers, with a view to retard the constitutional advance of British India. I have publicly referred to, and attempted to refute the correctness of these allegations on previous occasions—the last time during the visit to Bikaner a year ago of His Excellency the Viceroy—but, to our astonishment, these charges continue to be repeated—on what authority I am totally at a loss to understand. The Princes have lately also been solemnly warned not to interpose the bogey of their ancient Treaties and Alliances in the way of the freedom and emancipation of British India; whilst the demand has been enunciated to have our Treaties revised or scrapped on various grounds, including the argument that these Treaties are obsolete and that the Princes have no Sovereign rights.

15. Leaving our of consideration here, the petty Rulers, and any isolated expression of purely individual opiniosn of—at the most—a very small minority of Princes, I say without hestitation that if this is the genuine conviction of any sober-minded people in British India, the Princes as a body have been seriously misunderstood by some, and perversely misrepresenteds by others; and I challenge these totally unmerited, unfair and—I venture to add for reasons which will shortly be clear-ungrateful accusations.

16. From 1916 to 1921 I was Honorary General Secretary to Their Highness for the Annual Princes' Conferences held at Delhi, and from its inauguration in 1921 to 1926 I had the honour of being Chancellor of the Chamber of Princes. Since then-although I have not sought re-election as Chancellor—I have still retained the closest touch with the inner counsels of the Chamber of Princes as a Member of its Standing Committee, and I have attended every important Conference with the British Government as well as amongst ourselves. Speaking thus in all earnest, and with a full sense of responsibility, I am, from my personal knowledge, in a position to give the most unqualified and emphatic denial to all allegations regarding any such alleged mean conspiracy or unworthy attempts on the part of the Princes of India as an Order; and I assert without any fear of contradiction that—whilst all the 108 Members of the Chamber of Princes cannot necessarily be expected to hold the same views—far from the Princes as a body having expressed any hostility to the legitimate aspirations of , or having taken any other improper steps

with a view to opposing or checking the progressive realization of constitutional reforms in, British India, they have on various occasions not only made it abundantly clear that they have no desire to stand in the way of the political progress of their brethren in British India but they have also taken various opportunities, both in England and in India, of publicly expressing their approval and support of such constitutional reforms.

17. Without repeating all that has been said, I would refer such critics to the speech I made in London, in 1917 at the Luncheon given by the Empire Parliamentary Association, and particularly to my speech on the 7th March, 1919 at the Banquet to Lord Sinha, where I categorically gave chapter and verse not only of the opinions, publicly expressed or written, of some prominent individual Princes, but also of the views collectively voiced by the Rulers of Indian States in the Princes' Conference in support of the reforms then under contemplation. The Chamber of Princes had not then been instituted; but I think I can, without being guilty of any impropriety, safely add that on no single occasion has any such dishonourable proposal even been mooted in the Chamber. Colonel Haksar and Professor Rushbrook—Williams, on their return from their recent Mission to Europe, therefore only reiterated what had already been duly put forward on behalf of the Princes, namely that, in asking for a Committee to investigate into Indian State affairs—as indeed in regard to any other action that the Princes may have taken or urged—with a view to safeguarding the interests of their States and subjects, they were in no sense or degree hostile to the legitimate aspirations of British India.

18. In taking up this attitude, the Princes—in spite of some narrow-minded views taken by a few individuals in certain other quarters—were really influenced by their inborn loyalty and deep devotion to their beloved King—Emperor and their attachment to the Empire—as I have had occasion to remark more than once previously—and by their keen desire to see such measures adopted as would popularise and preserve the King—Emperor's Role in India, and would furthermore strengthen the ties that bind England and India together. Although many of the Princes were under no delusion as to the attitude of certain schools of political thought in British India—who even then desired to see the States wiped off the map of India—they were also influenced in taking up this attitude by their natural desire as Indians to see their Motherland rise to her full stature of Nationhood under the aegis of the British Crown.

19. Apart from certain other factors—which it is unnecessary to

refer to in detail here today, since they are matters purely between the British Government and the States—it will I trust be clear that the request of the Princes for such an investigation as is now being undertaken by the Indian States Committee was in no way based on any hostility to, or conspiracy against, British India, but with a view to safeguarding the rights of the States, their Governments and their people, and their internal autonomy and independence. This desire was also based on the instinct of self-preservation and self-defence—which lies buried deep in the human breast—as well as on the right of every individual, unit, or collective body to exist and to live their own lives in peace and security. Not only from people obviously ignorant or hostile and unfriendly to the States or their Rulers, but even from certain individuals from whom the States did not expect such irresponsible statements to be so made, have we heard the usual cries about the Treaties with the Indian States being no more than scraps of paper, and of no consequence, or that the States and their Rulers constitutionally possess no Sovereign rights or status. These light-hearted critics have even gone to the extent of saying that the States must go. Some speakers and writers have furthermore bluntly arrogated and reserved to themselves, and to the Government of British India of the future, the "right", to interfere in all kinds of matters—external and internal—appertaining to the States and thus to infringe our Sovereignty and to violate our autonomy—fiscal or otherwise. The States were also influenced by the apprehension thus caused generally amongst the States by such claims and threats, to seek safety and security for the future through such an enquiry at the hands of a Committee.

20. In view of such extravagant claims and random remarks which have been, and are being, indulged in British India, it appears necessary that there should be some plain, but dispassionate, speaking so that there might be no room for uncertainty or misunderstanding. Many an Indian State has existed not only long before anyone in British India claimed the right to meddle or interfere with them, but long before even the Moghal Empire established its away over the Country. The great majority of the Indian States have come into political and Treaty relationship with the British Government, not through conquest, but because such States, or the British Government, or both, desired to enter into such alliances for mutual benefit; and such Treaties did not therefore, generally speaking, grant, create or secure, but guaranteed many of the rights which were already fully possessed and enjoyed since long by the Indian States. Even Lee-Warner—whose doctrines cannot be said to be too favourable or

friendly to the standpoints of the State—refers with emphasis to the great respect paid to the Treaties, and to their sanctity and binding nature; and the same applies with equal force to subsequent official assurances, including pronouncements by different Viceroys right up to the present time. The most formal recognition has been given to these Treaties, which have been accepted by the British Parliament as binding on the Crown; and above all, there are many Royal Proclamations and gracious pledges and assurances given and reiterated by Queen Victoria, King Edward, and our present gracious King-Emperor, which—to quote the words of His Imperial Majesty in the Proclamation read out at the inauguration of the Chamber of Princes in February 1921—after expressing His Royal "determination ever to maintain unimpaired the privileges, rights and dignities of the Princes of India" contains the following significant words—

"The Princes may rest assured that this pledge remains inviolate and inviolable."

21. In these circumstances, it will be clear that, unless such Treaties and Engagements are modified or abrogated by the mutual consent of the Imperial Government and of the Princes, their provisions continue to have full force; and anyone suggesting the scarpping of these Treaties is, it will be obvious, guilty of making not only a highly injust, but an immoral, suggestion. History has been read in vain if it has not yet taught them that it is only brute force that will compel the States to submit to their Treaties being scrapped.

22. Just as the very existence of the States depends on a just of servance of their Treaty Rights, so are the States and their subjects equally concerned in safeguarding their Sovereign rights and internal autonomy, which vitally affects them in many matters of the highest importance—political, economic and fiscal- and I need say no more on the subject beyond quoting a small paragraph, again from Lee - Warner—

> ". . . Violence must be done to history, diplomatic engagements, legislative enactments, legal decisions, and long-established usage, if we are to discard ideas of suzerainty or sovereignty as inapplicable to the Native States of India, and incompatible with the future development of the Indian Empire."

23. The subject of interference and intervention in the internal affairs of States is too important and comprehensive to deal with adequately in the course of a few sentences, even if this was the right time and place to do so. Suffice it to say that the sooner such notions

are dismissed from the minds of all concerned including the refrain—"the States must go," the better it would be for the destiny of our Motherland. For the Indian States have no intention meekly to submit to any such demands; and they certainly will not go under without a struggle.

24. The territories of the Indian States occupy over a third of the total area of India, whilst their subjects comprise more than one-fifth of the population of the Indian Empire. The States are scattered over the length and breadth of India, and have been here for centuries, and demand the right to exist. India is the common heritage of the peoples of British India as well as of the Indian States; and the one will find the other to help and use; and it behoves both to respect the rights and liberties of each other, to refrain from interfering with their respective domestic affairs, and to derive the benefits which each one is in an undoubted position of offering to the other. I am one of those who, after giving earnest consideration to the matter, hold the view that in spite of some difficulties, which are only to be expected in all such matters, there is no reason why, with wise statesmanship and mutual toleration and good-will, both British India and the Indian States should not fit in any future scheme of Imperial for Indian Polity when India becomes self-governing under the aegis of our King-Emperor.

25. There is one other matter to which it is important to allude today. Side by side with the allegations made that the Princes and States are opposing arid obstructing the constitutional progress of British India, has been raised another bogey—in which it is surprising to find that some subjects of the Indian States, totally oblivious of all obligations of patriotism and gratitude to their parent states, have joined—namely, that the Princes are entering into another itrigue with the alien British Government, and have asked for this Indian States Committee, with the object of placing impediments in the way of the political advancement of their subjects, and to keep them out of their just dues, or in other words that the Princes are also conspiring against their own subjects. A greater and sadder travesty of facts it is hard to imagine !

26. I hold no brief for my Brother Princes; and today I am speaking entirely in my personal capacity as Maharajah of Bikaner. Human nature being what it is, and with different conditions prevailing in different States, it is inevitable that there should be found good, bad, and indifferent Rulers amongst our Order—as in every other community—and that their administration should similarly very according to the standards of life and the general atmosphere

prevailing in each State. No conscientious Ruler can have any sympathy whatever with any 'black sheep' in his flock, who bring discredit to the Princes and States; but from isolated cases, and a few instances of misrule, any sweeping generalization and insinuation that all Rulers are alike, cannot but be termed as a wanton and mischievous perversion of truth. Fair and honest criticism is beyond exception; but from column after column of malicious criticism and calumny indiscriminately hurled almost daily at the Order of the Ruling Princes in a certain section of the press one might almost imagine that we were not living in a civilized India, but in a barbaric land, where the hand of every Ruler was turned against his own people, where the Ruler was a tyrant, and ruling with an iron rod, oblivious to the interests and the well-being of his own people.

27. Whatever the motives which prompt some of our critics to make such assertions, they have forgotten one cardinal point, viz., that when the Princes ask that their Treaties should be maintained unimpaired, that the internal autonomy of their States should be respected, and that there should be an equitable adjustment between British India and the States in regard to matters—fiscal and financial—the Princes are not asking for anything for themselves to the exclusion of their people, but their demands expressly include their subjects. The term 'State' includes not the Rule alone, but the Ruler, his Government and his subjects, which are all component parts of, and all go to comprise, the 'State'. If any State were to lose its Treaty or Sovereign rights, not only the Ruler, not only the Government, but also his subjects all simultaneously and as a corporate body forthwith lose their independent status and Treaty rights. If the independence of a State goes, then Gentlemen, the subjects of the State, forthwith and simultaneously likewise lose their integrity and individuality. If the States gain fiscally, it is not only the Prince but the Government and subjects of the State who ought also to gain—and gain most—in all such matters. If the States lose in any such matters, that loss is shared by the subjects with the Prince and Government. Therefore, it is the Ruler as well as his subjects who stand to gain or lose together, and it consequently behoves the subjects of the Indian States to keep this fundamental point prominently in view. Any action of a bad Ruler, or of a bad Government, should not so blind a subject as to render him impervious to his own benefit, or to his own loss. In States where conditions prevail, contrary to this ancient ideal of the East as well as the present day ideal of the West, the sooner the ida that the State, as conceived by Louis XIV, belongs exclusively to the Ruler is put right, the better for our entire Order, the States and their subjects.

28. I will illustrate my point with a concrete instance. Amongst the various questions, which have been raised by us in the Chamber of Princes for the benefit of our States and subjects, there are some relating to very vital fiscal matters including Customs. As stated by the Prime Minister in his speech in the Legislative Assembly on the 25th August last:

> "at present the people of Bikaner, like those of other States, are also suffering from this disability in another form of double taxation, in that Customs Duties on goods imported into the States are also levied by the British Government at British Ports. As is well known, the Chamber of Princes has been earnestly representing these matters to the Government of India, with a view to the subjects of the States being made to pay such duty only once and that to the Government which has undertaken to pay for all their advancement."

One of the two equitable solutions of this important question is that the State should be given its proper share of the Imperial Customs Revenues levied at the Sea Ports. Another alternative would be some other satisfactory arrangement by which goods required for consumption in the States would without breaking bulk be admitted free of any Customs duty.

29. This is one of the matters which will doubtless be taken up by the Indian States Committee; and, should, as we all most sincerely hope, some such satisfactory results ensure, you, Gentlemen of this Assembly, do not require to be told by me that it is the subject of our State who will benefit first and foremost, and more than the Ruler of the State or his Government, as you would be saved from paying double Customs duty for an article imported into our State.

30. I am one of the foremost amongst those who eagerly look forward—as the Prime Minister has already publicly declared to you will my full authority—to the day when the Customs duty levied in the Bikaner State could be entirely abolished—which, I can safely state, would, in such a contingency be done as soon as we had paid off our public debt, recently constructed for remunerative Canal and Railway construction purposes which will be a mater of only a few years.

31. I trust that sufficient has been said by me to demonstrate the great importance to the Princes as well as to the people of the Indian States of the work undertaken by the Indian States Committee and how much it is in your joint interests that all such matters should be

thoroughly sifted and duly adjusted without delay; and I know that you, Gentlemen, will unite with me in the hope and prayer that the outcome of the deliberations and recommendations of the Committee will lead to a carefully conceived and permanently settled policy—in matters political as well as fiscal—framed on generous and sympathetic lines regarding the Indian States, and devoid of all diplomacy—secret or otherwise—for which there should be no room in dealings between friends and allies, and colleagues and partners, whereby the ties binding the Princes to the Crown and the Empire will be further cemented and strengthened, and still greater and lasting solidarity will prevail between the British Government and the States with their very real identity of interests. And let us also express the sincere hope that another direct benefit resulting from the appointment of this Committee, and a proper examination of all such important questions, will be to dispel the clouds of suspicion and mistrust arising in British India, and any doubts existing in the minds of any subjects of the States.

32. So much for the efforts made to render secure the present and future position of the Indian States, so far as the efforts of the Chamber of Princes and the Standing Committee, and—I confidently anticipate—the sympathy and support of His Excellency the Viceroy, the British Gove.nment and the Indian States Committee are concerned. But nothing that each one of them may do can completely and effectively secure the future of the Indian States. For, as I remarked in my speech when inagurating the Conference of Ministers held in Bikaner to discuss these very matters on the 16th August, 1926:

> "no one who think seriously and earnestly can shut his eyes to the fact that our future really depends largely, if not almost exclusively, upon the Rulers of States themselves, upon the extent we the Princes realise our great responsibilities and the sacred duty God Almighty has committed to our care, upon the manner in which we direct the affair of our States, upon the amount of care and thought which we bring to bear upon questions of vital importance to the well-being of our States and our subjects. Very difficult times unmistakably lie ahead of us . . . there is no use blinking the fact that the trend of certain schools of political thought is not in our favour. . . . Times are changing, and the Princes and States too have to adapt themselves to modern environments. Some of our States have every reason to be proud of their splendid achievements and of the high goal towards which they are so assidously working.

In some States on the other hand the need for reform will no doubt be apparent. It behoves us all—the Princes and their Ministers—to see to it that nothing which duty and prudence dictate is left unattended to. No doubt the future destiny of the Princes and States of India will be determined by the will of God; but if we discharge our duties properly and are not unmindful of our responsibilities, He in His infinite mercy will assuredly extend to us His protecting hand and guidance."

33. As I have previously remarked, the various Indian States are in varying degrees of advancement at the present moment, and thus no stereotyped model of Government can really be said to be effectively and completely applicable, or most suited, to each and every one of even the larger States, since every State must be the best judge of conducting its internal affairs in ways best suited to local circumstances, peculiarities, traditions, and sentiments, and to the different ideals and standards of administrative efficiency and education prevailing. It is also an irrefutable fact that reforms emanating from within, and on the initiative of the Governments of the States themselves and the steps taken by the Rulers of their own free will and accord, are far more likely to be successful and to lead to the most beneficial and lasting results all round.

34. The standard of education as existing in most parts of British India and that in the majority of the States does not bear any comparison. So too representative and popular institutions in British India have had a long—a very long—start of the Indian States. Whilst some of the, even then, most advanced States, such as Mysore, to there great credit, started Legislative Councils and other representative institutions—under whatever names and forms they were then known—it is only in the last decade, or at the most two, that such popular institutions have, if I mistake not, come to be established in some of the other States.

35. Any how as His Excellency Lord Irwin remarked in his speech at Rajkot that in proportion as our "administrations approximate to the standards of efficiency demanded by enlightened public opinion elsewhere, the easier it will be to find a just and permanent solution" of the difficulties and disabilities which the States have been suffering from.

36. But- whether we view them from the standpoint of the East or the West—there are some well recognized and all round accepted principles and functions of good Government and of Regal obligations and duties of Rulers to their subjects, over which there can be little, if

any, dispute—whatever the standard and conditions prevailing in any State, and wherever it is geographically situated. They form the Hall mark of every State worthy of being ranked as enlightened and progressive; and these to my mind are the essential preliminaries—the minima—which can inspire the general confidence of the public both within and without his territories, and which any Ruler (or State) should aspire to that wishes to put his house in order and to withstand the fierce light which beats upon a Throne.

37. It is in no vainglorious spirit, but with a feeling of devout thankfulness and profound gratification, that I and my Government feel happy, with our lands upon our hearts, to think that these are the general principles—the essentials—of good Government which we have humbly but earnestly tried to follow—with what measure of success I must leave to the judgment of posterity—which can be summarized as below:

I. For the Ruler of a State to have a fixed and well defined Privy Purse and a clear dividing line between his personal expenditure and that of the State.
II. Security of life and property by the employment of as efficient and uncorrupt a Police as possible for the maintenance of law and Order.
III. Independent Judiciary.
IV. The Reign of Law, including certainty of Law, its uniformity and approximation where possible with the laws of British India with such additions and alterations as local conditions may render necessary.
V. Stability of Public Services.
VI. Efficiency and continuity of administration.
VII. Beneficent Rule in the interests of the general well-being and contentment of the subjects.

These seven points are well worthy of being the watch words of internal reforms in the States, and of being adopted in the almanac of every Ruler or Government of an Indian State ŕeach point to be emphasized and specially remembered for each day in the week.

38. They do not differ from the Hindu ideal of Kinship so aptly placed before us by our own Shastras. I do not forget that at some places a King is described therin as embodying within him the spark of Divinity, but that spark is also hedged round with, and cased within a sheath of , stem behests and sacred commandments, which a Ruler is under an obligation to comply with by his Coronation Oath.

According to the formula of that Oath enjoined by the Aittreya Brahman, the King is sworn at the time of his Coronation with the following abjuration, which he has to repeat with Faith:

> "Between the night I am born and the night I die, whatever good I might have done, my heaven, my life, my progeny, may I be deprived of , if I oppress you."

In the Shanti Parva the King is asked to take the Pratigya mentally, verbally and physically:

> "I shall see to the growth of the Country, considering it always as 'God'. Whatever Law there is here, and whatever is dictated by Ethics, and whatever is not opposed to polity, I will act according to. I shall never act arbitrarily."

This is the ideal of the Reign of Law, which places Law above one's desire, caprice and fancy. It also clearly brings out how Law is supreme--superior even to the Kind. The King cannot arbitrarily create Law. He has to carry out the Dharma as is prescribed to him, and must subordinate his own wishes and inclinations to the paramount dictates of Dharma. Such is Dharmaraj, or the Reign of Law. Law or Usage was known as Pritha; and the King, or 'Parthiva' was one who not only ruled over the Prithvi (Earth) but who also upheld 'Pritha'—Usage or Law.

39. A Ruler cannot also afford to be oblivious of the other comandments prescribed to the King at the time of his Coronation according to our ancient ritual. Before he was asked to sit on the Throne, the Priest exhorted him thus:

> "To thee this State is given, thou art the Director and Regulator, thou art steadfast and will bear this responsibility of the trust so given for Agriculture, for well-being, for Prosperity and for Development."

Modern theories about Popular Rights, as conceived by Locke, of the Contrat Sociale as taught by Rousseau, and modern doctorines about the Rights of man and of Kingship as a Trust dependent on the concurrence of the people can find much support from the ancient Hindu Ideal of Sovereignty; and though it might not go to the length of laying down with Abraham Lincoln that "all Government is of the prople, by the people and for the people", the relations between the Ruler and the Ruled, defined by the Hindu Sages and Smritikaras left no room to the subjects of Indian States for undue apprehension or any need for a salvish appeal to the institutions and ideals of Western Polity for their common weal. Hindu Kingship is for protection, not for oppression. A Kshat-Triya ( -wound, and = to protect) Ruler was one who healed the wounds, or protected his subjects from aggression as well as oppression.

40. It is really remarkable and interesting to notice how the foregoing observations regarding the functions of good Government tally with a Note written informally by an honoured and esteemed friend, and a sagacious statesman recording an expression of his personal views about the general principles of good Government, which this distinguished writer says:

> "may be described as the task, firstly, of ensuring to the individuals composing the society governed, the opportunity of developing themselves as human beings, and, secondly, of wselding them into a compact and contented State. The discharge of this double function involves the necessity of finding and maintaining the due balance between the rights of the individual and those of the State to which he belongs."
>
> "Stated differently the ordered life of a community depends upon being regulated, not by the arbitrary will of individuals, but by LAW, which should expressly or tacitly be based upon and represent the general will of the community."
>
> "This is equally true of:
>
> Autocracy,
> Oligarchy,
> Democracy."

"And the efforts of Rulers therefore, whether they be One or Many should be directed to the establishment of the Reign of Law."

41. The need for the Ruler of a State to have a fixed and well defined Privy Purse and Civil List, and a clear dividing line between his personal expenditure and that of the State, is so obvious that it hardly requires any further remarks. The ancient Hindu Kings were similarly enjoined only to take a fixed su, or a definite percentage of the total income of the State; and the Civil List of an enlightened modern Ruler is normally also fixed in one of the two ways.

42. Unless such a principle is scrupulously and rigidly adhered to,

it follows that money which should be available for the development of the life of the community, and of its individual citizens, and for the general well-being and advancement of the State, is not forthcoming, which is bad for the State as well as for the Ruler and his Dynasty; and it is beyond dispute that no Ruler—as the custodian of the interests of his State and his people—can justify devoting a large percentage of the revenues of the State for his personal use. So urgent and important did I consider this measure of reform that, shortly after my coming of age, I, of my own free will and accord, introduced this system of a separate Civil List and Privy Purse on modern lines as long ago as April 1902; and it is a matter of no small gratification to me to feel that I was one of the pioneers amongst the Princes of India to do so; and furthermore that the Privy Purse expenditure in Bikaner has, during the last quarter of a century and more, been kept strictly and entirely separate from the State accounts. Under this arrangement only 5 per cent, of the Ordinary State revenues was, as you, Members of the Legislative Assembly, are aware, drawn upon for my Privy Purse, from which all my personal expenses, including the expenses of all my private establishment, etc., were defrayed on lines strictly laid down by me.

43. But it is not always easy to differentiate between personal expenditure and that incurred for Ceremonial purposes or for the Ruler in his position as Head of a State; and there was certain incidental expenditure which thus continued to be incurred by the State on my behalf. Although all such expenditure received the greatest personal attention—specially when the budgets were submitted to me—the matter continued from time to time to receive my earnest attention; and as a result of the orders issued at different times, action has been taken, with a view to the liability of the State for all kinds of expenditure—direct or indirect—incurred on my behalf, being definitely limited, and all such indirect items of expenditure have since 1925 also been transferred to the Privy Purse under the revised arrangements.

44. As the Prime Minister stated the other day in this House, the discussion of the Privy Purse, and Palace Budget, does not, under the present Constitution, fall within the purview of the Assembly; but, as he further informed you at the same time, I am always ready to take my subjects into my fullest confidence; and I have nothing to conceal. Therefore, a statement giving the broad details of the revised Civil List and Privy Purse arrangements has already been supplied to each Member of this Assembly along with the Budget Estimates; and I desire to express my gratification at the good reception which you have

accorded to the new arrangements. This statement gives the details of every such item of indirect expenditure which formerly was incurred by the State, over and above the 5 per cent, paid for my Privy Purse. From this you will observe that in my desire to have a definite percentage, and final cut between State expenditure and the expenditure incurred on my behalf, I have preferred—even at the risk of the percentage being temporarily a little higher than what I desire sincerely and most earnestly—to transfer to the Privy Purse some items, which could, perhaps justifiably, have been charged to the State.

45. I will not anticipate a fuller statement, which before long is, under my orders, to be expressly presented to the Assembly, giving you fuller details in connection with all such items. It will therefore suffice to point out that items such as my official tours and visits, and even my official residence in the Capital, viz., the Lallgarh Palace, and all existing Palaces and other Residences, kept for my use in the State, have now been taken over by the Household Department, the expenses of which will be defrayed by the Privy Purse—including all future additions and alterations in the Public Works Department and the Electrical and Mechanical Department work, furniture, etc. Similarly, I have preferred to include the grant so far set apart for Sumptuary Allowance. All such expenses incurred, directly and indirectly on my behalf, and including the five per cent, originally fixed for my Privy Purse, even now, amount to a little over 11 per cent; and with the State revenues fast rising, and with the further, and substantial, increase which we expect almost immediately from the Opening of the Gang Canal, I shall soon have the satisfaction of seeing all such expenditure kept at the definite figure of 10 per cent of the Ordinary revenues of the State—which is the percentage which I desire permanently to fix. of course, I am only speaking for our own State; and it is obvious that in some States, with smaller revenues, the percentage must vary and be larger.

46. There are several details in connection with the Privy Purse, such as extraordinary expenditure on occasions of briths, marriages, etc. which too are receiving my careful consideration; and as soon as we have been able finally to deal with such all items which I sincerely desire in the interests of the State and its subjects, as well as of my family the fullest information will be forthwith communicated to the Assembly.

47. The benefits of an independent Judiciary have always been valued most by me as an essential of good government. We were the

first State in Rajputana to establish the Chief Court in 1910, and with its establishment the idea of separating judicial ftom executive fimctions began tc assume shape. It was matured in 1922 with the creation of a High Court—again the first, and I understand the only one in my State in Rajputana; and you will be gratified to learn that this beneficient measure has now been launched with the creation of separate District Judge's Courts in the various Nizamats of the State. What I most eagerly desire, however, to achieve is the advancement of those nation building activities, which go to secure the welfare of the people; amongst which the highest place must needs be given to Education and Sanitation. I rejoice to see that there has been a general awakening amongst my subjects and a genuine desire on their part to take full advantage of the educational facilities provided for them. From the Budget placed before you by the Prime Minister you will have seen that a generous provision has been made for the experiment of compulsory Education during this year. Permissive legislation under which Education can be made compulsory within selected Municipal areas has now become ripe and this reform will have my cordial and sympathetic support when the necessary legislative enactment is placed before the Aseembly.

48. I am pleased to see that my Government is making adequate provision for the female population of my State, both as regards their education and health. A qualified Lady Inspectress of Girls Schools, who has won repute by her experience, has been appointed to take charge of the Girls Schools in the State and gratifying signs are manifest that my people have commenced to appreciate the necessity of female education. it is also encouraging to learn that qualified matrons and nurses are being provided in the District Dispensaries to look after the welfare of women. In this connection I am also pleased to learn that the Bikaner Municipality has already arranged a qualified Health officer and it is hoped that his vigilance will lead to the improvement of the sanitation of the City. You will be glad to learn that I have already approved of the scheme for Water Supply at my Capital; and steps are being taken for the appointment of an expert boring Engineer for sinking artesian wells. The work will be pushed on as soon as the possibility of tapping a plentiful source of underground supply is established whereby the one long standing cause of the defective sanitation in the City and the acute discomfort of my citizens will shortly be removed.

49. The interests of the health of my people, however, demand a radical improvement in our social customs and usages; and I congratulate Seth Shiva Ratan Mohta on his courage in introducing

the Bill for the prevention of early and unequal marriages amongst the Hindus. This social evil has ruined the health of the people and has been sapping the very foundations of the whole society by retarding the physical development of the race. The rate of infant mortality is likely to astound the stoutest heart amongst us and it is time we all woke up to this great social evil.

50. It is a matter of sincere pleasure to me that this bold reform has been proposed by a non-official member from amongst you. There are some matters no doubt where reform can proceed with greater propriety and better chances of assimilation, if it is inaugurated by the spontaneous will of the people. such intelligent co-operation on the part of my people will have, I am sure, the beneficial result of speeding up much desired reform in various directions. Every progressive government worth the name must provide itself with some machinary, by which it can inform itself of the trend of public opinion and of the needs, desires and aspirations of the people, and through which the people can make their voice heard. Government without popular consultation must at all times be difficult and may become impossible on occasions when new situations arise and unforeseen complications clog and paralyse the official wheels, I congratulate myself on the assistance and co-operation I have always received from my Legislative Assembly and have been for some time anxiously thinking of how best to enhance its usefulness and its power for good. Although under the constitution of the Assembly legislation can be undertaken without reference to the Assembly, I am glad to be able to assert that not in a single instance, in the past 13 years since the inauguration of the Assembly, has. my Government enacted any law without its being brought before the Assembly under the ordinary procedure. In connection with liberalising, where possible, and revising the Constitution and Rules of Business of the Assembly, I have much pleasure in announcing that this provision in the existing rules will be abrogated and that henceforth all legislation will be enacted only through the Bikaner Legislative Assembly. I have also asked my Prime Minister to convene an informal meeting with the non-official Members of this House, and to have a free and frank discussion with you with a view to elicit what further extension of your powers and privileges you desire which, I need hardly add, will receive my sympathetic and careful consideration. I am confident that by your continued loyal and unstinted co-operation the trust which I and my Government are placing in you will be fully justified and that you will serve your Sovereign and your State with the same steadfast fidelity and disinterested devotion as you have been

examplary in doing heretofore. I always bear in mind that the interest of the Ruler and the Ruled in a well-regulated State are identical and that they form component parts of one harmonious whole. They stand or fall together and the real good of the Ruler consists in promoting the good of his people. The strength of an Indian Ruler does not lie in the British bayonet, as alieged by some critics, but in the loyalty and affection of his own people; for his own people; for, as I stated at Shivpur, of all citadels protecting his Throne, none is so impregnable as the one raised on the hearts of his subjects. My welfare will always be in your continued prosperity and well-being. May the protecting arm of our Patron Deities Sri Lakshmi Narayanji and Sri Karniji-ever bless my State on its onward march to peace, progress and prosperity.

# Annexure 5

## Speech Delivered by His Highness the Maharajah on the 19th December, 1929, Proroguing the Bikaner Legislative Assembly

*Members of the Legislative Assembly,*

When you met last April, I was away on my annual and much—needed, holiday, and I am therefore all the more pleased to meet you on this occasion. Since then the General Elections have taken place; and, whilst I am glad to see some new members, you will all, I knowe, miss some old familiar faces.

We particularly mourn the loss of our highly popular and esteemed Revenue Minister, Mr. G.D. Rudkin, who so ably and conscientiously performed his duties and who was associated with us for a period of close upon seventeen years. The cruel hand of death removed him just when his valuable services were beginning to bear their first harvest of fruit. Death has been equally responsible for thinning your ranks among the non-official benches. Bt the demise of the late Thakur Heer Singhji of Bikaner, a promising life has been cut short; and we mourn the loss of a talented Chief who was inspired by loyalty to his Ruler and State and by a desire to render public service.

Amongst the new members I am glad to see Mr. Salusbury who, consequent upon Mr. Rudkin's death, has taken up the duties of Financial Commissioner, and is in charge specially of all work relating to Colonies and the Gang Canal. Mr. Salusbury has come to us from the Punjab with a high reputation as a capable and conscientious officer, intimately aquainted with Canal and Colonization work; and I have every hope that my people will find in him a just and sympathetic officer. Besides other popularly elected members who come to the Assembly for the first time, I am also pleased to see in the non-official benches here today representatives of the Canal Colony of Ganga Nagar. It is proposed to create a District Local Board for the colony which would serve the purpose of an electoral college and send popular representatives from that district. Pending the formation of a District Local Board, I had much pleasure, on the recommendation of my Government, in nominating to the Assembly five land-holders representing the rural interests of the Ganga Nagar Division.

In proroguing this Session, I do not propose to deal at length with matters of purely local interest to the Bikaner State. Great as is the importance attached to them by me and my Government, I have some observations to make today about, and to invite your attention to, certain matters of wider and the utmost importance to us of Bikaner, in common with the Rulers, Governments, and subjects of the Indian States in general. In order furthermore not to take up too much of your time I will, without reiterating the many important matters dealt with by me on previous occasions, merely invite your attention to the relevant portions of some of my previous utterances, such, for instance, as the speech which I delivered in this Council Hall on the 20th January, 1928; my observations when inaugurating the Administrative Conference on the 3rd October last; and the Interview which I gave to the Associated Press on the 2nd November in regard to the momentous and welcome pronouncement made by our popular Viceroy, Lord Irwin.

**Viceregal Pronouncement and Conference in England**

I feel sure that you, the Members of my Legislative Assembly, in common with my other subjects, will be in entire accord with me in welcoming the Viceregal Pronouncement, which is of such supreme importance to our brethren in British India as well as to us of the Indian States, and particularly the announcement of the intention of His Majesty's Government to invite before long representatives of different parties and interests in British India, and representatives of the Indian States, to meet them for the purpose of conference and discussion in regard both to the British Indian and the All-Indian problems.

6. I know that you, the loyal and patriotic subjects of the Bikaner State, will derive particular gratification at the just recognition by the British Government of the right of the Indian States, as a separate and independent entity in India, occupying the proud position of "perpetual Friends and Allies," and bound to the Crown by of fensive and defensive treaties, to have their due voice in the discussions and negotiations at such conference relating particularly to the wider question of closer relations in the future between the two parts of Greater India; and I am convinced that you will join with me in the earnest prayer that the proceedings of such conference will be marked by constructive, statesmanlike proposals, and an atmosphere, as I have previously said, of goodŕwill moderation, and toleration, and a due appreciation and understanding of the respective standpoints on the part of all concerned, so that, side by side with the due preservation

and maintenance of the respective rights of the Indian States as well as of British India, the way may be paved by a wide measure of general assent for the advancement and contentment, and above all for the unity, of All- India-bringing in its train a further accession of strength to the Empire.

7. I am also confident that you would like me to afford you this opportunity on this formal occasion of associating yourselves with me and my Government in tendering to His Excellency the Viceroy our grateful thanks for the noble and conscientious manner in which, as the Ambassador of Greater India, Lord Irwin has, with a rare courage and statesmanship of the highest order, fought India's battles and represented to His Majesty's Government the view-points of British India as well as the States during his recent mission to England, and of expressing our deep gratification at the success which His Excellency's earnest advocacy has won for him, of which the memorable mistrust of even those who are most sceptical or distrustful. And recent events have also amply demonstrated the genuine good-will and sympathy for India of His Majesty's Government—and particularly of Mr. Ramsay MacDonald and Mr. Wedgwood Benn—and their desire to do the right thing by us all. As I said in my Interview, more than this it is unreasonable for anyone in India to expect at this sage from the Viceroy, of His Majesty's Prime Minister, or Secretary of State for India; and it behoves us also to see to it that neither British India nor the States let down the Viceroy after his noble efforts and services in the cause of India, as the late Mr. Montagu—than whom Indian never had a truer friend—was unfortunately let down after the Montagu-Chelmsford Reforms.

8. Time flies, and, although it looks as if it was only a few months ago that we welcomed Lord Irwin to India, His Excellency will, in the natural course of events, be relinquishing the Viceroyalty in April 1931 ; and, in the interests of the two Indias, as well as of the Empire, and with a view to launching and ensuring the sucess of what we hope will be a further measure of libral constitutional advance for both British Indian and the States, it will be the earnest hope of all the sober elements throughout India that His Majesty's Government may be successful in securing the consent of Lord Irwin to stay on for a longer time as our Viceroy.

9. I ventured in my Interview last month to express the belief that good and not harm—will come to the States by such questions being seriously dealt with between the Imperial Government, the Viceroy and the Governments of the States, by separate negotiations, as well as by discussions at the Conference. I am aware that some

apprehension exists in the States on account of the fact that the Simon Commission has had no opportunities of properly eliciting the views and standpoints of the Indian States' Governments on the points involved, since they were not originally included in the Commission's terms of reference. But in my opinion there is no cause for anxiety on this point. In the first place, I am sure that we can confidently anticipate that a statesman like Sir John Simon, and his distinguished colleagues, will be the first to bear in mind the importance of doing justice to the legitimate claims of the States also, and of ensuring that the States too should receive fairplay; and secondly, it might in some ways be a decided advantage for the States to go to the Conference, not only with an open mind, but also unfettered by any compacts or previous commitments. We may further reasonably anticipate useful suggestios by the Simon Commission, after they have explored the various avenues, by which the interests of British India and the Indian States, where they conflict, might be satisfactorily adjusted, which would enable the two great constituent parts of India to settle down in peace and harmony to work out side by side their respective destinies in a spirit of friendship and co-operation. The States, which cannot be irrevocably bound by any schemes and proposals arrived at without their concurrence, will, we may rest assured, have the fullest opportunities of having their say—without which such Conference would be no conference at all. And so long as the case of the States is just and their attitude reasonable, I for one have nothing to fear from any such matters being dealt with by the Simon Commission or their being discussed at the Conference.

10. I desire to-day especialy to address you, the Members of my Legislative Assembly and, through you, my other subjects—whom you have the honour of representing her—in order to make more clear a particular point of high constitutional importance to the Indian States, viz., the claim put forward by certain so-called States subjects and institutions for the representation, as a separate and independent party, and on an equal basis, at the proposed Conference in England. Before I proceed further, it would perhaps be as well, with a view to obviate misunderstandings and minimise opportunities for misrepresentation, to make some necessary observations which deeply concern the States and their subjects, even if much of what I say to-day is a repetition of what I have said on former occasions. It is unpalatable to have to do so, but, as an old soldier of over 30 years' standing, I am a firm believer, where necessity compels, in a little plain speaking, which has its advantages and helps to clear the air.

**Bad Rulers**

11. In the first place let us at once, and freely, concede that a Prince who is a bad Ruler is a grave menace not only to his State and subjects, but also to his Brother Princes and the Indian States in general. For every such Prince does incalculable harm to his Order, and the sooner some wholesome check is put on the harmful activities of such a Ruler, the better for the Princs, the States and their subjects, and all concerned. it is Rulers of this type who afford opportunity to the enemies of the States and their Rulers for painting a picture of all the States, and all Rulers and their Governments, in the same colours. Human nature being what it is, it is impossible, as has been pointed out on more occasions than one in the past, to expedt every one of the 108 Rulers of States, who are Members of the Chamber of Princes in their own right, to be all of exactly the same mould; and it is, alas! inevitable that it is in the best interests of the Princes and States to see to it, and to let it be known by every means at their command, not only amongst the Princes themselves and the States, but to every one in the wide world, that such Rulers cannot, and should not, expect sympathy or support from their Order—in fact that such really bad Rulers—of whom we can thankfully and truly say there are only a few—should, so to speak, be ostracised and ex-communicated by their own Order.

12. If the criticisms in the Press and on the platform were confined to really bad Rulers, and the really bad Governments, of States, a public and inestimable service would indeed be rendered to the States and to the Princes and their Governments, no less than to the subjects of the States. But the present day methods adopted defeat their own objects. Gross exaggeration; the dissemination of falsehoods; deliberate distortion of facts; vituperation and vulgar abuse; branding the Princes as imbeciles, tyrants, traitors and oppresors, and "suckers of the very life-blood of their people," and as dishonest and unscrupulous miscreants—worse than criminals, guilty of every offence under the Sun—are only a part of the organised, vehement, spiteful and bitter propagands, and of the sensational, indiscriminate, and malicious campaign of wholesale and sweeping attacks on the Princes and Governments of the Indian Sates as a body, and are a picture of States and Rulers which, anyone inwardly acquainted with the States must realise, is painted either by those really ignorant of Indian States affairs, or by people whose deep personal prejudice and ill-feeling towards the Princes in particular and the States in general have warped their judgement and tainted their outlook—a state of affairs which cannot but be a matter of real concern to all

who have at heart not only the good of the States, but who would like to see a United and Greater India marching hand in hand on the road of progress towards their respective goals.

13. I read in an important Indian paper in Northern India some criticism on the political situation in British India from which I cannot do better than quote the following significant extract:

> "There can be no manner of doubt that there is a tremendous amount of intolerance in our public life to-day and that those who are or imagine themselves to be in a majority in any matter on which they are keen of ten go to extravagant lengths in parading their dislike of their opponents. We need scarcely say that this is not a healthy attitude and that it does not make either for strength or independence. Why cannot men believe that their opponents can be as sincere and patriotic as themselves?"

Change the work "Majority" into "opposition" and it is equally true of the attacks on Indian States and their Rulers. So much so that many do not hesitate even to write and speak of the Treaties of the Princes with the Crown as virtual scraps of paper and to advocate their being ruthlessly torn up. I ned not refer to our Treaties or innumerable Royal Proclamations and pronouncements on the subject; but here I will content myself by reminding such persons of the following words in His Excellency the Viceroy's Speech at the Chelmsford Club in Simla of only June last:

> ". . . then there are treaty rights of the Princes, inherited from the East Indian Company, and hallowed and confirmed by the successive declarations of the Crown. . . . I make no concealment of my view that in any proposals that my be made it is essential on every ground of policy and equity to carry the free assent of the Ruling Princes of India and that any suggestion that the treaty rights, which the Princes are accustomed and entitled to regard as sacrosanct, can be lightly set aside is only calculated to postpone the solution.that we seek."
>
> it is not by these methods that "the desire of wide statesmanship", to which His Excellency gave expression on that occasion, of seeing" a canvas set on which a picture of all India may ultimately be drawn" can be fulfilled.

**Internal Reforms in States and rights of States Subjects**

14. And now I come to the second point, viz., the urgent and

imperative necessity of such measures being honestly and energetically taken in States, with a view to introducing necessary internal reforms where they do not exist, and also for preserving and safeguarding the just rights of the subjects of Indian States and the liberty of their person and safety of property. Whether viewed from the culture and ethics of the East or of the West, whether the Government of a country be autocratic or democratic, the obligation undoubtedly rests upon a Prince and his Government to rule over his people wisely and well; and no single Ruling Prince in Indian can deny this responsibility imposed on him by God. A good Ruler must furthermore feel that his own conscience also imposes that responsibility on him. From the personal point of view too, and particularly in the interests of his Dynasty, a Ruler should naturaly be anxious so to govern his State as to reign over a loyal and contented people. It, therefore, follows that it is in the best interests of our States and of the Order of Ruling Princes that, where they do not already exist, internal reforms should be inagurated, about which I spoke at length in this very Council Hall on the 20th January, 1928. The urgency of steps being taken, where needed, by a Ruler to put his house in order in obvious; and it is not enough for such a Ruler to rest content with, and to sit complacently on, pious Resolutions of this nature. If they are to be of any avail, they have to be promptly translated into earnest action; and, as His Excellency the Viceroy said in a speech last June, all wise and liberal-minded Rulers will take account of the feelings of the subjects of Indian States.

15. It would however be a waste of time to deal here with the fantastic and false accusations so light-heartedly hurled against the Princes about their trying to perpetuate autocracy, absolutism and misrule, and similar other pernicious lies, to which I alluded in my speech at the Administrative Conference in October last; but let me here say in the most unequivocal and unhesitating words that nothing can be more absurd, or farther from the truth, than the allegations appearing in the Press and on the platform in British India that the Rulers and Governments of States, in fighting at the present moment for the rights of themselves and their subjects, are actuated by the desire to get a blank cheque for misrule and for oppressing their subjects. In the very nature of things the Princes and their Governments realise that there must arise occasions where intervention by the Crown, as the Paramount Power, is rendered inevitable. All that the Princes desire is that intervention, when rendered unavoidable, shall not be arbitrary, or based on inaccurate or one-sided reports, and that it must be resorted to not only with the

greatest reluctance, but after the most deliberate and sympathetic consideration by the Viceroy ŕas the Representative of the Crown—of the case of the Ruler or State concerned, and furthermore that such inter-vention must be resorted to for the sole purpose of the furtherance of the interests—present and future—of the Indian States and of the general Order of the Princes themselves—as Lord Irwin himself stated in His Excellency's speech in the Chamber of Princes in November, 1926.

16. There are assuredly other ways also of safeguarding the rights and securing justice for the subjects of States in the case of a bad or indifferent Ruler or Government; and I am voicing nothing but my sincere conviction when I say that the Chamber of Princes is destined to play an important part in the future—even though at the present day its utility is circumscribed by many limitations and restrictions. Nothing however in the immediate future will be more helpful or efficacious in this direction than the cultivation and growth amongst the subjects of States of a strong and suber public opinion, at the back of which there are not the self-styled leaders or disgruntled and disaffected so-called subjects—not infrequently leading the lives of political exiles, or at times men who have been deported from their States, or even convicted of grave offences, and who are inspired chiefly, if not entirely, by motives of vindictiveness against the Princes and States—but healthy public opinion backed up by bona fide loyal, patriotic and sober-minded subjects of the States, proceeding along peaceful paths with the sincere and laudable object of securing the political advance of their fellow-subjects, and framing their demands on constitutional and rational lines for the redress of genuine grievances and for the fulfilment of legitimate aspirations to share in the responsibility of administration. The strength of such wholesome and what must in time prove irresistible public opinion and the most effective and convincing method of securing internal reforms, and receiving the encouragement, good-will, sympathy and support, not only of the general public, but also of the Rulers and Governments of Indian States, lie in sobriety, moderation and reason, and not in the vehemence of declamation, or virulence of invective, or indiscriminate calumny, or wholesale abuse of the monarchical system.

17. I may perhaps be deemed to be old-fashioned and out of date; but I confess that I am a firm believer in co-operation and in carrying people with me, and as equally convinced of the dangers and drawbacks of non-cooperation. Although the statesmen of the older generation, like the Grand Old Man of India, the late Dadabhai

Naoroji, were before my time, I am old enough—and proud do I feel- to be able to claim personal friendship with some of the great sons of India of my generation, like the late Gopal Krishna Gokhale. It was my privilege, at his request, to have co-operated with him in securing the assent of my brother Princes with a view to a joint message being sent to the Prime Minister and people of Great Britain from the Princes and people of India immediately after the departure from our shores of Their Imperial Majesties the King-Emperor and the Queen-Empress after their memorable visit to India for the Coronation Durbar in 1911. And I cannot help feeling that if, instead of vituperation and abuse and indiscriminate calumny, there was more of moderation in thought and language, and greater co-operation and earnestness in appeal, inspired by loyal feelings and good-will, happier relations and happier results would have been manifest today and the pace in the direction of reforms in both British India and the States would have been considerably accelerated and the goal rendered more easy of attainment. And I am constrained to add that those who are endeavouring to stir up trouble and discontent amongst the ordinarily loyal and contented subjects of the States are doing a very great dis-service to the States subjects. As was rightly pointed out in a Resolution passed at a meeting of the loyal and bonafide subjects of a State which has recently been attacked a good deal:

"creation of estrangement between the Ruler and the ruled can never bring about the real good of the people."

18. I would just make a few more observations for the serious consideration of those eager and bona fide subjects of Indian States who, inspired by the best of motives for our States and people of our States, desire to see the pace of internal reforms accelerated. Let us not forget that the Indian States are at present in varying stages of advancement and that their administrations have attained varying standards and degrees of administrative efficiency, and the same applies to the subjects of the various States. Some of our States are extremely well governed, and as model States they can proudly hold up an exemplar even for provine es in British India to emulate. Others lag behind. To apply, or to expect to apply, at once the same standard of administrative efficiency to, or to desire the same degree of internal reforms in, each and every one of the States is to expect the impossible. To grant in the shape of constitutional reforms what may be feasible to the subjects of one of the most enlightened States like Mysore would be to create a situation which would neither be understood

nor be to the real benefit of the subjects of such States where altogether different circumstances prevail, and would, on the analogy of putting new wine into old bottles, almost certainly lead to serious dislocation of State business and to administrative confusion and chaos. Those of us, whether we be the Rulers and Members of the Governments, or subjects, of the Indian States, who earnestly desire to see every Ruler put his house in oreer—urgent and highly desirable as such a step is—must refrain from acting the role of impatient idealists and realise that the millennium cannot dawn by one fiat or useage, by a word of command from us, or a wave of our magic wand; and we must have patience and confidence both in ourselves and in the future, and derive gratification at seeing a change already being brought about which—believe me—is steady, even if it may appear gradual. And it behoves the subjects of the Indian States to be on their guard against intrigue by designing and mischievous persons to create unnecessary trouble between the Rulers and the ruled, and to alienate the allegiance and the affections of the subjects of States for their Rulers, and the steady effort to create dissensions between them; and it is equally necessary for the subjects of States to realise—what is conveniently forgotten by those who attack the rulers and Governments of States—that, side by side with the right of the subjects of States, the Rulers and Governments of States also possess certain undisputed rights, and that the subjects have also corresponding obligations and duties to discharge towards their States and Rulers; and that, in spite of occasional lapses on the part of the present day Rulers and Governments of States, there is much in the genius and indigenous system of rule in India, which has contributed many glorious pages to Indian History, and particularly to the History of the Indian States, and which has withstood the ravages od time and survived the wreckage of vast Empire. Surely it is our duty to conserve and improve, and not to destroy, this system of rule, which has in the past been peculiarly suited to our States in spite of the frantic efforts being made to uproot and exterminate it and to divert the ship of State into new channels uncharted and unfathomed. I have never claimed for the Indian States any immunity from criticism, or even correction, when occasion justifies it; and I trust that what I have said has made it amply clear that I am the last person to maintain that there is no need for reforms in some of our Indian States. Whether reform is to proceed on democratic or other lines is a point on which I shall not attempt to hazard an opinion. Democracy—which has its supporters as well as its detractors, has not been unknown in ancient India, where it was tried and found wanting. Some hold that it has not proved a sucess in the United States of America, and others maintain that signs have been unmistakably evident of a tendency to substitute the rule of an intellectual oligarchy instead. The terrors of mob mis-rule under Soviet Russia have been an eye-opener to the whole world. With the shining example of the success of limited monarchy in England no further argument need be advanced in favour of monarchy. The League of Nations has furnished to the world what potentiality there is in the combined strength of reason and forceful persuasion. Ostracism and ex-communication have of ten brought erring souls back to the fold; and the threat to place a ban of social outlawry has prevented aberrations from social conventions in the past. With the sanction of united civilization at its back the Leagues of Nations may, it is permissible to hope, triumph where armaments and militarism have failed. Similarly when Governments in Indian States cease to function for the benefit of the people and are tossed on the storm of angry passions, it is not democracy alone that can be the best salvage for towing the derelict safely to the shore. It behoves us all, the people and Princes of the States, through healthy public opinion and the loyal endeavours and support of all patriotic subjects of the States, with tact and sympathy and, above all, statesmanship and breadth of vision, to help to reclaim the wreckage of useful and time-honoured national institutions and to maintain a proper sense of perspective, and fidelity, loyalty and patriotism which the Indian States have a right to demand from every one of their sons—be he a Prince or a peasant.

**Claims and Credentials of Certain So-called "leaders" and "representatives" of Indian States and their Subjects**

Whilst on the question of the rights of States subjects and internal reforms in our States, I would take this opportunity of declaring in public what I have in conversation said in the past to some British Indian friends, viz., that I would not only welcome, but would be the first to acclaim, the convening in my Capital of a conference of bona fide All-India States subjects, if we could be certain that such conference would really comprise of the genuine representatives of various classes, communities and interests of the States in different parts of India, and if we could be assured that the proceedings of such conference would be conducted with dignity and decorum, with moderation and restraint, and in a spirit of fair-mindedness and reasonableness. I am aware that it is often alleged that the reason why the so-called States subjects Conferences are held in various parts of British India is that the subjects of States are not permitted to meet in Indian States territories. I will not attempt for one moment to defend the Government of any State which may be so ill-advised as to prevent the holding of any genuine conferences, really representative of the people, at which the real grievances of the subjects of the State or States, could be ventilated in a befitting manner. But there are other considerations which should not be lost sight of.

20. First and foremost, there is the duty, which falls on every Government in every part of the world, to maintain law and order and preserve the public peace and tranquility of the country. Liberty in certain circumstances is apt to develop into licence; and no Government worthy of that title can permit proceedings which are likely to create disorder or to cause a disturbance of the public peace through incitement and excitement offered to those who are ordinarily peace-loving and law-abiding subjects. There are alas ! too many cases to deliberate attempts to stir up trouble and create difficulties for Rulers and States Governments. As His Excellency the Viceroy has said in a public pronouncement:

> "I know of no reason by which the Government of any ordered State should be held bound to sit still with folded hands and watch the security of the interests committed to its charge thus stealthily undermined."

21. Another important consideration is that no Ruler or Government can lightly take the risk of the hospitality which they offer to the people of such gatherings to be abused by insults and indignities, and venomous and unfair attacks made by disloyal, disgruntled and discontented persons against the British Government, or the Princes and Governments of friendly States—an unhappy state of affairs which is a sad feature of so many of these so-called conferences.

22. It has of course been impossible for me, under present conditions, to attend any such conferences; but, with the knowledge of those presiding, I have sent some State officials to witness such proceedings; and I have of course felt it my duty to read the proceedings, and particularly the speeches, as reported in the Press, as also the various pamphlets, as well as the publications, issued under the auspices of such conferences.

23. The first thing that strikes one as extremely strange and significant is that such bodies, styling themselves as the Indian States' People's Conference, with their Headquarters at Bombay, have to go

to British India to find their presidents, like my friends Dewan Bahadur Ramchandra Rao and Mr. C. Y. Chintamani. If these institutions and persons really claim to speak for, and come from, and to be really representative of , bona fide States subjects, it is difficult to believe that they cannot get suitable leaders from the States subjects of anyone of the 108 Indian States to preside over their deliberations. However worthy such presidents from British India may be, it is inevitable that they cannot be intimately possessed of inside, personal knowledge of the States.

24. Incidentally, it is a pretty good indication of which way the wind really blows, that when, it was reported in the papers that the first President of the so-called Indian States' People's Conference in Bombay—Dewan Bahadur Ramchandra Rao—had accepted an appointment in the Mysore State, which was doubtless offered to him on account of his personal qualifications for the post, the so-called friends of, and newspapers supporting, the Indian States subjects should instead of taking it as a compliment, have forthwith proceeded to renounce one, who, out of the goodness of his heart-and, it has to be regretfully added, also by the wicked impositions of unscrupulous and designing persons, posing as aggrieved and injured States subjects—had been led to believe in the sincerity of their professions, and to denounce their honourable President's action in accepting the appointment as an "extremely deplorable and an extremely pitiable degradation", based on greed and selfishness and unworthy motives, and bereft of all noble-mindedness, and to enter "an emphatic protest" against his perfectly honourable and justifiable action.

25. The real feelings of such friends of the States are clearly manifest from the unconcealed offence felt at the visits to, or some complimentary remarks made regarding, the States or their Rulers and Governments by even such prominent British Indian leaders as Mrs. Besant, Pandit Madan Mohan Malaviya, Mr. Gandhi and Pandit Motilal Nehru.

26. Then if a Prince were to invite such a conference to his Capital, it would be equally necessary to examine the credentials of the office-holders of such conferences and associations, and equally essential would it be to examine the credentials of the various members and delegates, who claim to represent different States in different parts of India. As I have stated on previous occasions, my remarks are chiefly and inevitably confined to conferences such as those held in Bombay and Ajmer, in British territory, which I understand are supposed to represent the All—India and Rajputana States subjects respectively,

as we are not acquainted with the conditions of such conferences, held, as for instance, in Southern India, under the presidentship of Sir, M. Visvesvaraya. But then every one is of course aware of the advanced stage which the subjects of States such as Mysore, Travancore and Cochin have reached.

27. Speaking, however, chiefly for Rajputana and the neighbouring territories of States, is it irrelevant or unnecessary to ask why does not the executive body of the "Indian States' People's Conference" in Bombay publish a list or memoranda, giving the names, history and antecedents of the various gentlemen, who hold executive office, and similarly of the delegates and members, who claim to represent the States from various parts of India; and if they are to substantiate their claims as genuine leaders of, and bona fide, States subjects, it should, amongst other details, also be definitely stated regarding each such individual:

(1) Of what State he was a subject?
(2) Whether he still claims to be an Indian States subject or now is a British Indian subject?
(3) If the former, whether he is a born, or naturalized, States subject; and his claims to the same according to law?
(4) If no longer permanently residing in, or in the service of, State, the reasons and circumstances under which he left the State?
(5) Whether any such gentleman is a dismissed official, or was banished or deported from a State; and if so, the reasons and particulars of such dismissal, banishment or deportation?
(6) Whether he was so punished administratively or by a law court, and if so, the details of the same?
(7) By what communities and interests in the State was he elected, or nominated, as its representative?

28. Of the two gentlemen claiming to be delegates of the Bikaner State at the Indian States' People's Conference in Bombay last May, one was Mr. Bagarhatta—a totally strange and unknown name for a real Bikaneri to have—who supported a resolution regretting a policy of repression followed in certain States, both under Ruling Princes and under British Administration, and expressing its sympathy with the victims of such policy; and the second part of that resolution authorized the "Working Committee" with a view, to facilitate the proper ventilation of the grievances of the people of the States to receive all complaints, representations, petitions, and memorials, etc. The second name is that of Mr. Kanahiyalal Kalantri, whose name is

put down amongst the members of the Executive Committee numbering 70 gentlemen.

29. If we are not misinformed, Mr. Bagarhatta is styled the "General Secretary" of the "Rajputana States Peoples' Conference" and had, we are given to understand, in the papers to contradict the charge, preferred against him by his own colleagues, or the other gentlemen working in association with him in such anti-States propaganda, of being a spy of both the British Government and the Government of Bikaner. This gentleman has also the distinction of being the author of a particularly courteous, graceful, and, of course, strictly truthful attack on our popular and able Prime Minister, Sir Manubhai Mehta—a Statesman of not only Indian States, but All- India, fame—and, if rumour is true, he does not appear even to reside permanently in the Bikaner State. As regards Mr. Kanahiyalal Kalantri, it was necessary to ascertain his antecedents, as it appears that the Bikaner State has not even the honour of having any such person amongst its subjects;and he has apparently not even the remotest connection with the Bikaner State or its people.

30. You, gentlemen of the Non-official benches of the Bikaner Legislative Assembly—the real leaders and representatives of the people of this State—will, I am sure, particularly like to know further of the rights and claims of gentlemen of this type to represent and speak on behalf of our State, and of ourselves and the other subjects of the Bikaner State, and who—if their claims were met—on the strength of such pretensions would have received separate and independent representation at the Conference in England to be convened by His Majesty's Government. The examination of the credentials, even if ordinarily a pure formality, is one of the essential preliminaries even in democratic countries and institutions like the League of Nations and other formal, or International, gatherings. Still more obviously necessary is the close and careful examination of the credentials of such self-styled representatives and leaders of States; and it would be particularly interesting to know what vested interests or stake they have in Bikaner and what mandate or authority they have from the Bikaner State subjects whom they claim to represent. Have they had the honour of having been elected or nominated by the 130 old Chiefs and Nobles, or the great mercantile community for which our State is famous, or the agricultural masses of the State, or any other community, municipality or recognized body?

31. These are matters which ordinarily one would prefer not to touch upon. But the organised propaganda and systematic campaign conducted against the Princes and States generally, and the

constitutional principles involved of high political importance to the States, appear to render it necessary that the true state of affairs should now be really exposed.

32. Then turning to the proceedings of such institutions and bodies, even the executive officers do not hesitate to make wild and rash statements and the most gratuitous charges against the Rulers and Governments of States which, if challenged, they would often find impossible to prove or substantiate. As regards the delegates, I am informed that, more often than not, gentlemen claiming to speak for the States make no concealment of the bitter feelings which they personally entertain towards their own native land and their own Ruler. The constructive nature of their criticisms and suggestions; their patriotism and loyalty for the States; and the dignified restraint and courteous manner in which they refer to Rulers and Governments of States can, apart from the speeches made on those occasions, be seen at a glance from the subject-matter and wording of the resolutions passed at such conferences.

33. I am the first to admit that we should be Indians first and British Indians, or the people of Indian India afterwards; but this must surely be subject to the essential qualification that nothing should be said or done by us which involves disloyalty or harm to, or a violation of the rights of, the States, or anything which is contrary to the obligations entered into by the States with the Crown. But read what is said at such conferences and other occasions and it will show how far such so-called leaders of subjects of States are inspired by patriotism and regard for the welfare of their States and their fellow subjects. although the Princes and their Governments are fighting for safeguarding the sovereignty and inherent and undisputed rights of the States—such sovereignty being shared by the people as well as by the Rulers of the States—the so—called representatives of subjects have not hesitated to pass resolutions approving and supporting schemes and proposals which would in certain instances not only deprive the States of their sovereignty, but would furthermore involve a violation of the rights guaranteed to the Rulers and subjects of States by Treaties and otherwise, as for instance, their supporting a scheme where a definite position of subordination and inferiority was proposed to be assigned to the States vis-a-vis British India—and yet these gentlemen pose as special friends and guardians of the rights of the people of the States. Only last night I read in the Times of India of the 16th December about a recent meeting—of what is described therein as a "few representatives of Indian States peoples" in Bombay to protest against their exclusion ftom the Conference, in which Mr. Chudgar—who

took a prominent part in such activities in England—is said to have remarked that "the question which they were generally confronted with" (in England) "was whether the States peoples were really agitating or whether it was only a few disgruntled persons who were making the noise", and Mr. Chudgar then is reported as having made the following significant admission—"they had to admit to their shame that there was in fact no big organisation behind the movement."

**Can anything be more clear?**

34. This very leader writing in the Press under the plea of securing good government for the people of the States, and professing as one of his objects the removal of "absolute ignorance", or at any rate 'imperfect understanding", has advanced various pleadings and arguments, which, in effect, was a plea for over-riding the sovereignty of the States and violating the provisions of their Treaties. In the course of such pleadings he referred to one particular article of the Treaties of various States—an article in regard to the interpretation of which a difference of opinion exists between the States and the British Government and which is now engaging their attention. But this patriotic States subject has obviously found it convenient carefully to refrain from giving the text or substance of some important clauses in the Treaties. He has been good enough to make a similar allusion to our Treaty; but it would have been better ifhe had also quoted some of the other and more important clauses in the Bikaner Treaty, such, for instance, as the following:

"Article 1.—There shall be perpetual friendship, alliance, and unity of interests between,the Honourable" (East India)" Company and Maharaja Soorut Sing and his heirs and successors, and the friends and enemies of one party shall be the friends and enemies of both parties."

"Article 2.—The British Government engages to protect the principality and territoty of Bikaneer."

"Article 9—The Maharajah and his heirs and successors shall be absolute rulers of their countty, and the British jurisdiction shall not be introduced into that principality."

And what about the sanctity of those treaties in connection with which I have today already quoted a significant extract from His Excellency the Viceroy's speech of June last—about the same time when probably this article was being written in England—and what, above all, about the pledges and assurances to the Princes and States of India contained in the numerous Royal Proclamations by successive British Sovereigns, of which I will once again give today the following extract from the gracious Proclamation of our present beloved King-Emperor, which His Imperial Majesty was graciously pleased to issue at the time of the institution of the Chamber of Princes in 1921:

> "In My former Proclamation I repeated the assurance, given on many occasions, by My Royal predecessors and Myself of My determination ever to maintain unimpaired the privileges, rights and dignities of the Princes of India. The Princes may rest assured that this pledge remains inviolate and inviolable."

35. It was in view of such tactics and deliberate course of action that, besides referring to a few instances and details about the so-called friends and subjects of the Indian States, I said in my Administrative Conference Speech that the activities of such persons were not really so much concerned with the welfare of the States, but that their principal aim was to injure the Rulers of the States, and that in their bias and campaign against the Princes they were in effect trying to injure not only the Rulers and their Governments but also their subjects, which consisted not merely of the noisy elements and malcontents, but also of other communities and classes and interests with important stakes in the land. And it was for the same reasons that I referred in the same speech particularly to the gloatings and jubilations of such States" subjects" over any humiliation—real or imaginary—offered to the Princes and States with reference to any adverse points or recommendations in the Butler Report or elsewhere—indeed a sorry spectacle of the sincerity or political sagacity of such patriots and champions of the Indian States people.

**Untenable Claims of So-called "Representatives" and "subjects" to be represented at the Conference in England as Independent Party**

36. And now to revert to what I aluded earlier in my speech, namely the claim put forward by certain persons on behalf of the subjects of Indian States for the representation of their subjects as a separate and independent party, sitting and negotiating on an equal footing with the Rulers, at the proposed Conference in England. I referred to the subject very briefly in the course of my Interview when asked about the attitude of the Princes in regard to the invitation to a Round Table Conference by the All Parties Convention; and I was both surprised and sorry to see in a certain section of the Press my remarks on the subject described as bellicose. And numerous instances are

forthcoming of what I said having been deliberately misrepresented, misconstrued and distorted with the obvious object of causing mischief between the Rulers and the ruled in the Indian States, and allienating and estranging the loyalty, devotion and affection of States' subjects towards their Rulers, and creating—totally unnecessary and uncalled for—apprehensions and alarm in the minds of the bona fide, loyal subjects of the States. Various remarks and pleadings have been attributed to me in this connection which afford a temptation to expose such mischievous activities in detail; but, it would be infra dig and awaste of time and energy to deal with them at any length. There has also been a good deal of confusion of thought and ideas; and even the issues involved have been confounded. And though I am truly and devoutly thankful- and proud of the fact—that the deep-rooted and traditional loyalty of the people of Bikaner to their Ruler and State can be fully relied upon, I am anxious that such deliberately harmful propoaganda and other activities of those who pose as the friends of the Indian States and their subjects, but who in reality are inspired by anything but friendly feelings towards the States, should be appreciated and understood at their true worth. And I therefore, feel it a plain duty, speaking through you, the non-official members and real leaders and representatives of my subjects, to a wider audience of the loyal subjects of my State and other States, to refer to certain important details in this connection.

37. Perhaps, with a view to refreshing memories, it would be as well as to trace the history of the matters and to give below a few extracts from my Speech delivered on the 9th September, 1928:

> ". . . from a perusal of the Report of the All Parties Conference Committee, March 1928, it would be clear that amongst the principles enunciated by that Committee for determining the relations of the Indian States with the rest of India, it was laid down that the manner in which this fuller participation shall be effected between the Commonwealth of India and the Indian States in the common poilitical, economic and social life of the Common-wealth will be determined by an agreement between the Common-wealth and Governments and people of the States. To that proposal there were two distinguished dissentients—Mrs. Besant and Pandit Madan Mohan Malviya; and the latter proposed the deletion of the words "and people" as, among other reasons, they were inconsistent with paragraph 2, in which provision was made for the Commonwealth respecting Treaty Rights of the States, etc."
>
> "I do not wish to be misunderstood. I am all for the association of

the subjects with the Governments of their States. This is a policy which I and my Government have whole-heartedly and consistently followed. But the relations of all Nations and Governments, including the most democratic amongst them, are with the Rulers—in case of Autocracy—and with the Rulers and Governments—in cases of Constitutional Monarchy and Democracy. Thus, in matters affecting the States, the lawful authorities, with whom alone any such negotiations can be conducted, are the Rulers and the Governments of the States, whether such Governments profess autocracy, bureaucracy or democracy; and, except in the case of 'Mobocracy', no Government worthy of the name, could, for a moment, agree to such negotiations to be bilateral, and conducted on the one side with the lawfully constituted Government of the State or country and, at the same time, on the other side, with the millions of subjects of a State or country—an impossible and obviously utterly impractical proposal which would be nothing but Mobocracy—unbridled Mobocracy, leading to a state of affairs, which I have aptly seen defined as the 'chaos of mobocracy' !"

38. The All—Parties Convention passed a Resolution at Calcutta on the 1st January, 1929, from which the following is a relevant extract:

"This convention invites the Princes and peoples of Indian States to appoint representatives to confer with representatives of the Convention at a Round Table Conference with a view to discuss and agree upon the constitutional position and status of Indian States in the future Commonwealth of India and relations that should subsist between Indian States and the Central and Provincial Governments of the Commonwealth."

The Convention appointed "representatives, referred to in the foregoing Resolution, with power to correspond with the States and peoples organizations to appoint their representatives and to arrange for the conference not later than May next.

39. It was on the 10th August, 1929, that Pandit Motilal Nehru wrote a letter to His Highness the Maharajah of Patiala, Chancellor of the Chamber of Princes, extending to him, and through him Their Highnesses the Members of the Chamber of Princes, a most cordial invitation to appoint representatives to confer with the Committee of the Convention on the points mentioned in the resolution of the All—Parties Convention of the 1st January, 1929, already alluded to above.

40. Although no mention was made of the point in the invitation to His Highness the Chancellor, it was clear from what appeared in some newspapers that an invitation had since, or about the same time, also been actually conveyed separately to the "peoples" of the Indian States, and that some allegd States Subjects Conferences had already appointed so-called States subjects to represent the States independently, and on an equal basis with the Rulers and Governments of States, at such a Round Table Conference; and it needs to be borne in mind that the All—Parties Convention resolution moreover authorised direct correspondence with the "States and peoples organization" on such matters as the appointment of their representatives and arranging for the Conference.

41. This invitation was considered by Their Highnesses of the Standing Committee of the Chamber of Princes in Delhi in October last, and a reply was accordingly sent conveying thanks for the invitration and saying that, as the invitation was extended to Their Highnesses the Members of the Chamber of Princes, and the functions of the Standing Committee of the Chamber of Princes being well defined, that Committee did not fmd itself in a position to commit the Princes as a body to any decision in regard to such a matter, and adding that the invitation would therefore be placed before Their Highnesses the Members of the Chamber of Princes in February next when they meet in Delhi in connection with the Session of the Chamber of Princes.

42. It will thus be obvious that, in voicing my opinion on the subject in the Interview to the Associated Press last November, I was only giving expression to my personal views. At the same time it will be obvious that the Viceregal Pronouncement and the announcement of the intention of His Majesty's Government to convene a Conference in England will have a direct influence on the decision which Their Highnesses may arrive at in February next in the subject; and it was hence that I further expressed my personal opinion that a Conference such as that planned by the All Parties Convention had now become superfluous.

43. With reference to what I said in that Interview to make certain important points clear, I would first and foremost point out that it is an entire travesty of facts to allege that I said that the Princes had objections to sit with their subjects—as such—at any conference. Nobody is better aware than you, the Non-official Members of this Assembly, that not only do I almost every day sit in Conferences, Committees and on other occasions with my Ministers, Heads of Departments and other officers as well as my beloved subjects but

that I derive particular pleasure in doing so; and no Ruler worthy of the name can have the least objection to sitting with his bona fide subjects for the purposes of conference or discussion on suitable matters. But, apart from what I said in my speech of the 9th September, 1928, from which I have already quoted at considerable length, that is a totally different matter from expecting the Princes for one moment to admit the claim—put forward by the gentlemen and institutions alleging to speak on their behalf—for the States subjects, to sit and negotiate as a separate and independent party, and on an equal basis, at the Conference proposed to be convened in England. And it was for reasons such as these, which are perfectly obvious, that I said in my Interview that it was difficult to conceive that it was not apparent to the All-Parties Convention that it was in any case impossible to expect the Princes to depute the duly accredited representatives of their Governments so to sit and negotiate with the so-called representatives of their people, or that they could possibly have expected the Governments of the States to agree to be bound by any such action, agreement or decision of the so-called representatives of their subjects, whose credentials, I added, it would be interesting to examine and with which aspect of the case I have also dealt today.

44. From such action on the part of the All Parties Convention, as well as from the wording of the resolution, the impression would not be altogether unjustifiable, however remote from their intentions, that the people of British India intended to interfere directly in the internal and domestic affairs of the Indian States and to encroach upon their sovereignty and independence; and it may even be held to constitute an incitement, doubtless unintentional, to the members, however few, of such so-called States organizations to cut themselves adrift from their ancient moorings and to cease connection with where they belong.

45. Such an antithesis between duly constituted Rulers and Governments on the one hand, and the peoples of the Indian States on the other, being a new and novel idea, implying as it did a complete misconception of the relations between the Ruler and the ruled in our States, I ventured to add that the loyal and thinking subjects of our States would find it unacceptable even to themselves, who, as I remarked, have from time immemorial been accusatomed to regard their Rulers as their natural leaders and spokemen and the hereditary defenders of their rights and interests. Here let me add that if any Ruler has forfeited his right to such an honoured position, it is due to his individual actions and misfortune; but that cannot be rightly held to affect what, it can safely be added, is the general view point in many a State.

46. Even in British India, which made a start a great many years earlier than the Indian States in regard to the establishment of representative institutions and modern constitutional forms of Government, and with all the elaborate constitutional machinery now existing in British India, it is still the Central Government which actually nominates India's representatives to Imperial and International Conferences and gatherings, and which claims to conduct, and does conduct, all negotiations; and even in the Democratic countries of the West, where the constitutional system has been fully established, the "peoples" of such countries play no separate or independent part; and it is the Government which is responsible for such negotiations and settlements. True, in the fully developed Democracies of the West the Government is composed of the duly elected representatives of the people; but with their varying degrees of political advance, and the standard prevailing amongst their various Governments, it would be unfeasible to adopt such a procedure in the States today.

47. It was in view of these very grounds that an official announcement has since been made on behalf of His Excellency the Viceroy, and a similar reply was given by the Secretary of State for India to a question in the House of Commons on the subject, in which it was made amply clear that so far as the Indian States were concerned the questions which it is contemplated will be discussed at the Conference will be confined to broad questions of constitutional policy in regard to which the acknowledged Rulers of Indian States were the only people who could speak with authority.

48. The Viceregal Pronouncement had also made it amply clear that questions concerning the.intemal Government of the States will not arise at the Conference; and, as has also been officially pointed out, their discussion at such Conference is specifically precludeed, because such matters are within the purview of Rulers of each State, subject to the responsibility of the Crown, as the Paramount Power, for protecting the people against gross misgovernment.

49. In the criticisms of my Interview I have been accused of inconsistency, and of contradicting the views I expressed in my Legislative Assembly Speech on the 20th January, 1928, namely, that the term 'State' includes not the Ruler alone, but the Ruler, his Government and his subjects, which are all component parts of , and all go to comprise, the 'State'. It should, however, he obvious to any impartial and fair-minded individual that there is neither contradiction nor inconsistency in the observations made in separate context. The State undoubtedly includes the Ruler, plus his

Government, plus his subjects, who are all component parts of , and comprise, a State; but that is a very different thing again to the claims put forward on behalf of States; subjects; and it would have been more to the point if the advocates of the States subjects had justified their claim to independent representation as a separate body, and on an equal basis with the duly constituted Governments of Indian States and had enlightened us all as to how such separate, independent representatives were to be nominated and what States, communities and interests they could have legitimately claimed to speak and negotiate for.

50. It is all very well for such "friends" and "representatives" of States to speak of the memorable Viceregal Pronouncement as being "highly disappointing", and "absolutely" and "totally unacceptable" "from the exclusive standpoint of the people of the Indian States"—amongst other grounds because of "the mere fact that it has been welcomed by some of the leading Princes" which one worthless paper, pretending to speak on behalf of the States subjects, adds "does not at all improve matters"; or to accuse even our noble-minded Viceroy, Lord Irwin, of contradiction and insincerity—"doubting very much the sincerity of one who can enjoy hospitality at the expense of the starving States subjects"; or referring to the reasons for His Excellency's "refusal" of the "States Peoples request" as "utterly untenable" and having caused "widespread resentment"; or "strongly" repudiating and "resenting" what I stated in my Interview as "arrogant" and "preposterous"—which" cannot be too strongly condemned". But facts have to be taken as they are, and not as any single individual or body would have them to be; and no amount of superlatives of invective, forced or spacious pleadings, or abuse, or threats—that "this insult" will not be taken "lying down" by the "millions of States subjects" "ignored" and "betrayed", not only by the powers that be "but also by the British Indian leaders" whose attitude is "deplored" towards such States subjects, who, "have also unhesitatingly backed" such British Indian leaders "in the struggle for freedom"—will alter the real state of affairs.

51. In my Interview at the close of my observations on this subject, I expressed the hope that what I had said was a sufficient reply to the question asked as to why, if the Princes can attend a Conference convened by His Majesty's Government, they should be unable to attend the All- Parties Conference. Let me then add that had His Majesty's Government in disregard of the correct and constitutional position of the Princes and Governments of Indian States decided to invite the so-called representatives of States subjects to the Conference

as a separate, independent and equal party, it would, in my opinion, have been equally impossible for the Princes to take part in any such Conference; indeed I can see no surer method of breaking up this Conference so far as the duly constituted Governments of Indian States are concerned.

52. With reference to the question asked as to how it is that the British Government, or the Government of India, can invite, and sit side by side with, their own British Indian subjects, it need only be further pointed out, without citing facts which are obvious, that the Conference is to discuss largely questions affecting the British Government and their own British Indian people; and in any such matters affecting the Governments of Indian States would be equally happy and eager to sit and discuss similar internal questions with our own bona fide subjects.

53. The proposed Conference in England will be concerned firstly with the status of India as a whole in the Empire; secondly with the constitution of British India vis-a-vis His Majesty's Government; and thirdly with the relations between the Government of India and the Governments of the Indian States. The constitutions of the States are necessarily outside the scope of the Conference. That is a matter between the Ruler of a State and his subjects. In the constitutional structure of India the two Units are British India and the States. Each Unit will be represented at the Conference—the British Indian Unit by representatives of different interests and parties in British India, and the States Unit by representatives of the States taken as a group. Even the British Parliament—which has solemnly recognised the validity of the Princes Treaties with the East India Company and formally enacted that such Treaties "shall be binding" on the Crown—can claim no jurisdiction to examine the constitutions obtaining in the Indian States; and the admission of such jurisdiction at the Conference would be destructive of the internal sovereignty of the States, which naturally they dearly cherish. Constitutionally, therefore, the suggestion of a quadruple conference is inherently wrong, and hence the invitation only to the representatives of the constituted Governments of the Indian States; and that explains also why I ventured to add in the Interview that the Conference must be tripartite.

54. It should be apparent that these objections on the part of the Princes and States are due not to any personal feelings against British India or its leaders but because principles of far-reaching political importance are involved and because there are inherent constitutional difficulties as well. Nor should my remarks be misunderstood as

implying that I am opposed to British Indian leaders and the Rulers and. Ministers of the Indian States Governments coming together in a friendly way with the object of clearing misunderstandings, and comprehending each other's standpoints and for the purpose of frank and informal exchange of friendly views on matters of mutual interest. In common with other Princes, I and Sir Manubhai Mehta derived much pleasure from such informal talks with some of the more prominent leaders of British India in Delhi last Spring; and it is because I am a believer in the advantages of such a course that—when I was Honorary General Secretary to the Princes' Conference, the precursor of the present day Chamber of Princes—such informal and friendly talks were arranged on previous occasions, as, for instance, at Patiala in January, 1918, when the Montagu-Chelmsford Reforms were under contemplation, and about which I made a more detailed statement in my Speech in September, 1928.

55. In concluding the speech today, I would say to the overwhelming majority of the bona fide and loyal subjects of Indian States—have faith in your Rulers and Governments; they are fighting, and will continue to fight, your battles for you, their subjects, to the utmost power and ability; they are fighting for the whole State—consisting of you as well as their Governments and not for the selfish ends of the Princes or for any other unworthy motives. To the leaders of British India, I would, in all sincerity and good feeling, appeal once again to show, as His Highness the Aga Khan has said in his article in the London Times, the courage, the forbearance and the fundamental liberalism in regard to each and every party concerned; and to bear in mind that the adjustment of the relations of the Indian States to a Dominion India will need the patience, courage and tact that are essential to true statemanship. In spite of British Indians having not taken any particular steps to condemn the anti-State propaganda and compaign to which I have referred today, and in spite of at least the majority of them not having disowned publicly, and repudiated frankly and without qualification, statements of some of their firebrands, so unfair and hostile to the States, I decline to believe that the majority of moderate politicians and far-seeing statesmen of British India are not inspired by friendly feelings towards, or by the desire to see justice and fairplay meted out to, the States. As the other Times—the Times of India—observed in an article a little time ago, if interests clash it does not mean that one set of interests is to be swept away, or that one community need smother its individuality to suit the whole, and that constitution making being always a delicate task, a constitution must be made to fit the facts, and is not a thing to be laid down a

priori in the hope that facts will somehow or other fit themselves in, and that there is nothing to be gained—in fact everything to be lost—by minimising the difficulties inherent in the problem, but that there is everything to be gained by facing those difficulties with mutual effort and with the will to solve them. Under God's providence and with the good-will and sympathy of His Majesty's Government, the Government and people of British India, and the efforts of the Governments of Indian States I look forward to the day when a United India will be enjoying Dominion Status under the aegis of the King-Emperor, and the Princes and States will be in the fullest enjoyment of what is their due—in the words, in a recent letter to me, of a most distinguished statesman who is an old and proved friend of India—"as a solid federal body, in a position of absolute equality with the federal Provinces of British India and, as they have always been, loyally attached to the Crown."

# 4

# *Judicial Reforms Undertaken by Maharaja Ganga Singh Ji*

As is evident Maharaja Ganga Singh pioneered many reforms which made his administration of the State responsive to the changing times and attuned to the needs of the subjects. Not only rulers of other Indian States, but leaders and administrators in British India also were very profuse and wholesome in their appreciation of the many sterling qualities of the Maharaja which he displayed in abundance in various branches of civil and military administration.

Some semblence of judicial administration existed in Bikaner in the 1870's when three types of courts were set up in the capital. These were further augmented by courts setup at the Tehsil Headquarters where Tehsildars dispensed civil and criminal justice. A code of justice also came into being in consultation with the Agent to the Governor General of Rajputana. In the mid 1880's the Central Civil and Criminal Courts were abolished and replaced by Nizamat Courts of Bikaner, Reni and Sujangarh. An appellate court was also set up in Bikaner. It dealt with all cases and exercised original jurisdiction in those cases which were beyond the jurisdiction of the Nizamat Courts. In 1907 Maharaja Ganga Singh appointed a Commission to reorganise the entire judicial system after consulting the state of judiciary in other parts of British India as well. But it appeared that the findings of the Commission did not meet the approval of the Maharaja who was constrained to admit that the need of the hour was better supervision coupled with speedier and more efficient dispension of justice. What the Maharaja had in mind was the establishment of some sort of a Supreme Court having trained and qualified judges.

The Maharaja spelled out his views on judicial reforms in the speech delivered on 29th September, 1910 at a Durbar held at the Lallgarh Palace. (No. ) He declared that he had delayed the mention of judical administration to the closing part of his speech because it was the most important aspect of his proposed reform package for the State of Bikaner. At the same time he also set at rest all speculations and charges that he concentracted more on Executive side of the Administration at the expence of the judicial system of the State. If the executive aspect of the administration was dealt with first it was because initially it was a priority issue. Furthermore in the period of minority rule and the Regency phase the judicial system was handled competently by Sir Charles Bayley, when he was the Political Agent at Bikaner. Ganga Singh Ji remained convinced at that stage that even in the closing years of the 19th century, the judical system in Bikaner compared favourably with that of other States. The system did not merit radical changes, it was felt, but what was required was access of masses to justice. However, the Maharaja argued, what was good at one time could not remain to do so in the coming decades. As more and more people, especially the trading and banking communities of Bikaner, interacted more actively with British India, their aspirations and expectations in matters of judicial reforms increased.

As an initial step, Maharaja Ganga Singh announced the setting up of a Chief Court in Bikaner from the 1st October, 1910. The Chief Court was to be presided over by a senior judge who would be styled Chief Judge to be assisted by two other judges.

The advantages of having a Chief Court were many and varied. It would have sittings on all working days, would supervise the working of the lower courts more effectively and would have the benefit of qualified and trained judges. The Maharaja also made a very far-reaching pronouncement on the occasion:

> "I earnestly hope that, while strictly upholding the dignity of the law and dispensing the most impartial justice, our Chief Court will not in course of time tend to became a soulless body dealing coldly and frigidly with human affairs, but I trust that they will combine with law and justice the sterling qualities of equity, sympathy and good conscience, and also give due weight and consideration to the customs and useages and any special pecularities prevailing in our State, without which the contentment of people and the welfare of the State and its subjects cannot really be hoped for".

The establishment of the court was the first of its kind among the States of Rajputana. The Maharaja also assured the people that if need arose suitable modifications could be made in the structure of the Chief Court. A step in that direction was the abolition of the Appeal Court which reduced one stage of the appeal and mitigated the disadvantages arising from law's delay. Another decision was the stipulation that majority of decisions of the Chief Court would be deemed final—a step that would avoid unnnecessary delay. However, appeals in specified cases could still be referred to the Maharaja. This decision was based on similar practice in the Privy Council in England. To avoid frivolous and groundless appeals reaching the Maharaja for consideration, it was decided to impose a heavy court fee on appeals referred to the Maharaja Ganga Singh also held out that he was averse to aping institutions existing in the west or British India simply on the grounds that they were successful there. Local conditions and requirements would ensure that only what was best for the Bikaner State would be adopted from outside. Pending the appointment of a permanent Chief Judge it was decided that the 2nd judge, Munshi Kripa Shanker, M.A. would also officiate as Chief Judge while Babu Nihal Singh was appointed as the 3rd Judge. Both of them were experienced in Judicial matters with long experience in the Mahakma Khas and Appeal Court. Seth Nemi Chand was appointed 3rd Judge pending the appointment of the Chief Judge.

It was found that a lot of difficulty was experienced in the disposal of cases transferred from the courts of the Nazims at the Sadar and in the Districts to any other courts and the consequently serious inconvenience was caused to the parties and witnesses concerned. As a remedial step the appointment of an Assistant Nazim with First Class Magistrate's powers and having his Headquarters at Bikaner, was sanctioned. Such cases were to be referred to him as also original suits of the value of Rs. 1000. The said Assistant Nazim was; in addition, to act as sub-Registrar for Bikaner town as well with the stipulation that he would be available for going out to the Districts to decide on the spot similar transferred cases.

Other changes introduced were the abolition of Honorary Magistrates, Court at Bikaner and Nohar which had proved largely unsuccessful. An additional Naib-Tehsildar was also to be appointed to be attached to the Sadar Tehsil for the disposal of the Mal Mandi work which was previously carried on by the Munsiffs court.

In 1922 another landmark decision was taken with the establishment of a High Court of Judicature to replace the Chief Court.

Upon perusal and while summing up the new judicial system is was found to have many innovative features which merited attention. As mentioned earlier the Chief or High Court was to have one Chief Judge and two puisne judges. On the original side the court was to be presided over by one judge from whom appeal lay to the bench of the other two judges on the appellate side. All appeals lay to a bench of two or more judges and when only two judges sat on the bench, differences of opinion were referred to a full bench of all three. The powers conferred upon the court were considerable. It was empowered to pass any sentence authorized by law, except that no sentence of death could be carried into effect unless it had been confirmed by the Maharaja. From sentences of death, transportation for life, or imprisonment for a period of ten years or more, there was provision of appeal from the decision of the High Court to the Maharaja. In civil cases all orders and decrees of the High Court were final except where the amount or value of the subject-matter of the suit in the court of first instance was Rs. 10,000 or over and in cases involving rights and easements against the State when the Chief Court differed from the decision of the lower court. The Chief Court was also given the right of supervision and control of the lower courts. The executive and judiciary were thus completely separated—a reform of far-reaching importance and was a demand in British India as well.

The process of judicial reforms did not end in 1922 and continued into the fourth decade of the twentieth century. The policy of separation of powers was given a more definite shape by setting up of some separate Judicial Courts. These were the courts of district judges at Bikaner, Ganganagar, Sujangarh. Rajgarh, Suratgarh, Bhadra, Churu and Hanumangarh. This step led to releiving the revenue officers of most of their civil and criminal powers. Certain other anomolies were also emerging which clearly showed that the new judicial system was in need for further review. A glaring case was the fact that though the responsibility for maintenance of law and order rested with District and Second Class Magistrates; they lacked the requisite power and authority to carry out their duties. It was no surprise that the Home Minister stopped sending F.I.Rs. to them about crimes within their districts as they had nothing to do with the trial of these cases. Furthermore the District Magistrate had no control over the Police as different from the policy in British India. Similarly the Nazim was also deprived of the responsibility for prosecution of offenders against law and order. To improve the working and functioning of the Bar, a Legal Practitioner's Act was passed in 1925. This involved makinfg it compulsary for new entrants to pass a Law Examination and provision was made for the appointment of a Law Lecturer.

In his quest for continued reform in the judicial system, Maharaja Ganga Singh granted a new Charter to the High Court in November

1940. The major changes envisaged under this Charter were in the constitution and jurisdiction of courts:

i. District courts at Suratgarh, Rajgarh and Sujangarh were abolished to be replaced by courts of Munsifs. Now courts of the City Magistrate and court of second Munsif were created to replace the courts of the Additional District Judge, Sadar. and Honorary Munsif at Sadar.
ii. The powers of District Judges at Ratangarh and Ganganagar were enhanced and they were vested with the powers of an Assistant Session Judge empowered to try of fences punishable with death or imprisonment for life and to hear criminal appeals against sentence of imprisonment or of money in excess of Rs.100 passed by a Fist Class Magistrate and also against sentences passed by the Second Class Magistrates. All the Munsifs and City Magisatrates were vested with powers of a First Class Magistrate. The City Magistrate could also henceforth try cases under Municipal Act.
iii. The bench of Honorary Magistrates continued to exercise the powers of a Second Class Magistrate.
iv. The judicial officers in Ganganagar district were relieved of all criminal work. The Nazims were empowered to try non - cognizable cases on complaints and challans under sections 107, 108, 109 and 110 of the Criminal Procedure Code.
v. The Tehsildar of Ganganagar devision could not try criminal cases with the exception of non-cognizable offences on complaints. The Tehsildars at Lunkaransar, Surpura, Sardarshahr, Dungargarh, Taranagar, Nohar and Anupgarh were to continue to try civil suits also upto the value of Rs. 200.
vi. Experienced law graduates were to be appointed to work as Government Advocates and Public Prosecutors at various judicial courts, e.g. Ganganagar and Patangarh.
vii. A new post of Assistant Registrar, High Court was created to lessen the work load of subordinate courts.

A common allegation levied against Maharaja Ganga Singh was that he always cloaked his autocracy in the garb of internal reforms and in his designs he was aided and abetted by the British Government. The nature of his rule may be subject to debate but his commitment to reforms for the welfare of his people was never in doubt. He remained dedicated to organize the judicial system in Bikaner on scientific lines. His increasing insistance on the involvement and use of the services of technocrats and professionals in administration gave it a much needed fillup and helped the State to transform itself from a medieval State to a modern one.

## References

1. K.M. Pannikar—His Highness The Maharaja of Bikaner, Oxford, 1937.
2. Four Decades of Progress in Bikaner, Government Press, Bikaner, 1993.
3. Speech of Maharaja Ganga Singh at a Durbar held at the Lallgarh Palace (Relevant portion), 29th September, 1910.
4. Prabha Bhargava, 'Judiciary in the Bikaner State' in G. & L. Deora edited Maharaja Ganga Singhi Ji Centenary Volume, 1980.
5. Administrative Reports on the Administration of Bikaner State of 1909—10, 1010-10, 1939-40 & 1941-42.
6. See Also Speech of His Highness on Eve of Inaugration of High Court.

# Annexure 1

## The Bikaner State Rajpatra

**Extra ordinary**

**Bikaner, Thursday, 29th September, 1910**

**Speech delivered by His Highness the Maharajah at a Durbar held at the Lallgarh Palace on Thursday, 29th September, 1910, to announce various important changes introduced from the new of ficial year—1st October, 1910.**

*Judicial*

I have reserved all mention of the Judicial Administration of the State till now, not because it is a branch of our Administration to which I attach lesser importance, but because it is in this connection that I shall be making the most important announcement today.

I have of ten heard it said that an account of the fact that I have been devoting my energies to reforming the executive side of the Administration and to re-organising and improving the same, I have had no time to pay any attention to the Judicial system in the State. It has, I believe, even been wondered at and commented upon that nothing has till now been done in this direction.

I should like to take this opportunity of clearly stating that neither of these views is at all correct, and I think I shall be able to show you that the real facts are quite different. In the first place, after I asssumed the government of my State and whilst I was considering the question of introducing reforms in the administration, the chief point that I had to pay attention to was what part or parts of the State Administration required the greatest and earliest attention. The answer to that clearly was—the Executive Branch of the Administration. It was, therefore, this pressing reform which was taken up to begin with. But it would be quite a fallacy to imagine—as I am going to explain to you—that the Judicial side of the Administration was not taken into account.

The first thing we must remember is that the system of our Judicial Administration had then only comparatively recently been organised during my minority under the able guidance of Sir Charles Bayley, when he was Political Agent at Bikaner, and did not at the time stand in such immediate need of reform as the Executive Branch. Then, though comparisons are odious, our Judicial system even as it stands now will, it is believed, compare very favourably with that in most of the States. In fact, when you hear of what we propose to do now, you will notice that it is not the system that even now requires may radical change or reform. And finally, in the files dealing with the Introduction of the present system of administration and of the time when I was working out all the changes, there is to be found, in a note in my own handwriting, dated the beginning of 1902, an entry to the effect that the system of our Courts of Justice was a sound one and required neither change nor any remarks.

Yet any system however carefully devised will, after all, require some modification sometime or other by the very efflux of time, in order to meet the changed circumstances and the growing needs of the public. These changes have from time to time been made during my reign either in the shape of circulars issued by the Durbar, or as the outcome of the discussions at the Administrative Conference, or by the conferment of additional powers upon different judicial of ficers, by raising the status of various Sub-Tehsils into Tehsils and grouping and rearranging villages under various Tehsil and Sub-Tehsils courts for the convenience of the public.

Progress however being the law of human nature, nothing which is good today can be equally good for all times to come. The trading and banking communities of Bikaner, carrying on business in British India, have specially become accustomed to much higher principles of the administration of justice than those which have till now guided our Courts. Present day notions of law and justice are very different from what they used to be some 20 years ago, even among common people also whose standard of expecting justice from courts has considerably increased.

Five years after the present system of administration had been introduced and just before I proceeded on a holiday to England in 1907, I felt that the time had arrived for and that circumstances fully warranted, a further advance up the ladder of judicial efficiency. I, therefore, appointed a Committee to thoroughly go into the present judicial system and to submit their recommendations for additional improvements and reforms.

Though the Judicial Committee made several useful and sound proposals I felt that by adopting them alone, we would not be really progressing very far, and I was irresistably led to the conclusion that, if any substantial good was to be done to the public, and if we were sincerely solicitous—as we certainly are—for a greatly improved and more efficient and superior Judicial administration, the State must take some decisive and bolder action. By this remark I do not, I need hardly add, mean to cast any reflections upon any court, but what I do mean to imply is that the system of judicial administration was unsuitably placed under the chief supervision of a Court whose Judges were inseparably connected with the Executive side of the Administration and could, by force of circumstances, only devote two days in the week to judicial work—a step, which, however suitable and convenient in the early stages of the progress of our State, is obviously not upto the standard which our people have a right to expect now from the State.

Gentlemen, I have been engaged upon and given the present scheme my most careful consideration for more than the last two years and I have come to the conclusion that although the new proposals will be more costly—the annual expenditure being estimated at Rs. 32,000 on the Chief Court alone—it is the duty of the State to introduce the change forthwith in the interests of justice and of my subjects.

I had, in my speech in August last when instituting the Board of Revenue, expressed the hope of my being able to provide an independent Chief Court and I feel very great and genuine pleasure in now announcing the creation and establishment of a Chief Court in the Bikaner State with effect from the 1st October, 1910.

The rules of the Chief Court and my orders in connection therewith will be read out to you at the conclusion of my speech by Munshi Kripa Shankera, from which you will gather that the Chief Court will be presided over by a Senior Judge, who will be called Chief Judge, and two other Judges.

It is needless for me to dwell at any length upon the advantages resulting from the Chief Court for they are self-evident. You will now have a Chief Court sitting every day of the week to dispose of cases and to supervise and improve the working of the Lower Courts and the court will be presided over by fully qualified and trained Judges. I earnestly hope that, whilst strictly upholding the dignity of the Law and dispensing the most impartial justice, our Chief Court will not in course of time tend to become a soulless body dealing coldly and frigdly with human affairs, but I trust that they will combine with law and justice the sterling qualities of equity, sympathy and good conscience, and also give due weight and consideration to the customs and usages and any special pecularities prevailing in our State, without which the contentment of the people and the welfare of the State and its subjects cannotreally be hoped for.

Gentlemen, I believe that by sanctioning the creation of the Chief Court we have embarked on a momentous and novel experiment found no where in any other part of Rajputana. It is not unlikely that, after the actual experience of a year or more, some changes will be found to be necessary, but the State has reserved the full right and powers at all times for its Ruler to alter, modify or add to, the rules, constitution and composition of the Court. I shall watch over the work and progress made by the Chief Court with the greatest interest and sympathy and I pray that its career may be crowned with success and that it may before long not only become an established fact but also be found to be an invaluable and indispensable asset to the State and boon to its subjects! That the Chief Court will, in due course, bring our judicial system on a par with the efficiency obtaining in other departments I have no doubt.

It is the opinion of a large number of experienced and wise men, most qualified to judge, that one of the undesirable features of grafting western methods upon the Indian system of judicial administration is the great delay and the various stages and numbers of appeals before a party can finally attain redress and keeping this in view I have sanctioned the abolition of the Appeal Court which reduces one stage of the apeal and mitigates the disadvantages arising ftom law's delay.

With the provision of an independent, reliable and upto date Supreme Court, it has been held that delay could further be avoided by making the majority of the decisions of the Chief Court final and I am sure that, in the circumstances, this will cause no misgivings to the public but will, on the other hand, be appreciated by them. For the same reasons it seems unfair in the interests also of the State Administration that my time should be uselessly occupied in listening to, and disposing of , frivilous and groundless appeals, as has been the case in the past. In accordance, however, with the sentiments of the people and the principles governing such matters in our States, certain appeals in specified cases have still been allowed to come to me about which final orders will invariably be passed by me personally, but the preliminaries in connection with these will be gone through by the Members of my Council on lines somewhat similar to the system of appeals in the Privy Council in England.

As regards the raising of the court fee on appeals preferred in the Lower Courts, it is hardly necessary to add, that, when the State has gone to the length of providing a competent court with so much cost to itself, it is not unreasonable that those who would benefit by it should pay for the better and more speedy justice that they are sure to get, under the present reformed system. As far as the total cost of appeals is concerned, this will not affect the pockets of the parties, inasmuch as, instead of two appeals at half rates there will now be one appeal at full court fee.

Whilst on the subject of introducing reforms and changes, whether those referring to the past or the present—as on the instances of the Chief Court and the Board of Revenue—or the future, I should like one point to be very clearly understood and that is that I am strongly averse to introducing any reforms or changes in the Administration of our State merely on the lines of , or simply because they are in force in, British India or in this or that State. In fact I might go further and I state that some reforms eminating from the West, though they fully answer the purposes in that part of the world, are very far from being suitable for the requirements of British India—much as of the Protected States. There is no reason why we should thus blindly copy them nor are we of course bound in any way to do so. At the same time I hold it to be one of the first duties of a sympathetic and wise Ruler and a true lover of his country to adapt what is best from the West or from British India and other States, and by such additions and alternations as are found to be necessary and most suitable for local conditions, circumstances and peculiarities, to introduce the most suitable and practicable system that lies in his power; and this principle, gentlemen, I have always on leavoured to follow.

I hope I have said enough to convince you that our Chief Court is not an innovation solely on the lines of the British Judicial Courts but the natural outcome of the advance of our State and subjects and of the growth and assimilation of those principles of good government which have, I believe, so largely contributed towards the efficiency of our administratation and the prosperity of the people.

As to the appointments to the Chief Court the question of obtaining the services of a capable Chief Justice for the Chief Court is engaging my best attention and I hope the appointment will be made before very long. For the two other seats on the Chief Court I have had much pleasure in nominating Munshi Kripa Shankera, M.A., to be the 2nd Judge and Babu Nihal Singh to be 3rd Judge.

Munshi Kripa Shankera's valuable services to the State have been amply demonstrated in the Mahkma Khas, and his work in the Judicial line in the State is well known to the public and needs no introduction beyond my stating that he brings with him to the Chief Court a sound and practical knowledge of law. As to Babu Nihal Singh, he has, for the past 10 years, been actively engaged in the judicial line—first as

Nazim of Bikaner and for the past 8 years as Judge of the Appeal Court.

Pending the arrival and permanent appointment of a Chief Judge, Munshi Kripa Shankera will of ficiate in that capacity and and Babu Nihal Singh will officiate as second Judge, whilst Seth Nihalchand, who has for so long served the State in various capacities, has been selected as the most suitable officer available to officiate as third Judge until further orders.

In view of the difficulty often experienced in the disposal of cases transferred from the courts of the Nazims at the Sadar and in the District to any other courts and the consequent serious inconvenience to the parties and witnesses concerned, I have sanctioned the appointment, with effect from 1st October, 1910, of an Assistant Nazim with 1st class Magistrate's powers and having his headquarters at Bikaner, who will deal with such cases at Bikaner and will hear original suits of the value of Rs.1 000 as well as act as Sub-Registrar for Bikaner town and be at the same time available for going out into the Districts to decide on the spot similar transferred cases and to replace partly the Munsiffs Court at Bikaner which is now being abolished.

The Honorary Magistrates' Courts at Bikaner and Nohar which have unfortunately not been very successful in fulfilling the object for which they were established will now also not be necessary and will therefore be abolished with effect from the new official year.

For the disposal of the Mal Mandi work at Sadar, now carried on by the Munsiffs Court at Bikaner, an additional Naib Tehsildar is being appointed and attached to the Sadar Tehsil.

This ends the list of judicial changes and reforms and I thank it will be found, as I have said before, that it is not in any way changing but merely improving the present judicial administration and I hope all these reforms will be appreciated by the public, as being entirely in their own interests.

Before leaving the subject of the judicial administration of the State, I should like to express my best thanks to the State Council—both collectively and to each of the Members individually—for the manner in which they have kept going the judicial work of the highest court in the State, inspite of the drawbacks and disadvantages, to many of which I have already referred; and the Council will now, as I said in my Revenue Board Speech, be able to still more closely associate themselves with the administration of the State—their legitimate sphere of work.

# Annexure 2

## Speech delivered by His Highness of Bikaner on the even of Inauguration of High Court, 1992

*Gentlemen,*

The issue of to-day's Proclamation establishing a High Court of Judicature in Bikaner is a notable step in the history of the judicial development of the State and indeed may almost be said to mark its climax.

2. I have no desire to weary you on this occasion with too great detail of the past history of our judicial administration, but some mention of the chief landmarks of its progress may be of interest.

3. The first foundations of a regular judicial department on modern lines in Bikaner were laid in 1871 during the reign of His late Highness Maharajah Sri Sirdar Singhji Bahadur when separate Civil, Criminal and Revenue Courts were opened at the Capital. In 1884 in the memorable reign of His late Highness Maharajah Sri Dungar Singhji Bahadur the scheme was extended further and district courts were established in the four Nizamats the Executive Council of the State fulfilling the functions of a Court of Appeal.

4. During my minority the system of judicial administration was reorganized under the able direction of our old and valued friend Sir Charles Bayley, a former Political Agent, who did so much for the benefit of my State and people during his term of office as President of the Council of Regency.

5. For several years afterwards that system, which answered the requirements of the time, called for no immediate change. But progress is the law of nature and the growing needs and requirements of the people and altered circumstances rendered further organization necessary with a view to enhancing the efficiency of the Law Courts to the standard attained in other branches of the administration. The disadvantages of a system under which my Executive Council combined the functions of a judicial appellate Court with its normal executive authority also became more and more apparent as the number of judicial cases increased.

6. Accordingly in 1907 I appointed a Committee to go thoroughly into the question of judicial reform and to submit their recommendations. Though the proposals of the Committee did not in point of fact go so far, I, after considering their report, decided that the establishment of a Supreme Judicial Court, independent of the executive side of my Government, was the next essential and necessary step.

7. We are accustomed to hear it stated by those not well acquainted with the internal administation of Indian States even by men of eminence who might be expected to make a more intimate and careful study of facts—that in all the States the administration of justice is directly controlled by the Ruler, which statement carries with it the implication that the Rulers are in the habit of having cases decided according to their likes and dislikes. I hold no brief for all the States nor can it be claimed that the standard of efficiency is the same throughout the length and breadth of India but such sweeping and broadcast statements made in regard to all States, big or small, and even the most advanced, undoubtedly do a great injustice both to the Rulers and to their Governments. At any rate, I leave it to you, the officials and people of Bikaner, to judge how far such remarks are applicable or justified in regard to our own State and I am happy to be able to say on this occasion that throughout my reign I have scrupulously avoided any interference with, or the exercise of any control over, the course of justice in the various Law Courts of the State, otherwise of course thanby regular appeal legally preferred to me, and my policy has been and always will be, as far as lies in my power, to render the judicial courts of the State independent of my executive interference whatsoever.

8. Accordingly in pursuance of this policy I established on the 1st October, 1910 the Chief Court at Bikaner, presided over by a Chief Judge, with two other judges to assist. The Chief Court has now been in existence for eleven and a half years, and without entering on a lengthy review of its work during that period, I am glad to feel that this measure, and the greater independence of the judicial department resulting from it has given general satisfaction, and, I believe, also been popular with my subjects.

9. The time however has now come to advance another step, and to raise the Chief Court to the greater status of a High Court, and it is for the inauguration of this High Court that I have convened this Durbar to-day.

10. This change from a Chief Court to a High Court is no mere change in name only. It betokens greater powers, greater

responsibilities, and greater dignity. Some of these are embodied in the Proclamation which I have issued and which has just been read out by the Home Member, and others are shown in the rules which are being issued in amplification of that proclamation.

11. The change which will perhaps affect litigate most is the abolition of miscellaneous petitions or 'faryadis' which it has become the practice of almost every defeated party in a suit to present either to my Council or to the Chief Minister against the orders passed by the Chief Court. Such 'faryadis' will in future no longer be entertainable against the orders of the new High Court, whose decisions will remain final unless modified or reversed in regular appeal. An appeal will only lie as of right in civil cases where the property in dispute is of a value of Rs. 10,000 or over or where 'Jagir' lands are involved. In cases where a substantial question of law, custom, or established usage is involved, special permission to appeal on those grounds only may be granted by the Judicial Committee of my Executive Council, but no appeal shall be heard unless such special permission has previously been obtained. In all other cases it has been left to the discretion of the High Court to grant or to refuse permission to appeal as they think fit.

12. Although I have just referred to this decision about Faryadis as a 'change' it is hardly correct to use such a phrase. As a matter of fact, 12 years ago it was decided to introduce this change and a formal announcement was made and orders promulgated to that effect. A reference to rule 12 framed in connection with the institution of the Chief Court, issued in the Rajpatra dated the 29th September, 1910, will show clearly that except for the specific cases covered by rule 13 and in regard to appeal in Criminal cases provided for under rule 10, no other appeals from the orders and decrees passed by the Chief Court were declared to be permissible.

13. In my speech of the 1st October, 1910, when inaugurating the Chief Court, I had, with reference to this, made it clear that, with the provision of an independent and reliable Supreme court, it seemed unfair in the interests of the State Administration, as well as in the public interest, that my time should be uselessly occupied in listening to and disposing of frivolous and groundless and petty appeals but that, in accordance with the sentiments of the people and principles governing such matters in our States, provision had been made for certain appeals in specified cases to come before me as of old.

14. It cannot be really contended that after an interval of 12 years, and with a High Court in existence, there was greater need to do for

entertaining more appeals or for relaxing the provisions then made for limiting such civil and criminal appeals.

15. It is unnecessary for me to point out that there is nothing I and the Maharaj Kumar desire more then to be in close touch with my subjects and to have every possible and reasonable opportunity of acquainting ourselves with the grievances and sentiments of my subjects. But just as in administrative matters, work has been delegated, and powers and responsibilities allocated to the Ministers and Heads of Departments and other officers concerned with a view to decentralising and giving relief to the Ruler and enabling him to have more time and leisure to devote to important matters of State, affecting its welfare as well as that of its people, so also in regard to the judicial side of the administration, some delegation of authority and decentralization is essential if the progress and prosperity of the State is to continue and to receive the attention which it demands at the hands of the Ruler as well as the Heir Apparent and the Ministers of the State.

16. In all matters, of the two parties to a suit, one party is bound to be dissatisfied with the decision of a court and, whether out of genuine feelings, or with a desire to harass his opponent and to cause him as much loss as possible the defeated party—human nature being what it is—will often attempt to put of f the evil day of the execution of the decree passed by the court, by such further appeal and other attempts to cause his opponent loss by every means in his power. The defeated party would, therefore, in many cases no doubt prefer appeals and Faryadis and with but a faint, or even no hope of success, to explore as many avenues as are open to him.

17. There is at the same time the other side of the shield, and it is an undoubted fact that the party which has won its suit in the lower court naturally desire the decree to be executed in his favour, in a reasonably short time. It should be emphasized that with the inauguration of a Supreme Court of Judicature, such as the High Court, the time has certainly arrived when petty civil and criminal cases can all the more safely be left to a court of such standing for final adjudication and decision. It is only because, unfortunately in many cases due regard is not paid to enforcing the orders issued from time to time that this system of indicriminate appeals, and the entertainment and disposal of Faryadis in the Mahkma Khas has grown up, contrary to my intentions and contrary to the provisions of the orders and rules issued at the time. We are, therefore, not making any fresh departure but only conforming to what was decided 12 years ago in regard to not entertaining any such Faryadi petitions.

18. At the same time, as would be clear from the concluding paragraph of the Proclamation instituting the High Court, as was also provided in the rules issued relating to the Chief Court, power has been duly reserved whereby nothing in the proclamation or in the rules or regulations Issued from time to time shall affect the Sovereign powers and prerogatives of myself and my Heirs and Successors in regard to our entertaining any suits or appeals, creating any special tribunals for any purpose, or to pass any orders or to taking any other measures which might seem fit in the interests of justice and equity. By virtue of this power, in case of any grave wrong or injustice having resulted to any party and having come to light against which it is not permissible to prefer an appeal, it would still be possible for the Ruler or the State to enquire into his grievances in exceptional circumstances. But I must make it clear that it is not the policy of myself and my Government to let this provision be abused by permitting a reversion to the practice of entertainment of Faryadis as a general rule or to encouraging indiscriminate appeals by means other than those provided in the Proclamation, rules and regulations.

19. There is however, one point in this connection to which I must also allude here. In the old rules, published relating to the Chief Court, appeals were also permissible under the terms of Section 13(2) relating to easements and certain rights under certain conditions. The question of what provision, if any, will be necessary in this connection is engaging the earnest attention of myself and my Government and any necessary steps involving will be taken in regard to this subject in due course—if necessary, by the introduction of legislation in the Assembly.

20. In criminal cases, in the same way, special permission to appeal, with restrictions in cases where a double appeal has already been heard or where the High Court has confirmed the finding of the lower court has been substituted for 'Faryadis'. The right to appeal in cases of capital sentences or of imprisonment to 10 years or over has been left as at present, and in accordance with the sentiment and old-established practice prevailing in our State no sentence of death shall be carried into effect unless and until has been confirmed by me.

21. These are no light powers, but I have every hope that the Chief Justice and Judges of the new High Court will realise the importance of the responsibility that is being placed on them to see that justice is upheld throughout my State, and that they will prove worthy of their trust.

22. The Chief Justice will henceforth take rank precedence with

the Members of my Executive Council according to seniority of appointment and will have a right to be consulted on all matters affecting directly or indirectly the judicial administration.

23. Side by side with the improvement of the Bench steps are also being taken to improve the general standard and qualifications of the Bar practising in the State Courts, and as one of the first measures to this end my Government have under consideration a proposal to the effect that after one year from now no professional uncertificated Mukhtar, commonly known as 'Mukhtar Maqbula' should be allowed to plead in my Court higher than a Nazim's.

24. As for the personnel of the High Court, it is a matter of congratulation that its first Chief Justice will be Pandit Pyare Lal Chaturvedi whose services, we had the pleasure of obtaining from the Government of India nearly a year ago. Rai Bahadur Babu Nihal Singh, who has rendered valuable and faithful services to the State for a period extending now to 33 years, and who will bring with him a ripe and intimate knowledge of the custom and usage prevailing in the State, and Babu Lakshmi Narain, who entered the State Service a little over a year ago, are the two other Judges whom I have appointed. Pandit Bisheshwar Nath, who has for some time officiated as one of the Judges of the Chief Court, will, after being placed on Special duty for a certain period, be appointed to the responsible poet of State Vakil at Mount Abu.

25. I had hoped, simultaneously with the establishment of a High Court, to put into effect further measures for the greater separation of the subordinate judicial and executive branches of the administration but I have reluctantly been compelled to postpone these for a more financially favourable moment. The final separation of judicial and executive functions in the State necessarily means a considerable increase in annual expenditure and at the present time, when all our available funds are urgently required for the big railway and canal schemes which are now in hand, I have considered it best to defer this increase in expenditure. In this decision I have also been influenced to a certain extent by the consideration that in view of the serious unrest prevailing in various parts of India just now, the present does not appear to be a suitable time for introducing such a measure straight off even though all other circumstances permitted to it. Such ultimate separation has, however, both my sympathy and approval and is a goal to be worked up to.

26. It only remains for me now to declare the High Court of Judicature of the Bikaner State duly inaugurated and to invoke the blessings of the Almighty upen the important step which has today

been taken and also to express the earnest hope that this measure will lead to the further happiness and well-being of my beloved subjects and that the Judges of the supreme High Court, present and future, will in all their work be actuated by the highest motives and strictly adhere to the distates of equity, justice and good conscience and mete out even handed justice to all alike, whether rich or poor, high or low, without fear or favouritism.

27. Before resuming my seat I would like to take this opportunity of referring to a matter, to which I alluded in my speech on the 7th April, when opening the last session of the Legislative Assembly. It will be recalled that on that occasion I had, after referring to my indifferent health of the past few months, expressed the hope that a complete rest and holiday at Mount Abu would suffice but I had also foreshadowed the contingency of my having to proceed to England for some 3 to 4 months towards t he end of May, should urgent grounds of health necessitated my going to a different climate for a change and rest and for special medical treatment. As you are aware I, unfortunately, was laid up with another sharp and severe attack of fever on the very next day, which sadly interfered with my taking part in the festivities and rejoicings prior to our leaving for Rewa in connection with the auspicious Wedding of the Maharaj Kumar. In the circumstances I have, under strong medical advice, decided to proceed to England and I propose to sail from Bombay on the 20th May and, please God, hope to be back in India about the 7th September. During my enforced absence, which I greatly regret on both public as well as personal grounds, the Government of the State will be carried on by the Maharaj Kumar, assisted by the State Cabinet and Council.

# 5

## *Ganga Canal-Boon to a Parched Desert State*

One of the lasting contributions of Maharaja Ganga Singh was the construction of the 84 mile long Ganga Canal which brought the waters from the heights of the Himalayas to the parched deserts of Bikaner through the Canal. The vast and sandy expanse of Bikaner, in the middle of the Indian desert, was perhaps the driest and most arid portion of India. The average rainfall in most of the State was 12 inches and in certain zones even less. As Sardar K.M. Panikkar in his Biography on Maharaja Ganga Singh very aptly remarked. "No river flows through it (the desert); water sources are few and far between and the sand dunes that cover the land in unbroken monotony add to the barrenness of the schene a fearsome appearance". The early years of his assumption of full powers co-incided with the worst ever famine to visit the State of Bikaner within living memory. Ganga Singh was convinced that water had to be made available for cultivation and the live stock even as rainfall failed. During the days of famine, Col. Dunlop Smith, the Famine Commissioner had represented in vain to the Government of India to undertake an irrigation scheme which would include some portions of Bikaner. But the grim tragedy of famine had its benefits also as Lord Curzon, a visionary and genius in certain aspects of administration, woke up to the needs of the importance of canal irrigation which would ensure that the ryot was not dependent on a precarious and often capricious monsoon. But before the concept of canals took realistic shape in Bikaner, other steps were also initiated with varying degree of success attending them.

A powerful water pump at Palana and the digging of 'Kachha' and 'Pacca' wells were some early measures. But both the measures did not yield the desired results. Subsequently the State administration turned to construction of Bunds with two such Bunds coming up at

Madh and Gangapura respectively and the Pilap Bund was strengthened thrice and the inner side lined with 'Kankars' or pebbles.

Two new feeder canals were dig up to augment the water supply in the Kodamdesar Bund. Another Bund was constructed on the Gajner lake which was expected to serve the dual purpose of being a feeder to the lake itself as well as providing water for irrigation.

But the State Government in Bikaner stood convinced that ultimate solace lay in canal irrigation. Early representations to the Punjab Government yielded limited results as Bikaner was allowed the use of waters from the West Jamuna Canal to irrigate 460 acres of land in the Bhadra Tehsil. Later on even this facility was withheld by the Punjab Government so also was the reduction in water supply to the Northern and Southern Ghaggar Canals in 1906. As the area under cultivation diminished, the costs of the maintenance of the Ghaggar Canals went up. Thus the Ghaggar Canals became a liability to the State.

The interest evinced by Lord Curzon, Sir Denzil Ibbetson and Sir Michael O'Dwyer in the irrigation problems of Bikaner was heartening for Maharaja Ganga Singh. Thanks largely to the efforts of A.W.E. Standley, Chief Engineer and Secretary, Public Works Department, it was found feasible of irrigating large tracts in North Western Bikaner from the waters of the Sutlez. Thus when the Chief Engineer of Punjab, R.G. Kennedy, started preparing the Sutlez Valley Project, Maharaja Ganga Singh represented and pleaded his case for Sutlez waters to Bikaner and even rushed to Shimla to request Lord Curzon to intervene in favour of Bikaner. But Lord Curzon left India before the scheme could take off and Bikaner's case was considerably weakened. Bikaner was not a riparian State and Bahawalpur, one of the owners of the Sutlez waters, took strong exception to the participation of Bikaner in the Sutlez irrigation scheme. In 1912 Bahawalpur Ruling Council had argued that the Sutlez waters were barely sufficient for Bahawalpur itself and that Bikaner, which had no rights otherwise, would deprive it (Bahawalpur) of irrigation facilities to 50 per cent of its lands. The President of Bahawalpur Council categorically stated:

> 'I would beg leave to submit for consideration since it has been clearly established that a far greater supply of perennial water than is available is required for the irrigation of the lands of Bahawalpur—a riparian State with full rights to the same—that no part of the supply under this or any other project is surplus and

available for transfer to Bikaner—a State with no legal rights to any part of the supply'.

To complicate matters further the State of Bahawalpur was under a Regency Council and the Chief of Bahawalpur was a 'voiceless minor'. The Maharaja had represented that the Bahawalpur State had greatly over-estimated the areas which were fit for cultivation. In response to Bahawalpur's objections the project of 1905, which commanded nearly 181akhs of area in Bikaner, was reduced in 1913 to 6,40,000 acres, and in the project of 1914 to 5,00,000. This alarmed the Maharaja who stated that, Judged by every criterion—liability to famine, the excellent quality of land to be irrigation (3,300 square miles of the north-western area which could be commanded by the Sutlez waters consisting of level loam of the highest quality and an ideal country for irrigation) the difficulty experienced by the Punjab and the neighbouring areas from large-scale emigration in times of scarcity—the Bikaner State was more suited to irrigation than Bahawalpur. As regards to the rights of riparian States the Maharaja often claimed with certain amount of justification, that the paramount power was duty bound to make use of the Sutlez waters most beneficial to the overall interests of India.

The Sutlez Canal scheme finally appeared ready for take off only in 1920 when things had normalised after the end of the World War. It was on 4th September, 1920 that an agreement was signed between the Governments of Punjab, Bahawalpur and Bikaner on the sharing of the Sutlez waters. To implement the scheme the Bikaner State was fortunate to have at its disposal the services of the highly gifted Mr. G.D. Rudkin who was Revenue Minister of the Maharaja's Government from 1912 onwards. The problems confronting Mr. Rudkin were enormous. The area to be irrigated was a level plain of lightest loam where the water level was about 180 feet below the surface. The average rainfall was reduced further and stood at 6 inches. The fertility of the land was offset with the problem of the absorption of water by the parched land. Owing to fear of water-logging in British Indian territory, through 71 miles of which the canal had to run, it also had to be concrete lined which added considerably to the cost. Land tenure also tended to be a major issue. Though there were no jagir lands in that area, speculators had occupied a lot of land as a result the 'Khalsa' had shrunk to 700,000 acres by 1912 from a healthy 4,500,000 acres in 1904. This not only deprived the State of the necessary capital but also made the process of colonisation difficult.

The State Government, as a first step, stopped all further

encroachments. For the next step classification of all land was made into cultivable and waste land and then the waste lands were resumed in exchange for occupancy rights on the cultivated land. The cultivation were then given permanent tenures—an exercise personally supervised by Mr. Rudkin himself. The new comers to the State were treated with a certain amount of leniency and genesority. The settlement satisfied all parties.

Financing of the project was a major issue. The original estimate was for Rupees two crores which had to be revised to Rupees 3 crores. The expenditure involveed also included a loop line 157 miles in length to open up the canal area and the establishment of mandis, schools, hospitals, police station etc. The expenditure was further raised to over four crores of rupees. The procurement of loans on a massive scale was never going to be an easy task. Financial help from Government of India implied the interferance in the internal economy of the State. Even the sale of waste land in the canal colony could not wholly finance the project. But the Maharaja was undaunted at the prospect as his credit stood high and financers, both from within and outside the State, came forward and advanced the necessary funds as short term loans at rates which compared favourably with the rates paid by the Government of India itself. The total amount thus raised was Rs. 2,36,00,000.

In an characteristic gesture the Maharaja entrusted the task of bringing the limestone or Kankar (required for the concrete lining of the canal) from the quarries located within Bikaner itself, to the State Railways. This effected some economy though in cases the limestone was transported over 200 miles.

The entire work was completed by the autumn of 1927. On 26th October, Lord Irvin personally came to open the canal which was appropriately name Gang Canal after the Maharaja himself. (Nos. 1 and 2). In addition to the rulers of Kota, Datia, Kishangarh, Nawa Nagar, Palanpur, Sitamau, Wankaner and Danta the Governor of Punjab also graced the occasion. The great nationalist leader and visionary, Pandit Madan Mohan Malviya blessed the Maharaja on the auspicious day and termed him as a modern day Raja Bhagirath.

Cold facts and figures were inadequate in highlighting the magnitude of the work undertaken by the Maharaja. The length of the main Canal from the Headworks (Ferozepur) to Shivpur was 84-½ miles but with feeders and distributaries it ran into 568 miles. The capacity was 2144 cubic feet of watrer per second. 80 out of the 85 miles were lined with concrete, the cost of the lining coming to Rs. 78 lakhs. In the ultimate analysis the canal was to irrigate 6,20,000 acres but in the initial phase the area actually covered was 2,40,000 acres for the rabi crops and 1,36,000 acres for the kharif crops. The distribution of the waters to the three States of Punjab, Bahawalpur and Bikaner was done on a rotational basis with prior intimation to villages as regards to their turn to receive water on a six monthly basis. The final share of Bikaner towards the cost of the project was Rs. 310 lakhs. Before the water started flowing in the canal it was calculated that the area to be irrigated (1000 sq. miles) had to be colonised and the process was worked out in minutest details. The entire area was divided into squares of 25 bighas each, the length of each side of a square being 825 ft. The old inhabitants who were State tenants were granted prioriety rights on payment of a low rate of 'Nazrana' in order that their status might not be inferior to that of the new purchasers of the State land. In some cases, even the nominal payment was waived aside. The whole area was divided into 913 chaks or water courses of which 496 were given to the old inhabitants. The average size of each chak was 50 squares. The Gang Canal lead to the birth of 500 new villages and the population of the State jumped from 28,000 in 1921 to 180,000 in 1934.

A unique feature of the coming of the canal was the immigration to Bikaner of ryots from outside the State, notably from Punjab. It was a satisfying fact that among those who had purchased land in advance in the canal area a large proportion came from the British area in the Punjab. The cultivator in Punjab was most shrewd, thrifty and hard working amongst the cultivators in India. The ryots in British India were traditionally suspicious of the personal rule in Indian States and nothing short of physical compulsion could have made them emigrate to Indian States. That they did so on their own accord spoke volumes of the faith they placed on the ruling powers of Maharaja Ganga Singh.

The Gang Canal brought in its wake all round development in various other areas. A suitable number of marketing centres, which later grew into important trading towns, mushroomed around the canal area. The most important of these was Ganganagar, named after the Maharaja which compared favourably with similar trading towns of long standing in the Punjab. Industrial progress also kept pace with agricultural growth with the establishment of four ginning-factories, three pressing-factories, and two sugar-factories in the canal area. The more progressive of the villages in that area had a fair sprinkling of oil-extractors and four-mills. To keep abreast of scientific developments in the field of agriculture, an experimental farm was established at Ganganagar. Experiments were conducted with various types of seeds and the benefits of these experiments were passed on to the ryots. The cultivators were also provided with better quality of seed and fertilizer to improve their yield. A cotton laboratory was also set up which conducted new researches on the seeds of the crop, which was one of the staple products in the area. Easy credit facilities were also created in the colony so also were co-operative societies for the purpose of advancing loans at easy rates with the active support of the Government. The Maharaja was wise enough to realise that the new colonisers were accustomed to a great degree of self-government from their days in Punjab and hence the main townships were given Municipalities in neighbouring areas of British India. A district Board was also established on the British Model and it undertook a scheme for starting schools, opening rural dispensaries and constructing roads. The State Government respond to the Board's initiative by opening a High School in Ganganagar and proposed the upgrading of all primary schools to middle schools. The Government further appointed a colonisation Minister with wide ranging powers to oversee the growth of the canal area. (Also see Annexture No. 3).

## References

1. Mishra, S.C., 'Progress of Irrigation During the Period of Maharaja Ganga Singh' in G.S.L. Deora edited, Maharaja Ganga Singh Ji Centenary Volume, Bikaner, 1980.
2. Pannikar, K.M., His Highness The Maharaja of Bikaner, Oxford, 1937.
3. "Four Decades of Progress in Bikaner", A State publication, Bikaner,1937.
4. Report on the Administration of Bikaner (1926-27).
5. Speech delivered by Maharaja Ganga Singh Ji at Farewell Dinner to Mr. Standley, March 1926.
6. Speech delivered by Maharaja Ganga Singh Ji at Banquet in Honour of Princes and Guests at Ganganagar, Oct. 1927.
7. Maharaja Ganga Singh Ji's Speech at Opening Ceremony of The Gang Canal at Shivpur, 26th October 1927.

# Annexure 1

**Speech delivered by His Highness the Maharajah of Bikaner on the 22nd March 1926 at Farewell Dinner to Mr. Standley.**

*Ladies and Gentlemen,*

As soon as Mr. Standley informed me in August last that he proposed to retire in April this year, I gave orders, and had an entry duly made in my official fixtures, about a farewell dinner to be given to Mr. Standley and, I hope she will permit me to add, though she is not an official, Mrs. Standley. But during the state of uncertainty in which I was plunged some three weeks ago when I had to face the possibility of having to leave Bikaner for some months at very short notice, one of the things which caused me special concern was as to how I was going to manage to hold this function—full up as we were at the time with fixtures relating to the recent dual festivities. I am therefore more than pleased at being enabled to take this opportunity of testifying, in a befitting and public manner, to the high regard which I and my Government—and I am sure I can add everyone in Bikaner—entertains for Mr. Standley, the gratitude which we feel for his many valuable services rendered to this State and the people of Bikaner and the sincere regret which we feel at his forth-coming departure and at the severance of old ties and official associations of nearly a quarter of a century.

2. Shortly after my coming of age, one of the most urgent and complex problems which I had to face was how to improve the lot of my subjects and to minimise the evils and the dangers resulting from recurring famines and scarcities; and after out recurring famines and scarcities; and after our trials and ordeals during the famine of 1899-1900 which was the worst of its kind known during the last hundred years, actual experience also suggested how essential it was that something should be done—and done quickly. To know that there was little that could be done in regard to local projects—by which I mean bunds; for local irrigation, though even there I felt that there was some scope however small. But the most important thing was to make a determined and earnest attempt to secure the blessings of regular irrigation by means of a big canal from a river like the Sutlej.

Our former efforts to secure irrigation for that State had until then unfortunately proved unsuccessful. But one does not like lightly or easily to admit defeat; and if success is to be attained it is only by perserverance and by the working up of all the necessary facts and figures and by putting forward one's case in such a clear and cogent manner as to render it unassailable as far as lies within human power. It was thus that some twentythree years ago I asked the Government of India to help me by lending me the services of an irrigation expert. And, thanks to their sympathetic response and particularly to the assistance given me in the matter by Mr. Sidney Preston—the then Secretary to the Government of India in the Public Works Department, to whom also we are indebted for his share in the inception and the pushing forward of the Sutlej Canal Project we had the good fortune of securing the services on deputation in November 1903 of Mr. Standley.

3. That was one of those days for which we in Bikaner will always have cause to be grateful, because it marks the direct steps which by the grace of God have led to the successful inception and the carrying out of the Sutlej Valley Project from which we look forward to receiving irrigation in our State in about eighteen months' time from now. Mr. Standley with his usual keenness and vigour plunged into his task in a manner which was after my heart. We had preliminary talks and discussions; we toured all over the State looking for likely sites for irrigation projects, big and small; and we visited our Northern Frontier with a view to acquainting Mr. Standley personally with the lie of the land within our territories in close proximity to the Sutlej River. And it was not long afterwards that Mr. Standley was able, after taking levels, to demonstrate the perfect feasibility of irrigating our lands from that river. Thus, as I stated in my speech at Ferozepore at the recent ceremony which took place there, Mr. Standley is, so far as we in Bikaner are concerned, the Father of the Sutlej Valley Irrigation Projects. In the rainy season of 1906, I went to Simla with Mr. Standley accompanying me fully armed with the various facts and figures which Mr. Standley had worked up—expecting to have a tough fight before the claims of Bikaner to irrigation from the Sutlej were likely to be conceded. As it happened we had an easy walk over; and in this while we are greatly indebted to the Government of India and to the officers responsible for working out the first detailed project for our weir higher up the river at Harike, there can be little doubt that Mr. Standley's notes and figures played an important part in the preparation of the project and in the acceptence by the Government of India of the validity of Bikaner's claim to irrigation.

4. Within an incredibly short time of his joining us in, I think it was November, 1903, Mr. Standley also prepared in full detail, together with the necessary plans and estimates, his proposals for two irrigation bunds which in their turn were also constructed in an equally short time. One of these, the Pilap Bund, has proved successful as the large sheet of water which is stored there in the rains amply demonstrates, and if we could count upon a larger population and more certain rainfall annually irrigation could undoubtedly be secure from this bund, though, of course, it pales into insignificance in comparison with the Sutlej Canal. But I am hopeful that, when our of ficers concerned are more free from the care and work involved in regard to the Sutlej Canal Project and the colonisation of the area to be irrigated thereby, something practical will yet be devised for taking advantage of this source of irrigation, viz., the Pilap Bund. The Madh Bund, also in the Magra District was a project from which we and the experts we got from outside hoped to secure further irrigation. But as unfortunately happens in some cases, the soil forming the bed of the dam is porous and whilst a large amount of water comes into the bund it is not possible to stop it for sufficiently long to secure an assured supply for irrigation purposes. Indirect benefits have however accrued from this bund in that the level of the water has been raised which in its turn will lead some day or other to well-irrigation in the lands below the Bund and by no means an insignificant forest for these parts of the country is now growing up on both sides of the bund, of which the newly created Forest Department is already attempting to take advantage.

5. After irrigation, the next urgent and by no means a less important consideration in its own way for this State—is the storage of water wherever possible in this dry land of ours. And Mr. Standley was wholly and entirely responsible for inaugurating a scheme whereby a considerably enhanced volume of water is now being stored in the Gajper lake and other tanks. Well do I recollect taking him on hot afternoon in April just before proceeding on my annual holiday to Gajner when during the course of my inspections I pointed out to him that water in Gajner was received only from one direction, namely from the little river which lies to its West, and I asked him whether we could not do something which would bring about a larger supply of water for Gajner which in those days was, more of ten that not, difficult to fill except in years of unusually good rainfall. I think what was in 1904. And lo; and behlod, when I came back from Mount Abu after my usual summer residence there at the end of June, there were three distinct water channels of several miles length planned and

constructed and all ready, which during the rainy season that followed entirely proved their success by bringing in a considerably increased quantity of water into the Chaunda Sagar tank, and from that, when it overflowed, into the Gajner Lake. Mr. Standley's system was taken the fullest advantage of by us as regards Gajner with the result that we have now added something like 14 more square miles, if I am not mistaken in my figures, to the catchment area of Gajner and now we can confidently look to water coming into Gajner not only when it rains to its test but also to its North and East—the country to the South being too low to permit of any feeder channels being made in that direction. it is in consequence that it is happily now the exception and not the rule for Gajner not to be full and there will always remain another permanent memorial to Mr. Standley at Gajner in that I have called the main Channel into which the various other channels flow the Standley Feeder Channel.

6. Mr. Standley also made a feeder channel for the Darbari tank and we have since been able to extend that system by yet another channel made for the same tank and also by making some more channels likewise to increase the capacity of the Kodamdesar and Jogiro tanks.

7. And here I should like to digress for a moment to point out that inspections are no new things but tried and trusted friends of mine the value of which nobody appreciates more than I do; and though, I fear, they are extremely trying and introme at times to the officers concerned as, let me franky admit, they are to me, they are very necessary things—evils if you like—and I trust the result of that one inspection in April 1904 will lead to a moral being drawn by any officer who may be inclined to doubt or undervalue the necessity of and the benefits aceruing from such inspections. The very prompt and through manner in which the work of the various bunds and channels, not to speak of such an important matter as the taking of the levels for the Sutlej Canal Project by Mr. Standley will I trust also be emulate by those who follow him. As Mr. Standley found, the only way to reduce the number of inspections and the work connected therewith was to get on and to finish the things which rendered such inspections necessary.

8. To resume my narrative, although I was anxious and Mr. Standley was agreeable that he should continue his good work in Bikaner it was unfortunately not possible for him to be spared by the United Provinces Government; and greatly to our regret, Mr. and Mrs. Standley left us in 1906. But in the interval between that and his retirement in 1921 after a long and distinguished record of service

where he rose to be Chief Engineer and Secretary to the Local Government, we have had the pleasure of many visits from Mr. Standley and the benefit of receiving much help and valuable suggestions in regard to various matters, and particularly in connection with various important points as they arose relating to the Sutlaj Valley Project.

9. I need hardly dilate on the pleasure that I felt in being able to secure for the State the advantage of the further services of Mr. Standley consequent upon his retirement. And during the last four and a half years he has, as was the case during his former period of service, done much good and valuable work with the full details of which it is impossible in the time at my disposal to deal. I will there fore confine myself to making only a few observations by way of pointing out how valuable have been Mr. Standley's services during his second period of service here as they were during his first period of service. Under Mr. Standley's advice the new bund at Gajner has been created to afford protection to the Palaces there and to store further water which till now used to go to waste when the lake over flowed; two more channels have been dug further to increase the supply of the Kodamdesar tank; and other channels are under project for similarly bringing in an increased supply of water into the Gajner Lake and the Darbari Jogiro and other tanks; the Chaundasagar tank at Gajner is being raised by one foot; and last but not least Mr. Standley is just finishing a complete scheme for water-works in our Capital a part of which outside the City was conceived and carried out by Mr. Standley twenty years ago. A revision of the schedule of the Public Works Department rates has been effected and other reforms brought about with a view to organise the Public Works Department, whilst instructions have been fully and clearly laid down in regard to various matters which if carefully borne in mind and strictly followed by the Engineers who will have to deal with such work in the future, will save them and others concerned much trouble and difficulty and delays.

10. The Palana Colliery which has always been one of Mr. Standley's chief loves in Bikaner has again benefitted by his advice and experience and certain important and interest in experiments for briquetting our Palana cola will I hope lead to some substantial results in the not far distant future. Those who know Mr. Standley well do not need to be reminded of the thorough and conscientious manner in which he has always been wont to discharge his duties and to give of his best at all times. But I cannot regrain from giving one particular instance. We were then expecting Their imperial majesties,

the King—Emperor and the Queen Empress here in 1905 and the work which that Visit involved will be easily appreciated particularly when it is realised that the Lallgarh Palaces had then only very recently been completed and occupied by us and much remained to be done in regard to the interior decorations, putting in marble floors throughout the varandahs and court-yeards and in many other directions both inside and outside the Palace precincts. It would be indeed a revelation and a matter for prodound astonishment to many if they were to see the formidable list of works which Mr. Standley had to carry out between April and November 1905 not only at Bikaner but also at Gajner which up to then had hardly been touched by us. The expenditure involved even in those cheap days of labour and easy prices also amounted to a considerable sum. But nothing daunted, and full of confidence and pluck, Mr. Standley persevered and by his successful and systamatic method of work and the attention to detail which is so necessary to attain success and satisfaction and by frequently and personally inspecting each and every work every single thing was ready on the day when my Illustrious Guests arrived at Bikaner—even though almost from day to day to Mr. Standley's misfortune I went on adding more and more to his task involving very heapy work to be completed before the appointed date. But unfortunately the strain involved was too great for any human being—and it has to be borne in mind he was working single handed throughout the period—and I regret to say on the eve of the arrival of Their Imperial Majesties Mr. Standley had to take to his bed and to remain there till after the Royal Visit was over. But he had his special reward in the shape of a gracious souvenir with which Their Imperial Majesties were pleased to present him on my bringing to their notice his special enthusiasm and very arduous labours in helping to make the Imperial Visit a success.

11. Need I say more to explain how grateful we do indeed feel to Mr. Standley and how sad we are at losing his valuable services and at parting from such an old and great personal friend? We are not only parting with old friends but what to the State is more important the friends who throughout their official as well as social life have thoroughly and wholeheartedly associated themselves with the state its people and ourselves individually.

12. Before proceeding further, I should also like to take this opportunity of expressing my appreciation of the good work done by Mr. Jose, the present Executive Engineer of the Public Works Department who, especially in the past few months, has had to face exceptionally heavy work of a very trying and difficult nature. And

with the advice and instruction before him of Mr. Standley and the precept of his example I am sure that Mr. Jose will be able to give a satisfactory account of himself in the carrying out and completion of existing works in regard to which both he and feel happy at last to see day-light, and in coping with the work and responsibility that lie ahead of him in the post to which he is shortly to be promoted as State Engineer.

13. And now, Ladies and Gentlemen, the honour is getting late and I have detained you at sufficient length. So, I will conclude by once again renewing my regret at the impending departure and the official loss which we shall sustain by Mr. Standley's retirement. On the social side also our loss will be equally great and we shall miss very greatly too the presence of the gracious lady who is seated next to me. But we look forward to seeing Mr. and Mrs. Standley both amongst us again as my guests when we hope in October 1927, I may be vouchsafed the great pleasure and the realisation of one of my life's ambitions by opening the Sutlej Canal.

14. Our warmest good wishes will accompany Mr. and Mrs. Standley to England and we hope that they may be spared for a great many years to enjoy their well earned rest. ladies and gentlemen, I will ask you to join me in drinking to the health of Mr. and Mrs. Standley and in wishing them all good fortune.

# Annexure 2

## Speech Delivered by His Highness the Maharajah at the Banquet in Honour of the Princes and Other Guests on the 25th October, 1927, at Ganga Nagar, Bikaner State

*Your Highnesses, Ladies and Gentlemen,*

Tomorrow, by the grace of God, the Gang Canal will be opened by His Excellency the Viceroy; and waters from the Sutlej River will be released to irrigate these desert, but fertile, plains, parched with eternal thirst, unslaked from hoary antiquity.

2. As I shall be making two more speeches tomorrow, I am reluctant to inflict another speech on you tonight; but on the eve of this Great and Joyous Day for my State and people—and of course for myself—I cannot propose the toast of my Guests without giving expression to the real pleasure which I derive in offering them all a most hearty welcome.

3. No one particularly prizes old friendships more than I do, or rejoices at making new fiiendships; and my happiness today is enhanced by the fact that there are present here, in this distinguished Assembly, so many personal friends from amongst the members of the Fair Sex, my Brother Princes and the Cadets their illustrious Houses, and a galaxy of men of light and leading from amongst the High officers of the British Government and the Notables of British India, as well as the Chiefs and Nobles, and Ministers and other Guests, from the Indian States. To you all, Your Highnesses, Ladies and Gentlemen, I tender my sincere thanks for responding to my invitation, and for coming to this out-of-the-way place—some from thousands of miles across the seas—for "auld lang syne", and just to shake me by the hand in genuine sympathy and to share in my joy for our prolonged and ceaseless labours, extending over a quarter of a century, now being crowned with success by the mercy of Providence.

4. Amongst my Brother Princes I am highly gratified at seeing at my side my dear friend and illustrious neighbour, His Highness the Maharajah Sahib of Jodhpur, whose visit, accompanied by his Brother, Maharaj Sri Ajit Singh Sahib, has caused immense pleasure to me and to everyone in Bikaner. Not only are the Houses of Jodhpur and Bikaner closely allied by indissolubleties of flesh and blood, but I

have had the pleasure of knowing His Highness enjoying the closest friendhip with that noble and gallant Prince, His Highness' late lamented Father; and I am old enough to retain personal, grateful recollection of the courtesy and kindness which I received as a boy from His Highness' famous Grand-father.

5. Amongst other kinsmen we are delighted to welcome His Highness of Kishengarh, whose recent Accession gave widespread pleasure in Rajputana, and who has our best wishes for a long and prosperous Reign, and His Highness of Sitamau and his delightful Sons—a cultured Ruler, and active supporter of the Chamber of Princes, and a keen participant in all matters pertaining to the welfare and dignity of the Princes of India.

6. It also affords us all unalloyed pleasure in welcoming here today His Highness the Maharao Sahib, and the Maharaj Kumar Sahib, of Kotah. My personal friendship with His Highness—a wise and highly popular Ruler—dates back to 1889, when we both joined the Mayo College, Our two Houses, for long associated by friendly ties, are, by the grace of God, to be still more intimately united through matrimonial alliance between his beloved Son and my dear Daughter, to which His Highness and I have both given our blessings.

7. His Highness of Datia is no stranger to us through his visits to Bikaner and my visits to Datia and we have very pleasant recollections of His Highness' hospitality and of the excellent sport we enjoyed in his forests.

8. I have for 30 years known my valued and dear friend His Highness the Maharajah Jam Sahib of Nawanagar; and I will remember how it appealed to me as a youngster to meet for the first time—long before his Accession—that Prince of Sportsmen at the height of his fame as a great Cricketer. Since then we have seen much of each other, both during the Great War in France, and before and after that in India; and we have often visited each other, and worked shoulder to shoulder at many an important problem concerning our Order. It was furthermore His Highness who introduced me to my first and second, and only, lions—all that I can claim to my credit as a lion hunter—and my elder Son was similarly introduced to his first lion; and we shall never forget the happy times and the fine sport which we invariably enjoyed in His Highness' Capital and his sporting State. The part which His Highness plays at Imperial and International gatherings, and specially in our Chamber of Princes and the Princes' Standing Committee, has proved that His Highness possesses prowess no less renowned in the realm of politics than in the field of Sport.

9. The affectionate and brotherly relations existing between His

Highness the Nawab Sahib of Palanpur and myself are well-known and require no further reference. Highness' personal charm of manner and his magnetic qualities have won for him a host of friends all over India; and we have had the pleasure of welcoming him to our State on many an occasion in the past; and we are all delighted that His Highness has been able to be present at this epoch-making event. Our pleasure is enhanced by welcoming to my State for the first time the Heir-Apparent of Palanpur.

10. Fate decreed that, in spite of the warm friendship existing between us, and also of Visits proposed to be paid in the past, this should be the first occasion on which I welcome His Highness the Maharana Raj Saheb of Wankaner; and I sincerely hoep that this is the first of many visits which His Highness will pay to my State, I had the pleasure of being present in Wankaner, and congratulating His Highness in person, on the occasion of the Silver Jubilee of his Reign some three years ago, when the Guests present were able to see something with their own eyes of His Highness' enlightened and progressive Administration, and of the love and esteem in which he is held by his subjects.

11. During the course of our pilgrimages to the famous and ancient shrine of Sri Ambaji and our visits to Danta, I had opportunities of meeting the Maharana Sahib, and of renewing my friendship with his late revered Father with whom I was at school. During my trips to Danta State His Highness was good enough to offer me and my Family some splendid tiger shooting on one of which occasions Her Highness the Maharani bagged her first tiger—and one of the happiest of my recollections will be a prolonged hunt estending over no less than three hot weathers, when we were fortunate enough to exterminate a prolific family of man-eaters—totalling at least 9 tigers all told—who were taking a serious toll of the pilgrims and of the Danta State subjects; and it is specially gratifying to me that His Highness has been able to join me on this occasion.

12. It is also a great pleasure to see in our midst my old friends, the Nawab Regent of Loharu and the Rao Sahib of Alipura.

13. Whilst we all regret the absence of my esteemed friend, the veteran Ruler of Benares, We warmly welcome the Maharaj Kumar Sahib of Benares, and look forward shortly to again showing him some Sport in my State, and thus returning to a certain extent the hospitality we have enjoyed whilst shooting in the famous Chakia Jungles of Benares.

14. Turning to my Guests from British India, I trust that I shall not be considered guilty of making invidious distinctions, if I refer to the

pleasure which has been afforded to me specially by the presence here of my friends, Sir Bhupendra Nath Mitra—whose outstanding merit and ability have won for him the high position which he occupies—and Mr. Das, who has our best wishes in his laudable efforts to set up in India a much-needed modern school on the lines of Public Schools in England.

15. I am also particularly glad to see present amongst us today Sir Clement Hindley and Sir Austen Hadow. As I once said on one occassion in the Chamber of Princes, when I was Chancellor, there is no Department of the Government of India which has shown greater sympathy for, or maintained more cordial relations with, the Princes and States than the Railway Board. As the Head of a State possessing a Railway system of its own, I should like also to say tonight how pleased we are at Sir Clement Hindleys term of office being extended for another two years, which we are confident will prove as beneficial to Railways in India as to the Government of India.

16. Amongst the High British officers, I am also glad to see here another very old friend in Mr. Sams, whose delightful contributions to the Press, as for instance, the "Digressions of a Knight-Errant", many of us have enjoyed reading from time to time with keen relish.

1 7. As there will be no other opportunity, we must not fail tonight also to drink to the health of absent friends whom we shall be welcoming tomorrow; but who have been delayed owing to today's Ceremony at Ferozepore.

18. A most warm welcome also awaits His Excellency the Governor of the Punjab. Sir Malcolm Hailey, as the Head of the Punjab Government, which, with us, is one of the two partners in this part of the Sutlej Valley Irrigation Project, is an old and valued friend of many years' standing. Another old friend arriving here tomorrow is Sir Geoffrey deMontmoreney.

19. Tomorrow it will also be a real pleasure to meet and, indeed I may say, all of us of the Indian States, to welcome the Hon. Mr. C.C. Watson here who took over charge yesterday of the Political Secretaryship to the Government of India. He has long been connected with the Political Department; and we in Rajputana have known him for a quarter of a century; and wherever he has been, Mr. Watson has won universal esteem and popularity, and made fast friends with the Princes and people of the Indian States; and his frankness, sympathy and courtesy have secured for him the confidence of all with whom he has come in contact.

20. I shall spare for this evening the blushes of the officers of the Irrigation Department—including those serving in my State—as I shall

be referring to them tomorrow in great detail. But let me just say how much I, and everyone in Bikaner. appreciate their valuable services, and how sincerely pleased we are to see them all here.

21. To the Leaders of British India we also accord a hearty welcome! I am glad to see present here today my old friend—Pandit Madan Mohan Malaviya. I was closely associated with Pandit Madan Mohan Malaviya for a considerable period when we were endeavouring to found the Hindu University at Benares, to which the Hon. Pandit is nobly devoting so much time and attention.

22. Turning now to nearer Home, it is a great plesure, amongst British officers present from Rajputana, to welcome first and foremost my old and esteemed friend, the Hon. Mr. Reynolds, Agent to the Governor-General in Rajputana. If I have not referred to him before, it is because I feel confident that, as an old Rajputanite, he shares my sentiments and would himself wish, according to our Rajput ideas of courtesy, that the names of the Guests from outside be mentioned first; for we look upon Mr. Reynolds as one of ourselves; and I am sure that he reciprocates the sentiment. I believe that Central India was his first love; but I think it would be equally correct to say that, after his long residence, specially in later years amongst us, Rajputana has now become his second Home. Mr. Reynolds is no stranger to Bikaner; but I deem it an auspicious omen that his first visit to Bikaner after assuming charge of his high office and so soon after the birth of his son and heir, on which happy event, I am sure it would be in accordance with the feelings of his numerous friends present here tonight that I should offer him once again my warmest congratulations, coincides with the advent of the Gang Canal; and I feel that I am voicing the sentiments not only of us all in Bikaner, but indeed of all Rajputana, when I pray that the high hopes entertained of him will be realised in a full measure. I much regret the absence of Mrs. Reynolds in our midst on this occasion, but look forward to welcoming her here later in the cold weather.

23. Reference to the Agent to the Governor-General in Rajputana reminds me of one who, had he been spared today, would have particularly rejoiced at the Bikaner State's good fortune in securing this great Canal. His age would, in any case, have prevented him from being present here in person; though I am sure, he would have been present with us in spirit. But alas! the cruel hand of death claimed him only three months ago. I refer to a very dear and highly esteemed friend, and a most popular Agent to the Governor-General in Rajputana, the late Colonel G.H. Trevor. Though he retired more than 32 years ago, when I was only fourteen, it was a great pleasure to

take every opportunity of seeing him whenever I was in England; and I shall ever remain highly indebted for his loving care and for his securing for me a Tutor and Guardian possessing the Exceptional qualities of Sir Brian Egerton.

24. Last, but not least, I extend the warmest of welcomes to old Bikaneries whom—old friends—I rejoice to see amongst us here today. Amongst them I was looking forward most eagerly to welcome back amongst us on this happy occasion—my greatest friend in this world and my dear old Tutor and Guardian, Sir Brian Egerton. I can never repay the deep debt of gratitude which I owe to him for the affectionate care an conscientious attention which he bestowed upon me, and for the thorough administrative training which he imparted to me, and which has stood me in such good stead in the discharge of my responsible duties as Ruler of this State. Sir Brian had actually taken his passage, but he had unfortunately to give up all ideas of coming out here on the grounds of health. I know that his thoughts will be with us today, and specially tomorrow, and I am certain that no one in Bikaner could be more pleased at the advent of this Canal than Sir Brian Egerton.

25. The Egerton Family, I am happy to think, is however not to go unrepresented. For, at the Opening of the Gang Canal there will be present another very dear and old friend of myself and my Family, and indeed of everyone in Bikaner, in the person of Sir Philip Grey-Egerton- the head of the Egertons-and also a younger cadet of the Egerton Family in the person of Mr. Wille B. Egerton, Assiatant Private Secretary to His Excellency the Viceroy. I derive the greatest possible pleasure in welcoming Sir Philip in our midst, whom I think we are fully entitled to consider, as I am sure he also counts himself, and old Bikaneri. He has never failed to afford us the happiness of his presence in our midst on any occasion of importance, ever since he first visited Bikaner over 30 years ago. As an instance of his genuine affection and friendship for Bikaner and for us all I might add that he came out to India barely for five weeks only last April on the occasion of my younger Son's Wedding; and here he is back amongst us again to our delight

26. Another old Bikaneri, whose absence on account of advanced years we greatly regret, but who will I know also be with us in spirit, is Sir Charles Bayley—for several years a popular Political Agent in Bikaner, and also my Guardian. My State owes much to the reforms effected, and to the good work done, during my Minority, by Sir Charles, who will always be also remembered with gratitude, specially for the recoganisation of the judicial branch of our Administration.

27. His numerous friends will be as delighted as I am to see present here, Colonel Windham—without exception the most popular Resident—with whom the Bikaner State has had the pleasure of being officially associated, and whom the Jodhpur State has now the good fortune to claim as Vice-President of the State council.

28. Major-General Sir Charles Mac Watt and Colonel Watson have been closely associated with the State and myself and my Family, as Heads of our Medical Department; and they have known my children from their early infancy. Colonel Rawlins, my old comrade-in-arms in the China War, 27 years ago, was associated with our Troops both in peace and war for a considerable number of years, including the Great War when he served with the Bikaner Contingent from start to finish in Egypt and Palestine. To Mr. Standley, who first came to Bikaner as State Engineer in 1903 and who after retirement from British Service came back for some years to Bikaner as our Chief Engineer and Secretary to my Government in the Public Works Department, I shall be referring again tomorrow. His close association with the Gang Canal is well-known; and we are all very pleased that he has been able to come out with Mrs. Standley and that he will be present at the Opening of the Canal, to which he has devoted so much time and energy.

29. I am also glad to see here today Rao Bahadur B. V. Samarth, for sometimes my Foreign and Political Minister, and we shall have here tomorrow Lala Ram Lal, who has served as my Private Secretary with ability and who now occupies an important place in the Punjab Government Secretariat.

30. Your Highness, Ladies and Gentlemen, in once again extending to you all a most cordial welcome, I would ask you to overlook any deficiency in our arrangements. But I do beg you to believe that, in spite of the difficulties of organizing a camp at such distance from the Capital, I and all the Departments and officers of my Government, have attempted to do our utmost to provide for your comfort and enjoyment.

31. In conclusion, I would ask for the indulgence of my Guests for a minute or two longer in order to enable me to take this opportunity of expressing my deep appreciation of the work done by various officers and Departments of the State in connection with these Celebrations. Much heavy work has fallen on my Prime Minister Sir Manubhai Mehta. It is a great pleasure to me to have been able to secure his valuable services; and his Premiership will, I am sure, prove to be a great advantage to my State and my subjects; and even in the short time that he has been here, he has afforded me considerable relief.

32. Mr. Rudkin too has had to shoulder very heavy work. His valuable work as Revenue Minister during the last ten years is well-known to many of you; and tomorrow you will hear something further about what he has accomplished in connection with the important and difficult problems relating to the Gang Canal and Colonization in the Canal Area.

33. To each and everyone of my other Ministers, the Thakur of Sandwa, Master of Ceremonies, as well as the Master and Comptroller of the Household, and to the various other officers concerned, my acknowledgements are due for their share in making this Camp the success which we all hope and trust it will be.

34. There are certain officers and Departments on whom the brunt of the work has fallen; and I wish particularly to express my high appreciation of the excellent work done by Thakur Sheodan Singh, who during the illness of his superior officers has, almost single-handed, gallently stuck to his post in spite of bad health, and done the work not of one man but verily of some half a dozen rolled in to one. Major Dickson, who, in addition to his duties as my Private Secretary, has been my Secretary for the Gang Canal Opening Celebrations and who has worked ceaselessly day and night in seeing to the various arrangements for these Celebrations and for the comfort of my Guests, deserves a word of special tribute and thanks, also the entire Staff of the Private Secretary's office among whom it is a pleasure to me particularly to single out for special mention Rai Saheb Kanahya Lal, my Joint Assistant Private Secretary.

35. I am lost in admiration at the wonderful efficiency and promptness with which all in our Government Press have worked, and are still working and successfully opening with the extremely heavy pressure of business day and night under the able direction and guidance of the Superintendent, Babu Kishen Lal.

36. It is with great pleasure that I now give the toast of my Guests, Your Highnesses, Ladies and Gentlemen may we often meet again; and may I have many more opportunities of welcoming you to Bikaner! I raise my glass and drink to your health and happiness and wish you all every good fortune.

# Annexure 3

**Speech to be Delivered by His Highness the Maharajah at the Opening Ceremony of the Gang Canal at Shivpur (Bikaner State) on the 26th October, 1927.**

*Your Excellencies, Your Highnesses, Ladies and Gentlemen;*

My foremost feeling today is one of the deepest thanks-giving to the Almighty and of the most heartfelt satisfaction that the ambition of a lifetime is about to be fulfilled by securing for a portion of my State the inestimable blessings of irrigation.

Nearly two years ago at Ferozepur, where Your Excellency yesterday opened our Headworks, I expressed the fervent hope that it might be vouchsafed to me to witness the water flowing down the Canal in my State. Today that fervent hope and prayer is, by the infinite mercy of Providence, about to be fulfilled. With most men when they feel the pleasure of seeing one of the most cherished dreams realized, their first thought, I think, is to collect as many of their friends as possible to share in their rejoicing, and by that means to double their own pleasure. I am no exception to the general run of men in this respect; and my next pleasant duty, therefore, is to express my genuine gratification at seeing so many friends collected round me today on this occasion of such unparalleled importance.

To Your Excellency and Her Excellency Lady Irwin, I would express my wannest gratitude for honouring us with your presence on this great day for my State and my people. It is due to the grace of our beloved King-Emperor, and a manifest sign of the gracious interest which His Imperial Majesty is ever pleased to evince in the Princes and States of India, that an undertaking of such magnitude can be brought to a successful fruition for the benefit of the territories and subject of an Indian State under the King- Emperor's protection. It was for this reason, and in order to testify once again to my deep debt of gratitude to the British Government—without whose impartial and generous support this project could never have been launched—that I did myself the honour of inviting Your Excellency, as the Representative of our august King-Emperor, to perform the Opening Ceremony here today, and I beg to thank Your Excellency very much for your consenting to do so.

May I also respectfully add that on personal grounds as well it affords me the sincerest pleasure that this Ceremony is to be performed by Your Excellency? We welcome you here, Sir, no less as a man than as a Viceroy, who by his deep religions convictions has made a strong appeal to the religious sentiment of India; who by his transparent sincerity and unaffected simplicity and the earnest manner in which he has been whole-heartedly striving to mitigate, and if possible to eradicate, the greatest curse from which India is at presnt suffering-communal strife-has inspired general confidence and won universal respect and who during the short time he has been in India has, in more ways than one, already given practical demonstration of the fact that he is indeed a sincere friend of both the Princes and the people of India.

At the Banquet given in honour of Their Highnesses the Princes and my other guests last night, I took the opportunity of expressing the real pleasure which I derived in welcoming them on this memorable occasion, and the gratification that I felt at so many of my Brother Princes and other personal friends having been able to respons to my invitation and to be present here at this out of the way spot, 186 miles from my Capital. Today I will therefore only briefly repeat my welcome to all my guests and will once again beg them to overlook any deficiency in our arrangements and to believe that we have sought to do our utmost to provide for their comfort and enjoyment.

Today when, after nearly 29 years of striving and strenuous endeavour, at least some portion of my State is at long last to share, as a part of this great Indian Empire, in the benefits of irrigation, I like to carry my memory back and to remember with sincere gratitude not only those who are still labouring to make this Canal a success, but also those to whom we owe a deep debt for their assistance in the past-though they are no longer on the active list, and some alas! have joined the great majority. There are so many officers of the Government of India and of the Punjab Government who have contributed to this great achievement, to whom I would like to express my thanks and to pay a tribute. If I were to respond to the dictates of my heart, the list would soon become too long. But I must not fail on this happy occasion to reiterate our indebtedness to the late Lord Curzon, during whose vigorous and stimulating Viceroyalty a practical scheme for a big Irrigation Canal in Bikaner was first conceived in 1905; Lord Chelmsford, during whose Viceroyalty a definite Agreement regarding the Sutlej Valley Project was finally signed; Sir

Denzil Ibbetson, who, true to the best Imperial instinct, held and worked on the principle that Nature's gift of water should be used to the best advantage of the Country, whether dyed or yellor on the Map of India; Sir Michael O'Dwyer and Sir Edward maclagan for their equal fair-mindedness and sympathy; and to my old and valued friend Sir Malcolm Hailey, whose ready help and that of the Punjab Government throughout the period of construction I gratefully acknowledge, and who, with Lady Hailey, we are delighted to welcome here today.

Amongst the talented Irrigation Engineers, past and present, it is a great pleasure to recall the names of Mr. Sidney Preston, Mr. R.G.Kennedy, the late Sir Michael Nethersole, Mr. H.W.M. Ives, Mr. E.R. Foy, Mr. R.P. Hadow, Mr. A.G.C. Fane, Mr. T.B. Tate and Mr. F.H. Burkitt; whilst Bikaner will never forget Mr. A.W.E. Standley, whom I have on a previous occasion described as the Father of this Project so far as we in Bikaner are concerned; and it is nice to see him here today back amongst us alongside with some other old Bikaneris. I also wish to express my grateful acknowledgements for all that they have done, to all the other Punjab Irrigation Engineers serving under Mr. Hadow.

I must also express my gratitude to the officers of my own Government from top to bottom, without whose valuable services and loyal assistance little could have been achieved. The brunt of the work has fallen on the shoulders of Mr. Rudkin, our popular Revenue Minister, whose association with the State, I am happy to feel, dates back to 15 years when he came here as Revenue Commissioner. His expert knowledge, gained as a Punjab officer of the Indian Civil Service, of irrigation questions and colonisation, which were necessarily new to my Government, has been of the greatest benefit. He has enjoyed the fullest confidence of myself and my Government, and has proved himself to be a true friend, philosopher and guide not only of the old Bikaner agriculturists but also of our new Colonists in the Canal area. Mr. Rudkin has been ably assisted by his experienceed lieutenant, Rai Bahadur Lala Jai Gopal, now Revenue Commissioner, Ganga Nagar. On him too, much responsibility and work have fallen. Our thanks are due also to Mr. F.C. Glass, the Senior Irrigation Engineer in the State. He was employed on this Project as far back as 1906 he has carried out in turn the detailed survey of the Canal area in the State and the construction of the Feeder and all the Distributaries within Bikaner territory. There are two other officers whom I should like also particularly to mention today. Mr. Rustomji, the Finance Minister, who, with ability and cheerfulness, has never failed to respond to the huge calls of expenditure involved by this Project and the simultaneous construction of several extensions of the Bikaner State Railway; and Mr. Fearfield, the Manager of our Railway, for the great work accomplished by him and the other officers under him in transporting the kankar required for the lining of the Canal. In order to convey some idea of the magnitude of the task, I might perhaps observe that in the project it was originally proposed to line the Canal with limestone conveyed from the Punjab quarries near Ambala. In consultation however with the Punjab Irrigation officers it was ultimately decided to use instead kankar of a particularly suitable type from the Darbari quarries not far from Bikaner City; and our State Railway undertook to transport it from there to the Canal-and average distance of 250 miles, with a return journey for the empty wagons of an equal distance. It is calculated that the substitution of our kankar for the Punjab limestone has saved the State about one crore of rupees in expenditure. Over one million tons of kankar have had to be transported, involving a very heavy strain on the Railway, which deserves its full need of praise for this remarkable achievement. As a triumph of organisation it may be added that it was rendered possible for the record quantity of 600 tons of kankar—or one whole train—to be loaded by means of bin-shoots in five minutes.

My reference to the kankar used for lining this Canal reminds me that, in my anxiety to discharge my obligations to all concerned, I have not yet given any technical details and figures usual on such occasions. Statistics are at all times apt to be dull except to those immediately concerned; and a layman is, at the best of times, wise in eschewing technicalities. Mr. Hadow in his modesty has asked to be excused from responsing to our invitation to make a speech today. He alone could have portrayed such details in anything but drab colours, but he doubtless feels, as I do, that Your Excellency, and several of those present today, will have heard a good deal of such facts and figures yesterday at Ferozepur and will again hear more about them the day after tommorrow at Islam. But there are a few special points about this Canal which perhaps are worth bringing to Your Excellency's notice. In the first place practically for its whole length, from the Headworks at Ferozepur to the gates opposite to us here, a distance of 84 miles, this Canal is a canal lined, both bed and sides, with concrete. It is the first experiment of the kind made in India on this scale, and it will, I am informed, be the longest lined Canal in the World. If the experiment turns out to be a success, as we all trust it will be, it may be that this Canal will be a further milestone in the onward march of Engineering Science and a forerunner of other lined channels in India, thereby not only effecting a great saving in the water supply which can be utilised in irrigating additional lands but also avoiding the serious dangers of water-logging.

To those of you who are used to seeing large unlined Canals of the Punjab and elsewhere, this channel of the Punjab and elsewhere, this channel my probably appear to be a small one; but that is in part due to the fact that it is lined and can thereby bring down a greater supply of water for its size than an unlined channel. I say "in part" because as a matter of fact I too most heartily wish it could only have been larger; in spite of the expenditure we have incurred to economise the water, we have had to omit from the irrigation schemes—according to the latest computation—some 300,000 acres of good command land by this Project, or about 30 per cent of the area which should have been irrigated, because our water supply will not be sufficient. Great as is the task achieved, and great also the benefits accruing from it, this Canal, when measured in terms of the area commanded, touches, as a matter of fact, only a fringe of my territory in the North-West; or to be more precise, this Canal will serve to irrigate about 620,000 acres, or less than 1,000 out of the 23,315 square miles comprising the Bikaner State. However, to criticize one's child on the very day of its birth is not good manners; and I only mention this because there has been a tendency to confuse this scheme with that prepared in 1905, which contemplated Headworks at Harike higher up the river and actually commanded a far larger area in my State but which, for reasons which it would be inappropriate for me to touch upon today, was unfortunately abandoned.

But difficulties are made to be overcome and Hope runs eternal in the human breast; and the hopes of all Bikaneris, together with those of a considerable propertion of the British subjects in the Punjab, are anxiously centred on the Bhakra Dam Project, which we are happy to feel is on the waiting list of Irrigation Schemes before the Punjab Government. Although it will involve my State in much heavier expenditure as compared with the 1905 project, it is calculated to irrigate in my State alone may be possible for the Bhakra Dam Project to be sanctioned and takes in hand. At any rate, of this I am sure—that never will Your Excellency deal with an irrigation project which is more eagerly awaited and more sorely needed by the peasants than the Bhakra Dam Project. The appointment by Lord Curzon of an Irrigation Commission led to many far-reaching schemes being devised and given effect to; and all well-wishers of India and of Your Excellency will hope that one of the substantial services and permanent benefits to our Country from the deliberations of the Agricultural Commission, and one of the land-marks of your Viceroy, will be the great stimulus given to much needed irrigation works.

There is another broad feature in which our land and colonization problems have differed from those of the great colonization schemes of Crown waste which have been carried out with such success in the Punjab during the last 30 years. This tract in Bikaner is not a blank area of Crown waste. In it, for many years, before a canal scheme was even dreamt of , numerous villages of State tenants have been fighting a hard fight against Nature and eking out a precarious existence, entirely dependent on the mercy of the God of Rain. The fair treatment of these tenants so as to fit them in with any general colonization scheme has in the past few years given me and my Government much anxious thought, and I think we may claim that in the final decision arrived at they have been treated on the most generous and broad-minded lines possible. In place of their status as ordinary tenants they have been given full proprietary rights on payment of a small Nazrana, recoverable in instalments after irrigation, and even this has been waived in the case of some of the old original settlers. More than half the area to be irrigated has been so granted to these old tenants, or about three times the area that had been under their tenancy in 1910; and finally their holdings, including all classes of tenures which average in size about 60 acres, have been consolidated by squares on their own water courses. The opening of this Canal today by Your Excellency will, please God, turn these poor and struggling tenants of the past into stunly and prosperous land owning peasants of the future—their Country's pride.

As regards the remaining land to be irrigated by this Canal we have followed a new line of policy, which I understand has not been tried elsewhere, in that we have sold proprietary rights over nearly the whole of it in advance of irrigation to outside colonists, the leading representatives of whom I am very pleased to meet here today.

Your Excellency will thus release water today not into an uninhabited waste, which is to be colonised in the future, but into a tract where, so to speak, each man is waiting at the corner of his field watching for the water to arrive to enable him to cultivate it.

I have heard a criticism directed at this policy of selling proprietary holdings in advance of irrigation to the effect that, if we had waited, we should have got a better price. This is not the time or place to enter on a discussion of policy, but I have referred to it because that policy had neces sarily to be adopted by my Government in order to keep to the guarantee asked of us by the Secretary of State for India before according approval to the Sutlex Valley Project. I trust we shall be pardoned for a feeling of legitimate pride and gratification that we have done what we said we would and have been able to meet our financial obligations and to pay for our share of the cost of this great project by the sale of proprietary rights in advance, from our surplus revenue, and by floating our own loan.

It would perhaps be interesting to add that the cost to the Bikaner State of this Canal, including about Rs. 53,00,000 representing our share of the Headworks at Ferozepur, is estimated to approximate Rs. 3,00,00,000 as against the original estimate of Rs.2,01,00,000. Including the estimate in the current financial year, our total expenditure so far on this Canal and, during the last 7 years, on our various Railway schemes, already exceeds Rs. 4,78,64,000 and we have had recourse to a public loan of only Rs. 1,82,50,000. The Railway projects include the completion of a loop line to serve the area to be irrigated, 160 miles in length, including a small branch line to Anupgarh, which has yet to be built.

Though perhaps not unique in this respect, we have, instead of giving them common place names of insignificant villages or localities, called the two Main Branches of the Canal aftrer Sri Karaniji and Sri Laxmi Narayanji, the two patron Deities of our State; whilst this place, which will for ever be remembered by posterity as the auspicious site of this historic Ceremony, has been named Shivpur after one of the three Gods of our Hindu Trinity. Similarly the names of the more famous of my Ancestors, and of one very famous former Prime Minister—Maharao Hindu Mal—have been given to the more important villages—some of them destined in the days to come to grow into big Towns and flourising centres of trade through the advent of this Canal, which in response to popular request, I have, though not without difference, given my consent to be called the Gang Canal after my name; whilst two of the less important places have similarly been named after my two sons.

And now, Your Excellency, I must bring to a close a Speech which I fear has already run to considerable length. The successful launching of this Scheme will ever remain a standing monument to the solidarity of interests between the British Government and the Indian States, the credit for which, as I have already attempted to make clear,is due to the officers of the Governments of India and the Punjab and to those of this state. For myself, throughout these 29 long and anxious years I have patiently waited, fortified in the belief that God will not forsake us in this our greatest need, and unwavering in my confidence in the justice and good will of the British Government; and I have been constant to give all my trust, support and encouragement and the fullest powers to the officers of my State responsible for the carrying out of this great undertaking—happy in the consciousness of doing my duty by my State and my beloved people. I have humbly endeavoured in all earnestness to live up to the ancient Hindu ideal of Kingship. Etymologically a Raja is only he who pleases his people and keeps them well content; protection is the very kernel of kingly duties according to the Mahabharata, and of the sic citadels of a kingdom mentioned in our Holy Scriptures, the citadel of "ready service and the love of the subjects" is the one most impregnable. A righteous Ruler is enjoined always to conduct himself in such manner as to forego what is dear to him for the sake of doing that which benefits his people. The same wisdom we find treasured in the culture of the West in the precept:

> "The Prince exists for the sake of the State, not the State for the sake of the Prince."

Both by the tradition set up by my Ancestors and by my own upbringing I have been taught to live for my people, their hopes and aspirations have been my prime ambition and their well being my supreme reward. Your Excellency can therefore, well imagine my emotion and my joy at the propitious advent of life-giving waters from the Punjab to irrigate our arid plains!

Your Excellency, today is the closing day of our Hindu Festival of Dewali—the Feast of Lamps—always held as auspicious and a good omen for man in his longing for greater and greater light. Today Your Excellency will be lighting a new light, opening to my people a new life of Hope and Faith with the opening of the sluice gates here at Shivpur. In requesting Your Excellency to perform the Opening Ceremony of the Gang Canal, I am confident that this distinguished assembly will join me in humbly offering our devout thanks to the Great Architect of the Universe and in invoking His blessings upon this effort of ours for the good of my people. May the Flood gates you open, open the door to the perennial flow of Plenty and Prosperity to my State!

# 6

## *Maharaja Ganga Singh Ji and the Cause of Education*

Education was an area which was very dear to Maharaja Ganga Singh. Himself a very good student as his record at Mayo College, Ajmer testified, he was convinced that the foundation of a modern State rested on education and literacy in the society. He was fortunate that his predecessor, Maharaja Dungar Singh was also a far sighted ruler who had realised the importance of a sound education system and towards that end had introduced the scheme of State schools throughout the length and breadth of the State with the added stipulation that education should be made available free in the firm belief of the old Hindu Doctrine that knowledge should be open to all. At the same time the teaching of English was also introduced in schools.

The Maharaja extended reforms in education and went a step further from where Maharaja Dungar Singh had left it. When Ganga Singh Ji assumed full powers there existed in the State of Bikaner 29 educational institutions, 49 teachers and 1606 students scattered all over the State. At the time of his death in 1943 there were 141 government schools, 137 aided schools, 191 recognized private schools and a Degree College (Dungar College) with a total student strength of 29,803.

### School Education

During the spate of initial reforms in the State in the early twentieth century, a post of Director Education was created who was empowered with wide ranging powers. But it was not till 1918 that a comprehensive education policy could be formulated and put into effect. The salient features of the policy were:

i. Liberalisation in educational policy with the aim to popularise higher education;
ii. The Walter Nobles School to be elevated to Matriculation level.
iii. Increase in the faculty positions in Dungar Memorial College and the district vernacular schools.
iv. Primary education to be strengthened by the opening of new government schools and liberal aid be provided to private schools for the above stated purpose.
v. The government would undertake the duties of inspection, advice and training of faculty in educational institutions. At the same time women's education was to be encouraged.
vi. Sanskrit education to enjoy exaulted status in the State. Members from the local priestly class were to be taught the disciplines of astrology, grammer and vedic studies. Competant Sanskrit teachers to be employed to teach Sanskrit and the State was to provide all facilities.
viii. Local people were to be taught fine arts as well as provided vocational training at State expence.

Primary education came in for special attention of the Maharaja. As an initial step primary schools, District schools, girls' schools and hindi primary schools were established. Anglo-vernacular and vernacular schools were also set up. Such institutions were entitled to aid from the State Government. In 1928—29 further steps were taken with regards to primary education when the Municipalities were asked to setup primary schools and towards maintenance of these schools, the Municipalities could seek State assistance to the tune of 2/3rd of the cost. This experiment proved highly successful in Bikaner, Churn, Ratangarh, Sardarshahr, Rajgarh and Sujangarh. Montessari Schools also were started in the early 1940's.

Middle schools also developed during the reign of Maharaja Ganga Singh. By the close of the nineteenth century middle schools were limited in numbers. The major schools were Sadul High School, Walter Nobles School, Lady Elgin Girls School, Mohta Moolchand School, in addition to middle schools at Churn and Ratangarh. At the death of Ganga Singh Ji the number of middle schools had gone upto 24.

High Schools totalled eleven by 1942-43—an impressive increase in numbers from a solitary High School (Darbar High School)—which was functioning in 1898—99. Most of these schools had started as middle schools.

Dungar College remained the only college in Bikaner. It was started as an intermediate college in 1928 and and subsequently was raised to the status of a Degree College in 1935. A new building and a Boys Hostel were also constructed. The College was affiliated to the Agra University and since early days its students figured regularly in the University Merit Lists. By 1942 the College was ready to be elevated to the status of a Post-graduate College with societies like the Historical Society and Literary Society proving highly popular among students.

No mention of education would be complete without reference being made to women's education in the State. By 1898-99 there were only two girls schools in Bikaner—Lady Elgin Girls School and a private Girls' School attached to Mohta Moolchand School.

Keeping the purdah restrictions in view, a scheme was introduced in 1898-99 in which a provision was made to specially appointed lady teachers to visit the homes and imparting education to girl students there. Encouraged by the response to this scheme it was decided that every khalsa village having a population of 2000 or more was to have a girls school. Statistics bear testimony to the growth of women's education during Ganga Singh Ji's reign. At the time of his death there were 41 girls schools out of which 25 were government schools. The total enrolment of students in these schools crossed 4000. Among the popular girls schools was the Her Highness the Maharani Nobles Girls School started under the patronage of the Maharani Sahiba. It catered especially for daughters of the families of the nobles who were deprived of the benefits of education because of conservatism and the rigid purdah system. The classes were upto the Anglo-Hindu Middle standard and for examination purposes the school was affiliated to the U.P. Education Board. Another equally popular girls' school was the Lady Elgin Girls High School which was raised from a middle school to a High School in 1940. An exhaustive Adult Education Programme ensured the supply of trained lady teachers for the Girls' Schools.

**Contribution of the Maharaja to the University at Varanasi**

If education in Bikaner owned a lot to the tireless efforts of the Maharaja, his contribution to the growth and development of the premier University at Varanasi, the Benaras Hindu University, were laudatory and were an eloquent testimony to his concern for higher education in the society. The foundation stone of the great University was laid by the Right Honourable Charles Baron Hardinge of Penshurst, Viceroy and Governor-General of India on February 4, 1916.

In a cavity under the marble stone was a large copper plate which had a lengthy inscription the early part of which read as follows:

> *"The Universal Spirit be held the Ancient Law of Righteous Living Oppressed and cast into disorder by the rush of Time, and the family of the children of Manu, dwelling on this Earth, disorganized and unsettled, when five thousand years of the age of Kali had passed over the land of Bharata-Varsha.*
>
> *Then Blessed Mercy arose in the Supreme Mind and Auspecious Will, from which emanate great glories, to plant a new the seed of renovation of that Ancient Law and organization on the holy soil of Kashi, on the banks of the sacred stream of Ganga.*
>
> *And the creater and Benefactor of the World, the Universal Soul moving in all, brought together His Children of the East and of the West, and induced their minds to that unanimity which meaneth good and right understanding and directed them to raise this Home of Universal learning in the Capital Town of the Lord of the Universe.*
>
> *The prime instrument of the Divine Will in this work was the Malaviya Brahmana, Madana Mohana, lover of his motherland. Unto him the Lord Gave the gift of speech, and awakened India with his voice and induced the leaders and the rulers of the people into this end.*
>
> *And other instruments also the Supreme fashioned for His purpose—the high-minded and valiqnt Ganga Simha, Ruler of Bikaner."*

The objectives of the University when formulated reflected also in large measure the educational philosophy of Maharaja Ganga Singh as well. They were:

a. To promote the study of the Hindu Shastras and of Sanskrit literature generally as a means of preserving and popularising for the benefit of the Hindus in particular and of the world at large in general, the best thought and culture of the Hindus and all that was good and great in the ancient civilization of India;
b. To promote learning and research generally in Arts and Science in all branches;
c. To advocate and diffuse such scientific, technical and professional knowledge, combined with the necessary practical training, as is best calculated to help in promoting indigenous industries and in developing the material resources of the country; and

d. To promote the building up of character in youth by making religion and ethics on integral part of education.

Though the University bore the name of a particular community, it was a catholic institution. People from other religions were eligible for appointment in the University and students from other communities were admitted on its rolls without any prejudice. Though the Maharaja of Mysore was the B.H.U.'s first Chancellor, Maharaja Ganga Singh was its longest serving Chancellor.

The First, Prospectus of the University, prepared as early as 1904, laid out the conditions why the University was deemed as a Hindu University. It was felt that the Hindu Society, which constituted the largest segment of India's population, was in the early twentieth century utterly disorganized and disintegrated. Religion had become mainly the pursuit of a few persons here and there. Barring a few exceptions, men who were endowed with intellectual gifts were mostly absorbed in the cares of office or professional business, and scarcely ever thought of religion. The rest of the Hindu Society consisted of ignorant agriculturalists, petty traders, ill trained artisans, half-starved labourers; all formed a mass of abject humanity, oppressed by poverty and decimated by disease. Such deplorable conditions could be remedied only with a wide diffusion of knowledge—so ran the argument for the establishment of a Hindu University. One of the patrons of the University, Sir Goverdhandas Banerjee also supported the claims of a Hindu University on the grounds that what was truly admirable was the true Hindu ideals of life and thought which constituted the real landmarks of Hinduism and which enabled Hinduism to resist mighty revolutions that had swept over the country. Those ideals were permanent around which grew certain features which were transitory in nature. Quoting Manu on the occasion Banerjee stated:

> *"One set of duties (is prescribed) for the 'Satya' age; different sets for the 'Treta' and 'Dvapar' and again a different set for the 'Kali', according to the decrease in those ages".*

Maharaja Ganga Singh who had been associated with the Hindu University since its inception, as mentioned earlier, made many memorable speeches for the cause of the University during his very long association with it. One such early speech was delivered at the Town Hall of Calcutta on the 17th January, 1912 in his capacity of President of a public meeting organized to garner cash and support for the proposed University. The Maharaja used the occasion to make his pitch and dwelt at length about the idea of the University. He said that all the different streams were merged into one amalgated movement for propogating the concept of a Hindu University. He used the occasion to quote a passage from the King—Emperor's speech delivered earlier to the Senate of Calcutta University which read as follows:

> *"It is to the Universities of India that I look to assist in that gradual union and fusion of the culture and aspirations of Europeans and Indians on which the future well-being of India so greatly depends. I have watched with sympathy the measures which from time to time have been taken by the Universities of India to extend the scope and raise the standard of instruction. Much remains to be done. No University now-a-days is complete unless it is equipped with teaching faculties in all the more important branches of science and the arts and unless it provides ample opportunities for research. You have to conserve the ancient learning and simultaneously to push forward western science."*

The Maharaja stated that though this address was to the Senate of the Calcutta University, it was equally applicable to the promoters of the Hindu University or of the Muslim University. Commenting on the character of the proposed Hindu University, the Maharaja assured the gathering that the University would be a residential and teaching University which would seek 'to conserve the ancient learning and simultaneously to push forward western science', and 'to build up character without which learning is of little value'. It was also felt that as no country in the world was fully satisfied with the educational system in force, it was no surprise that similar feelings persisted in India as well. The reasons for this state of affairs in India, according to Ganga Singh Ji was the conviction that the intellect had been developed too exclusively and that character had been insufficiently considered and also that the then existing provision for higher education and research was inadequate.

The address was also used to promote the course of religious teaching the demand for which was increasing regularly as the conviction grew that character could best be built up when it rested on the precipts of a great and noble religion. Touching on the theme of denominational Universities, the Maharaja countered the claim that the establishment of such Universities promoted sectarian differences. He further argued that the nation was big enough to support a Hindu University as well as a Muslim University. Much good could be done by diverting the charities and activities by creating institutions which would appeal to them in a special degree. It was a fond desire, the Maharaja asserted, that there was every reason 'to hope and believe that with both the institutions broadly organised, soundly managed and sufficiently endowed, and with the spread of knowledge which they will foster and promote, they will contribute towards creating a spirit of mutual esteem and goodwill among the members of the two communities'. If the syllabus of the two Universities was based on morality, reverence and duty then the teaching would lead to tolerence and not estrangement.

In his concluding remarks the Maharaja said that both denominational Universities were to be open to students of all creeds and classes and the spirit of give and take was best reflected in the exchange of compliments and subscription between High Highness the Aga Khan and the Maharaja Bahadur of Darbhanga. (No. 1)

Maharaja Ganga Singh's association with the Benaras Hindu University was lasting and he served it in many diverse capacities. As early as 1916 he was accorded the signal honour of presiding over the series of extention lectures organized in the University. In his presidential speech he welcomed such opportunities as they provided him relief from the daily affairs of State administration. He was hopeful that the benefits of research in the University would be beneficial for the development of backward States. The theme for the extention lectures on that occasion was commerce with special reference to trade policies. Industrial growth was another theme for the lectures.

The Maharaja stated that sheer brain power was insufficient unless combined with earnest and continous effort. He also advocated a scientific approach to the study of commerce. Quoting the eminent Professor Lees—Smith on the occasion he said:

> *"The leaders of commerce and business need to be scientifically trained just as a doctor or a barrister or professional man is . . . Modern experience shows us that business requires administrative capacity of the very highest type. It needs not merely technical knowledge but it needs the power of dealing with new situations of going forward at the right moment and of controlling labour. These are just the qualities which Universities have always claimed as being their special business to foster."*

Ganga Singh Ji also concurred with Prof. Smith that if the control of commerce was to be in the hands of the youth than it was the task of the University to produce wide-minded enterprising men of initiative. Striking a sombre tone the Maharaja felt that though exports in 1915 stood at 244 crores and there existed 230 cotton mills in the country, these had to be compared with the situation prevalent in other countries.

The remaining part of his speech was devoted to the agriculture sector. He felt that this sector was most dependent on co-operation with other departments as the bulk of the vast population of India subsisted on agriculture and unfortunately famine and draughts caused by fickle nature of monsoons were calamities which overtook the land from time to time. The advantages of a co-operation were hence self-apparant and their own recommendation. Backwardness among the agriculturalists was further compounded with the problem of rural indebtedness. To remedy the above stated problems it was advocated that the qualities of foresight, thrift and self-reliance were to be developed in the agriculturalists combined with the acquisition of business habits. In this scenario the co-operative movement was seen as the ultimate answer. By 1913—14 there were already around 11380 co-operative societies in existence. The co-operative movement was seen as the main instrument of educational, social and moral reforms. The movement was also seen as most likely to release the agriculturalists from chronic indebtedness and freeing him from the necessity of incurring new loans at high rates. In conclusion the Maharaja graciously gave the India the watch-word of "Hope" and which he further defined as—(No 2)

> *"Let hope also be the watch-word of our University movement and may God bless and reward our labours".*

In 1920 Maharaja Ganga Singh paid another visit to Benaras University but because of indifferent health he did not make a customary long speech but in the course of his brief address he wished the University years of growth and prosperity. (No.).

In 1922 Ganga Singh Ji was nominated as Pro-Chancellor of the University-a richly deserved honour he held till 1929. In 1927 he was further honoured with the conferring of the degree of L.L.D. Finally in 1929 he was accorded the supreme distinction—he was elected Chancellor of Benaras Hindu University—a post he held till his death in 1943.

In December 1927 he revisited B.H.U. and delivered a major address which had all the hallmarks of his philosophy of education and his concern for Indian values. (No. 3) He started by dwelling on his long association with the holy town of Benaras which always exercised a peculiar fascination for him. Varanasi, to the Maharaja, was the home of Hindu Culture, the seat of Divine Learning and the heart of Hindu civilization. It was also the sanctum sanctorum of a pious Hindu as it was also the abode of Lord Vishwanath—the Father of the Universe. The sacred ghats on the banks of the Ganges, served as a fountain of inspiration to the pious imagination of the devotee. Referring to the men who shaped the destiny of the University, the Maharaja commented:

> *"The ambition of bridging the gulf between the old and the new, of bringing about an alliance between antiquity and modernity like a confluence between the Varna and the Assi has all along inspired the eminent pioneers of this noble Institution with a religious zeal that commands universal respect".*

It was a matter of satisfaction for the Maharaja that besides including a study of Hindu Religion, Ancient Hindu Polity and Hindu Civics in its curriculum on the side of Humanities, scientific subjects like Geology, Mining and Metallurgy as well as Industrial Chemistry had also found a place within the University's portals. The Engineering wing, with special reference to Electrical and Mechanical Engineering, had already started atracting students from all over the country.

While expressing satisfaction with the growth of other disciplines, the Maharaja felt constrained to remark that the agriculture faculty had not developed along the anticipated lines. He mused that the need of the nation was that two blades of grass should grow where hitherto only one blade grew. If and when the agriculture faculty developed than it would have to deal with problems of land cultivation and crop experiments, of improvement of the implements of tillage and of adoption of labour saving devices and the latest mechanical contrivances for the extraction of the maximum return from the soil at the minimum of cost. The Maharaja also used the occasion to seek financial help from patrons as the first corore already collected had proved insufficient. The Maharaja himself had donated Rs. 1,00,000 to the University in addition to a grant of Rs. 12,000 to be paid annually. If the resources proved inadequate, he reasoned, then certain pruning would have to be done more like a clever surgeon who knew where and when to apply the knife.

A major part of the second half of the Maharaja's address revealed his indeapth understanding of the philosophical approach to education and what constituted University education. Redefining the scope of the Hindu University, Ganga Singh Ji held forth the following profound views:

*"Our aim and endeavour should be the glory of God and relief of man's estate. If we ponder seriously, I am sure, we shall find that there is no real conflict between Religion and Science. It is no doubt true that undue emphasis of the claims of Faith may clash with, and drown the voice of Reason; and any scheme of studies which subordinates the claims of the rational faculty to the dictates of authority must end in stagnation and decay. We are living in a world of the wireless and aeroplanes and this era of scientific renaissance could not possibly have been ushered in by the schoolmen of the Medieval Ages, who delighted in logomachines about Form and substance, concept and name, Identity and Difference. The ancient Universities of Taxila and Nalanda hummed with polemical wrangles about the variety of the cosmos, nascience about the a cosmic reality, and the existence of a future world; but it is open to question whether they really contributed much to the advancement of our ascendency over Nature in the World. If we desire to understand the mysteries of Nature, we have to accost her and force her into a corner under the air-pump and extort or coring out her secrets. Bhartihari, the Royal sage, sang of the impossibility of weaving ropes from the rays of the sun or pressing out oil from sand. Our present day victories in the field of science have achieved even more . . . Science has not only anhilated space; she has longthened life, she has minimised danger, she has controlled lunacy and trampled disease." (speech on 9th December, 1927)(No. 3).*

## References


1. Sundaram, V.A., Benaras Hindu University, 1905-35.
2. Bhanot, S.K., 'Bikaner Rajya Mein Shiksha Ke Pragati' in G. St. Devra edited, Maharaja Ganga Singh Centenary Volume, Bikaner, 1980.
3. 'Four Decades of Progress in Bikaner' Govt. Publication, Bikaner, 1937.
4. Karni Singh, 'Relations of Bikaner with Central Powers, Bikaner,1968.
5. Powlett, Gazetteer of Bikaner State.
6. Ojha, G.H., Bikaner Rajya Ka Itihas, Vol. II, Ajmer, 1940.
7. Administrative Reports of Bikaner State, 1905-06, 1908-09, 1937-38,1939-42.
8. Maharaja Ganga Singh Ji's address at a Public Meeting at the Town Hall of Calcutta on the 17th January, 1912.
9. Extension Lecture delivered by Maharaja Ganga Singh Ji at Hindu University at Varanasi, 1916.
10. Speech at Benaras Hindu University by Ganga Singh Ji, March 1920.
11. Convocation Address of the Maharaja of Bikaner at the Hindu University, Varanasi, December, 1927.

# Annexure 1

## Benares Hindu University

**The following address was delivered by His Highness Maharaja Sir Ganga Singhji Bahadur, G.C.S.I. G.C.I.E. of Bikaner, as President of a public meeting held in support of the proposed Hindu University of Benares at the Town Hall of Calcutta on the 17th of January 1912.**

*Maharajas, Rajas, Ladies and gentlemen,*

I thank you cordially for the honour you have done me in inviting me to preside at this meeting, and I am very glad of the opportunity which the occasion of the visit of Their Imperial majesties has afforded me to avail myself of that invitation: for it enables me not only to identify myself with the movement we are assembled here to-day to support, which has always had my warmest good wishes, but also to testify to the fact that although we, Ruling Chiefs, come from our own territories outside the limits of British India proper, we are entirely at one with our brethren in British India where loyalty to our beloved King Emperor, Co-operation with the Government of India in the path of order and good government as also the true advancement and well-being of our mother-country and His Majesty's Indian subjects are concerned.

I do not propose to-day to trace the history and growth of the idea of founding a great Hindu University. Started some years ago, its progress till recently has been gradual. It is only in the last few months that the movement has become completely coherent and has advanced by rapid stages. The different schemes have been amalgamated. Public meetings held all over India and the large donations promised have made it clear that the University is no longer the ideal of the few but has kindled the enthusiasm of the many. The general approval and Sympathy of the Government have been secured and the University is on a fair way to being a settled fact.

For this we are indebted to the promoters of the scheme—some of whom we are glad to see are present here to-day whose energy and perservance have over-borne all difficulties. They wisely set themselves to secure the approval of Government and the co-operation of the Ruling Princes. We are gratefully conscious of what they have accomplished and of the manner in which they have accomplished it.

We are no less indebted to the Government and specially to His Excellency the Viceroy and the Hon. Sir H. Butler, the Member for education, for their help and sympathy towards what may fairly be called the united endeavour of a great community to achieve a grat and common object.

That our object is a great one I think to one can dispute. It would be superfluous to speak of the benefits of education. It is a necessary condition of a nation's prosperity and lies at the root of all progress. The Government have done much in the last fifty years to promote education of all kinds-primary, secondary and higher—and the recent announcement made by the command of His Imperial Majesty has given us a renewed assurance of the future spread of mass education. But deeply grateful as all friends of education are for this great boon from our Sovereign, they must be yet more rejoiced at the reply which His Imperial Majesty was pleased to make to the address presented by the Senate of the Calcutta University, a reply which is in fact a benediction on the aspirations of all who like ourselves, and the supporters of the Muslim University, are endeavouring to further higher education.

I cannot do better than quote from that significant speech to which it was my privilege to listen from the King-Emperor's own lips:

> 'It is to the University of India that I look to assist in that gradual union and fusion of the culture and aspirations of Europeans and Indians on which the future well-being of India so greatly depends. I have watched with sympathy the measures which from time to time have been taken by the Universities of India to extend the scope and raise the standard of instruction. Much remains to be done. No University now-a-days is complete unless it is equipped with teaching faculties in all the more important branches of science and the arts and unless it provided ample opportunities for research. You have to conserve the ancient learning and simultaneously to push forward Western science. You have also to build up character, without which learning is of little value. You say that you recognise your great responsibilities. I bid you god—speed on the work that is before you. Let your ideals be high and your efforts to pursue them unceasing and under Providence you will succeed.'

Although these words were spoken to the Senate of the Calcutta University, yet if His Majesty had been addressing the promoters of the Hindu University, or of the Muslim University, they could not desire a more gracious recognition of their endeavours in the past of for words of higher hope for the future.

Our Hindu University is to be a residential and teaching University which will seek 'to conserve the ancient learning and simultaneously to push forward Western science', 'to build up character without which learning is of little value;' it will be equipped 'with teachings faculties in all the more important branches of science and the arts' and will provide 'ample opportunities for research;' and it will be the aim and endeavour of our University 'to assist in that gradual union and fusion of the culture and aspirations of Europeans and Indians on which the future well-being of India so greatly depends.'

It is more than half a century ago that what Lord Morley has described as one of the most momentous steps in the history of British rule in India was taken. I refer to the establishment of Universities. It is difficult to over-estimate the importance of the existing University, or to praise too highly the work which they have done in the past and are doing to-day in diffusing learning and culture.

The British Government have always believed—and their belief has not been shaken—in the value of the spread of knowledge.

The recent unrest, of which all true patriots and well-wishers of India must hope we shall hear no more, has led not to discouragement and not to the discrediting of higher education, but to the desire by Government for more and better education.

No country in the world is however satisfied with its educational system, and it is not to be wondered at that there should have arisen a certain feeling of dissatisfaction in this respect in India also-a feeling which I believe I am right in saying has gradually resolved itself into a conviction that the intellect has been developed to exclusively and that character has been insufficiently considered and also that the existing provision for higher education and research in inadequate.

The proposed Hindu University will fill a great want by being a teaching and residential University providing for technical instruction and encourging research and by what is more important, including in its courses the teaching of religion.

The demand for religious teaching has of late years been steadily increasing, and side by side with it the conviction has been growing that character can best be built up when it rests on the precepts of a great and noble religion. Certain difficulties may at first present themselves as regards religious instruction, but no such difficulties should obscure the fact of its necessity.

The Hindus as also our Musalman brethren are proud of being the heirs of a great civilisation, a great religion, and a great literature. It is to foster and conserve these that the two new Muhammadan and Hindu Universities are now promoted.

But like everything new the proposal has provoked criticism. It has been said that denominational Universities are liable to promote sectarian differences. Perhaps I may be permitted specially to touch on this subject. I would say, and I think I can count on the support not only of this distinguished assembly but also of our community at large when I say it, that it is not in any spirit of hostility or unfriendliness to our Muhammadan brethren that this scheme has been launched—a scheme which, as a matter of fact, was mooted several years ago. Whatever the ideal may have been, India is big enough for two such Universities as are now before the public. Situated as we are at the present moment it must be conceded that much good can be done by diverting the charities and activities of the two communities towards the promotion of education by creating institutions which will appeal to them in a special degree. It is our earnest desire to work in a spirit of amity and concord an din such a way that the Muhammadan and Hindu Universities may be looked upon as sister institutions labouring to promote in their respective spheres the good of the children of our common country, and there is every reason to hope and believe that with both the institutions broadly organised, soundly managed and sufficiently endowed, and with the spread of knowledge which they will foster and promote, they will contribute towards creating a spirit of mutual esteem and good-willl among the members of the two communities. Based on morality, reverence and duty, their teaching will tend to tolerance and not estrangement, and with the spread of education of which this movement is a great landmark, both Musalmans and Hindus will recognise the common humanity which unties them and the common goal to which they are striving by different paths.

It is important to remember that both the Muhammadan and Hindu Universities are to be open to students of all creeds and classes, and the mutual exchange of compliments and subscriptions between His Highness the Aga Khan and the Maharaja Bahadur of Darb hanga and other instances where the Muhammadans and the Hindus have contributed towards the educational institutions and schemes of the sister communities augur well for the future.

While on this subject may I, as a true well-wisher of our country, express the earnest hope that any difference which may have divided the Muhammadans and the Hindus in recent times may at an early date disappear. I would not presume to dwell on the harm arising from such a state of affairs, but would again like to quote from the speech of His Imperial Majesty the King—Emperor in his parting message to India, where His Majesty, out of his noble solicitude for the well-being of his people, said:

> 'It is a matter of intense satisfaction to me to realise how all classes and creeds have joined together in the true-hearted welcome which has been so universally accorded to us. Is it not possible that the same unity and concord may for the future govern the daily relations of their private and public life? The attainment of this would indeed be to us a happy outcome of our visit to India.'

No object can be dearer to the heart of India, and loyalty and patriotism both demand it that every leader of men among the two communities should exert all his influence to bring about a consummation so devoultly wished for by every body.

A fear has also been expressed that the University is designed to lower standards and to gain popularity by making degrees easy to obtain. There is no justification for any such misgivings. It will be one of the most earnest aims of the University to keep up its standards and if possible to raise them higher than those of the existing Universities, so that its graduates may be regard as the flower of the youth of India.

The Hindu University movement is a purely educational one. Politics have not and will never have any part in our project, and our ambition is to turn out loyal oubjects of the King-Emperor and good members of society able to hold their own in life. Worked on broad lines it must maintain, as it has secured, the interest and confidence ot the Princes and people of India and the cordial co-operation of the Government. It is gratifying to see from the constitution of the proposed University that the promoters are fully alive to these needs, and it will be a privilege and an honour to the Hindu University to have His Excellency the Viceroy as its Chancellor. In this connection I am sure you will all be very glad to hear that His Excellency the Viceroy has very kindly authorised me to express his sympathy with out Hindu University movement and his good wishes for its success.

Before concluding I would like to join in the appeal to the Princes and people of India to subscribe liberally to the funds of the University. it is encouraging to hear that over 43 lakhs have already been subscribed. I hope this amount will soon be doubled and that before long a sufficient sum will be forthcoming to make the Hindu University not only self-supporting but the first educational institution in India, fully equipped with the most modern appliances and inspired by the culture of the East.

In his speech in reply to the address from the Senate of the Calcutta University His Imperial Majesty was graciously pleased to give to India the watchword of 'Hope'. Let Hope also be the watchword of our University movement, and may God bless and reward our labours!

# Annexure 2

## Your Highnesses, Members of the Hindu University Society, Ladies and Gentlemen, 1916

I thank you for the honour you have done me by asking me to preside at the Inauguration of this series of lectures which I take it are in the nature of University extension lectures. Although a Ruler of an Indian State has in the course of the day's work to deal with files and cases relating to such widely divergent and multifarious subjects as Land Revenue and Finance, Customs and Excise, Roads and buildings, Railways and Irrigation, Army and Police, Political Reforms and Legislation, Civil and Criminal Justice, education and public health and Sanitation, and so on—all of which tend to the welfare, advancement, and contentment of the people and to increase efficiency in the State Administration, I trust you have not selected me as an expert in the subjects which are going to be dealt with this morning. That commerce and industries—most important and vital subjects which a State can have to deal with—should also engage his serious attention goes without saying. But as the Indian States in common with the rest of India, are, on the whole, rather backward and vehind the lines in this direction—and though doubtless the question will, as time passes, receive daily increasing attention, and we all hope that in the next couple of decades or so great strides will be made—I cannot hold wishing that someone else better fitted then myself had to deal with these subjects today in his presidential address so as to do justice to them. Whilst therefore, asking you to forgive any shortcomings in my speech, I will only add that as one keenly interested in the establishment of our Hindu University and as a quiet—and I hope it may have been found a willing—worker in this great cause, it was with no small pleasure that I accepted the invitation to preside at today's function. And if I might be pennitted to strike a personal note, may I add that I take it as an intended compliments, on the part of Hindu University Society, to the famous and large Mercantile and Banking community of my State—the Seths and Sahukars—who figure so prominently and successfully in the field of commerce, industries and trade, not only in Bikaner but throughout the length and breadth of the India Empire.

I do not think that you would desire me to say anything by way of introduction as regards the gentlemen who have kindly agreed to lecture today. It is to my mind of far greater importance that your time should be taken up in listening to a discourse on the subjects from persons better qualified than myself and I instead of attempting to put forward something to you in an original form it will I trust be agreed that a few general remarks will be adequate for the purpose.

I need hardly remind you of what trade our people carried on in ancient times with distant countries. Though India was once famous for manufactures, it must be realised that we are now very backward in the matter of trade and industries and have much lee-way to make. It must be something before we can successfully compete, in friendly and healthy rivalry, with other countries in the more important manufactures but there is at the same time to no reasons why India should not ultimate succeed. And to take only two instances, it is at least encounraging to note that in the year 1913-14 our exports stood at 244 crores and our imports amounted to nearly 200 crores as against 18.75 crores and 14.05 crores respectively in 1954-55, whilst, without referring to other industries, since the first cotton mills was started in Bombay some 60 years, approximately 230 mills have been established in India. In this age of competition, however, it is brain power combined with earnest and contineous efforts which succeeds, and the first thing that is required is commercial education on sound and up-to-date lines for our youths. It is in this direction that a faculty of Commerce in our University will supply a much felt Prof. Lees—Smith has well said:

> The leaders of commerce and business need to be scientifically trained just as a doctor or a barrister or professional man is Modern experience shows us that business requires administrative capacity of the very highest type. It needs not merely technical knowledge but it needs the power of dealing with new situations of going forward at the right moment and of controlling labour. These are just the qualities which Universities have always claimed as being their special business to foster, and we, therefore, say that if you are going to fulfil any of the hopes . . . if you are going to take in your own hands the control of the commerce of this nation, then you must produce wide—minded enterprising men of initiative, men who are likely to be produced by the University Faculties of Commerce."

Turning now to the no less important subject of co-operation, I will only say that as the bulk of the vast population of India subsists on agriculture and as unfortunately famine and droughts in this country, caused by the riokie nature of our monsoons, are calamities which are bound to overtake the land from time to time, the advantage of co-operation are self-apparent and their own recommendation. In the present age of advancement the agriculturists are one of the few communities who have not progressed to an appreciable extent. Besides their backward methods of agriculture, the degree of their indebtedness must cause concern to all well-wishers of the Country and in addition to the measures which the British Government is taking to help them, co-operation is one of the golden remedies which will have very far-reaching results.

It is most essential to develop in the agriculturists the qualities of foresight, thrift and self reliance, combined with business habit and a due sense of responsibility and to stimulate the ideas of moral and economic progress. A co-operative society alone can best fulfil these functions. The progress already made is full of hope. The growth of the co-operative movement in recent years has been remarkable and in 1912-13, 11382 societies are reported to have been in existence a against only 843 in 1906-07. The societies have moreover been instrumental in giving a further stimulus to education and have also led to social and moral reforms. They are bound to be of the greatest assistance to the agriculturist in releasing him from the bonas of chronic indebtedness and freeing him fro the necessity or incurring new loan at high rates of interest.

Before resuming my seat I would add that we in India who desire to see a greater diffusion of knowledge among our people should derive encouragment from the speech delivered at Calcutta by our beloved King-Emperor when His Imperial Majesty was graciously pleased to give to India the watch word of "Hope". when speaking very shortly after that at the Town Hall in Calcutta at a meeting in connection with our Hindu University, I ventured to refer to this and to say:

> "Set hope also be the watch-word of our
> University movement and may God bless and
> reward our labours,"

Thanks to the sympathetic attitude of our great and popular viceroy and to the single minded zeal and indefatigable energies of my friends, the Maharajan Sahib or Durbhanga, Dr. Sundar Lal and Pandit Madan

Mohan Malviya and the other promotors of the scheme—OUR HINDU UNIVERSITY BILL has been passed. We had the lively gratification yesterday of seeing the Foundation Stone laid by His Excellency and as soon as the buildings which will adorn the site are completed, one of most cherished aspirations of our Community will have been realized by the Hindu University coming into actual existence in this our Holy City.

Some of you present here today will doubtless be joining our University when its doors are thrown open, and to you and to others who may hereafter flock to this Institution, I would like to say one thing. Whether in the world of commerce or in any other line that you may choose for yourselves, should you experience any drawbacks or difficulties, derive strength and confidence from the fact that, by the Grace of God, we have reigning over India a Sovereign whose gracious sympathy for our country and whose solicitude and affection for the Indian people are well-known—not only to us but throughout the world and that his governments both in England and in India will assuredly endeavour to satisfy the legitimate aspirations and to remove and real grievances of the people of India, with whom they are daily endeavouring to establish closer though and greater sympathy.

Terrible though war is, the titanic struggle that is now raging in the World, and the solid and united front which all parts of the British Empire have presented, have brought us all closer together and will bring about a still better understanding between India and England as also with the rest or the British Empire.

I. do not want to stand any longer between you and the learned lecturers and I have much pleasure in calling upon the Hon : Mr. Lalubhai Samaldass to deliver his address.

# Annexure 3

## Speech of His Highness the Maharajah of Bikaner at the Convocation of the Benares Hindu University at Benares on the 9th December, 1927

*Mr. Vice-Chancellor, Senators and Graduates of the Benares Hindu University, Ladies and Gentlemen;*

Let me thank you very cordially for inviting me to preside at your Convocation this year. It is a privilege which I highly cherish; and I rejoice at the opportunity which it affords me of renewing my acquaintance with this ancient Seat of Learning. I do not come to you as quite a stranger. It is now sixteen years that I was first intimately associated with the Scheme of founding a Hindu University when—charged with a message from that great and noble-minded Viceroy, Lord Hardinge, of sympathy and goodwill for the great cause—I had the privilege of urging the claims of an Academy that would enshrine whatever was of the best in ancient Hindu Culture before a large public gathering assembled at Calcutta. For years later, we had the satisfaction to see the seed then sown sprouting and giving promise of a healthy and vigorous life. Associated as I have been from the earliest commencement with all the preliminary vicissitudes that alternately helped or hindered the birth of this Great University, I was privileged to be present at the laying of its Foundation Stone at the hands of Lord Hardinge in 1916. In 1920 I was again in your midst and was able to atend the series of learned discourses, and to partake of the intellectual fare, so generously provided by the Academy. The ties which bind me to you are dear to me and they have brought me again before you this evening. If, except for occasional visits, I have not been able to come and see you more frequently, it was not because of any lack of interest but due to reasons of State and health, over which I had no control.

Benares has always exercised a peculiar fascination on me. I have always looked up to Varanasi as the home of Hindu Culture, the Seat of Divine Learning and the heart of Hindu civilization. The abode of our Lord Vishwanath—the Father of the Universe and the Creator—resplendent Kashi has always been regarded as the Sanctum

Sanctorum of a pious Hindu. Its sacred Ghats, constantly laved by the ripples of the sacred Ganga, serve as a fountain of inspiration to the pious imagination of the devotee; and the ancient Gyan-Vapi has even now not ceased to well up with memories of hoary traditions of antiquity. The ambition of bridging the gulf between the old and the new, of bringing about, an alliance between antiquity and modernity like a confluence between the Varna and the Assi has all along inspired the eminent pioneers of this noble Institution with a religious zeal that commands universal respect; and when I realise how this great idea has in such a short time—fructified in this imposing pile of edifices on the banks of the Assi, I feel convinced that the promotors of this new ideal of a residential Teaching University have not been mere dreaming idealists. The various Schools of Literature and Science housed in this noble array of buildings, which we see before us apread out in charming prospect, have all manifested signs of healthy and vigorous development, which is a good augury for the future. The progress already achieved by this young University, in spite of a decade of unparalleled financial depression and world turmoil, ought to satisfy the most impatient and ardent reformer; and the pious spirit of Faith and Hope with which its founders have braved an epoch of exceptional stress and storm must evoke our admiration and respect.

The Benares Hindu University has made ample provision for imparting advanced academic education in various branches which compares very favourably with the literary fare provided at the other Sister Universities in this country. Besides including a study of Hindu Religion, Ancient Hindu Polity and Hindu Civics in its curriculum on the side of Humanities, Scientific subjects like Geology, Mining and Metallurgy, as well as Industrial Chemistry, have found a place within its portals and useful provision is being made for cultivating a spirit of Original Research through the conveniences of well-equipped laboratories and finely assorted workshops. The School of Engineering is a special and strong feature of the Benares University which draws students in large numbers.

The Benares Hindu University has made ample provision for imparting advanced academic education in various branches, which compares very favourably with the literary forum provided at the other Sister Universities in this country. Besides including a study of Hindu Religion, Ancient Hindu Polity, and Hindu Civics in its curriculum on the side of Humanities, Scientific subjects like Geology, Mining and Metallurgy, as well as Industrial Chemistry, have found a place within its portals and useful provision is being made for cultivating a spirit of Original Research through the conveniences of well-equipped laboratories and finely assorted workshops. The School of Engineering is a special and strong feature of the Benares University which draws students in large numbers from far and near for practical training in Mechanical and Electric Engineering. Upwards of 2,000 students have been already enrolled on the lists of the various Schools and Sections constituting this large Unitary and Teaching University.

At the same time, though much has been done, it must not be forgotten that more yet remains to be done. The Faculty of Agriculture has yet to be added to the Course of Training. The art of making two blades grow where one grew before has a peculiar value for our Country which is mainly agricultural; and problems of rural reconstruction must engage through early and earnest attention of every true lover of the Country. Problems of land cultivation and crop experiments, of improvement of the implements of tillage and of adoption of labour saving devices and the latest mechanical contrivances forthe extraction of the maximum return from the soil at the minimum of cost must receive increasing attention in course of time. The deliberations of the Royal Agriculture Commission will throw new light on the several questions connected with Agriculture and Irrigation and they deserve—and will no doubt receive—adequate attention at the hands of the University authorities. Then there is the Faculty of Commerce which ought also soon to engage the minds of the organisers of this Great University. All these developments, however, mean money and the Hindu University is not suffering from any glut of this precious metal. The financial condition of the University has been causing some anxiety or several years past and this aspect has no less to be borne in mind. Your devoted and zealous Vice-Chancellor, my friend the veteran Pandit Madan Mohan Malaviya—to whom this Benares Hindu University is most deeply indebted and who has dedicated his life and life-work to this noble mission—has lately issued an appeal for a Second Crore. I join my faint but earnest voice to his impassioned and laudable appeal to all true Hindus and real patriots of the Country to contribute their mite towards the fulfilment of this high ideal. No philanthropic cause could be more sacred than the feeding and fostering of this Hindu University. If our private charities were more organised and better discernment and discrimination used in the selection of worthy objects for the countless charitable public Trusts that our benevolent countrymen have at their disposal, the collection of a Second Crore need not battle us as altogether beyond our reach. Strenuous effort is no doubt needed; but there is hardly any problem, however stupendous, that can appeal or stagger the soul of a real patriot, a true lover of Learning and a selfless seeker after Truth.

We cannot indefinitely feed our various Schools on mere Faith and Hope. They require the sinews of war and they cannot be kept long without adequate sustenance. However worthy our objects and ideals may be, prudence cannot allow them to outrun our financial resources. Should our appeal not meet with adequate response, then, instead of extending and filling out, it may be prudent—indeed necessary—to curtail our activities and endeavour only intensive culture for the time being till the financial prospects become more promising and cheerful. A clever surgeon is he who knows where and when to apply the knife. Pruning and weeling are useful operations that help the healthy growth of the plant. But I decline to believe that our Hindu community will sit with folded hands and allow such a measure to come to pass.

At the same time, it might be prudent to specialise the University in a few particular branches of study so as to save overlapping of functions and re-duplication of effort. The scope of the Hindu University ought to be defined so that each University could cultivate that Branch and excel in its equipment for that particular subject. Our aim and endeavour should be the glory of God and relief of man's estate. If we ponder seriously, I am sure, we shall find that there is no real conflict between Religion and Science. It is no doubt true that undue emphasis of the claims of Faith may clash with, and drown the voice of Reason, and any scheme of studies which subordinates the claims of the national faculty to the dictates of authority must end in stagnation and decay. We are living in a world of the wireless and aeroplanes and this era of scientific renaissance could not possibly have been ushered in by the ssSchoolmen of the Medieval Ages, who delighted in logomachies about Form and Substance, Concept and Name, Identity and Difference. The ancient Universities of Taxila and Nalanda hummed with polemical wrangles about the vanity of the cosmos, nescience about the acosmic reality, and the existence of a future world; but it is open to question whether they really contributed much to the advancement of our ascendency over Nature in this world. If we desire to understand the mysteries of Nature, we have to accost her and force her into a corner under the air-pump and extort or wring out her secrets. Bhartrihari, the Royal Sage, sang of the impossibility of weaving ropes from the rays of the sun or of pressing out oil from sand. Our present day victories in the field of Science have achieved even more. If Bhartrihari were to visit the world in his new incarnation today, he would stand aghast at the uses to which we have put the Solar and various other Rays in the service of man. Science has not only annihilated space; she has lengthed life, she has minimised danger, she has controlled lunacy and trampled disease. She restores eyes to the blind and hearing to the deaf. She has enlisted the sunbeam in her service to limn for us with absolute fidelity the faces of the friends we love and transmit the picture from across the Seas. She has harnessed the lightning for the conveyance of our message to the other end of the world and has enabled our vision to penetrate to the bowels of the earth to find out what priceless treasures are embedded below. It is in this Department of Science that much remains still to be done in our Indian Universities and this you can only achieve if you perfect your laboratories and study Nature in her manifold manifestations. Cultivate a spirit of Research, of Observation and Experiment and your conquest over the elements of Nature would be materially assured. Let me not be misunderstood. I do not discourage the study of Spiritual Dialectics; the problem whether our soul has three dimensions or four is no doubt fascinating; but it can hardly be disputed that as its name implies Metaphysics must come after Physics.

Equally insistent is the claim of Physical Culture. Any Scheme of Education in order to be complete, comprehensive and all embracing must include the culture of the body as well as of mind. "Sound mind in a sound body" has been an adage too much profaned as much by over-iteration as by under-observance. I am gratified to find that the claims of the human body have been receiving due attention from the Hindu University authorities; but what I do wish as a soldier to emphasise on this occasion is the value of regular Military Training. Besides serving as a course of healthy physical exercise, such a training would instil a love of discipline and an espirite corps among the alumini of this Great Institution. A spirit of comradeship, of sportsmanship and of brotherly sympathy is essentially needed at this juncture; and with a course of Military Training super-added to its academic achievements the Hindu University Corps would not only be of immense service to the Country, but as a Unit of the Territorial Militia could always place its loyal services at the disposal of His Imperial Majesty—our beloved King—Emperor.

Loyalty to your Country and your King is one of the primary civic duties enjoined by every writer on Jurisprudence. It is the foundation of law and order and as good citizens it should be your first concern to foster and uphold this cardinal virtue. Fidelity to the Sovereign is among the fundamental duties prescribed by the Hindu Dharmashastras and I charge you, Young Students of the Hindu

University, ever in your life and conversation you prove yourselves worthy of the proud alma mater which starts you on your life's career this day. Let loyalty to our beloved King Emperor be the priceless ornament in the character of every Graduate turned out by our University. It is up to you jealously to guard against this matchless jewel being dimmed or tarnished by seductive writings of the advocates of anarchy and chaos however fascinating they may be.

Let your Professors and Instructors at the same time remember that their object is not merely the imparting of advanced educational; it is also, if not more the formation of a sound and steady character. The value of a Residential University can best be demonstrated in the facilities it can afford for the building up of good character. Let your goal be the culture of "Self-reverence, Self-knowledge, Self-control; which three alone lead to Sovereign power". One cannot fail be struck with the mistaken notions bout liberty that of ten prevail in the minds of some young men. True Liberty consists in freedom to do what one ought not freedom to do what one wills, which only deteriorates into license and wanton depravity. Learn to control yourself; for moral self-government alone can prepare you for any higher form of political self-government. Cultivate the habit of self-reverenace. We have indeed every reason to be proud of our ancestors, our ancient culture and our glorious civilisation; but do not let any undue bias for antiquity deter you from your duty to posterity. Reverence for the ancient Aryavarta can never be incompatible with an eager solitude for the elevation and re-generation of Mother India. But with this end in view "Act, act in the living present"; and "above all to thine ownself be true; so that thou canst not then be false to any man". Service and Sacrifice ought to be the twin vows of your modern Brahmacharya. Our land has been well-known for its spirit of Chivalry. If that Age has gone from the present day Western World of Sophisters and Economists, let not that same canker eat up the vitals of our ancient culture. Never fail to set a high value on a habit of deference and reverence to your elders and of proud submission to rank and sex which is the true test of an abiding civilisation.

The value of high character and sub-lime moral ideals is incalculab at the present day. We are passing through critical times. An era of transition has ever been an era of trouble, travail and turmoil owing to the dethronement of old ideals and the effete in capacity of the new ideals to take their place. India is hovering between two worlds in our time; the one as dead as Queen Anne, the other yet 'too powerless to be born'. The greater is the necessity of wise caution and robust commonsense. We must live at peace with our fellow subjects—our Moslem brethren; for pray do not forget that though we are divided by Religion, we are all Indians first and foremost and Hindus and Moslems and everything else only afterwards. Our communal tension has unfortunately become a veritable cancer and must be radically cut off if we want to preserve our national life. Our popular Viceroy, Lord Irwin—a good, religious man—has sent forth in all earnest his exhortation for mutual understanding and racial reconciliation. Let not that sage counsel fall upon deaf years. Remember that Life is only a compromise. Let us all realise that the high road to national greatness lies along the old highway of steadfast well-doing all round and they who are the most persistent and work in the truest spirit of general well-being will invariably be the most successful. Success treads on the heels of only righteous endeavour.

Philosophers and Educationists have proclaimed how our environments and surroundings mould human character and shape our destiny; and in this respect you, fortunate alumni of the Kashi Vishwa Vidyalaya, are well-favoured and richly endowned. For what can be more holy than Kashi, which succeeded in attracting Lord Gautama Buddha whose first lesson on the Doctrine of Divine Mercy and Universal Brotherhood was initiated in the Deer Park at Sarnath. What can be more inspiring than the sacred Waters. Mother Gapga that are even now credited in this Iron Age of Doubt and Disbelief with supreme healing powers for all our ills, both of mind and body. You are now leaving your Brahmacharya Ashram. Go forth into the World out of the portal of this Great Institution with this rich dowry of Divine Inspiration and you will be admirably fitted to wed that "Stem Daughter of the Voice of God" Duty in the Great life's journey that lies your feet.

# 7

## *Maharaja Ganga Singh Ji's Participation and Role in the League of Nations*

THE SPRUNT IN Anti-British activities in the wake of the partition of Bengal in 1905 and the emergence of the extremist party under the inspiring leadership of Bal Gangadhar Tilak, Bipinchandra Pal and Lala Lajpat Rai left the British Government visably alarmed. If the British Government felt alarmed, the Native rulers also had cause for worry though on different grounds.

Since the early days of the East India Company it was its declared policy that the rulers of Great States like the Nizam of Hyderabad, the Maharaja Scindhia of Gwalior, the Maharaja of Indore and the rest were to be prevented from forming an alliance of any nature which would be harmful to the Company's interests.

It was in the wake of this that any State which entered into a subsidiary alliance with the British was debarred from having any relationship with other native states and all disputes between the States were to be decided under arbitration of the Company.

The events of 1857-58 further convinced the British that if an upheaval of such magnitude could take place without the assistance of the rulers, then the consequences were mind boggling if the Indian rulers were to unite or come together into a confederacy. Thus it was decided that the isolation of the native rulers was the paramount need of the hour and towards this end the political officers appointed in the States were vested with enormous powers—a situation very galling to the rulers. The rulers, in many instances, were over-ruled by the Political Agents who kept a very watchful eye over the rulers specially with regards to their relations with other rulers. But there was a school of thought in the British Government which felt that the stage of the isolation of the Indian rulers was over more so after 1857-58 and their prestiege and authority could be harnessed by the

Government of India for the preservation of its interests. It was in this light that Lord Lytton had suggested in 1876 the creation of an Imperial Privy Council for India composed partly of selected Ruling Princes and partly of officials. But the scheme did not materialise due to misgivings on both sides—the princes felt that their sovereign position would be lowered by membership of such an association and the officials on the other hand felt that the end of the 'isolation of Princes' would lead to widespread collaboration among the Princes. Lord Lytton had to rest contend with the award of a new title of "Counsellors of the Empire" to a few Princes. But this scheme never got under way. It never met, no one, besides the few selected rulers, was nominated to it, and it died a quiet death. But Lord Lytton succeeded in one endeavour when he brought together all the ruling Princes of Rajputana under his presidentship to discuss the proposal to setup the Mayo College at Ajmer. This was the first time the rulers of Rajputana assembled under one roof to consider the important subject of education.

The Chiefs' College Conference of 1904 and the consultation of the Ruling Princes regarding Imperial Services troops in 1905 were two crucial meetings convened in the time of Lord Curzon which involved the ruling chiefs. A change in the attitude of the Princes was discernible in 1904 when a confident group presented a note to the Viceroy which laid out that the Princes were collectively ready to render any service for the betterment of the masses in the public interest. But it was however, the far-sighted Lord Hardinge (1910-16) who clearly anticipated the possibilities of imperial co-operation and the benefits that lay in the close association of the Government of India and the Indian States. One Indian ruler who had clearly thought on similar lines was none other than Maharaja Ganga Singh who had submitted a minute to the Viceroy in which he advocated the creation of a machinery which would secure sustained and intimate co-operation between the two Indias. He was of the view that there was grave danger of the States being left behind and shut out altogether of the national mainstream. The Princes were not willing to be mere puppets and thus share the fate that had be fallen some of the European aristocracies. They felt that they had a legitimate sphere which was in no sense opposed, but only complementary, to the democratic element in British India. The States and the Princes were self-governing feudatories, argued the Maharaja further, who were unique in the whole of British Empire and they desired to justify and live upto that position which to them was of special pride. He also felt upset that questions related to the Indian States were raised inBritish India and they were in no position to voice concern at some of them even though they tended to be injurious to their interests. There was only one officer in the Governor-General's Legislative Council- the Political Secretary—who was directly connected with the affairs of the Indian States. Single-handedly the one officer was unable to protect the interests of all the Indian States who for all practical purposes, constituted one-third of the whole of India. The Maharaja's concluding remarks reflected his anguish at the state of affairs in which the ruling classes were to sit in the same councils along with the nominated or elected people. He commented:

> "The very existence of the States may be dangerously threatened and the true self-government of India by the Indians, the product of thousands of years of evolution on indigenous lines, may be lost altogether, the whole Government of India sinking to a drab dead level of democracy without any of the interest or distruction that is suited to the religions, the instincts and the imagination of the people."

It was around this time that the Maharaja propounded the idea of a federal chamber representing all the States—and if necessary, through the Governors and Lieutenant Governors who could sit with the ruling chiefs, the provinces of British India as well—would grow up with, at first, advisory functions only. The essential message of the Maharaja was the earnest desire that the States should have a formal voice of some kind in the Government of India.

Lord Hardinge responded favourably in 1914 when he declared that the Princes were his trusted colleauges and he desired to seek their collective opinion whenever possible on matters affecting their interests. Hardinge was equally appreciative of the fact that the Maharaja did not ask that the Chiefs should be associated with the governance of India outside their own states.

The war saw the Maharaja render active service in various threatnes of war—a gesture that was warmly appauled at home and abroad. It was during the war that the Conference of Princes was first summoned to meet in Delhi in the winter of 1916 and as Ganga Singh Ji was the prime mover in the organisation of the Conference he was entrusted by his brother Princes to act as its honorary General Secretary—a post he held for five consecutive years from 1916 to 1920. As the war entered its third year it was decided that closer co-operation between the Dominions and the mother country was a must and towards this end an Imperial Conference was convened in London. When the

Conference was summoned in 1917, Maharaja Ganga Singh was one of the three Indian representatives to be associated with the Secretary of State for India as India's spokemen at the conference.

Maharaja Ganga Singh's nomination as a Indian Representative at the Imperial Conference brought about a rare maturity of thought in him and marked his emergence as a astute statesman. Prior to his departure for London the Maharaja addressed an assembly of Princes—an address which electrified the whole nation. He asserted that all Indians—whether in British India or in Indian States—were citizens of the same mother country with comon problems and aspirations. He further hoped that the services rendered by the Indians in the war effort would bring the British Government and the British Dominions closer and the British sense of justice and fair play would prove equal to the occasion and the just aspirations of India would be given their due. The Maharaja's speech raised a storm—for the fIrst time the ruler of a great State at a banquet presided over by a Governor and attended by many ruling princes had given unequivocal expression to nationalist and patriotic sentiments. Nationalist newspapers hailed it as the dawn of a new era when Princes and peasants would work together for the greater glory of India.

Mr. Llyod George who was fully aware of the contribution of Indians to the war effort, accorded the Indian delegation the rights of full membership in the Imperial Conference. Llyod George was highly impressed by the Maharaja about whom he remarked that:

> *"Bikaner as he was familiarly and affectionately called—The Indian Prince—was a magnificient specimen of manhood of his country. We soon found that he was one of the wise men that came from the East. More and more we came to rely on his advice especially on questions that affected India."*

During his stay in the London, the Maharaja received the freedom of the city of London, a doctorate of laws from Edinburgh University and other marks of honour from the British public. At every opportunity the Maharaja put accross India's case and aspirations most forcefully. In a landmark speech delivered at a luncheon given by the Parliamentary Association (United Kingdom Branch) to the Indian Delegates in the House of Commons, Harcourt Room, on 24th April, 1917, Ganga Singh Ji made many telling points including the possibility in future of the concept of Autonomy. (No. 1) At the outset he made it clear that when he referred to India he referred to both—British India and the Indian States. While professing total commitment for the Empire he also added:

*"It is equally unnecessary for me to assure you that the welfare of the Empire, for loyal and patriotic reasons if also for motives of enlightened self-interest, is a matter of abiding interest and concern to us.*

*Subject always to these two qualifications and consideration which are ever upper most in the mind of every thinking and loyal Indian (and they form by far an overwhelming majority of our population) our aspiration is also to see our country under the guidance of Britain—and as Mr. Chamberlain said, with the help of Great Britain—making material advance on constitutional lines in regard to matters political and economical, and ultimately to attain, under the standard of our King Emperor, that freedom and autonomy which you in this country secured long ago for yourselves, and which our more fortunate sister Dominions have also enjoyed for sometime past".*

*"My Lords and Genglemen, it is any matter for surprise that India should be aiming at her political regeneration ? You have given education on Western lines to Indians and after centuries of close and intimate connections with Great Britain—the land of liberal traditions and popular institutions—we Indians would be foolish if we did not see much that was good in your political life in this country. And we would be still more foolish if, after grasping the good points of your national life, we did not desire to have grafted or assimilated all that was good in your institutions and system, where-ever and whenever our conditions permitted it".*

On the issue of India's desire for ultimate self-government and autonomy within the British Empire, the Maharaja conceded that problems persisted. But, he argued, if diversity of race was a hinderence than there were different races in Great Britain itself and Canada as well. About the unrest in the country the Maharaja identified two types of unrest—one unleashed by terrorists and anarchists and the other led by the intelligensia as an legitimate protest.

The former could be crushed by force but in the latter case if the Indians had a greater say in administration than unrest could automatically diminish. The Maharaja also referred to the 'Unchanging East' which . . . .

*bowed low beneath the blast,*
*In patient deep disdain*
*She let the legions thunder past,*
*And plunged in thought again".*

Maharaja Ganga Singh also set at rest any doubts that the States would not welcome reforms in British India. On the contrary reforms would also follow in Indian States though on different lines as internal conditions varied. The Maharaja ended his speech with the plea that in order to secure a proper place in the constitution of the Empire, there should be an institution of a Council or Assembly of Princes where important questions concerning the rulers and subjects of the Indian States on one hand and the British Government on the other, could be discussed.

The efforts of Maharaja Ganga Singh were warmly applauded by the ruling Princes at a Banquet given to the late Indian Representatives by them at Delhi on the 8th November, 1917. The Maharaja used the occasion (No. 2) to refer to the ground swell of goodwill towards the Indians among the people of Great Britain and how it was an happy augary for times to come when Indian aspirations would be realised.

**Paris Peace Conference and Membership of the League**

The 'great' war ended on 11th November, 1918. The next momentous question was the negotiation of a peace treaty. On 15th Nov., 1918 Maharaja Ganga Singh received an urgent telegram from the Viceroy urging him to proceed immediately to England, on the express desire of the British Minister, to participate in the Peace proces. The other Indian delegate was Sir (later Lord) S.P. Sinha. On 1st January 1919 the Maharaja was invested with full powers from the King—Emperor as one of the plenipotentiaries for the Conference. It was a great honour. Mr. Montague, the Secretary of State for India was the Head of the Indian delegation.

The vital question that faced the Indian delegation was that of representation of India on the League of Nations. The fact that India was neither independent nor self-governing was urged even in the British Empire delegation against India inclusion in the League. To counter this Lord Sinha and the Maharaja represented to the Secretary of State in which whereas Lord Sinha stressed the legal and constitutional aspect, the Maharaja concentrated on the political aspect. The latter stated with emphasis that the position of India could not be differentiated from that of the Dominions in the matter of representation on the League of Nations. Furthermore, the question of internal autonomy was not the test to apply for membership of the proposed League. The test was also not mentioned in the resolution of the Conference on the subject held earlier nor in President Woodrow Wilson's speech. Wilson's speech had stressed on the aspect of every civilized nation becoming a member of the League. Ganga

Singh Ji stressed that about Indian civilization there was never any doubt—a fact testified to earlier by the former Secretary of State for India, Lord Crewe, who while dwelling on Indian races had stated:

> 'races representing a civilization of almost untold antiquity races which have been remarkable in arms, and the science of government'. Lord Crewe had also referred to the Indian soldiers as 'high-souled men of first-rate training and representing an ancient civilization'. The Maharaja also reverted to President Wilson's observation that at the Paris settlement it was not the representatives of the Government but representatives of people who were to be accorded a place of honour as the settlement aimed at satisfying the opinion of mankind.

The meeting regarding the constitution of the League of Nations was held on 5th February, 1919. The British representative, Lord Robert Cecil, accepted the decisions on the understanding that India would in any case be included in the League by virtue of the signature of the covenant by the representatives of the British Empire and in view of the hope expressed by President Wilson in this behalf. Yet as Article VII of the draft proposals for the covenant provided only for the inclusion of such colonies as enjoyed full governing powers, it was feared that the Indian claim would fail to be accepted. The Maharaja again made hectic efforts through Lord Robert Cecil and ultimately his efforts were rewarded and India secured a foothold in the League of Nations as a member.

**Role in the League**

The Maharaja was invited to participate in the 1922 session of the League but because of family reasons declined the honour. In 1924 he accepted a renewed of fer for participation in the League. In addition to Lord Hardinge and Maharaja Ganga Singh, Sir Mohammed Rafique and Sir Stanley Reed were other members of the delegation with Maharaja Kumar Sadul Singh as substitute delegate.

One of the questions that merited the attention of the fifth Assembly was the replies and attitudes of member nations towards the matter of limitation of armaments as envisaged in the Draft Treaty of Mutual Assistance formulated in terms of instructions issued by the Leagues for implementing the provisions of Article VIII of the Covenant which enjoins "that the maintenance of peace requires the reduction of Armaments to the worst point with national safety". The replies of the member-states were not encouraging and bordered on hostility. While the British and French official stand was in favour of arbitration as a means of lasting peace, the Maharaja expounded the Indian viewpoint that vast frontiers inhabited with turbulent tribes had to be taken into account while discussing disarmament To resolve the issue an International Conference was summoned. Committees were appointed to prepare the background to the Conference and Maharaja Ganga Singa Ji was associated with the third committee whose task was the examining of the obligations contained in the covenant of the League in relation to the guarantees of security which a resort to arbitration and a reduction of armaments may require. The results of deliberations of this Committee were:

1. That an aggressor State (i.e. a State which refused to submit to arbitration) would be regarded as an International outlaw.
2. That all States members of the League shall refuse to have a financial and economic dealing with it.
3. That such a State shall be regarded as having no more rights than a common outlaw.
4. That if naval, military or air force was required to punish the aggressor, the signatory states may under the direction of the Council of the League, use their forces for the purpose.
5. The Maharaja was also associated with the issues of the traffic in and private manufactures of arms and the position of India in relation to International Health Organisation. On the former Issue it was proposed to convene an International Conference to deal with the matter. With regards to matters of health India had no member on the Board of the Health Organization of the League whereas it was a nation constantly ravaged with epidemics and diseases. Thanks to the efforts of the Maharaja a resolution was adopted by which the Health Organization was required to communicate its programme and a report of its activities to International Health Office at Paris where India was represented.

In 1930 a rare honour was conferred upon the Maharaja—he was selected as the leader of the delegation to the eleventh session of the League of Nations to be held from the 10th Sept., 1930 to 4th Oct., 1930. He was the first and last Prince to be honoured thus. Other members of the delegation were Nawab Sir Zulfiquar Ali Khan, Sir Ewart Greeves and Sir Deva Prasad Sarvadhikari. Sir Denys Bray and Sir Jahangir Coyajee were named substitute delegates.

During the session, the Maharaja's active participation was confined to the deliberations of the Third and Fourth Committees which dealt with disarmament and the Reorganization of the League Secretariat respectively. On disarmament the Maharaja rightfully stated that the machinery of the League was for the whole of the world and not for Europe or Asia.(No. 3) He was responding to a suggestion of M. Briand in the Assembly when the latter advocated the creation of European Union to deal with limitation of arms. The Maharaja also appreciated the role played by Sir Jahangir Coyajee in the Economic Committee where the latter advocated an indeapth study of recession and depression in trade and industry. Sir Jehangir also held forth that agricultural problems be treated at par with problems of industry and commerce, more so in case of countries like India where agriculture was the staple industry.

The speech which the Maharaja delivered in March 1931 to the Indian Prices also dwelt on length with his participation in the Imperial Confrence.(No. 4) The 1930 Conference was devoted mainly constitutional matters—a subject for discussions in the Round Table Conferences as well. The Conference focussed attention on attempting a definition of the attributes of Dominion Status. The preparatory work was done by the Conference on Dominion Legislation that had met in London in 1926. Its report had served as the basis for further talks on inter-imperial relations and other related issues such as the legislative powers of Dominion Parliaments, the provision of machinery for adjustment of disputes between self - governing members of the Commonwealth, the diplomatic representation abroad of the Dominions and so forth. A supplementary agenda dealt with economic co-operation between various units of the Empire. Replying to the British Prime Minister's speech, Maharaja Ganga Singh had stated with candour that the Indian States were one with the British Empire—the Constitutional problems not withstanding—and had no desire to severe links with the British Commonwealth of Nations. The occasion was also used to reiterate the resolve of the Indian States for demand of Dominian Status.

Another issue that was raised and merited attention was the issue of nationality and common status of the subjects of the various parts of the Empire. Speaking on behalf of the Princes and the States of India and obviating all future difficulties and misunderstandings, Ganga Singh Ji once more dwelt on the special status they enjoyed by virtue of the Treaties of perpetual alliance and fiiendship and other engagements negoaited in the second decade of the nineteenth century. Because of the said Treaties it way beyond dispute that the subjects of the Indian States were not British subjects, nor did British legislation, including that by the Government of India, apply to Indian States.

It was gratifying for the Maharaja when the Secretary of State wrote to him that whatever the recommendations of the Imperial Conference, they in no way prejudiced the position and Status of the Princes of India or their subjects.

## References

1. Panikkar, K.M., His Highness the Maharaja of Bikaner, A Biography, London, 1937.
2. Srivastava, Ram Saran; "Maharaja Ganga Singh's Role in the League of Nations' in G.S.L. Deora edited, Ganga Singh Centenary Volume, Bikaner, 1980.
3. Karni Singh, The Relations of the House of Bikaner with the Central Powers, 1465—1949. New Delhi, 1974.
4. Speech delivered by Maharaja Ganga Singh at a Luncheon Given by The Empire Parlimentary Association (United Kingdom Branch) to the Indian Delegates, in the House of Common, 24th April, 1917.
5. Ganga Singh Ji's speech at the Banquet given to Indian Representatives, 8th Nov., 1917.
6. Maharaja's speech at the British Indian Union Lunch, 3rd Nov., 1930.
7. Ganga Singh Ji Statement in the Chamber of Princes règarding work in League, 18th March, 1931.

# Annexure 1

## Speech delivered by his highness the Maharajah of Bikaner at the Luncheon given by the Empire Parliamentary Association (United Kingdom Branch) to the Indian Delegates, in the House of Commons, Harcourt Room, on 24th April, 1917.

*Mr. Lord Chancellor, My Lords and Gentlemen,*

It is with no small feelings of gratitude and pleasure that I rise to offer to the Lord Chancellor and Mr. Chamberlain and to you, my Lords and Gentlemen, of behalf of India and on behalf of the Ruling Princes, and on behalf of my collegues and myself, our respectful and grateful thanks for the extremely kind and generous terms in which reference has been made to us here to-day, and for the kindly welcome and reception with which you have honoured us. We particularly appreciate the signal honour which you have done us by going out of your way and establishing a new departure by giving us, a non-Parliamentaty people, this very kind and hospitable entertainment. It will be greatly appreciated in India, and believe me will evoke the warmest response in all parts of my country. (Cheers.) They will specially appreciate the courtesy you have done us, as coming from an Association like yours, so closely related to that great institution of this realm, known throughout the world as the "Mother of Parliaments"—an institution which it is the aim and ambition of all countries, old or new, to adopt, with such modifications as may be necessary to suit their own conditions.

2. Although it is my misfortune to have to make numerous speeches in the course of the year, I have no pretensions to be an orator, and, speaking before such a distinguished assembly of statesmen and the prominent public men not only of Great Britain but from all parts of the Empire, if I use my notes to a considerable extent, I must crave your indulgence.

3. Let me say at the outset that the fact that India has, for the first time, been invited to send her representatives to the Imperial War Cabinet and the Imperial War Conference has caused wide-spread gratification as a just but, may I be permitted to add, somewhat overdue recognition of her unflinching loyalty and devotion to her Emperor, of her position within the Empire, and of the services which,

as in the past, it has been bot her pride and her privilege to have rendered to her Sovereign and the Empire in the greatest crisis which we have had to face. (Cheers.) I have not come to England to urge the claims of India. It has been my honour to be selected amongst the representatives from India to give our local experience or views that my help the Empire to bring the war to a successful and glorious conclusion. I beg you to believe that the first consideration at the present moment in India of all concerned is to devote all their energies and all their rexources to the war. (Cheers.)

4. But as so much is written and said about the aims and aspirations of India, perhaps you would to-day desire me to tell you something about them.

5. It is hardly necessary for me to remind you that some two-thirds of the area of our country is British India proper, and one-third represents the territories of those independent Ruling Princes of India which enjoy and glory in the protection of His Imperial Majesty the King-Emperor, and which are proud to have come into the British Empire through treaties of perpetual friendship and alliance with the British Government or other similar engagements.

6. Incidentally, I may mention here that next year it will be exactly one hundred years since my own State and my ancestors entered into political relations with the British Government by concluding such a treaty of perpetual friendship and alliance (Cheers), and if, by the grace of God, the war has by that time been brought to a successful conclusion, we hope fittingly to celebrate the event.

## INDIA'S UNITED PURPOSE

7. To revert, however, to India and her hopes in regard to the future, I think I can sum them up in a few sentences, and here when I speak of India I refer both to British India and to the Indian States.

8. Our first and foremost consideration and constant care is at all times to render what little service we can to our Emperor and the Empire, for I hope it is hardly necessary for me to assure you that we are all deeply imbued with feelings of profound veneration and devoted attachment to our gracious Sovereign and his Throne. (Cheers) It is equally unnecessary for me to assure you that the welfare of the Empire, for loyal and patriotic reasons if also for motives of enlightened self-interest, is a matter of abiding interest and concern to us. (Cheers).

9. Subject always to these two essential qualifications and considerations which are ever uppermost in the mind of every thinking

and loyal Indian (and they irrefutably form by far an overwhelming majority of our population) our aspiration is also to see our country under the guidance of Britain—and, as Mr. Chamberlain said, with the help of Great Britain—making material advance on constitutional lines in regard to matters political and economical, and ultimately to attain, under the standard of our King Emperor, that freedom and autonomy which you in this country secured long ago for yourselves, and which our more fortunate sister Dominions have also enjoyed for some time past.

10. On our loyalty to the Sovereign and of our genuine desire to contribute our utmost towards the well-being of the Empire it is not for me to dwell on this occasion. I must leave that to you and to the future verdict of history, but I would venture with all modesty to express the hope that India and the Indians will not be found to have lagged beind in their efforts in the cause of the Empire. (Cheers).

11. As to our future aspirations, there are various matters of importance to us, such as a sound system of education, and industrial and economical development—still practically in its infancy in India—on which much could be said, but with the short time at our disposal I will confine myself to the political aspect, which it appears desirable in the interest of the Empire as a whole should be brought forward clearly and prominently.

12. My Lords and Gentlemen, it is any matter for surprise that India should be aiming at her political regeneration? You have given education on Western lines to Indians and after centuries of close and intimate connections with Great Britain—the land of liberal traditions and popular institutions—we Indians would be foolish if we did not see much that was good in your political life in this country. And we would be still more foolish if, after grasping the good points of your national life, we did not desire to have grated or assimilated all that was good in your institutions and system, wherever and whenever our conditions permitted it. (Cheers.)

## THE GOAL OF AUTONOMY

13. Regarding India's desire for ultimate self-government and autonomy within the British Empire, I am prepared to admit that it presents a difficult problem. But is the difficulty such as to be insoluble by British statesmanship and British good will and sympathy, or are the existing conditions in India so hopelessly irreconciliable with Indian aspirations as to render the question merely academic, not worth serious thought, but fit to be relegated into the background,

only to be brought out in a dim and distant future? Certainly there is diversity of race. But does not even the United Kingdom consist of three different races? And is not Canada inhabited by, at least, as great a diversity of races and nationalities? And what about South Africa? And when talking of different races and customs as existing in India, we must bear in mind that India is not a country but really a vast continent; it is not a State but an empire within the Empire.

14. Then unfortunately we have unrest and sedition in India, though people at a distance not fully acquainted with facts are apt in this connection to get a somewhat erroneous impressions. I know that it is, not necessary for me to point out that so far as section is concerned, it is confined to an extremely small percentage of the vast population of India—to the extremists and to the anarchists. The millions of the Indian people are loyal to the core. The unrest that exists is of two kinds, that which the seditionists attempt to spread, happily with small response, has to be faced and is being faced and suitably tackled by the authorities. And it is our earnest hope in India that we may gradually be in a favourable position to eradicate it. It is a concerous growth not peculiar only to my country. The other kind of unrest is what, if I mistake not, was so aptly described by a British statesman a few years ago as legitimate unrest, It originates from impatience at the rate, and the nature, of the political progress made in India. it is in the minds of people who, rightly or wrongly, hold these opinions but who certainly are as loyal as you and I are. I decline to believe that British statesmanship will not rise equal to the occasion. For it depends on the various complex and important Indian problems being handled with sympathy, with imagination and with a generous and broad-minded perspicacity and boldness by the responsible Ministers of the Crown, whether or not such unrest will die out or continue. And it is further the considered opinion of many who have given the subject a thought, that if the people of Indian were given a greater voice and power in directions in which they have shown their fitness, we should hear much less of unrest, agitation and irresponsible criticism. Certain it is that despondency and desperation would give way to patience and fortitude, for India has confidence in the world and good faith of Great Britain. The enemies of order and good government would then be without the lever with which they at present attempt to swell their ranks and to spread sedition.

## THE CALL FOR FURTHER ADVANCE

15. You have doubtless heard of the "Unchanging East" which

" . . . bowed low beneath the blast,
In patient deep disdain,
She let the legions thunder past,
And plunged in thought again."

16. But I can assure you that India at least has been and is, changing very rapidly and beyond conception, and that under the invigorating influence of Great Britain she is making truly remarkable and gratifying strides.

17. No reasonable—minded person will contend that India is ripe at the present day for self-government in the full sense of the term, but there are many who think that there is yet room for further political reforms and advance. On the part of Indians we need patience, a due sense of responsibility, and above all concentration on that which is attainable. To you we look for sympathy and help, readiness to recognize the changes which are taking place in India and to help Indians to achieve that further progress and in due time to realize her cherished aspirations. We are conficent that these questions will be considered in time and in such a manner as to permit of something being done at the conclusion of the war-not as the price of the loyalty of India, for no one knows better than she that loyalty has no price and that her adherence to Great Britain and the Empire is not due to any unworthy motives but because she feels that she can only realize her object within the great British Empire and with the sympathetic aid and assistance of the British people.

18. There may be difference as to the nature of India' demands, but there can be no difference as to their being perfectly reasonable and legitimate; and here I should like with your permission to read an extract from a speech made at Manchester only yesterday by my distinguished collegue Sir James Meston, who holds the high position of Lieutenant-Governor of the United Provinces, Speaking of the demands and yearnings of India, he said:

> "Its ideals at least are no unworthy. They are precisely the ideals which you yourselves have followed through the centuries and which you are now securing.
>
> "If wisely guided, this spirit will vivify India's pride in our Empire, her affection for England and that firm and unbargaining loyalty, which. . . is the proudest tradition of all that is best in India."

## THE STATES AND BRITISH INDIA

19. Perhaps I might mention here in case it be thought by anybody that the States will be alarmed at and resent political advance made in British India that we of the Indian States—and I speak for the Ruling Princes no less than our subjects—would rejoice at such progress, for after our concern for the Empire our greatest anxiety is to see our country progressing and prospering and our fellow-countrymen in India receiving what is their due. To show you that I am not speaking in an irresponsible manner, I would point out that at least 10 per cent, so far as I remember, of the important States already have representative government. Every year some States are being given representative government on generous and constitutional lines, and this shows that though we are autocrats we attempt not only to march with the times but also to do our duty towards our States and people. (Hear, hear).

20. And what can I say to-day in regard to that one-third of India in area and some one-fourth of its entire population consisting of the Indian States, the more imprtant of which are under the direct government of Ruling Princes and the other States under that of the Ruling Chiefs. Though not technically forming part of British India, we are proud of our unique position within the British Empire, having come under the suzerainty of the King-Emperor and in political relations with the British Government by the treaties and engagements to which I have already briefly alluded, and I venture to assert that we yield to no one, not only in British India but in the whole world, in our loyalty and attachment to the King-Emperor (Cheers). And as allies and friends no one has more at heart the best interests of the British Government. (Cheers).

21. Situated as we are we have naturally resented any undue interference in our internal affairs—and here we must gratefully acknowledge the sympathetic attitude of successive Viceroys of India as well as of the Government of India and, as I hope I may say to his face, that of the Right Hon. the Secretary of State for India. Although each State has preferred to be left free to manage its own internal affairs on the lines best suited to local circumstances, local pecularities, and local traditions and sentiment, and though different ideals and different standards of administrative efficiency exist, there is no diversity of views and thoughts in matters of Imperial concern. Again I prefer not to deal with such services as we may have been able to render during the preset crisis. But as regards our past services, it must be known to you that in the Mutiny the States all fought on the

side of and stood steadily for the British Government, just as a matter of fact did the greater number of the people of British India and some regiments of the Indian Army, even though it was called the Indian Mutiny and the Mutiny of the Indian Army. But as regards our utility in the Empire, It will suffice for me to give you the following short extract from the famous dispatch of 1860 from Lord Canning:

"The safety of our Rule is increased, not diminished, by the maintenance of Native Chiefs well affected to us. . . . In the Mutiny these patches of native Government served as breakwaters to the storm which would otherwise have swept over us in one great wave, and in quiet times they have their uses. . .

"And should the day come when India shall be treatened by an external enemy, or when the interests of England elsewhere may require that her Eastern Empire shall incur more than ordinary risk, one of our best mainstays will be found in these native States. It was long ago said by Sir John Malcolm that is we could keep up a number of Native States as royal instruments, we should exist in India as long as our naval superiority in Europe was maintained."

## A COUNCIL OF PRINCES

22. As to the future we have not got many ambitions. Assured of our possessions and of our position, rights and privileges by the gracious pledges given in the historic proclamation of Queen Victoria of 1858, pledges which have been equally graciously re-asserted by both his late Majesty and our present beloved Sovereign, we only ask for the privilege of being allowed further opportunities of serving our King-Emperor and the Empire, and for the continyance of the good will and sympathy of the great British nation in our endeavours to work out our own salvation in the best interests of the Empire, our States and our subjects.

23 .As Rulers governing such a vast area in India we, however, feel that if we are to keep abreast of the times, and of the conditions prevailing and likely to prevail in British India, and that if we are fully to secure and to retain our proper place in the constitution of the Empire, there must be developments. We feel that we must have a regularly assigned and more definite place in the constitution of the Empire by the institution, at an early date, of a Council or Assembly of Princes formed on proper lines, where important questions concerning ourselves, our States, and our people on the one hand, and the British Government on the other, can be discussed and settled

just as Legislative Councils exist in British India. I should perhaps make it clear that we have no desire whatever to encroach upon the affairs of British India, any more than we should relish any outside interference with our own internal affairs. These ideas, which have been maturing for some years, were definitely and officially brought forward by a large and representative number of Ruling Princes at a meeting convened by Lord Chelmsford at Delhi in October last, and the Viceroy's speech and the attitude of the Government of India lead us to hope that the question is receiving sympathetic consideration. (Cheers).

# Annexure 2

## Speech Delivered by Major—General His Highness the Maharaja of Bikaner, G.C.S.I., G.C.I.E., A.D.C., LL. D., at the Banquet given to the Late Indian Representatives by Their Highness the Ruling Princes, at Delhi on the 8th November, 1917.

*Your Excellencies, Your Highness, Ladies and Gentlemen,*

When even the poet was constrained to confess that 'words but half reveal and half conceal the soul within', a layman can hardly hope adequately to express his sentiments when he is moved so deeply as I am to-night. I am afraid that no words of mine can even half express my innermost of feelings and I can only beg Your Highness to believe that I am deeply conscious of the very high honour done me to-night. I am extremely grateful for this signal mark of approbation on Your Highnesses' part. I wish I could believe that I really deserved the opinions which you have been so kind as to express in regard to myself and my humble services whilst on my recent mission to England. I value them the more as they emanate from generous impulses and evidence your kindly feelings towards me.

I can assure Your Highnesses that no one could appreciate more than I do what a high honour it was for me to have represented Your Highnesses at the meetings of the Imperial War Cabinet and the Imperial War Conference. That honour was enhanced by the numerous tokens of Your Highnesses' approval of my selection and by the confidence which you were good enough to place in me and to which you gave public expression in the Banquet in Bombay on the eve of my departure for England in February last. By to-night's function, with which Your Highnesses have been pleased to honour my late colleagues and myself, you have added substantially to my gratitude which is rendered all the deeper by the distinguished representative of our gracious King—Emperor presiding over to-night's Banquet. To His Excellency we, the Ruling Princes, will ever remain grateful for specially securing our representation in the innermost Councils of the Empire. No less are we grateful for his desire to cultivate the closest personal relations with the Ruling Princes of India, for his unmistakable sympathy with ourselves and our States and for the kind words in which His Excellency has referred to our Order to-night. As His Highness the Maharajah Scindia has already said, we are particularly pleased that Her Excellency Lady Chemsford has been able to grace this function with her presence.

I also beg to tender my heartfelt thanks to His Excellency the Viceroy and to my friends, Their Highnesses the Maharajah Scindia of Gwalior, the Maharajah of Patiala, the Maharajah of Kapurthala, President of the Banquet Committee and the Jam Sahib of Nawanagar, on whom, as Secretary, much heavy work has fallen in organizing this Banquet, for the very generous terms in which they have so kindly referred to me. And in what words can I thank Your Highnesses for the most handsome present which you have given me as a token of your friendship and regard which I greatoyesteem. Need I say that this gift will ever remain amongst my most cherished possessions. I am not exaggerating when I say that the memory of these many incidents and of to-night's ceremony will be fondly treasured by the people of my State.

If it be permissible, on an occasion like this, for one guest to refer to his fellow-guests of the evening, I would wish to associate myself with all that has been said to-night about the great services rendered by His Honour Sir James Meston and the Hon'ble Sir Satyendra Sinha. And I would add that no one could have had more courteous colleagues or more conscientious and devoted fellow-workers in the cause of one's country. It is only when the whole story comes to be told that we shall realize in any adequate measure how much India owes to these two distinguished Statesmen. That the veteran Sir Satyendra Sinha, with his calm judgement and broad outlook, should have so wholeheartedly, and unsparingly fought the battles of India with earnestness, tact, and enthusiasm was only to be expected from a distinguished patriot of his reputation. And his services entitled him to the gratitude of all his fellow-countrymen. But further, I would venture to predict—and I do so in no irresponsible fashion—that the verdict of history will accord no less high a place in India's gratitude to Sir James Meston for the just, impartial and equally whole—hearted manner in which he espoused the cause and for the courage and ability with which he urged her claims. As I have already remarked on another public occasion since my return from England, no Indian could have been more loyal or true to India's interests than the liberal-minded gentleman, who, at present, presides over the destinies of the United Provinces and whose services we all hope will not be lost to this Country when before long he relinquishes charge of his present high office.

As for my humble share of work during this mission in England, I would only say that all through the time that I had the honour of representing Your Highnesses, considered myself answerable to you for all my public acts and utterances and that I consientiously endeavoured to the utmost of my capacity, to serve our Emperor, our Empire, our Order and the people of our States as well as the people of British India.

Nine months ago at the Banquet in Bombay, I was entrusted by Your Highnesses with messages of loyalty and devotion to His Imperial Majesty the King-Emperor, of friendship and good-will towards Great Britain as well as our Sister Dominions and Colonies, and with messages of our steadfast determination, in common with the people of Great Britain, to see this war through to a triumphant issue. That trust it was not difficult to fulfil; for wherever we went we found that the staunch loyalty of the princes and people of India, particularly as evinced by our participation in the present World—War had received, and was receiving, generous and sympathetic recognition. We were presented with the Freedoms of the City of London and other important Cities in Great Britain and as I remarked in my speeches on those occasions, we realised that these honours were conferred on us not as personal tributes but as a generous recognition of the unique position in the British Empire of the Ruling Princes of India and of the Services which, along with our fellow-countrymen, it had been our proud privilege to render to our beloved King-Emperor and his Empire. For evidently the purpose of honouring us was to recognize that India had become, and in a deeper sense than before, an integral portion of the British Empire, worthy of her copartnership and of her place in the great fabric which comprises the Dominions Over-seas.

The gracious sympathy and deep interest which Their Imperial Majesties have always been pleased to manifest in all matters relating to the Indian Empire, are a matter of common knowledge in this country. Similarly the knowledge of the equally gracious interest and solicitude evinced by Their Imperial Majesties for the Izzat and privileges of the Ruling Princes is our most cherished possession. From the telegram, which my late Colleagues and I jointly despatched to His Excellency the Viceroy on the day of our return to India it is already known that we were the receipients in England of the gracious messages which His Imperial Majesty communicated to the Imperial War Conference. India was honoured also by the gracious interest which the King—Emperor and the Queen—Empress were pleased to evince in our work. In that telegram we also reported the universal appreciation that was accorded to our inclusion in the inner councils of the Empire, the gratifying and cordial reception which was accorded to us by His Imperial Majesty's Ministers and the Statesmen of the Dominions, the spirit of friendliness and sympathy with which questions affecting the special interests of India were invariably approached, and the genuine desire shown to eliminate conflict of policy between India and other parts of the Empire. We added that the fullest opportunity had been given to the Indian Representatives, who accompanied the Secretary of State to every meeting of both the Cabinet and the Conference, of sharing in the discussion of every subject which came up. We alluded to India's participation in future Imperial Conferences being ensured by a Resolution as also to the high courtesy and consideration shown us by Mr. Austen Chamberlain, the late Secretary of State for India. I shall, therefore, not take up the time of this distinguished assembly by dilating on these topics.

While on this subject I must not omit to say that on various ocasions in England I promised to bring back to our Countrymen messages of sympathy and goodwill. In my speech at the luncheon at the Mansion House following the presentation of the Freedom of the City of London, I said that we would on our return tell our countrymen that they can confidently rely on Great Britain fulfilling her great mission and being true to her glorious heritage. The significant events since our return to India have happily made that promise all the more easy to fulfil. The recent pronouncement by the Secretary of State on behalf of His Imperial Majesty's Government and the sympathetic and statesmanlike speech by His Excellency the Viceroy early in September open a new chapter in the political history of India and cannot but have the most beneficial effect. This must be a course of genuine gratification to those who have at heart the best interests of the Empire and of this Country. I feel sure that I am voicing the sentiments of my Brother Princes in offerring my respectful congratulations to His Excellency the Viceroy on the courageous part he has taken in these great events. In consequence Lord Chelmsford, if I may say so, deservedly commands to-day the gratitude and confidence of every responsible person in India. In his speech on the opening day of the recent Legislative Session in Simla, after warning all communities, "British and Indian alike, the public leaders and particularly the Press representing every interest and every class that sentiment is a delicate plant which withers under the rūde breadth of uncharitableness", His Excellency made an eloquent appeal for mutual confidence, co-operation, and goodwill. In common with Your Highnesses I belong to no political party, our sole concern being with the welfare and strength of the Empire and of India. I would, therefore, venture strongly to express the hope that His Excellency's earnest appeal will meet with a warm response from all who have sincerely at heart the best interests of the Empire and this Country. I fervently pray that all classes and communities may realise their great responsibilities and sink their differences, bending all their energy to work, with greater mutual toleration and sympathy, for the moral and material advancement of India, the contentment and prosperity of which will contribute greatly to the strength of the Empire. For as that brilliant Viceroy, Lord Curzon, said in his speech at Calcutta in 1902 "We are ordained to walk here in the same track together for many a long day to come. You cannot do without us. We should be impotant without you. Let the Englishman and the Indian accept the consecration of a union that is so mysterious as to have in it something of the Divine, and let our common ideal be a united country and a happier people." In spire of all the horrors and misery which this terrible War has brought in its trail, it has, we may comfort ourselves, at any rate strengthened the ties that bind Great Britain and India together. Therefore, we feel more than ever that our destinies are intertwined. The common baptism of fire has brought us as near as brothers are—differences of race or creed notwithstanding. The King-Emperor's soldiers in Great Britain and India have fought side by side in common defence of justice and humanity against a treacherous and unscrupulous foe and the reality of their comradeship on all the battle-fields has come home to their people in their respective lands. There now exist between us a better understanding, a greater sympathy and closer ties of friendship and affection. Surely, these are happy auguries for the future and when under the dispensation of a just Providence, Victory is achieved by us we may well look forward to seeing India an honoured Member in the Family of Nations that form the British Empire, joining hands with England to achieve the triumphs of Peace which ultimately are more important than even the triumphs of war.

# Annexure 3

## Speech by Lieut.-General His Highness the Maharajah of Bikaner at the British-Indian Union Lunch on the 3rd November, 1930, in reply to the toast proposed by the Chairman, The Right Hon. The Marquis of Reading

*My. Lord Marquis, My Lords, Ladies and Gentlemen,*

On behalf of myself and my Collegues who have the honour of representing India at the Imperial Conference, may I first tender thanks for the compliment paid to us by the Committee and Members of the British-Indian Union; also to you, Sir, for your courtesy in making the time in a very strenuous life to preside today, and for your cordial references to myself? It was with special pleasure that I accepted the invitation to be present at this pleasant luncheon. It affords me an opportunity of reviving the friendship which, I think I may say, marked our relations during the five years of your Viceroyalty, when so many great events and movements stirred India—a period which happened to coincide with my own term of office as Chancellor of the Chamber of Princes to which you, Sir, have referred. It also gives me an opportunity of expressing my warm sympathy with the objects of the British-Indian Union. The years which have passed since the Union was established not long after the War have confirmed my appreciation of the importance of this Society and of the value of the work which it is doing. For the basic idea behind your activities is Union—you recognise that the unique association of Britain and India demands a friendly partnership inspired by mutual respect and trust, and you strive to fulfil that purpose by bringing together all who seek the closer unity of Britain and India. This is an object very near to my heart and at which I have aimed all the years of my life. My earnest hope is that the Union will go forward and flourish and that the common service we wish to give the Crown and the Commonwealth may be made more effective by the spirit of co-operation it is your purpose to develop.

There are other reasons which accentuate the pleasure I have in being here to-day. Your President is His Royal Highness The Duke of Cannaught, to whom I shall ever remain deeply indebted for many gracious acts of great personal kindness. Next to those of Their Majesties no name is held in higher honour and esteem, nay affection, in India than that of this distinguished son of the Great Queen Victoria. There are not, I suppose, many living today who have personal memories of the days of His Royal Highness' active work in India, when as Commander-in-Chief of what was then the Bombay Army he left a deep impress on its efficiency, and on the defences of the Harbour which made it secure in the anxious days of the War. After a long life devoted to the public service, His Royal Highness would be forgiven if he felt that his work is done and he is entitled to rest. But he knows no weariness in well doing; and the active interest he takes in the work of this Union, and in many other important bodies, shows how vivid is still his sense of duty, and how strong is his atachment to my own dear land. We recall with special gratitude the readiness with which he put all other considerations aside, and on behalf of His Majesty journeyed again to India to inaugurate the new Constitution embodied in the Government of India Act of 1919. He is indeed an inspiration and exemplar to us all. Other honoured friends of mine are intimately connected with the Union—particular Lord Willingdon, who leaves a fragrant memory wherever he serves. To them and all other workers who believe that the future of India can best be ensured under the Crown and within the Commonwealth, our thanks are due.

You will probably before many months have the opportunity of welcoming another great servant of the Crown in the person of Lord Irwin, whose term of office, unfortunately for India no less than for the Empire, is drawing toward its close. It is not easy for me to speak of one I have learnt deeply to admire and respect while he is still in office. But I cannot let the occasion pass without saying this. When Lord Irwin was appointed to the Viceroyalty the Government of the day sent India of their best. A man of the loftiest character, with an assured place in Parliament and the Cabinet, he accepted this new responsibility, and has filled it with the singleness of purpose which has stamped all his public life. We Indians, whatever our creed, honour all men who are staunch in their own faith, even though it differs from ours. Lord Irwin is above all things a Christian gentleman. We Indians who have been in intimate touch with the Indian scene, and who realise more correctly that critics at a distance—including some whose knowledge of India is now out of date—the extraordinary complications resulting from the surge for full nationhood which has arisen with such tremendous force, are in a position fairly to judge his policies and his work. With that knowledge, informed by the experience of thirty-two years of active rule since I came of age, and with a large stake in India, I wish to state my conviction that during these very difficult and anxious days Lord Irwin has been the ralying point of all who wish to serve India and the Commonwealth. High above conflict, underterred by damour, no matter from what side, he has pursued serene and unruffled the task of securing in India the widest attainable measure of unity and confidence whilst the path of constitutional progress is being mapped out. The greatest personal force leading to confidence and co-operation, without which little of value will be achieved, is the personal trust reposed in such a wise measure on all sides in the Viceroy; when he lays down his burden of office it will be with the knowledge that all man could do he has done to steer India through these very stormy water to the constitutional haven which we hope will be created by the Round Table Conference in London. Feeling this very strongly, I am cut to the quick to find his policies misunderstood and his motives misrepresented by many who, remote from the realities of the situation, cannot appreciate the special problems he has had to face. Nevertheless, I feel assured that when the dust of controversy is laid he will have high place in that band of great Englishmen who with a single eye to their duty turned neither to the right nor to the left in their determination to serve India and help her forward to her great destiny, and in so doing rendered invaluable services to the great Empire over which our beloved King-Emperor rules.

You will ask: What of the India to-day? What lies behind the developments of this year which have caused so many who love India and desire to serve her pain and anxiety? This Society knows no politics and identifies itself with no Party, either here or in India. But without trespassing on this forbidden ground, there are a few thoughts I would put before you. We are witnesses of the pangs of travail at the birth of nationhood. The seeds of these great forces were sown a century ago, when English was chosen as the medium of higher education. The soil has been continuously warmed and fertilised by vivid contact with English literature and English institutions. Stage by stage, sometimes too slowly, dome times perhaps quickly, India moved to the position when the demand for self-government inevitably arose, and the passion—I cannot use a less expressive word—for equal status in the world became the over-mastering desire of the hour, Rightly understood, this is not only natural, but should be the pride of all who have laboured in and for India. The political awakening of India is thus neither limited nor unnatural. It is the inevitable result of a hundred and fifty years' association with Great Britain. You cannot teach a people as receptive as ours British history and British literature without awakening in them desires. and ideals akin to your own. If sometimes the political evolution of India seems to lean to the extreme, the explanation is not a change of political faith, but the clouding of faith by pessimism. This cannot be banished by invoking the hope that maketh the heart sick, but only by a determination to translate these ideals into realities. The imperative need of the day, therefore, is for courage, and a sympathetic and imaginative understanding—not for distrust and timid caution. To me and my colleagues at the approaching Round Table Conference—from British India, as well as from the territories of the Ruling Princes—has been committed the great responsibility of welding these forces into a constitution which will place India firmly on the road to full political stature and an equal place within the British Commonwealth of Nations. We shall approach this task with the fullest sense of responsibility, in the spirit of service and the spirit of humility, but in the confidence that we can achieve success if we work in union and understanding. You will ask, as indeed I am asked wherever I go, what will be the ambition of India when she assumes these powers and all the onerous responsibilities they entail? Before attempting to answer that question, I would beg everyone to remember that there are two parties in British-Indian politics. There are those who are not unjustly described as extremists, aiming at the complete independence of India and the establishment of a socialist republic or some other form of government which has never been clearly defined. From them we are wide as the Poles as under. Then there is the great body of opinion, loyal at heart to the Crown, yet resolute in the determination to win for India as soon as may be feasible full responsible government and equality of dignity and status in the British Commonwealth of Nations, but which pursues the path of ordered progress and believes that India can best fulfil her destiny under the aegis of the King-Emperor.

The policy of the Princes and States at the Conference will be determined by their representatives now assembling in London and will necessarily be influenced by the circumstances that arise. But, speaking for myself, I shall indeed be surprised if the States do not lay emphasis on two essential conditions, which I have had occasion previously to outline both in India and since my arrival here. They are :

1. That India retains the British connection as an equal partner in the British Commonwealth of nations; and

2. That an equitable agreement is reached between all the parties concerned to govern the relations of the two Indias, ensuring for the States their due position in the future constitution as co-equal partners with British India, guaranteeing their Treaties and internal Sovereignty, and safeguarding their interests, including those of their subjects, on terms just and honourable alike to the States and British India.

Subject to recognition of these essential conditions, I am confident that the Princes and States will readily support all legitimate proposals emanating from their friends in British India. Further, I feel I may safely add that we shall cheerfully devote all our energies and influence, in co-operation with the representatives of His Majesty's Government and the Imperial Parliament, to securing for India that control of her own affairs and that fulness of stature in the Empire which I, in common with many others, sincerely believe to be in the best interests of Great Britain and of my Motherland. With that definition, I can only reply to the question in the words I used at the opening of the Imperial Conference the other day. . . . In spite of all that has happened, and is happening, India does wish to remain within the Commonwealth. The Princes and subjects of the Indian States, of course, retain undimmed their loyalty to the King-Emperor and attachment to the Empire, and the great majority of the people of British India are, I firmly believe, desirous at heart that their country shall occupy an honourable place in the British Empire. It is surely our common task to see that with the continuance of the British-Indian union this aspiration is satisfied, to the great and enduring benefit of all concerned.

# Annexture 4

**Statement by Lieutenant—General His Highness the Maharajah of Bikaner in the Chamber of Princes on the 18th March, 1931, regarding his work at the Assembly of League of Nations at Geneva and at the Imperial Conference in London, in 1930**

*Your Excellency; Your Highnesses;*

With the permission of Your Excellency and Your Highnesses, I propose, in order to save time, to make a joint statement regarding my work at the Assembly of the League of Nations and the Imperial Conference last autumn. I have no desire to waste your time in giving a very detailed account of everything that took place. Much of this information will be available in the Reports, and which almost entirely is not of immediate concern to us.

My having to leave India in August was inconvenient to me on both public and private grounds. But having had the honour and good fortune of claiming many of Your Highnesses amongst my valued, personal friends; and being the recipient of your trust and confidence; and, above all, having regard to a stem sense of duty and a call to render further service to our gracious Emperor and the Empire, as well as to our Motherland, I felt that I could not but accept the invitation even though it entailed my leaving Bikaner some two months earlier than if I were merely attending the Round Table Conference, which, as you are aware, did not meet till about the middle of November.

My clear duty, as also my natural desire, is to spend most of my time in my own State and with my own people. But the circumstances in which His Excellency the Viceroy and the Secretary of State were kind enough to extend to me an invitation to lead the Indian Delegation at the League of Nations, and to attend the Imperial Conference held in London last October, were exceptional. It was the first occasion when a Member of Your Highness' Order was being invited to undertake the responsible mission of leading the Indian Delegation to Geneva. The Imperial Conference also promised, as it proved, to be one of the most important of its kind since the Great War.

My Colleagues at Geneva were:

(1) Nawab Sir Zulfiqar Ali Khan; and
(2) Sir Edward Greaves who, I regret to say, had later to leave our Delegation and to return to England owing to serious illness in his family; and his place was taken by Sir Basant Mullick.

Our substitute Delegates were:

(1) Sir Deva Prasad Sarvadhikary;
(2) Sir DenyaBray; and
(3) Sir JehangirCoyajee.

The Indian Delegation to the Imperial Conference consisted, besides the Secretary of State and myself, of Sir Muhammad Shafi and as Substitute Delegates of Sir Geoffrey Corbett, and Sir Padamji Ginwala.

5. I left Home on the 14th August and sailed from Bombay by the "Narkunda" on the 16th August last. Two of my colleagues from British India who were to form the Indian Delegation to Geneva, viz., Sir Deva Prasad Sarvadhikary and Sir Jehangir Coyajee, were my fellow passangers, and I had several opportunities of discussing with them, on the voyage some of the questions that were on the Agenda of the Assembly. At my request His Excellency the Viceroy had been so kind as to place at my disposal, the services of Mr. G.S. Bajpai, Joint Secretary to the Government of India in the Department of Education, Health and Lands, as my Private Secretary at Geneva, and in London during the session of the Imperial Conference—to whom I am sincerely indebted for much valuable assistance.

6. I reached London on the 31st August, and after a short stay of four days, which was deemed necessary for the Delegation to meet the Secretary of State for India, I went to Geneva where Sir Zulfiqar Ali Khan, the other Delegate from India, who had been in ill-health, later joined us.

7. The session of the Assembly opened on the 10th September and lasted till the 4th October. As I had to return to London in time for the opening of the Imperial Conference on the 1st Ocrober, my stay at Geneva could not be prolonged beyond the 24th September, when Sir Zulfiquar Ali Khan took charge of my work. But the crucial stage of discussions of the more important questions was over before I left.

8. Your Highnesses are aware that the work of the Assembly is distributed among six committees. Each delegation has to allot different members to different committees, since it is physically impossible for anyone delegate to attend all. With the concurrence of my colleagues, I decided to sit on Committee No. 3, which dealt with Disarmament, and Committee No. 4, which was charged with the consideration of an important Report regarding the reorganisation of the League Secretariat, in which connection Mr. Bajpai rendered especially meritorious service. In addition, I had to be available for consultation with my colleagues who served on the other committees, as the Leader of the Delegation is responsible for the co-ordination of its activities and also for meetings of the British Empire Delegation.

9. For the sake of economy of time, I must resist the temptation to give an account of all the subjects considered and the work accomplished by all the committee. Viewing the last session in broad perspective, its most important preoccupations were Disarmament and Economic Co-operation among the nations of the world. I will not weary Your Excellency and Your Highnesses with what I said in the one and only speech which I had to make at Geneva. Its gist was, I understand, cabled out to the Press in India; and I append a copy of the same. I will only add that I, of course, took the precaution of safeguarding India's freedom to deal with the peculiar requirements of her frontier by drawing attention to their complexity, and to the inability of the machinery of the League to deal with them.

10. Connected with the subject of limitation of armaments, but in a sense wider in its scope, though perhaps less tangible in form, was the project of a European Union foreshadowed by Mr. Briand in the Assembly of 1929, and expounded at great length in the general debate in 1930. Its aim is European co-operation, in politics and economics, with a view to avoidance of a European conflict. M. Briand had disclaimed all idea of organising Europe in a spirit of antagonism to the rest of the world. There was nothing to which exception could, therefore, be taken in the principle of his proposal. But there was all the greater need, for this reason, for avoiding anything that might give rise even to misapprehension outside Europe that the machinery of the League, which stands not for Europe or for Asia, but for the world, was being utilised merely to promote European aims. This aspect of the matter I ventured to bring out in my speech; and the resolution finally adopted by the Assembly in regard to it reflects this caution, since the representatives of non-European States Members of the League can join the inquiries which may be inaugurated in

order to frame definite proposals for the realisation of Mr. Briand's idea.

As regards the economic field, the main work was done in the second Committee, where the proposal of the Indian Delegation for the continued and systematic study of depression in industry and trade, which is really periodical in character, was put forward with great ability by Sir Jehangir Coyjee, and adopted with the warm approval of the representatives of other important countries, e.g., Great Britain, the Dominions and Japan. By calling for the treatment of agricultural problems on a level of equality with those of industry and commerce, provision was made for the study of matters which are of special interest to countries like India whose staple industry is agriculture. The chief credit for this is due to Sir Jehangir; and I venture to think that it is also a matter of gratification to India.

12. A full account of our labours and our suggestions for the future will, I hope, appear before long in our report to the Secretary of State for India.

13. I desire specially to emphasize the very harmonious and friendly relations and the close co-operation, which existed between one and all of my colleagues and myself, who rendered excellent service in the cause, and for the honour, of India; and I beg to take this opportunity once again of expressing to them my sincere and deep gratitude for all their loyal help, friendly assistance and great coutesy.

14. I will now briefly review the work of the Imperial Conferencve which sat in London from the 1st October till the 14th November.

15. Though the Secretary of State for India is, in accordance with precedent and India's present constitutional position, the acknowledged leader of the Indian Delegation at the Imperial Conference, I desire most gratefully to state that Mr. Wedgwood Benn, whilst helpful in every way, and keeping in the closest touch with us all at all times, was, at the last Conference, good enough to give every possible freedom for independent and individual ***expression of views to his concogoes nause own convesin in*** meeting the legitimate aspirations of India, no less than his great courtesy, invariably extended to us, deserve our very especial gratitude and India's grateful and ungrudging recognition.

16. The range of subjects covered by the Conference was wide. The Imperial Conference of 1926 constituted a land-mark in inter-imperial relationship, by attempting a deflnition of the attributes of Dominion Status. The implications of this definition had to be further

* Appendix A.

studied and stated in the form of constitutional propositions, first by experts, and then by another Imperial Conference. The preparatory work was done by the Conference on Dominion Legislation that met in London in the autumn of 1926. Its report was the basis of the agenda of the last Imperial Conference as regards inter-imperial relations, and dealt with a number of highly important, but intricate, constitutional problems, such as the legislative powers of Dominion Parliaments, the provision of machinery for adjustment of disputes between self-governing members of the Commonwealth, the diplomatic representation abroad of the Dominions, and so forth. This group of subjects formed one important part of the agenda; the other related to closer economic co-operation between the various units of the Empire with a view to the promotion of economic prosperity. Between them, they occupied most of the time of the Conference.

17. The Indian Delegates were received with the greatest consideration and friendship both by His Majesty's Government,—amongst whom we are particularly in debted to the Prime Minister, Mr. Ramway MacDonald, and the Secretary of State—as well as by our fellow-Delegates from allover the Empire.

18. By the courtesy, and at the special request, of the Secretary of State I had the honour of replying on behalf of India to Mr. MacDonald's speech of welcome on the opening day of the Conference (a* copy of the speech is attached); and I prof ited by the opportunity to convey to the Conference on behalf of Your Highnesses a message of our staunch loyalty and deep devotion to the august Person and Throme of His Imperial Majesty the King-Emperor, and of our feelings of steadfast friendship and alliance to the Nations of the British Commonwealth.

19. In view of India's existing constitutional position, our interest in the discussions of the political questions related less to the present than to the future. But as we met practically on the eve of the Indian Round Table Conference, from which it was my earnest hope that India would emerge with her rise to Dominionhood assured, I felt that the time when the decisions on these auestions would acquire a practical value for us was not far off. I, therefore, followed the proceedings of the Inter-Imperial Relations Committee of the Conference with keen interest. The Secretary of State had designated Sir Muhammad Shafi and myself on this Committee. Sir Muhammad's knowledge of constitutional law and practice was of great assistance.

* Appendix B.

The recommendations of the Committee, and the conclusions reached in regard to them by the Conference, have, I believe, been published,.and I need not recapitulate them. The scheme devised for the institution of the Commonwealth Tribunal for the purposes of determining differences and adjusting disputes of a justiciable character, which may arise between the Dominions inter se, or between them and Great Britain, however, may not be without a bearing upon a similar problem that has been engaging Your Highnesses' attention; and I would invite the attention of Your Highnesses and Your Ministers to the detailed proposals.

20. I must add that some changes contemplated in the Nationality and Common Status of the subjects of the various parts of the Empire was dealt with. I do not think that the point seriously arose. But, as I had the privilege of representing the special interests of Your Highnesses and of our States at the Conference, I felt it my duty towards them to make the point clear in the hope of obviating all future difficulties and misunderstandings. The position of the Princes and States of India is not only unique in the Empire, but it may, I believe, correctly be stated to be without parallel in the history of the world. The Rulers of our States are proud of the position which they enjoy in the Empire in virtue of their relations with the Crown by means of Treaties of perpetual alliance and friendship and other Engagements. It was beyond dispute that the subjects of the Indian States were not British subjects, nor does British legislation, including that by the Government of India, apply to our States. Therefore, without going into further details relating to our Treaty relations—some points concerning which, I pointed out, are at present the subject of discussion between the British Government and the Indian States—I wrote a letter enclosing a note to the Prime Minister—of which copies were sent to the Secretary of State—in which I stated that I wished clearly to have placed on record that my presence at the Imperial Conference, or the absence of any remarks on my part should not be taken to imply any admission of any alteration in the status and Nationality of the Indian States and their Rulers and their subjects—whatever they may be—by the discussion of this, or other allied Inter-Imperial subjects recently before the Imperial Conference. I added that my observations might be held to be covered by the words—"local conditions or other special circumstances"—which were

* Appendix C.

* Appendix D.

* Appendix E.

dealt with in paragraph 8(4) of the original draft conclusions of the Committee relating to Nationality and Common Status. I attach a * copy of my Note.

21. Rreceived in reply a letter from the Secretary of State, in which I was assured that my memorandum was carefully examined by expert authorities in the light of the conclusions of the Imperial Conference, and that they were in general agreement that I was right in thinking that the recommendations and conclusions reached at the Imperial Conference would in no way prejudice the position or status of Princes of India or their subjects. The letter concluded with the hope that the above facts would remove any doubts that I might have had on the subjects. A similar reply* was received by me from the Prime Minister.

22. The economic side of our work was in the capable hands of Sir Padamji Ginwala, a former President of the Indian Tarrif Board, and of Sir Geoffrey Corbett. If I may say so, they expounded India's policy of discriminating protection with admirable lucidity, and proved prudent and faithful custodians of her interests.

23. The relations and co-operation between the various Indian Delegates at the Imperial Conference were, I gratefully acknowledge, as cordial and iliendly as those which existed between myself and my colleagues in Geneva.

24. I must here express my wann gratitude to the Prime Minister of the United Kingdom, who was President of the Imperial Conference, to the Secretary of State for India, and to all the representatives of the Self-Governing Dominions for the unfailing courtesy and kindness extended to us. It was a privilege to have worked with them, and the friendships thus formed will, I am sure, be warmly cherished by us all.

25. As one of Your Highness' Order who, as specially representing your interests, is answerable to Your Highnesses for his activities on all such Imperial and International occasions, I take this opportunity of also attaching to this Statement copies of the following letters bearing on my work during my recent triple Mission from:

(1) the Secretary of State for India, dated the 26th November, 1930*
(2) the Prime Minister, dated the 21st January, 1931 **
(3) the Secretary of State for India, dated the 21st January, 1931 +
(4) the Lord Chancellor, dated the 22nd January, 1931.++

* Appendix E.
* Appendix G. + Appendix I

26. Before concluding, may I, Sir take this opportunity of expressing my indebtedness to Your Excellency for the many kind letters and telegrams you were pleased to send me, which, during a long and very strenuous and anxious period, were a source of great encouragement and satisfaction to me; and if any little service that I may have been able to render to the Empire and to India and our States, in Geneva and in London, meets also with Your Highnesses' approval, I shall have further cause for gratification.

. ** AppendixH. ++ Appendix J.

APPENDIX 'A'

**(Speech as Leader of the Indian Delegation at the Eleventh Session of the Assembly of the League of Nations, on Tuesday, the 16th September, 1930**

The speech with which this discussion opened set in me unforgettable memories astir.. For, as a signatory to the Treaty of Versailles, I shared with myold friend, Sir Robert Borden, the historic privilege of assisting at the birth of the League of Nations. When I came to the Assembly six years ago, it was as the representative of the special interests of "Indian India", as distinct from British India—those Indian States which possess their own internal sovereignty and comprise the territories of the Ruling Princes of India, who rule over some seven hundred thousand square miles and some seventy-two million subjects—in other words, about a third of the vastness of India and about a fourth of her teeming people. Today I have the honour to stand here as the Leader of the Indian Delegation, thus symbolising the unity of India in its adherence to the League.

To the emphasis, Mr. President, which has been laid throughout this discussion on the need for making World Peace impregnable, India would have me add hers. The very diversity in which speech after speech has developed this theme is evidence of the intensity of the sentiment that inspires us. Our common purpose is to seek Peace and ensure it, and no array of difficulties, however great, must be allowed to dishearten us. Yet it was but a few years back that mankind still believed that glory was to be won through war. Happily, out of evil has come good, and the civilized world, tom by the suffering of those long years of war, is changing its whole outlook. And as I listened to the speech of my gallant friend, General Hertzog, I could not help calling back to my mind what I myself said six years ago: it is not among the ranks of those who have borne the burden of the fight that fire-eaters are usually to be found; for soldiers, after all, are the best judges of the horrors of war, the keenest to descry where its dangers lurk, themost impressive advocates of Peace. I myself am a soldier; I am descended from an ancient fighting stock from amongst the martial races of India; I have known war and its horrors. And there is today none who more deeply desires to see the whole force of our being dedicated to the service of Peace.

In that service much has recently been done; witness the Pact of Paris, the Optional Clause, the London Naval Treaty, to all of which India has adhered in that devotion to the cause of Peace with which she will set herself to the examination of the General Act ast the forthcoming Imperial Conference.

But the greatest task of all lies ahead. If the World is to be saved from the devastation of other wars, whose horrors would assuredly exceed the worst horrors it has known, there must be a limitation of armaments, real, universal, substantial. That there can be no effective security without such limitation, no one knows better than the soldier. No one knows better than the soldier the practical difficulties which stand in the way. But these we must face and surmount. And though India has special difficulties of her own and special need for vigilant preparedness along her vast frontiers, peopled as they are by war-like tribes against whom the machinery of the League affords no protection, she is ready to collaborate in all schemes of Disarmament compatible with her security. For the will to peace inspires, and ever will inspire her. Should anyone doubt it, let him read her philosophy with its embodiment of the most complete and consistent code of pacificism in the World.

With such ideas, India cannot but be friendly to the underlying aims of that European co-operation of which M. Briand gave so eloquent an exposition the other day. Nevertheless, may a word of warming come without offence, and yet not without force, from the East? M. Briand disarmed criticism, it is true, by disclaiming'all idea of organizing Europe in a spirit of antagonism to the outside world. Indeed, he described his plan as one of those regional agreements which, so far Ifrom impairing, are designed to fulfil the purpose of the Covenant. But is there not a danger in these early years of the league that a plan for the closer union of Europe may give rise to misapprehensions outside Europe itself as running counter to the basic conception of the Covenant that the League exists, not for Europe, not for Asia, but for the World? Any impression that Europe, better organized industrially, thanks to its mastery of the applied sciences, than most of the old, and some of the young, non-European countries, is seeking to consolidate its industrial position to the detriment—however unintended—of less fortunate parts of the world might conceivably lead to consequences which no member of the league could desire. It was indeed a happy instinct that prompted M. Briand to refer the whole question to the League, so that not merely Europe but all members of the League might be given an opportunity for considering how far the League machinery could fitly be adopted to the treatment of such regional problems. And does not the interdependence of the various countries of the world, and the organic connection between Industry and Agriculture, point insistently to the desirability of making all international co-operation in the economic sphere not sectional, oı regional, but, so far as possible, world-wide? For what effects one part of the world today must react sooner or later upon others. And what effects Industry must ultimately react upon Agriculture. Thus, although industry was the first to feel the effects of power-war depression, Agriculture is feeling it now, and, in its turn, is depressing Industry still further. The depression of Agriculture and the depression of Industry are indeed organically allied problems, and embrace the whole world between them. Hence, what seems to me at any rate needed is for the technical organizations of the Leaque to investigate the means whereby Agriculture and Industry alike can now be rescued and safeguarded hereafter against a recurrence of this world-wide depression. And although I mayself speak here with the difference of a layman. I hope that the Indian Delegation will be able to make concrete suggestions to this end in Committee.

Let no one, Mr. President, misunderstand the tenor of my remarks. Smooth words come easily enough to the lips. But without sympathetic criticism—where criticism is needed—there can be no progress. One and all, we are loyal to the League; of that our presence hare today is evidence. But is would be a poor sort of loyalty that fought shy of fearless introspection. It is not enough for us to serve the League blindly. We must serve it with that loyalty that comes of clear-sighted courage.

APPENDIX 'B'

## Speech at the Opening of the Imperial Conference, on Wesnesday, the 1st October, 1930

I have the honour, through the courtesy of my right honourable friend Mr. Wedgwood Benn, of addressing this Conference on behalf of India. For my colleagues of the Indian Delegation and myself, I desire to thank you, Sir, and the British Government most sincerely for the cordial welcome, as also the graceful hospitality, extended to us in common with the Prime Ministers and other representatives of the Dominions. As the spokesman today of the Indian Delegation, and through it of the Government, Princes and people of India, may I join the other speakers at this Conference in tendering our respectful and loyal greetings to Their Majesties and our assurances of unswerving devotion and attachment to the King—Emperor and his gracious Consort? As a former Prime Minister of Australia fittingly observed at a previous Conference, the Crown represents something more than the visible symbol of the Empire's unity, the centre of its loyalties and the link which binds the whole Empire together. To us Indians—and I speak for my fellow Princes as well as the great mass of my countrymen both in the Indian States and British India—there is something peculiarly sacred in our feelings of veneration for the Sovereign; and this is all the more so in the case of His Majesty King George V, whose life of selfless service in the cause of all the peoples ollis vast Empire fulfils all the ideals of true Kingship set forth in our Holy Scriptures.

Some of those present here today are attending an Imperial gathering for the first time. I myself am one of the exceptions, as I had to privilege of representing India at the Imperial War Cabinet and Imperial War Conference of 1917, and also at the few meetings of the Imperial War Cabinet in 1918-19 that preceded the Peace Conference. The new faces that I see amongst us today provide evidence of the change which is inevitable in human affairs. However, I venture to assert with confidence that whatever else these changes of personnel may signify, they mark no weakening of the spirit of devotion to the Crown or of attachment to the British Commonwealth of Nations. In 1917 I delivered to a similar distinguished Assembly a message of goodwill from my brother Princes especially entrusted to me at a Banquet in Bombay just before my departure from India, emphasizing their staunch loyalty to the august Person and Throne of His Majesty, their feelings of steadfast friendship and alliance with the Nations of the British Commonwealth and their determination, in the hour of crisis to be once more true to their traditions of co-operating to the full extent of their resources in the cause of the Empire. I desire to repeat that message today.

The tasks that face us today differ from those that confronted the Empire thirteen years ago. The War has left a heritage of problems, political and economic, that need for their solution all the resources of statesmanship and all our reserve of patience, of mutual goodwill and trust. In the examination of the various important problems before us know, Prime Minister, the Conference may count upon the Indian Delegation making its full contribution.

There is one important problem which, for obvious reasons, finds no place among the agenda of this Conference. I refer, of course, to the Indian constitutional problem, the difficulties of which have without doubt been accentuated by the emotional and spiritual forces that the Great War unchained. That problem is primarily once for Great Britain and India to solve together and is to be the subject of the Round Table Conference which His Majesty's Government in Great Britain are convening next month. And yet I cannot let this occasion pass without reminding all my colleagues of the supreme urgency to the Empire of an early and satisfactory solution of this problem on courage . . . and statesmanlike lines. To omit all reference to it today would be to fail in one's duty to the King-Emperor and to the Commonwealth. We also owe it to our colleagues from the Dominions to enlighten them on the one question which, I expect, each one of them has asked himself during the last few months. Does India with to remain within the Commonwealth? My answer, in spite of all that has happened and is happening in India, is "Yes". The Princes and subjects of the Indian States—whose interests I have the honour specially to represent here—of course retain their loyalty to the King—Emperor and attachment to the Empire undimmed. And the great bulk of the people of British India are, I venture to say, desirous at heart that their country shall occupy an honourable place in the community of Nations that constitute the British Commonwealth. If this aspiration can be satisfied—as it is may hope and belief that it may be—the future will be full of promise. The Indian States, as you may be aware, have their own special problems requiring consideration and equitable adjustment, but there is nothing in those claims inconsistent with the desire of the Indian States to help India forward towards its promised goal as an integral part of the Empire.

The King—Emperor's gracious sympathy and solicitute for the Princes and people of India is well known to us all. His Majesty's Government in this country are happily alive to the gravity of the issues involved and are animated by a sincere and sympathetic desire to promote a settlement in conformity with legitimate Indian aspirations and with the solidarity of the Empire. May I add in conclusion that India feels confident that, in the delicate task that awaits the Round Table Conference, she may count also upon the goodwill of the Great Dominions whose freedom in unity within the Empire represents the ideal of all that is best and—despite appearances—all that is most influential in contemporary Indian politics?

APPENDIX 'C'

**Note by Lieut. General His Highness the Maharajah of Bikaner, G.C.S.I., G.C.I.E., G.C.V.O., G.B.E., K.C.B., A.D.C., LL.D. with reference to the discussions on the subject of Nationality and Common Status at the meeting of the Heads of Delegations at the Imperial Conference, November, 1930**

I do not think that the point seriously arises here. But, as I have the privilege of representing the special interests of the Ruling Princes and States of India at the Imperial Conference, I feel it is a duty which I owe to my brother Princes and to our Indian States to make one point clear in the hope of obviating all future difficulties or misunderstandings.

The position of the Princes and States of India is not only unique in the British Empire, but I believe it would be correct to say that it is without parallel in the history of the world. The Rulers of the Indian States are proud of the position which they enjoy in the Empire in virtue of their relations with the Crown by means of Treaties of perpetual alliance and friendship and other engagements. It is beyond dispute that the subjects, of the Indian States are not British Subjects, and British legislation, including that of the Government of India, does not apply to the Indian States. At the same time, for international purposes and in relations with countries outside India, the subjects of the Indian States enjoy the same benefits as if they were British, or British Indian, subjects. Therefore, without going into further details relating to our Treaty relations—some points concerning which are at present the subject of discussion between the British Government and the Indian States -1 merely wish to have it placed clearly on record that, whilst I have no other particular observations to make in connection with the question of Common Status for the various component parts of the British Commonwealth of Nations, my presence here, or the absence of any remarks on my part, should not be taken to imply any admission of any alteration in the Status and Nationality of the Indian States, their Rulers and their subjects—whatever they may be—by the discussion of this, or other allied Inter-Imperial subjects now before the Imperial Conference.

I think my observations might be held to be convened by the "local conditions or other special circumstances" which are dealt with in paragraph 8(4) of the original draft conclusions of the Committee relating to Nationality and Common Status.

Sd/- GANGA SINGH
Maharajah of Bikaner.

The Carlton Hotel,
London: November, 1930.

## APPENDIX 'D'

**Copy of letter, dated London, the 13th February, 1931, from the Right Honourable W. Wedgwood Benn, D.S.I., D.F.C., Secretary of State for India, to Lieut.-General His Highness the Maharajah of Bikaner**

I am much obliged to you for writing to me on the 23rd January, from Marseilles and sending me a copy of a letter and memorandum which you addressed to the Prime Minister on the same date in regard to the position of Princes and their subjects, in the light of the discussion in the Imperial Conference on the questions of nationality and common status.

I have had your memorandum carefully examined by the expert authorities in the light of the conclusions of the Imperial Conference and I can inform Your Highness of a general agreement that you are right in thinking that the recommendations and conclusions reached at the Imperial conference in no way projudice the position or status of Princes of India or their subjects. This opinion, I hope, will remove any doubts that Your Highness may have had on the subject.

## APPENDIX 'E'

### Copy of letter, dated London, the 18th February, 1931, from the Right Honourable J.Ramsay MacDonald, Prime Minister, to Lieut-General His Highness the Maharajah of Bikaner

I duly received the letter which you wrote to me before you sailed from Marseilles at the end of last month, and the enclosed Note which you had prepared on the subject of the position of Princes and their subjects in the light of the discussions of the Imperial Conference on nationality and common status.

The note has been carefully considered, and I understand that Mr. Benn has now written to you endorsing your conclusion.

I trust that you had an enjoyable voyage home, and have found everything as you would wish.

APPENDIX 'F'

**Copy of letter, dated London, the 26th November, 1930, from the Right Honourable W. Wedgwood Benn, D.S.O., D.F.C., Secretary of State for India to Lieut-General His Highness the Maharajah of Bikaner**

Now that the Imperial Conference is satisfactorily concluded, may I send you this line to say how very grateful I am for you cordial and untiring co-operation in our task.

Indeed, I can say that the work has been done by my colleagues, and we can all look back with pride on the part which India had played in this Imperial Conference.

I personally shall always remember it as a very happy time.

APPENDIX 'G'

**Copy of letter, dated London, the 21st January, 1931, from the Right Honourable J. Ramsay MacDonald, Prime Minister, to Lieut-General His Highness the Maharajah of Bikaner**

I am, I hope, just in time, before you leave England, to say how very deeply I have appreciated the opportunity of renewing contact with you during this autumn and winter. First in the Imperial Conference, and as soon as it was over in the Indian Round Table Conference, we have had the benefit of your experience and statesmanship. The Imperial conference indeed has owed much to you before, seeing that, as long as 13 years ago, you took part in its deliberations; in fact, this year, as one of India's Representative again, you were the doyen amongst the Representatives present from every quarter of the Empire.

It is difficult for me to express how valuable the co-operation of Your Highness has been in the proceedings of the Indian Conference. Nor will I try in the small compass of this letter to say how sensible I am of what we owe to your help. There are still many problems ahead of us, and I am confident that Your Highness will still not be backward in lending your powerful aid in continuing the work on the line which the Conference has laid down.

I do not doubt that, before the great task which has been initiated in London in the past ten weeks is completed, we shall be brought again in contact, and I look forward to that occasion. In the meantime, pray accept my most sincere good wishes.

APPENDIX 'H'

**Copy of letter, dated London, the 21st January, 1931, from the Right Honourable W. Wedgwood Benn, D.S.O., D.F.C., Secretary of State for India, to Lieut.-General His Highness the Maharajah of Bikaner.**

Before you leave England, I must convey to you what a great gratification it has been to me to have been afforded the opportunity to make your acquaintance and to establish with you relations, I hope I may say, of friendship. The prizes of a political career are to be found, not in the office which it may be one's lot from time to time are to be found, not in the office which it may be one's lot from time to time to occupy, but in the ties of personal friendship which the tenure of office gives an opportunity to form.

And it will always be a source of peculiar gratification to me that I should have had the chance of coming to know intimately a personality so prominent in Indian affairs and one who had rendered, on many notable occasions, such great service to his country.

When I first met you, you were about to undertake the leadership of the Indian Delegation to the League of nations Assembly at Geneva. It was the first time that the task of leading the Delegation had been shouldered by an Indian Prince; and I can think of no one more worthy of this distinction or more fitted to uphold the dignity and the traditions of his Order in this Capacity. Your Highness had barely time to see the Assembly conclude its Session before it became your duty to sustain the role of one of India's leading Representatives at the Imperial Conference. You were the fust Indian Ruler to take part thirteen years ago, in the deliberations of the Imperial Conference; indeed you were the doyen of the representatives of all the various members of the British Commonwealth present at the Conference recently concluded; and I need not say of what value to India were your experience and sagacity in the proceedings of the Imperial Conference of 1930.

Hard upon the Imperial Conference followed the Indian Round Table Conference. It is not necessary for me to attempt to indicate the importance of the part you have played in this

Conference. The Conference indeed is not, in the fullest sense, yett completed; and we are still too close to the picture to get the prespective required for estimating to what degree the results achieved should be attributed to the efforts of this or that Delegate. But I am sure that there is no one who could fail to realise the conspicuous part played by Your Highness or be blind to the transcedent importance of the decision which you took yourself and have induced others of your brother Princes to take in choosing the path of Federation as the true road for India to follow towards the goal to which all her sons aspire for her.

I must add for my wife and myself and expression of the real sorrow with which we shall hear of your departure.

## APPENDIX 'I'

**Copy of letter, dated London, the 22nd January, 1931, from the Right Honourable The Lord Sankey, G.B.E., Lord Chancellor, to Lieut.-General His Highness the Maharajah of Bikaner.**

I hope that when this letter reaches you, own people in India will have given you the hearty welcome which you have earned so well.

Please accept my sincere thanks for the great part which you have played at the Round Table Conference. From first to last you gave us all a splendid lead. My own task as chairman for the Federal Structure Sub-Committee would have been doubly difficult without the assistance and advice which I owe to you.

May you take back many happy memories of the colleagues with when you worked in so great a cause; and may the future hold greater contentment and prosperity for the country whose interests we both have so much at heart.

# 8

## *Statesman Extra-ordinary Maharaja Ganga Singh and the Chamber of Princes*

THE DAWN OF THE 20TH centuty heralded a change in the political scenario of India with the whole of India engulfed in massive turmoil resulting out of the partition of Bengal in 1905. The boycott of British goods by the Indian National Congress and the emergence of extremist party under the leadership of Bal Gangadhar Tilak, Bipin Chandra Pal and Lala Lajpat Rai were acts which alarmed the British greatly.

On the other hand the Princes were experiencing a different set of problems in the administration of their Strates. Their grievance was that their authority was being systematically undermined by the British Government. The political department, headed by the Governor General, had come to assume supreme authority vis-a-vis the Princely States. The instrument of power of the Government of India was the Political Agent in the State who wielded tremendous power and treated the Indian States as mere isolated units. They ensured, rather successfully, that the Indian States remained isolated from the British India. Another area where the writ of the Political Agent ran large was that no inter-State relations were permitted without his concurrence or interfearance. Even social intercourse was frowned upon with disfavour. This high handed policy climaxed during the Viceroyalty of Lord Curzon who preferred to treat the Princes as mere agents of the Crown in the administration of their territory, thereby implying that the Princes had no inherent rights of their own. At the same time the attitude of the Indian National Congress, which had stepped up its anti-British campaign, was cause for alarm for the Princes who were uncertain about their future in India. The Princes started pressing for direct relationship with the Crown which would render them some internal security and at the same time a change was perceptible in the British attitude as it sought the co-operation of the Princes to suppress seditious and anti-British activities in India. This was thus the inauguration of a new policy of the Government of India towards the Princes which was based on trust, friendship and co-operation.

One ruler who was willing to seize the opportunity of the change in the attitude of the Government of India and strengthen the claim of the internal sovereignity of the Princes, was Maharaja Ganga Singh. He had for a long time been an advocate of an organization or institution of the Princes where they could voice their concerns collectively and ventilate their grievances. As mentioned earlier efforts made by Lord Lytton and Lord Curzon to force an association of Prince had came to naught. The same fate had be fallen the suggestion of Lord Minto of setting up an Advisory Council of rulers and big landlords to combat the political unrest prevailing in the country at that time.

Lord Hardinge was also sympathetic for the creation of an association of Princes. Maharaja Ganga Singh responded favourably in 1914 by submitting a Minute to the Viceroy in which he reiterated the demand for an association of Princes which would foster greater co-operation between the Government of India and the Princes. The Princes, as representatives and heads of their States, had a right to have a voice in the government, especially in matters relating to the sovereignity of their States. The services rendered by the Princes at the outset of the world war were warmly applauded in England and by the Government of India. The change in attitude of the Imperial authorities fascilitated the process of the convening of a conference of Princes at the earliest and it materilised in 1916. The Agenda for the meeting had among its issues the important matters relating to the ceremonial to be observed at the installtion of a Ruling Prince; the minority administration; the administrative training and education of minor princes etc. The meeting was the prelude to the establishment of the Chamber of Princes. The Maharaja was elected as the Conference's General Secretary—a post he held till 1921.

The Maharaja visited England in 1917 AD to attend the Imperial War Conference and Imperial War Cabinet meetings, the details of which find mention elsewhere. But the theme of his speeches there also was the grant of self-rule and autonomy to India. The Maharaja's speeches in England had a profound impact on the mind of Austin Chamberlain, the then Secretary of State for India, who asked the Maharaja to send him a Note on important issues regarding India which demanded immediate attention of the British Government.

As the Maharaja was in the process of returning to India, he despatched a Minute on 15th May, 1917 to Chamberlain from Rome which became famous in later years as the 'Rome Note'. The Rome Note was crucial in many ways. The Note cautioned the British that times were changing over which no single government agency had any control. Even the Princes, had they desired, could not check the pace of progress that was discernible in many fields in their States. Railways, Newspapers, Telegraphs and Postal facilities had broken the barriers between the Indian States and British India in the exchange of ideas. The influence of western ideas was also manifest in the middle class of professionals. At this crucial juncture the Maharaja exhorted the British Government and its leaders to display qualities of bold statesmanship. The solution to India's problems:

> 'require bold statesmanship. Timidity, timorousness, faint-heartedness abhorrent in peace or war in war is fatal'.

The Note further went on to strike a grim note that despite the unprecedented show of loyalty in the war effort by millions of Indians, there was an impending sense of pessimism and gloom with regards to internal reforms. If the British failed the Indians at that stage, the note argued, then the ranks of extremists and seditionists would automatically increase. Further those voices which had advocated patience and perseverance, would become dimmer with the passage of time. Ganga Singh Ji also argued that reforms and material advance were not demanded as a price of loyalty to the British cause during the war but an outcome of the coming together of the two because of the war. Quoting Lord Curzon's speech in London, in 1901, the Maharaja stressed on the emotive and sentimental aspect of the Indian character. Curzon had said:

> *"Depend upon it, you will never rule the East except through the heart, and moment imagination has gone out of your Asiatic policy your Empire will dwindle and decay".*

The Note also highlighted four main issues to be deliberated upon at the earliest. They were:

1. The extreme importance-indeed, the vital necessity—of a formal and authoritative official declaration being made by the British Government at the earliest possible opportunities to the effect that self-government within the British Empire is the ultimate

object and goal of British rule in India.

2. The advisibility of inaugurating, on liberal and sympathetic lines, further political reforms in the constitution and functions of Provincial Legislative Councils as well as in the Imperial Legislative Council in British India.
3. The desirability of greater autonomy being granted to the Government of India as well as to the Provincial Governments and a lesser degree of interference with both, in regard to matters which are not of great Imperial concern.
4. The vital importance to the Indian States, their Rulers and their subjects of establishing at an early date on constitutional lines "Council or Assembly of Princes to deal with matters which concern the British Government on the one side and the States, their Rulers and their people, on the other. (Appendix—Rome Note).

The Secretary of State for India made a declaration on 20th August, 1917 defining the goal of British policy in India as the establishment of a representative government. The role of Maharaja Ganga Singh came in for high praise in the second conference of Princes held in 1917. It was also a matter of concern for the Princes as the Secretary of State for India was personally coming to India to study the nature of political problems that were engaging the Government of India. It was anticipated that a greater measure of political power and the establishment of representative institutions in British India was bound to have grave repercussions in Indian States. While the other States might have shuddered with alarm at the anticipated developments, Ganga Singh Ji took a different view. He held that events in British India should have their counterpart in the States and strongly urged that a formal council or Chamber of Princes should be immediately constituted to deal with matters affecting all States and their relations with the Government of India.

The Montagu—Chelmsford Report recommended the setting up of a Chamber of Princes with a standing Committee. Thus a long standing demand of the Maharaja was finally accepted. About the composition of the Chamber the Princes had advocated that the following were eligible to be members:

a. the ruling princes of India exercising full sovereign powers, i.e. unrestricted civil and criminal jurisdiction over their subjects and the powers to make their own laws;
b. all other princes enjopying heriditory status of 11 guns and over,

provided that no State or estate having feudatory relations with any sovereign state shall be eligible for membership of the Chamber.

But the composition of the Chamber proved to be difficult. There were many big States whose powers were curtailed by treaties and in comparision smaller States enjoyed full sovereign status. The Maharaja was away in England at that time for the historic Peace Conference but still he kept in touch with events at home. He wrote to the Viceroy that all rulers enjoying a 11 gun salute and enjoying the title of His Highness should be eligible for membership of the Chamber. Ultimately the Maharaja was able to resolve the deadlock and it was stipulated that the membership of the Chamber included all eleven-gun States irrespective of the powers they enjoyed and also that of the nine-gun States which enjoyed full powers together with a reasonable and proportional representation of the smaller rulers. It was again at the suggestion of Ganga Singh Ji that the Chamber of Princes came into existence by a Royal Proclamation as the Parliament was not deemed competent enough to legislate in matters affecting the Indian States.

In 1919 the Princes Conference assembled at the termination of the war to congratulate the victor powers and renew their loyalty to the Crown. (No. 1)

A committee constituted under the chairmanship of Sir William Duke to oversee the formation of the Chamber, found Maharaja Ganga Singh Ji as one of its automatic members. Two issues dominated the attention of the Princes Conference in its closing stages. There was some objection to the use of the term 'sovereign' status of the rulers on the grounds that the use of the term might be used by the rulers and States against the Government of India's conception of paramountcy. But the Maharaja was able to prove such fears baseless.

Another issue that proved ticklish was the question of co-operation between the Imperial Service Troops 'maintained' by the States and the Indian army. The Imperial Service Troops had been mooted in 1885 when Indian States agreed to maintain troops to be used for Imperial Service. These troops were controlled by the ruler of the State and British Officers only served in an advisory capacity. The Imperial troops played a very important part in the World War. But there were problems of co-hesiveness. The British Officers looked down upon Indian Officers and even insisted that senior ranking officers of the Indian Army salute them. Indian Officers were not allowed the privilege of dining in the mess of the British officers.

Because sentiments were rising high in this matter the Maharaja took the initiative to resolve the issue to the general satisfaction of all. At the outset it was established beyond any iota of doubt that the 'Imperial troops' were solely the troops of the rulers and served the British interests only on voluntary basis. The troops would be rather disbanded than incorporated in the Indian Army—so ran the Maharaja's argument. It was further felt that officers commanding their Imperial troops would enjoy the same rank, pay and status of other serving officers of the Indian army. Here again the Maharaja had his way and the Imperial Service Troops' were renamed 'Indian States Forces'. Inspecting Officers were henceforth to be called 'military advisors'.

**Maharaja Ganga Singh Ji as Chancellor of the Chamber of Princes**

The Chamber of Princes was officially inaugurated by the Duke of Connaught on behalf of His Majesty on the 8th of February, 1921, in the historic audience hall, Dewan-i-Am, of the Moghul Emperors in the Delhi Fort. The address from the Chair stressed upon the aspect that change was inevitable and that the States were expected to play crucial role in the modernisation of India which would meet the aspirations of the people of India. The Royal Proclamation also stated:

> "My Viceroy will take its council freely in matters relating to the territories of Indian States generally and in matters that affect these territories jointly with British India or with the rest of my Empire. It will have no concern with the internal affairs of individual States or their Rulers or with the relations of individual States with my Government, while the existing rights of the States and their freedom of action will in no way be prejudiced or impaired".

The Viceroy was to be the President of the Chamber whereas the Chancellor and Pro-Chancellor were to elected annually by the members themselves. The Chamber was to have 108 Rulers who were members in their own right.

There were 127 non-salute states who were to elect 12 members to represent them in the Chamber. The decision of some leading States like Hyderabad and Mysore to stay aloof from the activities of the Chamber was a dampner in the efforts of the Princes to present a unified front. Maharaja Ganga Singh appeared to be the automatic choice of the rulers for the post of Chancellor of the Chamber and was voted for the post by a large majority. It was the unanimous opinion among the Princes that the Maharaja was best suited for the job, not only because of his vast experience of public affairs, but because of his previous knowledge of the working of the Princes Conference and his personal ability as well. The members also did not lose sight of the fact that the Chamber was the creation largely of the efforts of the Maharaja. A standing committee comprising of the rulers of Cutch, Gwalior, Patiala and Nawanagar was also elected to assist the Chancellor in carrying out the work of the Chamber. Factional rivalries, inevitable in public institutions, not withstanding, the Chamber did commendable work. It succeeded in 'codifying and thereby limiting the political practices which had eaten into the substance of treaties and in removing misapprehensions, in derfining many doubtful points in the relations between the States and the British Government'. One of the earliest decisions of the Chamber was the adoption of the term "Narendra Mandal' as the vernacular designation of the Chamber.

The powers of the Chancellor were not defined. There was no Secretariat and no finances—the Chancellor had to provide both out of his own resources. The Political Secretary, Sir John Thompson, had clarified in 1923 that with regard to the official position and duties of the Chancellor, it was the latter's prerogative to decide on the business of the Chamber in his capacity of being the Principal Officer of the Chamber. The Maharaja himself was not in favour of entrusting of the Chancellor with such powers as would commit the princes as a body for any definite act. He of ten reiterated that the Chancellor was at best a liaison officer between the Indian Princes and the Government of India. The Maharaja thus deliberately adopted a low profile and trended with great caution so as not to offend the sensibilities of other members.

From the start the Princes were at a disadvantage as they were not given to public speaking and were further handicapped by the fact that only the Princes were allowed to attend the sessions of the Chamber which were presided over by the Viceroy. The Maharaja devised a way out by organising informal meeting of the Princes which could also be attended by their ministers and other experts and in which vital questions could be discussed including those which were to come up in the formal Chamber meetings.

The early years of the Chamber coincided with the first civil disobedience movement of Mahatma Gandhi. The events at Jallianwalla Bagh and the dissatisfaction with the limited nature of reforms coupled with the purported anti Muslim policy of the British Government towards the Turks, generated a lot of unrest in the country. The success of the direct action (also known as non cooperation) alarmed the Government of India which was convinced that demand for further reforms would increase. Under pressure from the legislatures the Government of India inaugurated a policy of 'discriminating protection' as a result of which custom tariffs began to mount, and though this was a matter which affected the States, the Government of India neither consulted the States nor initiated steps to protect their interests. The Provincial Assemblies, acting independent of the Centre, adopted a policy of open hostility towards the Indian States. Such was the state of affairs that even the Maharaja started having some misgivings. In 1924 he made an impassioned appeal in the Chamber of Princes (No. 2) that there was no logic in exempting only. the Princes enjoying 19 gun salute from the payment of custom duties whereas on the other hand the less privileged States paid those duties. The Maharaja also tried to convince the Viceroy Lord Reading, that with the rapidly changing political scenario and rising unrest in British India, it was imperative that an infonnal Round Table Conference of Princes be convened so that the Government of India be apprised of the aspirations of the Princes and the difficulties they were to experience in the face of unrest in India. Other issues which Ganga Singh Ji wanted to be discussed at the Round Table were the technical questions like boundary disputes, acquisition by princes of non-residential property in British India, the employment of Europeans in States etc. More important was the question that the Government of India accepted practice appropriate to the lesser States had been applied indiscriminately to the larger ones, but it was equally claimed that use age and sufferance had created undefined rights, that the paramountcy of the Crown had overridden the rights of the States. With every assertion of the princes' rights, based on treaties or engagements, the counter claim of the paramountcy of the Government of India became more and more insistent. Another point, delicate in nature, was the table of salutes. The rank and precedence of Indian rulers was decided by the table of salutes orginally drawn up in the mid- nineteenth century. At the time of the preparation of the table many Strates were given higher rank to which they were not entitled either politically or militarily. An infonnal meeting of Princes on this issue was mooted. At the same time the Maharaja also advocated that States should enter into direct relationship with the Viceroy through only one intennediary instead of many, as was the tradition at that time.

Some of the achievements of the Maharaja during the Chancellorship phase related to settlement of issues connected with minority administration and ceremonials at the time of installation and investiture. Other questions, such as the disabilities of the States in regard to currency, salt, opium etc were referred to an expert committee. But the major achievement of Ganga Singh Ji was that the Government of India finally acknowledged that the sovereignity of the Rulers extended to the air and the authority of the States was also established over wireless and broadcasting in their respective areas.

In 1926 the Maharaja had moved a crucial resolution regarding joint deliberations in the Chamber of Princes (No. 3). The Resolution read as follows:

"That a committee be appointed consisting of Princes and Ministers, to consider in consultation with Representatives of the British Government and to report to the Chamber of Princes:

a. the best means of safeguarding the interests of the Indian States on occasions when an enquiry is undertaken into matters of common interest to the States and to British India, and;
b. what machinery should be devised for giving effect to the proposal contained in para 311 of the Montagu—Chelmsford Report regarding joint deliberations".

This proposal had been in the pipeline since 1918. In the committee to be appointed the Maharaja proposed the names of five rulers into the mover of the resolution and 5 ministers from various States.

After successive re-elections the Maharaja decided to step down from the Chancellorship in 1926. His work as first the General Secretary of the Princes Conference and later as Chancellor of the Chamber was greatly appreciated and his brother Princes presented him with a souvenir worth Rs. 75,000 in the form of an inscribed gold plate.

**Maharaja Ganga Singh as President of the Chamber of Princes Reorganisation Committee**

By 1938 it was clear that though events were moving at a very rapid rate all over India and political changes of far-reaching importance were taking place, the Chamber of Princes was riven with dissent and discord and was on the verge of bankruptcy. Under such adverse conditions it was felt imperative to restructure the working of the Chamber of Princes and a Princes Reorganisation Committee was formed in 1938 and Maharaja Ganga Singh was appointed as its

President—a honour which he accepted with great humility. The first meeting of the Committee was held in Bombay in June 1938 and the speech of the Maharaja struck a very cautious and sombre note at the outset which set the tone for the rest of the meeting.(No. 4). He lamented that the Chamber of Princes had lost its edge and was no longer in a position to exert influence for the purpose of obtaining recognition of the legitimate demands of the States. The disarray in the ranks of the Chamber of Princes was at all levels. The bigger States felt aggrieved that they did not get due importance in the Chamber whereas the smaller States felt they were totally excluded from independent functioning in the Chamber because they were discriminated against on basis of their size and resources or lack of them. The Maharaja also stressed that a common ground would have to be found in which both contending parties would be pacified and accommodated which would result in States like Hyderabad, Baroda, Kashmir, Travancore once more playing an active role in the activities of the Chamber and the smaller states would feel that they had a meaningful role to play in the Chamber.

Commenting further, the Maharaja said that the idea of the Chamber was mooted as a counter-part—not a counter weight—to the Montagu-Chelmsford Reforms in British India initially. Successive Government of India Acts had lead to great constitutional reforms in the Provinces and in the process the organisation of Indian States had become weaker. The weakness of the Chamber left many important issues, vital to the interests of the Princes, unresolved. They related to:

1. Commissions of Enquiry;
2. Successions of Heirs—Apparent;
3. Ceremonials;
4. Courts of Arbitration;
   and other less significant issues.

At the same time it was proposed that the recommendations of the Hydari Committee be considered to gauge the importance of the States interse and who should be permanent members of the Chamber. Political and economic interests should also be considered, it was advocated. The election process would also have to be revamped to eliminate suspicion. While concluding the Maharaja strongly urged that a Council of Ministers be constituted to examine the entire question of the reorganisation of the Chamber of Princes at the earliest.

## References


1. R.P. Vyas, 'The Role of Maharaja Ganga Singh in the Formation and Stabilisation of this Chamber of Princes' in G.S.L. Devra edited Ganga Singh Ji Centenary Volume.
2. 'Rome Note', 15th May, 1917 by Maharaja Ganga Singh.
3. Proceedings of the Meeting of the Narendra Mandal from 1921 to 1926.
4. K.M. Panikar, 'His Highness the Maharaja of Bikaner.
5. The British Crown and the Indian States (Directorate of the Chamber's Special Committee).
6. P.L. Chudgar, Indian Princes under British Protection.
7. Speech of Maharaja of Bikaner (3rd Nov., 1919) in the Princes Conference at the ternination of War.
8. Extract from His Highness's Speech delivered in Chamber of Princes (24th Nov., 1924).
9. Speech by His Highness the Maharaja of Bikaner in the Chamber of Princes (26th Jan., 1926).
10. Maharaja Ganga Singh's speech at the opening of Minister's Infonnal Meet. (16th August, 1926).

# Annexure 1

## Minute by Colonel His Highness the Maharaja of Bikaner, G.C.S.I., G.C.I.E., A.D.C., LL.D.

*Rome Note*

The well-being and prosperity of India and the ever increasing happiness and contentment of her people must necessarily be matters of very deep concern to every loyal Indian whether he be a British subject or a resident within the territories of the Indian States.

This is of as much importance to the Ruling Princes and Chiefs of India as it is to the British Government, for there is a complete identity of interests between the British Government and the States. We have a very large stake and vested interests of vital importance in the Country and our future stability and prosperity—may be our very existence—depend on the maintenance and strength of British rule in India. In fact, as I stated in my recent interview to The Times our future is bound up together and all that tends to the stability and popularity of the one tends to the stability and popularity of the other.

Then again conditions existing in British India and the attitude and feelings of its people find their inevitable reflext in our own States. Those of our States whose Governments have made considerable advance and progress are for obvious reasons anxious to keep abreast of the times. We cannot, even if we would, afford to ignore public opinion as also the various changes that may be going on across our borders in British India. Many of us are surrounded by the territories of British India. With increased Railway, Telegraph and Postal facilities, and the spread of education and Western thoughts and ideals, and with large numbers of our subjects carrying on trade and business in British India, there is—much more than formerly—frequent and intimate inter-change of ideas and opinions and greater contact between our own subjects and those of British India. And should there be any grievance and discontent in British India such feelings and even anarchy and sedition are Indian States and their Governments also.

In all matters prejudicial in any way to the stability of the British Government, the Ruling Princes and Chiefs have already amply shown that they can be relied on to stand solid on the side of the British Government and that they unhesitatingly throw themselves, unasked and uninvited, into the breach in suport and defence of the only rule under which we all realise that India can realise her aspirations and reach her goal. But in other matters the welfare and the steady political advance of India on constitutional lines is a matter of no small concern and importance to the Ruling Princes and Chiefs, not only because, as Indians, they have the good of their Country and their fellow-countrymen at heart, but because they feel that such a course would, in itself, popularise, strengthen and preserve British rule in India.

It is hardly necessary to state that a very heavy and grave responsibility lies, especially at the present moment, on the British Government and on British Statesmen, both in Great Britain and in India. As the Prime Minister remarked with such statesmenlike sagacity in his Guildhall speech on the 27th of April, Indian problems:

> "require bold statesmanship, Timidity, timorousness, faint-heartedness, abhorrent in peace or war, in war is fatal."

I would, therefore, venture with all respect and with all the emphasis at my command, to give expression to my prof ound belief and to strike a serious note of loyal and solemn warning that unless Indian problems—complex and difficult as they appear—are, at the golden opportunity which has now presented itself, handled in a sympathetic and generous spirit and with imagination, broad-minded perspicacity and, above all, with boldness by the responsible Ministers of the Crown in the two Countries, the results will obviously be as deplorable as they will be undesirable and unfair both for Great Britain and for India. If this golden opportunity is not properly and fully availaed of, a deep-rooted and widespread feeling of disappointment and grievance, discontent and bitterness, will inevitably spread throughout the length and breadth of British India. The force of that feeling no man can at present properly gauge, but there can be no question that compared with it the recent unrest and discontent would appear to be a trifle.

Signs and evidence are amply forthcoming that, in spite of the undoubted and irrefutable loyalty to the King—Emperor of the hundreds of millions of the people of India, there is, even in the minds of a considerable number of sober minded people, unquestionably and absolutely loyal to the core, a strong and growing undercurrent of uneasiness and impatience, of disappointment, despondency and even despair, specially in regard to the political future of India—feelings based on the utterances of, and view expressed—officially and unofficially—by some British statesmen and administrators and on the rate and nature of the political progress made upto now in India.

It is for all these reasons that I strongly feel it is to be my duty which I owe not only to India, but also to my Emperor and the Empire, no less than to the British Government, the Secretary of State and the Viceroy—to represent these matters while I am here especially on the mission—and it is again for these reasons that I further strongly feel that I should be laying myself open to charges of being even disloyal to the Sovereign and unfaithfull to his Government if I refrained from free and frankly bringing to notice these facts and possible dangers.

I am aware that I may be considered by some to be unduly pessimistic in making the above statements and in attempting to draw attention to these facts and possibilities. But I can only state that we, who are natives of the Country and thus have more opportunities than the Government themselves of ascertaining the real feeling and state of affairs, have no delusions on the subject. But at the risk of being scofed at as a pessimist, I should like to repeat that the feeling on the subject is more intense and whilespread than is commonly thought arid that the dangers ahead are very real. And, as I ventured to state in my speech on the 21st April at the Empire Parliamentary Association Luncheon, it will depend on how these questions are handled, whether the present "legitimate unrest", subsides and dies out or continues and increases, on the one hand, a really liberal, sympathetic and bold statesman like policy in the immediate as well as the near future will result in restoring confidence and giving patience, fortitude and hope to the people, who will then rest content and assured that they have some thing definite to look forward to. On the other hand, we may have to face the, by no means, imaginary creation of a second Ireland in India. This would mean that the ranks of the Extremists, and even of the Seditionists, would be swelled beyond measure, instead of being diminished, and that those of us will be entirely discredited who have been staunch Imperialists and loyalists and who have counselled patience and faith in Great Britain and her being true to her mission in India. God forbid that the latter results should ensue, but if British statesmanship fails to rise fully to the present occasion, it is a question for the earnest consideration of His Majesty's Governments both in Great Britain and in India whether the Indian people and their leaders will be held solely responsible at the bar of history for what I honestly and firmly believe will in such circumstances surely come to pass.

No one in a sane frame of mind or with any sense of responsibility or a stake in the country would urge that rash or dangerous steps should be taken which may jeopardise the stability of British rule in India. Much less would he urge what, under present circumstances, might be impossible of accomplishment or attainment—specially in regard to so important a question as that of political reforms aiming ultimately at granting to India self-Government within the British Empire.

One of the most important questions for serious and immediate consideration is whether what has been done so far and what may be proposed to be done now or in the immediate future in the direction of political reforms and advancement is all that was and is possible of accomplishment or attainment, or whether there was and is yet room for further progress and action.

In my speech at the Empire Parliamentary Association Luncheon, I stated an incontrovertible fact, viz., that India has been and is changing very rapidly and beyond conception and that under the invigorating influence of Great Britain she is making truely remarkable strides. So rapid has this progress been that even officials who left the country only a few years ago would find it difficult fully to realise it. With education on Western lines imparted to Indians by the British Government and after countries of close and intimate connection with Great Britain—famous throughout the world for its freedom and liberal traditions and popular institutions—and with the advance made in recent years, political problems have necessarily come more and more to the front. Owing to the war and the honourable part which India has had the proud privilege of playing in it, a further strong impetus has been given to Indian aims and aspirations. With the generous and sympathetic recognition throughout the Empireh of India's services and with the re-construction and reconstitution of the empire the tapis, hopes are not unreasonably entertained that India may also look forward to further reforms and material advance—not as the price of loyalty but as the logical result of the Empire having through this crisis been brought closer together and of the better understanding that has prevailed owing to the loyal co-operation of the various parts of the Empire.

Extreme conservatism and excessive caution can produce as much harm as rash and precipitate action. India is a land where sentiment and imagination play a great part. Strike the right clard and touch the imagination and you get results for exceeding all anticipation from a people well-known for their grateful responsive nature. Lord Curzon in his speech at the Guildhall when receiving the Freedom of the City of London in 1901 said:

> "Depend upon it, you will never rule the East except through the heart, and moment imagination has gone out of your Asiatic policy your Empire will dwindle and decay."

Though a great deal can be written on various important matters the only four points that I propose specially to deal with on this ocasions are:

(1) The extreme importance- indeed, the vital necessity—of a formal and authoritative official declaration being made by the British Government at the earliest possible opportunities to the effect that Self-Government within the British Empire is the ultimate object and goal of British rule in India.
(2) The advisability of inaugurating, on liberal and sympathetic lines, further political reforms in the constitution and functions of Provincial Legislative Councils as well as in the Imperial Legislative Council in British India.
(3) The desirability of greater autonomy being granted to the Government of India as well as to the Provincial Governments and a lesser degree of interference with both, in regard to matters which are not of great Imperial concern.
(4) The vital importance to the Indian States, their Rulers and their subjects, of establishing at an early date on constitutional lines "Council or Assembly of Princes to deal with matters which concern the British Government on the one side and the States, their Rulers and their people, on the other.

With the time at my disposal, this Minute does not pretend to deal exhaustively with the various details and points connected with these most important subjects. But it is hoped that the matter dealt with will suffice. If I have failed to make any point clear or if any further elucidation is required, I shall on being informed be only too happy to submit further details at the earliest possible date.

After apologising for having already taken up so much space with these preliminary—but I hope it will be agreed necessary and important—remarks I now propose to deal separately with the points named above.

**I. Declaration regarding Self-Government**

This idea is not a novel one and has been brought forward on many occasions and by men in various walks of life. The extreme advisability and importance and urgent necessity for such a course are based on three considerations:

Firstly, it will go a very long way in dispelling the uneasiness, impatience, disappointment, despondency and despair, at present so markedly noticeable and to which I have already referred in paragraph 7.

Secondly, the ranks of the Extremists and even of the Seditionists and Anarchists will be considerably diminished if not entirely done away with. With such an authoritative official statement, people can await with patience, fortitude and hope, the fulfilment in good time of—to them—the most important aim and object of British rule in India resting content in the thought that the political future and the regeneration of their Country is now assured and fully secured, and?

Thirdly, there will be something definite as regards the policy of the Imperial Government to guide the members of the Indian Civil and other Public Services.

The whole question is whether or not this is the goal of British rule in India. I submit that there can be but one answer and that is emphatically "Yes". If the granting, when the right time comes, of self-government within the Empire is not the goal of British rule in India, then it is impossible to conceive what the goal is.

It is hardly necessary to state that the desire for self-government in any educated people is a simple elementary fact of human nature or that according to Western ideals self-government is government by the people, that is, democracy as oposed to autocracy or beaurocratic government—in other words representative government. In Lincoln's words it is "government of the people, for the people, and by the people." The idea of representative government is by no means new to India. Without any desire to enter into any controversial details, it is an undoubted fact that in the olden days, India, contrary to the general ideas now prevailing, had a good deal of representative government in various forms long before it was known in the West. It is a matter of common knowledge that in the village—the unit of national life—the Panchayat or village Council regulated, and in some cases still regulates, its own affairs. And in regard to higher institutions, records are forthcoming to show that large bodies of men existed and advised the King in regard to various public affairs. Several Committees or bodies dealt with taxation, land revenue, irrigation and tanks and such important matters, whilst the existence of what are now municipal or local self-governments is to be traced in bodies which were then entrusted with town improvements and matters of local interests. As Sir James Meston pointed out in his Guildhall speech:

> ". . . When Boadicea was filling this land with her fierce revenge . . . at that time India was a settled continent with a mature civilisations, with wealthy cities, jewelled shrines, Monastic Orders, and civil institutions which still have something to teach us. Three centuries before the Romans invaded England our great Emperor Ashoka was issuing edicts from his resplendent Capital at Putna; he was summoning his Council of a thousand Elders . . . he was perfecting the civil administration of his giagentic kingdom, . . . At a time when our ancestors were wandering in the woods and forests India was a highly developed, cultured land. . . ."

However that may be intimate contact with English civiliation and the close study of English literature. English history and "English" political ideals for over a century and a half, have all been tending to stimulate strongly among the educated classes in India a desire for national liberty and self-government in the sense of representative government. British Statesmen, it is safe to contend, will not cavil at our conviction that the possibilities of securing the greatest possible good for the greatest possible number of people are vastly greater under a system of government which is a carried on in consonance with the wishes and opinions of the people and where possible, with the advice and consent of its subjects or their chosen representatives. Nor, it can equally confidently be asserted, will the dispute the claim that the ruler and the ruled have an equal interest in the well-being of the State and that, therefore, the ruled as they prove themselves fit should have a progressive voice and share in the government of their own ountry.

For the last thirty odd years, large sections of our educated people have formulated their political ideal for India, as self-government within the Empire. As a class they believe that their ideal of self-government, in its Western sense of representative government, can be realised only if India remained an integral part of the British Empire. I can best describe this ideal in the glowing words of that illustrious Indian patroit, the late Gopal Krishna Gokhale, who, for many years before his death, enjoyed the equal confidence of the British Government and the Indian people:

> "I want our people to be in their own country what other people are in theirs. I want our men and women, without distinction of caste or creed, to have opportunity to grow to the full height of their stature, unhampered by cramping and unnatural restrictions. I want India to take her proper place among the great nations of the world, politically, industrially, in religion, in literature, in science and in arts. I want all this, and feel, at the same time, that the whole of this aspiration can, in its essence and its reality, be realised within this Empire."

The realisation of this ideal is not possible without political self-government, and yet there are some Englishmen who, while acknowledging, and indeed even encouraging, the legitimatising of the ideal deny this ideal as suited to Asiastics, while others regard those who strive to obtain the machinery for its realisation, as dangerous and even disloyal.

Step after step has been taken and is being taken by the British Government which inevitably tends towards the same end. The spread of the English language and Western education; the extension of railways and telegraphs; the creation of a sense of unity among the various peoples; and the steady admission of Indians to some of the highest offices of State, are all preparing the way for representative government. And however divergent may be the views of some Englishmen and Indians on various subjects, there seems to be on the whole, an apparent agreement as stated by Lord Sydenham in an article in the Nineteenth Century in December 1916, that:

> ". . . British rule in India can be justified only if, in addition to the maintenance of law, order, and equal justice, it is directed to leading the people always onward, and upward, bridging over the innumerable rifts which divide them, and smoothing the path to nationhood and self-government. . . ."

Going back to earlier times, we find that John Bright in a speech at Manchester in 1877 said:

> "I believe it that it is our duty not only to govern India well now for our sakes and to satisfy our own conscience, but so to arrange its government and so to administer it that we should look forward to

the time when India will have to take up her own government and administer it in her own fashion. I say he is no statesman—he is no man actuated with a high moral responsibility . . . who is not willing thus to look ahead and thus to prepare for circumstances which may come sooner than we think and sooner than any of us hoped for, but which must come at some not very distant date."

Lord Curzon in a speech at Calcutta in 1902 said:

". . . We are ordained to walk here in the same track together for many a long day to come. You cannot do without us. We should be important without you. Let the Englishman and the Indian accept the consecration of a union that is so mysterious as to have in it something of the divine, and let our common ideal be a united country and a happier people."

Without labouring to detail what both India and the British Empire would lose were India no longer to form part of the British Empire, for the purposes of this Minute, be sufficient perhaps to say that our ideal of self-government within the Empire is also the result of what, I believe, Lord Hardinge termed "reasoned attachment."

And here I make no apologies for giving a verbatim quotation from the memorable speech on the subject which excited universal admiration in India, delivered as President of the 30th session of the Indian National Congress in 1915, be my present colleague Sir Satyendra Sinha who said:

"It is, however, unfortunately the fact that a few years ago unhappy statements and even actions of responsible statesman gave rise to a widespread suspicion among large classes of people in all parts of India that there was a change of policy—a deliberate intention to retrace the steps. That this suspicion is not wholly without foundation will appear from the estimate of an eminent French publicist who cannot be charged with either lack of sympathy for the British administration of India or an excess of sympathy for the Indian reform party. This is what M. Chailley says: "Had England taken as her motto 'India for the Indians', had she continued following the ideas of Elphinstone and Malcolm to consider her rule as temporary, she might without inconsistency grant to the national party gradual and increasing concessions which in time would give entire autonomy to the Indians, but that is not now her aim." (The italics are mine). Does any reasonable man imagine that it is possible to satisfy the palpitating hearts of the thousands of young men who, to use the classic words of Lord Morley, "leave our universities intoxicated with the ideas of freedom, nationality and self-government," with the comfortless assurance that free institutions are the special privilege of the West? Can any wonder that many of these young men, who have not the same robust faith in the integrity and benevolence of England as the members of this Congress, should lose heart at the mere suspicion of such a policy, and driven to despair, concoude that "the roar and scream of confusion and carnage" -is better than peace and order without even the distant prospect of freedom."

Fifteen years ago, Lord Morley said: "the sacred word 'tree' represents, as Englishmen have thought until today, the noblest aspiration that canimate the breast of man." And today, millions of Englishmen are fteely sacrificing their lives in order that others may be free: therefore, an Englishman will be the first person to realize and appreciate the great insistent desire in the heart of India, and I for myself say with all the emphasis and earnestness that I can command that if the noble policy of Malcolm and Elphinstone, Canning and Ripon, Bright and Morley, is not steadily, consistently and unflinchingly adhered to, the moderate party amongst us will soon be depleted of all that is fine and noble in human character. . . .

. . . I appeal to the British nation to declare their ungrudging approval of the goal to which we aspire, to declare their flexible resolution to equip India for her journey to that goal and to furnish her escort on the long and weary road. Such a declaration will be the most distinguished way of marking their appreciation of India's services and sacrifices—her loyalty and her devotion to the Empire. Such a declaration will touch the heart and appeal to the imagination of the people for more than any mere specific political reforms. These latter may fall short of the high expectations raised by utterance of the responsible English statesmen as to the future place of India in the Empire and they may cause general disappointment.

But an authoritative declaration of policy on the lines I suggest will, without causing such disappointment, carry conviction to the minds of the people that the pace of the administrative reforms will be reasonably accelerated and that henceforth it will be only a question of patient preparation. . . ."

We may surely take it then, that the ideal or goal of British rule in India undoubtedly is, and must be self-government within the British Empire.

The Indian ideal of self-government within the British Empire is based, not merely on a sentiment of Nationality, or mere attachment to England—which there undoubtedly is—but on a reasoned conviction that the retention of India within the Empire is essential both for India and for the Empire.

. Now however much prejudiced or ill-informed critics may say that this ideal is only preached by a small class bent on securing power for itself, evidence is forthcoming that the Ruling Princes are themselves becoming inspired with the same ideal and are steadily taking steps to give effect to it. The Rulers of some of these States are representatives of the fighting races of India, such as Sikhs and Rajputs.

I submit that there are really no inseperable difficulties and insoluble problems in the way, nor are there really any dangers in which the British Empire would be exposed by the declaration of such a policy, nor is there anything in existing conditions in India irreconcilable with Indian aspirations of which renders such a declaration impossible.

It has been said that such a declaration would commit the British Government, future Secretaries of State and Viceroys to a definite line of policy and that the people of India would after that always be clamouring for more powers and reforms and never be satisfied with what they were given and that there would be constant dispute as to when the clamouring for more powers and reforms and never be satisfied with what they were given and that there would be constant disputes as to when the country would be ripe for the grant of self-government and whether the time had not arrived. If I have understood these objections correctly, I would submit with all due respect that if self-government within the Empire is the goal of British rule in India (and there cannot really be two answers to this question) then there can be no possible harm, but on the contrary, a great deal of good in publicly and officially avowing at the earliest possible opportunity that such is the goal. The results and effect will be beneficial in an inestimable degree and the question of committing future public servants of the crown does not arise. I would even go so far as to say that I can see much harm and very serious danger in posponing such a declaration, but not one single benefit. As regards the other apprehension, so long as the British Government goes on conceding judicious, generous and timely political reforms in a sympathetic and broad—minded spirit they can afford to disregard any unreasonable clamour. Even with free and representative institutions developed to such a remarkable extent in Great Britain, clamour for more powers and greater political reforms is by no means rare there and India or any other country could hardly be expected to be an exception. People will undoubtedly want more power. But not conceding to the people of India liberal measure of reforms or refusing to make an authoritative and official statement of this kind, which would calm and fortify the people, well, it is submitted, certainly not make clamour of agitation less, on the other hand, it will add to the "loyal unrest" and of course swell sedition.

It is not suggested that any time limit should be assigned and the question of when complete self-government may be conceded will be still for the British Government to decide on generous and broad statesman like lines. But I would, at the same time, respectfully urge that the beneficial effects and results should not be marred by the declaration being hedged in with too many restrictions and qualifications which would bear the appearance of a want of trust and a lack of sympathy on the part of the British Government.

I have also heard the apprehension expressed that the effect on the Indian Army of such a declaration might be undesirable, should this view really be held by any responsible officer, I would venture to state that whilst no such danger is at all perceptible to our Indian mind, on the other hand, the fact should not be lost sight of that the classes from which the soldiers of our Indian Army are recruited do not all find employment in the Army alone. While some brothers will be in the Army, others may be following legal or even political careers, and they are all bound to exchange views and make comparisons when they meet on furlough, etc. With education and Western ideas spreading over the country, Indians whether in the Army or in other civil employment, will all naturally desire to see their country materially advancing. If the bulk of the people are discontented and defeated and, in the absence of any such declaration, see no political future for their country, the discontent and unrest is sure gradually to spread to the Army as has happened in other countries before now. Thus any withholding of the declaration is far more likely at a future date to cause an undesirable effect on the Army rather than the issue of such a statement.

We have also heard of India consisting not of one nation but of a series of nationalities and races with varying customs and languages. I do not purpose to repeat here what I said on the subject in my speech at the Luncheon in the House of Commons. I will, therefore, only add that what struck us, Indian Representatives, very greatly during the sittings of the Imperial War Cabinet and Conference, was the fact of the varying and extremely divergent nationalties forming the populations of Canada, South Africa and some other parts of the Empire—where they enjoy full self-government. No differences in India in the way of nationalty, or race or caste, can be greater than the differences existing, for instance, in Canada between the English Canadians, French Canadians, German Canadians and so on, or in South Africa where we have Englishmen, Dutchmen and I understand, some negro races. The point cannot too often be emphasised when we talk of different races and customs to be found in India that India is not a country but a vast Continent not a State but in itself an Empire within the Empire.

Sedition, as I stated in the same speech, is happily confined to an extremely small percentage of the vast population of India and cannot affect the right and,claims of the hundreds of millions of the loyal subjects of His Majesty and King—Emperor. Political unrest will surely die out should a bold, statesmanlike and generous policy be adopted in regard to this declaration and to future political progress. If British statesmanship was able to concede full self-government to South Africa within some 8 years after the South African War—a fine stroke of statesmanship and imagination which turned an enemy people into loyal supporters—the claims of India, after centuries of action and loyal services to the Throne and the Empire, at least to a declaration about self-government in the future within the British Empire cannot, it is submitted, fairly be ignored.

Unless I am mistaken, there was a large number of people in England who doubted the wisdom of granting self-government to South Africa. There may be, and undoubtedly are, similar doubts about even this declaration being made in regard to India's political future, but in the minds of those intimately in touch with Indian affairs and conversant with conditions now prevailing there and who have the best interests of the Emperor and the Empire no less than these of India at heart, there is not the least doubt as to its being in the immediate future, a measure pre-eminently fitted to allay unrest and misgivings and to produce the most beneficial results, which will stand the Empire in good stand at some critical time in the distant future. In fact it will avert unhappiness and discontent and possible danger. The beneficial effect which it will produce cannot be exaggerated and it will touch the imagination and arouse the deep and heartfelt gratitude of every Indian.

I would, however, point out that the declaration, whilst being simply and briefly worded without being hedged in with numerous narrow and petty restrictions and qualifications, should not be in the form of a mere statement by a Secretary of State or other high official at, say, some Parliamentary debate or in some despatch, but should have all the stamp' and weight of authority and formality in the shape of a gracious Proclamation by the Sovereign or at least on behalf of His Majesty's Government in England under the authority of the King—Emperor. Few documents have done more good and better service to the Empire in dispelling fears, suspicions and alarm than the gracious Proclamation of Queen Victoria widely known in India as our Magna Charta. It is a similar authoritative and solemn official statement which will further give courage and hope to India, and what is more fitting than that it should be made during the reign of a Sovereign so universally and personally beloved throughout the Indian Empire and whose gracious sympathy for India is a household word. I would venture to suggest that this declaration should be made at the earliest possible moment No good purpose can be served by delaying it. On the contrary the beneficial effect it will produce and the discontent and alarm that it will dispel render it all the more essential that it should be proclaimed now, before the war is over say on the King Emperor's next Birthday or on some other suitable date in the near future.

If side by side with the definite official declaration that self-government for India within the British Empire is the object and goal of British rule in India, the reservation was made, that it would be granted at such a time as, in the opinion of His Majesty's Government, India and her people have shown themselves to be fitted for it,—I would respectfully submit that it would provide for everything and that no further qualifications or stipulations would be really necessary.

Although not coming under this head, I would take the liberty of further suggesting that, at the same time, a declaration should also officially be made announcing His Majesty's pleasure about the grant of proper British commissions to Indians in the Army.

II.– Further Political Reforms both in the Imperial Legislative Council as well as the Provincial Legislative Councils

The first point for consideration in this connection also is what are the intentions of Great Britain regarding India's political future". The subject of self-government for India within the Empire has already been dealt with at length. If there is no intention under any circumstances of letting India have self-government in any form or of helping her to advance politically on the lines on which other members of the British Empire have already progressed, then the raising of these points or their consideration is superfluous. But if, as India sincerely trusts confidently hopes, Great Britain does desire to carry out her mission in India to the full and if Great Britain and his Majesty's Government is really anxious and desirous of seeing India making reasonable politically progress towards such a goal, then the favourable consideration of further political reforms and advances a matter of urgent and serious import.

It is often stated by critics unfriendly to Indian aspirations or ignorant of real facts, that the India people have not shown such fitness or sense of responsibility as to justify material political advancement or hopes for ultimate self-government and much capital is often made even of the political "legitimate unrest."

A calm and impartial consideration of last history in this connection will, however, it is submitted, reveal certain facts, which, it appears desirable, should be brought prominently forward, before any suggestions as regards the future are made. I believe that Council reforms were carried out in India mainly in 1861, in 1892 and lastly in 1909. officials as well as non-officials have testified in recent years to the rapid strides India has made in the past and is making at present. But even assuming that the progress has not been as rapid, as Indians contend, can it really be seriously stated that India did not make any progress at all in the 31 years between 1861 and 1892 to warrant any further advance or concessions being made in between? Nor can it be said that the political progress of India was so unsatisfactory and slow as to have compelled the British Government to postpone taking further steps during the 17 years between 1892 to 1909. An examination of the powers possessed by the Imperial Legislative Council prior to 1909 and the real conditions existing in regard to local self-government such as the control of municipalities and local boards will show that the Indian non-official members had, as a matter of fact, very little voice or power. Had a start been made on liberal and broad lines from, say, the time of Lord Ripon, it is clear that the progress as well as the capability of the people would have been very greatly developed and there would have been, through actual experience and sharing of responsibilities, greater advance at the present date.

Informed and educated public opinion considers that the progress could have been accelerated had there been a large infusion of sympathy in the policy of administration and consequently the people feel that they have legitimate grounds for dissatisfaction and grievance with the nature and the rate of advance so far made. Those of us who have also the best interests of the British Government at heart, find it difficult to meet the allegation that the British Government never grants any political concessions until, at the eleventh hour, agitation and public clamour force their hands, and that what is given with a bad grace and not in a generous or sympathetic spirit.

Some unfortunate statements of persons in responsible and high quarters have further tended to fan this feeling. Colour is further lent to such beliefs by one or two quite recent instances in regard, for instance, to the questions of creating a High Court in place of the present Chief Court in the Punjab and of establishing an Executive Council in the United Provinces. Both these questions, though recommended by the Government of India were in the first instance negatived by the Secretary of State or His Majesty's Government in England and it is a matter of common knowledge in India that, in spite of such refusal, both these changes are ultimately to be made. Incidentally, it may be added that it is such matters that have greatly strengthened the agitation and demand in India, and, I understand, also in certain quarters in England, for abolishing the present India Council which assists the Secretary of State at the Indian Office, for the feeling is growing in India that apart from a great deal of under interference in ordinary administrative affairs (with which I shall deal later) the whole work done in the Secretariats of the Government of India is practically all gone over again in the various Departments of the India Office, and that at times the India Council taken as a whole is not as liberal and sympathetic in its ideas as India may reasonably expect.

Examining also the power and previleges at present enjoyed by the Imperial and Provincial Legislative Council in India, a careful analysis will, I venture to submit show that they do not as a matter of fact have any real voice or wield any real power. All that they can be said to have got at present is a certain amount of influence. Though this has been a considerable advance as compared with the system in force before 1909, the fact nevertheless remains that the reforms of 1909 were considerably overdue. And taking into consideration and substancial progress of India it is universally held that the powers enjoyed, specially by the non-official members of such Assemblies, do not go far enough, that the regulations and the rules of business of such Legislative Councils can well and quite safely be made more liberal and that some of the petty restrictions with which they are hedged in, could, without any danger, be considerably relaxed.

It has been stated that some of the non-official members are irresponsible both in their criticism and their suggestions but until the people are saddled with more responsibilities and given some real power, this cannot be remedied; and even then some irresponsible members will always be found in every country, just as, I believe, I am not wrong in stating, they are still to be found even in the British Parliament since the 1909 reforms, there has been a marked and satisfactory change for the better in many directions in the Indian legislatures, to which teste money has been given in warm terms on many public occasions by Lord Minto and Lord Hardings. I regret I have not got copies of such speeches with me but I would beg to quote the following from Lord Hardinge's speech at a state Banquet in Bikaner in November 1912:

> " . . . but I should like to say how pleased I was at your creation of a People's Representative Assembly. Its powers will be not unlike those enjoyed by my Legislative Council; and judging from my own experience, I do not think they will be abused, and I can honestly testify to the great advantage it has been to the Government of India to hear quiestions affecting the moral and material interests of the people frankly discussed. In my judgement the enlarged Councils have done nothing but good, and have been of great assistance in legislation, and I am confident that Your Highness will have the same experience in Bikaner. I tender to Your Highness my warm congratulations upon granting to your people so liberal and progressive a measure."

In regard to further political reforms and advance in British India, it has been said that it is yet too early after the 1909 Councils reforms to think of anything substantial being done after the war. In this connection, there are two points which I would respectfully beg to submit for consideration. If even in normal times the British Government were in a position after 17 years to make substantial advance in 1909, then at the present moment after such eventful 8 years which have changed the face of the world, it could hardly be contended with conviction that the time has not yet come for taking any further step. Moreover by the time that any post-war reforms are actually given effect to, it will be nearer 10 than 8 years. In view of the rapid advance already made and the fact that the majority of people in India regarded the 1909 reforms as considerably over the, it appears highly necessary as well as advisable, that further and substantial instalment should follow immediately at the end of the war. After a war of such magnitude, in which Great Britain and the whole of the civilised world are fighting in vindication of justice and rightconsness, liberty and freedom, for great and small nations, and in which, it has been the good fortune and privilege of India to have rendered loyal assistance to the utmost of her power, India naturally expects that her place and position as an integral part of the Empire, which represents the best ideals of freedom and liberty, should be assured for all time to come. No one will dispute that Great Britain should rule India through the sentiments and affections of the Indian people. Apart from all considerations of avoiding the impression that any reforms and concession have been exacted by agitation and clamour, it is an accepted maxim that he gives twice who gives quickly. Substantial progress will have to be made sooner or later—if not immediately at the end of the war, a very few years after that. What will be gained then by delay when the conclusion of the war presents an ideal opportunity which will strike the imagination? If this question is not dealt with imagination and in a bold and statesmanlike manner, it will, however incorrectly, inevitably be regarded in India as an indication of the deliberate desire of His Majesty's Government to put back the hand of the clock and of their policy to deny to the Indian people any real voice or power in their own affairs.

Without going into details, it may be mentioned that even 10 years ago the Government of India in their despatch to the Secretary of State themselves recommended wider reforms than were ultimately sanctioned by Lord Morley. In regard to some such matters at any rate, it can still less be contended that it is too early to make any further advance at all. After 8 years' actual experience, and considering the undoubted success that the new Councils have been, it could not, it is submitted, be really asserted that there is no room for further and larger development. Everything would therefore appear to point to its being essential that there should be further development on generous lines both as regards the legislative and the executive Councils of the Local Governments as well as those of the Viceroy.

No reforms leaving intact the Imperial Council, either executive of legislative, would be considered substantial or satisfactory by the people, specially after such times as the present, and I feel it my bounden duty to point out that in such a case the disappointment and sense of grievance will indeed be very acute.

The subject is too large and important to permit of its being dealt with exhaustively in a Minute of this nature. Nor do I feel conpetent to define the precise nature and extent which such further reforms should take. It however, seems to me imperative that before any final decision is arrived at by the British Government all these questions should in their various aspects and details, be thoroughly investigated by a committee of representative and liberal minded statesmen in sympathy with the ideals of popular government, who would, after careful investigation, be able to report what specific measures can immediately be adopted and by what steps in the future the ultimate goal can be reached in India. It would appear equally necessary that India should be fully represented by some of prominent men being also appointed to the Committee and that care should be taken to obtain and considers into Indian opinion on the subject.

There may be difficulties in bringing this Committee together while the present submarine and other difficulties connected with the war exist, but if, side by side with the declaration already referred to, it is also stated that such a Committee will be appointed to consider the question of constitutional reforms and progress in India, any unavoidable delay would not be of much consequence.

I would, however, venture most strongly and earnestly to urge that the declaration of policy as well as the announcement of the appointment of such a Committee should be simultaneously made without any loss of time.

**III. Greater Autonomy being granted and a lesser degree of interference with the Government of India on Provincial Governments.**

There is perhaps no need to write at length on this subject. Not only the people of India but I believe I am not incorrect in stating, both the Government of India and the Provincial Governments will welcome greater autonomy and freedom of action and a lesser degree of interference in regard to administrative and other matters which are not of Imperial concern or of first rate importance. In India it is felt that in all matters at the present moment there is need for greater decentralisation and of the delegation of considerable powers by the Secretary of State in Council to the Government of India and similarly by the Governor General in Council to the Provincial Governments, and that only in matters of high policy and of Imperial and great concern should there still be retained the strict control in matters of detail that is at pesernt exercised by the India Office.

Whereas in India it is held that at times undue and unnecessary regard has been paid generally to prestige, the fact seems to have been lost sight of that, under the existing relations between the India Office and the Government of India, the prestige of the latter in the eyes of the Indian public suffers considerably by the exessive control by the Secretary of State and from the want of decentralisation. Indian opinion further holds that except in matters of Imperial of first rate importance, the control of the future to be exercised by the India office should be in the way of influencing the main lines of the policy of the Government of India and of co-ordinating Indian policy with that of the Empire.

The instance already cited in regard to the action taken in England in connection with the establishment of a High Court in the Punjab and the Executive Council in the United Provinces are both illustrations in point and show, if I may respectfully further add, the inadvisability and danger of too much interference with the people responsible for carrying out the administration on the spot.

**IV-A Council or Assembly of Princes**

This Minute has I fear already run to very considerable length and as, in any case, I intend submitting a note so His Excellency the Viceroy specially on this subject together with some other points connected with the Indian States, I do not think I need here refer to the subject in detail. I will, however, send a copy of my note when ready.

# Annexure 2

**Speech Delivered in the Princess' Conference by His Highness the Maharajah of Bikaner, on the 3rd November, 1919, in seconding the Resolution moved by His Highness the Maharajah Scindia of Gwalior, on the victorious termination of the Great War.**

I beg to second the resolution moved by my old and valued friend, the Maharajah Scindia of Gwalior. I heartily associate myself with what His Highness has said, and am happy to join him in the tribute which he has paid to our splended Indian Army, to Lord Hardinge, to Your Excellency and the Government of India, to His Excellency General Sir Charles Monroe and the other Commanders-in-Chief in the various theatres of war; also, in view of the part which our own troops have been privileged to take in the war, to the officers, services and departments of the Imperial Government, not forgetting our friends of the Political Department and the British Officers associated with our troops.

At the victorious termination of the world-war, which so completely absorbed our attention and energies during the five dreary years of its duration, it is but natural that our thoughts should turn to the future—to the period of regeneration that has already begun and of reconstruction that lies before us. It is true we have the problems of our individual States and of our own peoples to attend to, Important though they are, the ordeal of the Great War from which we have emerged, and the comradeship which it occasioned, have necessarily left their mark upon our perspective. Consequently the things which a few years ago loomed large on our horizon have now, as a matter of course, to suffer diminution in stature—we cannot but regard them now as somewhat parochial affairs.

The close association in danger, the participation in adversity, as also the sharing of the ultimate triumph have united us—the Imperial Government and the Indian States—more closely than ever, and have led to a better realization of our respective difficulties and anxieties, our hopes and aspirations, our standpoints and ideals. They have brought home to us, better than anything else ever could, the very real identity of interests which exists between the British Government and the Indian Princes—a fact which, I venture to assert, can never be over-emphasized. Unless I am greatly mistaken, it is considerations such as these that have led His Highness the Maharajah Scindia to touch upon the Imperial aspect of our relations. Doubtless to them are also attributable some of the remarks which are today fallen from Your Excellency's lips, as also the welcome and highly gratifying announcements which you, Sir, have just made of the decision of His Imperial Majesty's Government in regard to matters of the highest import to us. Some old-time arrangements, having served their purpose will for many years, naturally stood in need of adjustment and reform, and therefore, the decisions announced must be productive of the highest good.

The end of the war leaves with the Princes the gratifying feeling of a solemn duty loyally and conscientiously performed also to the utmost of their capability and resources: with the Imperial Government it leaves the will and determination to allow nothing to remain undone which is calculated further to strengthen the bonds that already unite us.

And so we are, surely, entitled to look at the future with high hopes and to assume it to be full of bright augury. As for the relative position of the British Government and the Princes, the paramountcy of the former is beyond dispute and the relation of the latter as Allies and Friends is as freely admitted as it is clearly defined. Guyided as we are, in Your Excellency's eloquent words, by candour, loyalty, liberality and goodwill, there is no need between us for that evil thing—secret diplomacy. We devoutly hope that an era of peace and prosperity lies in front of us for many a year to come. But should fortune be fickle; should we have to face once again external aggression or internal trouble; should we have to fight the Bolshevik menace or to repel the invasion of a foolish or arrogant foe; the British Government and the Ruling Princes will assuredly continue to stand together, shoulder to shoulder, united in their loyalty and devotion to their Gracious King-Emperor. Whatever betide and come what may, the union shall abide and stand evry strain.

Maharaja Sri Ganga Singhji, Chancellor being escorted by Dr. S. Radhakrishnan, Vice Chancellor to dais to deliver the Convocation address at the Baneras Hindu University, 1941.

# GREAT MEN OF THE EAST.

## INDIAN PRINCES FOR THE COMING CONFERENCE.

**By D. COMPTON JAMES.**

The round table conference to discuss the future constitution of India is likely to have far-reaching effects on the history of that troublous country. At present two-fifths of India is governed by 700 native princes whose powers, as between state and state, vary to an extraordinary degree. Much misconception exists concerning these princes. During recent years a few of them have appeared in the news in no favourable light, and there has been a widespread tendency to take it for granted that they are, in the [illegible], capricious and dissolute rulers. Nothing could be farther from the truth. Generally the Indian princes are hard-working monarchs. A few lead lives that are definitely austere.

Hyderabad, the premier state of India, is governed by the Nizam, of whom it is said that he is the wealthiest man in [illegible]

The Maharajah of Bikanir (left) and the Maharajah of Patiala.

world. The colossal fortunes of English and American magnates shrink into insignificance when one considers the enormously valuable personal possessions of the Nizam of Hyderabad. He possesses gold and jewels the value of which no one can even estimate. One of his jewels is a life-size parrot carved from a single emerald.

Notwithstanding his incredible wealth, the personal habits and needs of the Nizam are extremely simple. He is a strict Moslem, and that alone implies no small degree of austerity. Ris[illegible] at 5 a.m., he works all day at the complex business of administering a huge territory populated largely by illiterates. His charities are many, including a grant of pensions to the ex-royal family of Turkey and large donations towards the building of a mosque in London.

Hyderabad is one of the best governed states in India. The Nizam is the titular head of the constitution. He has, and exercises, the power to amend or veto its acts, and in addition the power of life and death over criminals. Never satisfied to be a mere figurehead, he has [illegible] himself personally responsible for the control of certain branches of the activities of his Government.

After the rather startling escapade of his heir-apparency, the Maharajah of Kashmir has settled down to hard work of governing his state. As "Mr A." he was not a very impressive figure, but it must be remembered that clever crooks have made dupes of many notable men, and that the higher a victim's rank the more plastic he is likely to be in the hands of blackmailers. Since his accession to the throne of Kashmir, Sir Hari Singh has shown sound judgment and full appreciation of his responsibilities. One of the first laws he passed made it possible for a debtor to require the production of a moneylender's books for at least six years back in order that the court might be able to decide as to the equity of debt and interest. Prior to the passing of this law extortion and misery had been rampant in the state.

The Maharajah of Patiala, Chancellor of the Chamber of Princes, and head of the Sikhs, approximates more closely to our idea of an Eastern potentate. He is tall and heavily built, handsome in a florid way that is pleasing to the Indian eye. He, too, possesses some remarkable jewels, including the second largest emerald in the world, which he wears as a belt buckle. He is a very able ruler, and his conduct of the Chamber of Princes—at best a difficult task—has earned high praise from Indian civil servants and those who come into official contact with him.

"Ranji" is a name well known in England. It is the cricketing name of that delightful personality the Jam Sahib of Nawanagar. After his amazing exploits on the cricket field, the Jam Sahib has shown equal ability in the government of his state. He has revived the trade of the ancient port of Kathiawar, moribund at the time of his accession, until Bombay has had to look to its laurels. In spite of his long association with England "Ranji" does not always see eye-to-eye with the Government of India, and when he does not he can be very outspoken. He is rated as the cleverest of the Indian princes, and whenever he expresses an opinion his words are accorded very serious attention. Curiously enough, he is still a bachelor, the only one among all the ruling princes of India.

Bikanir is governed by a Maharajah whose energy is inexhaustible. For centuries it was a sandy waste with only two rivers, each of which lose themselves in the sand. Under its present ruler the revenues of the state have more than tripled and large areas have been brought under cultivation by irrigation schemes. The Maharajah of Bikanir is also noted as a big-game hunter.

The Gaekwar of Baroda is not very well known in Europe, but some of his possessions are almost household words. He owns two of the most historic diamonds in the world, the Akbar Shah, which belonged to the great emperor of that name, and the Eugenie, which was given to Queen Catherine the Great by Potemkin. He also has a durbar carpet made entirely of jewels.

A book could be written about each of the princes of India and still their possibilities would not be exhausted, so rich are their states in legend and custom. In the near future their status will be thoroughly reviewed, and it is probable that on the recommendations of the conference the new government of India will be based. Truly, a momentous occasion for the 700 rulers of India!

A newspaper cutting depicting the Maharaja of Bikaner and the Maharaja of Patiala.

Above we give the first of a series of cartoons, specially drawn for "The Times of India", of the delegates from India who are attending the Round Table Conference.

A caricature of the Delegates to Round Table Conference at London. Maharaja Ganga Singhji is shown as a central figure.

Maharaja Ganga Singhji addressing the Princes at a meeting of Chamber of Princes at Taj Mahal Hotel, Bombay, 1936.

Maharaja Ganga Singhji at a dinner hosted by the Indian Princes in his honour on his

A group photograph taken during the visit of Maharaja Ganga Singhji to Mysore State – 1928.

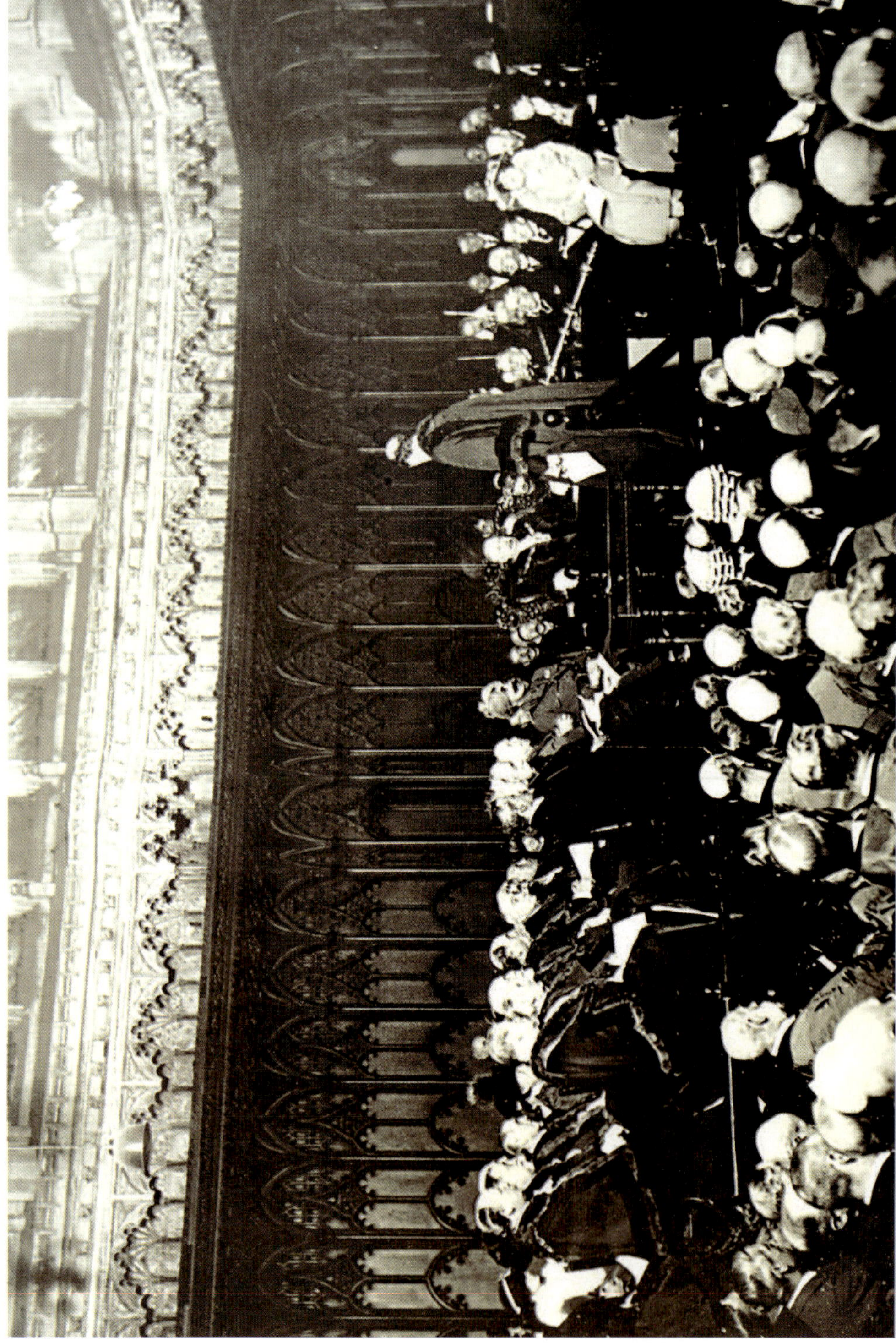

Maharaja Ganga Singhji inspecting a Guard of Honour during the 1st World War, 1915.

Maharaja Ganga Singhji with members of the delegation to the League of Nations held at Geneva in 1930.

Maharaja Ganga Singhji addressing the members of the Press during the Silver Jubilee celebrations of King George V at London in 1936.

Maharaja Ganga Singhji with Girija Shankar Bajpai, ICS, who was the secretary to the Indian delegation to the League of Nations, held at Geneva in 1930.

# Annexure 3

## Extract from His Highness' Speech delivered in the Chamber of Princes on the 24th November, 1924

Furthermore, the logic is difficult to justify that only Princes enjoying permanent salutes of 19 guns and over should be exempted from the payment of customs duties whilst the Rulers of smaller or poorer States should have to pay them, and the only logical conclusion, I submit, is that at least all Princes who are Members in their own right of the Chamber of Princes, should enjoy this courtesy and compliment. In fact, I would personally go even further and say that—even though monetary considerations are not, as I have said, the basis of this recommendation—the smaller and the poorer the states, the greater the necessity for this exemption and courtesy. Indeed, I would go still further and say that, if it is a matter of practical policies, not only the 108 Princes who are in their own right Members of the Chamber of Princes, but also all the more important of the Ruling Chiefs—and in this term I do not include the petty Chiefs with practically no powers and possessions—should, if possible, also enjoy this privilege and courtesy.

# Annexure 4

## Speech Delivered by His Highness the Maharajah of Bikaner in moving the resolution regarding joint Deliberations in the Chamber of Princes on the 26th January 1926.

*Your Excellency; Your Highnesses;*

The Resolution which stands in my name reads as folows:

"That a Committee be appointed consisting of Princes and Ministers, to consider in consultation with Representatives of the British Government and, to report to the Chamber of Princes

(1) the best means of safeguarding the interests of the Indian States on occassions when an enquiry in undertaken into matters of common interest to the States and to British India, and

(2) What machinery should be devised for giving effect to the proposal contained in para 311 of the Montagu-Chelmsford Report regarding joint deliberations."

2. It is necessary that I should at the outset give a brief history of the subject; and in this connection I would first remind the House that in the 'Outlines of the Scheme' prepared by the Committee of Princes which was elected by Your Highnesses in November 1917, with the express object of formulating proposals in connection with the necessary and important reforms affecting the States—which it is gratifying to find are all embodied in Chapter X of the Montagu-Chelmsford Report—the following paragraphs bearing on the subject under discussion are published in the Explanatory Note:

"Committee of Reference for matters of Joint Interest."

"This proposals has reference to the protection and guardianship of Imperial interests and matters of common concern to British Provinces and Indian states in regard to which the States have hitherto had no voice. There are important subjects dealt with by the Government of India which are of common interest both to British India and the Indian.States. A change in the tariffs, a modification in the currency policy, readjustment of the salt tax, a decision of questions of emigration and immigration, the efficient and progressive administration of the Posts, Telegraph and Railway Departments, all these affect the peoples of the States almost as much as they to those of Btitish India. The effects of these decisions are not less real or onerous for the reason that they operate only indirectly on the people of the States."

The following was the actual proposal contained in the 'Outlines of the Scheme' which the Princes on the Committee, after obtaining the views and suggestions of their Brother Princes, placed before Lord Chelmsford, who was then Viceroy, and Mr. Edwin Montagu, who was then Secretary of State, at Viceregal Lodge in Delhi in February, 1918:

"In view of the long felt need that the Indian States should have an adequate voice in matters affecting them either in their individual relations with British India or in matters which affect them jointly with British India, a Joint Committee shall be constituted composed of representatives nominated by the Chamber of Ruling Princes and an equal number of delegates selected by the Government of India from the Legislature concerned. To this Committee shall be referred for expression of opinion all questions coming before any Legislature, Imperial or Provincial, the determination of which may affect the interests of all or any of the States in India. The reference in each case shall be answered and the report of the Committee duly considered before a final decision is taken by the Legislature concerned."

In the course of the discussion, which then ensued, it will suffice to mention, as then explained by me that "the scheme put forward was only an outline and that it must necessarily be elastic. The Ruling Princes were not in a position to make definite suggestions, but they did not want to be mixed up with Legislative or other bodies in British India, since the outcome of that might be mutual interference in one another's affairs. The main point was that facilities should be given for consultation in some form of other."

Ultimately the proposal found a place in para 311 of the Joint Report fro which the following extract will suffice for the purpose:

"Our last proposal is intended to provide some means of deliberation between the Government of India and the Princes on matters of common interest to both, and so to ensure that as far as possible decisions affecting India as a whole shall be reached after the views of the Darbars have been taken into account. In the past in certainly has occasionally happened that the States were vitally affected by decision taken without reference to them; and yet no machinery for such collective consultation with them has higherto existed, It seems to us that they have a clear right to ask for it in the future. We have abandoned for the present all consideration of suggestions that the Ruling Princes, or some representatives of their Order, should be members of the Council of State, Not only would this at the present stage infringe the doctrine of non-interference on the part of the Princes in the affairs of British India, but we are satisfied that few, in any, of the Princes themselves are ready for such a step. On the other hand, it seems to us that, when a Council of Princes has been established, and when a Council of State created, the machinery will exist for bringing the senatorial institutions of British India into closer relations when necessary with the Rulers of the Native States. Matters affecting the native States generally, or the native States and British India in common, or the Empire, might, as we have seen, be referred to the Council of Princes . it would thus be possible for the Viceroy, when he thought fit, to arrange for joint deliberation and discussion between the Council of State and the Council of Princes, or between representatives of each body."

When the various reforms proposed in Chapter X of the Joint Report were placed on the Agenda of the Princes' conference in January 1919, His Excellency the Viceroy in the course of his opening speech referring to this particular question said :

"Your Highness will recollect that in dealing with the constitution of British India we have proposed in the Joint Report a council of State, which, to use the words of the Report, "shall take its part in ordinary Legislative business and shall be the final Legislative authority in matters which the Government regards as essential." "What we have in view is to provide means of deliberation between the Government of India and Your Highnesses on matters of common interest by joint deliberation and discussion between the Council of State and the Council of Princes or between representatives of each body. Such joint deliberation would take place only at the instance of the Viceroy and it will be obvious that in making use of the provision the Viceroy would attach the greatest weight to any wishes which Your Highnesses might from time to time express in the matter. The arrangement would be permissible only and at the outset I suggest that simplicity and freedom from restrictions will be a supreme merit of a scheme, which rightly used, may well hold a rich store of benefit for this great country which we all love and in which the Princes and Chiefs have a joint heritage with the peoples of British India."

The Princes at that conference resolved:

"that this Conference recommend that the consideration of the question of the means to be provided for joint deliberation between the Government of India and the Princes on matters of common interest to both, should be postponed until the Chamber of Princes and Chiefs has been established and until the result of the proposals made for the introduction of Reforms in British India is definitely known."

This is where the matter now stands. The pre-occupations of the War and its after-math have in themselves kept us all more than occupied. The Chamber of Princes only came into being in February 1921, when at the same time effect was given to the memorable Declaration of the Policy of His Majesty's Government of the 20th August 1917 for constitutional advance in India by the inauguration by His Royal Highness the Duke of Connaught of the Council of State and the Imperial Legislative Assembly. And although the Princes and States would have found it beneficial to their interests had some machinery been devised and effect been given before now in regard to the question of joint deliberations, the delay might perhaps also bring some compensating advantages. We have had breathing space to watch the working of the Chamber of Princes and the Princes' Standing Committee on the one side, and the working of the Imperial legislatures on the other; and there is little doubt that we shall now be in a better position to consider the question fully in all its bearings and to devise some machinery for giving effect to the objects with which this Resolution has today been moved.

In the meanwhile I may observe that the matter has not been lost sight of. In my speech, when taking part in the debate in this Chamber in February 1923 in regard to the Indian States (Protection against disaffection) Bill, I ventured to make the following observations:

"I cannot help thinking that if there were some suitable machinery in existence at the time when this unfortunate arose, where by joint deliberations could have been held between the representatives of the Imperial Government, of the Princes and of the Imperial Legislatures for the purpose of discussing matters of Imperial or joint interest, some at least of the difficulty and misunderstanding which surrounded this matter, might have been avoided to the great advantage of every body concerned."

After referring very briefly to the past history of the case I added that I had raised the point in our Standing Committee in November 1922 and expressed the hope that a scheme would be evolved and discussed in the Chamber before long, which would meet with such cases and emergencies in the future.

I think, however, that there can be no question that the time has now arrived—and if anything is overdue—when all of us concerned should give this matter, which so closely concerns the interests of the Princes, their Governments and their subjects—and I venture to add the interests of the Imperial Government—the earnest, considered and urgent attention which it now demands.

Important decisions taken by the Government of India or by His Majesty's government, and the policy formulated and the line of action followed in British India, very often closely affects the Indian States and their interests. These range over a wide field, some of which even directly and other often indirectly affect the Indian States.

I do not think I need take up any more time in dilating upon the necessity for joint deliberations. Nor need I dwell at length on the need for considering and devising the best means of safeguarding the interests of the Indian States on occasions when an enquiry is undertaken into matters of common interest to States and British India. The difficulties experienced by the States in getting the evidence of their Ministers and others concerned recorded before the Fiscal Commission are of recent origin. Such Commissions and Committees are not infrequently appointed by the British Government—for instance one such Commission, viz., the Currency Commission has not yet concluded its labours—and deals with matters which closely affect the States and their subjects. Enquiries by Royal Commissions or Committees appointed in India generally also have a direct or indirect bearing on the problems of Indian States. And here I am sure that it would be the desire of the Princes of India—both those present here and those who have been unable to come—that I should tender to Your Excellency our very sincere and grateful thanks for your acceding to the request which I submitted to you as Chancellor for the representation of the Indian States on the Indian Sandhurst Committee by the nomination of Major Zorawar Singhji of

Bhavanagar.

In certain quarters the view is held that the only adequate method of safeguarding the interests of the Indian States on occasions when an enquiry is undertaken into matters of common interest is that His Excellency the Viceroy should be pleased to provide for the representation of Indian States on the personnel of all Royal Commissions as well as on all Commissions and Committees of enquiry appointed in India, to investigate matters in which the States are concerned. The advantages of such a procedure are obvious; and I think I have sufficiently spoken on this aspect of the question already. In some other quarters the apprehension is entertained that it might be unwise for the Indian States and dangerous as regards their Constitutional position and sovereign rights, for them to take part in such Commissions and enquiries by direct representation. But I submit that the wording of my Resolution is not only non-controversial but that it will serve the very object we have in view, viz., that the Committee which I moved should be appointed, consisting of Princes and Ministers, should consider in consultation with representatives of the British Government what are the best means of safeguarding the interests of the Indian States when such enquiries are undertaken in matters of common interest; and any dangers to the Princes and States will no doubt be duly taken note of by such a Committee in the course of their investigations and, we hope, also adequately provided for.

It only remains for me to emphasize that in moving this Resolution regarding joint deliberations, and the consideration of the question as to what would be the best means of safeguarding the interests of the States in enquiries of Common concern, we are actuated by no unfriendliness whatever to our brother Indians in British India, nor are we actuated by any desire to retard the advance of constitutional progress therein. It has already been publicly declared on our united behalf in the past that we have no desire to encroach upon the domestic affairs of British India, any more than we want anybody from outside our States to interfere with the affairs of our own States and our Governments. All that we desire is to safeguard the interest of our States and our subjects where they directly or indirectly involved and this is the object and the scope of my Resolution which, I am confident, will be in accord with Your Highnesses' views.

In asking for the concurrence of this House to this Resolution, I also propose that the following be appointed on the Committee:

Princes:

1. His Highness the Maharaja of Jammu and Kashmir;
2. His Highness the Maharaja of Patiala;
3. His Highness the Maharaja of Alwar ;
4. His Highness the Jam Sahib of Navanagar; and
5. The Mover.

Ministers:

6. One representative of the Mysore State;
7. Sir Manubhai Mehta of Baroda;
8. Colonel K.N. Haksar of Gwalior;
9. Sir Prabha Shankar Pattani of Bhavnagar; and
10. Professor Rushbrook-Williams of Patiala.

# Annexure 5

## Inaugural Speech Delivered in Bombay, on the 6th June 1938, by General His Highness the Maharajah of Bikaner, G.C.S.I., G.C.I.E., G.C.V.O., G.C.E., K.C.B., A.D.C., LL.D., President of the Chamber of Princes Reorganisation Committee

*Your Highness the Chancellor, Your Highness, and my other Colleagues on the Chamber of Princes Reorganisation Committee;*

In view of the supreme importance to us all of the questions which are to engage our attention and of the fact that the present is a time even more than normally critical for the entire body of the Princes and States of India, I would ask for your permission to make certain preliminary observations. In asking for your indulgence for detaining you for, I fear, some little time, I trust that by the time we finish our labours it will be found that what I am going to place before you in this speech, far from involving a waste of the time of Your Highnesses and of the Ministers present, has, on the contrary, saved time and in some ways facilitated the work before us.

2. Our principal task, as I conceive it, is to endeavour to formulate a scheme which, by the grace of God, would once more bring about real, and, I pray, lasting, harmony and unity amongst the States, both big and small, especially in the Chamber of Princes—a unity which I am sure everyone of Your Highnesses and the Ministers present here desire as ardently as I do; and I am no less certain that you all are equally anxious to see the Chamber restored to its original potential utility. And I am most anxious, as far as it lies in my power, to dispel the doubts and the clouds of suspicion and mistrust which unfortunately exist at this moment.

3. I am deeply conscious of the honour done me and the mark of confidence shown me by His Highness the Chancellor and my brother Princes on the Standing Committee by their apponting me to be the President of the Chamber of Princes Reorganisation Committee. But I have of ten wished that these heavy responsibilities had been laid on some other shoulders and that it had been possible for me to take part in the work of our committee as one of the other working members.

4. When we met in Delhi in February last it was my intention to press that His late Highness the Maharajah of Patiala should be appointed President of this Committee, but by that time His late Highness was unfortunately too ill even to be present. And his untimely demise—which we all so deeply mourn and which is an irreparable loss not only to the Chamber of Princes but to the whole Princely Order—has, to my great regret and that, I am sure, of all of you, deprived us of his valuable assistance in the delicate and inricate task with which we are faced.

5. I am, however, happy in the thought that His late Highness of Patiala's heart was set as firmly and deeply, as is mine, on the restoration of harmony amongst the States, and that, in spite of his serious illness, His late Highness kept in close touch with me on this question until a few days before his widely lamented demise.

6. It would have been more approprate if His Highness the Maharajah Jam Sahib, our present Chancellor, could have accepted the Presidentship of the Committee; but in his modesty he desired that the task should be undertaken by me.

7. Therefore, when the strong desire was expressed by His Highness the Maharajah Jam Sahib and the other Princes present in Delhi that I should undertake these duties, I felt that lowed it to my Order and to the States to accept the invitation. And I am sure that I shall not be appealing in vain when I beg for the friendly co-operation and cordial assistance of Your Highnesses and my other friends on this Committee in the labours that lie before us.

8. For my part, I would assure Your Highnesses, and you gentlemen, that all my efforts as President of this Committee will be solely directed to the attainment of our common object, namely, the restoration of unity amongst the States—never more needed than in the present anxious times—so as to make of our Chamber of Princes a strong body, capable effectively of securing the interests of the Princes and the States as a whole, and that I shall put forth my best endeavour to help in the formulation of proposals designed to meet the legitimate claims and aspirations of the bigger as well as the smaller States.

9. Copies of the Resolution, passed in Delhi on the 17th February last, by the Princes' Standing Committee, have already been circulated to you all. But I would ask for the further indulgence of Your Highnesses and the Ministers present in reading out its full text, which, if I may say so, summarises the position effectively and will, therefore, bear repetition here, if only for the sake of elucidating the weighty reasons which led the Standing Committee to take this important decision.

1. "The position in which the Indian States find themselves today is unquestionably one of extreme gravity. Their difficulties have grown and accomulated during the past years till they have become complex and serious; and this at a time when the States are passing through one of the most critical periods in modern history.
2. British India has become more organised and more able effectively to press its claims on the British Government, whilst the Chamber of Princes, as an effective organisation of the States, has, lately, through diverse reasons, lost much of its effectiveness to safeguard their interests. This has been chiefly due to lack of unity amongst the Princes and the consequent inability to take concerted action.
3. The necessity first of cordial unity and next of collective deliberation and concerted action has been rendered all the more imperative in view of the recently enacted Constitutional Reforms which so vitally affect the States. Indeed, the need for unity amongst the States as a whole was never more pressing than it is at the present moment. And the great political value of the combined action of the States cannot be over-emphasised.
4. Confronted with all these difficulties on the one hand, we fmd on the other that the one instrument which we had had created, viz., the Chamber of Princes, has lost its edge and is no longer able to exert united influence for the purpose of obtaining recognition of the legitimate demands of the States and of securing for them the weight and attention to which the importance of the States entitles them.
5. A few of the bigger States chose to stand aloof from it from its very inception. Several other Rulers of the bigger States went out of it in recent years. As a result we have been officially told more than once that its executive body, namely, the standing Committee, cannot be regarded as possessing the authority to speak in the name of the States as a body, more particularly the larger States.
6. This impression of disunity has been deepened in all minds by the present system of elections. The evil has undeniably tended to eliminate a force obviously of great political value, namely, the association, in a position of responsibility, of some of the most important States.
7. There is dissatisfaction at both ends of our ranks. While the bigger States have felt that the present Constitution of the Chamber did not give due weight to their position and their

extensive interests, some of the smaller States have felt that, regardless of the attributes which they unquestionably possess in common with other States who have been admitted, they have been arbitrarily excluded from the Membership of the Chamber in their own right. There is between them all the common ground of identical interests, but there is and has been an absence of united action through a medium combining those definite and well-marked interests.

8. The time has now come for an earnest and determined effort to formulate a scheme whereby the bigger States might once again be closely associated with the Chamber of Princ es, and its strength further enhanced by the admission in their own right to the Membership of the Chamber of Princes of such States as are entitled thereto on certain defined tests, so that it might once again become a forum for joint deliberation and an authorised organ for articulating the united opinion of all the States and for concerted action. Thus alone can it discharge the functions for which it was originally created. Such a scheme must be preceded by an investigation which must embrace a convincing description of the trend of events during the past years, a frank exposition of the causes which have tended to weaken the position of the Chamber, and by focussing those trends and causes the investigation should lead up to the formulation of proposals which, by their reasonableness, would elicit a large measure of support.
9. The Standing Committee therefore resolves that a Committee be appointed to formulate proposals for the reorganisation of the Chamber of Princes, and invite the following Princes to serve on the Chamber of Princes Reorganisation Committee.
10. The Committee further resolves that, with the permission of the Rulers concerned, the following Ministers be associated with the Chamber of Princes Reorganisation Committee-".

10. It will, I trust, be agreed that the whole of the Resolution of the Standing Committee, which I have just ventured to read out, deserves our closest and most careful attention. But I should like, if I may, especially to emphasize three important points, which form the crux of the problem:

(1) It is clear that dissatisfaction with the present unfortunate state of affairs is not confined only to the bigger States, who desire and I submit not unreasonably—that due weight should be given

to their position and their extensive interests. Dissatisfaction exists also among some of the smaller States, who have felt that, regardless of the attributes which they unquestionably possess and which as I have felt all along, clearly entitle them to Membership in their own right of the Chamber of Princes, they have so far been arbitrarily excluded from that privilege.

(2) I have the strongest reasons, therefore, for hoping that if we succeed in formulating a scheme by which confidence will be restored in the minds of the bigger States, not only will unity once again be brought about, but that the result will be that all the bigger States, with hardly any exception, will willingly associate themselves with the activities of the Chamber. The resulting position will be even better than it was in the past, and joint deliberations and concerted action amongst the States as a whole will once again be assured.

(3) Our scheme of reform must also provide for, and facilitate, the entry of such other States as, on certain defined tests, are clearly entitled to the Membership of the Chamber in their own right, so that the Chamber may gain a further accession of strength.

To this end, it is incumbent on us, as the Resolution of the Standing Committee states, to examine the causes which have tended to weaken the position of the Chamber and to propose means whereby such harmful and disquieting factors can be eliminated.

11. Here, may I digress for a moment to make one other preliminary observation? I trust that it is unnecessary for me to assure Your Highnesses and the Ministers that nothing is farther from my intention than to say anything, in my opening remarks or in the course of our discussions, which might have even the semblance of a controversial or partisan character. Still less do I desire to score any debating points. For, I feel that I shall be voicing the sentiments of the Members of this Committee when I say that the scoring of debating points is totally unsuitable in all cases where the interests of the Princes and the States are concerned; and the matters which we have now under discussion are, in any case, of far too great importance, and the times for too critical, for us to indulge in any such really fruitless triumphs.

12. If we are to achieve the object for which this Committee has been appointed, it will, I am sure, be agreed that it would be neither wise, nor desirable, nor even expedient, for any of us to take up an attitude of intransigence or to resort to hampering technicalities. We must rather look facts in the face, for we shall be unable to solve the problem if we ignore facts and the state of affairs which unhappily

confront us today.

13. It is undeniable that a situation has developed which has made the question of the reorganization of the Chamber of Princes urgent and vital. Whatever the causes—and it is no part of my duty or that of Your Highnesses and the other Members present here to apportion blame—the irrefutable fact unfortunately stares us in the face that most of the larger States have dissociated themselves from the activities of the Chamber and have thereby rendered our organization weak to the point of being dangerous to our interests.

14. I will not take up time by referring to the earlier days when the States in the Chamber were happily united and it went from strength to strength, and with it the prestige and the honour and dignity of the Princes and States, and when, in many ways, the rights and interests of the States were not only effectively safeguarded, but in several important directions lost ground was regained. In 1931, for instance, all the States in India, except Indore and perhaps Mysore, were associated with the work of the Chamber; Hyderabad, Baroda, Kashmir, Travancore and other big States, which have now definitely withdrawn from our activities, were supporting the Chamber with contributions and by the active association of their Ministers. That, alas is not the state of affairs today.

15. The States that have thus withdrawn from the Chamber represent very large political, financial and other interests. The process of withdrawal has been continuous and uninterrupted. A few of us of the bigger States who have so far continued to remain in the Chamber have done so, not because they dissociated themselves from the views and anxieties, generally speaking, of the other larger States who have gone out, but because they have so far felt that if they also withdrew the situation would become even more critical and the death knell of the Chamber itself may be sounded—a calamity, which, it is superfluous for me to say, cannot but have the most disastrous results for the States, both big and small. And some, like myself, have not been without hope that when, at long last, the time came for this question to be taken up by the Princes, as it happily has come now, timely and effectual measures will be taken and the impending calamity averted.

16. May I here also emphasize a further point, which perhaps has been lost sight of in the heat and strife of party politics—which, I venture to say with all respect, are such outstanding and marring features of the Chamber politics of the day, and have brought ridicule on us in British and British Indian Circles and, instead of enabling our Chamber to be the organ of a united Princely Order, have

unfortunately tended of late to make it weaker and weaker as each year passed by? I would remind all concerned that, to some extent, the Chamber of Princes was conceived as a counterpart—definitely not as a counterweight—to the Montagu—Chelmsford Reforms in British India. It was apprehended that a devolution of power to the Provinces even to the extent contemplated in the Act of 1919 might adversely affect the interests of the States; and it was, therefore, considered essential to have an organisation for the Princes and States to safeguard their rights and interests. By the Government of India Act of 1935, the Constitutional Reforms in the Provinces have gone far beyond the stage contemplated in the Act of 1919, while our Organisation has unquestionably not only become weaker, but disorganised. An examination of the Constitution of the Chamber including, of course, its Executive body, has thus, I submit, become inevitable from this point of view alone.

17. I have often wondered whether the seriousness of the situation and the extreme weakness of the Chamber of Princes at the present moment have been widely and seriously recognised, or the painful and glaring fact that, at least during the last 30 or 40 years, and certainly since 1916 when the Princes Conferences first began to be held, followed in 1921 by the institution of the Chamber of Princes, the prestige of the Princes has never stood so low as, alas! it does today. It was not so low even during Lord Curzon's Viceroyalty. And I submit that it is for Your Highnesses and the Ministers to give to this disconcerting aspect of the question too your earnest consideration and to examine the casuses that have contributed to this unhappy state of affairs. If that is done, the great deterioration which has taken place will leap to the eye.

18. I would urge with all respect that we should not shut our eyes to such glaring and incontrovertible facts as that the Chamber and its Standing Commttee have at the present moment really ceased to be the accredited spokesmen of the States. As most of those present here must know, we have been actually told more than once that the Chamber, and with it, naturally, the Standing Committee, as they exist today, are not representative of the States.

19. We can leave alone earlier instances. But Your Highnesses and the Ministers present do not need to be reminded that when last year, during the Session of the Chamber of Princes, the officiating Chancellor, His Highness the Maharaj-Rana of Dholpur, preferred the request—and that too in writing—that a Resolution be discussed in the open Chamber on the question of the Federal negotiations, he was informed that the Chamber of today was not representative

enough to put forward proposals of such a nature on behalf of the States as a whole—and this in spite of the Resolutions passed in the full and formal Sessions of the Chamber of Princes in 1931 and 1932, to the effect that the Federal Constitution in its completed form and the draft bill relating thereto should be examined by the Chamber as well as by each individual State and that the discussions and negotiations undertaken by the representatives of the Chamber would be subject to the final confirmation and ratification by the Chamber as well as by each individual State.

20. All this, if the States had continued united and to act in concern, would have been impossible.

21. Again, when His Highness the late Maharajah of Patiala addressed the Political Secretary requesting that the representatives of the Chamber may, in accordance with previous practice, be associated with the trade negotiations with Britain which were then under contemplation, the reply received was, I gather, that the views of the States should be communicated to the Government of India through individual representations.

22. In fact, on these and other not infrequent occasions, we have been clearly told that the Chamber and its Standing Committee, as matters stand at present, have ceased to represent the States as a whole and especially the bigger States.

23. These, Your Highnesses and gentlemen, are significant facts which cannot be denied and which, I submit, in themselves are sufficient to dispel any doubt that may still be felt with regard to the imperative necessity of a serious consideration of the problem and of our making a serious effort to reconstitute our Chamber, so as to make it once again an organ of our joint deliberation and concerted action.

24. One injurious result of this lack of unity and of the present state of affairs has been that many important matters, which might have been dealt with and brought to a satisfactory conclusion in the past few years, still remain pending. Take for example, questions of supreme personal importance to the Princes and their Dynasties, like:

(1) Commissions of Enquiry;
(2) Successions of Heirs—Apparent;
(3) Ceremonials, which involve matters relating to the honour, dignity, and prestige of Rulers and States;

or matters of no less importance to us, such as:

(4) Courts of Arbitration;
(5) Armies and the defence of our States, with which are connected Schemes for Internal Security;
(6) Censorship of telegrams in times of emergency, so necessary in these troublesome times;
(7) Sovereign rights of the States in Cantonments and other Ceded Areas;
(8) Retrocession of jurisdiction over railway lands; and
(9) Several other matters of political and economic importance affecting the vital rights and interests of the States.

I need not take up time by mentioning other instances some of which at least are of equal importance.

25. Another result of the withdrawal of most of the bigger States is that the finances of the Chamber today are in a very critical condition; in fact it can fairly be said that the Chamber is at present on the verge of bankruptcy.

26. I would beg Your Highnesses and gentlemen to believe that behind the proposal for the reorganisation and reform of the Chamber of Princes there is no Machiavellian scheme nor any deep-rooted plot that I know of on the part of any of the bigger States or individuals. Nor is there any intention or desire on the part of anyone—least of all on mine, your President—that we should rush through this important matter or, as has been suggested, to formulate a scheme exparte, and so on. Nor, again, is there may faction, party, or section of the Princes that I am aware of who are out to reorganise the Chamber "nearer to its own heart's desire".

27. Any proposals on the subject that have been put forward in any detail will, I think you will all agree, necessarily have to be examined; and, since none of us would, I am sure, desire a rambling and prolonged discussion, it might be the opinion of this Committee that we should take some such scheme as that put forward by the Hydari Committee as a basis of our discussion, and examine its merits and weak points. The problem is at once a complex and a delicate one; and obviously no scheme of this nature can claim to be perfect. To this matter I have been giving anxious thought for a long time; and in some of the proposals that have been put forward I have myself detected certain details which seem to require further consideration. For instance, taking certain well recognised tests which are officially applied for the purpose of gauging the importance of States inter se, I cannot conceive a scheme to be wholly satisfactory which excludes some important and larger Principalities. Personally, I should have

liked to have seen included all the 17 Gun, and other important, States amongst those who, it has been proposed by the Hydari Committee, should hereafter have permanent seats on the reformed Standing Committee.

28. But let me emphasise that it has never been proposed by anyone that no alternative scheme should be discussed here by us. That, it is perfectly open to anyone of Your Highnesses and the Ministers to do, should you so desire; and I—and I am sure everyone else—would welcome it, provided that any alternative scheme is practicable—i.e., gives due weight to two essentials, namely, the number of lives affected, and the magnitude of economic and political interests involved. Without satisfying these tests any scheme must obviously fail to achieve unity. It is, I submit, our clear duty to see to it also that the scheme adopted effectively deals with and provides a practical remedy for eradicating the root causes which have done incalculable harm to our Chamber, and led to the secession of most of the bigger States—causes which, to the knowledge of many of us, have furthermore actually prevented sveral other Princes, including those of the so-called smaller States, from attending the Chamber and facing the unpleasantness and other attendant evils of elections and the canvassing and propaganda connected therewith. I for one—and I am sure I can say the same on behalf of many of us here—shall be very glad to give any such alternative proposals the most earnest and careful attention.

29. Nothing contained in the Resolution of the Standing Committee is more correct or—bearing in mind the objects in view—more to the point than the statement in paragraph 6 to the effect that disunity has been deepened in all minds by the present system of elections and that this evil has undeniably tended to destroy a force obviously of great political value, namely, the association in a position of joint responsibility of some of the most important States.

30. Eliminate the present most harmful, and what undoubtedly, is at the same time, for the Princes, most undignified, system of elections and the canvassing and propaganda attendant thereon, and we shall-it is my firm conviction—have eliminated at least 80 per cent of the evils which have led to the non-participation of several States and which, God forbid, if continued, will, as surely as night follows day, lead to many more States going out; and such withdrawals will by no means be confined solely to the bigger States. The only result, I gravely fear, can be the death, without even a decent burial, of the Chamber of Princes, which we were able to get established at the sacrifice of much time and trouble.

31. One essential and wholesome remedy of this fundamental evil would be open voting where votes have to be taken or recorded. This would effectively do away with canvassing as it exists today, and its consequent evils.

32. I have heard it said that convassing and propaganda are only to be expected in any democratic system, and that elections and voting which obtain in the Chamber are part of such a system. I trust that I shall be absolved of the charge of being personal or controversial, if I say, in the interest of the izzat and dignity and the good name and well-being of the Princes and States, that this argument, pushed to its logical conclusion, would mean that we should also have wholesome checks and safeguards on no less democratic lines in regard to elections—i.e., make ourselves amenable to the discipline provided elsewhere, e.g., in British India, and even in democratic England, whereby elections in certain contingencies can be impugned, and after enquiry by legal process declared to be null and void and so on. Just imagine the indignity of deposits, their forfeiture, and the ignominy of the verdict of corrupt practice, etc. !

33. In order that we may be enabled to formulate the best scheme possible and one which is likely to elicit the largest measure of support amongst the Princes and States, big as well as small, and fairly satisfy the legitimate claims and aspirations of both categories of States, as well as dispel the suspicious and apprehensions which are unfortunately entertained in certain quarters, it is essential that all points of view should be fully placed before this Committee—as they are actually represented today in its personnel. And as time is of the essence, it is imperative that any flaws in, or any objections to, any schemes discussed by us during our deliberations, should be ventilated here and now, instead of being raised at a subsequent date. Otherwise, valuable time would be lost, and interminable difficulties would be experienced and obstacles would arise in our path. I would, therefore, as your President, beg to all the Princes and Ministers to speak out frankly. I feel sure I am also voicing the feelings of all present here when I appeal for constructive proposals and, in view of the vital importance of the matter, for the avoidance of obstructive tactics.

34. Faced as we are with a serious situation, when our position is threatened from many quarters, I would also request, with all the earnestness, I can command, that personal rivalries and party feelings may be eschewed, at least while we are engaged on our present task.

35. His Highness the Maharajah of Dewas (Junior), whom I had the pleasure of meeting here the other day, and His Highness of Bilaspur are unfortunately unable to assist in our labours as they have

had to proceed to Europe owing to ill health. I regret that His Highness the new Maharajah of Patiala, who had been added as a Member of this Committee, and His Highness the Nawab of Bahawalpur have been prevented from coming owing to urgent matters demanding their presence in their States. His Highness the Maharaj-Rana of Dholpur was also invited to serve on this Committee; but I greatly regret that he was unable to accede to our request in the matter. In order to make our Committee still more representative and to carry further confidence, some more Ministers too have, with the consent of the Standing Committee, been added, namely:

Nawab Aliyavar Jung, Hyderabad;
Sardar C.S. Angre, Gwalior;
Qazi Sir Azizuddin Ahmed, Datia;
Sardar K.M. Panikkar, Patiala;
Mr. V.M. Pawar, Dewas (Junior);
Rao Bahadur Y.A. Thombare, Sangli; and
Colonel Zorawar Singhji, Panna; as also
Mir Maqbool Mahmood.

36. In connection with the question of devising the best scheme possible for the reorganisation of the Chamber of Princes, it should have been unnecessary for me to have to refer to one other detail. But to my great surprise I have heard it suggested that the present move is a plot on my part to secure once again the office of the Chancellor!

37. May I remind you all that I have persistently refused to stand for the Chancellorship ever since I relinguished that Office in 1926—in spite of a very large number of my brother Princes having at the time strongly pressed me not to give it up, and on many subsequent occasions to stand again for the Chancellorship? I would also invite attention to what I have frequently said and written—both in public and in private—in this connection, making it clear that I had no ambitions, nor the least desire, in all ordinary circumstances, to stand again for the Chancellorship, and that, if I could have consulted my own personal wishes, I would have long ago asked to be excused from standing for election even to the Standing Committee.

38. Consequently, no one need have any fear that there is a danger of my desiring to stand against anyone for the unenviable post of Chancellor! And I do beg that, both now and later on, this all important question of the reform of the Chamber will be considered irrespective of any personalities and on a plane higher than that of

party politics.

39. I now turnto the question of the admission, in their own right, to the Membership of the Chamber of Princes, of certain other smaller States. That is a matter on which at least I hope there is not going to be much divergence of opinion. As you are aware a Criteria Committee was appointed some time ago to consider what tests should be prescribed which would entitle more States to be admitted. That Committee has unfortunately not yet met. of its five Members, His late Highness of Patiala, is, alas ! no more; Thier Highnesses of Dew as (Junior) and Bilaspur are in England; and His Highness of Wankaner and I are the only two Members present here. Thus, my hope cannot be realised of holding a meeting of the Criteria Committee here after we have finished our labours in connection with the reorganisation of the Chamber. The labours and recommendations of the Chamber of Princes Reorganisation Committee will, I have nodoubt, help to simplify the task of the task of the Criteria Committee when it meets later on.

40. Contrary to the impression which has been created, I have every sympathy for the smaller States. I have written and spoken publicly on many occasions on this question. I am all in favour, and have been so for the last five years and more, of the admission of certain smaller States on clearly defined tests which have yet to be settled. The only difference between myself and some others is as to the means by which this should be done. I have held all along that to deal with this question first would be to lessen the chances of such admission and, what is far more serious to us—not only those who are already Members, but also those who seek to become new Members, of the Chamber—would be calculated by itself to bring about the complete disruption of our Chamber. Once the necessary reform has been carried out and confidence restored in the minds of the bigger States, I am in a position positively to state that there will be no objection on the part of the bigger States to the admission of such smaller States as are clearly entitled to be admitted.

41. When there is dissatisfaction amongst both the bigger and the smaller States with the present state of affairs, and the causes which have contributed to that have to be examined and proposals formulated which would elicit general support, a Committee like ours, which has to deal with the reorganisation of the Chamber, could not possibly ignore the interests of the smaller States. For, no reform, of the Chamber could be complete or equitable which ignored the interests of the smaller States as well. And to think only of the bigger, and not of the smaller, States would, I repeat, be unfair, and to this I

personally could never be a party. For, without desiring to bring in any controversial matter I am constrained to remark that, in spite of the impression to the contrary which has been created amogst the smaller States, I have, as of old, still the greatest sympathy and friendship for the smaller States, whose battles I have unceasingly fought for the last 22 years and more, and whose cause and legitimate rights and interests I have unfailingly championed all the time, and I hope God may enable me to do so to the end of my days, whatever the outcome of our present discussions. I challenge anyone to prove anything to the contrary.

42. I may, on further consideration, decide to address my friends of such States in greater detail on this matter; but in the meanwhile I would invite attention to the concrete facts and figures which will be found in a Circular Letter No. 5—8 F., dated 4/7th August, 1931 which in itself categorically proves how unfounded are such charges which have been preferred against me of lack of sympathy with the smaller States.

43. As for the proposed Committee or Council of Ministers I entertain the hope that on this point too there will not be much difference of opinion. I think every fair-minded person, Prince or Minister, who has given the matter any serious thought will feel profoundly thankful that the Hydari Committee was constituted when it was, and will gratefully appreciate the valuable work which it has done and the incalculable services which it has rendered to the Princes and States, both big and small. I wonder where we should have been in regard to Federal problems without the labours of the Hydari Committee. We have also gratefully to bear in mind the great assistance rendered by the Government of Hyderabad to all the States in making available, so freely and generously, much material, including matters on which legal advice had been taken by them, bearing on the general question of Federation, the Instrument of Accession, and the Limitations and Reservations to be made by the States in regard to the Federal Legislative list.

44. I am, therefore, in hopes that we shall also be able to agree in a statesmanlike manner to the proposal to establish a Council of Ministers, which, in addition to dealing with Federal questions, will also be able to render valuable assistance in other matters of no less importance to the States.

45. The Ministers' body, in its turn, will I am equally convinced need the support of the Princes in regard to certain matters, both federal and non-federal.

46. There seem to prevail certain erroneous ideas about the position

taken up by, and the view point of , the bigger States. As President of this Committee, it is not right that I should say anything which might appear to be in a partisan spirit. But it is certainly my clear duty to place before Your Highnesses and the Ministers certain important facts relating to the dissatisfaction of the bigger as well as the smaller States.

47. It has been stated that the bigger States in their attitude towards the Chamber are actuated by considerations of mere prestige and dignity, and that, in keeping themselves aloof from the Chamber, they are not influenced by any logical reasoning—in fact, that there is no real gulf to be bridged between the bigger and the smaller States, and that, therefore, there is no necessity for any stress to be laid on the importance of getting the bigger States back into the Chamber. I venture to say that a moment's consideration will reveal the fallacy of, as well as the lack of political sagacity in, holding any such views. Some of the observations which I have already made in my speech today, and the facts which stare us all in the face, will in themselves be sufficient to establish that. I have even heard it said that, if the bigger States refrain permanently from participating in the activities of the Chamber, and that if they decide to take other steps to safeguard their own interests, the loss will be theirs and not that of the smaller States, and that the Chamber will still continue to function without any serious consequences to the States, still less to the smaller States.

48. I will not attempt here to deal with such strange arguments. But in fairness to the big States may I say just this much? It is not any exaggerated notions of prestige or dignity that are responsible for the attitude of the big States—an attitude which, in the interests of unity and the well-being of the Princes and States as a whole, I am sure nobody regrets more than the big States themselves their having been compelled to adopt in view of the State of affairs which at present exists. All that they ask, in the light of the actual experience of the past few years, is that effective measures be brought into force to ensure that due weight is given to their extensive interests and that, being in a minority, their votes should not be swamped, and their voice should not be stifled,by the preponderating votes and numbers of the smaller States, also that some matters which have brought about the present state of disruption, and not only that, but which have adversely reflected on the dignity and fair name of the Princes and States, should be put right.

49. I would assure everybody that the bigger States are as anxious, as should be all the other Princes and Ministers, that that great Institution of such benefit to the States, namely, the Chamber of

Princes, should not only be preserved, but strengthened and made even more effective, for the purpose of safeguarding the common rights and interests of the States and their Rulers.

50. When things reached a crisis, a small Committee of Ministers, which was appointed to go into the very question now engaging our attention, had, amongst other proposals, suggested that in the Chamber of Princes itself, as in the proposed Committee of Ministers, no resolution should be considered as having been carried by a majority unless that majority also included 50 per cent, of the States (present and voting) which have been allotted two or more than two seats in the proposed Upper House of the Federal Legislature. But some of us thought that this would only accentuate the unhappy differences between the bigger and smaller States; and, I am sure, everyone will be glad to learn that such a proposition does not today form part of the expectations and wishes of the bigger States.

51. There was, I am aware, an apprehension in the minds of many that the principle of "one State, one vote" in the Chamber of Princes was also in danger of being altered.

52. May I, for a moment, digress and remind those who may not be aware of the fact that, when discussions were taking place between the Officers of the British Government and the Committee of Princes relating in the Constitution of the Chamber of Prineves a little before it was inaugurated. His Highness the late Maharaja Scindia of Gwalior —to whose sympathy, sagacity and support the Chamber and the States, both big and small owe so much—and I opposed plural voting, and from the very commencement very strongly urged that each State, big or small, should have one vote each in Chamber; and in this we were heartily supported by His Highness the late Maharajah of Patiala, as will be clear from the Official proceedings of the 14th August, 1920.

53. Today, no part of any scheme or proposals which the bigger States are likely to favour urges plural voting; and I trust that this will reassure all who may have doubts on the subject that the principle of "one State, one vote" is not in any way to be interfered with.

54. Before concluding, May I, in all friendness, and with the utmost sympathy towards the smaller States, earnestly plead that every one of us should do the best possible for the sake of unity? Unity is the crying need of the moment. All other matters are of comparatively secondary importance.

55. During the last three or four days the air has been thick with rumours of all kinds. I sincerely hope, in the interests of each and every one of us, and, above all, for the cause of the Princes and states

and their subjects, that such rumours are false. But I have been told that this Conference is likely to break up without achieving the much desired goal. I have heard it waid that no decision is possible at this moment, and that there must be another meeting of the Chamber of Princes Reorganisation Committee some suggest in February next, and some in the early autumn.

56. Let me in all earnestness sound a note of friendly caution that if we proceratstinate or delay the decision, the cause will suffer, not of the bigger States alone, nor of the smaller States exclusively. The entire Order of Princes and all the States will undeniably suffer from any such delay. Remember, I pray you, that opportunity does not often knock at the door. If we do not come to a fair and satisfactory decision at this psychological moment it may be too late. In the ordinary course of events, we should before very long receive the Revised Instrument of Accession and the comments of the British Government on the safeguards, limitations and reservations which the States have proposed in regard to Federation. This meeting may succeed in delaying tactics; but the British Government will not wait for our answer until such time as we attain unity, and Federation is a problem in regard to which, above everything else, we must have unity and the closest consultation and co-ordination.

57. Are the States to be diunited even at this critical juncture in a matter of such vital importance on which the fate of the States—indeed their very existence—in the days to come depends? Are we going to permit matters so to shape themselves that posterity will blame us for our intertia and lack of vision? There is a vast difference between rushing matters through on the one hand, and shutting our eyes to obvious dangers and losing valuable time and opportunities which will not recur, on the other hand, and between saving the situation while there is yet time and suicidal delays. Surely, none of us would have it said about outselves—"Nero fiddled while Rome burnt".

58. On the outcome of our deliberations and decisions in this Committee; on whether or not we are able to evolve a scheme to attain the object in view—so vitally and urgently necessary in the interests of the Princes and States as a whole; on Your Highnesses present here, and on the rest of the Princes who are Members of the Chamber, contributing their full quota to the restoration of unity for all time and the creation of an effective Organisation representative of all the States; and on you gentlemen, the Ministers who are present here, and on your colleagues in the other States, will depend not only the existence of the Chamber of Princes, but, for reasons which

should be obvious, the very destiny of the States in the days to come.

59. Every one of us can assist in the achievement of our goal. Times are already difficult for the Princes and States. They will become critical as days go by. Let each one of us see to it that we do not add to our embarrassment by treating important matters lightly or by disregarding the dangers which beset us all- whether we come from the bigger or the smaller States. Let it not be said by posterity that we, the Princes and Ministers concerned, who have been entrusted with this task on behalf of the entire Order of the States, have been unmindful of our duties and responsibilities, and that we have thrown away a golden opportunity while there was yet time to put matters right, so that every State and Ruler could benefit.

60. I pray that the Almighty may guide our thoughts and inspire our action, and that, as the result of our labours and recommendations here, the Chamber may once again be made an effective Organisation representative of all the States, and that, under God's blessings, it may emerge a stronger and more virile body, and that lasting unity may be achieved—to the inestimable benefit of the Rulers and States of India.

# 9

## *Maharaja Ganga Singh—the Butler Committee and Round Table Conferences*

ONE OF THE MAJOR reasons Maharaja Ganga Singh decided to lay down the reins of Office as Chancellor of the Chamber of Princes was his belief that prolonged absences from Bikaner and preoccupation with affairs elsewhere were preventing him from devoting sufficient time to the administrative problems of his State. One of the steps the Maharaja took to resolve the problem was the appointment of Sir Manubhai Nandshankar Mehta as Prime Minister of the State. Sir Mehta had served with distinction the State of Baroda and was universally respected by Princes and Ministers of the Indian States as a hard working and honest worker.

1926 was not a very satisfying year for the Indian States. The theory of paramountcy worked on relentlessly and this was cause for concern and alarm for the Princes. The sulleness in the Indian States mood was matched with open hostility in the British India. The Congress Party was buoyed with successes in the elections in the Central Assembly and was agitating for more reforms. The Princes once more felt that with every step in political advance in British India, the rights and privileges they had long enjoyed because of past treaties and engagements were likely to be diminished. In these circumstances the Princes once more pressed for an immediate examination of their rights vis-a-vis the British Government. The British Indian jurists were of the view that the relationship of the Indian States was not with the Crown but with the Government of India and hence their past treaties had no validity—an assertion that distressed the Indian States greatly. The new Viceroy, Lord Irwin, was looked upon as a true friend of the Princes and sympathetic to their needs. It was at his initiative, taken at Simla in 1927 that the Indian States Inquiry Committee (the Butler Committee) was appointed in 1928. The Maharaja was hopeful that not only would the existing rights and privileges be confirmed by the Butler Committee but the relations between the States and British India would also be defined in proper perspective. The Committee was well received in Bikaner and the Maharaja tried his best to lay down this ground rules for the working of the Committee and the response of the Indian States to its proposals. Addressing the Chamber in 1928 (No. 1) the Maharaja delivered a speech full of candour but without malice and laced with due humility. He cautioned the members of the Chamber that times were changing very rapidly and public opinion was a factor one could ignore only at his own peril. There was a sizeable section of the intelligentsia which was of the opinion that while the Princes were anxious to enforce their rights against the British Government, as against their own people they recognized no obligation or duties; that good government was of no concern to them, that their interest lay in securing as much of the State revenue as possible for their own personal pleasures. This led to co-relation of internal reforms to the reassertion of their sovereign rights. Ganga Singh Ji said that all questions on the issue of sovereign rights were irrelevant until good government was ensured in their States. He repeated the theme that the strength of the princes could come only from the quality of their internal administration, from the love and affection in which their subjects held them. He also referred back to a speech made in 1926 in which he had put the entire issue in its proper perspective thus: "Times are changing, and the Princes and States too have to adopt themselves to modem environments. Some of our States have every reason to be proud of their splendid achievements and of the high goal towards which they are so assiduously working. In some States on the other hand the need for reforms will no doubt be apparent. It behaves us all the Princes and their Ministers—to see to it that nothing which duty and prudence dictate is left unattended to. No doubt the future destiny of the Princes and the States of India will be determined by God; but if we discharge our duties properly and are not unmindful of our responsibilities. He in his infinite mercy will assuredly extend to us His protecting hand and guidance". Some newspapers responded favourably to the efforts at internal reforms in States like Bikaner.

The Maharaja quoted one as writing in its editorials:

> *"If the Ruling Princes were . . . anxious to promote the welfare of their subjects, add to establish the rule of law, . . . there will be no section of Indians which would express feelings of hostality towards the order, or advocate its abolition, or regard it as an obstacle in the way of India's*

*attaining the goal of democratic freedom".*

At the same time Ganga Singh Ji was of the firm belief that the Princes should be left independent to conduct their internal affairs according to conditions prevalent in their States: "of conducting its internal affairs in ways—best suited to local circumstances, peculiarities, traditions, and sentiments and to the different ideals and standards of administrative efficiency and education prevailing."

In 1929 Maharaja Ganga Singh made another significant declaration in the Chamber of Princes seconding a Resolution moved by the Maharaja of Patiala in response to the issues raised by the Butler Committee. The resolution covered two core issues—(i) that the Princes and States of India can have nothing to do with any proposals having for their object the adjustment of equitable relations in India of the future between the Indian States and British India, which as has been urged by a section of British Indian politicians, have as their goal the complete independence of India, and thus the severance of the British connection; and (ii) the Princes' attitude towards and sympathy for, the legitimate aspirations of our brethren in British India for attaining full nationhood under the aegis of the Imperial crown.(No. 2)

The much awaited Butler Committee Report was finally published in April 1929 and was a disappointment for the Indian States in more ways than one. One redeeming clause of the Report was that the treaty relationship of the States, being with the Crown, could not be transferred without the consent of the States to any British Indian authority over which the Crown had no full control. The Report on the whole was a justification of the past and present practices of the Government of India. In response to the demand of the Princes of an definition of paramountcy, the only reply the Committee gave was that paramountcy was, 'paramount'. To add to the discomfort of the Princes it was also feared that the Parliamentary Commission, appointed to conduct an inquiry into the success of the Montagu-Chelmsford, would also recommend a further political advance for British India.

The Princes met in Bombay to device a strategy to counter the Butler Committee Report in June 1929 prior to the departure of Lord Irwin, the Viceroy for England. The meeting was historic as the Chiefs stood steadfast in their resolve of the defence of their rights and privileges as laid down in the Treaties.

In October 1929, the Maharaja used the occasion of the annual Administrative Conference to talk at length on the Butler Committee and other related issues.(No. 3) The first half of the speech was expectedly devoted to the review of the working of the various departments like education, medical, industries, revenues, agriculture etc. The remaining part of the Report was devoted to the Butler Committee Report and a detailed appeal to Indian States subjects in the wake of the publication of the above mentioned Report.

About the Butler Committee Report the Maharaja admitted that it was not upto the expectations. But it was too early to comment as the report of the Simon Commission was awaited. The silence of the Princes on the Butler Report was not to be construed as their weakness, Ganga Singh Ji added, as the Report and its implications would have to be examined in the Chamber of Princes for which a special session would be convened. The Maharaja also cautioned the Princes and the subjects to remain calm and not get carried away by provocative statements by the politicians and Newspapers in British India who termed the Butler Committee Report as a slap on the faces of the Princes and members of the Chamber of Princes.

In a subsequent appeal to the subjects of Indian States which formed the concluding part of the speech, the Maharaja once again stressed that the internal sovereignity and independence of the Indian States was essential for the very existence of the States in the future. On this issue there was no dispute with the wishes of the people of British India who were equally desirous of full autonomy.

The Maharaja expressed anguish and anger at certain individuals and professed leaders of masses who were organising unauthorized conferences of Indian States and claimed to speak on behalf of the oppressed subjects of the Indian States who were reeling under the autocratic rule of the despotic rulers. (This was with reference to States 'People's Conference founded in December 1927). The Maharaja had no objection and instead he welcomed valuable assistance from the subjects in administration provided progress in education and political outlook was achieved. Under existing circumstances, it was argued, the steps proposed by the States' People's Conference would lead to disruption of the Indian States. The leaders of the States' Conference described the Princes as attempting to:

1. Perpetuate autocracy, absolutism and misrule,
2. Stem the rising tide of nationalism in British India and the increasing power of public opinion in their own states;
3. Secure a blank cheque to oppress their subjects and to squander public money; and
4. Work generally against their subjects and the best interests of

their subjects, 'altogether ignoring' them.

The Maharaja concluded his speech by stating:

> *'I whom the Almighty has been pleased to ordain to be the Ruler of the Bikaner State, can never forget that I am, at the same time, the first servant of the State and the first servant of my subjects'.*

The same sentiments were again expressed by the Maharaja in our subsequent interview held on 2nd November, 1929 .(No. 4)

Towards the end of 1929 Lord Irwin was able to convince His Majesty's Government to host a Round Table Conference in London, attended by all interested parties, to resolve the 'Indian problem'. The Maharaja assured his brother Princes and the Governments of Indian States that the Round Table Conference was to their interests as well. He was on record stating.

> *"The princes realizing fully well that they are bound to their brethren in British India by ties of blood, race and religion, have no desire to hamper the attainment of Dominion status by British India or be a drag on its constitutional advancement. . . . Any attitude of undue incompatability on the part of the princes would be both unpatriotic and unreasonable."*

Ganga Singh Ji had of late started stressing upon the concept of Federation as solution to all ills in India.

> 'Ever since 1918, the Princes have been asking for some means of joint deliberation on questions of common concern affecting British India as well as the States. Custom duties; excise, salt and opium; railways and means of transport and inter-communication, including aerial navigation; post and telegraphs; wireless and radio broadcasting; as well as the fiscal and financial problems of coinage and currency, banking and exchange—these are all questions affecting and demanding joint deliberation between the constituted government of the two constituent parts of the country'.

As the Round Table Conference was scheduled for November 1930, the meeting of the Chamber of Princes preceeding the Conference assumed great significance and it was in that Conference the Princes were to shape their strategy for the Round Table meet. Maharaja Ganga Singh delivered three masterly speeches in the Chamber to set the tone for the conference. In the introductory speech delivered on 27th February, 1929 in which the Maharaja laid down the ground rules for deliberations. of the Chamber he concluded his speech by making the following observation about India-originally made by Mr. Ramsay McDonald:

"There is an old world, old in civilization, in philosophy, in religion and in culture, which has been hitherto weak in the material powers that have characterized Western peoples, but that world, wrapped in slumber as was thought, has now become awake and is beginning to understand what natural self-respect is. Taught and tutored very largely by us, it is bringing our own ideas home to us and asking us to honour the effects of our actions and to grant it not by charity, but because our hearts are enlightened—the freedom that we have been nourishing for ourselves for so many generations". (No. 5)

One problem which was agitating the Princes was the provision in the Butler Committee of the right of the paramount power to intervene in the States. The Maharaja, initiating the discussion on this issue, had conceeded that intervention was justified in certain well-defined cases because the British were committed to protect the States from external aggression and internal rebellion. But there was justification in the allegation of the Princes that 'legitimate intervention in the interests of the State more often than otherwise degenerated into petty interfearence, intended to exhibit the power and increase the prestiege of the political officers.'

The concern of the Princes was justified as the Butler Committee was deliberately evasive and vague about the limitations on intervention. Ganga Singh Ji opined that the Princes should be vested with the full powers to represent against unjustified intervention by the Government of India. (No. 6)

Intervention, according to the Maharaja, also led at times to political death of an able ruler. Whart was also objectionable was the Butler Committee's assertion that intervention was justified in the interests of India and in face of popular agitation, the Government of India could intervene in the administration of the States as well. This, it was felt, made intervention dependent upon circumstances over which the rulers had no control.

Another important point on which the Maharaja led the discussion was the doctrine of usage and sufferance which was often applied by the Government of India against the States. The princes claimed that usage was valid only under certain definite conditions, that it must have developed in the State concerned, that it must have a certain extension in space and in time, that usages which developed during minorities etc., should not be considered as binding. The practice followed by the Government of India often was to apply the precedents which developed in and were appropriate to the lesser States to the major States too. Some officials like Sir Robert Holland recognized that 'a body of useage influencing the relations with the States had come into force through a process which, though benevolent in intention, was to some extent arbitrary'. Thus while on one hand the Political Agent was contending that 'usage lighted up the dark corners of the treaties' and any attempt to define or limit its operation was not necessary and undesireable, the Maharaja was appealing for a rectification of the procedure and a liberalisation of policy in a manner consistent with the position of the States and their special relations with the crown.(No. 7)

In a subsequent dinner speech (No. 8) on 12th May, 1930 the Maharaja once again stressed upon the fact that there was no conflict of interests between the Indian Princes and the leaders in British India as far as the question of grant of Dominion Status to India was concerned provided:

a. as long as there was no gross maladministration in their States, there should be a constitutional guarantee that there would be no interference with their internal sovereignity;
b. a guarantee that questions connected with the personal and dynastic status of rulers would be dealt with exclusively with the Viceroy;
c. a guarantee that no legislative enactment passed by the British Indian Legislature would extend to Indian States unless their concurrence had been secured through joint deliberation;
d. a guarantee that the Indian States would not be asked to contribute to Imperial burdens without regard to existing treaties.

With the Round Table Conference round the corner in an interview on 19th July, 1930 Maharaja Ganga Singh issued an appeal to moderate leaders and statesmen in the Congress to suspend agitations in India till the Round Table Conference was held.(No. 9) He exhorted those leaders to ensure that in any future set-up of India, the Indian States would be accorded an honourable position.

The Round Table Conference got under way on 12th November, 1930 at St. James Palace, London. The Maharaja, as a prelude to the

Conference, had suggested that the representatives from British India should sit in joint session with the representatives of Indian States. But the representatives of British India had come to the Conference suspicious of the Indian States and were convinced that they would oppose self-government Dominion Status to India. (No. 10)

The proceedings opened with due solemnity and Sir Tej Bahadur Sapru opened the case for India. He made a great plea to the Indian States to join hands with their brethren in British India to establish an All India Federation which would re-unite the common motherland into a great nation. The Maharaja, who represented the interests of the Indian States, replied to the speech of Sir Tej Bahadur Sapru. (No. 11) He did not leave the Conference long in doubt of the position he would adopt. He also welcomed the idea of a Federation, provided there were legitimate safeguards for the interests of the States. He however claimed that the establishment of a unitary State, with a sovereign parliament sitting at Delhi, for which the people of British India were clamouring was impossible. The reason behind this was expressed by the Maharaja thus:

"Our starting-point, therefore, must be a recognition of this diversity, our unity must be sought not in the dead hand of an impossible uniformity but in an associated diversity." He further argued that in matters of a Federation in India there was no historical precedence to guide the conference. However, he favoured giving it a chance provided deep thought was given to its composition.

'We, however, recognize that a period of transition will necessarily intervene before the Federal Government is fully constituted, and that federation cannot be achieved by coercion of the States in any form. The Indian princes will only come into the Federation of their own free will and on terms which will secure the just rights of their States and subjects.' As on previous occasions the Maharaja stressed on three developments of the existing administrative machinery as essential for the smooth working of any new system. They were as before:

1. treaty rights of the Princes exist and must be respected.
2. that they are with the Crown and could not be transferred to any other authority without the agreement of the princes.
3. treaty rights could only be modified only with their free-assent. Maharaja Ganga Singh also demanded the establishment of a Supreme Court and an Indian States Council to adjudicate upon matters regarding rights of the Indian princes. His speech took everyone with surprise. Whereas on one hand it was whispered

> in the British Indian Camp that the princes were being used by the Crown to water down the grant of self-government, on the other hand some disgruntled element in Britain alleged that the declaration was the outcome of an unholy alliance between Brahmin ministers of States and Brahmin seditionists of British India. The Government of India was totally unprepared for the Maharaja's declaration and stated that it had no ready proposals on the issue.

The Conference accepted in principle the idea of a Federation and central responsibility and entrusted the task of workingout the details to a committee—the Federal Structure Committee—headed by Lord Sankey.

The path of the Princes joining the Federation was never easy. Though Maharaja Ganga Singh had been one of the staunchest advocates of the idea of a Federation, the scheme of Federation as propounded in the Draft Instrument of Accession led to great disillusionment among the Princes and even Ganga Singh Ji started having serious reservations about the Indian States joining the Federation.(No. 12) The Draft failed to live upto the expectations of the Princes and when the Viceroy categorically stated that:

> *"the terms now indicated must be regarded in all essentials as incapable of further relaxation since they represent the furthest joint to which, after the fullest consideration of all issues involved. . . . His Majesty's Government have found it possible to go to meet the wishes or apprehensions expressed by States".*

The dreams of the Princes were shattered. The Maharaja issued a Pamphlet titled "To Federate or not to federate—The Vital Question before the States and their Reply'—in which he discussed the issue at length. The main argument earlier was that the Federation would comprise of the Indian States, already sovereign, and British Indian Provinces who enjoy power only by devolution or grant, on equal basis. The Princes' stand was that the States were being levelled down to the position of the Provinces instead of the other way around as was practical. Furthermore the Draft was too rigid, it was argued, with too many federal subjects. Ganga Singh Ji was appreciative of the Viceroy's standpoint when the latter had declared in Udaipur that the decision of the Princes entering the Federation is:

> *"One that has of set purpose been left to the free and unfettered judgement of*

*individual rulers concerned".*

Another point that rankled the rulers was with regards to questions of customs and taxation—they stood to lose substantially in these areas upon joining the Federation. The appointment of Federal officials in States or supervision of internal administration by Federal agencies was also not to be appreciated by Rulers as would be the case once the Federation came into being.

As a parting comment Ganga Singh Ji also quoted extensively from the pronouncements of Congress leaders like Nehru and Rajendra Prasad who were openly inciting mass movements against the Rulers under the agencies of the Praja Mandals.

The advent of World War—Two saw relations between the Rulers and the movement called All India States Peoples' Conference (which claimed to be the voice of the people in Indian States) deteriorate further with certain of the latter's leaders advocatring non co-operation with the British in the war effort. But Bikaner and other States held firm in their commitment to assist Britain in the war effort.(Nos.13 & 14) At the same time it was announced that the matter of Federation would be revived only after termination of the war. This announcement was greeted with relief by the rulers.

In a subsequent speech in March 1940 Maharaja Ganga Singh expressed the view that the end of the war should once more reopen the issue of the future of the Federation with the three contending parties (Indian States, British India and Government of India) meeting on footings of equality and coming to an tripartite agreement. (No. 15)

## References

1. D.N. Mishra, 'Maharaja Ganga Singh of Bikaner—An Assessment of a Statesman in G. S.L. Deora edited Centenary Volume.
2. K.M. Panikar, 'His Highness, The Maharaja of Bikaner'.
3. Maharaja Ganga Singh Ji's speech in the Chamber of Princes regarding the appointment of the Indian States Committee. (23rdFeb.,1928).
4. Maharaja Ganga Singh Ji's Speech in the Chamber of Princes (13th Feb., 1929) on relations between Indian States and British India.
5. Speech by the Maharaja of Bikaner in the Administrative Conference (3rd Oct., 1929).
6. Interview of Maharaja Ganga Singh with Associated Press of India. (31st Oct., 1929).
7. Maharaja Ganga Singh Ji's Speech in the Chamber of Princes (27th Feb., 1930).
8. Speech of His Highness of Bikaner in the Chamber of Princes. (28th Feb., 1930).

9. Speech of Maharaja Ganga Singh Ji in Chamber of Princes on 'Usage and Sufferance'. (1st March, 1930).
10. Dinner Speech of Maharaja Ganga Singh (12th May, 1930).
11. Interview of Maharaja Ganga Singh with Associated Press of India (18th July, 1930).
12. Speech by Maharaja Ganga Singh Ji at Indian Round Table Conference, London, (17th Nov., 1930).
13. Speech of Maharaja Ganga Singh at Indian Round Table. (8th Jan., 1931).

# Annexure 1

**Speech delivered by His Highness the Maharajah of Bikaner in the Chamber of Princes on the 23rd February, 1928, in moving the Resolution regarding the appointment of the Indian States Committee and Internal Reforms in the Indian States.**

*Your Excellency; Your Highnesses;*

Opportunity was taken, during the last Session of this Chamber, to express our gratitude at Your Excellency's decision to convene the informal Round Table Conference, which met at Simla last May, where questions of great Importance to the States were discussed—we trust to the mutual advantage of the British Government and of Indian India. Your Excellency's advantage of the British Government and of Indian India. Your Excellency's appreciation of the benefits accruing from such free and frank informal discussions was particularly pleasant for us to hear; and we in our turn came away happy from that Conference, full of grateful recollections of Your Excellency's courtesy and sympathetic understanding and appreciation of our standpoint; and we hope that that meeting was only the first of several more to be convened from time to time both during Your Excellency's Viceroyalty, and thereafter.

2. To-day I am privileged to move a vote of thanks to Your Excellency, and to the Secretary of State, for the prompt appointment of the Indian States Committee, which was one of the specific requests we placed before you in Simla last May.

3. Questions of vital moment to the States will be dealt with by the Indian States Committee. They are not without their complexities, in as much as the position of the Indian States within the Empire is acknowledged to be unuque and without a parallel in history, and for the right understanding of certain problems connected with which neither International Law nor the Federal or Municipal Law of any country supplies any clear guide. But I feel sure that I am voicing the sentiments of this House—and indeed of the Indian States generally—when I repeat what I said in another speech a few days ago that it is a matter of congratulation and gratification, and as much in Imperial interests as in our own, that such important work is to be carried out by the Indian States Committee during the Viceroyalty of Lord Irwin—

who is proving himself so successful in unlocking closed doors and opening up sealed hearts—and that His Excellency has at his side, as his Political Secretary and Chief Expert Adviser, a sympathetic Political Officer like Mr. Watson, of whom high hopes are entertained by us. Indian India no less rejoices at the appointment as Chairman of the Committee of our old and esteemed friend, Sir Harcourt Butler.

4. To me personally also, it is a source of particular gratification to see the Indian States Committee appointed. For, as early as 1915, at the desire of that great and popular Viceroy, Lord Hardinge, I wrote a Minute on various important matters concerning the Indian States, in the course of which I urged the necessity of convening at an early date a Conference:

"for the consideration, in all their various aspects, and settlement,of such points. . . ."

But Lord Hardinge unfortunately left India shortly afterwards.

5. In the interval the Princes' anxieties were reduced considerably by the hopes raised from the various reforms which were urged by us. But various causes and factors—which I need not touch upon to-day-intervened; and the actual experience of the working of the reforms relating to the Indian States, as outlined in Chapter X of the Montagu-Chelmsford Report clearly indicated to us that our expectations had not bee fully realized and that somthing more was needed. I am one of those who hold the conviction that it is still possible to raise a noble edifice upon the foundations then laid, which can fully meet our various requirements, and prove of advantage to the States as well as to Empire. Particularly do I hope that, different though it is in certain aspects from our conception and ideal, this Chamber of Princes—in itself a unique body without parallel, where the Sovereign Rulers of the Indian States under the benign protection of the King-Emperor, meet in friendly conclave with His Imperial Majesty's exalted Representative in India—will yet prove to be one of the most beneficial links in the chain that unite the Princes of India with the Crown, and play an important part in the future destinies of the Indian with the Crown, and play an important part in the future destinies of the Indian States. But in the circumstances briefly alluded to by me, it became my duty, as Chancellor or Your Highnesses' Chamber at that time, to explore further avenues with a view to securing adequate safety for the Indian States.

6. As Chancellor I had already officially put forward before Lord Reading in 1922 a proposal for an informal Round Table

Conference—a request which it was ordained for Your Excellency to accede to fully five years later—and in August 1924—after important consultations with some prominent fudian States' Ministers, whom I had informally invited for the purpose—I placed, again as Chancellor, before the Viceroy as definite request for the appointment of an Indian States Committee.

7. I will not reiterate to-day all that I said only a few weeks ago in my speech in the Bikaner Legislative Assembly regarding the Indian States Committee, nor need I allude again to all the allied details dealt with by me when I had the honour, in November 1926, of moving in the Chamber of Princes a resolution of welcome to His Excellency Lord Irwin. I will therefore only refer to a few points in connection with the first part of my resolution. The need for overhauling, re-adjusting, and keeping up-to-date, the old machinery governing the Imperial relations with the States is obvious. Sir, I am an optimist; and—whatever the difficulties—I do not believe that they are insurmountable; and I have a invincible faith in the power of honest, open statesmanship—devoid of all diplomacy and secret reservations and manoeuvres. No political ill is hopelessly incurable if only it if rightly diagnosed and skilfully, as well as sympathetically, treated. As remarked by Your Excellency when opening this session and recently at Jodhpur:

> "if there be on both sides good will and a common desire to find for the various problems a solution, which will conduce to mutual properity and progress, we can face without anxiety whatever the future may have in store."

8. Whatever the faults of shortcomings in the past—on ether or both sides—one fact is really beyond doubt or dispute, viz., that, except perhaps in a few matters of minor detail, the interests of the British Government and of the Indian States are identical and that the future destiny of both is indissolubly interwoven. It is irrefutable that trust begets trust; and what henceforward is necessary—and what Your Excellency has yourself appealed for—is mutual trust and confidence and reciprocal goodwill, and a mutual appreciation of each other's standpoints and difficulties.

9. When I had the pleasure of welcoming Sir Harcourt Butler and his eminent colleagues to Bikaner the other day, I referred to my writing to Sir Harcourt and saying years ago that, finding ourselves, as we did, in the hands of such good doctors as the late Lord Minto and Sir Harcourt, one might almost have said that the wounds of the past had healed, and that unless there was to be in the near future a

change in the treatment, the wounds were not likely to open again. To-day I am particularly anxious to avoid, as far as possible, any reference to controversial matters; still less do I wish to refer on this occasion to the causes which in recent years led to a change of treatment and which retarded our progress. But I feel that this distinguished Assembly will whole-heartedly share with me the hope that history will again repeat itself, and that Sir Harcourt Butler will, with the willing co-operation of his colleagues, and the sympathetic and strong support of His Excellency the Viceroy and the British Government, once again be instrumental in totally removing such malignant growths and thus help in bringing about a permanent and complete cure. I will, therefore, leave this subject after saying that the Chamber of Princes looks forward with hope and faith to the recommendations of the Indian States Committee, and to their being considered and discussed in this Chamber, before His Excellency the Viceroy and the Secretary of State and the British Government take up the final solution of the various problems involved.

10. I wish that my task in moving the second part of my Resolution was as simple as in dealing with the fIrst part. No one is more conscious than myself of the difficult and delicate points involved; and it is only under a strong sense of duty to our Order, and because in my judgement it will be highly injurious to the interests of the Princes and their States to delay, that I venture to place this Resolution before Your Highnesses for your earnest and favourable consideration. For reasons which will be obvious, I feel sure that this House will believe me when I say that I do most heartily wish that there was at the moment some one else in my place speaking and moving this Resolution!

11. As from more points than one it is of the utmost importance to the Princes and their States that there should be no misunderstanding, nor any apprehension, in any quarter—including in the minds of those about to-day as regards the exact meaning and scope of this Resolution which have promoted me to move it- and which I hope Highnesses to accept it—I would beg for the indulgence to Your Excellency and of Your Highnesses if I take up your time and recall certain details connected with this very matter which will make it clear that the subject matter of this Resolution does not come up before Your Highnesses to-day for the first time, and that there is really nothing new which I am springing on Your Highnesses to-day in the shape of a surprise. Indeed I should be sorry for the sake of our Order if I felt that this very important matter has not already been engaging the attention of those or Your Highnesses who look well ahead.

12. Speaking here as I am before some Princes riper in age and experience than myself, I would first beg Your Highnesses to absolve me from any intention of being dictatorial, or of being guilty of lecturing to any Brother Prince much less to this distinguished Assemblage, or to our Order.

13. The second point that I wish to make clear is that nothing in my Resolution, or in what I say to-day, is meant to imple—or can really be held to imply—that the condition of affairs in all, or even the majority of , our States is the opposite of satisfactory.

14. Our States and Governments as well as our subjects, it is true, are in various stages of advancement; and local circumstances and conditions and that standard of administration must likewise vary—and late though our States were, compared with British India, in starting on modern lines of administration and education—we can look with satisfaction upon the fact that some of our States are very well administered and have attained a high level of advancement and development, which may well be the envy not only of other States, not so fortunate in possesing the same natural resources, but which would—I make bold to add—compare favourably with some parts even of British India; whilst many Rulers of our States have, to the best of their light and according to the conditions prevailing in their States, been devoting the best years of their life, and much of their time, to the service of their States and in promoting the welfare of their subjects. In some of the advanced States the essentials of good Government are already clearly forthcoming. Such Rulers and States will have nothing more to do so far as the terms of this Resolution are concerned. It is possible that in some States—should they deem my Resolution, and the submissions which I make to-day, worthy of attention—the necessity may be appreciated of applying some or other of the important internal reforms, which for some reason or other it may not have been found possible higherto to give full effect to; whilst in some other States again, if my Resolution is instrumental in bringing these important matters prominently to the forefront, and if it leads to their consideration in earnest, my labours will not have been in vain; and I venture to predict that not only the particular State, or States, but our entire Order will thereby be the gainers.

15. The third point which I wish to emphasize is that I had devoted particular care in wording this Resolution; and the same applies to framing this speech, so that nothing should be said which might justly be taken as compromising the internal independence and autonomy of our States or our rights and position. I need hardly assure Your Highnesses, as well as the other Princes not present here to-day, that

I am not blind to certain obvious aspects of the question under discussion, and particularly to the danger of any arising from, or any wrong interpretation being placed on, this anything that might be said in this hall to-day, either by me in speech, or by any of Your Highnesses in any debate that may follow. I would venture in all modesty to express the hope that the record of my ten years' special work undertaken on Your Highnesses' behalf—for the first five years as Honorary General Secretary to Your Highnesses for the annual Princes Conferences, and for the second five as the first Chancellor of the Chamber of Princes—will show that there is no one, within or without our Order, who attaches greater importance to safeguarding the rights and interests of the States as well as the Izzat and dignity of the Princes, or who has opposed more strenuously undue interference in our internal affairs. We naturally cherish, and desire to preserve intact, and to render secure for all time, our internal autonomy and independence; and we resent—and, I venture to state, rightly resent—undue intervention or interference from any source outside our States in our internal and domestic affairs, or any encroachment on our Sovereign powers. It would be out of place on this occasion for me to refer at length to the delicate and vaxed question of such interference, or to go into details of what can be said to amount to—what i have always understood to be the official phraseology—"flagrant injustice" or "gross" or "intolerable" "misrule", in which extreme, and happily rare, cases interference has been claimed to be justifiable or unavoidable.

16. Nor have I lost sight of the fact that from time to time in the past, claims have been advanced from varous responsible quarters on behalf of the Government of India as regards both the need and the justification for intervention—claims more wide, more frequent, and more insistent, and I would respectfuly add—some of them at least based on grounds which it would appear difficult constitutionally to justify or substantiate.

17. Bur for the purpose of this Resolution I would first recall the important words used in regard to this subject by His Excellency—our present, popular Viceroy—in his inaugural Address in this Chamber in November 1926, when, after assuring us that the realised "to the full the sanctity and the binding nature of the treaties and sanads" and that he would do all in his power to observe them. His Excellency, in his reference to "another aspect of the relations" of the Princes with the British Government, on which he did not think that in practice we should find ourselves in disagreement, state:

"The general policy of Government remains, as it has been in the past, a policy of non-interference in affairs that are internal to the States. It is only in extreme cases that the Paramount Power will intervene, and I can assure Your Highnesses that any such action which it is ever thought necessary to take, will be taken only after the most deliberate and sympathetic consideration, and with the greatest reluctance. Its sole purpose will be the furtherance of the interest, present and future, of the Indian States, and of the general Order of the Princes themselves."

His Excellency further was good enough to offer us his confidence, and observed that he knew he could count on ours; for indeed our mutual confidence is more than ever necessary at this juncture of Indian political development. With this assurance, and with this appeal of mutual confidence, in our minds, we can safely proceed on our task of discussing this Resolution; and, when explaining the wording of some of the clauses of my Resolution, I shall have something more to say, which I trust will further reassure Your Highnesses that we need not—on the score of this Resolution alone—be afraid of intervention, or dictation, from the British Government, or any of the local Political Officers, in regard to questions of Internal Reforms. On the contrary I would venture in all seriousness to say to Your Highnesses that by accepting, and acting on, this Resolution, we should be definitely minimising the risks of and checking, intervention, from the British Government of from any other quarters, inside or outside our States.

18. There is one more subject which I feel it important to dwell upon in these introductory remarks. It may well be asked "What are the grounds for this Resolution, and where is the necessity of moving it in the Chamber of Princes—why not instead deal with such matters in the Princes' Informal Meetings?" The answer which I give, with all respect and in all friendliness, is that such a Resolution is based on the very instinct of Self-preservation and self defence, and that it appears necessity that it be discussed in this Chamber of Princes for the future well-being and strength; and indeed I would in all earnest go so far as to say that it is imperatively necessary for the very existence of our States as well as for consolidating the position of the Rulers and their Dynasties. That it will also promote the well-being and contentment of our subjects, which so many of Your Highnesses really have at heart, and which is so essential for our own security, also goes without saying. But here I am specially emphasizing the grave risks which the Rulers of States themselves will run personally, and which

they will fortheremore leave as a bad legacy to their children and their children's children, in the near or distant future, if, where such reforms are necessary, no heed is paid to this matter of such vital importance to the entire Order.

19. As will be obvious, and as has repeatedly been pointed out by several Princes—including your humble servant—as well as some of our most able Ministers, at the Princes' Informal Meetings, and in the reports and recommendation of various Ministers' Committees, there are two ways of consolidating, strengthening and safeguarding the future position of our States, including our own position and that of our Heirs and Successors. Both ways are equally important, if not interdependent. One is to ask—and we have a right to ask—the Imperial Government to continue to respect and maintain, and take such steps as will effectively render secure, for all time, our Treaty and other rights, and of internal Sovereignty and may be found mutually satisfactory and effective for the purpose, and, where need by, by revising their policy and improving the political machinery governing our own relations with the Crown. For this we have made every effort through the Chamber of Princes and our Standing Committee and let us hope that under the blessings of Providence, and with the sympathy and support of His Excellency the Viceroy, the Secretary of State and the British Government and the Indian States Committee, our apprehensions may be finally laid at rest and our aims fully achieved.

20. But, Your Highnesses, as I remarked in my recent speech in the Bikaner Legislative Assembly, nothing that each one, or all, of them may do can completely and effectively, and by itself, secure the future of the Indian States. For, as I remarked in my speech on the 16th August 1926. when inaugurating the Conference of Ministers held in Bikaner to discuss the future position of the Indian States:

> "No one who thinks seriously and earnestly, can shut his eyes to the fact that our future really depends largely, if not almost exclusively, upon the Rulers of States themselves, upon the extent we, the Princes, realise our great responsibilities and the sacred duty God Almighty has committed to our care, upon the manner in which we direct the affairs of our States, upon the amount of care and thought which we bring to bear upon questions of vital importance to the well-being of our States and our subjects. Very difficult times unmistakably lie ahead of us . . . There is no use blinking at the fact that the trend of certain schools of political thought" (in British India) "is not in our favour. . . . Times are

changing, and the Princes and States too have to adapt themselves to modern environments. Some of our States have every reason to be proud of their splendid achievements and of the high goal towards which they are so assisuously working. In some States on the other hand the need for reform will no doubt be apparent. It behoves us all—the Princes and their Ministers—to see to it that nothing which duty and prudence dictate is left unattended to. No doubt the future destiny of the Princes and States of India will be determined by the will of God; but if we discharge our duties properly and are not unmindful of our responsibilities, He is His infinite mercy will assuredly extend to us His protecting hand and guidance."

21. It will thus be obvious that certain important measures for the purpose of securing, and consolidating, the position of the Indian States can only by undertaken by the Rulers and Governments of the States themselves; and Your Highnesses do not need to be told by me that in such cases where even the essentials of good Government are not manifest, no other course of action will stem the tide of public opinion in such States, which in such circumstances must ultimately sweep everything before it. Nor do Your Highnesses need to be reminded by me that the strength and the safety of a Ruler and his State do not for all time lie in the bayonets of the British Government or of his own Army, but can only be permanently secured and maintained if his rule is broadbased on the loyalty and affection and the contentment and co-operation of his own people. Hence the imperative and urgent necessity, where required, of putting our houses in order. Many instances are forthcoming of the disastrous results—disastrous not only to the Sovereign personally, but in my humble opinion disastrous not only to the Sovereign personally, but in my humble opinion disastrous in many ways to the State as well as to society—to the mightiest Sovereign of some of the greatest Powers and Empires on the face of this Earth, who failed to detect the sign of the times and rushed headlong to their doom, or the doom of their descendents, through unwise autocracy. I need only mention Louis XIV—at one time the mighty Emperor of the great French Empire and his Successors.

22. Let me not be misunderstood. As I have already said there is much in many of our States which we can be proud of , and which some of the less advanced States can well emulate; and although, in view of the fierce light that beats upon a throne, the occasional and sad lapses of a Ruler gain undue prominence and widespread

notoriety, a greater truth was never stated than by that conscientious Viceroy, Lord Chelmsford, in his remarks during a discussion in the Princes Conference on the 20th January, 1919, when he said that he did not believe that there was much misrule in the Indian States.

23. Human nature being what it is and with different conditions prevailing in different States, it is impossible to expect all the Rulers of our States to be of one uniform quality; and occasional lapses are, alas! inevitable. But such painful relevations, Your Highnesses will agree, do no good to the Order as a whole or to the States as a body. Similarly the crippling beyond measure of the State finances, and the attendant neglect to find sufficient funds to ensure good Government for the State and for the purpose of advancing the happiness, prosperity and contentment of its subjects, has an adverse effect on us all in matters fiscal and financial as well as Political. And in this connection I am tempted once more to quote from His Excellency's recent speech at Rajkot:

> "... the more your administrations approximate to the standards of efficiency demanded by englightened public opinion elsewhere, the easier it will be to find a just and permanent solution" of the difficulties and disabilities from which the States have been suffering."

24. It is in view of all such, and other, considerations of the highest import to us and to posterity that, after the most anxious and deliberate consideration, and on the unanimous suggestion and advice of all my Brother Princes on the Standing Committee present in Simla last May, and of some of our ablest Ministers and other well-wishers, whom I consulted, I have consented to move this Resolution to-day which, if the States are fortunate enough to receive Your Highnesses' general support and consent in passing, will carry with it greater formality and great weight, not to be expected at our Informal Meetings. For, the attendance there of all the Princes present in this Chamber cannot always be counted upon. The Resolutions of the Chamber have, of course, no binding force on any State, but they none-the-less carry great moral weight, and will, it is hoped, lead to their receiving a greater measure of serious attention and prompter consideration, than any resolutions informally passed at our Informal Meetings. Also, from the short narrative of events which followed it will be noticed that although this all important subject has from time to time, and for several years past, been considered by us at Informal Meetings, it has not received the widespread, earnest attention, nor

have the results achieved hitherto been as effective or as satisfactory, as the importance and urgency of this very far-reaching questions demand.

25. At our Informal Meetings in February, 1921, a small Committee of Princes and Ministers was for the first time appointed during my first year of office as Chancellor, to go into such questions affecting the future position of the Indian States and to consider what was necessary for the Governments of the Princes to do internally for strengthening the position of their States. Unfortunately we were meeting then at a time of great rush, which coincided with the visit of His Royal Highness the Duke of Cannaught for the purpose of inaugurating the Chamber.

26. Without going into the details of each and every subsequent occasion when we discussed such measures, I will specially remind Your Highnesses of one very important discussion in our Informal Meetings, held in Delhi on the 7th November, 1921, when His Highness the late Maharajah Scindia of Gwalior appealed to the Princes to leave no stone unturned in setting their houses in order. He particularly referred to the changed spirit of the times, and to the attempts made by a certain class of people in British India to excite feelings of disaffection in the minds of the subjects of our States. His late Highness expressed his conviction that unless the Rulers retained a hold upon the affection of their people, attended to their legitimate grievances and took a personal interest in the efficiency of their administration, there was a great danger threatening the existence of their entire Order; and he observed that the problem of the future would get more and more complex and difficult, and that unless wisdom and care were brought to bear upon their solution, their successors would find their position rendered extremely insecure.

27. His late Highness of Gwalior again returned to the same subject in a subsequent informal discussion in November, 1924. In supporting his remarks I ventured to urge that we must seize time by the forelock, and that we must act—while there was yet time—and put our house in order, and thereby ensure the preservation of our States and Dynasties.

28. The Ministers' Report drafted at Bikaner in August 1926, and presented in Patiala in February 1927, also laid particular emphasis on the needs of essential Internal Reforms; and I have already aluded to my inaugural remarks when opening the Ministers' conference in Bikaner in August 1926.

29. His Highness, our present Chancellor, in addressing a circular letter to the Princes last year in regard to the Committee Meetings in

Bikaner and Patiala also invited Your Highnesses' attention to this important matter. But unfortunately as the question could not be adequately dealt with in the course of such a brief circular letter, some serious misunderstandings arose. I earnestly hope all such suspicious and doubts will be finally laid at rest by to-day's discussions as also by some further observations which I shall shortly be making when explaining the wording of the various clauses of this Resolution.

30. I will conclude my general observations by quoting the following five, out of many, relevant and significant extracts from a third party—a responsible, leading Indian Newspaper, which in its editorial on my Legislative Assembly Speech said:

1. "If the Ruling Princes were. . . anxious to promote the welfare of their subjects, add to establish the fule of law, . . . there will be no section of lndians which would express feelings of hostility towards the Order, or advocate its abolition, or regard it as an obstacle in the way of lndia's attaining the goal of democratic freedom."
2. "There is no doubt that the present fiscal arrangements are grossly unfair to the subjects of Indian States."
3. "The demands of the Indian Princes are in essence similar to those of people in British India, namely, the freedom to manage their own affairs without outside interference. They would meet with considerable support ftom Indian Publicists if the Indian Princes follow the general principles in the discharge of their responsibilities enumerated by His Highness. . . ."
4. "If these Internal Reforms are introduced and carried out in the right spirit, the Rulers of States will have the united support of their subjects and people in British India in any effort they may make for preserving intact their treaty rights."
5. "Rulers who with to increase their power and fortify their position should know where the real strength lies."
   (in, viz., the loyalty and affection of their people)

31. I will now deal with and explain Clauses (3), (4) and (5) of the resolution. Speaking generally first, I have attempted to avoid the use of such ambiguous terms as are likely hereafter to lead to difficulties as to their exact meaning and scope. For instance, "efficiency" of administration, or of anything else, is an extremely wide term, and we cannot have outside judges, or umpires reviewing and adjudging what does or does not constitute "efficiency".

32. Secondly, whilst on the subject of efficiency, I would invite

special attention to the famous declaration of policy, which a widely respected and popular Viceroy, Lord Minto, made at Udaipur on the 3rd November 1909, when he had Sir Harcourt Butler, as his Chief Political Adviser. Lord Minto on that memorable occasion said:

> "I have always been opposed to anything like pressure on Durbars with a view to introducing British methods of administration—I have preferred that reforms should emanate from the Durbars themselves, and grow up in harmony with the traditions of the State. It is easy to overstimate the value of administrative efficiency—it is not the only object to aim at, though the encouragement of it must be attractive to keen and able Political Officers, and it is not unnatural that the temptation to futher it should for example appeal strongly to those who are temporarily in charge of the administration of a State during a minority."

33 . The third point in my general observations regarding, Clauses (3), (4) and (5) to which I wish to invite the attention of all concerned is that whilst the Princes of India are not unmindful of the altered circumstances prevailing in the world to-day, and will, it is earnestly to be hoped, be found to be keenly alive to their duties and responsibilities, they are not in any way conceding by to-day's Resolution, or debate, that they would willingly accept the views, or boiter dicta, of any outside party as to what is, or is not, sufficient or adequate, or what should, or should not, be done in their States in matters which come purely within the purview of their internal autonomy. Nor do they accept that a uniform standard of administration, to suit the diverse conditions prevailing among the various States in varying stages of progress, is possible of attainment, and that therefore every State and its Ruler must be the best judges as I remarked in my recent Legislative Assembly speech:

> "of conducting its internal affairs in ways best suited to local circumstances, preculiarities, traditions, and sentiments, and to the different ideals and standards of administrative efficiency and education prevailing."

34. The degree of political consciousness awakened in the various States varies immensely in direct proportion to their education and contact with political ideals of the West. No wise man would accordingly dispute the claim of the government of each State to be the best judge of the measure, and the manner and the pace, of such

internal administrative reforms, as may be most suited to promote the progress and the prosperity of their States and subjects. It has been said that an Englishman's house is his own castle. This applied with all the greater force to the Rulers of the Indian States; and therefore it is essential that they must remain paramount masters in their own homes; and all such reforms, when and where found to be necessary—and as occasion demands—must for lasting success depend upon their spontaneously emanating from withing and on the initiative of the Ruler and the Government of the State concerned.

35. It is important that here I should also make it clear that what I am to-day urging on the earnest attention of my Brother Princes, and what was proposed to be laid down by me in this Resolution, is in no way contrary to the terms of the memorable declaration, by our valued friend, the late Right Honourable Edwin Montagu of the 20th August, 1917, when, as Secretary of State for India, he stated in the House of Commons that as the responsibility for the welfare and advancement of the Indian people lay on the British Government and the Government of India:

> "the British Government and the Government of India . . . must be the judges of the time and measure of each advance and they must be guided by the co-operation received from those upon whom new opportunities of service wit thus be conferred and by the extent to which it is found that confidence can be reposed in their sense of responsibility."

The British Government cannot therefore reasonably expect the States to go further than the declaration made by the British Government—as far as it applied to them—in regard to the advance of constitutional reforms in British India. Although the Resolution, as I had originally drafted it, has been altered by me solely out of diference to the recently expressed wishes of some of Your Highnesses whom I had informally consulted in the matter, it is necessary not only in fairness to myself, but also to the interests of the Princes and States of India in general—that I should make it clear that—although I do not regard the revised wording of this Resolution as equally satisfactory for the safety or our States and the best interests of our Order—these observations equally apply to the revised Resolutions as placed before the Chamber of Princes to-day.

36. Para (3) of the Resolution makes it clear that a Ruler and his Government alone must be the best authorities to judge of what methods are best suited to promote the porsperity of their States and

subjects. At the same time, I would venture-speaking as I am to my Brother Princes—respectfully to point out in a frank manner that the consequences to a Ruler, who is unmindful of. or indifferent to, marching with the times, and who does not make the best use of the opportunities open to him, are likely to be most disastrous to himself, his Dynasty, and his government in the near or distant future. But this is a subject on which, in view of what I have already said to-day, it is unnecessary for me to dwell upon further.

37. Turning now to Clause (4) of this Resolution, it is impossible also to ignore the wisdom of the political philosphy which teaches that any reform, in order to be real and enduring, must both be spontaneous and emanate from whthin; and it needs no labouring on my part to demonstrate what an impossible position would otherwise be created for a Ruler and his Government—as well as, I venture to state, the British Government—if it were to be otherwise. Reforms, like constitution, must grow from within; it is impossible to expect them to last otherwise. Genuine administrative reform can thrive and prove of any real value only on the initiative of the Ruler and the Government themselves, and if the motive force behind it is spontaneous, and not forced from outside quarters. At the same time, and subject to these necessary besafeguards, I would venture to urge most earnestly that the aim and endeavour of each one of us ought to be to bring our individual administrations up to the generally accepted progressive ideals of beneficent Government.

38. I trust that I have said enough to show that the Rulers of States in generally endorsing this Resolution are not binding themselves to "any catastrophic changes" and that they are in no undue danger of having their policy dictated from outside, or of subjecting themselves to the risks of undue interference, from the Government of India of its officers, or anyone else outside their States.

39. In order further that all suspicious and doubt may be dispelled so far as this Resolution is concerned, I would add that only a visionary or an idealist can hold the belief that the results seeming from the general acceptance of this Resolution to-day by Your Highnesses in the Chamber of Princes will forthwith lead to every thing being put right and in absolutely perfect order, or to every reform being established at one full sweep or a wave of the magic wand. The chief obj ect of this Resolution is to get the Princes' attention concentrated on the essence, as well as the subject matter, of this Resolution and to bring prominently to the front, and to get the idea steadily to permeate into the minds of those of our Order who have—from whatever causes, avoidable or unavoidable—lagged behind, and by honest precept,

persuasion and friendly advice to try to get them for the common good, and of their own free will and accord, to put their houses in order, where such necessity exists.

40. Taking now sub-paragraphs (a) and (b) of Clause 5 of this Resolution, I would ask Your Highnesses to persue carefully their wording, which I venture to assert in such as to encourage even a small State, or one however backward, to accept without any misgiving or misapprehension. The words "a definite code of law" need not frigthen even the most conservative amongst us; for, whether there are laws and codes, either original or enacted afresh and based on the laws of British India or any other States, it is obvious that, if there is even a resemblance of the administration of justice and of codes and laws in a State, they must be based on some principles of justice ; and I should indeed feel alarmed as regards the future of our States if there was anyone amongst us so autocratic, or so bold, as to assert that such codes and laws must be ignored and the term 'justice" so degraded as to disregard the legitimate liberty of person and the safety of property, or that they must be administered by a judiciary which is not independent of the executive in the dispensation of strict and impartial justice, but that it should be subordinate to the orders of the Executive Government or the will and caprice of the Ruler as regards conviction of people irrespective of their being innocent or guilty, or in awarding decrees in civil suits, irrespective of the ordinary canons of law, equity and commonsense. And it also follows that the judiciary must also feel secure in their tenure of office—so long as they discharge their duties and responsibilities properly. What is necessary is that our judiciaty must be charged with the administration of justice to the rich and the poor alike- without fear or favour, and equally to all our subjects; and that there should be a proper and adequate judicial branch of the Administration in our States providing for adequate modes of redress as well as for appeal.

41. In essence, what I am urging to-day, and which I feel Your Highnesses will agree with me, is that there should be the 'reign of law' prevailing in our States and not the 'reign of desire'.

42. As regards paragraph 5(b), what is proposed is that there should be a settlement upon a resonable, and, I would venture to point out, a definite, basis of the purely personal expenditure of the Ruler, as distinguished from the public charges of administration. I wish to make it clear that I do not talk of any fixed amount or of any percentage, or of any other allied details. All these must necessarily and rightly vary according to the conditions prevailing in each State and particularly according to the revenues of the State concerned.

The main point as regards the Civil List and Privy Purse of a Ruler is that is should be settled on a reasonable and definite basis, to enable the Ruler to maintain his position and dignity and that as larger a proportion as possible may be available for the development of the life of a community and of its individual citizena.

43. It is difficult, here also, for me to conceive that anyone of us would be disposed seriously to contend the equity or the need for the Ruler of a State to have a fixed and well-defined Privy Purse and Civil List, and a clear dividing line between his personal expenditure and that of the State. The reasons for the same are so obvious that they hardly require any further rmarks. The ancient Hindu Kings were similarly enjoined by our own Shastras and our own Nitis, only to take a fixed sum or a definite percentage of the total income of the State; and the Civil List of an enlightened Ruler of modern times—even, I gather, in Western Countries—is consequently fixed at either a definite sum or at a definite percentage of the total ordinary income of the State.

44. It will be generally conceded that it is not always easy to differentiate between the purely personal expenditure of a Ruler and that incurred for ceremonial purposes by the Ruler in his official position as the Head of the State; and it is obviously quite impossible to lay down any hard and fast rules on the subject. The various circumstances prevailing in each State—with which the Ruler and his Government are best and closest acquainted—must supply the test in the consideration and settlement of such questions by the Ruler and his Government; and so long as a sincere effort is made to draw that a definite line of demarcation—where it does not exist -between the purely personal expenditure of a Ruler and the public charges of administration, all other points pale, comparatively speaking, into insignificance. It must also follow, where the percentage of the State revenue is the guiding principle, that there can be no uniform standard applicable to the various States. For it is indisputable that whereas a certain smaller percentage would be a resonable and definite basis for a big State with larger revenue. it follows obviously that with a State—say of a revenue of 1 lakh of rupees—a fixed percentage, say 10 per cent, would by no means suffice even for the reasonable personal expense of the Ruler—much less if he is to keep up his position and dignity. It therefore follows that such percentage in the smaller States with smaller revenues must necessarily vary and be larger.

45. I would like to emphasize that Your Highnesses are not being asked by the Chamber or me or anyone else to give any opinion

whatever to-day on the various details of such settlements of Civil List and Privy Purses or what the percentage should be. This is a matter entirely for consideration and settlement in accordance with the conditions and circumstances and other factors prevailing in each State. Here again it is impossible to conceive however that any Ruler can seriously contend that he is justified in spending the greater proportion of the revenue of his State on his personal expenditure and on his pleasures and enjoyment—to the detriment of the interests of his State, his Government and his subjects. And as some Princes asked some questions on another point, let me also add that this Resolution here refers solely to the revenues of the State, and does not of course in any way refer to the purely personal income of a Ruler derived from private sources. Any Ruler who derives a private income from sources independent of the ordinary and extraordinary revenues of the State, such for instance as inheritance, bequests, or from private estates outside the State, or savings from his own Privy Purse, etc. need not trouble to take such details into consideration for the purpose of this Resolution.

46. I believe that, except for isolated cases, there is, in accordance with either our ancient, or modern, ideals, real differentiation made in our States between the Ruler's personal expenditure and State expenditure; and Your Highnesses, in accepting Clause 5(b) of this Resolution, would not be departing in any way from the ancient ideals of the Dharma of a Prince or the modern ideals of the duty of a Ruler, in regard to this important detail-upon which so much will depend, as far as the future of our States, and our own Dynasties is concerned. For it is on this score and because of the thoughtless acts of a few amongst us, that our entire Order is most frequently assailed.

47. I feel sure that Your Highnesses will agree that it is far, far better for all of us to take time by the forelock and to bring about such essential reforms in the interests of good government, as and where they are needed, on our own initiative and of our own free will, rather than have to do so under the force of public opinion, or other circumstances.

48. I would venture to add that in States where there is no Reign of Law, no independent judiciary fearlessly administering impartial justice, and where there is no clear cut line and proper distinction between the personal expenditure of a Ruler and the charges of administration, we also suffer in various fiscal and financial arrangements. For instance, I believe that our claim to a share in the customs revenues derived by the Government of India from British Seaports would be on a still stronger footing if we were able to

demonstrate to all concerned that the proportionate amount to which our State is entitled from customs duties levied in British India would not be frittered away on the personal pleasures and expenses of a Ruler, but that it would benefit the tax-payers of our Indian States just as the revenue derived in British India in the shape of customs in undoubtedly devoted by the Government of India for the benefit of the British Indian tax-payer.

49. In commending this Resolution, and particularly paragraph (5), I feel that it is necessary to invite Your Highnesses' particular attention to the fact that you are not signing a blank cheque, or committing yourselves carte blache, to any undue encroachment upon your legitimate rights or prejudice to your interests. After all when we come to view it from the Eastern standpoint or that of the West, there can be very little that in essence is different in the Eastern standard of Kingship and beneficent Government from the modern ideals of good Government; and before concluding my speech I would, in support of my statement, refer to some of the well-recognised and generally accepted principles and functions of good government, and of Regar obligations and duties of Rulers to their subjects, over which there can be little, if any, dispute—whatever the standard and conditions prevailing in any State, whatever its revenues and resources, and wherever its geographical situation. Several of Your Highnesses are not totally unacquainted with an important Note, written entirely in our interests, and purely informal as an expression of his personal views, by an honoured and esteemed friend and sagacious statesman. I quote some extracts from it here not because of any desire to flatter but because I venture to think that when Your Highnesses come carefully, and even critically, to examine the principles enuciated therein, with which no reasonable person, with a wise apprehension and looking far ahead to the days to come, and with due regard to the best interests of his State, himself and his Dynasty, will really be in disagreement.

50. As said in this Note:

> "The functions of Government may be described as the task, firstly, of ensuring to the individuals composing the society governed the opportunity of developing themselves as human beings, and, secondly, of welding into a compact and contented State.
>
> ** *
>
> II. Stated differently, the ordered life of a community depends

upon being regulated, not by the arbitrary will of individuals, but by LAW. . . .

* * * *

X. Every Government should have some machinery by which it can inform itself of the needs and desires of its subjects, and by which these can make their voice heard.
This machinery need not be strictly representative (or elective) in character, but its essential requisite is that it should maintain a close connectin between Government and Governed.

****

XII Perhaps the principal necessity for a personal Ruler is that he should be able to choose wise counsellor, and having chosen them that he should trust them, and encourage them to tell him the truth, whether or not this is always palatable."

* * * *

52. When referring in my Legislative Assembly speech to the widely accepted principles and functions of good Government—be it noted so far as my State and my Government were concerned and as an expression of my own opinion—I adumberated the following seven points:

I. The necessity for the Ruler of a State to have a fixed and well-defined Privy Purse and a clear dividing line between his personal expenditure and that of the State.
II. Security of life and property by the employment of as efficient and uncorrupt a Police as possible for the maintenance of Law and Order.
III. Independent Judiciary.
IV. The Reign of Law, including certainty of Law, its uniformity and approximation, where possible, with the laws of British India, with such additions and alterations as local conditions may render necessary.
V. Stability of Public Services.
VI. Efficiency and countinuity of administration.
VII. Beneficent rule in the interest of the general well-being and contentment of the subjects.

Of the above points, II, III and IV are covered by paragraph (5) (a) of this Resolution; whilst point I, is covered by paragraph (5) (b). Point II, referring to security of life and property is partly covered by paragraph (5) ( a), whilst the necessity of as efficient and uncorrupt a Police as possible for the maintenance of Law and Order requires no addumberation—difficult though the ideal is, as compared with what one may expect in this difficult world of ours. Continuity of administration and its efficiency similarly needs no illustration—subject to the remarks I have already made above in regard to 'efficiency' and similarly nothing in particular is necessary to be stated here for purposes of this Resolution in regard to point VII-Beneficent rule in the interests of the general well-being and contentment of the subjects-specially when we look at such principles from what has been stated above.

53. To secure good Government, we must obviously have competent machinery which is an essential of success; or, in other words, Public Services, to which capable honest officers would be attracted under a sense of security of tenure in accordance with the Civil Service Regulations of the State concerned and the contract of their service—so long as they discharge their duties with loyalty, honesty and efficiency.

54.1t is unneccessary to add that these principles do not differ from the Hindu ideal of Kingship so aptly put before us by our own Shastras. Whatever difference of opinion there may be as regards the method of giving effect to them, I do not believe that there is really much, if any, difference between any one of us here as regards the general principles of good Government or the essential need of the States on their own initiative and in their own interest to put their houses in order.

55. As His Excellency remarked in his recent speech at Jodhpur, the solicitude for the welfare and prosperity of our subjects:

> "should be alike the pride and reward of every Ruler who has the interests of his State at heart. With the rapid spread of education the problems which the Princes of India have to solve are daily becoming more complex, criticism of their administration more and more insistent and the highest standard of Government more generally demanded by public opinion. It is wise to recognise and not to ignore the forces which are at work and to realise that a Prince who neglects to discharge with humanity and justice the sacred trust, which he has inherited, is not only sacrificing the interests of his subjects and his State, but is weakening the position

of the Order to which he has the honour to belong. . . ."

56. Let us demonstrate to the world by the manner in which we deal with this Resolution—both here and hereafter—that Indian Kingship and our ancient oriental culture provide for just as good government as any system of modern rule or of Western democracy.

57. In conclusion, I must apologize for having taken so much of Your Excellency's and Your Highnesses' time in moving this Resolution. But I feel confident that it will be appreciated that the grave importance of the matter will be taken in extenuation. I would venture earnestly and solemnly to repeat that, just as the ultimate decision to be arrived at by the Imperial Government on issues now before the Indian States Committee is a matter of life and death for our States, sao in my humble judgment it is equally a matter of life and death for our States, and for us ourselves and our Dynasties, what action we take, not only during today's debate, but also the action which each Ruler and State, if, and where, he finds the necessity for such action, will take upon our decision today—if, as I hope, my Resolution is accepted by Your Highnesses. We can but hope and pray that a just and equitable solution will be found by the Indian States Committee and be supported by the Imperial Government, which would reassure the minds of the Princes, and that through the wise action taken by ourselves today and hereafter in regard to the aims and objects which this Resolution has, I trust, prominently placed before Your Highnesses, the strength and prestige will be advanced not only of the Princes and States, not only of the Great Indian Empire, but also of the greater British Empire, and that we—the Princes and our States and subjects—will thereby be enabled to take our proper and rightful place as "perpetual Friends and Allies" and enabled without encroachment, without menace, and without anxiety or vexation, to work out our destinies under the aegis of our beloved King-Emperor to whom we are bound by ties of the most steadfast loyalty and deepest devotion.

# Annexure 2

**Speech delivered by His Highness the Maharajah of Bikaner in the Chamber of Princes on the 13th February, 1929, in supporting the Resolution moved by His Highness the Chancellor (Maharajah of Patiala) regarding the attitude of the Chamber of Princes towards proposals relating to the equitable adjustment of relations between the Indian States and British India.**

*Your Excellency; Your Highnesses;*

It is not necessary for me to speak at any great length in supporting the very important resolution which has just been moved by His Highness the Chancellor. It was only the other day-namely on the 9th of September last at a dinner, which I gave in Bikaner in honour of my Prime Minister, Sir Manubhai Mehta, on the eve of his departure for England to take part in the Princes' work there connected with the Indian States Committee-that I took the opportunity of explaining at considerable length the views and sentiments and the attitude and outlook of the Princes and States on the various important matters prominently before us at the present moment, views which, I believe I am not incorrect in saying, are held not exclusively be myself, or shared by only a small number of the Rilling Princes of India, but by at least the great majority, if not—as I would fain hope—by our entire Order, and which furtheremore represent sober opinion in our Indian States.

At the same time, in regard to a resolution so important as the one now under discussion, and which must of necessity cover a wide field and diverse subjects, it is the duty of everyone, whether belonging to the States or British India, to make as clear as possible the terms of this resolution as well as our attitude in regard to its subject-matter so as to leave no room for any honest misunderstanding or deliberate misrepresentation. it is also best for us all to be perfectly frank. It pays invariably, at least in the long run; and leaves no room for imaginary calculations or false expectations.

His Highness the Chancellor's resolution moved today on behalf of the Chamber of Princes covers two important points. It attempts to make it clear:

1. that the Princes and States of India can have nothing to do with any proposals having for their object the adjustment of equitable relations in India of the future between the Indian States and British India, which, as has been urged by a section of British Indian politicians, have as their goal the complete independence of India, and thus the severance of the British connection; and
2. the Princes' attitude towards, and sympathy for, the legitimate aspirations of our brethren in British India for attaining full Nationhood under the aegis of the Imperial Crown.

It should not be necessary to labour the first point. Honour and good faith demand that all parties concerned should pay scrupulous regard to treaties and engagements, which have created mutual rights and obligations—and here may I in all friendliness add that the States insist upon British India also respecting our Treaties and Rights. The Princes of India have all along assessed at a very high value the sanctity of plighted faith; and in doing their utmost to live up loyally to the high moral qualities of integrity of word and sacredness of compact, they have of ten cheerfully carried on the struggle and borne heavy sacrifices. Thus it will be clear that apart from our feelings of personal loyalty and attachment to His Imperial Majesty the King-Emperor, we are intimately bound to the British Crown through our Treaties and Engagements, which in themselves render it impossible for the Princes even to countenance, much less to lend their support to, any such fantastic and impossible proposals which aim at complete independence and the severance of the British connection.

Moreover, it is my honest conviction, as I am sure it is that of Your Highnesses, that India can find no ampler scope for its continued constitutional advancement or greater security for its future well-being than in the Commonwealth of the British Empire. As a single instance in support of my argument, it will suffice to point to the sure shield offered to us all in India, with our extensive sea coast, by the might of Britain's Navy, not to speak of the defence and protection of our far flung frontiers guaranteed to India by the British Army. And where else for the orderly and peaceful development of our country can we look for all the resources and facilities which the most powerful Empire in history can offer us?

In this connection I would refer to the significant pronouncement made on the subject not long ago by General Smuts with reference to similar talk about the complete independence of South Africa and its breaking adrift from the Empire. He pointed out, so far as I recollect, in much stronger language, that without the British Navy behind them, the independence of South Africa would not be worth much for any length of time.

We the Princes and people of the Indian States are ourselves Indians; and we do most sincerely with our Motherland and fellow countrymen well and we do equally sincerely look forward—as proudly as any British Indian—to the day when our united Country would attain to the full height of its political stature, as in every way an equal, and fully trusted, member of the committee of Nations within the British Empire, and as much respected as any other self-governing British Dominion.

This has already brought me to the second point of our Resolution. As I have pointed out on more than one occasion, many Princes have within this Chamber and without, and not only in India but also in England, gone out of their way not merely to express their sympathy with the legitimate aspirations of British India, but we have, as occasion demanded, further urged that generous and liberal measures be taken early to accelerate the constitutional advancement of British India within the Empire.

And today we have in this Resolution again reiterated that we adhere to our policy of non-interference in the purely domestic affairs of British India and have repeated our assurances of sympathy with its continued political progress—be that towards Dominion Status, or Self-Government under the aegis of the British Crown, or whatever other system compatible with our ideal might be desired and found most suitable for British India. But it would obviously be futile and in vain for any section in British India to seek to make terms with the Indian States, the Princes and their subjects for any readjustment in the future policy of this Country unless the basis of such negotiations was without mental reservation of any kind, or if the Dominion Status now asked for, is ultimately to be only a cloak for the goal of separation and complete independence.

And here, Sir, may I be permitted to say with what gratification I read, as I am sure was the case with my Brother Princes, the words addressed by Your Excellency a few days ago in the Imperial Legislative Assembly giving as assurance to British India that the memorable Declaration of 1917 stands, and will stand for all time, as the solemn pledge of the British people.

When a few weeks ago in informal discussions amongst ourselves the proposal was mooted for this Resolution to be moved by His Highness the Chancellor, some of us naturally also took into consideration the question as to whether such action on our part was capable of being honestly misunderstood in the Country; but-as was pointed out during such deliberations—when the text of the Resolution was read as a whole it was not only clear that we were not thwarting in any way the consitutional advancement of British India, but that far from opposing, we were really lending our moral support to, the leaders of British India who, for instance in Calcutta last December, succeeded in getting rejected the Resolution moved by an extreme section of politicians for complete independence. And it is in this spirit that we all trust that our actions and deliberations today will be viewed by all impartial and fair-minded men in British India.

Before concluding I would incidentally also observe that proof of the wisdom and justification of Your Highness' decision last Monday to throw open to the Press and the public the meetings of our Chamber in their entirety is forthcoming in a most practicable manner much earlier than might ordinarily have been the case. For, there can be few resolutions and discussions like the one now engaging our attention which, unless undertaken in the fullest light of publicity, are more capable of producing misunderstanding, or even misrepresentation, and of creating suspicions in the minds of the people and the Press of British India. It requires no great powers of imagination to realize what might not have been said in regard to our discussions, and even our motives, in taking up this subject today. It will be easily perceived that had our sittings been held in seclusion and our proceedings not been available to the Press and the public, all kinds of rumours—even distorted versions—would have gone round; and, through ignorance and alarm, and in some cases the deliberate perversion of facts, the wildest canards would have like a snowball gone round and gathered strength, when the Chamber of Princes, as well as individual Rulers taking part in today's debate, would not only have been represented—but believed by many an honest individual in British India—as thwarting India's constitutional advancement. Today, with our deliberations taking place in public, with the reporters of the Press present in this Chamber, and our proceedings freely available to all the sundry both in British India and our States, the Chamber of Princes as well as each one of us are in the strong position of being able conclusively to show to the entire World that nothing has been done by the Chamber of Princes contrary to their of repeated declarations. Except those who are not open to reason, every fair-minded person in British India will now be in a position to understand that we stand for evolution and not for revolution and that we stand—and stand unflinchingly, steadfastly and irrevocably, and regardless of all sacrifices—for the maintenance of the British connection, as well as for the adequate safeguarding and correct recognition, of the Treaties, rights, privileges and prerogatives of ourselves and our States.

# Annexure 3

**Speech Delivered by His Highness the Maharajah inaugurating the Administrative Conference on Thursday, the 3rd October, 1929.**

*Sir, Manubhai Mehta, and Gentlemen,*

It affords me very sincere pleasure to inaugurate this Session of the Bikaner State Administrative Conference and to see this body meeting once again after a lapse of some years—meetings which I hope will henceforth be regular annual events.

**Associating the People with Administration**

The past history of the Administrative Conference, in common with that of all great public institutions, has been a somewhat chequered one; but the central idea of associating the people with the administration of the State has never been lacking. A happy blending of all that is best in the democratic idea of Government of the people, by the people and for the people, with all that is again, best is benevolent autocracy—in the right sense of the term—and not merely an apish imitation of things Western—some of which are not always necessarily suited to the East—has ever been my aim and endeavour; and the very variety and multiplicity of the suggestions and proposals put forward, by official and non-official members alike, and carried out during the last quarter of a century of the existence of this Conference, is a proof of how jealously and zealously I and my Government have fostered the spirit of self-expression among my people, how readily they have been taken into our fullest confidence, how pleased we have felt in taking advantage of their views and advice, and of what weight we attach to their opinions and deliberations.

**Personal Touch Between the Ruler and the Ruled**

I have always felt that there cannot be too much or enough of contact between the Ruler and the ruled in an Indian State. The Indian State Administration is distinguished from other forms of Government in the sister Provinces of British India by the one main fact that it is a living rule; it is not an automation but has a soul. Personal touch between the Ruler and the ruled is a marked factor of success peculiar to Indian States, which has to be nursed with fostering care and parental solicitude. I have been alway eager to give my subjects greater and greater opportunities of coming into personal and intimate contact with my officers. There is no room for any 'sun-dried bureaucracy' in an Indian State.

**History of Administrative Conference**

The beginning of this Conference dates back to 1905, when it was called the Revenue Conference, and when matters relating purely to Land Revenue were originally discussed. This Conference was convened by me with a view to bringing the local Revenue Officers and my subjects in closer touch and thus bringing the gulf between them. I was so pleased with the success that attended the first Conference that I decided to make it an annual fixture. And the Conference soon grew from strength to strength from 1905 to 1908; several reforms, big and small, and important schemes of great potential value were taken in hand as a result of the discussions held at these annual Conferences; and as a full measure of latitude for frank discussions from every standpoint was allowed, we were enabled to do things in days, which it would have taken months, if not years, to accomplish in the ordinary course of official routine—and to do them better at that. Committees and Sub-Committees were formed to draft rules, regulations, and even laws, as also detailed schemes of reform, and such proposals were laid again before the Conference.

In this way many important questions were settled and measures introduced conducive to the welfare of the State and its subjects and calculated to improve the relations between the State Officers and Departments and my people.

Feeling that more might be done for the people's happiness and for bringing them and the District Authorities in particular into more intimate touch, and for raising the general efficiency of the administration, and realising that the scope of the questions and measures discussed at these Conferences had become so wide as to embrace the administration as a whole, resulting in many important changes and reforms being introduced and in some old rules and regulations being revised that brought up-to-date and in many other measures being taken to improve the conditions of the various classes and comunities of my subjects, the name of this Revenue Conference was changed in 1910 into that of an Administrative Conference.

In 1908 some non-official gentlemen were also nominated as members of this Conference; and thus it was in that year that the first seed of Representative Government was sown in the Bikaner State.

To give you an idea of the work done I may add that the number of questions and proposals discussed and disposed of at these Conferences were as below:

| | | |
|---|---|---|
| In 1905 | ... | 49 |
| In 1907 | ... | 68 |
| In 1908 | ... | 105 |
| In 1909 | ... | 114 |
| In 1910 | ... | 100 |

It was perhaps only to be expected that in course of time the number of such subjects to be discussed should decrease, although the fact that only 9 such questions were brought up at the Conference in 1911, and only 13 in 1912, naturally caused me considerable disappoitment.

I had always hoped that it would be found possible to extend the functions of the Administrative Conference, and to turn it into a truly representative body when the time was ripe for it. Thus, when in September, 1912, various boons and concessions were conferred on the people on the occasion of the celebrations connected with my having completed 25 years of my Reign—the 'Silver Jubilee', as it was popularly known in the State-I announced my intention to institute the Representative Assembly. This Assembly was duly inaugurated in November 1913, which of course is now known as the Bikaner Legislative Assembly; and in consequence it was then felt that there would really be no scope for an Administrative Conference so constituted, since opportunities were open to elected representatives of the people of expressing their views and of putting forward their proposals during the Sessions of the Assembly. Thus the holding of these Conferences was discontinued from 1913. No one at the time, official or non-official, had really first-hand experience of the working of a Legislative Assembly; but it is only right to add that within a few years of the inauguration of the Legislative Assembly actual experience showed that a mistake had been made in discontinuing these Conferences, since details in many directions, which often received attention on the suggestions of the non-official members, could not be dealt with in the same manner in the local Legislature. Perhaps the paucity of the Agenda had at least an indirect influence in the decision arrived at. Anyhow it was soon realised that the Administrative Conference filled a distinct want and had a sphere of usefulness peculiarly its own, in no way overlapped by the activities of the Legislative Assembly. But for our pre-occupations during the Great

War and its aftermath, the Administrative Conference would have been revived earlier; and, although an attempt was made in 1921, once again the paucity of the Agenda and the lack of enthusiasm shown generally by officials as well as non-officials in the Conference of March of that year clearly indicated to me that it was no good attempting to force the pace, and that the Conference could not again be a success unless and until all concerned really took interest, and an active part, in it.

I had however never failed during this interval to keep prominently before my Government the urgent necessity of reviving these Administrative Conferences, and of repeatedly urging the great advantages to all concerned accruing from such Conferences. It is thus that I derive particular gratification at the fact that the Conference has once again been resuscitated; and I have particularly to thank my trusted Prime Minister, Sir Manubhai Mehta, for the enthusiasm and energy with which he has brought about this meeting. The fact that, in spite of comparatively short notice, the Agenda this year contains no less than 41 questions, covering a wide and useful field of subjects, in itself leads me to hope that the apathy displayed at one time both by officials and non-officials has become a thing of the past; and I have every hope that under the sympathetic encouragement and wise guidance of the Prime Minister and the able and loyal support of the other members of my Government and of other Officers of the State, this Conference will not only become a regular annual fixture, but that it may resume its old functions and be yet one more powerful source of contributing towards the happiness and contentment of the people of the Bikaner State and in drawing the Government and the Officers of the State into the closest touch with my beloved subjects.

Whilst every care has been taken to ensure that this Administrative Conference does not in any way become a rival of , or replace or supplant, the Legislative Assembly with its clearly defined functions and scope of doing good in its own field, every endeavour has also been made to derive the maximum of benefit from this Administrative Conference; and several innovations have been made on this occasion. The number of members has been largely increased, the proportion of non-official membes having been raised from 10 to 1921 to about for times this number today. All non-official members of the Legislative Assembly, both elected and nominated, have been made eligible as ordinary members of this Conference.

At the last Conference of 1921, out of a total number of 37 members, 10 were non-officials, including the Chiefs and Nobles,

Seths and Sahukars, and Vakils. This year 77 members have been invited to participate in this Conference, of which 38 are officials and 39 non-officials. The former consist of the Prime Minister and five other members of my Government; the Chief Justice and the two Puisne Judges of our High Court of Judicature; 20 of the high officials, Secretaries and Heads of Departments and some of the more important officials, the four Nazims and the four District Judges; and the officer of the Court of Wards. The non-official members comprise of one Rajvi, four chiefs and Nobles, 12 Seths and Sahukars, one other leading citizen, 17 non-official members of the Bikaner Legislative Assembly, besides ex-officio members and other non-official members of the Assembly already invited to this Conference to represent their respective interests and 4 members of the Bikaner Bar.

In any Administrative Conference, there will always be certain points of purely administrative technique, which are most fitted for preliminary discussion by the various officials with the members of my Government to enable frank and free discussions and heart to heart talks taking place in the first instance between the various Officers of the State and to enable even junior officials to put their points of view before their seniors without any hesitation and to encourage them to voice the practical difficulties they meet with in actual administrative work. But on some of these subjects too, an opportunity will be open to non-official members to take part and to join in the discussions at a later stage.

**Rural Reconstruction and Industrial Conferences**

At this year's Conference, another new departure has been made which I feel sure will be welcomed by the non-official members, and for which valuable suggestion I am particularly grateful to the Prime Minister. It is proposed to hold, side by side with the Administrative Conference, Economic and Industrial Conferences, for which purposes the main Conference will divide itself into two Committees or Sub-Conferences.

The Economic or Rural Reconstruction Conference or Committee will discuss all questions of:

(1) economic interest for the welfare of villages; and
(2) The development of rural economy, such as:

a. Agriculture;
b. Co-operation;

c. Sanitation;
d. Education;
e. Medical relief in Villages for men as well as women;
f. Conciliation and mediation in litigation;
g. Redemption of debts;
h. Prevention of further fragmentation of holdings; and
i. Consolidation of agricultural holdings;

whilst the Industrial Conference will deal with questions connected with:

(1) Urban developments;
(2) Advancement of Industries;
(3) Cottage Industries;
(4) Factory Legislation;
(5) Relations between Labour and Capital;
(6) Municipal Taxation;
(7) Customs and Octroi;
(8) Regulation of Compulsory Education in towns, etc.;
(9) Sanitation; and
(10) Medical relief for men and women.

All these Committees or Sub-conferences, on which non-official members will be strongly represented, will, I trust, as has been made sufficiently clear, be an adjunct to the main Administrative Conference; and the Prime Minister, as your President, will elucidate all further details in connection with such work.

And now I should like to take this opportunity of addressing particularly the officers of the State present here today, specially as it is a long time since such an opportunity has occurred and when I look round I see so many new faces. And here I feel that all present will join me in the regret and the sorrow that we feel in missing many faces familiar and dear to us. Prominent amongst them I would mention the heavy loss that my Government has suffered this year by the loss of two loyal, able and old servants and Ministers of the State—the late Khan Bahadur, Mr. Rustomji and Mr. Rudkin—and also of another very high officer, the late Chief Justice, Rai Bahadur Chaubey, Pyare Lall.

**Advice to State Officers**

I have often spoken on some of these subjects before, but I trust repetition will do no harm today. First and foremost would I would like to impress upon all State Officials the extreme importance of greater sympathy and closer touch with the people. There is a great need for this to be demonstrated not only by the high officers but also by the District Officers and those lower down in the official rank of precedence who come most in contact with my subjects. I once in this very place talked of the necessity of the officials guarding against turning themselves into frigid human machines, who just follow red-tape and regulation without in any way thinking of how much a little touch of sympathy, a little word of advice, a little hint to a petitioner as to where was the right place for him to go to, the help by means of a chit or otherwise in directing him to go to the proper quarter—what a lot all that would do. May I hope that this point will be borne in mind not only by the District Officers but that you, gentlemen, who are higher up will also pay special attention to this at headquarters, as well as when you go out in the districts on tour? And here, gentlemen, let me once again emphasize the supreme importance of your undertaking regular and frequent tours in the interior of the State.

The second subject that I wish to touch upon today is the need for our all being on the alert to check bribery and corruption as well as intrigue, in every way possible. I am perfectly aware that bribery and corruption are impossible altogether to stop; but it is not impossible at least to keep them within check; and if all officers will do their duty properly and will at once and severely deal with any deliquents, I feel sure that much could be done. I have reasons to believe that when cases of this kind come to notice, leniency is not infrequently shown, which, it will be obvious, is entirely misplaced. I appeal, therefore, to all officers to try their utmost to eradicate and at least to keep within check as far as possible this great evil. I trust that these evils are not so rampant in our State as in some other places, but that is no reason for relaxing our efforts.

Then I would appeal for greater co-operation and co-ordination in the field of administration between Departments and Officers, which is essentially necessary, and it is with one such object that I have resuscitated this Administrative Conference. Here in this gathering you will all have opportunities of free and frank talk and friendly exchange of ideas and of informal discussions. My subjects, whom I have always considered a part of my Government, will have ample opportunities to ventilate their grievances and to suggest remedies; but to the officials I would specially say today that I look to cooperation between Department and Department, between officer and officer, and their staff, as much as between the State and its subjects. Unless we have co-ordination and co-operation, the results are bound to be poor. Human energy is apt to suffer as much from friction as from waste. Our efforts at administrative improvements are often needlessly spent through a number of agencies without any endeavour at co-operation. We have not, many of us, still learnt to apply the art of

conservation of energy and division of labour to our administrative problems. In the economy of administrative effort co-ordination and marshalling of forces are no less important than concentration of energy. If the suggestions of one officer at any healthy experiment are handed over to the officer in charge of that Department, we save at least some wastage involved in reduplication of effort. Administrative Conferences help to secure such co-ordination so that the results achieved by one are utilised and made a fresh point for further eleboration on the part of the officer controlling the Department concerned. Such healthy coŕordination along with equally helpful co-operation is a great asset and of ten the key to success in the art of government.

You, the official members of this Conference, do not require to be reminded that the task of administration is getting more and more complex every year. I have already endeavoured to rule for the benefit of my people. Two years ago, for instance, I enjoined the rigid separation of the Executive machinery from the Judicial Tribunals of the State; and I trust my subjects have already commenced to appreciate the merits of an independent Judiciary altogether untrammeled by the traditions of the Executive Departments. It rests in your hands to take this justice almost to the doors of the people's houses and to make such justice easy and expeditious to attain. I have also sanctioned the Village Panchayat Act, so that petty letigation could be avoided or settled promptly by your own village elders. I expect my officers to move about freely among my people and to bring home to their minds the benefits of such facile adjudication through arbitration and conciliation of the village Panches. The administration of justice should be both prompt and cheap. Laws' delays have been proverbial; and costly litigation spells ruin.

You have to raise my people in their fitness for administration of local and Municipal affairs and gradually to awaken their political self-consciousness. Our Municipal Government requires to be fostered with sympathy and a real desire for improvement. Let not the finger of scorn be allowed to be pointed at the lethargy and apathy of our citizens for Municipal Government.

My Government is also shortly evolving a new law for District Local

Boards. We must begin with the rudiments of administration and commence our reform with the foundations in our villages and districts. I wish you during your present sessions to devote your special attention to the problems of rural reconstruction. The village is the unit of our political system; and the economy of village life presents us with problems not less intricate than those of our towns and the Capital. Problems of Agriculture, Irrigation, Agricultural holdings, and Agricultural improvement, of Animal husbandry, the improvement of breeds of cattle and their preservation, Relief of Agricultural indebtedness through Co-operative Societies and Land Mortgage Banks—all these questions deserve your attention.

There are moreover the Nation-building Departments-Education, Medical Relief, Sanitation and Hygeine, and last, but not the least, the revival of Industries—both in Rural as well as Urban areas—which ought to claim the attention of this Administrative Conference.

With your concurrence we have passed the Compulsory Primary Education Act—a measure of fundamental importance for the task of Nation-building. It is for the Municipalities and other Local Bodies to make a suitable gesture and to indicate their readiness to avail themselves of this beneficial measure which is the only 'Open Sesame' for any permanent progress and advancement of our country.

I attach equal importance to the revival of industries in our State. And you will be gratified to observe that I have invited our Captains of Industry and eminent businessmen to take a prominent part in this branch of the Conference. of all our industries, Agriculture is of course by far the most cardinal industry for the uplift of the rural masses. If to this sheet anchor of our rural economy we fasten some subsidiary cottage industries to keep the cultivators engaged in the slack season so as to help them further to earn their living, our object would to a great extent be achieved. Bikaner wool has attained a wide repute for its purity and excellence in the market. Until we have a large Woollen Manufactory and an extensive Carpet Factory, the art of weaving excellent blankets and lois from our superior wool should form the backbone of our cottage industries. Bikaner unfortunately is not blessed by Nature with abundance of Agricultural resources; it is pastoral country. We have no rich minerals embedded in our sands; but the geological survey of the State is not so disappointing. There are untold possibilities in the lignite mines at Palana; and I am gratified to learn that the development of coal and carbon products has been engaging the attention of my officers. Moreover there is excellent building stone, gypsum, ochre and china-clay which require careful developing. I look to you, Seths and

Sahukars of Bikaner, with your business talents and your purse, to co-operate with my Government and to help the growth—economic and material, moral and intellectual-or our State so as to set an example to our neighbours. The ultimate good of our State and its people must be our common goal.

Before continuing some of my other observations, I should like to touch upon a few more points. I referred a little while back to the separation of the Executive from the Judicial; and the Honourable Judges—the Chief Justice and the other Judges of the High Court—are the best authorities to say how independent in reality the Judiciary has been made by us and how little or how much of interference they have experienced from the Executive. But since a certain section of correspondents and newspapers are always talking of that as a farce, my Government would, I have no doubt, be delighted to take up the challenge and dare them to prove it and also in what way the Executive is interfering with the independence of the Judiciary. Whilst speaking on this subject I might also refer to an important detail. On the 21st March 1928, the Prime Minister issued a confidential circular, which I think it would do no harm, but great good, if I today made public. In that circular, the Prime Minister said that it had been brought to my notice that recommendations were at times made to, and attempts made to bring undue influences upon, the Judges, Magistrates and Munsiffs so as to affect the course of justice by people of influence, both official and unofficial, and the Prime Minister went on to point out in this circular that the independence of the Judiciary is the one characteristic and distinguishing feature of a perfect administration; and he emphasized once again that I considered it essentially necessary and desirable to stop this evil of using official or other personal influence to affect the course of justice. The Chief Justice of the High Court was therefore requested to ask all judges, Magistrate and Munsiffs promptly to report to the High Court the name of any person so endeavouring to approach the Judges, Magistrates and Munsiffs; and a request was also preferred for the names of such persons to be communicated every month to the Prime Minister for necessary action.

Well, gentlemen, the Executive cannot do more. And if there is any attempt to tamper with the independence of the Judiciary by sources other than, and unknown to, the Executive Government, it is for the distinguished Judges of the High Court and the other learned Officers administering justice to deal with the evil and to bring it to the notice of my Government when they can be assured of the fullest co-operation on the part of my Government I should also like to impress on all officers—Executive or Judicial—the need for the greatest care i n the selection of State servants not only the Gazetted officers but also the Establishment—clerical or otherwise. The consequences and the harm arising from an inefficient and incapable staff and favouritism in selection are obvious.

Another point which I wish to emphasize in connection with the employment of officers and subordinates is the claim of the people of Bikaner to receive priority. I have made many speeches on this subject before and have made it abundantly clear that to me and my Government there is no question of partiality or favouritism for Bikaneris, which would be unfair to anyone outside—be he an Indian or an Englishman. To us, every officer in our service—Bikaneri or non-Bikaneri—is entitled to the fullest consideration and protection and support; and where a Bikaneri is not qualified by education or otherwise to fill in a post—whether it be that of an officer or a subordinate—it is essential in the interests of the State that the best man for the post should be got from outside irrespective of class, creed or race. But where all other points are equal, there is the prior claim of the Bikaneri to receive the first preference in appointment; and this is the point which I wish to emphasize today. I have lately seen even Chaprasis going about who are not Bikaneris. I cannot believe that officers cannot find Bikaneris even for such posts. I had a talk with the Prime Minister on the subject a few days ago; and was very pleased to find that he had already taken notice of what is not obviously becoming to a certain extent an abuse of power by the officials concerned and that he is already providing in the new Rules for the definite claims of Bikaneris to receive prior consideration; and I understand that a statement is also to be compiled showing what new recruits in the upper or lower ranks have been recruited from Bikaner and otherwise. In this connection, I would remind officials that at one time the necessity was felt for statements of appointments made to be specially submitted by all Departments in which reasons had to be expressly given as to why a Bikaneri was not appointed. I will not attempt to anticipate any further action or orders that may have to be issued by Government on the subject; but I would ask that all concerned in all Departments will bear this important fact in mind.

I have just said that all officers, whatever their nationality, religion, race or place of residence, can be assured of the fullest support and the fairest treatment and consideration at the hands of my Government. I need not impress upon even those officers who are new—for they ought by now to have found out from officers who have been longer in the State Service—that no one is a greater champion of their rights and no one fights with greater enthusiasm and energy their battles than myself so long as they serve their State and subjects in a loyal, honourable and efficient manner; but at the same time it is a doctrine of my faith that whilst we must give the fullest support in every way to all deserving officers, we must not be misled by any false or empty notions of prestige to support those who by any act have forfeited our trust.

The few remaining points I wish to bring forward here today can be summed up in a few words.

For the last two or three years—and specially this year—you have all seen the terrible ravages by locusts. It is not a new danger. We have had periods of locusts invading our State, as they do other countries and other parts of India, but in all my experience I do not wish to imply any blame, I merely ask whether, in view of the security which we enjoyed from locusts for a certain number of years, we have not been lulled into a false sense of security or forgotten some of the essential precautions—some of the steps that the village people and officials used to take—to cope with the menace before it got beyond control. This is a point which I have asked the Prime Minister to discuss with you, gentlemen, officials and non-officials.

There are two comparatively insignificant, but in their own way important, points to which I should like the District Officers, and in particular the officers of the Revenue Department, to pay special attention, and to direct the attention of their subordinates, to the same.

Go to any part of the State and see how many places there are, even in our sandy tracts, where certain kinds of Rabi crops can be sown—provided there is rainfall late in the season, such as in September. There is rapeseed and even mustard which at least can be grown. Those who are new may scoff at the idea but they have to remember that till comparatively recently, and within the lifetime of many people, Rabi was hardly known in the entire State—not even in the North, where in good years of rainfall, long before irrigation, lacs and lacs of maunds of wheat and other Rabi crops have been sown. We must therefore not be dazzled by the benefits accruing from irrigation in the Gang Canal areas—and I hope further from the Bhakra Dam—by not troubling to grow Rabi and all efforts must be made and the people encouraged and exhorted by our officers to grow it, wherever it can be grown.

The second point relates to tree planting. You have to go to any village in the worst and sandiest part of our State and you will see in the villages, and near the tanks and wells, very fine old trees. How many new trees do you see now? Surely it is upto the District Officers to teach the present genemtion the advantages and benefits of following in the footsteps of their fore-fathers and at least doing what was done of yore inthis connection and even doing more now.

Unfair Allegations by Certain Newspapers.

Finally whilst addressing the officials I feel it necessary also to utter a warning to those officers as well as those non-officials who are the real leaders of public opinion in the Bikaner State who, by habit or temperament, may evince extra sensitiveness on the subject of attacks in the Press. I need not dilate upon the fact that there are newspapers and newspapers, and criticisms and criticisms. An officer who discharges his duty by the State and its subjects honourably, honestly, conscientiously and justly, has nothing to fear from such attacks. If he does not so discharge his duties, he will not only have to face such public criticism in the Press, but also the displeasure of his superior officers and the disapprobation of his Government Any Ruler, Government or officer who objects to, or disregards, honest and fair criticism, inspired by honourable and laudable motives, fails in the proper discharge of his duties. For an honest and efficient Press is the 'Fourth Estate'; and wholesome criticism is good for us all in more ways than one. One of the functions of an honest and honourable Press is not only to criticise where criticism is really called for, but also to instil fresh ideas and to help to take a Ruler, Government or official out of any ruts into which he may have driven deep through force of habit or imperviousness to light. It is thus, I trust, clear that I am not referring to the honourable and respectable section of the Press or to fair and just criticisms and helpful suggestions. But all officers, who proceed undaunted on their appointed task and who discharge their duties without fear or favour, should not pay the slightest attention to being attacked by a certain type of local correspondents and a certain section of the Press, who have brought the name of the Public Press into the mire, and who have indeed strayed far away from all that is honourable, best and noble in the traditions of journalism and journalists. Therefore, I say to each and every one of the officers present here—and I ask you to repeat it to the officers serving under you—"Benefit by honest and honourable criticism, but ignore and treat with contempt ignoble attacks of the tainted newspapers." See how, in season and out of season, and without the slightest discrimination, the Rulers, Governments and Ministers of all States—good, bad or indifferent—

are indiscriminately and sweepingly attacked by such newspapers and correspondents—not infrequently accompanied by vulgar abuse. These newspapers and journalists live and thrive because there are unfortunately amongst the Rulers, Ministers and other Officers people who, through defects in their administrations or Public Services, or through temperamental weakness, allow themselves to be blackmailed; and it is on such blackmail that such unworthy editors of such unworthy papers and the correspondents of the same elk subsist, and indeed often make quite a profitable living—further augmented by a large number of copies subscribed in the States, not only by people who are "again the Government" but also—human nature being what it is—by a good many other people, who derieve amusement and find dull moments livened up by reading such spicy stuff and scandal. Even though it is not often difficult to discriminate between truths and falsehoods, the danger remains of the ignorant masses being often misled and of much mischief and disaffection being thus wantonly created amongst the subjects of the States. Many authentic instances of numerous falsehoods, published in such papers—not infrequently contributed by local men posing as patriots and champions of States subjects—and even obvious attempts at blackmail, could be cited without difficulty.

During April and May last, when there was shortage of water in our newly constructed Gang Canal, there appeared in a notorious paper published in a British Indian centre in Rajputana, with unconcealed glee, a paragraph—inspired in all probability by a local 'patriot' obviously gloating over, what he felt was assuredly, the discomfiture and humiliation of the Government of Bikaner—stating that discontent was growing in the Gang Canal Area on account of sufficient water not being available, together with the publication of the rumour that" satyagraha" was to be performed in the Canal Area! The same paper produced a perfect gem of journalistic fairness and honest criticism by referring in the same connection in another of its issues to my "wasting lakhs of rupees of the public money on the construction of the Gang Canal !" There was the same kind of jubilation manifested by another paper of the same type. But did the honest, just and patriotic local correspondents—whose hearts so bled for the poor and oppressed people of this State, and whose sense of justice and fairness, specially to the authorities of their own State, were so pronounced—ever write a single line, or did such newspapers at any time publish any statement, to explain that this shortage was due to an Act of God and not in any way to any sin of commission or omission on the part of the Government of Bikaner or of its officers, nor inherently connected with any defect in the Canal project? Did they ever refer to a communique issued shortly afterwards by the Prime Minister, in which copious extracts and facts and figures were reproduced from a communique on the same subject issued by the Punjab Government, and which made it abundantly clear that an investigation by the Punjab Government into this question had revealed the fact that the supply of water this year at Ferozepur, where the Canal Headworks are situated, was the worst on record during the last 28 years, that such shortage of water was due to the exceptionally unfavourable conditions of snowfall—which they did not expect in the future except at long intervals—and that such shortage, as well as the consequent natural disaffection of the Colonists, was not confined to the Gang Canal Area in the Bikaner State alone but that it was shared by all the colonies in the entire Sutlej Valley Project, including British territory in the Punjab?

Similarly, did such newspapers and correspondents publish one single line, in fairness to our State and Government, about the various concessions regarding the suspension of payments due from colonists in the Gang Canal Area, estimated at some Rs. 25 lakhs or more, which it was my pleasure to sanction, as a special measure, in July last—in view of the losses the new settlers had suffered on account of the recent comparative failure of the crops in the Punjab and of its not being found possible, owing to such unusual shortage of water in the Sutlej River last Summer, and of the unavoidable delays in finishing certain masonry works in certain Canal Areas, to arrange for an equitable supply of water to all chaks during the two crops, whereby the capacity of such purchasers to pay instalments of the purchase money of the lands sold had been somewhat impaired?

In the same connection it may perhaps amuse you, gentlemen, to hear that about the same time my Private Secretary received a letter from the Editor of one such paper, who said that he had received "serious complaints with regard to the settlement on the bank and near the so-called Great Ganga Canal," that it seemed, amongst other things, and besides other great sufferings of the poor inhabitants, that "the atrocities inflicted by your staff on the poor settlers are horrible"; but this gentleman went on to say that "before publishing the allegations we wish to visit the place ourselves" and asked if we would make necessary arrangements and let him know at an early date when, the Editor added that, he would come up himself for the "tedious task" as he did not want to write anything "alarming with regard to States, most of whom Are our patrons".

To take another very recent instance, some of you may have read the very vulgar attack, in the worst of tastes, on no less a personage than our distinguished and popular Prime Minister, Sir Manubhai Mehta, who has rightly made a name throughout the length and breadth of India as one of the foremost statesmen and most capable of administrators of modern times produced in our Indian States; and yet a person, styling himself as the "General Secretary of the Rajputana States Peoples Conference," has been good enough to tell the world at large that Sir Manubhai has proved a hopeless failure as a reformer and administrator in Bikaner and that the people of Bikaner have not in the least been benefited by his experience, qualifications and outlook. So, Gentlemen, if you are attacked by such scurrilous papers and correspondents you will at least find yourself in distinguished company!

Then again take this Administrative Conference, with the brief history of which I have already dealt today, and the facts of which are well-known to the officers and people of the State who have been any length of time in the State service or who have resided in the State all their lives. Such facts should also surely be known to such expert correspondents of such papers, which papers—if they laid claim to any sense of responsibility or fairmindedness—should, it would not be unreasonable to expect, in their turn have verified facts before attacking the Government and assigning to them all sorts of false and dishonourable motives. A paper printed at Beawar in British Rajputana published a letter from its own correspondent, in which, in addition to certain other mis-statements, it was asserted that no just recommendations were to be expected from this "farcial invitation" to State officials and non-officials to attend this Administrative Conference; and that rumours were on the other hand afloat that this device was only hit upon to find new avenues of taxation and for the enhancement of existing taxes! a vernacular paper in Delhi took up this parrot cly in an open letter to me and, after repeating more or less the same things, improved upon them by stating that it was almost certain that additional taxes and cease, will be levied on the people under this pretext and then proceeded positively to assert that in view of the affairs and policies of the Indian States, it would not be improper to say that "the rumour surely contains some truth in it" and finally, I was warned that the results of such an Administrative Conference would be prejudicial to the State as well as to the people!

Although it is by no means an offence to enhance the revenues and resources of a State by all fair and legitimate means, I have had the curiosity to have a statement prepared in the Secretariat of the total number of questions taken up in the various Administrative

Conferences held in the State ever since the first meeting convened some 23 years ago. As a result I have been informed that out of a total number of 4 79 questions so discussed—which dealt with diverse details relating to Administration; Agriculture; Begar;

Customs and Excise; Education; Extradition; Finance; Irrigation; Jails; Judicial; Malmandi; Medical and Public; Police; Works of Public Utility; Revenue Settlement; Social Reforms; Trade and Industries; Planting and preservation of trees; etc.—only five questions had any relation; direct or indirect, with taxation or otherwise raising revenue. of these five, one was a proposal made by a Nazim in 1909 regarding imposing an export duty on tobacco; the second in 1909 by a Tehsildar proposing to levy a wheel-tax, which matter was taken up alongwith the general question of making the Bikaner City Municipality self-supporting; the third was a proposal made in 1911 by a distinguished Pardeshi Member of the Government of the time to award a prize for the best essay on the means of improving the resources of the State, in the fourth case, a local cess was proposed in 1912 for the construction of village ranks; and the fifth question related to a proposal made in 1912 for a change in the scale of fees fixed in the execution of certain class of civil decress. But in all the five cases no official action, as it happened, resulted with the exception of the wheel-tax imposed subsequently when the Municipalities were made self-supporting.

In the Agenda of this Conference—and it is necessary to emphasize that such Agenda consists entirely of points suggested by, and at the discretion of , individual officers, irrespective of whether they relate to their own Department or are considered by them to be matters in the general interests of the State and its subjects—out of 41 questions so far placed on the Agenda, there is not one single question relating to taxation or enhancement of the State revenues. Such then is the veracity, and fairmindedness of such correspondents and their newspapers, and such is the credit and reward given to the Governments of States which are honestly trying to do their best for their subjects by promoting their welfare through reviving the Administrative Conference and receiving suggestions for improving the Administration in various directions from officials and non-officials alike at such Conferences!

Such newspapers attack on the heavy taxes levied in the State as also about new taxation; but my Government would be very glad if such correspondents and newspapers will enlighten us, as well as the world at large, as for what these accusations and charges are based on and what the new taxes are.

**Butler Report**

I will now for a few moments refer to a subject of more than local importance to us. As the Report of the Indian States Committee, commonly known as the Butler Committee, was published in April last, it may perhaps be expected that I should take this opportunity of saying something on the subject. The time is neither ripes, nor suitable, for any public pronouncement by me or by my Government on the many issues of such great importance to the Indian States dealt with in the Butler Report. Since, however, the silence of myself, in common with that of the Princes, might be misunderstood—and even deliberately misrepresented by a certain class of people—it would perhaps be as well if I said a few words in explanation. From time to time the speeches made by some Princes during the last two years would have made clear the reasons for the appointment of the Butler Committee, as also the hopes of the Princes and their Governments of thereby securing and safeguarding the rightful position of the States in the body politic of India, as well as their aspirations and anxieties in regard to certain important matters whereby the States and their subjects were adversely affected under present day conditions. It will be recalled that I too dealt with such matters in my speech delivered on the 20th January, 1928, in our Legislative Assembly, and again in another speech delivered on the 9th September last at a farewell dinner given at the Palace in honour of the Prime Minister on the eve of his leaving for England to take part there in the proceedings of the Butler Committee.

Efforts were not wanting, ever since the publication of the Butler Report, to stampede the Princes, individually and collectively, forthwith to pronounce their views on the Report. But I venture to say that the Princes have displayed no small measure of wisdom and political sagacity in not following the tactics, adopted at times in British India, by rushing to the Press and on the platform. Apart from there always being the risk of having to repent at leisure any hasty action taken, or pronouncement made, on the subject, statesmanship and prudence demanded that the Princes, who do not believe in non-eo-operation, should also safeguard against the dangerous consequences on the one hand of jeopardizing diplomatic and political negotiations with the British Government on matters constitutional, political and fiscal, and on the other of unnecessarily coming into conflict with British India and alienating the sympathy, or incurring the hostility, of sober public opinion in British India.

The Butler Report—though by no means lengthy—required in

the first instance much time and care for a calm and dispassionate study of its various proposals and recommendations and of all the implications involved. And then, pending an examination in detail of each and every problem and point dealt with in the Butler Report, which in its turn necessitates much spade work on the part of the Princes Standing Committee as well as the Special Organization of the Chamber of Princes—which has to be re-established at an early date—it was obviously necessary that there should be an opportunity for the Princes and Ministers of the States to meet and discuss at length the more important details and to settle the broad outlines of the future course of action which it may be deemed desirable to follow. Such an opportunity occurred towards the end of June when a Conference was held in Bombay and over which—in the unavoidable absence of His Highness the Maharajah of Patiala, the Chancellor, and His Highness the Maharajah of Kashmir, the Pro-Chancellor, of the Chamber of Princes—the duty devolved upon me of discharging the functions of the Chancellor. In accordance with the decision arrived at, and the mandate given, the Princes of the Standing Committee immediately afterwards met His Excellency the Viceroy at Poona on the 28th June and communicated to Lord Irwin the tentative views of the Conference regarding the various findings and recommendations of the Butler Committee. And as it was also deemed advisable to make public such tentative views, the resolutions passed at the Bombay Conference were also, under similar authority given by that representative body, published immediately after the Poona meeting, which sufficiently clearly conveyed what, in the opinion of the Princes' Conference, constituted the satisfactory, as well as the unsatisfactory, features of the more important findings of the Butler Report.

By far the most important subject to be found on the Agenda of the next session of the Chamber of Princes—which, according to the present programme, is to be held from the 25th February to the 1st March—will be the consideration of the Butler Report; and now that the proceedings of the Chamber of Princess are happily open to the public; and therefore reported in the Press also, it will be possible for anyone belonging to the States or British India interested in the matter to acquaint himself with the details of the interesting and important debate on the subject which can confidently be anticipated in the Chamber of Princes.

Since it will be in such a debate in that Chamber that the authentic and carefully considered and mature views of the Princes and States will be expressed, it would obviously be improper for me to anticipate such a debazte or even to attempt to give expression to any views—necessarily tentative at this stage—which I and my Government may have formed.

Moreover, the Report of the Simon Commission is still awaited; and their recommendations are bound to cover certain details in which both British India and the States are interested, such, for instance, as fiscal matters and those of common concern to the States as a whole as well as British India.

I referred a little while ago to the need for a calm and dispassionate study on the part of the Princes and their Governments of the contents of the Butler Report. Still move important is it that the wide field covered by the Butler Report should, at the present juncture as well as in the future, be examined and dealt with in as calm and dispassionate an atmosphere, and in as calm and dispassionate a manner, as is possible by all parties, directly or indirectly, and wholly or partially, concerned in the various problems now before us. Their solution in each and every detail is not going to be so simple or easy as some may imagine. It will require not only a proper grasp of the correct constitutional position of the States and a full appreciation of each other's standpoints and difficulties, and no small amount of statesmanship, tact and sympathy, but also a reasonable amount of 'give and take', and reasonable compromise on all sides, in the cause and service of India as a whole. Any hasty or ill-advised word or act might well disturb the harmoney so essential for a happy and equitable solution—just, fair and honourable to all concerned. British India, no less than the Indian States, has to make its contribution towards this goal. And here I should like to express my feelings of grateful appreciation—shared I am sure by my Brother Princes and the States in general—of the restraint, moderation and sympathy with which, with but a few exceptions, the leaders and the respectable Press of British India have during the last year or so, and particularly since the publication of the Butler Report, dealt with problems concerning the States in general and those arising out of the Butler Report in particular.

Whilst speaking of the Butler Committee Report, I will say this much more on this occasion. By the very nature of things it would have been expecting the impossible to have hoped that every thing in the Butler Report would be seen eye to eye from the standpoint of the States; and consequently it is not really surprising that there should be some divergence of views even in regard to important matters, where the standpoint of the States differs from the recommendations of the Butler Report. In this connection I would remind you once again of the resolutions passed to the same effect by the Princes at the Bombay Conference in June last. They indicate in broad outline those features which have come as a disappointment to the States. But will all that—speaking personally for myself—I do not share such views expressed in certain quarters, as for instance that the Butler Report is "staggering" or that it is "a slap on the face of the Princes". I have always had a high personal regard for my old friend Sir Harcourt Butler, and whilst fully realising some of the disappointing features of the Butler Report. I cannot bring myself to attribute them to any lack of sympathy for the States on the part of Sir Harcourt, and I feel that it is possible to ascribe such unsatisfactory features to the extremely difficult nature of the questions involved and to the fact that the States are in this respect sui generis and that there is no parallel to their position in History. And being an optimist, and having confidence in the righteousness of the cause of the State and in the good faith and the honourable and equitable treatment of such questions by His Excellency the Viceroy and His Majesty's Government, I sincerely feel that there are great potentialities of benefit to the States arising from the appointment of the Butler Committee; and I share the view expressed by the Prince's Conference in Bombay that any such unsatisfactory features and questions now at issue between the British authorities and the States, as also between the States and British India, can be solved in personal discussion with His Excellency the Viceroy and by recourse to frank and friendly negotiations of a diplomatic and political nature rather than by any legal steps or by any caucus of non-co-operation.

Whilst it would, as I have said, be both premature and unwise to attempt to deal in anything like detail with the provisions of the Butler Report, yet in the attempt to contribute my own little quota towards the much desired goal, I trust that I shall not be found guilty of any indiscretion if I were to refer today to certain important aspects which strike me as deserving of being prominently and urgently pressed to the attention of the leaders and people of the Indian States as well as to those of British India; and I need hardly add that my remarks, and my appeal, are intended for the respectable and moderate elements, including the Press, of British India as well as of the States; since it is hopeless to appeal to the extremist element whom, alas, some are to be found, to a greater or lesser extent, in every class, community and country.

# Annexture 4

**Interview granted on the 2nd November, 1929, to the Associated Press of India by Major-General His Highness the Maharajah of Bikaner, G.C.S.I., G.C.I.E., G.C.V.I., G.B.E., K.C.B., A.D.C., LL.D., in regard to the important official pronouncement made by His Excellency the Viceroy, as published in the Gazette of India, Extraordinary, dated the 31st October, 1929.**

I have only a couple of hours ago received a full copy of His Excellency the Viceroy's important Statement but I say without hesitation that as a partriotic Indian devoted to his Motherland, as a Ruler of an Indian State who, in common with his subjects, has a real stake in the Country, and as a Ruling Prince deeply attached to His Imperial majesty the King-Emperor by inalienable ties of unflinching loyalty, I sincerely welcome the momentous declaration authoritatively made by His Excellency the Viceroy to the effect that it was implicit in the declaration of 1917 that the natural issue of India's constitutional progress as there contemplated is the attainment of Dominion Status, and that before the stage of a Joint Parliamentary Committee was reached His Majesty's Government propose to invite representatives of different parties and interests in British India as well as the representatives of Indian States to a Conference for the purpose of seeking, the greatest possible measure of aggrement in regard both to British Indian and all-Indian problems, so that it may be possible for them eventually to submit to Parliament such proposals on these grave issues as may command a wide measure of general assent.

2. This statesmanlike, courageous, and timely action is a further manifest of the gracious sympathy and abiding solicitude of our beloved King-Emperor for the Princes and people of India, on whose behalf His Majesty, as Prince of Wales, made such an earnest appeal for greate: sympathy on his return to England after his first visit to India, and to whom, as Emperor, His Majesty was further pleased, a few years later, to deliver at Calcutta the heartening message of faith and hope. Those who have the privilege of knowing well our popular Viceroy were fully assured of the genuine sympathy and noble

sentiments which Lord Irwin entertains for both British India and the Indian States. But His Excellency's recent announcement must surely afford the amplest proof to every one of his transparent sincerity of purpose and the conscientious manner in which he has faithfully discharged his duties during his recent mission to England as India's Ambassador. The fair, liberal, and business—like manner in which the Labour Government tackled the Egyptian and Iraq questions so soon after their coming into power had led me to think that His Majesty's Government appreciated full well the saying that "great empires and narrow minds go ill together", and encouraged me in the belief that problems connected with British India and the Indian States would be dealt with in the same liberal and statesmanlike spirit and with the same breadth of vision and imagination so necessary in regard to questions of Imperial indeed world wide—significance; and we, of India-to whichever of its two great parts we belong—have indeed good reason to be grateful to the Viceroy as well as His Majesty's Government, and the Secretary of State, Mr. Wedgewood Benn, for thus paving the way for the attainment by India of its full political freedom as an equal and honourable Member of the British Commonwealth of Nations.

3. With the Report of the Simon Commission still under preparation and the impossibility of anticipating, it is nor reasonable to expect more at this stage, and it is now for India—Indian States as well as British India—to demonstrate to the world at large, that they are jointly and severally capable of dealing successfully with, and solving, the problems involved in a practical and business-like manner, coupled with reasonableness and good-will and with mutual toleration and sympathy and a due appreciation of each other's claims and difficulties.

4. There must inevitably be some disappointment at the prospect of some delay in holding the proposed Conference in England, which is might not be found fensible to do before the Summer of 1931; but a severe European Winter is not the most favourable time for the settlement on amicable lines of problems of such grave import to all concerned. A few months are of comparatively small importance in the life-time of a nation or a country; and it is perhaps all to the good that not only British India but also the Indian States should have ample time calmly and carefully to study the proposals of the Simon Commission before partaking in the Conference.

5. The minds of the Indian Princes who gathered in Delhi last week were never "exercised" as to the effect which the forthcoming announcement would have on the Indian States as I have seen it stated

in some papers. Far from feeling any apprehensions, the Princs and Governments of the Indian States will I feel sure welcome the proposed Round Table Conference, as it will on the contrary, it is hoped, fmally set at rest all the doubts and apprehensions entertained in the States and clarify the special position of the States within the Empire. The Princes, realising fully well that they are bound to their brethren in British India by ties of blood, race and religion, have no desire to hamper the attainment of Dominion Status by British India or to be a drag on its constitutional advancement. Nothing is further from their desire than to break up the Country into two discordant halves waring against each other in fratricidal feuds; and they as earnestly look forward to the unity of India as their friends, the political lenders of British India. Any attitude of undue imcompatibility on the part of the Princes would be both unpatriotic and unreasonable. They have in the past repeatedly emphasized their sympathy with the legitimate aspirations of their fellow-countrymen in British India, and they went a step further at the Bombay Conference in June last when they cordially welcomed the attainment of Dominion Status by British India as an integral part of the British Empire. In my speech at the Administrative Conference delivered only a month ago, after expressing the hope that the rumours were true about the Round Table Conference to be convened by the Imperial Government, I went on to state that the sympathy and support of the Princes would be forthcoming in a very substantial and practical manner at such Conference. Though various important details have yet to be considered and agreed upon, the Princes are not unmindful of the full implications of Dominion Status now happily assured to India. They have openly given expression to the belief that the ultimate solution of the Indian problem and the ultimate goal'—whenever circumstances are favourable and the time is ripe for it-is Federation, which word has no terrors for the Princes and Governments of the States. Ever since 1918, the Princes have been asking for some means of joint deliberation on questions of common concern affecting British India as well as the States. Customs duties; excise, salt and opium; railways and means of transport and inter-communication, including serial navigation; posts and telegraphs; wireless and radio broadcasting; as well as the fiscal and financial problems of coinage and currency, banking and exchange—these are all questions affecting and demanding joint deliberation between the constituted Governments of the two constituent parts of the Country. The policy hitherto pursued in the absence of joint deliberation has been not only unjust to the interests of the States but has benefited the

Government and people of British India at the expense of the States.

6. The Princes thus have for long been anxious for an equitable and satisfactory settlement as regards the future position of the Status in the polity of India of the future. This was one of their chief objects in asking for the appointment of the Indian States Committee; but in the Butler Report this aspect of the Indian States problems has not been dealt with, and I anticipate that good—and not harm—will come to the States by this question being seriously dealt with between the Imperial Government, the Viceroy, and the Governments of the States, by separate negotiations, as well as by discussions at the Conference. The wisdom of having the Butler Committee appointed will now be more apparent.

7. What the Princes have all along contended, and attached importance to, is a just recognition of the correct position of the States and adequate guarantees and safeguards for the preservation and maintenance of the Princes' honourable position as "Perpetual Allies and Friends", and for their rights and privileges as such in any new polity devised for the governance of the country; and they naturally lay especial insistence upon an obvious point, namely, that in any new arrangements under the Dominion form of government any adjustment of their future relations with British India should be settled only with their free consent on terms just and honourable and satisfactory to the States as well as to British India. The States cannot be expected to agree to any proposals involving a violation of their Treaties or infringement of their Sovereign rights and internal autonomy and independence. British India and the States have indisputably existed side by side for a great many years as two separate parts with mutual advantage and it is impossible to believe that they cannot so exist in the future without anyone desiring to encroach upon the rights of the other or wanting the States to merge their separate entity. The Princes and States will therefore, be gratified at nothing that the scope of the Conference is to be confined only either to British Indian, or All Indian, problems, and that questions purely of domestic concern affecting the internal autonomy of the States have been wisely eliminated.

Asked about the attitude of the Princes in regard to the invitation issued by Pandit Motilal Nehru to a Round Table Conference, His Highness said:

8. I am glad in a way that you have asked this question. Desirous as I am of not touching on any controversial matter on this happy occasion, I should have preferred to say merely that a Conference such as that planned by the All Parties Convention has now become

superfluous, but perhaps it would be as well to make certain important points clear.

9. I fully appreciate the importance of evolving, with the free consent of all the parties concerned, a suitable constitution for India which would for the future guarantee and protect their several rights and interests; but in my view such a Conference, if it is to be of any value must be tripartite; and it is on these grounds that the Princes will, I am sure, welcome the Conference proposed by the Imperial Government. The Princes and States have made it abundantly clear that they stand solid for the British connection, and they cannot attend a Conference held in the absence of the other party to our Treaties. But whilst ignoring the British Government, and not including any of their representatives in the invitation, representatives of the "peoples" of the Indian States appear, in accordance with the terms of the All Parties resolution, to have also been invited. It is difficult to conceive that it was not apparent to the All Parties Convention that in the circumstances it was in any case impossible to expect the Princes to depute the duly accredited representatives of their Governments to sit, and to negotiate, on an equal basis, with so-called representatives of their peoples as a separate and independent party; nor could they have possibly expected the Governments of the States to agree to be bound by any such decisions of the so-called representatives of their subjects—whose credentials in regard to such claims it would at least be interesting to examine. Such demarcation between the duly constituted Governments of States and their people was, to say the least, unfortunate; and implied a complete mis-conception of the relations between the ruler and the ruled in our States, which the majority of the bonafide, loyal and thinking subjects of our States would themselves find unacceptable, since they have from time immemorial been accustomed to regard their Rulers as their natural leaders and spokesmen and the hereditary defenders of their rights and interests. Here I wish to emphasize that in all their efforts in the past to secure the just rights of their States, the Princes and States as a body have as I said in my speech last month, wholeheartedly worked in the best interests of their subjects as the custodians of their rights and they will endeavour honourably and consistently to bear in mind their duties towards their people and to do their best for them in all future negotiations. But the Treaties of the States have been entered into between the British Government and the Rulers as the representative of their people; and as such the Rulers and their Governments, who have every right to stand on their constitutional rights, will note with satisfaction that this correct distinction has been

drawn in the Viceregal statement and the Prime Minister's letter by making it clear that the invitation of His Majesty's Government will be extended to "representatives of different parties and interests in British India and the representatives of the Indian States."

10. These remarks are, I trust, also a sufficient reply to the question asked in the Press as to why, if the Princes can attend a Conference convened by His Majesty's Government, they should be unable to attend the All Parties Conference.

11. In conclusion, I beg respectfully to share in the Viceroy's hope that the Pronouncement may evoke response from, and enlist the concurrence of , all sections of opinion in India. I earnestly pray that His Excellency's hope will be fulfilled by the determined efforts of the leaders and people throughout India, wherever and whoever they are, breaking through the webs of mistrust, which have not only clogged the relations between India and Great Britain, but between British India and the States. It will be the duty of every one to contribute to the success of the Conference by constructive, and not destructive, proposals. Whatever mistakes have been made on any side, or by any individuals, in the past, now with the prospects once again bright for India, we ought, each and every one of us, to remember the eloquent and moving appeal made by His Royal Highness the Duke of Connaught in 1921, "to bury along with the dead past the mistakes and misunderstandings of the past, to forgive where you have to forgive and to join hands and to work together to realise the hopes that arise from today" and thus bring about, in His Excellency the Viceroy's words "the touch that carries with it healing and health" by which we may all contribute to the good of Greater India and of the. Empire.

# Annexure 5

**Speech containing General Observations made by His Highness the Maharajah of Bikaner in the Chamber of Princes on the 27th February, 1930, During the Introductory Debate on Agendum No. 11 (1).**

*Your Excellency; Your Highnesses;*

It was my privilege in the earlier part of my speech, when moving the Resolution in this Chamber on the 23rd February, 1928, regarding internal refonns in the Indian States, to tender our grateful thanks for Your Excellency's kind and sympathetic assistance in securing the appointment of the Indian States Committee; and today I beg to associate myself whole-heartedly with this Resolution which thanks Your Excellency once again.

I feel sure that I am echoing the sentiments not only of this Chamber, but of the Princes and States as a whole, when I beg, with all respect, to state that it is indeed our good fortune and highly gratifying that there should be in India a Viceroy like Your Excellency who will deal with matters of such vital importance to the States.

The resolutions to be passed at this Session, and the debate during the next few days on—to use a shorter term—the Butler Report, are intended to give an indication of the general views and feelings of this Chamber in regard to the various important details and recomendations contained in the Butler Report.

In regard to what are considered in the States as the satisfactory features of the Butler Committee's Report, resolutions were passed at the Conference of the Princes held in Bombay last June welcoming them. As for what the States regard as unsatisfactory features—some of which cause us deep concern—it will be the hope of all, inspired by loyal and patriotic feelings for the States, that the negotiations, which we propose should be carried on, will, with Your Excellency's valuable support and sympathy, result in matters being put right and justice being done to the States, who from a variety of causes feel anxious and regards several such important matters.

After the Round Table Conference, when concrete proposals are to be framed by Your Excellency's Government and His Majesty's Government, it will indeed be an added source of satisfaction and encouragement to the States if-as I have said on a previous occasion—in the interests of the two Indias, as well as of the Empire, and with a view to launching and ensuring the success of , what we hope will be, a further measure of liberal constitutional advance for both British India and the States, His Majesty's Govemment may be successful in securing the consent of Your Excellency to stay on as our Viceroy for a further period.

This resolution also affords us an opportunity of referring generally to certain aspects and details, which do not form the subject of specific resolutions to be moved hereafter during this Session.

As regards the Butler Committee's Report, I will say this much further on this occasion. By the very nature of things it would perhaps have been expecting the impossible to have hoped that the Butler Committee would see everything eye to eye with the Indian States; and consequently it is not really surprising that there should be some divergence of views, even in regard to important matters, where the standpoint of the States differs from the recommendations of the Butler Report. In this connection, I would once again invite attention to the Resolutions passed on the subject by the Princes at the Bombay Conference in June last. Speaking personally for myself, I do not share the views as I have heard expressed by some, as for instance that the Butler Report is "staggering" or that it is "a slap on the face of the Princes". I have always had a high personal regard for my old friend Sir Harcourt Butler, and whilst realising some of the disappointing features of the Butler Report, I cannot really bring myself to attribute them to any lack of sympathy for the States on the part of Sir Harcourt; and I feel that it is possible to ascribe some such unsatisfactory or indecisive features to the extremely difficult nature of the questions involved, and to the fact that there is no parallel to the unique position of the Indian States.

Rather than looking upon the Butler Report as the end of things, I personally look upon it as the beginning of things—from the consideration of which, and from the negotiations resulting from which, final settlements on lines equitable and fair to the States might reasonably be expected to ensue.

But with all that it will be obvious that the Butler Report is not the authoritative verdict of a tribunal and that the States cannot be expected to treat its recommendations as final.

There is a saying—particularly in that part of India from where I come, viz., Rajputana, which applies to all men of honour and self-respect throughout the world, of whatever country, race, or religion—that a man, worthy of the name of a man, fights his utmost to defend four things, namely—(1) his honour and dignity; (2) the honour, dignity and safe-keeping of his lady-folk and family; (3) his lands—which term, broadly interpreted, embraces not only his territorial possessions, in whatever form, but also his rights and his inherent, vested interests of all kinds; and (4) his weapons and his horses.

Leaving aside today certain points legal and otherwise—which at present do affect the dignity of the Members of our Families and which need attention—the Princes and States, I need hardly say, are very much interested in questions affecting the honour and dignity of the Princes and their Families and in safeguarding their territorial possessions, and Treaty and other rights and the interests of their States and subjects.

For a satisfactory, just and honourable settlement of the points that are at issue between the Indian States and the British Government, or between the States and British India—some of which form the subject of specific resolutions today and the two days following—the first thing that appears to my mind is that none of us should be hide-bound by red tape, or tied by past precedents, and past usage and political practice. Usage is forming the subject of a separate resolution, which has also been allotted to me to move later on during this session. Red tape is, as we all know, a word that is a hardly annual and the subject of jokes, relating to most of , if not all, the Governments of the world, where official procedure at times receives prior consideration at the expense of the head and the heart. As Mr. Lloyd George remarked, when he was Prime Minister, in his speech at the Guildhall in regard to India in my presence in 1917 , when the Imperial War Cabinet was in session:

> "Minds running the same course for a long time are apt to get rutty; and the weightier the mind the deeper the ruts. You require fresh minds to lift the cart out of those worn furrows."

We sincerely and gratefully appreciate the very sympathetic policy of Your Excellency, ably supported by a sympathetic Political Secretary—in the person of my old friend Sir Charles Watson. But one cannot help regretting that the good work and the good atmosphere created between 1916 and 1918 had not been continued longer without interruption and further utilised to the mutual benefit of Imperial and States' interests, and had the work and problems relating to the States been tackled and continued on right lines, a happy consummation would have been rendered all the easier of attainment within a very short time afterwards. For the demand of the States contained nothing unreasonable, and could, in my humble estimation, have been settled at the most within some two years or so. But this, alas, is a case of lost opportunities, which, in Imperial interests also, is, I respectfully submit, no less to be deplored. The policy as regards the States, instead of being carefully conceived, settled and framed upon generous, liberal, and sympathetic lines is handicapped at times by old precedents and prejudices and is apt to undergo changes at the whim and fancy of those responsible for the conduct of affairs of the Indian States, and is specially liable to be varied by so many diverse elements and according to the personal predelictions and idiosyncracies of the Viceroy, the Political Secretary or the Secretary of State and his Council, of the time being. In the case of some not in touch, or in sympathy, with the States, or who—what I venture to submit, and in the opinion of the States—misread the situation, or fail to grasp the points involved, much harm can be done; and with one stroke of the pen former carefully considered policies based on close personal contact of the States and a true realization of the position and rights and circumstances of the States, are changed and new policies inaugurated, which lead to mutual mistrust, disappointment and difficulties, which successors, however sympathetic, find it difficult—in view of notes and policies recorded—to get away from at least for some time to come.

Had it been otherwise, there would, in my humble estimation, have been no necessity for the Butler Committee to be appointed; or for the heavy expenditure which the States had to incur in being forced to fight for their just rights; nor would either the British Government or the Indian States have had to bear all the trouble, disappointment and discouragement which have resulted. New fangled theories about the ultimate powers regarding Paramountcy, and such matters, before the appointment of the Butler Committee, and the extravagant and exaggerated Imperialist claims, inconsistent with the plighted word and good faith of Great Britain, or sound statesmanship, advanced on behalf of the Paramount Power—claims more wide, more frequent, more insistent and, I respectfully submit, based on varied and not infrequently untenable grounds and opposed to constitutional and historical facts and to the provisions of our Treaties and other Engagements, and in direct contradiction of the solemn and clear pledges and assurances in the famous gracious Proclamation of Queen Victoria, repeatedly reiterated and affirmed by successive British Sovereigns in numerous Proclamations—have not helped to ease the situation or to allay the anxieties of the States, or their Rulers, Governments and people.

As regards precedents, which not infrequently are created, and then followed and quoted—without the States having had any voice in the matter—I think I can best, without taking up too much time of Your Excellency and Your Highnesses, sum up the feeling of the States by referring to a speech made in 1917 by General Smuts while speaking about the future Constitution of the Empire, which I have quoted before, and which other Princes have since done me the compliment of quoting in their turn. General Smuts said:

> "Do not try to think of existing political institutions which have been evolved in the case of European developments. The British Empire is a much larger and more diverse problem than anything we have seen hitherto and the sort of constitution we read about in books, the sort of political alphabet which has been elaborated in years gone by, does not apply, and would not solve the problems of the future. We should not follow precedents but make them . . . I am sure, if we disabuse our minds of precedents and preconceived ideals, we shall evolve, in the course of years, the institution and machinery that will meet our difficulties."

I respectfully beg to urge—and I feel Your Excellency will agree—that this is equally true and desirable as regards the relations of the Paramount Power with the Indian States and that this very sound principle—enunciated by a great Dominion Statesman—will be found to be of mutual advantage to Imperial interests as well as to the States. If we could go ahead in the future with imagination, and regardless of precedents, and do what is just, right and equitable to all parties concerned, it would assuredly result in further strengthening the ties that bind the Princes and people and States of India to the Crown.

If regardless of past precedents, we act on principles of right versus wrong, and are inspired with a vidid imagination and a broad outlook, it must be productive of the greatest benefit all round. As an example I would quote the instance of Sir Henry Compbell Bannerman, when he was Prime Minister of England, and his Government, who succeeded, in spite of strong opposition in granting Dominion Status to South Africa, which proved of inestimable value to the Empire during the Great War, when South Africa voluntarily and willingly fought, side by side with the other countries comprising the Commonwealth of British Nations against those who thought that might was right. Truly has it been said that little minds and a great Empire go ill together; and I feel that I am voicing the confident and earnest hope of all of us here that in regard to the States—big and small, rich and poor, important and unimportant—Your Excellency and Sir Charles Watson will leave a legacy to your successors which will prove a source of unalleged gratification to the States and end the perpetual anxiety and worries to which the States, under the present system of flux and drift, are subjected to.

There is one other point about which I would also ask for the indulgence of Your Excellency and Your Highnesses to make an observation or two and that is on the subject of diplomacy. I beg with all modesty, to quote an extract from a speech which I made on the opening day of the Princes' Conference in November, 1919, in supporting a resolution moved by my dear and lamented friend, His Highness the late Maharajah Scindia of Gwalior, on the victorious termination of the Great War, in the course of which, after alluding to the Imperial aspect of the relations between the British Government and the Princes, and referring to the future" with high hopes", and as "full of bright augury", I ventured to urge in the following words that there was no need between the British Government and the States to have resort to displomacy:

> "Guided as we are, in Your Excellency's eloquent words, by candour, loyalty, liberality and goodwill, there is no need between us for that evil thing—secret diplomacy. We have stood together in the past and weathered many a storm. We devoutly hope that an era of peace and prosperity lies in front of us for many a year to come. But should fortune be fickle; should we have to face once again external aggression or internal trouble; should we have a fight the Bolshevik menace, or to repel the invasion of a foolish or arrogant foe, the British Government and the Ruling Princes will assuredly continue to stand together, shoulder to shoulder, united in their loyalty and devotion to their gracious King—Emperor. Whatever betide and come what may, the union shall abide and stand every strain".

As for the future, I can best quote from a recent speech by Mr. Ramway MacDonald, the present Prime Minister of Great Britain, regarding Egyptian affairs which is also applicable to India and the Indian States:

> "There is an Old World, old in civilization, in philosophy, in religion, and in culture, which has hitherto been weak in the material powers that have characterized Western peoples, but that World, wrapped in slumber as we thought, has now become awake

and is beginning to understand what national self-respect is. Taught and tutored very largely by us, it is bringing our own ideas home to us and asking us to honour the effects of our actions and to grant it—not by charity, but because our hearts are enlightened—the fteedom that we have been nourishing for ourselves for so many generations. The great danger . . . then, is that we may be too long in performing this act of recognition."

Your Excellency, and Your Highnesses, that is the spirit that animates British India, as well as the Indian States, and I will conclude my speech by again quoting a few words from another recent speech by Mr. Ramway MacDonald, which precisely sums up my feeling as regards the negotiations now to ensue between Your Excellency and your Government and the Indian States as well as in regard to the important points arising out of the Butler Report and the Round Table Conference and other matters, namely:

"I will be optimistic until the end."

## Annexure 6

**Speech Delivered by His Highness the Maharajah of Bikaner in the Chamber of Princes on the 28th February, 1930, in Moving the Resolution Regarding Intervention, Agendum No. 11 (5) Part 1**

*Your Excellency; Your Highnesses;*

The following is the Resolution which I beg to move:

> "That this Chamber considers that the time is now opportune for defining, by just consultation between the nominees of His Excellency the Viceroy and those of this Chamber, the bases of Intervention in.the internal affairs of the States."

This Resolution was, of course, drafted before Your Excellency's reference to the subject in your inaugural speech last Tuesday; but although we shall doubtless experience some difficulties if, as we hope, effect is given to this Resolution by Your Excellency, we feel that the subject is of much tremendous importance that every possible avenue must be explored—at least to simplify and clarify matters; and that an attempt must be made to define the doctrine of intervention, not on the basis of the recommendations of the Butler Committee, but after joint deliberation with the representatives of the Princes. If, after such consultation between the nominees of Your Excellency and those of this Chamber, it is found impossible to define the bases of the right of intervention, or to come to a satisfactory conclusion, we shall at least have probed fully into the question and each done our best. As Your Excellency will, I feel sure, further agree, nothing but good has come in all cases where we have discussed questions in a frank and friendly manner with the object of arriving at a solution, or at least a compromise—honourable and fair to all concerned.

The principle, namely of contractual necessity—not any vague Imperial necessity—as the correct test of the occasion for intervention, which we had urged was easily intelligible—could easily be understood by the Princes and their people as well as by the British Government. The Butler Committee failed to make the position at all definite and rest content with that confession of their inability when they remarked that paramountcy must ever remain paramount. It was a counsel for despair. But we are not without hopes that, even if our efforts during the proposed consultations are not entirely successful, we shall make some satisfactory advance on the present state of affairs; and if we can even lay down in what cases there should be no intervention, that will be something gained.

There are instances forthcoming—I fear, not rate—so far as the past is concerned, of interference even with the private, family and domestic affairs of Rulers. Heirs—Apparent of Rulers have been placed in a position of even exercising veto and control over the action of their fathers, who have not abdicated but who have been unfortunate victims of circumstances and at times of panicky and hasty action; and thus the impossible has been attempted, viz., setting up two Sovereigns in one State, just as it is impossible to put two swords in one scabbard.

It was a matter of frequent occurrence some 20 to 30 years ago, and I fear not unknown even in recent times, when Prime Ministers and the other Ministers of States have been supported by the Political Officers and encouraged to act against and insult their Rulers.

Cases are not wanting—dating back not to antiquity—when Political Officers have interfered, or attempted to interfere, in support of rebellious or otherwise guilty Nobles of our States, regardless of the inherent rights and susceptibilities of their Sovereign Rulers. Indeed, about the time when I came of age, a veteran Political Officer expounded to me the strange doctrine that his policy always was—be it noted that it was not the declared policy of the Paramount Power, but the personal policy of an individual Political Officer—in variably to support the State against the Nobles during periods of minorities and, similarly, invariably to support the Nobles against their Rulers immediately the minorities cease. This obiter dictum, regardless of rights and wrongs, needs no further comment.

It has been within my experience soon after I came of age to have been forced during my early days to dismiss proved and loyal men—who had served the State for a great many years, without the slightest inquiry or investigation or without the slightest opportunity being given to such loyal and deserving officials the single chance of repudiating the allegations made against them by intriguers in our States, or the charges preferred against them by such Political Officers—because the Political Officers held the view that they were "mischievous" men and "did not mean well in the least."

We have had official letters of enquiries addressed to me and to my Prime Minister asking for explanations and even for files on petitions submitted to the Resident at Bikaner regarding even Police Jamedars and Constables against their dismissal by the Departments concerned and such matters.

We have been asked, on acount of a petition similarly to the Resident from the gardener at Gajner, to furnish explanation of what the case was about; and we have had a letter from the Political officer who was in those days accredited to our State asking why the butcher, who was a Bikaner subject, but who supplied meat to the Residency, had been dealt with in some matter according to the law and recognised practice, usage and custom of the State. The explanation of my Government was actually demanded by the Resident in regard to the most heinous of fence of our failing to supply a camel sowar required for the benefit of the domestic menials of the Residency; and ultimately, we were threatened by the statement that it was fortunate that the "explanation"—in effect of course a reply—sent by my Political Department had" arrived in time to render it unnecessary for" the Political Officer "to take any further steps in the matter." ?

When, shortly after my coming of age, in 1902 I tried to inaugurate a system of Administrative Reform and to introduce almost the identical Secretariat system followed by the Government of India themselves, I first had great difficulty in getting the Political Officers, whom under the then conditions I had to consult, to agree to this scheme, which was a distinct improvement on the old system carried on during my minority—which worked very well and which is still in force; and for years afterwards, I was pestered with questions and asked to "furnish" "reports" as to the manner in which the system was working—as if it was totally strange and untried and dangerous Administrative scheme which we were resorting to.

In 1904—when, like members of a criminal tribe, asking for leave of absence, Princes were required to take permission before leaving our States—I was in different health and I had proposed to proceed on a purely private and informal visit to Bombay for a change. But I actually received a letter from the Resident advising me to defer my visit for another 10 days as the Agent to the Governor—General could not anticipate the orders of the Government of India twice asked for, and because the delay showed that there may be some difficulty. My health was not of course taken into account in the least. Later I was graciously informed that there was "no objection" to my proceeding to Bombay. In the meanwhile, I had however dared the Political authorities to arrest me or stop me forcibly from going to Bombay, as of course I intended carrying out my original programme.

I trust that I am not digressing too much if I express the hope here that during Your Excellency's Viceroyalty a change may be effected whereby questions relating to the Princes and States, instead of being viewed from the standpoint of whether or not there was any "objection", would be viewed with the single aim and object of meeting the reasonable demands of the Princes and States for safeguarding their legitimate rights and interests, and making the Princes' and States' position more secure and more happy, and thereby enabling the States to make more marked and rapid progress all round and further strengthening the relations that exist between the Crown and the States, which have stood the test of the fiery ordeals of great wars and rebellions, and have proved that the Princes and States are whole-heartedly inspired with the single object of being true to their Treaties and obligations and worthy of the high position they are privileged to occupy as "perpetual Allies and Friends" of the Crown.

Some references have already been made to this most important and intricate subject in the general discussions which took place when the Resolution thanking Your Excellency for the appointment of the Butler Committee was moved yesterday; and for my part I think I cannot do better than quote a relevant extract from a speech I made on this very subject the other day in the Bikaner Legislative Assembly:

> "in the very nature of things the Princes and their Governments realise that there must arise occasions where intervention by the Crown, as the Paramount Power, is rendered inevitable. All that the Princes desire is that intervention, when rendered unavoidable, shall not be arbitrary, or based on inaccurate or one-sided reports, and that it must be resorted to not only with the greatest reluctance, but after the most deliberate and sympathetic consideration by the Viceroy—as the Representative of the Crown—of the case of the Ruler or State concerned, and furthermore that such intervention must be resorted to for the sole purpose of the furtherance of the interests—present and future—of the Indian States and of the general Order of the Princes themselves., as Lord Irwin himself stated in His Excellency's speech in the Chamber of Princes in November, 1926."

I am sure, and I am confident so are my Brother Princes, that nothing is further from the policy or intention of Your Excellency personally and the present Political Secretary than that intervention should in any case be arbitrary; and we are grateful to Your Excellency for your assurance that the unpalatable task involved in intervention or interference is resorted to only with the greatest reluctance. One of the most important things that is urgently called for is that the Prince and his Government concerned should have the fullest opportunities of making their representation on the subject; and if, as we hope, such consultations as are contemplated under this Resolution .lead to some further details being satisfactorily worked out in this connection also, it will be one of the additional advantages of our jointly examining the question.

As I said yesterday, policies and political practice are of ten liable to change with a change of the Viceroy or the Political Secretary, and in some cases even with a change of the Political Officers accredited to our Courts. And unfortunately sad cases have in the past occurred involving not only humiliation to the Ruler concerned, but often—however benevolent the intention—grave injustice and irretrievable harm to the dignity and prestige and, indeed, the entire career of the Ruler. These cases sometimes place the British Government in a most embarrasing and unenviable position, specially when they recognise later on that their action was hasty and arbitrary, at times based on one-sided reports and versions; but matters often are then found to have gone too far to permit of a satisfactory and honorably settlement—on considerations of Prestige and other grounds, it is too late to rectify the wrong done.

It will be easily realized that Intervention, and the result of the action taken after Intervention leading to the deposition, or abdication, of the Ruler concerned, means at times the extinction of the Public career of a Ruler and amounts to his political death. As a parallel I might cite the instance of a man wrongly hanged for murder, and if it is afterwards discovered that the man was innocent, it is too late to bring the unfortunate person back to life.

As in the case of Treaties, so in the case of Intervention, there have been two distinct schools of thought practically ever since our entering into Treaty relations with the British Government. In the case of Treaties some urged that Treaties were dead letters and therefore may be violated or ignored. Others attached importance to plighted word and the good faith and the honour of Great Britain. Similarly some authorities were emphatically against intervention, whilst some favoured intervention. But I trust that I shall not be considered to be irrelevant, or out of order, if I gave a few extracts from what have been said by some of the highest and most eminent British authorities of the past, in regard to both Treaties and Intervention, which in some cases are interdependent or difficult to separate.

In regard to Treaties, the following three extracts will I trust be sufficient for the purposes today:

(1) Extract from Sir John Malcolm's "Instructions to his Assistants":
"On all occasions where they are referred to treaties and engagements should be interpreted with much consideration to the Prince or Chief with whom they are made. There is often, from opposite education and habits, much difference between their construction and ours of such engagements; but no loose observation, or even casual departure from the letter of them, ought to lead to serious consequences, when it appeared there was no intention of violating the spirit of the deed, or of acting contrary to pledged faith. When any article of an engagement is doubtful, I think it should be invariably explained with more leaning to the expectations originally raised in the weaker than to the interests of the stranger power."

(2) Extract from Lord Auckland's minute on the Orchha Case, dated 2nd January,1842:
"I cannot, for a moment, admit the doctrine, that because the view of the policy upon which we may have formed engagements with Native Princes may have been by circumstances materially altered, we are not to act scrupulously upto the terms and spirit of those engagements."

(3) Extract from Lord Hasting's Pronouncement to the Nawab of Karnatic:
"A treaty plighted the public faith of the nation, so that it must be my duty to maintain its terms according to their true spirit, which ought always to be construed most favourably for the party whose sole dependence was on the honour of the other."

(4) In referring to the internal independence and autonomy of the States, the Marquis of Hastings again recorded in his Journal as long ago as the 1st February, 1814, or over 116 years ago—
"This formidable mischief has arisen from our not having defined to ourselves or made intelligible to the Native Princes, the quality of the relations which we have established with them.'
***I*n our treaties with them we recognise them as Independent Sovereigns.** Then we send a Resident to their Courts. Instead of acting in the character of Ambasador, **he assumes the functions of a dictator; interferes in all their private concerns; countenances refractory subjects against them;** and makes the

most ostentatious exhibition of this exercise of authority. To secure to himself the support of our Government, he urges some interest which, under the colour thrown upon it by him, is strenuously taken up by our Council; and the Government identifies itself with the Resident not only on the single point but on the whole tenor of his conduct. In nothing do we violate the feelings of the Native Princes so much as in the decisions which we claim the privilege of pronouncing with regard to the succession to the Musnud. . . . It is supposed that by upholding the right of primogeniture we establish an interest with the eldest son which will be beneficial to us when he comes to the Throne. . . . He, too, will in his turn **have to feel our interference in the succession as well as in minor instances**. With regard to the latter it might be argued that some interest of the Company is always really involved. The simple existence of such an interest is not the true question. What should be considered is whether the matter be of a proximity or magnitude to make the presecution of it desirable at the expense of the disgust and estrangement which you sow by the procedure."

(5) Even Lord Dulhousie, than whom any more zealous upholder of the rights of Paramountcy is difficult to imagine, while admonishing the Resident at Hyderabad for his proposal to intervene on alleged maladiministration remarked:

"But so long as the alleged evils of His Highness' Government are confined within its own limits and affect only his own subjects the Government of India must observe religiously the obligations of its own good faith. It has no just right to enter upon a system of direct interference in the internal affairs of His Highness' Kingom, which is explicitly forbidden by the positive stipulations of treaty, which would be utterly repugnant to the wishes of the Sovereign and is unsought by the people. over whom he rules."

In the passages on which the Butler Committee rely, the circumstances in which intervention would be warranted have been detailed—a very different thing from leav ing the right of intervention wholly dependent upon the individual discretion of the Political Officer. The Committee, moreover, have really propounded a new doctrine; they have suggested an extension of the scope of intervention beyond what the Government of India themselves have claimed so far. They contend that the right to intervene may be exercised in the interests of India as a whole, and even in order to suggest changes in the traditional forms of administration in case of popular agitation. These are really new principles and new claims. They are dangerous principles, for they make intervention dependent upon circumstances over which a Prince may have no control. To make one case—extreme, but no inconceivable—would popular agitation in India in favour of the substitution of the form of Government in which the Prince was to be excluded from all effective participation in the Government of his State, supported by agitation within the State, instigated from British India, justify intervention? Surely our traditional institutions and usages cannot be exposed to changes demanded by uninformed caprice and clamour—often by persons noisy in the extreme, but really either in the minority, or not really representative of the various classes and communities of the bona fide subjects of the States. The risk is not fanciful for no one can prophesy how far popular agitation in India against Indian States—much of it based on misconception or even malicious misrepresentation—may go, and what changes in our policy it may demand. A popularised Central Government in British India, even though it may have no concern with the Princes, could, and is bound to, influence indirectly, perhaps, but substantially, the discretion of future Viceroys. Even if intervention has a less drastic purpose, e.g., to ensure cooperation in a matter of interest both to British India and the States, would not a pupularised Central Government have a position of substantial advantage over the States in influencing the decision of the Viceroy?

20. British India is more vocal than ourselves. The Provinces have been vociferously clamouring for greater provincial autonomy, more freedom from interference by the Central Government and less restrictions upon their own authority. They ask for a gift of new rights. The States ask for a restoration of their original status, what actually belonged to them. If the British Indian Legislatures and Provincial Governmentrvention with their administration from the powers that be, the States have a greater justification in claiming for a restoration of their own original internal autonomy, so as sufficiently to safeguard it from encroachments in the near, or distant, future. Such a happy consummation will bring in its train substantial political and other advantages of the highest mutual importance which are obvious. Moreover-what, comparatively speaking, is of no small consideration—it will conduce to the peace of mind of all concerned and to the increased efficiency of our respective work in the task of administration, untrammelled by unnecessary interruption and

worries and anxieties, so far as the relations of the Crown and the States are concerned.

21. The extreme importance as well as the urgency of the matter must be my plea for inflicting myself on Your Excellency and Your Highnesses at such length to-day for which I tender my apologies.

# Annexure 7

**Speech Delivered by High Highness the Maharajah of Bikaner in the Chamber of Princes on the 1st March, 1930, in Moving the Resolution Regarding' Usage' and 'Sufferance'. Agendum No. 11 (5) Part 2.**

*Your Excellency; Your Highnesses;*

I now rise to move another Resolution allotted to me, viz., :

"That this Chamber is of opinion that the doctrine of Usage and Political Practice, as expounded by the Indian states' Committee, is neither sound in its conception nor fair in its application to the relations subsisting between the Crown and the Indian States. That doctrine has in the past been the cause of serious and unjustifiable encroachments upon the internal sovereignty and autonomy of the Indian States which are recognised in Solemn Treaties, Engagements and Sanads.

A course of practice followed with respect to. indificual States by the Political Department of the Government of India in certain eventualities, which has neither been consistent nor uniform, or to which from time to time exception has been taken by the States concerned, or, which arose during minority, joint administration or any such interregnum, when the Government of India held the position of trustee with respect to the State concerned, cannot afford any basis for intervention by the Government of India to the prejudice of the acknowledged rights of the States."

2. On every question of importance, whether or not there are provisions in our treaties, which the Butler Committee agree are of continuous and binding force, usage is quoted in support of some course of action which conflicts with our claims, Now the questions which naturally arise are:

(1) What is this usage?
(2) How did it originate and what has been its age?
(3) It is governed by deflnite principles based on law and equity?

(4) Had the States agreed to it or had a voice in it?

As it is now enforced, it is difficult to answer these questions.

3. The Resolution which I commend for the acceptance of this Chamber does not deny the validity of usage. All that is contended is that unless the particular usage which is quoted as authority, fulfils the conditions I shall attempt to enumerate, it cannot be considered as valid usage, With Your Excellency's and Your Highnesses' permission I shall refer in some detail to these conditions which are most important.

4. First, the States contend that a usage, unless it has been consistently and uniformly followed over a considerable period. has no validity at all. The mere fact that on one occasion a Ruler allowed a case to be decided in a particular manner or agreed to it, does not of itself create a usage. I will make my meaning clear by means of an example. Let us supose that a Ruler asked the advice of the Resident, as his friend, on one occasion about the appointment of a Prime Minister and that the Resident's advice was followed. That by itself does not create a valid usage under which the Paramount Power could claim that on all future occasions the Resident's advice should be sought before appointing a Prime Minister, Nor can any such matter apply to, or bind, the other States. As regards the claim of age or antiquity, the usage complained of could not have been older than the British Rule which is by no means ancient.

5. Secondly, even continuous usage does not create any right if the Ruler concerned submitted to, or accepted, the practice under protest or compulsion. Usage is valid only so long as the consent of the Princes whom it affects is forthcoming—and willingly forthcoming. When a Ruler protests against a particular practice, or is forced to do something under unusual circumstances against his inclination or better judgement, obviously he is not a consenting party, and the usage ceases to be valid.

6. The third condition is equally important. Any usage which goes against the express provisions of a treaty can have no binding force.

7. Usage can be allowed to grow up only when the treaty itself has made no provision. When the treaty or any other formal agreement, by which the relationship of any particular State to the Paramount Power is governed, provides in clear terms for such cases, usage can have no place. It is in this sense that the picturesque, but unconvincing, statement of the Butler Committee that the picturesque, but unconvincing, statement of the Butler Committee that usage lights up the dark places of the treaties is understood. When the treaties

themselves are luminously clear there is no need for the rush-lights of usage.

8. The fourth condition is that no usage can be valid which grew up at a time when the Government of India, either owing to the minority of the Ruler, or owing to the circumstances, exercised internal control over the State. It is ageed on all hands that on such occasions the Government of India stand in the position of trustees. It is a clear and universally accepted canon of equity that a trustee cannot derive benefit at the expense of the beneficiary, however long he may be in possession as a trustee.

9. The second part of this resolution states that usage which developed owing to the local conditions of one State should in no case be considered binding on another, merely on the ground that usage is valid where it originated. I submit that this proposition has only to be staed to gain the acceptance of all reasonable people. Usage develops as a result of local circumstances. Such usage may be valid in the State in which it grew up. But it does not follow that its validity extends to another State, differing in the circumstances of its historical growth, of its treaty rights and of its methods of administration.

10. It is important to emphasise that in the framing of such "usage" and "political practice" the States had no voice. The Viceroys in their most fonnal pronouncements, as well as the Government of India and their Officers, in speeches and in writing, have on more than one occasion clearly admitted the validity of the claims of the Princes and States that they had no voice whatsoever in the framing of such "usage" and "political practice"; and they have equally clearly admitted that such "political practice" and "usage" have had a corroding influence upon the Treaty Rights and the Internal Sovereignty of the States.

11. On the 22nd September, 1919, Mr. (now Sir Robert) Holland, then acting Political Secretary to the Government of India, pointed out to the Princes' Committee at their very first meeting—the precursor of the present Standing Committee that:

> "there had been in the past a constant development of constitutional doctrine under the strain of new conditions as the British Power had welded the country into a composite whole. That doctrine, as for instance in the case of ' (various matters), "had been superimposed upon the original relations of many States of the Indian body politic and had not been inspired by any desire to limit the sovereign powers of the Indian Rulers. The Rulers' consent to such new doctrine had not always been sought in the past, partly

because it was often evolved piecemeal from precedents affecting individual States, and partly because it would have been impracticable to secure combined assent within a reasonable period. It was admitted, however, that, while the justice and necessity of the new measures was clearly seen, their effect upon the treaty position was not appreciated at the time, with the result that a body of usage influencing the relations with the States had come into force through a process which, though benevolent in intention, was nevertheless to some extent arbitrary".

12. Lord Chelmsford in his speech at the opening of the Princes' Conference on the 3rdNovember, 1919, made the following observations regarding the revision of political practice:

"Thers is no doubt that with the growth of new conditions and the unification of India under the British Power political doctrine has constantly developed. In the case of extraterritorial jurisdiction, railway and telegraph construction, limitation of armaments, coinage, currency and opium policy, and the administration of cantonments—to give some of the more salient instances—the relations between many States and the Imperial Government have been changed. The change, however, has come about in the interests of India as a whole and I need hardly say that there has been no deliberate wish to curtail the powers of Princes and Chiefs. We cannot deny, however, that the treaty position has been affected, and that a body of usage, in some cases arbitrary, but always benevolent, has insensibly come into being. Some of Your Highnesses have therefore asked that the Darbars should for the future have a voice in the formulation of political practice. The Government of India entirely concur in the justice of this claim, and with the approval of His Majesty's Government hare decided to accede to your request, in regard to that portion of our political doctrine which can be expressed in the form of general principles, in so far as it is based on considerations other than treaty rights. From the point of view of Government also it cannot but be of the greatest advantage that devisions as to political practice which may have a bearing on the States' prerogatives should be taken after formal and collective discussion with Rulers."

"It is a pleasure to me to be able to inform Your Highnesses of the intention of the Government of India and of His Majesty's Government to adopt your proposals for the appointment of a Standing Committee. . . ."

13. Again, in his official letter to the Princes of Rajputana on the subject of simplification of Political Relations, dated the 27th March, 1920, Sir Robert Holland, then Agent to the Governor-General in Rajputana, wrote as follows:

"It must be admitted frankly that in the past there was in some cases undue interference in the internal affairs of the States. To explain fully the reasons for this would necessitate recapitulation of much of the past history of Government relations with the States. So early as 1820, Colonel Tod remarked that the result of his benevolent intervention in the internal affairs of Mewar had been to throw the local machinery of administration out of gear and to weaken the hands of the Ruler. Later, practices now perceived to be iconoclastic and subversive of tradition, were initiated, though with the best intentions, by officers in charge of minority administrations, and these crystallised into principles for universal application. Precedents, evolving under special circumstances in individual State, were declared, without proper scrutiny, or due consideration, to be applicable to the States as a body. The Princes felt that their Treaty rights were being encroached upon and in the absence of facilities for mutual discussion of grievances and common representation of their point of view, they feared lest the development of the practices which they saw growing up might seriously prejudice the exercise of their sovereign power within their States."

14. An important point which I wish to make as regards usage, and indeed as regards all that concernes the Rulers and States as a body, with special reference to liberalization of the policy towards the States and making it more sympathetic in matters political and fiscal, is that, contrary to the tendency manifest in official quarters, the benefits should accrue not only to the Princes of the larger States but also to the comparatively smaller States and their Rulers. For, equity and justice demand that at least as much, if not greater, attention should be paid to the lesser and consequently weaker Rulers and their States.

15. I now come to the term "sufferance" which is to be found in clause (1) (b) of the terms of reference of the Butler Committee, and which I might as well quote here:

"to report upon the relationship between the Paramount Power and the Indian States with particular reference to the rights and obligations arising from:

(a) treaties, engagements and sanads, and
(b ) usage, sufferance and other causes ;"

I have heard it described that the above mentioned insertion of the word "sufferance" was the product of an ingenious legal brain, and a brilliant attempt at diplomatic strategy for the purposes of concolidating Imperial interests to the prejudice of the States.

16. The Butler Committee in para 40 of their Report recorded that:

"Usage and sufferance have operated in two main directions. In several cases, where no treaty, engagement or sanad exists, usage and sulferance have supplied its place in favour of the States. In all cases usage and sufference have operated to determine questions on which the treaties, engagements and sanads are silent; they have been a constant factor in the interpretation of these treaties, engagements and sanads; and they have the consolidated the position of the Crown as Paramount Power.

17. Sufferance and other things have certainly gone far to consolidate the position of the Paramount Power; but the Indian States feel that this was done at the expense of the internal Sovereignty and the legitimate interests of the States, and is yet another case of the undermining and infringement of their Treaty rights.

18. What however sounds anomalous, and is indeed astounding in the extreme is to say or imagine that the all powerful Paramount Power with the whole might and the immense resources of Great Britain as well us of the great British Empire behind it could possibly be placed in a position of equality with, or on the same footing as, the Indian States in regard to sufferance. The use of the words quoted above, stating that sufferance has also supplied its place in favour of the States, by which we understand that the Committee meant to imply that in some cases the Paramount Power too suffered loss of legitimate and legal rights to the undue benefit of the States by sufferance and that sufferance also affected the position of the Paramount Power. It that is so, we submit a contradiction of what follows where the Committee say that sufferance has also consolidated the position of the Crown as Paramount Power.

19. To content that sufferance on the part of the Paramount Power has invariably affected their rights to the benefit of the States is really iudicrous in the extreme; and it can I submit reasonably be contended that it was not the result of force majeure applied, or of unwilling

submission to anything else done, by the Indian States.; which the States are obviously not in a position to do—but the result of deliberate and carefully considered action on the part of the Paramount Power, who have, ever since our Treaties, always had experts carefully to vet and deal with constitutional and legal matters affecting their relationship with the States; and had had available to them at all times—besides most efficient officers responsible for the political aspect of such questions—the advice of the highest and ablest legal experts not only in India but also in Great Britain. No such thing in the shape of expert legal and constitutional, or political and administrative, advisers, and careful political and legal vetting and examination of all matters affecting the relations of the States with the Paramount Power was, in the very nature of things, possible, much less available to the States, until very recently, and even then in an extremely minor degree as compared with all that the Paramount Power could command at all times ever since they entered into Treaty relations with them.

20. I am not a lawyer, much less a constitutional lawyer and therefore I merely speak as a layman so far as the legal aspect of the matter is involved. And we are fortified with the legal opinion of some of the most eminent Counsel in Great Britain, who gave us the benefit of their opinion—not as our advocates—but as some of the most prominent constitutional lawyers in Great Britain. But I believe, however, that I am not wrong in saying that the word" sufferance" meaning passive acquiescence, or implied consent, in Municipal Law, is operative only if it is no induced by fraud, force, undue influence, or mistake. It is suspended during minority when the person supposed to have acquiesced has no consenting mind. Judged by these tests, the inroads of Political Practice cannot really be justified under the term "sufferance" which presupposes full understanding of all the implications of a new theory and implies silence or acquiesence without the aplication of one's "judicial mind" to all the consequences involved.

21. Whilst it suited the Government of India at one time to issue a Resolution in regard to the Manipur tragedy in 1891 by which, with one stroke of the pen, all international status and privileges were forthwith and summarily denied to the States, yet, I submit, is it not surprisingly strange that where it suits the advocates of Paramountcy being paramount and supporters of the Imperial interests being at all times supreme—regardless of justice and equity—we find phrases relating to European international relations applied without demur, hesitation and with impunity to the Indian States in their relations

with the Paramount Power, as is clear from what I have already quoted in regard to the plea of sufferance on the part of the States? I submit that nothing can be more illogical, inconsistent or unfair.

22. There is great danger to our States—not subject to Municipal Law—from the misapplication of juristic doctrines imported from Municipal Law, Doctrines of usage, sufferance, acquiescene and waiver all presuppose full knowledge of the correct relations and the willing surrender of rights. Usage to be perfect depends on the ancient and uninterrupted asertion of rights and cannot be matured in face of various protests by the States from time to time; and no right can be acquired by usage or sufferance unless there has been such a degree of acquiensence as can amount to evidence of agreement and asquiescence in specific acts.

23. Joint action on the part of the Princes and States was obviously out of the question in the then existing conditions when no Chamber of Princes existed; and even in the latter period of our treaty relationship, few people in most States indeed realised what the treaties meant, or possessed even a scanty knowledge of English, specially so in Rajputana, and Central and Northern India. Even 40 years ago, when I came to the Throne, the number of people in the whole of my Capital, possessing even a superficial knowledge of English could be counted on the fingers of one hand. No properly organised Foreign Offices then existed in States with expert legal and constitutional and political advisors; and even when we made a beginning, our protests and our objections went in vain. In the training imparted to minor Princes, various doctrines—including such astounding doctrines as that the Princes were the agents and intermediaries of the British Government, and not the Sovereign Rulers of their States possessing internal autonomy, and justifying all kinds of intervention—were drilled into the young Princes; and no attempt was made to explain to the young Rulers the true constitutional position of themselves vis-a-vis the British Government, This all round ignorance and, in the then circumstances, the impossibility of really grasping the facts or the situation involved, combined with the arbitrary acts and rulings of the British Government—through undue influence, which the Princes and their Governments were unable obviously to resist—as well as the encroachments during minority administrations, have often been discounted in appraising the correct rights or appreciating the dangers, past, present and future, affecting the States. A moment's thought will reveal that it was impossible at the time for the States, and even the most sugacious of our statesmen, to foresee or realise

the far-reaching, and yet remote, effects of such detraction from the Sovereign rights of the States or to forestall the building up of the political practice or case-law—all converging upon the admitted infringements of treaty righs. Otherwise, there would certainly have been more frequent and more insistent protests in the past century.

24. Thus matters regarding sufferance between the British Government and the States cannot be judged as, for example, between two totally independent European States, fully enlightened and advanced, with up-to-date paraphernalia available for legal, constitutional and other Governemental machinery and advice. Had it been otherwise, and if really there is any force in the argument regarding sufferance, which we respectifully beg to contradict, what, for instance, is the need for revising the political practice in various directions and on diverse subjects as has been done during the last 11 years? Irrespective of such practice being unjust and unfair to the Princes and a clear encroachment on their Treaty Rights, sufferance alone would have sufficed to force it upon the States. What again was the necessity for admitting the rights of the Rulers of the bigger States to be styled "Princes" after they had been forced to put up a fight on the subject when we were officially informed at meetings and in correspondence some 15 or 16 years ago that we were in no way entitled to the term "Princes" but only to the term "Chiefs", which applied to the feudatories of our Indian States as well as to the head of negro and other wild races? Why similarly was the wrong redressed and the Princes' claims in regard to precedence modified, during Lord Hardinge's Viceroyalty, at least to a considerable extent—though some details have yet to be gone into—vis-a-vis certain High British Officials, who upto some 15 years ago to the humiliation of , the Princes had been given precedence above some of the greatest Ruling Princes in India, dating back specially to the Viceroyalty of Lord Curzon? Why then is there any necessity for an attempt, through mutual discussion and consent, to modify political practice, since it might similarly be urged that Princes through sufferance had given up all claims to any such redress? Where was the necessity for the institution of the Chamber of Princes to safeguard the interests of the Rulers and States of India, and why was the announcement made regarding various other reforms, to which I alluded yesterday in a speech, which were recommended in Chapter X of the Montford Report and accepted by the Imperial Government as well as the Government of India? Why again the need for rectifying and liberalising past political practice when some States under compulsion, or through ignorance or otherwise, had sent explanations and reports

about the non-appearance of a camel for the Residency menials, the prosecution as an ordinary criminal case of the Residency butcher, or the trial of a gardener of the Royal Palace, or the dismissal by the Department concerned of Police constables and other employees? Surely under the plea of sufferance all these things could be insisted upon today.

25.1 might here as well refer to the frequent manner in which innovations in theories are silently introduced in the legislative enactments of the Government of India, which are not previously even brought to the notice of the Governments of the States concerned. Mark for instance the phraseology in which the Indian States were referred to in such Enactments prior to 1890 or more than 13 years after the assumption by Queen Victoria of the title of the Empress of India. In spite of the unqualified assurances given publicly in Parliament by the then Prime Minister—Lord Beaconsfield—that such an assumption of the Imperial Title need cause no misgiving and that it would by no means affect the rights and status of the Indian Rulers, a change has been arbitrarily introduced in legal Enactments of the Government of India describing the relations of the Indian Rulers with the Crown; and the same untenable argument is a advanced in regard to other matters—political and ceremonial. In regard to such Enactments as were intended to have a bearing even on the territories of our States—and here I do not talk of the rights and wrongs and the legality or otherwise, of such Enactments—as regards our States, we find them described, correctly then, as applying to the

> "dominions of Princes and States in India in alliance with Her Majesty".

A sudden change came over the Imperialistic mind and authority in 1895, or 18 years after Queen Victoria's assumption of the title of Empress, when a new phraseology was applied and the Rulers were, I understand for the first time, referred to as being

> "under the suzerainty of Her Majesty."

No previous consultation with, much less the consent of, the States had taken place or been obtained. The innovation was not even communicated to the Indian Rulers; and the relationship of feudal suzerainty was thus smuggled into Legislative Enactments without even our knowledge. Is silence under such circumstances also to be interpreted into sufferance ?

26. To proceed a stage further, new legal fictions need legal acumen and intellect of an acute mind in order to be detected, and their remote consequences fully comprehended. Even where the States understood the implications of a theory, they had not the courage to raise their feeble voice in protest against the advice of Political Officers accredited to their Courts; and their silence, even under these circumstances, has been interpreted as acquiescence or suferance. Thus, for instance, their treaty and other rights—which have been safeguarded by Parliamentary Enactments and successive Royal Proclamations as "inviolate and inviolable"—are imagined as abrogated, though, specially in the past, they have not always had the means or facilities or environments to lodge their emphatic, but respectful, protest in time. And yet we go a stage further, and in the first Act dealing with the Government of India Act of 1915, we find for the first time the spectre raised of treaties being defunct. Section 132 of that Act, for instance, makes only such treaties made by the East India Company binding on His Majesty "as are in force at the commencement of this Act." This proviso did not exist in the older Act of 1858; and—in spite of Queen Victoria's Memorable Pronouncement announcing to the Princes that all Treaties and Engagements made with them by, or under the authority of , the East India Company were accepted by Her Majesty and will be scrupulously maintained, and in spite furthermore of the Parliamentary enactment to the effect that "all Treaties" made by the East India Company "shall be binding on Her Majesty"—is intended to imply that Treaties can thus cease to be in force. No exception could have been taken to this limitation if the modification of Treaties was meant to be such as had been agreed to by mutual consent; but if Treaties are taken to be rescinded or modified even by usage or sufferance, by a stroke of the pen, or by the insertion of a paragraph in legislative enactment, independently of our consent, it becomes a dangerous innovation to which strong exception must be taken.

27. And one is left wondering what really did the supporters of those, who urged the plea of sufferance, imply the Governments of the States to do. Did they expect us to resist any such encroachments on our Treaties and other rights by resort to arms, and thus prove ourselves unworthy of our ancient and religious tradition towards the Crown, or did they expect us, on the basis of international status, already denied to us, to send an ultimatum to the Government of India and to declare war upon them if they did not rectify all such matters within a specified time?

28. Your Excellency, this rectification and revision of all such matters and past mistakes, which we have now undertaken, even though it is not without its handicaps at the moment, is surely and clearly a recognition by the British Government of the wrongs committed in the past and their sincere desire to rectify them now and hereafter.

29. And only it is under the present day policy of sympathy and greater trust in the States that we are jointly endeavouring to rectify past mistakes and wrongs instead of having them presented to us as 'settled facts' sanctified by "usage" and accepted by "sufferance."

30. I would respectfully submit that I am not wrong in urging that sufferance of all things should, in no circumstances, be even considered—much less allowed—to stand as any argument so far as the relations between the Crown and the Princes are concerned.

31. We feel that Your Excellency and the Imperial Government will agree that what is far more important is that the interests and the rights of the States should be duly and adequately safeguarded; that justice should be done to them; that, where any mistake has been made or wrong done in the past, immediate steps should willingly and generously be taken to rectify them—whether they relate to political or fiscal matters as also questions involving the honour and dignity of the Indian States and their Rulers—and we earnestly urge, and confidently hope, above all, that in the near future, through a policy of absolute justice and impartiality, equity and fairplay, the plighted word of great Britain will be upheld, no matter what the question is that is involved, and that faith will be kept at all costs with the Princes and States.

# Annexure 8

## Speech Delivered by His Highness the Maharajah at a Dinner given on the 12th May, 1930

*Ladies and Gentlemen,*

I have asked you all to this dinner tonight with the express object of thanking each and every one of you, Gentlemen, as well as those who for unavoidable reasons are not present here tonight, and including the officers and men working under you, for the capable and energetic manner in which you have all carried out your respective duties and contributed to the success of the various functions and arrangements connected with the Wedding of my dear daughter. Let me congratulate you on the same and assure you of my grateful appreciation of your labours. Without desiring to make any invidious distinction I would desire specially to commend the able services of Major—General Thakur Hari Singhji of Sattasar on whom fell the heaviest brunt of work and responsibility.

2. I am leaving tomorrow for Bombay to enjoy the remaining portion of my much needed annual holiday, and from there I hope, as usual, to proceed to Mount Abu. I shall, therefore, be away from the Capital for some weeks; and as I shall, in all probability, be visiting Simla in July to attend some important meetings, and will, shortly afterwards, have to proceed to England on official business, and as another opportunity may not occur for some time, I propose tonight to detain you for a few minutes in order also to allude to some questions which are at the present moment prominently before the public in British India as well as the Indian States, I fear there is little that will be new in what I say tonight but a little repetition often helps to keep certain matters clearly focussed in our minds.

3. It is obvious that the situation with which India is faced at present is most delicate and anxious—indeed critical. There is already enough of trouble; and, I have no desire to say anything that may be considered to be controversial. And just as we of the States desire to be free from outside interference in the internal affairs of our States, I need hardly add that the last thing I wish to touch upon today is any matter which is purely the domestic concern of British India. At the same time if it

is within the competence of anyone to say or do anything which might remove misunderstandings and clear the position it is assuredly his duty to contribute his own little quota in order to render some service to our Motherland, to the Empire, and to our beloved King-Emperor.

4. The sad state of affairs in British India is clear to us all. If I allude even briefly tonight to the troubled situation there, it is not only because we of the Indian States are both directly and indirectly deeply concerned, but because of our love for our beloved Country. The position as regards the Indian States may, however, not be equally clearly visualized except by those who have intimate knowledge of the matters now engaging the attention of the Rulers and Governments of our States, or those who have made a careful, close and continuous study of the problems which face us.

5. It is necessary for the purpose of a brief review, that I should carry you back at least some 13 years, when I had the honour, as the first representative of the Princes and States, to attend in London the Imperial War Cabinet and the Imperial War Conference in 1917. Some political memories are notoriously and conveniently short, whilst with a certain class of individuals and newspapers it is even more convenient, than merely forgetting past facts, deliberately, alas! to misrepresent and even to distort facts. And at present with certain schools of political activities, both in British India as well as with some so-called leaders and representatives of our States it seems to be the fashion, moreover, to tar every Ruler and Government of Indian States with the same brush and to abuse and attack them indiscriminately and as a body. Thus, enjoying—as I am proud to feel that I do—the confidence and friendship of the great majority of my Brother Princes, and being placed in a position where, in common with some of the other Princes, we, as members of the Princes Standing Committee and the Chamber of Princes, have to shoulder the especial responsibilities in regard to the Indian States affairs it is inevitable that I should have been singled out for especial attention and abuse by such individuals, parties and newspapers, and as an instance of such deliberate misrepresentation I would refer to the veiled and grossly unfair reference to me at the last session of the Congress in Lahore.

6. But I am not inflicting this speech on you tonight, Ladies and Gentlemen, with any desire to make any personal references, or to vindicate myself. My past record and actions, apart from my numerous public utterances, will, I would hope, speak for themselves; and I am perfectly content to be judged by the verdict of history and posterity

when the dust of controversy has been laid, and it is possible for things to be viewed and judged impartially and in their right perspective by all concerned.

7. You, the Minister and other Officers of my Government, however, will recall that on more than one occasion in public—and of course on numerous occasions in confidential, official discussions and conferences—it bas been my privilege to have urged the claim of India, and particularly of British India, to a generous measure of constitutional advance. My speeches and action during the Sessions of the Imperial War Cabinet and Conference, as also when I was in England in 1918—19 at the time of the peace Conference, were at the time misunderstood by some die-bards both in England and in India. These matters I dealt with in my speech when inaugurating the Session of our Legislative Assembly on the 21st October, 1919. Subsequent events have, however, I make bold to say, not only justified all that I said and did, but I would venture to add that to all impartial and unprejudiced minds they have proved to the hilt that I was neither disloyal to the King-Emperor or the British connection—as some suspicious and reactionary persons thought in India as well as in England—nor disloyal or unpatriotic as regards my Mother Country and my brother Indians of British India. And all I need say Mother on the subject, so far as I am personally concerned, is that I have consistently and unflinchingly followed the dictates of my conscience and done the utmost that lay in my power to serve India and her sons—regardless of their being British Indians or the people of our States; and that is a line of policy which I shall follow equally strictly in regard to the discussions and negotiations at the forthcoming Round—Table Conference in England and, please God, to the last day of my life.

8. As with individual Rulers, so also the Ruling Princes as a body have been, and are being, attacked in the most unfair and unscrupulous manner and represented as being unpatriotic and traitors to their Motherland. They are accused of a desire to retard the constitutional advance of British India, and are represented as being obstacles in the way of British India's progress towards its appointed goal and are suspected of being in deep conspiracy, and having entered into an unholy alliance, with the British Government to deprive India of its birth-right. The most public and unqualified avowals of their sincere sympathy with their fellow-countrymen in British India have in certain quarters, been treated with scant courtesy and mischievous attempts are being made to cast doubts upon their sincerity—of which they have given ample proof already. These

malicious and totally unfounded attacks continue to be hurled at them in season and out of season, so as to create bitterness and ill-feeling between the two great and component parts of India—regardless of all considerations as to the great harm that was being done by such attempts at impairing unity. Upto the last moment, and indeed even till now, some individuals and newspapers have refused to grasp the hand of friendship offered by the Princes and States.

9. But, of late, events have marched with considerable rapidity. The unqualified support given by the Princes and States to the official Pronouncement made by our popular Viceroy, Lord Irwin, last October—making it unmistakably clear that the goal and policy of the British Government was Dominion Status for British India—and the announcement regarding the Round Table Conference to be convened in England, should in itself have left no room for doubt—even in the minds of the most sceptical or suspicious. Since then, however, during an open Session of the Chamber of Princes which met last February the Princes in no ambiguous language have once again given their sympathy and support for all the legitimate aspirations of British India and their hearty co-operation at the Round-Table Conference. The Princes also had some informal conversations last March with the leaders of British India representing various political parties, including the non-official European group. They have deputed two of the foremost Ministers of their States—our Prime Minister, Sir Manubhai Mehta and Colonel Haksar, Director of Special Organization of the Chamber of Princes—to sit informally with the presentatives chosen by the British Indian leaders themselves at an Informal Conference—for the purpose of exploring the "greatest possible measure of agreement "in regard to the future constitution of India.

10. I need hardly explain that my observations tonight of course represent my personal views and sentiments; but I think I can safely say that I am not voicing anything for different from the views and sentiments entertained generally by the Princes and States in regard to such matters. It is our earnest hope that the informal discussions which will take place in Simla next month between the two Ministers of our States and the chosen representatives from amongst British Indian leaders, will help greatly in the two constituent parts of India better appreciating and understanding each other's rights and position, standpoints and legitimate aspirations, and that such informal conversations will ultimately lead to a saving of a great deal of time and anxiety—so far as the States and British India are concerned at the London Conference where, when the time comes

for final and formal negotiations, we hope" an agreement will be arrived at, honourable and beneficial alike to British India and Indian States.

11. Let me add one word more about such informal discussions. I was surprised to learn from private letters from friends in England that the very open and harmless, informal discussions with the leaders of British India, and, in particular, the appointment of two of our Ministers to hold further informal conversations with the representatives of British India for the purpose of finding in a friendly manner the possible lines of agreement before the Round-Table Conference, was misunderstood as implying any weakening of the position, which the Princes have consistently taken up, of standing solid for the Crown and the British connection. As I have already said, amongst the leaders who met us at these informal discussion were also members of the Non-Official European group. And if my memory does not fail me, I believe, I am correct in saying, that the suggestion for such further informal discussions between our representatives and those of British India emanated from a distinguished Non-Official European Member of the Imperial Legislative Assembly, Need I add that there can never by any question of any weakening of the link with the Crown, which we must highly treasure and wish to retain unimpaired; but our sincere efforts to contribute our quota towards the peaceful solution of the difficult problem of constitutional advance and our natural desire—subject of course to the two well-known and essential conditions—to give the utmost support and assistance to our brother Indians is a matter which I think leaves really no room for serious misunderstandings or misgivings?

12. Much capital- deliberate and, I fear, mischievous—is being made in India of these two essential provisos, which the Princes made in the Chamber of Princes as well as on other occasions—and which I foreshadowed in my speech on the 9th September, 1928,—viz., firstly, that the Princes stand solid for the British connection and that their sympathy, support and co-operation offered to British India is essentially based on India remaining an integral part of the British Empire under the aegis of the Crown, and secondly that the Treaty and Sovereign rights and internal autonomy of the States must be adequately safeguarded for all time.

13. I must confess my utter failure to comprehend how these two obvious and essential conditions can be regarded by any reasonable and impartial person as dishonourable on the part of the Princes or unpatriotic to British India, with the people of which, as I have

previously observed, we are bound by ties of blood, race and religion.

14. It should be obvious to anybody, that the one characteristic and past tradition of which, more than anything else, a true Indian—be he a resident of British India or of our States—can legitimately be proud, in his loyalty, reverence and devotion to the Sovereign and his scrupulous adherence to his plighted word and the faithful discharge of the obligations of honour and good faith. Apart fro our Treaties, through which we occupy the proud position of "perpetual Allies" and "Friends", we are also particularly and personally attached to our gracious King-Emperor, who has always been pleased to evince the most gracious regard for our rights, honours and dignities, and—as in the case of the people of British India—to display the most genuine interest and sympathetic solicitude for the Princes, Peoples and States of India. Thus both Dharma and honour make absolutely clear to us the path which the Princes have unflinchingly followed When viewed in the right perspective such an honourable and loyal attitude on the part of the Princes and States of India, is no impediment in the way of constitutional— and I sincerely hope a liberal, prompt and early—advance of British India towards Dominion Status as an integral part of the Empire.

15. Turning now to matters of vital interest to the Governments and peoples of the Indian States, I would in the first instance, without repeating what I have said in my speeches on previous occasions, invite attention to the debates which took place recently on the subject in the Chamber of Princes, which will in themselves make the position clear. But the vast maority of the loyal subjects of our States need have no apprehension that their interests are not being carefully watched and safeguarded to the utmost of our ability.

16. There are in reality only a few points on which avenues of common agreement between the Indian States and British India have to be explored. They can be broadly outlined under three heads—

1. The Indian States seek the full restoration of their Internal Sovereignty; and barring certain necessmy safeguards for preventing gross misrule, they are not prepared to aquiesce in any undefmed residuary or ultimate powers of the new Dominion government. The problem presents little difficulty if the British Indian political leaders themselves are anxious to disclaim a right to succeed to the present exaggerated claims of the Government of India in regard to "Paramountey".
2. The Indian States ask for joint deliberation on all matters of common concern,. This right had been acknowledged by the

Joint Report on Reforms of 1919; it has been again emphasised by the Butler Committee; and the best constitutional guarantees have to be provided in order to make such joint deliberation an essential, and not a mere form, of legislative enactment and executive action. In no Federal system can there by any taxation without joint deliberation.

3. The Indian States consider it essential that a Supreme Court of Justice should be established for the adjudication of all suchjusticiable matters that might be at issue between them and the Government of India—a claim in which the British Indian leaders have themselves already lent them their full support.

17. In advancing to the Dominion form of Government certain necessmy safeguards and guarantees will be indispensable. The Indian Princes only ask for such additional gurantees for their own legitimate rights and interests. For instance, they ask for:

(a) a constitutional gurantee that there would be no interference with their Internal Sovereignty as long as there is no gross mal-administration in their States;

(b) A guarantee that questions connected with their personal and dynastic status will be reserved matters for consideration and decision by the Viceroy alone as the representative in India of the Crown;

(c) a guarantee that no executive action or legislative enactment passed by the British Indian Legislature will extend to Indian States unless their concurrence had been first secured through joint deliberation;

(d) a guarantee that the Indian States will not be asked to contribute to Imperial burdens without regard to their Treaties and without taking into consideration the total contribution made by the States as a whole body in men, money and cessation of territory; and that if any such contributions have to be asked for, they will be obtained with the free consent of the States;

(e) a financial gurantee that the Indian States shall not be exploited for the benefit of British India and that the revenues of fiscal measures like Sea-Customs, Excise, Posts and Telegraphs, and other combined income, to be raised only after joint deliberation, shall be equitably divided with the Indian States; and

(f) a guarantee that the common ministerial services would be equally manned by people from British India as from the Indian States.

18. We do not yet know the exact dates of the Indian Conference in London; but, ladies and Gentlemen, I am one of those who is firmly convinced of the sincerity and sympathy, and the good will and ftiendship for India which has inspired His Majesty's government in regard to the declaration made regarding Dominion Status and of their genuinely desiring to do the utmost within reason to further the cause of India at the Round-Table Conference; whilst, if I may be permitted to say so without presumption and in all respect the sincerity, the sympathy and the affection which Lord Irwin entertains for India, whom he is genuinely anxious to serve, is beyond doubt. I may be considered old-fashioned but—as an Indian, yielding to no one in his patriotism and love for his Country—I cannot help lamenting the rejection of the hand of friendship offered by Lord Irwin, Mr. Ramsay MacDonald and Mr. Wedgwood Benn and His Majesty's Government, and the refusal on the part of an important political party—at the present moment, of all times—to participate in the discussions and negotiations at the Round—Table Conference in London where the future destiny of India will be settled.

19. Even though it is unfortunately true that, in the past, the constitutional advance of British India might well have been accelerated and there has been displayed at times a sad lack of imagination and breadth of vision in the handling of the Indian problem, the present seemed the most propitious juncture for making up for lost time and opportunities, when—if all the political parties in India had firmly supported the Viceroy and His Majesty's Government and had agreed to go to England, unitedly to put forward reasonable and legitimate demands—the claims of British India would have been irresistible, if advanced with sagacity, moderation, decorum, and restraint. Instead of that, we see British India divided and a state of affairs brought about in India, which no one can predict what it will lead to, and which, in my humble opinion, must do us all untold harm. Had the Round—Table Conference failed through any unreasonableness or lack of sympathy on the part of His Majesty's Government or of the British Parliament, there would have been sufficient time to reconsider the position. Another golden opportunity has been lost to India. However, in the interests of India as a whole, we can only pray that the efforts of other leaders in British India, imbued with patriotism and sobriety will receive the maximum support from all persons and parties who have the good of India at heart, that

the harm done may be retrieved, that India may yet come into her own as an equal and honourable Member of the British Commonwealth of Nations, and that the Round-Table Conference will be followed by an era of peace and prosperity, to which our beloved, but sorely distressed, Motherland is surely entitled.

## Annexure 9

**Interview granted on the 18th July, 1930, to the Associated Press of India by Major-General His Highness the Maharajah of Bikaner, G.C.S.I., G.C.I.E., G.C.V.O., G.B.E., K.C.B., A.D.C., LL.D. in regard to the publication of important correspondence between His Excellency the Viceroy and Sir Tej Bahadur Sapru, K.C.S.I. and Mr. M.R. Jayakar, M.L.A.**

I would ordinarily decline to express any public views concerning the purely domestic affairs of British India—an encroachment to which its Leaders and people would be as entitled to object as would the Princes about any attempts in any quarters to interfere with the internal autonomy and domestic affairs of our Indian States. This however is not an ordinary occasion, and as happily it is consistent both with my loyal duty to our beloved King-Emperor and my patriotism to my Mother Country, I gladly accede to your request that I should express my views, for what they are worth, on a question of such momentous importance, not only to India but indeed to the British Empire to which the Princes and States are so sincerely attached.

2. As mentioned in the Statement issued by the Princes of the Standing Committee of the Chamber of Princes recently issued in Simla, repercussions of what may happen in the next few months which may well prove the most critical period in the history of India including the results of the Round Table Conference in London, will affect alike India as well as the Empire. They will also affect our States; and the present political situation in India cannot but cause the gravest anxiety to the Princes and States who, through Treaties of alliance and friendship, are bound by indissoluble ties to the Crown, and have ever been inspired by deep rooted feelings of unflinching loyalty and devotion to the King-Emperor, by friendship and attachment for the British Empire, and by the most patriotic feelings for their Countly. I desire to-day once more to reiterate the expression in the Princes' Statement of their full confidence in, and respectful tribute to, Lord Irwin who as grasped the realities of the situation with the instincts becoming a far-seeing statesman and is sincerely attempting to serve at one and the same time the best interests of India as well as

of Great Britain. When petty feelings have been laid aside and facts are possible to be surveyed dispassionately and in their true perspective, Lord Irwin will I am positive by the verdict of History be assuredly accorded a place amongst the greatest of India's Viceroys and as one who has so constantly reflected the genuine regard for the sentiments and susceptibilities and the very human expectations of the Princes and people of India by attempting to translate into action the earnest plea of sympathy for India graciously advanced by the King Emperor a quarter of a century ago and which His Imperial majesty was pleased to reiterate the other day at the opening of the India House.

3. With these important considerations in view let me first say that I concur with what has been stated in their letter to His Excellency by my friends Sir Tej Bahadur Sapru and Mr. Jayakar about the imperative necessity of some immediate steps being taken, in view of the political situation unhappily prevailing in India, and with their laudable endeavours to do all in their power to bring about a return of peaceful and normal conditions in India. I earnestly pray that their hope and belief will be justified, thanks to the sympathetic action and—if I may respectfully add the far-sighted statesmanship of Lord Irwin in permitting them to interview Mr. Gandhi, Pandit Motilal Nehru, and Pandit Jawaharlal Nehru. The only point about which I disagree with them is where they have modestly stated that if they fail in this attempt the responsibility will be theirs, for I make bold to say that they will leave no stone unturned, and if their attempts now fail, the responsibility for failure of such private negotiations will solely rest on the shoulders of those Congress Leaders who might take up an impossible position or are found to be obdurate; and such unreasonable attitude must surely result in rallying once again on the side of the British Government the liberal and moderate. Leaders as well as the Commercial community and many others who would indeed be justified in the circumstances in coming to the conclusion that the Congress Leaders were merely bent as destruction all round.

4. In the past I have not hesitated for one moment to express publicly the views which I hold strongly as to the great blunder and the grave harm that would enaue to India by launching at this moment of all others the non co-operation movement and by rejecting the hand of friendship of fered by His Majesty's Government and Lord Irwin, Mr. Ramsay MacDonald and Mr. Wedgwood Bean; and it is hardly necessary to refer to the extreme impropriety, not to speak of the grave implications, of processions and demonstrations, such as those recently insisted upon by Congress workers in Bombay in

honour of the serious offence of the recent mutiny by some men of the Garhwali Regiment, however much one deplores the resultant heavy casualities. Nor do I minimise the dangers of the spirit of lawlessness and defiance of authority that is being fostered.

5. It is obvicusly impossible for the British Government to approach the Congress Leaders for a cessation of the non-co-operation movement. I have now taken active part in the administration of my State for thirty-two years, and am a firm believer in strong rule. Any challenge to the supremacy of a Government—whether it be the British Government or the Government of an Indian State—must inevitably be taken up. Revolution, or forces moving towards revolution, must be put down; and no Government worthy of the name can abdicate its functions. But it of course follows that side by side with firmness the rule must be beneficent, just and sympathetic and at the same time tempered with mercy; and it is no less essential that we should not be handicapped by any false notions or mistaken considerations of prestige. I recall a significant passage in the Late Nizam of Hyderabad's letter to Lord Minto in 1909, when, in discussing measures necessary for the suppression of sedition then existing, he expressed himself as a great believer in conciliation and repression going hand in hand. It therefore follows that wise, statesmanship and the interests of India as well as of the Empire demand that every avenue possible should be explored and every opportunity wisely, tactfully and sympathetically taken advantage of to bring about more cordial and closer relations between the Government and the people. As I pointed out at the Guildhall thirteen year ago, when the honour of the Freedom of the City of London was conferred upon me, people who hold that India can be ruled at the point of the sword do a grave injustice to both Great Britain and India and that the retention of the British Connection in which I, in common with my Brother Princes, am a firm believer—must rest on much firmer foundations than force and be based on principles of justice and equity, humanity and fairplay.

6. Again in 1917, I ventured to bring home the fact that India even then was changing very rapidly and beyond the conception of those who—the strength of former residence or service in India or who, while residing in England all the time, have had official connection with this country—and who pose as critics of those who have the burden and responsibility and the duty of carrying on the King-Emperor's Government out here. It is imposible for them really to be aware of the remarkable changes going on, or appreciate the situation as it now exists in India.

7. I own a house and spend a month or two every year at the seaside in Bombay—admittedly the present storm—centre in India—and, thugh I was ill for part of the time, yet throughout my stay there last May and June, I kept my eyes and ears open, and was able to go about and see things for myself, and I also met frequently several loyal moderate and liberal friends amongst British Indian Leaders. I can thus claim to speak with some authority based on first hand knowledge and personal observations when I testify to the extremely grave situation and the unmistakable depth and force of the widespread National awakening. The movement has taken a firm hold on people of practically all classes and communities of Indians, at least in the Bombay Presidency, including a very large percentage of the commercial community and even those who do not entirely see eye to eye with Mr. Gandhi and others politically.

8. No doubt with all the power and resources at the command of Great Britain a great Government like the British Government with a mighty Empire at its back, can ultimately crush, or at least for the time being keep this movement under control. But even then the struggle is not likely to end as quickly as some may imagine and the situation it is apparent is apt to get worse before it gets better—not only in Bombay but also in other parts of India. In the meanwhile there will be created in an everincreasing degree intense and widespread feelings of bitterness and hatred the incalculable harm arising from which it is impossible fully to foresee at the present moment. Such a policy, in such circumstances, would not succeed even in our Indian States where the Rulers are, so to speak, autocrats and the people not so advanced as in British India. Indeed those who advocate such unwise and impracticable course appear circle from which all parties may ultimately find it difficult satisfactorily to extricate themselves.

9. It has to be borne in mind that many, including for instance the commercial community, are not really disloyal to the Crown or to the British connection. Though I do not profess to lay the slightest claim to be a fiiancial or ecnomic expert, I feel it may duty incidentaly to state here that there is also a vetry widespread and bitter feeling which is by no means confined to British India alone but is manifest in purely commercial and totally non-political circles even in our Indian States as regards the one shilling six pence ratio. Anyhow various reasons—some valid and others imagined—have contributed to such feelings of unrest and even of despondency and despair. It is in view of these important considerations that I have for some time past, favoured private negotiations such as those now proposed by

Sir Tej Bahadur and Mr. Jayakar and why I now venture respectfully and unqualifiedly to welcome the acceptance by His Excellency the Viceroy of their suggestion which I profoundly believe to be in the best interests of the Empire and this is what a wise Ruler of an Indian State would also do in similar circumstances.

10. I have had the honour of serving three successive British Sovereigns, both in peace and war, and my first campaign dates back thirty years to the reign of the great Queen Victoria; I am descended from a long line of soldiers, and I and my State and my subjects have vested interests and a very real stake in the Country. I trust therefore that I am justified in claiming that I speak not as an alarmist or one dabbling in politics, but with a full sense of responsibility as a true friend and well-wisher of Great Britain, and as one who has never departed from the traditional loyalty of his House, and as belonging to the Order of Princes to whom Treaty obligations and plighted word are of paramount consideration. And I would like to take this opportunity of expressing the earnest hope that the fullest support will be extended, both in England and in India, to the Viceroy and his Government, in their efforts to bring about a more satisfactory state of affairs in India, thus helping to ensure a better atmosphere at the Round Table Conference, the results of which are bound to influence, for good or for bad, the future destknies of India and the Empire. Tremendous issues are at stakel and never has there been greater need than today for bold statesmanship and courageous action; and if the Round Table Conference is to do good and satisfactorily to solve the problems of India including the Indian States, it is of the utmost importance that the Indian problem should not be considered on any pre-conceived lines and that it should be handled on absolute non-party lines, by which alone can we, under God's providence, hope to see India and Great Britain once again firmly united and standing shoulder to shoulder, for all time, against all foes to the mutual advantage of both.

11. I would also venture to appeal to our friends in British India to exercise patience and not to be alarmed, or to be put off, by anything which they might rightly or wrongly regard as likely impediments to the success of the Conference, and above all to rely upon the Viceroy and His Majesty's Government who, in spite of their having to face innumerable difficulties, are undoubtedly sincere in their sympathies for India, and, as Sir Tej Bahadur Sapru and Mr. Jayakar have rightly stated, they are no less anxious to explore every possible solution of the problems with which we are faced. However, much it may be desired to have a more definite pronouncement about the aims and

functions of the Round Table Conference it is difficult at this stage for the Viceroy and His Majesty's Government to say much more. But attention might here be invited to the Viceroy's assurance in his reply to Sir Tej Bahadur and Mr. J ayakar to the effect that it is his earnest desire as well as that of his Government, and no doubt also that of His Majesty's Government, to do everything that they can in their respective spheres to assist the people of India to obtain as large a degree as is possible of the management of their own affairs. In the words of one of the foremost of India's sons, my Right Honourable friend Mr. Sastri, we must all applaud the tone of sincerity and helpfulness of the recent speech of the Viceroy in the Central Legislatures, the magnanimity of whose words should dispel all hesitation and bring the best men of India to discover a lasting solution of her problems on this occasion of unparalleled promise, and it behoves us not to be unmindful of the rare opportunity offered and the tremendous responsibility placed on all Indians. As I said in a speech a couple of months ago, if all the Indian parties and communities, concerned unitedly put forward reasonable and legitimate claims at the Conference, and if they were advanced with sagacity and moderation and decorum and restraint, they would really prove irresistible. Should happily for India a suitable response be made by the Congress Leaders to the efforts of Sir Tej Bahadur and Mr. Jayakar, it is inconceivable that the response by the Viceroy and the British Government would not also be generous and such as would satisfy all reasonable-minded people.

12. One last word about the States. I am glad to feel that the cloud of suspicion and distrust against the Princes, and States has been removed and that it is at last being realised in almost every responsible quarter in British India that the Princes have no intention of standing in the way of British India attaining her legitimate goal. But only the other day, with reference to several unauthorized and incorrect reports relating to the recent Princes Meetings in Simla, I noticed it stated, amongst certain other not very generous remarks, that the Princes attitude at the London Conference regarding British Indian affairs would be the chief test as to whether or not they would agree to serve as the Ulster of India. There is really not the alightest ground for alarm in British India as regards the importance attached, and the emphasis very rightly laid, by the Princes and States—as has now been acknowledged by more authoritative sources than one-upon the solemnity and binding character of our Treaties, and the relations of the Princes and States being with the Crown, and therefore in future with the Viceroy and not the Governor-General, or its natural

corollary that such political relations with the Crown cannot and should not be transferred to anyone else without the express and free consent of the Princes. These are matters which might ultimately and profoundly affect the future—or indeed the very existence—of the States, but these are obviously their clear and inviolable rights. But with mutual respect for each other, and a due appreciation and understanding of the respective standpoints, and a just recognition of their rights, claims and aspirations, the closer association between British and Indian India for the purpose of co-operation in all India concerns ŕwithout infringing the Sovereignty of the States—are matters on which there is really no cause for anxiety or alarm to British India. As has already been made abundantly clear, the Princes and States stand solid only upon two essential conditions, namely:

1. that equitable and satisfactory agreement is arrived at between the parties concerned for the position of the States in the future constitution of India on terms just and honourable alike to the States and British India; and
2. that India retains the British connection as an equal partner in the British Commonwealth of Nations under the aegis of the King-Emperor. For the rest, I have not the least doubt that the Princes and Sates as a body will be prepared to be judged by their attitude at the Round Table Conference which, I am positive, will not only be fair but helpful to British India.

# Annexure 10

**Speech by Lieut.-General His Highness the Maharajah of Bikaner, G.C.S.I., G.C.I.E., G.C.V.O., G.B.E., K.C.B., A.D.C., LL.G., at the Indian Round Table Conference, delivered at St. James's Palace, London, on the 17th November, 1930.**

*Mr. Chairman,*

We meet in no ordinary times to attempt no ordinary task. In our immediate concern is the peace, happiness and good government of three hundred and nineteen millions of people, look in got whatever Government may be established for some relief from their present distresses, who I venture once again to assert—certain unhappy circumstances notwithstanding—are loyal to the core. What then would be the results if from any irresolution on our part—from unreason on one side, or reaction on the other, from timidity in one party and a refusal to recognize the essentials of constitutional government in another—we blenched from the work and failed of our duty to secure the greater contentment of India! It goes without saying that a very heavy responsibility rests on each and every one of us taking part in this Conference, and that the issues involved are really tremendous. It is impossible to minimise the magnitude of the task that lay before us; nor do I desire to under-rate the complexity of some of the problems involved. I am an optimist but there is no use in shutting one's eyes to facts. I have seen in Bombay and elsewhere during my travels in British India how the masses in the districts are being affected and I wish I could adequately express the gravity of the situation. I have always declined to be moved by threats of dire consequences, nor have I submitted to being dictated to at the muzzle of the pistol. But undue regard for preconceived ideas and false notions of prestige or exaggerated fear of some possible consequences have, I feel it will be agreed, also to be guarded against; and I, for one—and here I feel that I speak for my Order as well as for the representatives of British India who are gathered round this ancient hall-refuse to be made fearful by the difficulties ahead. Rather I find in them an inspiration to put forth the uttermost that is in me, in a spirit of confidence and of courage. The very immensity of the work makes it worth doing well.

His Majesty the King-Emperor was pleased to remind us at the opening of this Conference that "the last decade has witnessed a . . . quickening and growth in ideals and aspirations of nationhood which defy the customary measurements of time." I venture to appeal to you, Prime Minister and other Members of His Majesty' Government and to our Colleagues here representing the British Political Parties, to take their courage in both hands, to throw their hearts over the fence and follow boldly after, in the conviction that the greater our vision and determination, the greater is our success likely to be and the richer in consequence the harvest which we all- British India and the Indian States, and Great Britain and the Empire—shall reap. The ultimate attainment of Dominion Status under the Crown is unherent in the Declaration of policy in 1917, and has more recently received authoritative endorsement. Let us hitch our waggon to that star, fully realising that our sister States did not reach the end of one stride, but after evolution based on experience-that in the intervening stage certain safeguards and guarantees are imperatively necessary for the security of the body politic and all parts thereof -but looking straight on. Nothing worth having can be attained without facing some risks. These were taken when Lord Durham laid the foundations for the proud position which Canada enjoys to-day as the premier Dominion in our great Commonwealth-to the mutual benefit of Great Britain and Canada. Similar risks were run when Sir Henry Campbell-Bannerman secured Dominion Status for Sourth Africa with the happiest results, for which we had every reason to be frateful during the Great War only some five years later. I am equally convinced that if this Conference will but do the right thing by India, justly and managnanimously, my Country will be a willing and contented partner in the Commonwealth. She will then be only too glad, side by side with the benefits of an honourable and independent position internally, to have all the power and resources of our mighty Empire always at her back. No half-hearted measures, and no tinkering with the constitution will, I beg you to believe me, meet the situation. Many of our troubles in the past, and our troubles of the present, have arisen from these causes. Moreover when, in response to irresistible demands, some constitutional advance was made, it was often too late; and it wore the appearance of having been conceded with a bad grace and wrested from the British Government. So there never was a time in the history of India and of the Empire when courage—courage in thought, in aim, in constructive statesmanship-was more needed than now, when the great ambitions stirring India are struggling for constitutional expression. If is the spirit of courage, confidence, imagination and liberal statesmanship, that I pray our deliberations may be guided.

From what standpoint then do we of the States approach this great task? I speak primarily for myself, though I believe I shall have the general agreement of the Princes and the Ministers representing our Indian States at this historic gathering. We are here specially to present the policies of the Indian States. First and foremost in those policies is an unflinching and unqualified loyalty to the Throne and Person of His Majesty the King-emperor of India. With the traditions of centuries of kingship and with the instincts and responsibilities of hereditary rule ingrained in our being, the kingly idea and the monarchical system are bone of our bone, flesh of our flesh. Even if we were tempted to weaken from this principle—which is impossible-the thought of the intense devotion of the Imperial House of Windsor to the interests of India would re-kindle our faith. Three notable and encouraging messages from His Majesty still ring in our ears—the earnest plea for sympathy in dealing with Indian problems made at the close of the Indian tour as prince of Wales; the Watchword of hope given six years later at Calcutta; and the pledge that the Princes' privileges, rights and dignities are inviolate and inviolable renewed when the Chamber of Princes was inaugurated. In this threefold spirit of sympathy, hope andjustice, encouraged by the gracious words addressed to this Conference when it was inaugurated on Wednesday, wer bend with the greater optisism to the work that lies before us.

Linked with the devotion to the Crown is an unfaltering adhesion to the British Commonwealth of Nations. The old idea of Empire as signifying dominion over palm and pine has vanished; the concept of Empire as overlordship based on force was never true and now has not even the pale shadow of reality. The unity of the Empire was signally vindicated in the Great War; the basis of that unity was re-shaped at the Imperial Conference of 1926 when it was declared that the constituent States are autonomous communities within the British Empire, equal in status, in now way subordinate one to another in any respect of their domestic or external affairs, though united by a common alegiance to the Crown. Our attachment to the Empire or Commonwealth, call it what we may, is no mere matter of sentiment. It is based on the profound conviction that not only can each constituent State reach its full expression within these bonds ad under the Crown, but a higher development, politically and economically, that it could attain as an isolated independent unit.

Thirdly, we stand without compromise on our treaty rights and all that they involve. Those Treaties are with the British Crown, and obviously cannot be transferred to any other authority without our free agreement and assent. But do not conclude from this that I am one of those people who think that things never change. The States rightly maintain that Treaties concluded in honour and friendship are binding untill they may be amended, and they can only be amended by negotiation and honourable agreement on both sides. Nor must it be concluded that we of the Indian States are under the belief that changes in British India will have no reflex action on ourselves and on our relations with our own subjects. The territories of the Indian States are so interwoven with British India, so many of the more enterprising of our traders have business in the new commercial centres on the seaboard which have grown up under the Pax Britannica and the opening of the Suez Canal, that we must be influenced by the development of political ideas and institutions beyond our Frontiers. But this is our affair, We know our States and our people; we live amongst our own folk and are in the most intimate contact with their needs and possibilities. We shall know how and when to adjust our system to any changing conditions; but we will do it in our own time and in our own way, free from all external interference.

Is there anything in adherence to these principles either opposed to, or inconsistent with, the fullest development of India until she takes her equal place as a constituent State in the British Commonwealth with the other Dominions, welded into an indivisible whole under the aegis of the Crown? I say No-a thousand times No. It is sometimes said that there are two Indias, British India and the India under the rule of her own Princes. That is true is a political sense; but India is a single geographical unit and we are all members one of another. We the Princes, are Indians—we have our roots deep down in her historic past we are racy of the soil. Everything which tends to the honour and prosperity of India has for us a vital concern. Everything which retards her propserity and shakes the stability of her institutions retards our own growth and lowers our stature. We claim that we are on the side of progress. One of the most welcome signs of the times is the material weakening of the idea that the Princes are opposed to the political growth of British India, and would range themselves—or allow themselves to be arrayed-against the realization of the just hopes of their fellow countrymen in British India. We have therefore watched with the most sympathetic interest the rise of that passion for an equal position in the eyes of the world expressed in the desire for Dominion Status which is the dominant force amongst all thinking Indians to-day. Those of us who have grown grey under the responsibilities of rule and the practical work of administration-and thirty-two years have passed since I assumed the active governance of the State of Bikaner-deplore some of the expressions of this urge. We appreciate the fact that when contacts are broken under the impulse of revolutionary fervour, they have to be re-knit in blood and tears, and a weary path of suffering and loss trodden before society marches forward again. But behind these untoward developments, which we hope and pray is only a passing phase, lies the struggle for equality springing from our ancient culture and quickened by years of contact with the liberty-loving and constitutionally-minded British people.

It is, I submit, our duty to bend our energies to the task of satisfying this righteous demand without impairing the majestic fabric of law. How best can this be achieved? My own conviction is that if we are to build well and truly, we must recognise that associated with this geographical unity India is a land of some diversity. Our starting point therefore must be a recognition of this diversity; our unity must be sought not in the dead hand of an impossible uniformity but in an associated diversity. For these reasons, the establishment of a unitary State, with a sovereign parliament sitting at Delhi, to which the whole people would look in small things as in large, is to my mind impossible. There would be no room in such a constitution for the Indian States; moreover such a government would crack under its own imponderability. Would it not mean the harnessing of the most advanced to the chariot wheels of the least developed, and the slowing down of the general tide of progress? We of the Indian States are willing to take our part in, and make our contribution to, the greater prosperity and contentment of India as a whole. I am convinced that we can best make that contribution through a federal system of government composed of the States and British India. These two partners are of different status. The Indian States are alrady Sovereign and autonomous of right having the honour of being linked with the Crown by means of Treaties of “perpetual alliance and friendship” and unity of interests; British India derives whatever measure of authority it may posses by devolution. But it will not be beyond the wealth of experience available at this Table to devise a means of linking these differing units into a powerful federal administration.

As to the question whether, if a federal government is devised for India, the Princes and States will enter into association with it, the final answer must obviously depend on the structure of the government indicated and on other points involved, such, for instance, as certain necessary safeguards—constitutional and fiscal—for the preservation of the rights and interests of the States and their subjects. Federalism is an elastic term: there are several forms of federal government. Conditions in India are unique. We have no historical precedents to guide us; and the position of the Indian States is, I believe I am correct in saying, absolutely without parallel. All these and many other grave questions of policy and of detail will have to be examined and defined and settled first in Committee and in informal discussions. But, speaking broadly, the Princes and States realise that all All-India Federation is likely to prove the only satisfactory solution of India's problem. A federation, on the lines I have attempted to sketch on other occasions, has, as I have previously said, no terrors for the Princes and Governments of the Indian States. We howeverrecognise that a period of transition will necessarily intervene before the Federal Government is fully constituted, and that Federation cannot be achieved by coercion of the States in any form. The Indian Princes will only come into the Federation of their own free will, and on terms which will secure the just rights of their States and subjects.

I would not venture on the impertinence of even suggesting what course is best for British India. As we demand freedom from interference in our own affairs, equally we shall refrain from thrusting our oars into matters which are not our direct concern; the arrangements between the Central and Provincial Governments in British India are matters primarily outside the purview of the Indian States. If our co-operation is sought, it will, I am sure, be gladly and freely and honestly given. Our duty is to contribute so far as we can to the evolution of a system of government which will lead to the close and effective association of the Indian States with British India whose constitution is to be hammered out here. At the same time the rights in certain directions of the Rulers of the Indian States arising from their Treaties require to be more precisely defined. The Princes and States naturally want to know where they stand. However, sincerely desirous of making their contribution to a happy settlement they will obviously find it difficult to enter into new bonds so long as their rights are left tottering on the shifting sands of expediency deemed paramount at the moment. I think I can best elucidate what is referred to by quoting from a speech I made in the Chamber of Princes on behalf of my Order, on the 27th February last:

"New fangled theories about the ultimate powers regarding

Paramountcy, and such matters, before the appointment of the Butler Committee, and the extravagent and exagfgerated Imperialist claims, inconsistent with the plighted word and good faith of Great Britain, or sound statemanship, advanced on behalf of the Paramount Power—claims more wide, more frequent, more insistent and, I respectfully submit, based on varied and not infrequently untenable grounds and opposed to constitutional and historical facts and to the provisions of our treaties and other Engagements and in direct contradiction of the solemn and clear pledges and assurances in the famous gracious Proclamation of Queen Victoria. repeatedly reiterated and affirmed by successive British Sovereigns in numerous Proclamations—have not helped to ease the situation or to allay the anxieties of the States, or their Rulers, Governments or people."

The princes and States fortified by the legal opinion obtained from some of the eminent counsel in Great Britain have found themselves unable particularly to accept such claims on the principles enunciated in this connection by the Indian States Committee, and have already taken up the matter with the Viceroy and British Government, starting with the basic recognition that our Treaty Rights exist and must be respected; that they are with the Crown and cannot be transferred to any other authority without our agreement; and that they can be modified only with our free assent, three developments of the existing administrative machinery are essential for the smooth working of the new system and indeed of any system. It is an open matter of complaint that our Treaty Rights have been infringed. I need not stress this point, for it has been publicly admitted by no less an authority than the Viceroy and Governor—General of India that the Treaty Rights of the States have been encroached upon, and that in some cxases an arbitrary body of usage and political practice has come into being. The time has passed when issues of this importance can be decided ex parte by any government. We therefore attach the utmost importance to the establishment of a Supreme Court, with full powers to entertain and adjudicate upon all disputes of a justiciable nature as to rights and obligations guaranteed under our Treaties. This is another point which I need not labour, for it is a principle to which the leaders of political thought in British India have, I believe I am right in saying, lent their full support. Next we claim that in the questions which arise concerning the purely internal affairs of the States their case should not go by default. That will be of still greater importance ill the future. The King's Viceregent in India is even now burdened with many and grievous responsibilities, which will be weighted under the new system of Government; and here I would once again like to be associated in a respectful tribute to and to express our deep admiration and gratitude for, that great Viceroy, Lord Irwin. We think that it will be impossible for any mean, however able, amid these grave pre-occupations, to give adequate personal attention to those questions affecting the States which come up for day-to-day decision, and for which he will be directly responsible to the Crown. For these reasons some of us press for the appointment of an Indian States Council, to work with the Political Secretary and to advise the Viceroy of the day. Thirdly, there will be the need for the classification of those administrative questions which are of common concern to British India and the Indian States. This classification will require the previous consent of the States. As we advance further on the road to Federation there are other issues which will need safeguarding; as they are in the nature of details they are not our main concern today.

With this contribution to the common task before us I have done. Before I sit down, may I ask forgiveness if, as an old soldier, I have unwittingly given offence to anyone by any bluntness of speech? I am inspired by one thought—service to my beloved King—Emperor and devotion to my Motherland. Akbar, the greatest of the Moghuls, when he set out on the crowning adventure of his crowded life, placed his foot in the stirrup of opportunity and his hands on the reins of confidence in God. I would commend to you on the threshold of our great enterprise—the conquest of anarchy and reaction in Hindustan and the assurance of her contentment and prosperity as a co-equal partner in our great Commonwealth—the words of Abraham Lincoln in circumstances not altogether remote from these:

> "With malice toward none; with charity for all; with firmness in the fight, as God gives us to see the right, let us strive on to finish the work that we are in."

# Annexure 11

## Speech by Lieut.-General His Highness the Maharajah of Bikaner, G.C.S.I., G.C.I.E., G.C.V.O., G.B.E., K.C.B., A.D.C., LL.D., at the Indian Round Table Conference (Sub—Committee No.1—Federal Structure), delivered at St. James's Palace, London, on the 8th January, 1931

*My Lord Chancellor,*

Whilst there are advantages in speaking last there are also certain obvious disadvantages, for on behalf of myself and our Indian States delegation I should like to have been the first to pay a respectful tribute to you, my Lord Chancellor, as our Chairman, and to my old and esteemed friend Lord Reading, for the great contributions which you have made here. (Cheers). We have been sitting in this Committee now for well over a month and it is not for me to refer at length to the courteous and painstaking manner in which you have presided over us and helped us in our deliberations, and the way in which you have shown that you are working in the interests not only of the Empire, but in India. (Hear, hear,). If I may respectfully say so, Lord Reading's attitude is not only the attitude of a great stateman, but he has evinced the courage of a great man who has not been afraid to exhange his views and openly make such an announcement. (Cheers), Lord Readings's speech and the attitude of the Liberal Party will, I am sure, be a matter of profound satisfaction and gratitude throughout the length and breadth of India. (Cheers). Though our relations were not strictly those of chief and colleague, my connection with Lord Reading was particularly close from his arrival in India until February, 1926, when I declined to stand again for the Chancellorship, for during that time I was Chancellor of the Chamber of Princes. We were all very gratified to hear the promising observations made by Lord Peel, and we hope that the coping stone will be placed and some marked changes be forthcoming before too long in the mind of the Conservative Party. I can quite understand the caution of Lord Peel, with whom I have also had the privilege and pleasure of personal contact; and we all know that the great party which Lord Peel and Sir Samuel Hoare represent here is led by that broad-minded statesman

Mr. Baldwin. (Cheers).

There have been so many notable speeches made on all sides in this debate during the last few days that it seems almost invidious to single out anyone of them; but, if I may say so with all sincerity, we were greatly struck by Sir Tej Bahadur Sapru's lucid and masterly address—(cheers)—with which I find myself largely in agreement, as I am sure we all do on this side; and I have been much impressed also by the speeches of two other friends, Mr. Jaykar and Mr. Jinnah. And before I go farther may I say how pleased I am, and I am sure we all are, to have heard the statement made at the beginning of our proceedings today by the Lord Chancellor—(applause)—with regad to the forthcoming declaration by His Majesty's Government. Although opportunities will be forthcoming later on in a more ample measure in the plenary Conference, I feel it will be the desire of all of us from India, whether we come from the States or from British India, to take this opportunity of expressing our sincere gratitude to His Majesty's Government, and particularly to the Prime Minister, who is the Chairman of our Conference, and to the present Secretary of State, Mr. Wedgwood Benn, of whose great charm, courtesy, and—although the word is not always popular I am old-fashioned enough to like it—sympathy with India we have had such ample proof . (Applause.) Finally, my Lord Chancellor, I would conclude my preliminary observations by saying that I for one do not quarrel over words. When we talk of Dominion status or self-government—call it what you will—with necessary and adequate safeguards such as all reasonable parties and persons from British India have realised must be emphasised and put in any constitution, especially during the transitional period, may I say it is the passionate desire and earnest demand of all sober and loyal India, including those sitting opposite us here today, that we should have a really substantial measure of advance in India. (Cheers). Have all due safeguards, by all means, and provide for all reasonable guarantees; but for heaven's sake let us now get on, for the mutual benefit of India and of the Empire. (Applause.). I should like to make one last observation in this connection, in supplementing what Mr. Jayakar has said as to the immense waste of time, energy and talent which has taken place. As one who was Chancellor for five years, and who did the same sort of work for five years before that, I can testify to a similar waste of time, energy and talent in regard to problems connected with the Chamber of Princes also, where we have very often had to fight for matters of really no great importance, and when there was so much of the utmost importance otherwise before us.

I think it was Sir Samuel Hoare who asked what proportion of the States was likely to enter into the Federation. After our present discussions and negotiations, if the settlement turns out to be, as I hope and as I am confident it will, just and fair, and if the rights of the States are safeguarded, and they can feel secure in entering such a Federation, I consider it not only likely but very probable—and I speak as one who has had particular opportunities of gauging the feelings of the Princes, or of the great majority of the Princes and States, as Chancellor of the Chamber of Princes for a long time and as one who has kept in touch with them before and since-that at least 75 per cent. Of the States, if not more, will come into the F ederation-( cheers)- and that they will come in immediately-(applause)—and that more of the rest will follow shortly afterwards; and, as we gain experience of the working of the Federation, and as confidence is established in the minds of the States, I have no doubt that the edifice we are now building will be very greatly increased and added to, to the mutual benefit of India, the States and the Empire. With regard to responsibility at the Centre, I desire to offer my whole-hearted support to the idea. (Cheers). The Princes have made it clear that they cannot federate with the present Government of India, and we are not going to make an sacrifices and delegate any of our sovereign powers unless and untill we can share them honourably and fully with British India in the Federal Executive and Legislature. We cannot come in with responsibility to Parliament, though we realise the necessity of safeguards and guarantees, especially during the transitional period, which is another matter. With regard to finance, I would first of all invite attention to the fact that early in this sub-committee I raised the question of appointing a Financial sub-Committee. It will be-recalled that I did not press the point, on Sir Bhupendra Nath Mitra pointing out that such an inquiry would take a very long time, and that we should have to prolong our stay here indefinitely. But I should like it to be clearly understood that if we have not riased this point again during our deliberations, the States have nevertheless certain very definite grievances and questions to raise as regards the manner in which they have been affected in the past and- I say this in no unfriendly spirit -exploited for the benefit of British India, and in certain cases for other reasons. Federation has undoubtedly changed the position somewhat, and the States will have to consider finally what claims they are to put forward, or what other proposals for an equitable adjustment and satisfaction of their rights in regard to the various issues they have riased, such as those relating to sea Customs, railways, currency and coinage, posts and telegraphs, double income-tax, and so on. Perhaps these matters will have to be gone into very fully and very impartially, and the terms of reference for such an inquiry drawn up in consultation with the States. Before final details and treaties and agreements regarding federation can be entered into by the States, I think when other details are being worked out a Committee will have to be appointed to examine these matters, consisting of representatives of the Crown, of the States and of British India, and of experts. In this connection the question of the contributions of the States and other matters, both direct and indirect, such as ceded areas, will also have to be considered, and I would invite attention to the observations of my friend Sir Mirza Ismail in regard to certain remarks made yesterday by Sir Bhupendra Nath Mitra regarding the cost of maintaining the Political Department, tributes, and so on.

Now it is not for a soldier and a layman like myself to go into such technical details, but, whilst supporting the claim that finance must also, with resonable safeguards, be handed over to the Federal Government, I would wish particularly to emphasize the effect of certain fiscal, financial and administrative measures upon the States, in which connection the exchange rate of Is. 6d. has specially to be mentioned. I alluded to this in an interview which I gave when an announcement was made by Sir Tej Bahadur Sapru and Mr. Jayakar, who were conducting negotiations with Mr. Gandhi last July. I should like to say that at one time, not very long ago, something like three-quarters of the Marwari Bazaar in Calcutta consisted almost entirely of the subjects of my State, who trade and carry on business in British India. I believe I am not very far wrong in saying that that is the case now. Several of my subjects who are engaged in this trade and commerce in British India-any many of them are not in the least interested in politics, but are concerned with business-have told me that they, and the subjects of other Indian States as well as of British India, have been very adversely affected by this new rate of exchange of rs. 6d. I have no hesitation in saying from my own personal observations and interviews with friends in bombay, where I have a house-friends with whom I have had opportunities, as the Secretary of State is aware, of coming into close contact during the present turmoil-that the commercial and the mercantile community who have joined in this non-co-operation movement have done so largely owing to such grievances, and especially to the rate of exchange. Yesterday we had the testimony of an English commercial representative in India, Mr. Gavin Jones, who opposed the measure. He referred to the effect on agriculturists, and I know that is so because in our newly-colonised settlement our agriculturists are being especially hard-hit now. Subject, therefore, to due safeguards, as I have said, the federal India, consisting of the States and British India, should have financial autonomy, and I submit that the time has come when neither British India nor the States should be treated as infants but should be made free from all attempts to keep them tight within leading strings; that the desire should cease, which I have heard rather humorously expressed as the British Government wishing to retain the position of a grandmother looking after us. Not only have people to buy experience, some dearly even in social life, but even in States that has to be done, and at times it may be necessary to let them burn their fingers a little. The instance of Australia was cited; I had noted it before, I do not think that because Australians have got into financial difficulties there is any question of taking away their Dominion status and powers.

With regard to the political portfolio, which is a reserved subject. I have some observations to make, particularly with reference to foreign relations. As in the matter of defence, it will be dealt with separately, and I might add that we, the Princes, claim an equal voice and share with British India in that matter. So we claim the same voice in regard to foreign affairs. No doubt a Defence Committee will have to be set up in India, and on that Committee we want to be represented. The States, talking of defence, naturally desire to keep their armies intact as under present arrangements, though they will of course gladly and wilingly continue not only to place them at the disposal of the King-Emperor, but of the Federal Government for the defence of India as now. But in regard to foreign relations a Committee, we think, should also be set up to advise the Viceroy and the Princes, and on that Committee we would like also to be represented. Sir Muhammad Shaft referred to a separate Political member in-charge of the Indian States portfolio which at present is in the hands of the Viceroy. I know that in a certain number of States this idea is favoured. It is a hardy annual which has been before us prominently, at least since 1918 when we were considering the reforms which ultimately took shape in Chapter 10 of the Monford Report. As Lord Reading knows, the majority of the States still favour the Viceroy retaining the political portfolio. We desire in particular this close association with the Viceroy. The matter, however, has to be more fully considered. We also realise that questions relating to the affairs of the States will have to come up in some way in the Federal Legislature. There, no doubt, no great difficulty will arise in establishing contact with the States who federate; but, as to the representation of the States in some form or other, possibly we can devise a system without necessarily having a wholetime independent Member in charge of the political portfolio, to which several of us see serious objections.

We realise that the Viceroy is a very busy man, and he will not have his labours lightened when the Federation comes into being. We realise that at present, in consequence of the Viceroy being so busy, order are sometimes passed by the Political Secretary in the name of the Viceroy. Many of us intend taking up this question further with a view to ensuring that a definite policy shall in future prevail regarding the States, which should not change according to the personal views and idiosyncracies of individual Viceroys or Political Secretaries. And, in order to provide for the interests of the States being more fully protected and safeguarded against any hasty or arbitrary action, and to ensure successful resistance to any undue pressure by other departments, also to advise the Viceroy on personal and dynastic matters relating to the States, some of us are of the view that a small Indian States Council might be instituted to deal purely with the affairs of the Indian States, not federal affairs necessarily, to *assis* the Political Secretary and to advise the Viceroy. We have already taken steps in this connection. But, of course, this will not fetter the ultimate discretion of the Viceroy. Mr. Jayakar referred to the Indianisation of the Political Department. I should like to take this opportunity of clearing up a misunderstanding, which, I am happy to say, is not general. There is an idea which I was surprised to find prevails in certain parts of British India. I remember some two or three years ago in Bombay a paper—to which I will not give prominence, as it is not worthy of it, by mentioning its name—published the same lie. It stated that the States had opposed the Indianisation of the Political Department. I can tell you that that was not so during my ten years of Chancellorship, using the expression loosely, because for five years before that, when Conferences were called, I was Secretary to the Princes at the Conference. I have had my memory refreshed on this matter by asking the Director of our special organisation, Colonel Haksar, whether any such communication was issued on behalf of the Princes, and I am not aware of any such statement or speech being made. I cannot answer, any more than any of you can, for any individual views which might, unknown to me, have been expressed by some Princes; but we have no objection to the Indianisation as such of the Political Department. We want to see the best men who are suited for the work and who are fully qualified in the Political Department. We want to see the Political Department become the Corps Diplomatique like the Corps Dilplomatique here. But beyond that, naturally, if there is Indianisation in the Department—and I believe it has already begun and it is the policy of the Govemment of India—the subjects of our Indian States must also be eligible, subject again to ability and qualification.

Talking to some of my friends, I was amazed to fmd that they seemed to think the Princes are standing aloof from and do not wish to associate in close and friendly relations with our brethren of British India. Now let me tell you that ever since 1907, as I can personally testify, we have taken up a friendly attitude. When the Morley—Minto Reforms were under discussion, several of us, including myself I am proud to say, warmly supported and personally worked for an Indian member being appointed to the Viceroy's Council, which, as we know, resulted ultimately in the appointment of our great Indian leader and friend the late Lord Sinha. Since then, as we see, there are three other friends present here who have been Members of the Viceroy's Council. The Princes have always gone out of their way to show special consideration towards and to pay special attention to the Indian Members of Council. I think those of our friends in British India who have come most in contact with us will remember that not only have many of the Indian Members of the Government of India visited many of us, including my State, but we are always glad to have the pleasure, which I and several others have had, of their company on social and other occasions in Delhi, Simla, Bombay, and so on. The final observations I wish to make on this subject of the Political Department are also in the hope of clearing away certain misunderstandings in another direction. I want to take this opportunity of making it perfectly clear that it is not because of the slightest unfriendliness towards any individual members of the Political Department that the States feel that there is need for a revision of the present system and machinery. Many of us remember, and I am old enough to remember, Political Officers to whom the States are indebted for a great deal of invaluable assistance and help in the days when they were considerably more backward than they are now. We have had the pleasure of claiming many Political Officers not only as our friends but as our intimate and personal friends, and I trust it will not be considered presumptuous on my part if I refer to two very distinguished officers here: Mr. Reynolds, who is Agent to the Governor—General in Rajputana; and Sir Richard Glancy, who was Agent to the Governor—General in Central India. There are many other Political Officers and others in London now whom I need not mention. As I say, it is not with the persons but with the system that we feel dissatisfied. There is need now of overhauling the machinery, including, we hope, a more clear definition of the functions of the Political Officers, which question we have taken up with the Viceroy already.

Turning to a few miscellaneous subjects, I do not wish to go into details about certain technical matters—they have been dealt with sufficiently by other speakers—but personaly I must confess to my dislike of the term "dyarchy" or system that represents such a thing, because, according to an old Indian saying and I think that is not different from what you have in the West: You cannot have two Sovereigns in one State, just as you cannot have two lions—as we say—in one cage—one of the must be a very tame lion for the two of them to be together—or two swords (as we, the fighting class, say) in one scabbard. I would mention one of the special advantages of a point made by Sir Tej Bahadur Sapru in regard to reserve Ministers all falling with the Federal Executive Government—say, defence or foreign relations—and those which come under the full category of federal subjects. The point to me personally appears to be this; that if the Viceroy finds that a Minister has been a failure and if he feels that he is obnoxious and deliberately obnoxious to the country, or if he desires a change, he might appoint another in his place. Very often, I am sorry to say, in India, British India in particular (and we of the States are considered autocratsy) too much regard is paid to prestige, and it is found difficult to change an officer who holds high position. To me personally, therefore, one of the advantages and special merits of Sir Tej Bahadur Sapru's scheme is that even if Reserve Minister went out with a Government that had a vote of censure passed upon it, that would give the Viceroy an opportunity, if he felt it necessary, to appoint other men in their place.

Now, coming to the more direct questions of the States entering the Federation, I was truly glad to hear Mr. Jinnah say that there were potentialities in a Federal scheme, and I was more than gratified at the special reference which was made to the value of British India, and (I say this with all modesty) at the reference by Lord Reading to the value to the whole of India of the States expressing their willingness to enter a federation, in which connection Lord Reading was good enough to quote a speech of the Prime Minister in the Conference upon the effect of our willingness to consider a federation, and that more was now possible to be done for India in the way of constitutional advance that otherwise. Equally gratifying to us has been the response made by many other British—Indian friends, and in fact we feel that we can justly state that our willingness to enter a Federation has commended almost unanimous consent. I need hardly add it is my firm belief that, in spire of doubts and suspicions, the Princes and the States will do all that they can in reason to bring such a Federation into operation. I would point out that the States cannot really be grouped amongst the Minorities, such as they are known in British India, and that they really in effect and constitutionally are not only outside India, but also are one of the two great entities in India who are now entering into a Federation. What is more important, they are the only part of India which, even now, is independent and sovereign. a satisfactory settlement of the rights of the States has necessarily to be borne in mind. The agreement of the States and the Princes' Chamber is also very necessary. There are questions which are outside the orbit of the present discussions, such as those relating to paramountcy, with regard to which negotiations are being carried on with the British Government through the Viceroy. I made a little allusion in more detail to these questions in my speech at the first Plenary Session of the Conference. We have also to settle the exact terms and methods under which the States will enter into federation. These terms and details will also have to be carefully embodied in treaties between the Crown and individual States, and possibly by further treaties or conventions between British India and ourselves. Those details are naturally amongst the matters that have to be worked out. It follows that if we enter a federation, as I sincerely hope will be the case, the States must have their reasonably adequate representation in the Federal Executive. I will not go into further details. We shall have to see equally to the interests of the smaller States being safeguarded, as of course it behoves us of the more important States to see that no States are left in any unfair position or at a disadvantage.

Sir Samuel Hoare asked a third question, which was with regard to the numbers of the representatives of the States in the two Federal Legislatures. I shall have occasion to refer to this at length, should it be necessary, when we consider the Draft Report. In this connection we have to bear in mind that certain factors might affect the position, such, for instance, as the special seats that may be allotted to Minorities, in regard to which, if the Report has been submitted, I must confess that I have not had time to see it yet. Of course, finally, there is the question of the powers of both Legislatures. However, for the purpose of ensuring that the Upper House may exercise a steadying and stable influence on any possible rash, or otherwsie undesirable, acts or proposals of the Lower House, I think that it is necessary, not only that we should have in effect a strong Central Government, but that the Upper House should be vested with certain powers for this purpose. The safety of the States in the Federal

Legislature is subject to treaty and other safeguards. One of the important points for the States is to ensure at the beginning that the Legislature keeps strictly to the subjects which are at present defined as Federal, although it is quite possible when we come finally to consider our proposals, a few Subjects, not of the first importance, might be added to the Federal list, to which we might be agreeable. In regard to the safety of the States in the Federal Legislature, there is the treaty safeguard, the fair, just, and equitable settlement of questions, and of course the number of representatives.

Furthermore, we have already made it clear, so far at least as His Highness the Ruler of Bhopal and myself are concerned, that, subject to the necessary safeguards, we leave it to the Crown and British India to settle what majority will be necessary for throwing out a Government, and the procedure in thatr connection. We have made it clear, and it is a matter which I shall ask permission to refer to at a little greater length later today before I conclude, that we have no desire to dominate British India, nor have we the least idea of entering into unnecessary conflict with British India. With regard to the Federal Government, even although it may be considered to be an anomaly, I do not see, and I feel that I can say for our whole Delegation that we do not see any alternative except that the States must have a voice in any vote of censure, or in any action of the Legislature which may lead to the downfall of the Government. We would have preferred any other feasible alternative, but there does not appear to us to be any, and I do not think that any has been put forward from any other quarter. We personally, not only have no desire, but, as has been made clear by myself and other speakers on this side, do not wish to have any discussions in regard to the purely domestic affairs of British India. I am personally against it for reasons which have already been made clear. I am also against what we think will be, not only an unsuitable, but an undignified procedure, of walking out and walking in, not in the sense in which we have seen it in the case of certain parties in the British Legislature, but literally walking out when purely British Indian subjects are being discussed. It was for those reasons that I ventured to throw out the suggestion, should such a scheme be possible, that when purely British—Indian subjects were being discussed, the name of what I might refer to as the two British—Indian Upper and Lower Legislatures might be called differently with only the members for British India sitting in these two Houses; that separate sessions should be called for that purpose, and Federal subjects only should be brought up for discussion in the Federal Houses. If that scheme is possible, no one will welcome it more than myself, and I am sure that I can say the same for Their Highnesses and the Ministers representing the States' Delegation; but whether it is feasible or not is a matter for us all further to explore.

I shall be glad if any proposals to that effect could be brought in by which we shall be absolved from having even to listen to or to take part even without voting in, such purely British—Indian affairs. There again, I should like to see the list of the purely Central subjects or the British India subjects, because, as has been brought out in this debate, it may be that a matter appears at first purely to concern British—India, which may directly or indirectly turn out to have a bearing on the States. When such matters, directly or indirectly affecting the States do come up, of course it is essential that the representatives in the Federal Legislature of the States should be present, but these are matters of detail which I hope can be settled in India. I hope that we are not coming back again for further Conferences in England, even in the summer, much as I am sure that many of us would be delighted at the prospect of meeting many old and very dear friends. I think that the time has come, as my friend, Mr. Sastri says, when a return visit is due from His Majesty's Government, including the Prime Minister and the Lord Chancellor, as well as my friends of the Conservative and Liberal Parties, including our distinguished Viceroy.

There is a point which I wish to make clear in all friendliness, and I beg that I may not be misunderstood. We wish to make it clear that we, the Princes and other Delegates of the Indian States, have no desire whatsoever to in stand the way of India's progress, and particularly of British India. We shall sincerely wish British India "Good-speed" and I may add, not light-heartedly but seriously, that many States who have not acquainted themselves with details of federal Constitutions, will heave a sigh of relief. If that is your desire, and you want us to stand out, say so. But do not put the blame on the States for that. We shall have to rely, if you want us to stand out, on your treaties, and on the good faith of Great Britain and of British India and on the other necessary safeguards and adjustments, including fiscal and financial adjustments, so that the States may continue to exist, but beyond that you have our best wishes. The other alternative, of our not taking part in some of these matters, is, I think, absolutely impracticable and unfeasible—a scheme of having two Executives. I wish to make it clear that the States, contrary to what we have heard, have no desire whatever to play any part of domination over British India, in case it should be insinuated—I say this again in all friendliness—that the States are not going to do any dirty work or resort to any mean or dishonourable tactics at the bidding of anyone.

I challenge anyone here or in India to say that the States in a Federal India or under a Federal system of the Executive Government or Federal Legislature will really be in conflict, bloc against bloc, unless there is a proposal on the part of one of the States to break away from the Empire, into which the States will not and cannot be expected to agree. Secondly, I disclaim any such attitude on the part of the States unless there is any desire to encroach upon the Treaty and other Sovereign rights of the States, except in so far as may be willingly and mutually agreed in the revised Treaties regarding Federation; and, thirdly, unless their very existence is threatened. I do beg all to remember that India is not only the Motherland of our British Indian brethren, but also ours, and generally our interests are identical. But there is no remedy, as we say in India there is no medicine, for suspicion. First it was said in a section of the press and platform in British India that the Princes were conspiring with the British Government in an unholy alliance to keep British India out of its rightful due in the way of legitimate constitutional advance. I, in common with other Princes, challenge that statement, and I ask people to wait and see the results of this Conference. Now that we have shown in an unmistakable manner our intentions—and I hope we have proved them—which frustrated one of the hopes entertained in certain quarters, where the break-up of the Conference was desired, new inventions and suspicions are coming to have play, and dishonourable motives of a fresh kind are, I regret to say, assigned to the States.

I am speaking in a friendly manner, but quite frankly. a few days ago I saw in the mail from India a cutting from a vernacular Indian newspaper which stated that the Princes were scheming for perpetual depotism. I have also heard of suspicious at work which, I am afraid are liable to poison the minds of even the most friendly leaders of British India, whom I and we, many of us, hold in the highest esteem. The suspicions are to the effect that the States, in entering a Federation, are doing so with the intention of dominating British India, that the domination and power of Great Britain are only to be transferred into the hands of the Indian States, and that we are in a conspiracy with the British Government or with the Liberal, Conservative, or Labour or other Parties to prejudice the interests of British India. Now, I am very sorry to take up your time, but I do consider it of the utmost importance that we should make certain observations to dispel this cloud of suspicion, and, I hope, create not only a correct understanding, but a friendly atmosphere in matters where the closest and frankest co-operation in all sincerity between the States and British India is necessary if we are to return home and tell our people that we and the British Government and the great Parliamentary Parties have succeeded in what we set out to do. I think this cloud of suspicion should, if possible, be dispelled before our Conference holds another Plenary Session.

I therefore venture to ask permnission, again not in any unfriendly manner, nor as offering any threats or giving any ultimatums, to make the position of the States clear. I would invite attention to my speech on the first day that this sub-Committee met, namely, December 1st, and I would point out that it was not we, the Princes and States, who asked to be permitted by British India or the Crown to enter the Federation, but at the first Plenary Session of the Conference it was on the cordial invitation and earnest appeal of our friends of British India and to join an All-India Federation. A further appeal was made to us not to confine our vision merely to the Indian States, but realising that we want inIndia to confine our vision merely to the Indian States, but realising that we want in India to move forward—to have a vision of an India which will be one single whole, each part of which may be autonomous, and may enjoy absolute independence within its borders, regulated by proper relations with the rest of the Federation. Such a Federation, it was put to us, would be the solution of the difficulties of India and show the way to her salvation. A further declaration was publicly and freely made, that the Association of the Indian States with British India would be welcome for three reasons; (i) that they would furnish a stabilishing factor in the Federal constitution; (ii) that the process of unification would begin at once; and (3) that in regard to matters of defence the States would furnish a practical experience which is wanting in India at present. It was thus that we were asked to join this larger Federation, the details of which had yet to be worked out, and which was not present in the minds of the Government of India when they wrote their dispatch. The Government of India spoke of it vaguely as a distant ideal. It was a declaration also on the part of British India that Federation was now a really live issue. I need merely add finally that it was equally frankly stated that if we could come to some such solution nothing better could be achieved at this Conference.

I had the honour and privilege of stating on behalf of the Princes and States of India at the First Plenary Session of the Conference that whilst it was impossible to minimise the magnitude of the task before us or to under-estimate the complexity of some of the problems involved, I, speaking not only on behalf of myself, but on behalf of my Order, refused to be made fearful by the difficulties ahead, but rather, I said, that we should find in them an inspiration to put forward the utmost that is in us in a spirit of confidence and courage. I said that the very immensity of the work made it worth while. At the same time I made it clear that in pressing the policy of the Indian States—and after an interval of six weeks it is as well as refresh our memory, particularly in view of the fact that we have hardly had breathing space or time for thought—we felt, first and foremost, that our discussions and proposals were based upon our deep-rooted and unfaltering loyalty to the Throne and person of the King—Emperor, and upon our obligations of honour and plighted word. Secondly, we said that they proceeded from the prof ound conviction that not only can each constituent part reach its full expression within the Empire and under the Crown, but a higher development politically and economically can be reached in that way than India could attain as an isolated and independent unit. Thirdly, we stood without compromise on our Treaty rights and all that that involves—rights which, concluded in honour and friendship, are binding until they are amended, which only be done by negotiation and willing agreement on both sides. I also added in my speech on November 17th, as to the question whether, if a Federal Government could be devised for India, and the Princes and States would enter into association with it, that the final answer to that question must obviously depend on the structure of the Government indicated, and on other points involved, such, for instance, as certain necessary safeguards, constitutional and physical, for the preservation of the rights and interests of the States and of their subjects. I need not go any farther into the details of that speech, but I concluded by saying that a Federation on the lines I had attempted to sketch on previous occasions had no terrors for the Princes and Governments of the Indian States, and that whilst we recognised that a period of transition will necessarily intervene before the Federal Government is fully constituted, Federation cannot be achieved by coercion of the States in any form, that the Princes would only come into the Federation of their own free will, and on terms which would secure the just rights of their States and subjects.

I would also remind everyone that while stating that we, the Princes, were Indians who had their roots deep down in our historic past, we were racy of the soil, and everything that tended to the prosperity and honour of India had for us a vital concern, just as everything that retaded her prosperity or shook the stability of her institutions, retarfded our own growth and affected our own stature. Whilst claiming to be on the side of progress, we have never made any concealment of the fact that our willingness to consider entering into a Federation was dependent on two essential conditions or safeguards. The first of these was that India retains the British connection as an equal partner in the British Commonwealth of Nations; and the second, that an equitable agreement is reached between all the parties concerned to govern the relations of the two Indias, ensuring for the States their due position in the Constitution as co-equal partners with British India, guaranteeing their Treaties and internal sovereignty, and safeguarding their interests, including those of their subjects, on terms just and honourable alike to the States and to British India. I also explained at the first meeting of this Committee on December 1st that in making this ready and sincere and willing response to the invitation of British India to federate, we made it perfectly clear that we were prompted by three important considerations. The first of these was our devotion to the Crown and friendship for the Empire. For that reason we considered it necessary to give our earnest attention to the subject, even if some sacrifices were involved on our part, as we have willingly offered to make some sacrifices ourselves during the past few years. Secondly, that as Indians we were naturally desirous of assisting our country in every reasonable manner, including our fellow-countrymen in British India, as well as the portion comprising the territories of the Indian States, in becoming closer members of the British Commonwealth of Nations under the aegis of the Crown, and to rise to their full stature and be masters of their houses. Thirdly, that in the long run Federation might also prove of some benefit in certain directions to our States and subjects. The States, however, wish—and I made that clear—to secure the fulest freedom in their own affairs, and to retain their sovereignty and internal autonomy—or in some cases, where there has been arbitrary decision by an agent of the Crown, to regain it—as implied by Treaties, sanads, and other engagements. These include not only the important States, but the smaller States, whose interests, as I have made abundantly clear throughout our discussions here and elsewhere, it is equally our duty to safeguard. We laid the greatest emphasis on the States being co-equal partners, and we made it clear that we would not and would not accept any position of the slightest subordination or inferiority to British India, and that we desired to share equally, and with honour, with British India any sovereignty or Dominion status which British India might enjoy on a Federal basis I must apologise for taking up so much of your valuable time, all the more so as I know that we are pressed for time; but, as I have said, it is well, in view of the issues at stake, and with matters standing where they are, that such points and details should not be lost sight of. I venture to say that these are essential statements of conditions and matters of principle to which no reasonable and fair-minded person, be he a resident of Great Britain, or of British India, or of the Empire can reasonably take exception. These are questions of the most vital importance to the Rulers, subjects, and governments of the Indian States; indeed, they may affect the very existence at some future date of our States. It has also to be remembered that the Princes are not free agents, but they are trustees of their States, their subjects and their dynasties. We cannot lose sight of the existence and rights of our subjects, in the great majority of cases very dear to us, to whose interests many of us have devoted our whole lives and all our energies, in spite of allegations about our being the most terrible and tyrannical autocrats, and the calumny of certain so-called Indian States' subjects, and Indian States' subjects' Conferences and other bodies masquerading in the garb of being bona-fide State subjects' several of whom have even extreme revolutionary tendencies. I do not wish to pursue the subject farther here, but for the information of anyone who wishes to go into the matter I would direct his attention to a speech which I made in Bikaner in October 1929, when I opened our Annual Administrative Conference. Subject to such essential safeguards, I beg you all to believe that our thoughts are for a united India, and I would earnestly plead, as has been pleaded in the case of relations between Great Britain and India, for a greater measure of trust, friendship, co-operation, good will, and sympathy, in the relations between the States and British India and thus bring about a better understanding. Let me add that if we could always be sure that the leaders and representatives in the future Federal House could be of the type of our friends sitting opposite us here, then the States would have no anxiety, but we cannot, as I have said, take any risks. We have to bear in mind the possibility of power falling into other hands, and it cannot be ignored that it has been openly stated in the Press and on the platform by a certain political school of thought in British India that they wish to see the States disappear from the map of India. Hence the necessity for certain safeguards, but I trust that I have made it clear that there is nothing that we want to gain unfairly, and nothing is farther from our minds than to dominate our brethren in British India. We want to work as willing and co-equal partners if our assistance is desired. I shall touch later upon the question of the numbers of States' representatives in the Federal Houses. I do not want to start now a discussion on the details, because there will be further opportunities for all of us; but I do express the earnest hope that the Upper House will not be limited herely to one hundred, or anywhere near that number, as it will add greatly to our difficulties in securing the representation of the various interests in the Indian States and especially those of the smaller States.

In conclusion, I am constrained to refer to some criticisms of Mr. Gavin Jones, and certain other criticisms which I have seen in a certain section of the Press and among certain people of India. It really makes my blood boil to hear attacks levelled which are so unfair and unfounded on a Viceroy of the type of Lord Irwin, whose recent triumph in Calcutta after his speech at a dinner given by a European Association, has, we understand, led to the position of the Government of India being properly understood and better appreciated, and the difficulties of the Viceroy and of the Government of India better recognised. However, defective the present system of Government may be, and no one is more painfully aware of it than the Princes, I do sincerely feel the very greatest gratitude on the part of all in England and in India is due to Lord Irwin, but for whose personality the position in India would not only have been ten times as bad, as has been said by other speakers, but possibly twenty times as bad. I support also the most eloquent and moving plea made by Sir Tej Mahadur Sapru. I can personally testify from my observations in Bombay to how the boys and girls of India are now being carried away and are going to goal for the freedom of their country. However, misguided are the tactics of certain political parties, with which the Princes, in common with many of our friends on the other side, do not agree, I trust, Sir, that you will not consider me out of order if I express the hope that it may be possible soon to grant a general amnesty to all political prisoners except those guilty of serious crimes or offences. Finally, if I may venture to quote again what I said on the 17th November last, it is impossible to exaggerate the magnitude of the task that lies before us or to over-rate the complexity of some of the problems which are involved. It is no use shutting one's eyes to facts. I can testify from personal observations in British India how the masses, even in districts apart from what are known as the Intelligentsia, are being affected and deeply affected. I have always declined, as I said at the Plenary Session on the first day of the Conference, to be ruled by threats, or to be dictated to at the muzzle of a pistol, but I pray you all let us not be made fearful by difficulties ahead. As I said on a previous occasion let us find in them an inspiration to put forth the uttermost that is in us in a spirit of confidence and of hope. The very immensity of the work makes it well worth doing well. If only this Conference will do the right thing by India justly and magnanimously I am convinced that my country, as has been said before, will be a willing and contented partner in the Commonwealth, and that she will be only too glad, with all the benefits of an honourable and independent position internally, to have the powers and resources of a mighty Empire always at her back. I repeat that no half-heatred measures, and no tinkering with the constitution, will meet the situation. Many of our past and present roubles have arisen from such causes. Do not let us repeat the mistake of doing things too late, or of giving them the appearance of having been conceded with a bad grace and wrested from the British Government. The issues involved are too great for India, for England, and for the Empire, for that to be done. Courage in thought, in aim, and in constructive statesmanship, were never more needed.

My Lord Chancellor, Your Highness, and Gentlemen, a great opportunity and a great future lies before the Empire, British India, and the States. In a spirit of confidence, imagination, and Statesmanship, let us tackle the task before us. This Conference must not, and I pray that it shall not fail.

# Annexure 12

## Speech Delivered by General His Highness the Maharajah of Bikaner, G.C.S.I., G.C.I.E., G.C.V.O., G.C.E., K.C.B., A.D.C., LL.D., at the Conference of Princes and Ministers, held at Bombay, on the 10th June, 1939

*Your Highness the Chancellor, Your Highness, Ministers and Gentlemen,*

Before I deliver my speech on Federation I feel sure I am voicing the views of Your Highnesses and all present here when I give expression to the lively. gratification with which we have received the most encouraging telegram from His Exalted Highness the Nizam which we have just heard read out and at the presence of my old friend, Sir Akbar Hydari, and other Ministers from Hyderabad. Mr. Madhav Rao of Mysore. and other Ministers from Hyderabad, Mr. Madhav Rao of Mysore, and Dewan Bahadur Gopalaswami Ayyangar of Kashmir. The large and representative gathering present here today is evidence, as His Highness the Chancellor has just observed, that the Reform of the Chamber, as agreed upon in such a happy manner last autumn, has already begun to bear fruit resulting in unity which is so essential today.

I am grateful to His Highness the Chancellor for the opportunity given me of addressing this meeting on the vital question that is now under our consideration; and before I proceed further, I would ask for the forgiveness and indulgence of Your Highnesses and the Ministers present if I detain you at some length.

But I feel a very special personal responsibility today. For, as you are aware, it fell to my lot at the request, and on behalf, of the Ruling Princes present in England, who had previously discussed the matter thoroughly, to reply to the invitation of the British Indian Delegation and to express the willingness of the States to consider their entering Federation subject to certain essential conditions and safeguards.

To say that the decision which the States will arrive at as to whether, or not, they will enter the Federation will have a far-reaching effect on the future destiny of each of our States would be but a commonplace observation. But, if and when Federation should come about, and should any of Your Highnesses decide to accept the scheme of

Federation as now evolved, it would be only fair to me, and to my brother Princes and other Colleagues with whom I was associated at the Round Table Conference, that the facts should be plainly put before you all, so that none should be able to say that I did not explain the position or utter a timely note of warning, and in order further that in the case of the States so acceding to the Federation, it should not be possible for them to throw the blame upon me and my Colleagues for the evils and misfortune that in my considered opinion will assuredly follow on the acceptance of the Federal Scheme as now evolved and on the terms offered.

In public and in private, in my speeches and notes, I have consistantly taken up the attitude that we must await the completed picture and then decide as to whether we shall, or shall not, accede to the Federation. For reasons which I shall ask to be permitted to refer to briefly later on today, I was one of those who, on various weighty grounds, strongly supported the scheme of Federation of the type that we had envisaged and advocated, subject to certain essential safeguards and provisions being forthcoming in the Act and in our Draft Instrument of Accession for the due maintenance of our Sovereignty, and the safety and continued existence of our States as separate entities.

I have always urged that only when we see the completed picture should we come to a definite and final conclusion, and that if on a calm and dispassionate consideration of the pros and cons we came to the conclusion that the scheme of Federation as presented to us was not beneficial or acceptable to us, we should then clearly say "No", and explain the weighty reasons for which we decline to enter this Federation, so that the world may know that we were not rejecting it in haste or on flimsy grounds.

That time has now come. The completed picture is now before Your Highnesses, and His Excellency the Viceroy and the British Government expect from you and unequivocal reply by the end of July.

Since the First Round Table Conference in 1930, long and weary negotiations between the States and the British Government have been dragging on for no less than 9 years. On each occasion and at every stage the States, through the Hydari Committee, in our personal discussions with the Representatives of His Excellency the Viceroy and in other ways, have been repeatedly pointing out the various unsatisfactory features of the Bill, now the Government of India Act, and of the Draft Instrument of Accession and other important Documents such as the Instruments of Instructions, and have laid stress on the safeguards and conditions that we considered essential in the interests of our States. For some little time past, however, I have been obsessed with the foreboding and the growing gloomy conviction that the outcome of these negotiations will not be what we desire, and that the scheme of Federation as evolved will not be what we envisaged or advocated or are prepared to accept—indeed very far from it.

The time for negotiations has now gone. For His Excellency the Viceroy, in his letter forwarding the Draft Instrument of Accession and other connected papers, has plainly told Your Highnesses that:

> "the terms now indicated must be regarded in all essentials as incapable of further relaxation since they represent the furthest point to which, after the fullest consideration of all the issues involved. . . . His Majesty's Government have found it possible to go to meet the wishes or apprehensions expressed by States."

His Excellency further emphasised that:

> "there is no prospect of any substantial variation of the terms now indicated in the direction of allowing a less measure of accession than what is shown therein or of modifying or adding to the limitations specified."

It is now up to Your Highnesses, and the Ministers representing the Princes, who to our regret have unavoidably been prevented from attending this Conference, to act fearlessly, decisively and boldly in the best interests of your respective States, Dynasties and subjects, so that no Prince may in the days to come be held not to have been true to his sacred heritage and trust. Let it not, I beg of you, be said of anyone of us that we had thrown away, through a defeatist attitude, or by being stampeded into hasty or ill-considered action, all that it cost our Ancestors so much to win for themselves and to hand down to us. I would respectfully say that a defeatist attitude, or being stampeded into a line of action detrimental to the best interests of our States, would ill-become Princes who are born Rulers of men and leaders of Armies; and we have to remember the proverb:

> 'The Gods won't help those
> who won't help themselves',

or, as is said in our own language:

'Himmat-i-Mardan, Madad-i-Khuda'.

Pray also remember the duty which each of us individually owes to other States and our brother Princes, and that whatever individual action we finally decide upon in regard to the Federation will also have a direct bearing and effect on other States and the States as a body.

We have also to remember that the responsibility for coming to a decision as to whether, or not, we shall accede to the Federation is now that of the Rulers themselves. Our Ministers, and notably the Hydari Committee and the Gwalior Conference, have nobly done their duty in shifting the facts and placing the necessary material before the Princes. And in coming to a decision I beg that we should entertain no mistrust of others, and absolute frankness is essential in putting forward clearly our views without any ambiguity or mental reservations. Plain speaking is essential, and one unambiguous verdict is called for. Unity is the crying need between the bigger and the smaller States—who can be assured of the sympathy and support of the bigger States—and it is necessary that the Princes should speak with one voice here.

It is in this spirit of mutual trust and absolute frankness that, as a matter of my plain duty to my brother Princes and the States, I ask to be permitted to express my views in an unambiguous manner.

As many of Your Highnesses and Ministers are aware, I have made no secret of my own views and attitude. They are known in the highest quarters.

Ever since October last, when my Prime Minister, along with those of the other important States in Rajputana, saw the Resident at Mount Abu and had explained to them the contents of the Revised Draft Instrument of Accession and the limitations and safeguards which the British Government were prepared to concede to the States, i.e., ever since the completed picture was placed before me, it was with a sense of profound disappointment and regret that I came to the reluctant conclusion that on all grounds—constitutional, political, fiscal and financial—the scheme of Federation evolved was highly detrimental and likely to prove absolutely unacceptable to the States.

In coming to this conclusion I was not influenced by any personal considerations or matters exclusive to the Bikaner State. Indeed, so disappointing and unsatisfactory did we deem the completed picture that I and my Government did not even consider it worth while to take the trouble of having a communication addressed to the Government of India about any special rights or exclusive claims of

Bikaner, as for instance in regard to Excise, with particular reference to our Canal Colony, or the special rights of the Bikaner State, as for instance in regard to Minting and Coinage.

Some Ministers, and even Princes, have in the past few months asked me how it is that I, who supported Federation at the Round Table Conference and afterwards, am not now in favour of it Some persons have even made the amazing observation that the Princes took a leap in the dark without knowing what they were doing, when—subject, as I have already said, to certain essential safeguards and conditions-they expressed their willingness to consider entering the Federation at the First Round Table Conference.

With due deference I would venture to say that such Princes and Ministers cannot have carefully studied the speeches and declarations made, and the conditions put forward, by the Princes and Ministers of the Indian States Delegation at the Round Table Conference and the Federal Structure Committee and on subsequent occasions.

This, as I have already said, was done not only after frequent deliberations amongst the Princes at Meetings of the Indian States Delegation to the Round Table Conference, but after consultation with their responsible Ministers.; and legal advice was also obtained from time to time as found necessary.

Nor was I alone in adopting the attitude that I did at the First Round Table Conference, for which I feel that there is nothing for me to apoligise. Great Rulers like Their late Highnesses of Baroda, Patiala and Nawanagar, and those still happily with us like Their Highnesses of Bhopal and Indore, and Ministers of eminence like my mend, Sir Akbar Hydari-to name only a few—held the same views as I did.

We were of the opinion that under certain essential guarantees and adequate safeguards Federation seemed a satisfactory solution of the difficult situation with which all concerned were faced in 1939, even if some sacrifices within reason were to be made by the States for furthering the following objects:

First, their duty to the Crown and their friendship for the Empire, whereby they hoped, in view of the grave situation prevailing in India, to render further service to their beloved King-Emperor;

Secondly, their natural desire, in every reasonable manner, to assist their Motherland in attaining Dominion Status as a co-equal and honoured member of the British Commonwealth of nations, and to help their brethren in British India to rise to their full stature under the aegis of the Crown, just as the States were desirous of ensuring the fullest freedom in their internal affairs and of retaining intact their Sovereignity and autonomy and separate entity, as guaranteed by Treaties, Sanads and other Engagements; and Thirdly, because we felt that, in the long run, such a Federation might also prove of some advantage in certain directions to the States themselves and their subjects, especially in fiscal and financial matters which vitally affect them, but in which they have at present no voice.

I need not detain Your Highnesses and gentlemen by examining at length how far, under existing conditions, the objects we had in view are likely to be attained or furthered. These, I find, have been dealt with in a very clear and logical manner in a pamphlet, which doubtless Your Highness and gentlemen have received, headed "To federate or not to federate'—The Vital Question before the States and Their Reply."

Suffice it to state that the reasons which originally prompted the States to express their willingness to enter an all-India Federation under certain essential safeguards no longer hold good; on the contrary, the conditions at present obtaining in the country—which have undergone a marked change for the worse in the past year—emphatically enjoin that the States should steer clear of the scheme of Federation as now presented to us. Many essential safeguards consistently pressed by the States have not been provided. The Revised Draft Instrument of Accession and connected Documents are fundamentally defective and unsatisfactory in varous directions.

The States had urged that in the unique position of India where the two component parts are the States, already Sovereign on the one side, and the British Indian Provinces, which would enjoy power only by devolution or grant, on the other, a special constitution should be evolved which should be suitable not only to British India but to the particular position of the States which has no parallel in history. But the States are being levelled down to the position of Provinces instead of the Provinces being levelled up where found necessary—a point on which we also laid especial emphasis, Moreover, the scheme of Federation proposed is to rigid, with too many Federal subjects and with little scope or freedom left to the federating units.

A perusal of the list of Federal subjects appended to the first Federal Structure Committee Report will reveal that in regard to the subjects agreed to be made Federal, the proviso was often made that they were to be Federal only for policy and legislation, and not for administration.

Then, in regard to currency and coinage, the proviso was made—

"subject to adjustment with the States concerned of such rights as are not already conceded by them";

whilst in regard to development of industries, it is important to note that it was agreed:

"Development of Indistrues to be a Fedeml subject in cases where such development by Federal Authority is declared by order of the Federal Government made after negotiation with and consent of The federating units";

Whereas now the powers of the Federation as regards industries not specified for limited accession will be very wide and might well extend to rationalisation in all its forms and even to nationalisation.

As for Customs duties, it was specifically laid down:

"Customs on external Frontier of Federated India";

whereas now cordons and barriers can, in certain eventualities, be set up between the boundaries of even two Federating States.

All these simpulations have in effect now been thrown to the winds.

All these factors, individually and collectively, enjoin that, in the interest of our obligations to the Crown, to India, and to ourselves, and to our States and people, the Princes should forthwith decide and declare that they cannot, and will not, under the existing circumstances, enter the Federation of the type and under the conditions now offered to them.

The element of stability which was one of the advantages generally expected to accrue from the States entering the Federation will no longer be forthcoming. For we shall be in a hopeless minority in both the Federal Executive and the Federal Legislature.

Unity between the two Indias—one of the chief objects of Federation, and a most laudable ideal—is obviously unachievable at the present moment when we bear in mind certain recent political events and the bitter hostility to the States in so many quarters in British India.

I have heard doubts expressed whether the States would be acting loyally to our beloved King-Emperor in refusing to accede to the Federation. I make bold to say that under the existing political conditions it would, for reasons which are obvious, be a positive act of loyalty for the Princes to stand out of such a Federation, and certainly not an act of disloyalty.

We have only to see what heppened, for instance, when the Princes—true to their traditions of loyalty and devotion to the Imperial Crown—offered to place at the disposal fo the King-Emperor all the resources of their States together with their personal services during the International crisis of September last.

Talking as we are to-day amongst ourselves, might I contrast what is happening in India with the recent triumphanl tour of our King-Emperor and the Queen-Empress in Canada? Contrast the wonderful loyalty shown and the mignificent welcome given to Their Majesties in Canada with the position where, although the Provincial Governments are in effect His majesty's Government and the Ministers take the Oath of Allegiance to the King-Emperor, the Congress Governments will have nothing to do with Their Majesties' visiting India.

Are these attitudes to which we of the Indian States can possibly subscribe?

And consider for yourselves what the position of the States will be in an All-India Federation of the type now evolved and see how frequently the States, with their inherent loyalty to the Imperial Crown, will come in direct conflict with the representatives of British India in the Federal Legislature and doubtless even in the Federal Executive, should any of our States Ministers, even by convention, be given seats in the Federal Cabinet.

It is well-known that His Excellency the Viceroy did his utmost to get better terms for the States but that unfortunately his efforts were not crowned with success.

History is repeating itself; for it is no less well-known that at the time when the Draft of the Government of India Bill was under consideration, our late Viceroy, Lord Willingdon, and the Government of India pointed out to the authorities in England that some of its provisions would be totally unacceptable to the States. But their advice was, as in this case, thrown aside. Otherwise the Princes and Ministers would not hae been placed under the painful necessity of coming to the decision which they did in the momentous meeting held in Bombay in February 1935.

We are no less grateful to His Excellency Lord Linlithgow for not having brought any pressure to bear on the Princes in his letter forwarding the Revised Draft Instrument of Accession and connected papers and also for his having made it clear in his recent speech at

Udaipur that the decision as regards entering the Federation is:

"one that has of set purpose been left to the free and unfettered judgement of individual Rulers concerned", as well as for the assurance which His Excellency gave at Jodhpur that:
"neihter in the case of Jodhpur nor in the case of any other State will any pressure in regard to that devision be brought to bear upon a Ruler."

It is not for me to make a detailed examination or criticism of the Draft Instrument of Accession or of the Government of India Act. But take for instance some important details in the financial and fiscal field. The amazing provisions and restrictions regarding customs duties in the States have come as a total surprise to us. Whatever pious hopes the Davidson Committee might have expressed on the matter, it had been made abundantly clear that the States must be free in regard to customs duties, which imports and duties form a very considerable source of revenue for many a State. For instance, when the question arose in the Federal Structure Committee on the 9th December 1930, I on behalf of the States expressed my entire disagreement with certai points raised by some British Indian Delegates, and clearly said"

"I disagree entirely, we have the right to raise our tarrifs."

"You are asking us to do something which we cannot possibly agree to. We have the right, those of us who have customs duties, to put on whatever tariffs we like. . . . That is a power which we are not going to surrender."

And yet limitations have been most arbitarily proposed to be imposed on the Sovereignty of the States in regard to customs duties, which, so far as I can recollect, have not only never been accepted by the States but not even discussed with them.

Then again it is abundantly clear that the taxable capacity of the people of the States would, under the proposed arrangements, be advantages from industrial development would go to the Federation. The possibilities, therefore, of the expansion of revenue in the States have become extremely limited and there will be little, if any, money left with both the richer and the poorer States, the bigger or the smaller Sates, to find the necessary funds for metting the demands in conformity with present day conditions and requirements for nation-building activities-such as Education, Medical relief, Sanitation, etc.—or for reforms in the administration, and the scheme as it now stands will effectively cripple the economic resources of the States in a manner which the States had not contemplated before.

Thus, far from the possibility of the States' joining Federation proving beneficial to them in the long run, it is already clear that our acceding to the Federation will prove deterimental even in the short run!

Another point has to be borne in mind. It was because we realised that the Federation must have the necessary funds and a balanced budget that the States gave up pressing their claims for a share in the maritime customs and in posts and telegraphs and such things. But apparently there is no limit to the demand for more and more money to be squeezed from the States for the Federation. And now direct taxes and duties and still greater calls are being made upon the States which will still further impoverish and cripple their resources.

Only recently the smaller States have been urged to combine in regard to certai administrative matters, such as the Judiciary and the Police, etc. because of their limited financial resources. But on the other hand in the proposed scheme of Federation they will have little if any money available for increased expenditure for providing additional sums for such necessary purposes. The inconsistently is glaring.

It is obvious that the States, without any adequate safeguards for the maintenance of their Sovereign position and the preservation of their Treaties and Engagements, and with the contemplated financial provisions, will be worse off than British Indian Zamindars, whilst the Princes, although Sovereign in their own States, will be reduced to the position of Governors or Subas of Provinces.

Sometimes small things point to bigger things. Only recently in an Official communication received from the Government of India in regard to Rules under the Motor Vehicles Act we have yet another foretaste of what to expect under Federation. No exemption has been made for the Princes; but, to quote the words used in the Official communication, "the Central Government propose to ask Provinces to issue executive instructions to the effect that no action is to be taken against any Ruling Prince for driving without a licence. "What if the Provincial Governments do not accept the Central Government's proposals? What if they choose to arrest a Ruler for any non-observance of the provisions of the Act? will no the Central Government and the Paramount Power be as helpless to protect us as in regard to agitations fostered from without and the jathas marching from British India into our States?

The further danger to which I would invite the attention of Your Highness and Ministers present here is the amazing attempt to nullify the provisions of the Act by denying to the States under Section 6(2) the right to have our own administration of the subjects to which we are asked to federate and by refusing Administrative Agreements expressly provided for under Section 125 of the Government of India Act at the desire of the States. The immediate and inevitable result of the present proposals would be the introduction of Federal Officials into the State for direct administration, or, even if administration is entrusted to a State, of federal supervising and controlling authority by inspection and issue of directions, etc. The projection of the executive authority of the Federation into the States and the possibility that, in the collection of excise duties and other taxes, the Federal Agents would directly operate within the territories of the Rulers endanger not merely the administrative autonomy of the States, but would ultimately create a dual allegiance undermining the sovereignty of the Rulers and the loyalty of their people.

I would also invite attention to what has been said on the subject by the Hydari Committee, i.e. that the proposed Administrative Agreement "falls far short of what has been contemplated throughout the Federal discussions" and that "the result will be that on all matters accepted as Federal, there will be the possibility of administration being wholly carried out by Federal Officers not subject in any way to the control of the Ruler of the State."

I trust that enough has been said to show that the States are not going back on what they were prepared to accept but that what had been promised and agreed to is not being implemented and that new arrangements have been proposed as in regard to Customs which have never been accepted.

There are certain other points to which I would like, with the permission of Your Highnesses and the Ministers, to refer. I am constrained to allude to the trouble created by British Indians in various States which, if continued, would have certainly led to a form of civil war. Mahatma Gandhi's recent pronouncement is certainly likely to improve matters and the relations between the States and British India. But with all respect to that great Indian leader and world figure, Mahatma Gandhi, it is permissible to say that no one can foretell when there will again be a reversal of the policy and a revival of Satyagraha and attempts at direct interference in the internal affaris of our States.

It was only as lately as 1934 that Mahatma Gandhi wrote to Mr. Kelkar:

> "It is my conviction that any attempt on the part of the Congress at interference can only damage the cause of the people in the States."

The Congress policy of non-interference in the internal affairs of the States was, however, reversed shortly afterwards. And even after Mahatma Gandhi's recent prouncement, Mr. Rajendra Prasad, the President of the Congress, who is widely respected as a British Indian leader holding moderate views, speaking at a meeting in bombay on the 4th June, said:

> "If the States continue these methods and refuse to change with the times I am afraid the Indian National Congress will be compelled to change its policy towards the Indian States and actively support and take part in the struggle of the States people."

I am far from saying that we must not move with the times. Indeed, no well-wisher of the Indian States could but urge with all respect, and with equal emphasis, on Your Highnesses and your Ministers the necessity of putting our houses in order where such a step is necessary, and, of course, of removing promptly and in every reasonable manner possible the legitimate grievances of our people. But we cannot be expected to tolerate outside interference or to submit to outside dictation.

I would venture also to emphasize both the wisdom and the necessity of having, where it does not already exist, a clear cut line between State expenditure and the personal expenditure of the Ruler. The exact amount and percentage of the Privy Purse or the Ruler's Civil List must necessarily vary according to the revenues of the States. For the Ruler of a richer State can well be content by taking as his Civil List a smaller percentage of the ordinary revenues of the State than would be possible for the Ruler of a State with a smaller revenue to do, if he is to maintain his position and dignity with any degree of decency.

Mr. Pattabhi Sitaramayya, who is taking an active interest in the internal affairs of the States, in interpreting quite recently Mahatma Gandhi's intentions and decision regarding the suspension of Satyagraha in the course of an interview has said with reference to the period for which Satyagraha was suspended that:

"Mahatma's indefiniteness may mean anything from a moment to infinity.
When the light dawns on him, he will summon one and all to the firing line.
Political movements develop like natural cateclysms giving but little notice of the onset."

And Mr. Pattabhi Sitaramayya's oration was couched in the following terms:

If the Princes and their Dewans fail to make a suitable response to this humble appeal from Mahatmaji, now that they have got the long rope they will duly get the short shrift."

This in other words might perhaps not unjustifiably be interpreted as:

"Give the dogs enough rope and they will hang themselves!"

One matter of the most supreme importance to the States must also not be lost sight of . The provisions of the Government of India Act for the purpose of safeguarding the rights and interests of the States and the dignity of the Princes have even today proved completely ineffective.

As that soldier-statesman Sir Sikander Hyat Khan, the Prime Minister of the Punjab, stated in a speech at Sholapur the other day with reference to the trouble created in the States and with special reference to the agitation and trouble created by persons from outside in the Hyderabad State:

"It is a subtle move to demoralise the States and minorities by creating the impression that the Paramount Power cannot be relied upon to implement its pledges or treaty obligations to the Indian States."

Sir Sikander went on to add:

"In this connection the responsibility of the Paramount Power is particularly great, and the eyes of law-abiding India are critically set on Delhi and Simla to see how far they would permit the territories of an Ally of the British Crown to be invaded by the subversive elements from British India. Let us hope that this is not an earnest of what is in store for the States and other law-abiding units under the Federal regime."

We have needed every reason to be profoundly thankful to the Almighty that we have had a warning already; and if after the failure of the provisions provided for the protection of the Princes and States we blindly jump into the Federation, we shall have only ourselves to blame.

Then again, the prospects of constitutional crisis after crisis arising at the bidding of the Congress High Command or as a result of the steps taken in pursuance of orders received by the Congress Governments, which would lead to the suspension of the Constitution, are not very pleasant.

Now, as regards the future, I freely and frankly admit that the scheme of federation that the States had advocated and were prepared to accept had much to commend itself. Given certain conditions, it might have worked well. But at the present moment, neither the Congress, nor the Muslim League, are enamoured of the scheme. Even non-Congress Governments are opposed to it, as will be clear from Sir Sikander Hyat Khan's recent speech at Sholapur. In fact we have been told that the States will enter the Federation at their peril; and if we are so ill-advised as to do so, we must be prepared to face the bitter hostility and wrath of British India and of all the important political parties that count for anything in the Country.

As we are all aware, threats have also been held out to the British Government of mass civil disobedience in the event of Federation being forced upon India. To cite but one recent instance, Pandit Jawaharlal Nehru wrote thus in an article:

> "If British folly seeks still to impose it "(Federation)" upon us, it will mean deadly conflict and break-up of much that we have in India today. The ultimate result may be good or bad for us, but it will not be the functioning of Federation.
>
> And so I think that Federation cannot come. It is dead, and there is no magic protion that will give it life."

What then, I would ask Your Highnesses and Ministers to consider, will be the advantage to any State which enters such a Federation? Nobody wants it. It is obviously and clearly detrimental to the States. Why should the States then make sacrifices and part with some of their Sovereign powers for Federation of this kind, which will positively be harmful to the States?

I would also remind Your Highnesses of yet another important detail, viz., that once you are in the Federation you cannot get out of it. Secession is absolutely impossible. You will, therefore, be perpetually doomed.

Yet another point. Alarmists are not wanting who say that if the States stand out, there will be a Federation exclusively of the British Indian Provinces. That is a hypothetical position which does not alarm me in the least. In the first place, without the security and stability which the States would have brought into the Federation on their entering it, it is inconceivable to me that the British Government and Parliament would vest such an exclusively British Indian Federation with the same powers. Moreover, even if, for the sake of argument, that was feasible, I maintain that the States will be no worse off than they are today. In fact, States entering the Federation will be worse off than those who remain out of it.

It has also been urged by some that we should here and now reject the present scheme and put forward another scheme. No one has asked us to put forward an alternative scheme, and it is not for us to propose one at this stage. There will be time enough to consider any such scheme and our future course of action when the time comes and when we are approached.

Meanwhile I venture to counsel with all the emphasis at my command that we should confine ourselves to saying that the scheme of Federation which is now before us is unacceptable to us. Let us profit by the saying:

"Once bit, twice shy", and

for the present:

"Let well alone."

His Excellency the Viceroy in his letter forwarding the Draft Instrument of Accession and connected papers has himself said in paragraph 5:

> "I am now asking Your Highness to inform me at any time within the next six months whether you would be prepared to execute an Instrument of Accession on behalf of your State within the terms indicated in documents (1) and (2) mentioned in the preceding paragraph."

Only in yesterday's newspapers you will have ready that Colonel Muirhead, Under-Secretary of State for India. in answering a question in Parliament said:

> "The Rulers of Indian States . . . had been asked to say within 6 months whether they were prepared to accede to Federation on the terms proposed."

In the circumstances, by our putting forward any other terms we may only be courting a rebuff.

In conclusion I would invite especial attention to a couple of extracts from what has been said in the Report of the Hydari Committee to whose President and Members the Princes and States of India owe so much. In the concluding paragraph of their Report it is stated:

> "The Committee regrets ... to have to record its unanimous view that the drafts circulated, on the basis of which accession is offered, are fundamentally unsatisfactory in the directions noted by it."

The Committee are no less unanimous in what they have said in paragraph 10 of their Report namely:

> "In general, the Committee feels the extreme difficulty of its position in undertaking the responsibility of advising acceptance of the drafts to the individual Rulers to whom its Members owe allegiance ifit is unable to associate with that advice an assurance that the terms do not involve an impairment of their Treaty rights except with their consent."

I must apologise for having detained Your Highnesses and gentlemen at such length. But my excuse must be the supreme importance of the question and the disastrous effects upon the States which as sure as might follows day would result, should the Princes be so ill-advised as to accept the scheme of Federation now before us. I do beg to Your Highnesses and the Ministers to ponder carefully over the question and to give such a fearless and unequivocal lead and to come to such a definite decision that our successors and posterity may not blame us, nay curse us, for having left them such a bad legacy, but that they may, on the contrary, bless us for having, under God's guidance, had the courage and the foresight to save the States from untold harm and terrible disaster.

# Annexure 13

**Speech Delivered by General His Highness the Maharajah of Bikaner, G.C.S.I., G.C.I.E., G.C.V.O., G.C.E., K.C.B., A.D.C., LL.D., at His Highness' Birthday Durbar at the Fort on the 22nd October, 1939.**

*Chiefs and Nobles, Ministers, Officers and Gentlemen;*

It is unusual for me to make a speech at this Durbar; but today I desire to address the Chiefs and Nobles and the Civil and Military Officers and my other subjects present here in regard to the life and death struggle in which the British Empire is at present engaged.

As His Imperial Majesty the King—Emperor said in his broadcast message to the Empire at the outbreak of the War, twice in the lifetime of many of us we are faced with a War of such magnitude. The forces of savagery and barbarism have been unleashed over a great part of Europe by the criminal desire of a single individual, already intoxicated with power, to dominate the nations of the earth, despite all efforts by His Majesty's Government for a peaceful solution of all outstanding questions.

If I have not addressed my people earlier on this matter, it is for two reasons.

This supreme occasion demands deeds and not words; and I trust that the record of the past six weeks will demonstrate that we have not been idle.

Moreover, I was absolute confident that in my desire to render the utmost service possible in every direction to His Imperial Majesty the King—Emperor in keeping with the best traditions of loyalty and devotion to the British Throne, which have been the outstanding characteristic of my House, State and people, I had with me, heart and soul, all my Chiefs and Nobles, the Martial Classes of my State and my other beloved subjects, and that we all stood united as one by the Empire, in the protecting shade of which we of Bikaner along with the rest of India have flourished in prosperity and contentment for well nigh a century and a quarter.

As you are aware, as soon as I thought that War was imminent I offered, on the 26th August last, to place at the command of His

Imperial Majesty the King—Emperor the personal services of myself and my son, the Maharaj Kumar, and those of my Troops and the entire resources of the Bikaner State.

Immediately on the outbreak of the War I reiterated these offers.

In spite of the serious famine with which we are faced and which threatens to be of unprecedented severity, and to combat which also we are devoting our energies and resources, we have made a preliminary contribution for War purposes of 1 lakh of rupees from the State, of Rs. 50,000 from my Privy Purse and L 1,000 from Her Highness the Maharani to be devoted to whatever purposes His Imperoial Majesty the King—Emperor may decide.

We have, in addition, offered to augment the fighting strength of our Camel Corps, the Ganga Risala, by sending three additional Companies from the Sadul Light InfantIy, thus doubling the fighting strength of the Corps.

Already we have raised nearly to its full strength a 2nd Batallion of Infantry for our own Army and we have offered to raise for the British Indian Army 5 Battalions of Infantry which is equivalent to I whole Infantry Brigade and I Infantry Battalion in addition. In order not to leave out of consideration any matter, big or small, in regard to which we in this State might be of further service, and realising that in momentous times like the present it behoved all to do their "little bit" in every direction possible and that "every little helps", we have made certain further important offers in other directions also. And we have constantly in our mind the thought of what else we can do to render service to our beloved Emperor in this second Great War.

With a view to enable the State and the people of Bikaner to make the maximum contribution within their power and the resources of the State towards the successful prosecution of the War, we have also instituted a War Board which, besides attending to all activities of the State connected with the War, would especially deal with the work of recruitment for the British Indian Army whenever the British Government decide to avail of our offer. Until today I understook the duties of the President of the War Board. Now, however, that the work is fully organised and the more urgent and important'matters relating to the War have been dealt with, I am appointing Maharaj Mandhata Singhji to be the President of the War Board.

We are ready with a complete scheme of recruitment for the British Indian Army and we are also ready to bring into existence, as soon as we knowthat our assistance in the matter of recruitment is required, District bodies for the purpose of recruitment and other War work.

So far I have spoken only of the local aspects of the question.

As was only to be expected, the Princes and States of India have, without exception, rallied round the Imperial Throne and the Emire in this great hour of trial. And we of the Indian States thank God and can take pride in the fact that, despite the Princes having problems of their own which require satisfactory solution, Our loyal offers of service and co-operation in this War are unconditional and unqualified, that we have made it clear to the world that our loyalty demands no price, and that no sordid motives of bargain or barter have any place in our throughts and acts.

It is strange that a certain section of opinion in British India seems to regard the Princes' offers as something wanting in decency and they have been described as "gushing exuberance". The Princes of India are not concerned with supporting any political creed or doctrine, nor have they on this occasion reaffirmed their loyalty to the King—Emperor or offered to fight in this War for the sake of democracy or any other political doctrine.

As has been so aptly described by the popular and energetic Chancellor of the Chamber of Princes, His Highness the Maharajah Jam Sahib of Nawanagar, where the King—Emperor leads the Princes follow, anxious to do all that they can in support of a righteous cause.

Let me add that the Princes stand with their swords drawn round the King—Emperor's Throne, ready to risk their lives and to stake their all in conformity with the teachings of Religion, their Treaty obligations and their magnificent traditon of loyalty, which is also the proud heritage of their Motherland. They are once again proving themselves true friends of the Empire which they love in its hour of need. And let me also add that nothing will deter them in the task which, as a matter both of duty and of free choice, they have set before themselves.

It is often said by those who have but a superficial knowledge of Britain and her people that, in the ease and luxury of a benign peace, the British Nation has become decadent and is no longer the Imperial Race, vigorous, dynamic and hardy, ready to face and fight the dangers that threaten her everywhere. But this War, I am certain, will demonstrate how sadly mistaken such a judgment is. For myself I entertain no doubt. Britain today stands where she did, strong in her sense of duty, strong equally in her sense of fair play and justice.

As a meeting of the Standing Committee of the so-called States Peoples' Conference held at Wardha on October 11, a statement was issued in which, claiming to speak on behalf of the subjects of the Indian States and after associating themselves fully with the statement issued by the Working Committee of the Indian National Congress on September 14 and with the Resolution of the All India Congress Committee on the War passed on October 10, it was stated that the people of the States were wholly unable to give their support to the War under existing conditions, and the threat was held out that they may have to resist the impositions forced upon them. The Princes were warned that the Standing Committee, speaking on behalf of the people of the Indian States, could not accept the commitments made by the Princes and that the Rulers of States could expect no co-operation from their people.

Wherever may be the conditions in certain isolated States and regional areas, it can safely be stated that the views referred to above certainly do not represent, but are most decidedly contrary to, the views of the people in the vast majority of States.

So far as the body which styled itself "the Indian States Peoples' Conference" and professes to speak for all the people of the Indian States is concerned, an examination of the credentials of its members would beyond doubt lead to some interesting revelations as to their title to speak for the subjects of the States. It would further be pertinent to enquire the source from which they derive their authority, the mandate which entitles them to speak for the people of the States. The influence which this body wields in the States can be guaged from the fact that it would not secure a man of standing from the States to be its President, but has to resort to the expedient of electing a British Indian leader.

As for Bikaner, no one is in a better position to speak than you, I see in this Durbar Hall. And the fact that we have already raised a 2nd Infantry Battalion in this very short time, whom we saw at Parade this morning, and that recruits are tumbling over each other eager to enlist in the British Indian Army, is in itself a direct contradition of such ridiculous pretensions and statements.

One need not confine one's remarks to the territories of the Indian States. In spite of the manifestation in certain quarters of the lack of support and spontaneous co-operation which are to be expected at such critical times, the widespread offers of collaboration and help to the Empire given by various classes and communities in British India and their expressions of unconditional loyalty to the King—Emperor are a matter of the liveliest gratification.

Unless in nearly 60 years of my life and my close association with them in both Peace and War I have entirely misjudged them, and am wholly wrong in an appreciation of the mentality of my brother soldiers in British India, it can safely be predicted that, whatever the views, policy and decision of any political parties, the martial races of India will once again as eagerly, whole-heartedly and loyally fight for the King—Emperor and the Empire as in the days of old. And I take this opportunity of appealing to my brother soldiers, Sikhs, Muslims, Jats, Mahrattas, Rajputs and others of the fighting classes to spurn all blandishments, threats or cajoleries on the part of anyone that may be made to traduce them from the straight path of Dharma and duty, and to remain steadfastly loyal to our King—Emperor and unflinchingly to rally round the British Flag with faith and enthusiasm.

This would also not be an unsuitable opportunity of stating that the States must strongly repudiate the claim of any political party in British India, however influential and important, to speak or to act for, or in any other way to represent, the views and standpoints of the Indian States and their people.

You will have read with great interest the very important pronouncement recently made by His Excellency the Viceroy. His Excellency has made it clear that the natural issue of India's progress and the goal of British policy today is, as in the past, aimed at the attainment of Dominion States for India. Dominion Status was till recently, I believe I am right in stating, accepted as a satisfactory solution of the aims and aspirations of India. It amounts to virtual independence and is accepted by the great Dominions in the British Commonwealth, such as Canada, Australia and South Africa. With this I venture to think India should feel content at the present moment. And as an Indian, who has had the honour actively to work in the past for securing to our Motherland what is her rightful place in the comity of nations comprising the British Empire, I most earnestly wish that the response by all the people and parties of India and their co-operation in this War would be free of all bargaining and without cavil, and such as would enable every Indian proudly to hold up his head and to feel that India, with her ancient civilization and culture and her great traditions, was, in the spiritual and moral sense also, discharging her duty in this war in a manner commensurate with her greatness.

In the meanwhile, His Excellency the Viceroy has announced the intention of establishing a Consultative Body representative of all major political parties in British India and of the Indian Princes, over which the Governor-General would himself preside, and which would have as its object the association of public opinion in India with the conduct of the War and with questions relating to War activities. In this measure I have no doubt that His Excellency will receive a ready response and co-operation from the Princes and people of the Indian

States.

There is one other subject of great importance to the Princes and States of India to which I wish especially to allude on this occasion. It has already been officially announced that owing to the War and the necessity for concentration on the emergency that confronts us, all work relating to Federation has been suspended.

In his recent statement His Excellency the Viceroy has, on the authority of His Majesty's Government, further given an unqualified assurance to the effect that at the end of the War His Majesty's Government will be very willing to enter into consultations with representatives of the several communities, parties and interests in India and withe the Indian Princes with a view to securing their aid and co-operation in the framing of such modifications as may seem desirable in the Scheme of Constitution envisaged in the Act of 1935, which has met with such severe opposition and criticism from different political bodies and communities, including the Indian States.

I do not conceal from you the fact that this decision has come to me, as it has doubtless come to many other Princes and persons connected with the States, as a great relief. For the States, including several important States, have felt very grave anxiety and concern regarding some aspects of the Federal Scheme as it had been evolved. At a time when all our efforts should be concentrated on winning the War, which may last for four or five years, it is only right that matters of such a highly controversial nature should not be causing anybody any uneasiness. The Princes have been handicapped in placing before the public their objections to the Scheme of Federation as presented to them for acceptance as the negotiations were confidential. But this opportunity may be taken of publicly stating that the attitude of those Princes and States, who considered the terms offered to them as fundamentally unsatisfactory and thus unacceptable, was determined not by any desire to perpetuate, as has been alleged, their so-called absolutist form of government, or inspired by any selfish considerations to secure adjustments in their individual cases, but by the fact that some of the conditions, if accepted, would have proved highly detrimental to the States and their Governments and people, as the world will know when the right time comes. And it is gratifying to feel that at the end of the War all such objectionable features will undergo review and revision.

Before I conclude, it is necessary to emphasise that Great Britain today is fighting not for any Imperialistic purposes or for any unworthy or selfish ends. We are fighting to resist aggression, whether directed against ourselves or others, to break the boundage of fear daily encroaching upon the world. And we must not forget that should Hitler win this War, all talks of freedom and democracy for India will vanish like thin smoke, and brute force and the doctrine that "might is right" will reign supreme in which the slightest difference of political opinion might, as I said in a speech a little over a year ago at the time of the Czechoslovakian crisis, easily lead to the scaffold or the firing squad, in place of the liberty which India, along with other parts of the Empire, enjoys today under the aegis of the British Crown. God forbid that this should happen.

It is my profound conviction that in these troublous times when everything is so much subjected to revolitionary changes and upheavals, the great Empire over which His Imperial Majesty reigns offers the one stable element, the firm rock on which a peaceful world order could be raised, the one institution in which, under a beneficent spirit of peace, human effort in every direction could find its fullest realisation. In rallying round the Empire now, when its safety and security are challanged by a powerful foe, we are therefore not only acting in accordance with our sacred duty, but defending what each one of us holds dear, and what each of us wants to transmit without diminution to our successors.

In the interests, therefore, of our own country and of ourselves, even if not on a higher plane, it must be the prayer of all sober-minded people that God may grant a speedy and complete victory to the arms of His Imperial Majesty the King—Emperor and his Allies which will be of lasting benefit to India and to the world.

# Annexure 14

## Speech Delivered by General His Highness the Maharajah of Bikaner, G.C.S.I. G.C.I.E., G.C.V.O., G.B.E., K.C.B., A.D.C., LL.D., in the Chamber of Princes on the 11th March 1940, in supporting the Resolution Regarding War

*Your Excellency, Your Highnesses;*

I deem it an honour and it affords me the most genuine pleasure to support this Resolution.

The mighty struggle in which the Empire has been involved has now been in progress for over six months; and any impartial and unprejudiced person who has followed the happenings in Europe for the past year or two must in fairness recognise that the War is not of the seeking of Great Britain, but that it has been forced upon the Allies who had no other alternative but boldly to take up the challenge.

His Majesty—Government have made it clear beyond doubt that the sword, which has been unsheathed after so much provocation, willingly be sheathed after fully, demonstrably and unquestionably vindicating the principles which Germany has so lightly challenged, and after ensuring that the sense of fear which has hung like a threatening cloud over the peaceful peoples of Europe and Asia, and indeed the world, and which cast its everlengthening shadow on the life of every Nation is for once and all banished. They have proclaimed in no uncertain terms that in this War they have no selfish or Imperialistic motives. To allege otherwise, as some people in British India do, is not only preposterous, but a travesty of truth.

No words of mine are needed to emphasize the unbroken record of the unswering and inalienable loyalty of the Princes to the Person and Throne of their beloved King-Emperor and of their. unshaken friendship and faithful attachment to the Empire. These have over and over again been unmistakably demonstrated and tested both in the piping times of peace and under the fiery ordeal of War during the past century and more of the Princes' relations with the Imperial Crown.

The attitude of the Princes and States and, I unhesitatingly add, that of the people of the States, who, with but a few negligible exceptions, are whole-heartedly supporting their Rulers in their War Services, has been the subject of much hostile critism and even of sarcasm in certain quarters in British India; but that leaves as entirely unmoved. The Princes have before them the clear path of duty, and this they will tread unflinchingly and without a moment's hesitation as becomes those who have the honour to be perpetual Allies and Friends of the British Crown.

It is not my practice ordinarily to refer to certain types of criticism, but perhaps I might be permitted to make an exception paid to me by a Congress Newspaper which, in commenting on a speech I made at the last New Year'a Day Banquet, was good enough to remark that, although my utterances on the subject of the War had thrown a certain amount of doubt on my qualities of satesmanship, even my worst enemy had never challenged my Imperialism. I can afford to ignore the first part of the criticism; and although many interpretations can be placed upon the term "Imperialism", I must repeat that I felt honoured by being attacked for my Imperialism, if by Imperialism is meant devotion to the King-Emperor and attempts to render every possible service to him and his great Empire at all times, and especially in grave times like the present when the Empire has been forced into this gigantic struggle.

My references in that speech to our great navy and to the fact that we had on the Western Front as finely trained and gallant an Army as the heart of any soldier could desire were especially singled out for comment; and the fantastic suggestion was made in that editorial that I spoke as if the whole Empire belonged to me. That ridiculous suggestion can also be ignored; but I certainly maintain—and I feel that it is also the view of my brother Princes—that we, the Princes and people of the Indian States, are of the Empire and with the Empire and that we do not in consequence look upon the British Navy and the Army as foreign, and we take a pride in our thus whole-heartedly identifying ourselves with everything that redounds to the glory and safety of the Empire.

The Newspaper in question went on to refer to me as an elderly gentleman who was living in imagination all over again the days of his youth in contemplation of a decadent system. Your Excellency and Your Highnesses, I pled guilty to the charge of being an elderly geneltmen, but I do not think the blame of getting on in years can fairly be laid on my shoulders!

I can assure our critics and opponents that, as against the regrettable atitude adopted by the Congress, the Princes are once again firmly determined directly to render the utmost possible assistance within their power and resources to their Emperor and the Empire in this War also—is men, in money and in material—and what is more, this contribution of theirs is purely and entirely voluntary and spontaneous. And, further, many a Prince is a eager as he was 25 years ago to risk his life on the battlefields for the King-Emperor and the British Flag, and is praying that an opportunity may afford itelf at an early date when he and his Troops can flight for the common cause.

These semtiments may not be appreciated by those who are out to bargain and barter or who are given to bluff and bluster.

But the Princes of India, true to their tradition and holding fast to the ties that they so dearly cherish with the Crown of England, are ready to stake their all, and indeed welcome every sacrifice necessary to ensure, under god's blessings, a just peace based on a decisive victory to the Imperial Arms.

# Annexure 15

## Speech Delivered by General His Highness the Maharajah of Bikaner, G.C.S.I. G.C.I.E., G.C.V.O., G.B.E., K.C.B., A.D.C., LL.D., in the Chamber of Princes on the 12th March 1940, in seconding the Resolution Regarding the Political Situation in India

*Your Excellency, Your Highnesses;*

I beg to second this Resolution.

During the last 10 years and more the Princes have made their position unmistakably clear in relation to constitutional reforms in India. From at least the time of the First Round Table Conference they have publicly and unequivocally stated that they welcome and sympathise with their brethren in British India in their desire to achieve Dominion Status under the aegis of the British Crown. I myself an one of those who have, both in England and in India, personally urged on many occasions such claims of my Motherland and my fellow-countrymen. I, therefore, welcome the announcement made by Your Excellency on behalf of Ris Majesty's Government that the goal of British policy in India is the attainment by India of the full status of a Dominion. The Princes are, however, doing nothing more than their duty to their States and to their people in emphasizing that essential guarantees and safeguards for the preservation of the Sovereignty of the States and for the protection of their rights and interests arising from Treaties, Sanads and Engagements and otherwise, be adequately and effectively provided in a manner fair and acceptable to the Princes.

I trust we shall not be misunderstood; but it needs to be stated that the rights of Sovereignty and autonomy which the States enjoy, and which are guaranteed to them by their Treaties and other solemn Engagements with the Crown, constitute a condition precedent and should be an integral part of any arrangements which are arrived at for the future. This may sound obvious as the Princes have missed no opportunity to emphasize it again and again. It is, however, necessary to repeat it in the most unmistakable terms, once again, as a tendency has recently manifested itselfin certain important political quarters to consider the future of India without taking the States into account. No solution which omits to take into consideration this fundamental fact of the complete freedom of the States in regard to such matters and their unchallengeable equality with British India can obviously be acceptable to the States.

It was recognised during the entire course of the federal negotiations that in matters affecting India as a whole there were not two parties but three, that is, the Crown, the Indian States and British India, and that any agreement must be tripartite and must be negotiated freely so far as the States were concerned.

Not many months ago, from all that one read and heard, it might however almost have appeared as if the Indian States were not in the picture at all and that it was for the principal political party in British India to settle the future of the whole of India in direct negotiations with the British Government, as if the Princes and States were goods and chattel to be exchanged or transferred without their having a say in the matter.

As observed the other day by the Right Hon. Sir Akbar Hydari, the veteran statesman of Hyderabad, the Premier State of India, the Treaty relationship of the States is with the Crown in the United Kingdom and this special relationship cannot be transferred to another authority without the free and willing consent of the Princes. This is a point to which the Princes attach the greatest importance.

We sould, therefore, once again say respectfully, but with all the emphasis at our command, that any scheme of government for India which affects the States must also include as an integral part of it an effective machinery for the fulfilment of the Crown's obligations to the Indian States. The Princes very dearly and greatly cherish their relations with the Imperial Crown; and for the States it is vitally important that the Crown should continue in effective possession of the necessary power to guarantee to the States the protection stipulated for in our Treaties.

The Princes are putting forward these essential conditions for the preservation and the integrity of the States, not for the sake of the continuance of their personal power or for maintaining unchanged the nature of their Governments as has been unfairly suggested in certain quarters; and obstruction to the progress of India or the adoption of a negative policy in that connection is the last thing that they desire. What the Princes are anxious to secure is freedom from intervention or dictation by outside bodies. So far, thank God, no difference of interests between the Ruler and his people has, generally speaking, arisen in the States as the Princes and States have been prepared to meet the legitimate aspirations of their people.

Nor, unless the Crown fails in its obligations to the States—a contingency not to be contemplated—can the Princes be asked to give up what is legitimately theirs. The States have all these years faithfully and scrupulously discharged their Treaty obligations; and the Crown's obligations to the States have been recognised in the most solemn and unequivocal manner by successive Sovereigns of England; and holding to the faith in the plighted word and in the justice, honour and fairplay of Britain, the Princes of India feel assured that their rights and privileges would also be fully safeguarded by the Crown and its August Representative in India.

Your Excellency and Your Highnesses, I have a high regard for Mahatma Gandhi personally, whom I have the pleasure of knowing. He is held in universal esteem and respect, not only in India but throughout the world, as a great man who has in many ways worked wonder for his country. But in matters which affect the life and death of the States it is permnissible with all due respect and deference to venture to express disagreement.

It has been alleged in Congress circles that the Princes are an Imperial creation; that they are vassals of the Crown and have no status apart from the Crown; that the question of the Princes is a red-herring drawn across the path of India's progress for Imperialistic purposes; that the problem of the States is a bogey raised by the British Government; and that if the Crown parts with the power it today enjoys over the whole of India, naturally the Princes have to look up to the successor of the Crown, namely, the whose people of India, for the preservation of their Sovereign status.

I may here be permitted to state that many States, big as well as small, owe their existence to the strong arm of their former Rulers, and that too, long before the establishment of the British Empire in India. They have come into political relationship with the Crown by Treaties of Alliance and Friendship and other Engagements; and we have not the least doubt that Your Excellency and His Majesty's Government will agree that their unassailable position and their claims cannot be dismissed in this airy fashion, which ignores irrefutable historical facts.

If one might point out in all friendliness, it is British India which is the creation of the British Government. For no one can deny that before Great Britain extended her sway over India, the whole of this country was in the possession of Indian Rulers.

The allegation has also been heard that the Princes are unfriendly to the Congress. But that is not a correct statement of the position. The Princes at the Round Table Conference and till much later had given clear proof of their friendliness to and trust in, the Congress by expressing their readiness to work with the Congress for the benefit of India and the Empire. But it is a fact that it was the Congress which has of late shown active hostility to the States. Some of its foremost leaders have expressed the view that they do not want the States in the Federation, and that they would tear up the Tr ties of the States as if they were scraps of paper, and even that they would like to see the States done away with. All this has naturally caused grave misgivings in the States.

In conclusion, I would say that all that the Princes press for is that their legitimate interests and time-honoured rights guaranteed solemnly by the Crown should be protected. Subject to that essential condition they will, I am confident, be found to work willingly, sincerely and wholeheartedly like other true sons of the Motherland for the ordered progress and freedom of India under the aegis of the British Crown.

# 10

## *The Issue of Federation and Constitutional Reforms*

THE ROUND TABLE CONFERENCE convinced Maharaja Ganga Singh that the future course of events lay in the proper representation of the States in the proposed Federation and what safeguards were necessary to ensure that the interests of the Princes would not go by default. At the outset the Maharaja was keen that his Prime Minister, Sir Manubhai Mehta, would look to the affairs of the Federation while he would concentrate on the administration at home which he had neglected for long. But after 1932 he was convinced that he would have to personally intervene in the matters of the proposed Federation as it involved the tricky process of creating a consensus among the members of the Chamber of Princes. The questions of minting coins, increased supply of postage-stamps; revision of salt agreement and jurisdiction on railway lines were to be sorted out with the Government of India as under the new constitution those subjects would pass under the Federation.

There were two more problems which were causing concern to the Maharaja. One such problem related to the stand of some of the so called 'senior States' of Rajputana who were unwilling to accord Bikaner the status of a senior or important state. The other was the allocation of seats in the Federal Upper House. Maharaja Ganga Singh had always personally held that there should be no differentiation between sovereign states and that as far as possible there should be equality of votes for the units in the Upper House which was designed to enshrine the federal principle.

The return from the Round Table Conference was devoted to explaining to the people who mattered the need of a Federation / and why members of the Princely order should cease to resist the formation of the Federation. (Nos. 1-3) He cited three major reasons why the Indian States should join the Federation—

1. they would furnish a stabilising factor in the Federal Constitution;
2. that the process of unification would begin at once; and
3. that in regard to matters of defence the States would furnish a practical experience which is otherwise wanting in India at that time.

About the component elements of the Constitution which the Conference framed was the British Indian Princes, with their responsible and unitary governments on one hand and the Indian States, already sovereign and autonomous on the other. It was also proposed that the States, as co-equal partners with British India in the Federal Legislature, would send their representatives to the two Federal Legislatures, the Senate and the House of Representatives, where Federal matters would be dealt with. The States, it was also clear, would not vote upon purely British Indian subjects; both would share the responsibility of the Executive to the Legislature. It was also proposed to set up a Supreme Court to enforce the Constitution. The Indian States also wanted the Supreme Court to be empowered to resolve the disputes between the States and the Government of India.

Irked by constant pin-pricks by leaders of British India in the print media, Maharaja Ganga Singh made a press statement in September 1931 in which he made the final position and stand of the Indian States with regards to the Federation in clear terms.

"When the Princes and States were last year invited to join a Federation, they generally and gladly expressed their willingness to consider the question on terms of equality with British India, and even to make some sacrifices, on the condition that India remained under the Crown and that the sovereignity and autonomy of the States and their Treaty Rights were adequately safeguarded".(No. 4)

Around the same time the Maharaja made a series of very crucial speeches at the Federal Structure Committee meetings which left the Government of India and leaders of British India in no doubt as to the hardening of the stand of the Princes as represented by the Maharaja.(No. 5). At the outset he made it clear that Talukdars, Jagirdars etc. could not be classified as independent rulers as was made out in some parts of British India. Furthermore in case of nomination of members to Houses, there should be no discrimination between British India and Indian State. On matters of revenue the Maharaja made two observations:

1. that the Federal Government would derive its revenues by indirect taxation and will not be empowered to impose direct taxation on the Indian States or to demand any fresh contribution; and
2. that there would be no discrimination against the States and their subjects in regard to taxation or in any other matter-a point on which there was unanimity of opinion.

   Once the Federation came into being, Maharaja Ganga Singh expressed the View that there could be only three points of conflict between British India and the Indian States. They were—

   (i) If there was a proposal to break away from the Empire, which the scheme under consideration providing for India being placed on a footing of equality and partnership with other parts of the Commonwealth happily rendered it unnecessary to touch on;

   (ii) If the very existence of the States was threatened, or there was any danger to the existence of the States or any desire to encroach upon the treaty and other sovereign rights of the States, except in so far as may be willingly and mutually agreed upon—on which point he (the Maharaja) declined to believe that any serious proposition of that kind could be put forward on the part of the majority of their British Indian friends, and

   (iii) There were fiscal and financial matters regarding which we (the Princes) hoped that, by previous fiscal enquiry as well as the discussions which would take place, there all such matters would have have been satifactorily settled before the States entered into Federation, and on which matters the Princes demanded in fairness to the States mutual satisfaction on all such points.

Maharaja Ganga Singh also reiterated that on the one hand the Indian States would resist all attempts at interfearance in their internal affairs on the other hand they also sought to convince the British Indian Provinces that the States would not interfere in their affairs as well. As regards distribution of seats in the two houses he referred to a Resolution which read:

> 'The distribution interse of seats amongst the States in the two Houses should be left to be settled by the States. Failing agreement, the points in dispute should be referred to an expert committee to be appointed by the Crown'.

The Maharaja further claimed that population could not be the criteria for determining the status and number of seats to be alloted to a State. He quoted the instances of Udaipur whose population was less than that of many Rajput States but in terms of prestige and importance it ranked much higher. Therefore, it was advocated that other factors should also be taken into consideration like sovereignity and internal autonomy, relations with the Crown and the political importance of the State concerned.

With reference to the Constitution of a Supreme Court as envisaged in the Federation, the Maharaja was of the considered opinion that it should be called the Federal Court instead of the Supreme Court on the grounds that it was to be used for Federal purposes. On the question of the jurisdiction of the court, the Maharaja's views were in confirmity with the views of Sir Mirza Ismail. They were:

> "The Federal Court should have exclusive appellate jurisdiction from both the State and Provincial High Courts only in cases in which a point of Federal law is involved or in which any issue arises under the Constitution".

Ganga Singh Ji wanted the following phrase to be appended to the above statement:

> "Except in matters which though Federal are administered by the States themselves".(No. 6)

Events moved rapidly after 1932. There was a sharp divide visable in the attitude of the Princes towards the issue of Federation. In a frank and forthright speech before the Indian States Enquiry Committee on 21st March, 1932 Maharaja Ganga Singh admitted the schism that had taken place among the Princes and stated that though he stood committed to the notion of the Federation, his brother rulers could not be coerced to join the Federation. He once again stressed that the final acceptance of the idea of Federation was based on, among other conditions, the fundamental point that read as follows:

'On the profound conviction that not only can each constituent part attain its full strature within the Empire under the aegis of the British Crown, but a higher development, politically and economically, than an isolated unit'; (No.7 also see No.9).

The Maharaja also suggested that one way of resolving the deadlock would be to increase the quota of the seats of the Indian States in the Upper Federal House to 125. At the same time, he also argued that all the 109 States who were members of the Chamber of Princes in their own right, should have equal and individual representation as Governments in the Upper House.

After the Second Round Table Conference the Maharaja favoured the representation of Ministers in the ensuing Conferences as they were to be of technical nature and the Ministers were more adept at dealing with such matters. (No.8) Soon after the White Paper on the Federation was issued. It caused great disquiet among the Princes and again it was left to the Maharaja to sooth the ruffled feathers (No.9). He argued forcefully in the Chamber of Princes that the White Paper was not the final word and, as was rightly pointed out in certain directions, the proposed constitution lacked certain safeguards the Princes were insisting upon, then the Chamber would represent to the Majesty's Government on that score. He also underlined the fact that the Federal Executive would not be permitted to encroach upon the sovereignity of the States beyond such details as mutually agreed upon.

In 1935 the Maharaja had another occasion to address the Chamber of Princes on the important issue of Indian Constitutional Reforms. (No.10). He noted with satisfaction that the Joint Parliamentary Committee had done the right thing by the Princes by stating that there would be a legal differentiation between the functions of the Viceroy and of the Governor-General. Under the new proposed constitution of the Federation certain matters relating to the States, which were till then dealt with by the Governor-General in Council, could not be exercised on behalf of the Crown by any Federal Authority save in so far as they fell within the Federal sphere. Thus the rights and interests of the Indian States weti to be entrusted to the care of the Viceroy. The Maharaja further pledged that if certain safeguards in the Constitution were provided for the Princes and Indian States, then the Princes were willing to make certain sacrifices and to delegate to the Crown, for the specific purpose of Federation, a part of their sovereignity in regard to certain limited matters, which sovereignity they would share with British India in the Federal

Legislature.

The year 1937 was a significant landmark in the life of Maharaja Ganga Singh as it marked the Golden Jubilee of his reign. Over the years he had established a special rapport with successive Viceroys and maintaining past traditions the then Viceroy, Lord Linlithgow, paid a State visit to Bikaner to mark the Golden Jubilee. The Maharaja in his welcome speech appreciated the Viceroy's efforts of appointing a special Representative to discuss with the Princes and ascertaining their views on the proposed Federation.(No. 11). He also stressed the fact that as British Indian States had recently become autonomous and the Indian States were already sovereign, they could become equal partners in the new Constitution. The Princes, the Maharaja added, had long traditions of administration and a guarantee of freedom in internal administration would lead to socio-economic and political development of the States. Continuing in the same vein, in a Banquet Speech around the same time Maharaja Ganga Singh attributed the meaning 'utterly evil' to the term autocracy as propounded by many leaders of British Indian Provinces with reference to the rule of Princes in the Indian States. His reasoning was that autocracy stood for personal rule: a ruler could be either benevolent or despotic. He further argued that a benevolent ruler could be a true servant of the State whereas, by the same hardstick, popular government may well carry elements of autocracy.(No.12)

## References


1. S.R. Purohit, 'Samvaidhanik Vikas Mein Yogdaan' in G.S.L. Deora edited Centenary volume.
2. Rome Note.
3. Dr. Karni Singh, "The Relations of the House of Bikaner with Central Powers'.
4. Maharaja Ganga Singh Ji's speech at Municipal Board upon return from Europe (9th Feb., 1931).
5. Speech of His Highness, the Ruler of Bikaner at State Banquet at Lallgarh. 11th Feb., 1931.
6. Maharaja Ganga Singh's Speech at State Banquet at Bikaner, 9th March, 1931.
7. Press Statement by His Highness of Bikaner, 3rd Sept., 1931.
8. Six Speeches of Maharaja Ganga Singh at Federal Structure Committee, 15th Sept. — 22nd Oct., 1931.
9. Banquet Speech by His Highness, the ruler of Bikaner, 15th Nov., 1931.
10. Banquet Speech of Maharaja Ganga Singh at Lallgarh in honour of Members of the Indian States Enquiry Committee, 21st March, 1932.
11. Farewell to Heir Apparent on eve of latter's visit to Africa, 25th Oct., 1932.
12. Maharaja Ganga Singh Ji speech in Chamber of Princes, 25th March, 1933.
13. Speech by His Highness Maharaja Ganga Singh Ji in Chamber of Princes on

the subject of allocation of seats in Federal Structure, 25th March, 1933.
14. Ganga Singh Ji's speech in Chamber of Princes on the Silver Jubilee of the reign of his Imperial Majesty, 22nd Jan., 1935.
15. Maharaja Ganga Singh Ji's speech at State Banquet in Honour of the visit of Viceroy to Bikaner, 6th Nov., 1937.
16. Golden Jubilee Speech by Maharaja Ganga Singh Ji at State Banquet, 16th Nov., 1937.

# Annexure 1

## Speech by Lieut. General His Highness the Maharajah of Bikaner, G.C.S.I, G.C.I.E., G.C. V.D., G.B.E., K.C.B., A.D.C., LL.D., Delivered in Reply to the Address of .Welcome on his Return from Europe Presented by the Municipal Board, Bikaner, on the 9th February, 1931.

*Mr. President and Members of the Municipal Board,*

I thank you warmly for the loyal Address which you have presented me and for the very kind terms in which you have referred to my efforts during my recent triple mission to Europe to be of service to the King-Emperor and the Empire, and to the Indian States and British India.

I also wish to take this opportunity of expressing my sincere gratitude to the Chiefs and Nobles and other public bodies and communities of the State who have been so good as to send me special messages of welcome and congratulations.

Need I tell you how I rejoice to be back Home and how happy I am to be once again in my own State and amongst my own people after an absence of six months all but one week? I will not detain you by referring in detail to our work at the Assembly of the League of Nations in Geneva where I had the honour of leading the Indian Delegation, or what was done in London at the Imperial Conference—important as were their proceedings to the pence of the World and to the great British Empire to which we are so proud to belong. But looking back on these crowded months, you as Indians, and particularly as subjects of Indian States, would naturally be most anxious to hear something at first hand from me of what was accomplished at the Indian Round Table Conference in London and especially as to how it will affect our States and you, their subjects, as also our fellow-countrymen in British Indian with whom our fortunes are so closely interwoven.

I will not repeat, or dwell at length on, what has already been publicly said in the joint statement issued on Friday to the Press immediately on landing in Bombay by all the Princes and Members of the Indian States Delegation and the Delegates from British Indian whose signatures it bears and who travelled on the 'Viceroy of India'.

I will content myself by inviting your attention to its contents and, although I do not expect I shall have much to say that has not already been said by me in my speeches and interviews in England, I will straightaway proceed to express in the most unequivocal language at my command that I have returned full of hope, confidence and bright promise for India, and profound gratutide to the Almighty, at the substantial measure of general agreement and the great success achieved at the Round Table Conference in spite of so many obvious difficulties and diversities of interest. It cannot be over-emphasized that we, the Princes and States of India, and our colleagues from British India, working in the closest harmony, encouraged to go ahead through the gracious interest and solicitude of His Imperial Majesty the King-Emperor, and aided by the good-will and sympathy of the Prime Minister and the Secretary of State for India and Lord Sankey and other Members of His Majesty's Government, as well as the Delegation from the Imperial Parliamant, have been able to accomplish a work fraught with immense potentialities for the good of our beloved Motherland, and that we have rought back with us very substantial gains for our whole Country and our Countrymen, which will enable India to hold up its head and to take its due place as a co-equal and honoured partner of the British Commonwealth of Nations.

The Round Table Conference has had further results of incalculable value in having brought England and India closer together, just as it has brought the States and British India closer together, and in having demonstrated beyond the shadow of a doubt, at first-hand something of the new forces that, animate political thought in India-not only British India, but that which is also whole-heartedly supported by Indian India. The position in India and the Indian standpoint is now more clearly and more widely understand and, I feel sure I can add, appreciated; and British Public Opinion has undoubtedly undergone a remarkable change in favour of India Furthermore, His Majesty's Government and the British statesmen representing the important political parties in approaching the problem have, without ignoring the real difficulties, tackled them with a single will to find means by which the natural claim of Indian political thought may be speedily and substantially recognised, and results mutually beneficial to Great Britain and to India can best be achieved. In other words, those who have longed to see the Conference bear fruit for the true healing of nations may take a new hope.

It was our considered view that the time had arrived when we, both of the Indian States and of British India, must be captains of our own souls, monarchs of our own Fate; and it was our natural and srong desire that we should be masters in our respective houses. Sometimes this is expressed by the phrase "Dominion Status" and at other times by the term "Responsible Government". I thank God that we have placed both within India's grasp. The frame work of the Constitution fashioned in London establishes Responsible Government in India, meaning by "Responsible Government" and Executive chosen from those who have the support of the Federal Legislature, and which will hold office only so long as they retain that support. Such a Government leads, as surely as night follows day, to Dominion Status.

But we have done much more than that. We have provided a machinery whereby the two Indias, British Indian and the Indian India of the States,—which, though of the same flesh and blood, have hitherto been as under—are now to be linked in a federal whole, one and indivisible, each separate entity free to work out its own destiny in accord with its traditions and experience, but united in the common purpose of securing the greater good of our Motherland as a whole. Some of us of the Indian States—and this no doubt applies also to British India, though just at the moment I speak with particular reference to us of the States—have for the last decade and even more dreamt dreams of a United India taking her full place amongst the Free Nations comprising the Empire; and I, in common with some other Princes and Ministers, have gone into this subject at many a Conference and meeting and dealth with it in many a Note an speech, within and without the confines of our States. Indeed, although the time was not ripe for it, a Federation between the States and British India was considered in Bikaner, as long ago as December 1917, at meetings of Princes and Ministers when political reforms in the States were under consideration, and which were later dealth with in Chapter X of the Montford Report. But few of us dared hope to see it realised so soon, That dream has now become a practical reality; and let me say in all sincerity and candour that, looking on this work. I—and I am confident you too—find it good.

At the same time one can realise that those amongst the States who have not looked so far ahead, or made themselves familiar with the implications of Federation and with Federal Constitutions in various parts of the world, feel some natural misgivings as to possible adverse effects on the Sovereignty and autonomy of our Indian States and the interests and well-being of States subjects. The work of a Conference, such as that in which we have participated, proceeds stage by stage, sometimes going forward, sometimes seeming to move backward; and it is at times difficult even for those directly in contact with the scene to see the wood for the trees. How much more difficult then for you and others who remained behind in India and who see these proceedings only through the brief and at times the distoring mirror of the cable? Let me, before inviting your attention to further details. at once give expression to my conviction that there is really no ground for any valid apprehensions in regard to such matters in the minds of the Rulers and Governments of our States—big and small—as well as of our subjects whose interests have been consistently and constantly kept in view by the Rulers and Ministers of the States Delegation at the Conference. The inherent Sovereignty and autonomy and the Treaties and other rights of the States and their subjects have been duly safeguarded and will be maintained intact—"inviolate and invoilable" to quote the words of the King-Emperor's Proclamation of 1921—except only to the extent to which we may be prepared voluntarily to delegate them to the Federal Executive and the Federal Legislature, in which the States rightly claim an equal voice, and in which such portion of their Sovereignty as they delegate will be equally shared by the States in common with British India. The matters in regard to which any such delegation is to be made will be found in the last of Federal subjects already published with the Report of the Federal Structure Sub-Committee.

Perhaps apprehensions in the minds of some connected with the States have been further accentuated by exaggerated rumours of dissensions amongst the Princes and other Ministers of the Indian States Delegation, and probably a speech made during the concluding stages of the Conference—which however represented only the personal view of the speaker, and which, if necessary, will doubtless further be dealth with when these important questions come up for discussion in the Chamber of Princes next month. I have also seen hints in the Indian Press regarding a manifesto opposing Federation alleged to have been issued by one or two of the younger members of our States Delegation. as a matter of fact, not only did the Indian States Delegation in London do full credit to the States, but there was excellent and remarkable team work; and, as one of the Representatives of the States on the Federal Structure Sub-Committee, upon whom the brunt of the work fell and the heaviest measure of responsibility rested. I have no hesitation in declaring—and I feel sure my brother Prince and Colleague on the Committee, His Highness the Ruler of Bhopal, will fully Support me in this statement—that no one could have had better colleagues to work with; and although differences of opinion on minor points here and there were only to be expected, it would be impossible to conceive of any five Members working in greater harmony. And I am sure that you will all be glad to have confirmation from me, of what was only to be expected of a statesman of his eminence, that our Prime Minister, Sir Manubhai Mehta, who proceeded as one of the Delegates to the Round Table Conference representing the Special Organization of the Chamber of Princes, played a most useful and dignified part in our work and assisted us with many valuable suggestions and advice of great benefit to the States. This is however by the way; and let me add that the interests of the States, including those of what are known as the smaller States, have been clearly kept in view and equally safeguarded. My deep sympathies with, and my efforts to be of servcie to, them during my term of Chancellorship of the Chamber of Princes, and before and after that, are I trust too well known to necessitate my saying anything further. Though it is earnestly to be hoped that at least the major portion, if not all, of the States will in the common interests, and, I would add in the interests of the States themselves, come in, entry into the Federation will be entirely optional and voluntary by means of Supplementary Treaties to be made with the Crown by each individual State, big or small; and there is of course no question whatsoever of the States being bound by what was provisionally worked out at the Conference; nor was there the slightest suggestion on the part of anyone of any States being forced or coerced, directly or indirectly, to enter into Federation or of their hands being forced in any way.

I will now, if I may, briefly review a few of the more important features of particular interest to the States and their subjects, and at the same time make any observations that may be especially called for. As you are aware, at the first Plenary Session of the Conference an earnest appeal was made to the Indian States Delegation by our friends in British India to join an All-India Federation. Such a Federation, it was put to us, would be the solution of the difficulties of India and pave the way to her salvation. It was further declared publicly and freely that the association of the Indian States with British India would be welcome for three reasons:

1. that they would furnish a stabilising factor in the Federal constitution;
2. that the process of unification would begin at once; and
3. that in regard to matters of defence the States would furnish a practical experience which is otherwise wanting in India at present.

There were questions involved of the most vital importance to the Rulers, Governments and subjects of the Indian States. Indeed some of them were such as might affect the very existence at some future date of our States. In considering this appeal the Princes were not free agents, but trustees of their States, their subjects and their Dynasties. As I observed in one of my speeches in the Sankey Committee, we have to bear in mind the existence and rights of our States subjects, which, in the minds of the great majority of Princes are very dear to us and to whose interests, I added, many of us have devoted our lives and energies—in spite of allegations made to the contrary by certain people of whom the less said the better. We are also the trustees of the rights and privileges and the honour and dignity of our States which our Ancestors had won and our forbears preserved, and which we must hand down unimpaired to our Successors. You in common with the subjects of other States have grievances, particularly in regard to fiscal and financial matters, which we have striven in vain so far to redress. Therefore, whilst anxious to serve the wider interests of our Motherland, we had to be sure that these rights and privileges were secured, and restored where infringed upon. So when I had the privilege of responding to this appeal at the request, and on behalf, of the Princes and States at the Plenary Session of the Conference on the 17th November, I made it clear that our acceptance of the federal idea must be based on three fundamental conditions- fust and foremost, on our unfaltering loyalty to the Throne and Person of the King-Emperor and our obligations of honour and plighted word; secondly, on the profound conviction that not only can each constituent part reach its full expression within the Empire and under the Crown, but a higher development, politically and economically, than as an isolated unit; and thirdly that our Treaty rights, and the rights of our subjects, were scrupulously observed. I had already made it clear in my previous speeches in this connection that an equitable agreement must be reached, between all the parties concerned, to govern the relations of the two Indias, ensuring for the States their due position in the future constitution as co-equal partners with British India, guaranteeing their Treaties and their internal sovereignty, and safeguarding their interests including those of their subjects, on terms just and honourable alike to the States and British India. Subject to these conditions, a Federation in which the Indian States would enter as co-equal partners, and without the slightest suggestion of subordination or inferiority to British India, had—as I had publicly stated in the past—no terrors for the Princes and Governments of the Indian States and that we would be glad to co-operate. And it was subject to these essential conditions—conditions and matters of principle to which, as I said in another speech, no reasonable and fair-minded person, be he a resident of British India or Great Britain or the Empire, can reasonably take exception—which we always carefully bore in mind, that I and my colleagues worked in the Conference and in the various Committees; and it was with this firm understanding that we were able to go confidently forward.

And it was a matter of profound satisfaction to us that the justice and reasonableness of these conditions, after a little heart-searching here and there, won the sympathetic support of our British Indian Colleagues and I desire here, if I may, to pay a sincere and grateful tribute to them for the same. When we expressed our willingness to consider entering into such a Federation we were prompted by three important considerations. The first was our duty to the Crown and friendship to the Empire, and we considered it necessary to examine the subject even if some sacrifices were involved on our part in view of the present grave situation in India. Secondly, we were naturally desirous in every reasonable manner to assist our country becoming a co-equal and honoured member of the British Commonwealth of Nations, and to help our brethren in British India under the aegies of the Crown to rise to their full stature, just as we of the States are desirous of ensuring the fullest freedom in our own affairs and of retaining our Sovereignty and autonomy as implied and guaranteed by our Treaties, Sanads and other Engagements; and thirdly we were of the view that in the long run such a Federation was likely also to prove of some advantage in certain directions to the States and their subjects.

Now the component elements of the Constitution which the Conference framed will be the British Indian Provinces, with their responsible and unitary governments on the one hand, and the Indian States, already sovereign and autonomous on the other. The States, as co-equal partners with British India in the Federal Legislature, will send their representatives to the two Federal Legislatures, the Senate and the House of Rrepresentatives, where Federal matters will be dealt with. But the States have made it clear that they have no desire either to listen to or vote upon purely British Indian subjects. Both the partners will be represented in the Executive; both will have a voice in the decisions of the Federal subjects; both will share the responsibility of the Executive to the Legislature. This Constitution will be no rigid organism like a dead language, but will contain the seeds of expansion from within under proper conditions, and will be protected and interpreted on purely juridical principles by a Supreme Court, which is all the more essential now from the standpoint of both the States and British India.

We of the Indian States also want the point examined as to whether the Supreme Court cannot also be utilized for the settlement of any disputes arising between Agents of the Crown and a State, or States, regarding Paramountcy and such other matters, or failing that to have the benefit for the purpose of the suggested Commonwealth Tribunal proposed at the Imperial Conference of 1930. This is of course in addition to certain provisions which will have to be made for the more satisfactory and equitable settlement through arbitration in matters which are non-justiciable. The suggestion was made by some British Indians that the jurisdiction of the Supreme Court should be extended to the judicial side of the administration of the States. Since the States possess their own judiciary and independent High Court, or other final appellate Courts, such a course would obviously be incompatible with the internal Sovereignty of the States, big or small.

It is already clear that the broad details and principles only have been tentatively agreed to in England—highly important and encouraging though they are—and the remaining details—some of great importance—have to be worked our now in India. The Princes and people of India are, in any case, deeply distressed at the fact that they will so soon be deprived of the benefit of the presence of a great statesman and a great benefactor like Lord Irwin. That he will not be able to lend to us all, in the important task that lies ahead to us in this connection, the benefit of his sage counsel and support will be a further grievous loss. But we have the consolation of feeling that in his successor, Lord Willingdon, we shall have in our midst a statesman already well acquainted with India, and whose noble services to, and sympathy for, her cause justify our hoping that he will prove to be worthy successor to that great and popular Viceroy, Lord Irwin. Amongst the outstanding points may be mentioned, for instance, the proportion of representation of the States and of British India, and the allocation of such seats amongst the various States concerned, in the two Federal Legislatures, which also depends on their total Membership. The more important States will, it is obvious, enter individually; the rest by being grouped together. The settlement of these details will, we know, not be without their difficulties; but this is a matter which concerns the States only and not British India. And when the number of members for the Upper and Lower Federal Houses and the percentage of the States representatives in the two

Houses has been definitely agreed upon, the allocation of seats will have to be settled by discussions in the Chamber of Princes in consultation with those few States which at present do not avail themselves of their right of Membership of the Chamber, as well as with representatives of the smaller States; and in case of any dispute arising the matter will doubtless have to be finally referred for discussion to the Viceroy. And here I wish to emphasize that no ordinary Federation known at present could alone afford us a safe or sure guide in regard to Federation in the unique position of India where the two component elements are the Sovereign and autonomous Indian States on the one side, and British India and its Provinces on the other, which at present only enjoy power by devolution or delegation, and that only since comparatively recent times. In view therefore, of the fact that the position of the States in India and in the Empire is without parallel throughout the world and in history a special Constitution has to be framed to meet such special circumstances. As regards the States representation they have claimed an equal number in the Upper Federal House and a smaller percentage with weightage in the Lower House. It is abundantly clear that Federation cannot be achieved by coercion of the States in any form, and that the Princes would only come into the Federation of their own free will on terms which would secure the just rights of their States and subjects. Clearly the Princes and their Governments could not be expected to, and would not, accept any position of the slightest subordination or inferiority to British India, and they rightly and validly claim to share equally, and with honour, with British India any Sovereignty or Dominion Status which British India might henceforth enjoy as a result of the Federation. In thus claiming an effective voice and representation in the Federal structure, the States therefore urged and stressed the importance and need in justice to themselves and their subjects that the representation of the States in the Federal Legislatures cannot be based merely on area or population, but that regard must also be had to their Sovereignty and internal autonomy, their relations with the Crown, their political importance as one of the two separate great entities of India, and also—to quote from the Simon Report—"their existence and influence and the Crown's obligations in regard to them".

And here it is necessary to make clear the position taken up by the Princes and States throughout the Conference and all its difficult and anxious negotiations and deliberations in which—if I am not considered immodest, I would like to claim in all truthfulness for the States that—the part which they have played was patriotic and constructive and that they lent the whole weight of their influence and support with a single eye to furthering the cause of their Motherland and thus also helping the cause of the Empire. No unworthy motives influenced the Princes in expressing their willingness to enter into a Federation. Immediately after my speech at the first Plenary Session of the Conference, where as I have said it was my privilege on behalf of the Princes and States to come to the support of our Country and our fellow-countrymen in British India, I had the gratification of learning from various prominent people in England—including from Members of His Majesty's Government as well as our Liberal and Conservative colleagues of the British Parliamentary Parties, that our attitude had been instrumental in entirely changing the position and had immediately facilitated the task before the Conference and rendered it possible for a greater advance in the direction of the establishment of Responsible Government to be made than would otherwise have been practicable; whilst it was a source of genuine satisfaction to us to hear from the lips of the Prime Minister of England himself the following words—

> "The declaration of the Princes has revolutionised the situation. Supposing we had met here without the Princes, supposing the Princes had come and had said nothing, or supposing they had said, "We are here merely as spectators." What a different situation would have presented itself to us. The Princes saying what they have said has at once not only opened our vision, not, only cheered our hearts, not only let us lift up our eyes and see a glowing horizon, but has simplified our duties. The Princes have given a most substantial contribution in opening up the way to a really united federated India."

And this is what the Prime Minister said in his speech on the last day of the Round Table Conference in London:

> "Your Highnesses, I can add nothing to the tribute that has been paid to you by previous speakers regarding the magnificent part that you have played in making that possible. Before you came the structure of the Indian constitution was in doubt. Many people, as was said this morning, were doubtful as to whether British India alone could bear central authority. You came. You made your declaration. You shewed your patriotic interest in Indian affairs and your very wise vision regarding the future, and your words made it possible for us to build up a constitution and to put political

weight upon it of the nature of an All India Federation. That has been a great achievement and a great work for which both India and Great Britain are grateful to Your Highnesses".

Tributes of a similar high order were paid to the Princes and States, both in Committees and in the Conference, by the different Parliamentary parties, to whom—and particularly to Lord Reading—we all owe a sincere debt of gratitude; and this response of the States was undoubtedly instrumental for the gratifying change of view in the ranks of the Conservative Party also, as announced at a later stage by Lord Peel. The States can fairly claim also, with all modesty, that the support given by Mr. Lloyd George as the Leader of the Liberals, and by Mr. Baldwin as the Leader of the Conservatives in the last debate in the House of Commons, was largely influenced by the same considerations. And yet is it not astonishing how no sooner one cloud of suspicion disperses, than another cloud gathers. First it was alleged in certain British Indian quarters that the Princes were conspiring with the British Government in an unholy alliance to keep British India out of its rightful due. That statement was challenged in Indian by me in common with some other Prinres. When it was insinuated that the Prinres at the Round Table Conference were going to serve as Ulster of India, I pointed out in an interview given on the 18th July last that there was not the slightest ground for alarm in British India on the score of the importance attached, and rightly attached, by the States, to the solemn and binding character of their Treaties adn their relations with the Crown, or in regard to other essential safeguards, which were obviously clearly called for and their inherent and inviolable right; and I asked people to wait and see the attitude of the States at the Round Table Conference, which, I said I was positive, would not only be fair but helpful to British India. It is therefore sad, after all the experience and joint association of British India and the States in England in the past few months, still to find suspicious publicly ventilated in certain quarters in India—in the Press and on the platform—to the effect that the Princes, in consenting to enter the Federation, were influenced by the desire of dominating British India and that the domination and power of Great Britain was only to be transferred into the hands of the India States, and that the States were scheming for perpetual despotism. I thus took an opportunity in the Sankey Committee of begging all to remember that India was not only the Motherland of our British Indian brethren but that it was also the Motherland of the Princes and that our interests were generally identical, and I made it clear that the States had no desire whatsoever to stand in the way of India's progress, that it was not we, the Princes and States, who begged to be permitted by British India or the Crown to enter the Federation, but that, as briefly outlined by me, we had shown our willingness to do so only on the cordial invitation and earnest appeal of our friends of British India. So far as the States were concerned, questions in dispute between them and the Agents of the Crown, such as those relating to Paramountcy, and some other matters of a nature personal to the Princes—including questions affecting the honour and dignity of the Princes, their Consorts and their Families—were such as could be taken up, and which indeed have already been taken up, between and the Viceroy and the British Government. And without the least desire to show any unfriendliness or lack of sympathy with British India I added that, if so desired by British India and Great Britain we would be perfectly willing to keep out of the Federation—until such time as our help was required—and that we would still sincerely wish British India god-speed; but if such was the desire of British India, whilst we did not want to stand in the way, we also did not want to have the blame put upon us for any consequences that might follow. I pointed out that, in such a contingency, we would rely upon out Treaties and on the good-faith of Great Britain and of British India and on other necessary safeguards and adjustments—including fiscal and financial adjustments—so that the States may continue to exist. I also made it clear with regard to other unfounded apprehensions entertained that the Princes and States were not going to do any dirty work, or to resort to any mean or dishonourable tactics at the bidding of anyone. I emphasized that the States, if they were wanted to join the Federation, would, in the Federal Executive or Legislature really not be in conflict with British India, block against block, and that the only time the States as a body would come in conflict with British India would be either if there was any proposal of anyone to break away from the Empire to which the States would not, and cannot be expected to agree, or if the very existence of the States was threatened, or there was any desire to encroach upon the Treaty and other Sovereign rights of the States except in so far as may be sillingly and mutually agreed upon in the rivised Treaties and Conventions relating to Federation.

The only other possible point of conflict with British India would be in regard to fiscal and financial matters; and the subjects of the States have certain very definite grievances in relation to such matters as Sea-Customs, Railways, Currency and Coinage and Exchange, Posts and Telegraphs, Double Income-tax, and so on. Without putting the matter too strongly, we feel that we have been exploited in the past for the benefit of British India through being called on to pay dues which we had no voice in framing, and from the revenues of which the subjects of our States, as the tax-payers, derive no benefit. The position will, to a certain extent, be improved in the Federal System; and the States will now have to reconsider their claims and policy in regard to such matters in the light of the Federal scheme evolved, since they will be able to make their voices heard and their influence felt. But, as a preliminary to the establishment of the Federal System, I took the opportunity on more than one occasion in the Sankey Committee of making it quite clear that it was essential that these, and all other financial and fiscal issues, between the States and British India, must be examined by an Expert Committee consisting of Representatives of the Crown, of British India, and of the States, and of experts which will have to be appointed minutely and impartially to investigage the whole position and to prepare the basis of a settlement just and honourable to all concerned.

Then there is the question of the Is. 6d. ratio, which many of you, whether engaged in industries and commerce in Bikaner and in other States, or in British India, regard as most prejudicial to your interests, and to which I also drew prominent attention in my interview of the 18th July last, as also in England, Whilst on the subject let me add that any grievances of British India in this connection, in which the people of the States are united with their fellow, countrymen, will, let us hope, be put right by the establishment of a Reserve Bank and by the financial and fiscal autonomy we have secured.

Incidentally I may add that a self-styled friend, posing as a great patriot and champion of the Indian State and their subjects, but one who can see nothing whatever that is honourable or good in the patriotic response made by the States and in the strong fight they have put up for India, and who besides the States generally, seems particularly to have a pet aversion to this State and all connected with it, has, in the course of a recent article, which could not have been better written by the worst enemy of the States and of their subjects—been good enough to assign some amazing and highly discreditable motives to the Princes. With the activities and notorious manner of their attempting insidiously to stir up hatred and discontent against the Rulers and Governments amongst the

States subjects, I have dealt in the past on various occasions and I would specially invite attention to my speech here of the 3rd October, 1929. I would have preferred to-day not to make any reference to such petty minded and pervesely prejudiced individuals—who, posing as friends of the States subjects, have already done, and will if they have their way continue to do incalculable harm and mischief to them and their States—were it not for the fact that I wish to take this opportunity of uttering a serious word of caution to all concerned as to the attempts which, there is little doubt, will in any case be made in various quarters to cause a spilit between States and States, and between States and British India, in—let us hope and pray the forlorn—attempt to undo the good work which we have done and in order to deprive India and its people of what they have already gained at the Round Table Conference.

I was asked on more than one occasion at the Round Table Conference what proportion of the States was likely to enter into the Federation. I had no hesitation in saying that if the settlement is just and fair, if the rights of the States are safeguarded, and if they can feel secure in entering such a Federation it is not only likely but very probable—and I spoke as one who has had considerable opportunities of ganging the feelings of the Princes and States, as Chancellor of the Chamber of Princes for a long time and as one who has kept in touch with them before and since—that at least seventy-five per cent. of the States, if not more, will come into the Federation, and that they will come in immediately; and that most of the rest will follow as experience is gained and confidence is established; and though it is dangerous to prophesy I venture still to adhere to that opinion.

Before making one or two further observations which aply both to British Indian and our States, I would like to point out the great opportunities and field which have been opened out, far beyond the limited confines of our respective States, for playing a prominent part in shaping the destinies of our Motherland, to the cadets of the various Reigning Houses and to the Chiefs and Nobles and other notables and public men, along with other State subjects.

Gentlemen, I fear I have already detained you long enought; but my statement to-day would be lacking in an essential detail if I failed to make at least a brief reference to the question of the declaration of the rights of the States subjects raised in the Conference by some British Indian Leaders, whose sincerity of purpose and good intentions I am the first to recognise. These matters did not, and could not, really come within the purview of the Conference since they related to the Indian States and their subjects, which matters are naturally the concern of the Rulers, Governments and the people of the States, and of them alone, But I would invite attention to what I said in this connection at the rust Plenary Session of the Conference, which was to the effect that whilst the States must be influenced by the development of political ideas and institutions beyond their Frontiers, this is their affair. We know our States and our people; we live amongst our own folk and are in the most intimate contact with their needs and possibilities. We shall know how and when to adjust our system to any changing conditions; but we will do it in our, own time and in our own way, tree from all external interference. And in order to make the position clear, I took another opportunity at the Conference of making a few brief observations, when I pointed out that a good Ruler—whether he be a constitutional monarch, or what is known as an autocrat—is not only the servant of his people, but also their protector, whose duty it is to safeguard all the rights and liberties that are due to them, just as it is the duty of a Ruler to safeguard the corresponding rights of the State. I repeated what I have said previously, that any Ruler, if he is a bad Ruler—be he in the East or in the West—was best soon eliminated in the interests of all concerned; but that when all that had been said and done; people who posses intimate experience of the working of the States—some modern, some old-fashioned, each possesing different standards of Government, different stages of political advancement, which also applies to their subjects—know that there were not really anything like the number of bad Rulers in India that we have had depicted in false pictures. I went on to remind them of what we have done in this connection in our own State, with which no one is better acquainted than you, the subjects of our State, and of which you and we—my Government and I—alone are the best judges. And I invited attention, amongst other pronouncements on the subject, to my speeches in the Legislative Assembly of the 20th January, 1928, and at the administrative Conference on the 3rd October, 1929, and also to the Resolution which I had the proud privilege of moving some two years ago in the Chamber of Princes, which was unanimously accepted by the whole Chamber. I went on to state that this very important question of mutual benefit to the States and their subjects was thus clearly before the Princes; and I would only add to-day that reforms which emanate voluntarily from within the States, and on the initiative of the Rulers and their Governments, and in close harmony with the people of the Sates and the circumstances prevailing therein, can alone be efficacious and be found to be satisfactory in the long run; and that in such matters, whilst in some States there my unfortunately be much left to be desired, any undue forcing of the pace cannot but have the most unsatisfactory results for all concerned. I hope that I may be enabled to have another opportunity are long of dealing at greater length with this important question, so far as I and my Government, and you, my beloved subjects, are concerned.

Turning now to the safeguards proposed during the period of transition—and the length of that period depends on us Indians of British India and the States—some of which will doubtless need further examination, and which we have been assured will be so framed and exercised as not to prejudice the advance of India through the constitution to full responsibility for her own Government, I will only mention to-day what was pointed out in the speech of Mr. Ramsay MacDonald in closing the Conference, namely, that such safeguards are either expressed or implicit in every free constitution from the rising sun to the setting sun, and that if we Indians were drafting our own constitution without any outside assistance or consultation we could not do so without ourselves embodying safeguards in it.

And now, Gentlemen, in bringing my speech to a close, let me express my satisfaction at the release of some of the leaders of public opinion in India in order to secure for the scheme evolved at the Conference free and full consideration by all sections of opinion in India, and to echo the words of the Manifesto issued by us on landing in India on Friday, namely, that it is our hope that an atmosphere of complete peace will be created for the consideration of these questions of high import, and that the release of other political prisoners, who are not guilty of any serious offences, will follow—a course which both in the. Sankey Committee, and even long before that I have expressed my conviction on more occasions than one would be likely to produce in a large measure the most beneficial results for Great Britain and India.

In conclusion, I will venture to re-echo His Excellency the Viceroy in saying that if only distrust can be replaced in India by a spirit of mutual confidence and co-operation—and this I venture to say applies as much in regard to the relations of Great Britain and India as to the relations, present and future, between the States and British India—then, even in spite of the world crisis, we may see the dawn of a new optimism and the opening of new ways for the development of India's economic strength. I would also earnestly appeal for co-operation. We have provided the foundations of a responsible and stable government for the whole of India. None of us is satisfied with every detail; nobody charged with a task of this importance ever was. But we have done a great work; let us carry it forward to completion in a great spirit. Big issues and small men-like a great empire and small minds—go ill together, as I ventured to remind them in England, and as I now venture similarly to remind all concerned in India. Let us put aside all minor considerations and anything that may be mean or petty; but united now and henceforth throw into the task that we are in the utmost of which we are capable to ensure the contentment and prosperity of three hundred and twenty millions of our fellow Countrymen who look to us for guidance and direction in the attainment of their ideals. Surely so noble a purpose should, and shall, inspire in each and all of us a spirit of service and of sacrifice for the welfare of our beloved Motherland; to maintain and strengthen the honourable and lasting friendship between Great Britain and India; and through these twin forces to buttress even more securely the peace of the world.

# Annexure 2

**Speech delivered by His Highness the Maharajah of Bikaner at a State Banquet at Lallgarh on the 11th February, 1931.**

*Ladies and Gentlemen,*

I do not quite know whether or not to thank my dear son for getting me up on my hind legs to have to make another Speech after the very long speech which I had to inflict on several of you only on Monday last. I think I might well have been given a respite, specially as since the 9th September upto the 19th January I did nothing but listen to one perpetual stream of oratory, from morning till late in the evening, at the League of Nations including its Committess, at the Imperial conference including the committees and at the Round Table Conference including its Committees, till one almost felt that one could not eat, drink, or sleep, without having to be lulled asleep by speeches. I am happy, however, to have to say that I did not open my mouth more than twice upto the beginning of the Round Table Conference in London—although one speech at Geneva and one in the Imperial Conference were inevitable. The reason, I trust, need not be explained, viz., that I am not fond of hearing my own voice, much less of inflicting it on others. But alas! matters all changed with a vengeance and I found to my cost that at the Round Table Conference the number of days I did not open my mouth could, unfortunately be counted on the fingers of one hand—whilst equally unfortunately for myself and others I had at times to make as many as two and three long speeches in one day.

However to be more serious I do thank the Maharaj Kumar for the very dutiful and affectionate sentiments which have inspired him to break the rule for which all the same I am a not sure that he should be admonished—and I am happy to feel that he is inspired by the same feelings as many of you, my loyal friends and Officials, without whose loyal co-operation and support & I and my Government would be nowhere.

I should however really be grateful in one way to the Prince for having given me the opportunity of saying one or two things which could more properly be said here. And today speaking before so many of the fair sex I wish particularly to pay my quota of respectful tribute to the Womanhood of India, so gracefully and effectively represented at the Round Table Conference by two of the most accomplished and charming of our Indian sisters—Begum Shah Nawaz and Mrs. Subbarayan. The manner in which they deported themselves and took their due and prominent part in the Conference, and their speeches at the Conference particularly full, if I may say so, of patriotism and commonsense when they urged the claims of India to attain her just dues, were such as moved us all immensely.

I do not know that there is more for me to say to-night to supplement my speech of last Monday, beyond summing up my impressions of the last few days since my return home. So far as I can judge from conversation in British India, in the short time available, and from glimpses from the Newspapers of what is happening, there seems to be still a considerable amount of ignorance of the real work and of the very liberal and gratifying character of what has been achieved at the Round Table Conference.

Our greatest consolation is that we, of the States and British India, were doing a big work in a big way. Whatever the result, we have the satisfaction, so far as we are concerned, of knowing that a great occasion was faced in—may I say with all modesty—a great and constructive spirit by all concerned.

It is the work of the Delegates who have returned from the Round Table Conference to spread knowledge and to explain the various details, including safe-guards, which need to be better understood. But what is more important is that the great constructive work, and progress made, and the reulst achieved, should be appreciated at their proper value.

We have now done the first part of our work; and for the immediate moment great issues lie in other hands.

I venture to say that more active and effective official publicity is one of the greatest and most urgent needs of the moment. The Delegates to the Round Table Conference were only few and their opportunities now in India are limited.

India has really gained far more than the mere substance of independence. Let us hope and pray that moderate and mutual understanding and goodwill will prevail for the common benefit of India and of the Empire.

# Annexure 3

## Speech Delivered by His Highness the Maharajah at the State Banquet of the Princes and Other Guest on the 9th March, 1931, at Bikaner

*Your Highnesses; Ladies and Gentlemen;*

In proposing the toast of this evening my first duty, and a very pleasant one at that, is to offer the warmest of welcomes to Their Highnesses, my Brother Princes, and to my other Guests; and to give expression to the great pleasure which I derive in having them in our midst. I think I may modestly claim that a gathering so distinguished and so numerically large has not been witnessed or surpassed in the State in the past, except on the occasions of the Wedding of my children. But for the time at my disposal since I returned from England to India last month, I should have hoped to welcome a still larger number of Princes, Members of their Royal Families, their Ministers and other distinguished Guests from the Indian States on the one hand and our friends from British India on the other, today. I rejoice, however, at the presence of so many of my Brother Princes, accompanied by Members of their Royal Families, their Ministers and High Officers.

2. I ask forgiveness for not referring to the Princes in the strict order of Precedence; and I ask forgiveness likewise for not referring in great detail to each and every one of my distinguished and honoured Guests amongst the Princes, their Families, their Ministers and the Guests from British India.

3. But first and foremost I wish to refer to my oldest friend and dear Brother, His Highness of Nawanagar. Time will not permit me to say all that I would like to say about him tonight but we all know the very great, important and distinguished part which His Highness the Jam Sahib has played in the Chamber of Princes and in the matters appertaining to our Order and to our States.

4. Next I refer to another very dear and old friend of mine, His Highness the Maharana Raj Sahib of Wankaner, who, I am glad to see, is accompanied by that delightful young Prince, whom I am proud to claim as my Nephew.

5. Then there are my Brothers, Their Highnesses of Datia, Tajpipla and Sangli, who also need no introduction to you all here tonight.

6. Amongst the younger generation of Princes whom we all, I am sure, particularly welcome and whom we wish to see taking their due place in all seriousness and in all earnestness amongst us as those upon whom will fall the mantle, the duties and responsibilities of carrying on where we of the older generation leave offl; and helping us—now that we at this end are getting old and decrepit and infirm—to darry on, during our time and after us, the task which we have undertaken for the benefit and for the rectification and preservation of the rights of the Princes and States of India.

7. Here amongst the younger generation we see my Nephews, Their Highnesses of Dungarpur, Jhalawar and Narsingarh—whose lamented Fathers I had the honour of claiming as my personal friends.

8. Another Nephew of mine, Hig Highness of Rampur, we welcome for the first time after his Accession and we share with him in the bereavement which he and the Royal Family of Rampur have suffered and we as an Order of Princes of India have suffered by the lamentable and premature demise of my Elder Brother, His late Highness of Rampur.

9. His Highness of Danta is another Nephew of mine, whose revered Father I had the pleasure of knowing and who was a school-fellow of mine; and I feel sure that you all share with me the gratification which I derive at the active part that His Highness is taking in matters relating to the Princes and States, including the workthat comes before us in the Sessions of the Chamber of Princes.

10. We welcome also the young Princess of Wankaner and Rampur and the Ministers who have come independently of the Princes present here, amongst whom I feel delighted to welcome today at least two Members of the Gwalior Government in thew persons of my old friend and comrade, Sardar Sir Appaji Rao Shitole, and Major Hashmatullah Khan; whilst I hope Major=General Rajwade will be arriving here tomorrow; and we regret that illness has prevented Nawab Sultan Ahmad from also coming on this occasion. Then I must mention also the name of the Political Secretary of Bhopal, Qazi Ali Hyder Abbasi, who has come here at my invitation; although, I feel sure that you all regret with me the unavoidable absence of my Brother, His Highness the Ruler of Bhopal, who played such a magnificent, important and useful and, may I add, most careful, parts in safeguarding the interests of the States at the Round Table Conference and whose association with myself I shall to my dying day look back upon with the greatest pleasure and satisfaction.

11. With reference to the Guests from the States I desire also to mention tonight the name of that public-spirited gentleman and philanthropist Seth, Sir Hukam Chand of Indore.

12. We are delighted no less to welcome today our friends from British India. Owing to recent conversations between His Excellency the Viceroy and Mahatma Gandhi and the Session, which is now going on, of the Imperial Legislatures, and above all the great need for not letting get cold the great work we left off in London at the Round Table Conference, I much regret that several of my British Indian friends and erstwhile colleagues whom I had hoped to welcome here on this occasion are not present here. I am glad however that my friend, Mr. Ghuznavi, who has the distinction tonight of being the sole representative from amongst the British Indian leaders, is at least able to be present here. And I desire on behalf of myself- and I am sure on behalf of Your Highnesses and the other Ministers and others who come from the States—to thank him for all the trouble that he has taken to come for barely 36 hours, to be with us on this occasion. I hope in the course of the next day or two also to welcome Sir C.P. Ramaswami Aiyer and Sir Parasuram Patro, and I trust also Dewan Bahadur Ramawsami Mudaliyar, in our midst.

13. Apart from the great pleasure which I feel in welcoming my Brother Princes and the other guests here, I think it is a matter of mutual satisfaction to us to think that we shall here be enabled without being rushed to have opportunities of informally discussing important questions which will shortly be coming up before the Chamber of Princes in Delhi next week, and especially matters relating to Federation for which we could not possibly have had available to us the same amount of time in Delhi before discussions begin at the informal meetings of the Princes and in the formal session of the Chamber of Princes.

14. I consider, Your Highnesses, Ladies and Gentlemen, the presence here today of my Brother Princes and other guests as a good augury for the success of the work which we shall shortly have to tackle in Delhi. And I desire particularly to refer to Federation and all the issues involved therewith which the Princes and Ministers of the States will have to consider in Delhi with the object of ensuring for the States their due position in the future constitution of India as co-equal partners with British India guaranteeing their Treaties and their internal Sovereignty and safeguarding their interests, including those of their subjects on terms just and honourable alike to the States and British India.

15. Even more auspicious Do I look—as I am sure Your Highnesses,

and you, Ladies and Gentlemen, will agree—upon the satisfactory settlement brought about by His Excellency the Viceroy in the course of his recent conversations with Mahatma Gandhi. I feel equally sure that I am voicing the sentiments of the Princes and all present here when I take this opportunity of once again giving expression to our warmest congratulations and sincere flicitations to that noble Viceroy, Lord Irwin, on the great personal triumph which he has achieved, which is the crowning act of his Viceroyalty, and upon the remarkable patience and generous statesmanship and the great courage which he has displayed through these discussions, as indeed throughout the momentons and troublous five years of his Viceroyalty.

16. The obvious need for the happy termination of the recent most unhappy intemencene warfare in India was apparent to any sensible person. But, in spite of the innumerable congratulatory messages which Lord Irwin has received from all parts of the world and from all classes and communities, in spite of the views which we the Ruling Princes of India—who have a very real stake in the country—hold, in spite of the views which British Indians holding the most moderate views and of proven loyalty hold, and in spite of the views expressed by the Members of the British Parliament and the views of the European non-official community in India upon this magnificent achievement of Lord Irwin, ill—informed and unfair criticisms of some extremists and die-hards in England—and I have no doubt also in India to whom we too have a good handful, but I am referring chiefly here to the die-hards of England—who, unmindful of the best interests of India, of Great Britain and of the Empire, believe apparently in the doctrine of Martial Law and "No damn nonsense" (begging the ladies' pardon), and who strangely enough would seem to favour indicriminate shooting and causing blood-shed all round, bringing in its train intense and widespread feelings of bitterness and hatred, and doing irrevocable harm to Great Britain and India affecting the well-being and prosperity of the two peoples. Trqnauility and ordered progress of the country and peace with honour apparently seem to make no appeal to such persons.

17. History is again repeating itself. After the Mutiny, when there was a need for settling down the country and giving pardon to those offenders not guilty of serious misdemeanour the term"Clemency Canning" was coined as meaning reproach to Lord Canning by those who thirsted for everybody's blood as some slight compensation for the terrors of the Mutiny—a term which is now looked upon happily as the greatest compliment that could be paid to the memory of that great Viceroy of that period, Lord Canning. And I feel sure that all

the unfair criticisms and attacks made upon Lord Irwin in the past, or those now being made, or which may hereafter be made, will be appraised at their right value by the historians of the future, who, I am confident, as I am sure you are all confident, will have nothing but unstinted parise to bestow upon his noble, courageous and unselfish Viceroy, who, without looking to right or left, has pursued the clear path before him in the interests of England and India.

18. Surely, Your Highness, Ladies and Gentlemen, whether we agree or disagree with the Civil Disobedience movement—and most of us of course disagree with the same—or whether we approve or disapprove of some of the activities of certain Congress and other extremists leaders, the healing of wounds and the promotion of peace and good-will all round is at all times worthy of the best efforts of all human beings, and especially those placed of high positions and who are responsible for the carrying on of the Governments, such as those of Great Britain and of India.

19. For myself, and I feel sure I can add for all of you here, I would express the earnest hope that in the future India will have done with all the turmoil and trouble of the past and that we shall all proceed in constructive work—the States, British India and the Britishers—all working together to achieve the common goal for the common good.

20. Looking from the personal point of view, one advantage, which I feel will result nom the present truce—which we might call peace as it surely has reached that stage now—will be that Congress leaders and representatives of the Governments of our States will be brought in closer contact and to work hand in hand for the glory of India and the Empire. My experience in the past has been that a great deal of the unfriendly attitude and criticisms of States, their Rulers and their Governments which we have heard of and read is due to ignorance and lack of personal contact with and knowledge of the States and us all who represent the States, and of the real condition of affairs prevailing in our territories. This was evident even in the case of some Moderate and Liberal representatives of British India at the Round Table Conference. But our close association in London recently was,I am happy to feel, responsible for removing many such wrong impressions and suspicions and for bringing about a better apreciation of each other's stand-points and good qualities and mutual good-will and co-operation. The same, I venture to predict, will result from the association of the representatives of the States with the leaders of the Indian National Congress and other leaders, who I am glad to think will now similarly be participating in the second phase of the Round Table Conference shortly in India.

21. Your Highnesses, Ladies and Gentlemen, just as in common with those other Princes who have made ourselves intimate with the Federal question I have said that Federation has no terrors for us, I make bold to say that I personally have no misgivings—nor I feel sure is there any need on the part of the Princes and States as a body to entertain any misgivings—as regards what may be said on stray occasions and as stray words by stray individuals in the Press or on the platform in British India in connection with the internal affairs of our States which are outside the scope and purview of the Round Table Conference, or anything which might at first sight appear hostile to the State. Whilst it is the obvious duty, whether looked at from the point of view of both the East and the West, of the Rulers and Governments of our States to rule over their people well and in the best interests of their States and their subjects. attempts by outside authorities to interfere with what are the domestic, and the purely domestic, affairs of the State cannot but the productive of the greatest harm in more directions than one, apart from any righteous indignation or resentment caused to not only the Rulers and Governments of such States, but I venture to add even the vast majority of the loyal millions comprising the bona fide subjects of the Princes of India. I venture therefore to say that it therefore behoves British India as much as it behoves the Indian States to see to it that nothing is done or said on the part of either side which might be taken as undue interference in the purely domestic affairs of either side, or which is apt to disturb the harmonious and happy relations which have been brought about largely through our work and association at the Round Table Conference in London between the two great Indians, which, though certainly situated in one country and comprising as they do people of the same flesh and blood, are undoubtedly and irrefutably—geographically, politically and constitutionally—two clear and separate units or entities. Any closer association of these two great parts of our country can obviously come about only voluntarily and by the good-will and consent of both parties, and not through coercion or threats which would only retard matters, and, as I have said, do harm all around.

22. I need not reiterate what has been said by me and others in regard to the sweeping accusations and wholesale charges indiscriminately made against Rulers and Governments of States without regard to truth, justice or facts. No fair-minded person could possibly believe that all States and Rulers of States are bad, just as I fear it would be equally untenable to maintain that all Rulers are good or that all Governments or States carry on their duties as they

should. I feel sure, without repeating all that I have said in this connection on former occasions in India as well as in England, that Your Highnesses will be the first to agree with me that it is the duty of every wise Ruler and every good Government worthy of the name to see to it that, where the need is found for the introduction of necessary reforms and for effecting improvements called for it any direction, this should be done and done voluntarily and without loss of time. But I venture to feel that the greatest caution and circumspection will be needed by both sides in regard to any such matters. When I say both sides I refer to the States vis-a-vis British India and to British India vis-a-vis our States.

23. To our British India friends of all parties I venture especially to emphasize the need for sifting the wheat from the chaff, of testing the many statements and stories, often deliberate and malicious inventions, before accepting their veracity and to satisfy themselves as to the truth of any allegations against the Rulers of Governments of States before they accept them as facts.

24. Numerous instances could be given of incorrect facts and figures having been quoted and published which, it is a surprising, are accepted by many people in British India as being correct, but which it would be the easiest thing to refute, were it not for the fact that so many deliberately false and malicious things are said and written that it would be a sheer waste of time for the Governments of States to engage themselves in contradicting them and explaining away such false statements and which in the circumstances are best treated with the contempt which they deserve. Similarly, except in cases of very serious charges, or matters which may be considered of sufficient importance, it would equally be a waste of time, energy and money to prosecute the individuals or some of the papers that tarnish the fair name of Journalism and journalists. Then again, the claims and titles of individuals and institutions, posing to be the subjects of States and to speak for them, have to be carefully borne in mind. In other words, their credentials must be scrutinised and examined before their claim to speak for, or on such matters, could be accepted as valid. To all these I have alluded in my previous speeches in considerable detail, to which I would invite the attention of all those who may care to pursue the subject further. Much could be said about the political views and the activities of certain so-called leaders of States subjects, or of those who claim to be members of the institutions of bona fide subjects of the States, which would show directly how much such leaders and institutions are in conflict with the real views and sentiments entertained by our bona fide subjects. But when all

that has been said and done, if one were to believe all that such so-called leaders, representatives and institutions connected with our States claim to represent, one would imagine that a veritable reign of terror prevailed throughout the length and breadth of each and every Indian State, that their Ruler, inspired with the most unworthy motives, are blind not only to the interests and well-being of their subjects but also to the interests and well-being of their own children and their children's children;—in other words to their own Dynasties—Rulers who, if one would believe all these, were plunging head-long into disaster, to which such malicious, wicked and shortsighted policy would assuredly lead all Rulers who might be so ill-advised as to follow such a course or to take such a view. Assuredly and happily, there are not many such States but only a very few to be found in our midst.

25. With reference to the claims of Fundamental Rights of our subjects, of which we have heard and read so much lately, one would almost imagine that the need for Fundamental Rights exists because there are no such rights at present recognised or in existence in our States. I am ready, so far as I, my State and my Government are concerned, to take up the challenge. I utterly fail to conceive how it can be interpreted that what I said in my speech here on the 9th February that last was all that it is represented, or, rather I should say, misrepresented, to have been if justice or truth is really to prevail. My attitude on the subject speaks, and my words uttered on that occasion printed now in cold type speak, for themselves.

26. In an after dinner speech like tonight's I would not venture to take up the time of Your Highnesses, Ladies and Gentlemen, by reiterating at length all that I said on various occasions on the subject of the essential principles of good government; but may I invite the attention of all who care to read them to my speeches of the past on the subject, and particularly to my speech in the Legislative Assembly on the 20th January, 1928, in which I referred especially to the seven essentials of good government which were:

1. A fixed well-defined Privy Purse and a clear dividing line between the Ruler's personal expenditure and that of the State;
2. Security of life and property;
3. An independent Judiciary;
4. The reign of Law;
5. The stability of Public Services;
6. Efficiency and continuity of administration; and
7. Beneficial Rule in the interests of the general well-being and

contentment of the subjects of the States.

And in regard to each of the seven points, I herewith offer a challenge to any such so-called State subject or leaders or repred sentative of State subjects or institutions to prove that there is no fixed well-defined Privy Purse and a clear demarcating line between my personal expenditure and that of my Family and of the State. If there is one matter in which I and my Government take particular pride, it is in regard to those strict principles which are observed and enforced in this connection. I similarly ask anyone to prove that there is no security of life and property in my State; and likewise, that the Judiciary of the State from the High Court downwards is, so far as the Ruler and the Government of the State are concerned, not a perfectly independent Judiciary. Likewise let anyone prove that the reign of Law does not supervene in my State; that there is no stability of Public Services, except for those who are evil-doers or oppressors of my subjects, or that efficiency and continuity of administration is not paid regard to by me and my Government, or that my Rule and the administration of my Government is not in the interests of the general well-being and for the contentment of my subjects.

27. Speaking here to-night before a large gathering of the Rulers, their Royal Families, and their Ministers and other individuals of our States, who I hope I may justly claim to be a sporting lot, I feel sure that my Government would be glad to back up my challenge with a sum of rupees one lakh, which I will further supplement with a sum of another lakh of rupees from my Privy Purse against a lakh of rupees placed also on the bet by our critics: and anyone who forfeits that sum, let him give that sum for the benefit of some public institution or other beneficial work of public utility in the Bikaner State. We would accept that challenge.

28. I am also prepared further to take up another challenge by making at the earliest moment possible a still more detailed statement in regard to the policy of my Government and myself in connection with our subjects, on which I have already made many public and clear pronouncements. But this requires a little time in order that such a statement may be exhaustive and that it should deal not only with one or two particular classes of my subjects but, as far as possible, with each and every community, class or interests which comprise my subjects; and in order further that it may be just to all concerned, it is equally essential that such a statement should also embrace the corresponding rights of the States, the Rulers of States, and the Governments of States as well as the obligations of such subjects

towards them. As I said in my speech here on the 9th February, I hope I may be enabled to have another opportunity before long of dealing with this important question, so far as I and my Government and my subjects are concerned. While preferring to leave out all mention of the motives and aims inspiring certain gentlemen posing as friends or representatives of States subjects, I recognise—and I gladly recognise—as I am sure do my Brother Princes, the sincerity and honesty of purpose of some British Indian friends who have spoken on the subject in England and in India.

29. Your Highnesses, Ladies and Gentlemen, I have come to the end of my speech; but before I conclude, may I be permitted to say that the work that lies before us all, whether we belong to the Indian States or whether we belong to British India, is of much utmost importance to our common Motherland and will demand such a vast amount of time, work, thought and preparation and attention to details that I venture to think that the time and energy which at present both sides have occasionally been frittering away and dissipating in dealing with such spiteful and false propaganda against the States might well be devoted to a better cause, the promotion of the common interests of the people of both the Indias, and of building up a great and constructive scheme which will secure for India, including the Indian States, their due and rightful measure of constitutional advance and independence and which will enable the whole Country finally to take its place as an honourable and equal partner in the great British Empire, to which we are all proud to belong, rebounding to the glory of Great Britain and India.

30. Your Highnesses, Ladies and Gentlemen, it is with the most sincere and genuine pleasure that I now ask you to drink with me to the health, prosperity and long life of my Brother Princes, the Members of their Royal Families and of my Guests here including my friends, present or absent, of British India, and to couple with the toast the happy termination of the activities upon which we are engaged, which will bring the two great Indias into a whole and happy one, contributing to the happiness and well-being of our country and of the Empire.

## Annexure 4

### Statement to the Press by Lieut.—General His Highness the Maharajah of Bikaner on the 3rd September, 1931

Whilst I appreciate your countesy in asking me for an expression of my views, I am reluctant to respond. We are meeting to implement the general conclusions of last winter; I venture to think that we shall best further that work by throwing outselves into the task together, rather than possibly clouding the atmosphere by individual expressions of opinion. That is especially the case when, for more than a fortnight whilst on my way to Europe, I have been out of intimate touch with all that has happened in India and Great Britain.

We are dealing with the governance of three hundred and fifty-one millions of the human race. There are diverse conditions, and persons holding different political views, in British India; the Princes and States represent varied traditions, systems of administration and stages of development. But I am emboldened to hope that, behind inevitable divergencies, there lies a general determination resolutely to pursue a great deal. The vision of a United India. embracing British India and the Indian States in one great federation under the Crown, equal partner in the British Commonwealth, still grips our imagination.

As our objective is a United India, carrying the co-operation of all the loyal and patriotic men, the participation in the Round Table Conference of the Congress, through its representative. Mr. Gandhi, is to be welcomed.

I must not anticipate the case of the Indian States which will be put forward at the Conference and in Committees—and especially in the Federal Structure Committee—by the Indian States Delegation, embracing, besides the other distinguished persons, that veteran Prince His Highness the Geokwar of Baroda, and the Chancellor of the Chamber of Princes, His Highness the Nawab of Bhopal. Today, for special reasons, I would much rather not discuss any matters which may appear in the least degree controversial. No more unpleasant duty ever fell to me than to be compelled to issue a statement to the Indian Press last June on developments which had occurred since we separated in London. But my duty to my Emperor and to the Order of Indian Princes, and the insistent demand of several of my friends, compelled me to put personal considerations aside; for questions full of import to the future of the States were involved, and there was risk of some of the smaller States, perhaps not fully seized of the implications of a Federal Scheme, being led into grave decisions at short notice. However, I may safely say this ; whilst it would be idle to disguise the fact that, through a combination of circumstances into the details of which it is not necessary to enter, a certain measure of alarm was created in regard to the possible consequences of federation, it is possible that the telegraphic reports from India have exaggerated the differences between the Princes in respect to the Federal Scheme so far as it has been shaped.

With a wider study of the Scheme tentatively evolved, and a better appreciation of all that was done and urged on behalf of the States, both large and small, during our last Session, I have little doubt that many of the fears entertained have been dispelled; and I am confident that the contribution to be made in the near future by our Delegation will go a long way in further enlightening public opinion in the States. I have, throughout my life, dating back even before my long term of office as first Chancellor of the Chamber of Princes, as also in the particular discharge of my duties as a Member of the Federal Structure Committee, always borne in mind, and fought for the legitimate rights and aspirations of the smaller States, which have to be safeguarded as zealously as the interests of the larger States—a task in which I am happy to feel we have the sympathy and support especially of the Chancellor of the Chamber of Princes.

So far as the States are concerned, the position can be put in a nutshell. The crux of the question to my mind is this. When the Princes and States were last year invited to join a Federation, they generally and gladly expressed their willingness to consider the question on terms of equality with British India, and even to make some sacrifices, on the condition that India remained under the Crown and that the Sovereignty and autonomy of the States and their Treaty Rights were adequately safeguarded. Provided that the remaining principles and details are dealt with as satisfactorily as the various questions discussed so far, and the Princes, through essential safeguards, feel that the future existence and Sovrreignty of the States as a separate entity are not threatened, I am as sure today, as I was when we last met, that the great majority of the States will join the Federation. Otherwise, of course, no Ruler—who stands as a trustee of his State and subjects and the custodian of their rights—will feel free to enter a Federation.

I am confident that from this position the States as a body will not resile, even though there are yet many practical difficulties to be faced, in regard to which it is to be hoped the majority of our colleagues from British India will not place any insuperable obstacles. We of the Indian States Delegation will again earnestly endeavour to make our contribution to the progress and prosperity of India and the welfare of our fellow-countrymen, and thereby to render yet another service to our Kind-Emperor, to whom we are so firmly attached by ties of the deepest loyalty and unflinching personal devotion.

# Annexure 5

## Speech by Lieut.-General His Highness the Maharajah of Bikaner at the Federal Structure Committee Meeting on the 15th September, 1931

I do not propose, My Lord Chancellor, to make a speech today generally on the important questions affecting the States. Doubtless an opportunity will occur later, perhaps on questions such as that of the relative representation and percentage of the States in the Federal Legislature; and similar opportunities will also occur, I have no doubt, when we take up questions such as that touched upon by my friend Sir Tej Bahadur Sapru with regard to questions of confederation, and so on.

But today, Sir, before I begin to represent what I believe will be the general view -and the provisional views, subject to the completed picture—of the Indian States Delegation; and any other Princes and Ministers having particular views of their own will of course be free to express them—may I just say a word or two. On the 7th September it was my privilege, in the absence of the revered and esteemed leader of our Delegation, His Highness the Maharaja Gaekwar of Baroda, and of His Highness the Chancellor, to express the very great pleasure and satisfaction which we derived from the presence of you, Mr. Lord Chancellor, here as Chairman of our Committee, to whom we all owe so much. I also generally desire to join in the words of welcome to the new members of our sub-Committee, and particularly to Mahatma Gandhi, who represents the most important political party in India, which unfortunately was not represented last time; and similarly to join in the words of welcome extended by some of mv other colleagues to my old friend Pandit Madan Mohan Malaviya. I feel sure that in doing so I am voicing the general sentiments of the Indian States Delegation.

I would also just point out that, whilst I am, personally speaking, in general agreement with many of the details mentioned by Sir Tej Bahadur Sapru and Sir Muhammad Shafi, it has to be realised that it is not, by the very nature of things, in the power of any of us who are on the Indian States Delegation to dictate policy to all Rulers and

Governments of States in regard to certain matters which are covered by Head II. In the circumstances, therefore, it will inevitably be a matter, largely at least, for the States concerned to decide.

Before I go further to particulars, may I also say one word which may have to be amplified later: that is that there appears to be a general confusion in the minds of many here as regards what really are the States. We hear of 500 and 600 States. When I am talking of the States today, I should be understood as referring to the States proper, and not so much referring to what are in Aitcheson's Treaties—I am quoting from authoritative works of reference—referred to as the petty States, Talukdaris, Jagirs, and so on, though it is the duty and the care and the desire of our Delegation to safeguard all the reasonable interests of all concerned.

I have already taken an opportunity, since arriving in England, to voice the sentiments, which I have all along entertained in regard to the smaller States; and my past record of services in the Chamber of Princes and elsewhere has shown the sympathy which I have always evinced for them, and my desire, as well as my fights in the past, to safeguard all their legitimate interests.

With these observations, Sir, coming to Question I, I think there can be little doubt. I am glad to see that Sir Tej Bahadur Sapru and Sir Muhammad Shafi, who have spoken before me, recognise the case of the States, and I am particularly indebted to Sir Tej for supporting what I had said during our last session, that we have here to devise a special constitution for the States, as—to quote the words used today by Sir Tej—there is no parallel to the States in the constitutions of the world. As to Question I, Sir, and the method of selection of States' representatives for the Federal Legislature, so far as the Upper House is concerned, there will have to be nomination by States as Governments.

And in the Lower House it is a difficult matter for any of us on this side to lay down anything definite; but it is obvious that the States, big and small, are at present in various stages of advancement, political, social, economic, administrative, and so on, and, in the circumstances, I have no doubt that it will be according to the conditions prevailing in each State. That is to say, if there are Legislative Assemblies, the actions of the Governments of the States concerned will doubtless be based on lines different from those in States where there are no Assemblies. We hope in time the majority of the States will have such institutions. But the method of sending representatives to the Lower House will inevitably have to be left to each State according to the conditions prevailing therein.

For my part may I say that, having a Legislative Assembly, and having had it since 1913—I have not had time to go into that question in detail; and much will depend on what the final scheme evolved here is, and on the completed picture—I have no doubt that we shall have some method by which the Bikaner Legislative Assembly will have a voice in the selection of our representative in the Lower House. (Applause.) But I am giving you my personal views; I want to make that clear. His Highness of Bhopal wishes me to say that he shares exactly my sentiments in regard to his State, where he also has a Legislative Council.

As regards representation by groups of States, there are certain questions which may come up for discussion at a later stage. If there are any of the important States—by which I mean in the upper category of States, big and small- which have to be grouped, those are points, like some other points, on which we shall have to have discussion and settlement later on amongst the States with the assistance of the Viceroy. The question of how the groups will do it is a point which will have to be discussed then. If I may say so, I am particularly glad to hear what Sir Tej has to say on this matter; I hope he has expressed the general sentiments of our friends from British India. I am referring to his statement that the question of the distribution of seats inter se, and so on, is a matter for the States to consider with the British Government, or, as I prefer to say, with the Viceroy as representative of the Crown.

As regard the method of selection in case of nomination, our views are that whilst the method will be based on lines analogous to those obtaining in British India it is possible that there will be certain necessary modifications to meet local conditions; and the rules will have to be made in this connection by the individual States or groups of States federating.

Sir Tej Bahadur Sapru has already cleared up one point, namely that in case there are officials from the States in the Upper House there will be a difference, and the case of official ministers, and so on, who may resign, will also have to be provided for.

Questions (iii) and (iv) do not concern the States, but question (v) deals with the provision to be made for the representation of special interests other than communal interests. We feel again that that is largely a matter for British India; but we feel that the numbers should be included in the quota of British Indian representation. We shall doubtless have further opportunities of discussing the question of special interests later on.

With regard to the qualifications for membership of the Upper and Lower Houses, it is important that, in our own interests, our representatives should have proper qualifications, so that the members we send will not be treated as inferior. From that point of view it will be very useful to us to know finally the details of what is to be settled or proposed in regard to the representation of British India.

On the question of the Oath of Allegiance, I do not think it is necessary for anyone on this side to speak even a word in support of our well-known loyalty to the King-Emperor. Many of the Princes have even risked their lives on the battle-field for their King-Emperor. As, however, it is a question of the sovereignty and internal autonomy of the States, and of their being a separate entity, this question has to be examined to see that there is no change in the status of the States. What we consider of special importance to us is that no form of the Oath of Allegiance, or anything in that connection, should detract from allegiance of a subject of an Indian State to the Sovereign of the Indian State concerned.

With regard to Question (viii), the provision to be made for nominated members, we take it that that is meant to provide for Crown representatives. I have nothing special to say at present on that subject, except that we do not want questions of paramountcy and matters of personal concern to the Princes—dynastic questions, and so on—to be included in that.

# Annexure 6

## Speech by Lieut-General His Highness the Maharajah of Bikaner. G.C.S.I. G.C.I.E. G.C.V.O., G.B.E., K.C.B., A.D.C., LL.D., at a Banquet held at Lallgarh on the 15th November, 1931.

*Ladies and Gentlemen*

I have to make a statement- in as brief terms as possible—about the work at the Rond table Conference. But before doing so, there is another subject which I shall allude to to-night.

It is not without prolonged and anxious consideration that I feel, it a duty to-night to refer to a matter of considerable delicacy—a matter which, in view of the turn which events have taken, has become one of grave import, not to one State, or to the States as a body, but, I venture to say, to the whole of India—whether comprising British territory or the territories of the India Princes. In all ordinary circumstances it is improper for any reference to be made to the internal affairs of anyone State or individual Rulers of States. However, under the exceptional curcumstances of to-day, I have no doubt that I am giving expression, not merely to the personal feelings of myself and my Government, but that I am voicing on behalf of the people of Bikaner generally, our respectful and sincere sympathy and earnest concern at the recent happenings in the States of Jammu and Kashmir. Apart altogether from the cordial relations which have existed between the two States, and the personal friendship between myself and the present Ruler and His Highness the late Maharajah of Kashmir, any such events could not but cause us great anxiety.

Only the unwise rush in and talk of matters with which they are not fully acquainted, Although upto the time of my leaving India for London in August last I had a very shrewd idea as to the various intitial troubles in Kashmir, I have yet fully to grasp all the intricate details of the past three months. It would be as impertinent on my part to say anything in priase of my Brother, Hig Highness the Maharajah of Kashmir, as it would be improper to apportion any blame to those responsible for the Government of Jammu and Kashmir. But, whatever the real facts, two things seem to stand out very clearly beyond all controversy.

First and foremost is the sympathetic and friendly attitude of our popular Viceroy, Lord Willingdon, to whom not only the Ruler and State of Kashmir, but, I would respectfully add, all Princes and States of India owe another debt of gratitude; and, secondly, that—whatever the facts and inner history as regards the earlier happenings in Kashmir, there is ample and incontestable evidence forthcoming—by the fact of outside agitation in, and of Jathas from, the neighbouring British Indian Province of the Punjab, wanting to march on and to force their way into Jammu and Kashmir—of clear interference, or attempts at interference, by persons from outside the State of Jammu and Kashmir, in the sovereignty and the domestic and internal affairs of Jammu and Kashmir. Things reaches such a stage that there has not only been disturbances of public tranquillity and affiyas in the territory of an Indian State, but there has been lamentable bloodshed, and even loss of life. And His Excellency the Viceroy, we gratefully recall, has had to issue an Ordinance, known as the protection against Disorcer Ordinance, 1931, prohibiting the entry from British India of Jathas or other bodies for such unlawful purposes into the terrotories of the Jammu and Kashmir State or indeed the territories of any other Prince or Chief in India.

Whilst I repeat that troubles of such a grave nature, affecting my Brother Princes and our Brethren of our Sister States, must always be matters of close and anxious concern to the Rulers, Governments and people of every States, I would rather to-night deal with certai sinister aspects and very grave consequences, which, I fear, are bound to arise sooner or later, if such an unfortunate condition of affairs is not put a stop to or in future cases in encouraged by those whose first care and anxiety should be for the prosperity and well-being of India as a whole, and for peace and harmony to prevail throughout our Motherland. As a Hindu Prince I am equally anxious to avoid saying one word which might give to my observations on the subject a communal colouring. But, rightly or wrongly, the Hindu-Muslem question has loomed large in the Kashmir troubles; and it does not require any deep thought or great perspicacity to realise the far wide repurcussions that are bound to follow, with all the serious consequences that they will bring in their train, in other States as well as in British India. As His Highness' Mohammedan subjects are largely preponderant in Kashmir, the Ruler of which State is a Hindu, so there will be found several States, which could be mentioned straight of f, of which the Rulers are Moslem, but where the population is overwhelmingly, or at any rate very largely Hindu. If such troubles have, unhappily, arisen in Kashmir, on any grounds of religious fervour, or under the influence of communal or other feelings, surely the Mohammedan Rulers of these other States will be the last to feel any particular gratitude towards any outside people who may have been responsible for having stirred up religious fanaticism and hatred in the Kashmir State; and I venture, in giving expression to-night to my thoughts on the subject, to join the prayer of the hundreds and thousands of thinking people in British India and in the States that the Kashmir State troubles may soon be a thing of the past, and the similar troubles affecting both the States, and British India may never be heard of in future.

Ladies and Gentlemen, I have so far successfully avoided giving Press Interviews and I was anxious as far as possible, to refrain from making any public statement in regard to the round Table Conference for various public reasons. My friend, His Highness the Ruler of Bhopal, Chancellor of the Chamber of Princes, will be returning to India before long; and on him will naturally devolve the responsibility of fully placing before the Princes and States and the general public the results of the Conference, including what has been achieved by the State Delegation. And it will be obviously improper for me in any case to anticipate anything His Highness may have to say that I will not attempt it. Moreover, anything I say from personal knowledge can only relate to events upto the 23rd October when I left London. Although I have kept in telegraphic touch as regards more important work done since leaving England, it has been obviously impossible, specially during the voyage, to acquaint myself fully with all the necessary details and everything that has happened during the last 3 weeks at the Round Table Conference. Furtheremore, the thousands of words in the daily cabled versions and Press news pouring in across the seas do not make it easy to grasp what really is happening or to guage with any accuracy the turn which events may daily be taking.

At the same time, I have received several communications from my Brother Princes asking for information about our work in London, and several other friends have also advised me that my silence may be misunderstood and even misrepresented in certain quartes. I will therefore ask you, Ladies and Gentlemen, for your further indulgence, whilst I make a brief statement of my personal views, though I believe they are shared by the great majority of my colleagues in the Indian States Delegation and many of my Brother Princes.

It is a matter of sincere regret to me that I had, through circumstances beyond my control, to leave London earlier than I desired. I think I can claim without egotism that it is not my practice to leave work unfinished; but I had no option in the matter.

As many of you are aware, I have, for some years past been in indifferent health. During a considerable part of my stay in Europe last time, and again this time, I was daily undergoing drastic medical treatment concurrently with carrying on the heavy work which we had to face at the Round Table Conference. The strain involved was practically continuous and very great, necessitating working from early morning upto late hours almost every night, of ten through the week-end. During the last Session my health, as you know, was considerably impaired. I have also not been able to obtain a proper holiday and rest since March 1930, and even then I was only enabled to avail myself of a much shorter holiday than usual. The doctors were therefore insistent that I must have immediate rest if I was to avoid a breakdown, and also that, after having undergone such treatment, I should not run the risk of another chill in the cold and foggy November of England.

Moreover, I have been absent from my State on Imperial Missions and Duty for some nine, out of the last eighteen months; much of my time in India between February and August last was also taken up with public work, as also for some time before I proceeded to Europe last year; and there are, as you know, some important and urgent matters connected with my own State, including certain items in the new Budget which commences in November—particularly in view of the changed economic conditions. Furthermore, in the general interests of the Princes and States, I have had to place at the disposal of the Chamber of Princes the services of my Prime Minister, Sir Manubhai Mehta; and, in the Committee and Conference in London, besides much other important space wor, Sir Manubhai, with Colonel Haksar, is one of the two Ministers particularly representing the Special Organization of the Chamber of Princes. It was therefore, all the more necessary in the interest of our own State that at least one of us should return to Bikaner.

Even though a few questions were still pending, most of the important work, in which the States are vitally concerned, had already been dealt with -especially that relating to constitutional and political issues, regarding which the task was allotted to me by His Highness the Chancellor of placing in the Federal Structure Committee the views of our States Delegation.

I have come away full of confidence in my colleagues of the Indian States Delegation—which I assert remains a strong and substantially united body—and in our Chancellor, His Highness the Ruler of Bhopal, to whose energy and ability I desire especially to pay ungrudging tribute, and who may confidently be relied upon to direct the policies of the States, and do everything possible to safeguard their interests until the Conference ends.

I should also like to express my gratitude which I am sure is shared by my Brother Princes and other Colleagues of the States—to many members of the British Indian Delegation, representing different communities and so many varied interests, who showed friendly feelings towards, and comprehension of, the special position, Sovereignty and other rights of the Indian States, and sought to make their entrance into the Federation easy. I do not wish to make any invidious distinctions; there are so many names I could mention. But I would particularly refer to a few—Mahatma Gandhi, Pandit Madan Mohan Malaviya, Sir Tej Bahadur Sapru, Mr. Sastri, and Mr. Jaykar, as well as, Sir Muhammad Shaft, and Sir Sultan Ahmed, and Sir Maneckji Dadabhoy, Mr. Gavin Jones and Sirdar Ujjal Singh.

Turning now to some important details of our work, I desire, first and foremost, to make it clear that only the pressing reasons—both public as well as personal, which I have already mentioned, and nothing else, were responsible for my having to leave England when I did. It has nothing whatever to do—as I have heard it suggested—with anything connected with the Round Table Conference, much less with any so-called differences of opinion amongst the Members of the States Delegation.

These differences have been exaggerated and partly misunderstood, and were, comparatively speaking, of a minor character. I can best illustrate this by a concrete instance. From the few Indian Press reports which I have so far perused, it might appear that there was a very serious difference of opinion between myself and Sir Mirza Ismail, the Prime Minister of Mysore. I am happy to say that my personal relations with my old friends, Sir Mirza Ismail and Sir Akbar Hydari of Hyderabad, remain as cordial as ever; and it was particularly gratifying to me to receive a very charming letter from Sir Mirza on the eve of my departure ftom London, in regard to a point of disagreement, which arose not with me personally—but with the views held by the majority of our Indian States Delegation. Sir Mirza, as he explained in his letter to me, was impressed with the need of achieving the end of view as quickly as possible by a short cut—namely, the appointment straightaway of an imperial tribunal instead of—as preferred and thought desirable by the States Delegation—the Princes and States attempting, in close co-operation with His Excellency the Viceroy, so settle the somewhat complex problems of the distribution inter se amongst the States of the seats in the two Federal Houses. Anyhow, as Sir Mirza has said in his letter to me, the incident is happily closed. It will thus be seen that this minor disagreement was, after all, no more than a question of ways and means. Certain honest differences of opinion, even between one and the same Delegation, are inevitable in such work as we had to face. But the Indian States Delegation has, I repeat, on the whole, worked with remarkable unanimity and good feeling.

Even though the Sankey Committee was this time larger, and with some new Members, we had to go over some of the old ground again, and certain proposals were made by individual Members from British India which it was impossible for the States to accept, I have returned to India in no way disapointed with the results of our labours. In the interests of our Motherland and the Empire, and indeed, if we were to look carefully ahead, in the interests of all concerned, a Federal form of Government—with India as an equal partner in the British Commonwealth, and, in their turn, the States and British India also as equal partners—is the only one which can give India the unity of purpose and that equal status which we all so ardently desire. As I said before leaving London, I am still of the opinion that, if the final conclusions are just and equitable, the majority of the States, I have no doubt, will enter the Federation. But it is impossible for any Prince or State to make up their minds finally on the subject until they see the picture completed, and are satisfied that it is just and equitable. Speaking broadly—and subject to a further examination in regard to certain outstanding details—the scheme, so far as it had advanced when I left London, can be regarded as having dealt satisfactorily with the constitutional, and fiscal and financial issues, as also those connected with the Federal Court. But, as I have said, there are a few important matters still left; and in the draft constitution, as also elsewhere, adequate provisions and satisfactory safeguards will have to be provided to protect the interests and the Sovereignty and internal autonomy of the States in all matters, other than those which may be specifically and mutually agreed upon to be made federal, and in regard to which the States would be prepared to delegate their Sovereignty to the Crown for the specific purposes of Federation—which Sovereignty the States will share with British India in both the Federal Executive and Legislature. And the views and standpoint of the Princes and the States Delegation have been made absolutely clear as regards the maintenance intact of the Sovereignty and the Treaty and other rights of the States—big as well as what, for the sake of convenience, are called, comparatively speaking, the Smaller States.

There is another very important question which—as I have made clear on more than one occasion in the course of our proceedings—

is of very direct and immediate consquence to the success of the Federal Scheme so far as the Princes and States are concerned, and upon which will also largely rest the final decision of the States as regards entering Federation—viz., the number of seats to be reserved in the Upper and Lower Federal Houses, and the adequate and due representation of the States, and particularly the Smaller States, including the individual representation of the States who are Members of the Chamber of Princes in their own right. I myself have repeatedly clearly emphasized that nothing less than 125 seats for the States in the Upper House is likely to satisfy their ligitimate claims as a body. I learnt from a telegram I received recently that this point was again pressed by His Highness the Chancellor when the draft Report of the Sankey Committee was under consideration. This question, after further consideration in the plenary Session of the Conference, will doubtless be taken up again in the Session of the Chamber of the Princes next Spring.

Here I might further add that His Highness of Bhopal, with due regard to the Mandate from the Princes, and especially the Chamber of Princes, consistently and cordially joined with me—both in public as well as in private—in extending his support to the claims of the Smaller States.

With regard to the Federal Court, I have been asked certain questions of the gravest concern which will have a very important bearing on the future Sovereignty and integrity of our States, and particularly in regard to the suggestion emanating from certain British Indian quarters that the jurisdiction of the Federal Court should be extended to both the State Law Courts and to certain administrative matters which are of internal or domestic concern to the States. I would remind you all of what I said on the subject in my speech on the 9th February, 1931, on my return to India from the first Session of the Round Table Conference, namely, that the acceptance of any such proposals would obviously be imcompatible with the Sovereignty of the States. From a recent telegram I gather that the point was mooted again in the Federal Structure Committee by one or two British Indian delegates; but the Indian States Delegation were opposed to it, and, as was to be expected, the proposal was turned down.

I do not desire, at least at this stage, to refer to the Patiala-Dholpur alternative Schemes. It was a sufficiently unpleasant duty for me to have had to deal with this matter in my interview to the Times of India on the 23rd June last, when there was a danger of the Princes and States—and specially the Smaller States—being stampeded into action, which would have made all the Princes and States as a body look entirely rediculous, and all of them lacking in statesmanship and political perspicacity. But I am prepared to say this much; the more I study the objections and criticisms levelled against what the Indian States Delegation worked for last year, and has been and is working again this year, the less do I see any valid grounds for any such objections. Indeed, there is nothing new in the criticisms, or what are described as constructive proposals, which had not already been thought of, borne in mind or urged by us in London, at one time or the other.

Nor do I think it profitable to take up any time in dealing with the proposal regarding the States confederating amongst themselves, which will be totally inaceeptable at least to the vast majority of the important States. If however, for any reasons—good or otherwise—the Smaller States—or for the matter of that any States—specially prefer to confederate amongst themselves, that is of course a mater entirely for them; and such States as favour Confederation will doubtless first carefully weigh the pros and cons, and consider whether they are prepared to have a new super-sovereign power or authority imposed upon them in the shape of the Chamber of Princes, or its Standing Committee, or to invest the Chamber of Princes—which, important and useful as it is, is at present only an advisory and consultative body—with executive and legislative powers and authority, as well as with the powers of 'sanction', But I wish to make it clear that at least the Bikaner State—together with several other important States—will have nothing to do with Confederation, the principles of which are neither practical nor desirable for the end in view.

In conclusion, I desire to pay a very warm and grateful tribute to the Prime Minister, Mr. Ramsay MacDonald, Lord Sankey and Sir Samuel Hoare; as well as the British Parliamentary delegates. Though there has apparently been a short recess inevitable as a consequence of the Election, the dislocation of work, at least upto the time I left, was hardly noticeable. Mr. Ramsay MacDonald gave of his best; Lord Sankey, as usual, guided the work of the Federal Structure Committee with the calm, understanding wisdom and the great sympathy and sagacity which has throughout distinguished his work; whilst in Sir Samuel Hoare we found a new Secretary of State for India who, though new to his Office, firmly siezed the reins, and evinced his close grasp of the Indian problem.

Ladies and Gentlemen, our task is not yet complete. But if we all take our courage resolutely in both hands, and above all adopt as our watchword the inspiring Message of Hope which His Imperial Majesty the King-Emperor graciously gave to India when he came to announce in person his Coronation some twenty years ago, there are no obstacles which cannot be surmounted with mutual good-will and sympathy and confidence in each other and an unbending determination to overcome them. There will be difficulties ahead, inevitably associated with the task of framing the principles of a constitution—a very special constitution, if it is to be successful, to meet the unique position of the Indian States, which is without its parallel in history. And there will doubtless be further differences of opinion. But "where there is a will, there is a way" and behind all difficulties and differences, we can find a common purpose. That purpose is the resolution to place a united India firmly on the road to equal partnership in the British Commonwealth, loyal to our beloved King-Emperor, and to each other seeking through our very diversities by association in a common whole,the service of our Country and the welfare of its teeming millions.

# Annexure 7

## Speech Delivered by His Highness the Maharajah of Bikaner G.C.S.I., G.C.I.E., G.C.V.O., G.B.E., K.C.B., A.D.C., LL.D., at the Banquet at lallbarh in Honour of the Right Hon. J.c.C. Davidson, c.H., c.B., M.P., and the Members of the Indian States Enquiry Committee on the 21st March, 1932

*Mr. Davidson, My Lord; Ladies and Gentlemen;*

In rising to propose the health of the Chairman and Members of the Indian States Enquiry Committee, I desire to express the pleasure which I and my Government and my people derive in welcoming them to Bikaner. It is however a matter of disappointment to me that all the members of the Committee, and particularly my old friend—that popular and distinguished Political Officer Sir Reginald Glancy, have not been enabled to come here. I would also like, if I may, to include Lady Hastings in the welcome which we are offering.

Although the whole State has been plunged into deep mourning and grief owing to the irreparable loss which I and my Family have recently suffered, by the demise of my beloved and never-to-be-forgotten younger Son, Her Highness the Maharani and I were determined to ensure, so far as we and our Family were concerned, that nothing should be permitted to come in the way of the Committee visiting our State.

Thers are many weighty obvious and public reasons which have influenced us in coming to this decision. But at times like the present, when India is once again passing through one of the most critical periods in her history, when questions of the most vital importance to the whole Country are under consideration, and when we are living in an atmosphere of no small amount of suspicion and mistrust, and even misrepresentation and invective, I might perhaps be permitted to say a few words.

However great the sense of personal loss and sorrow may be, Duty and the interests of the State and of the subjects committed by Providence to the care of a Ruler most always take the first place, regardless of all personal considerations. Willing co-operation is the creed of the Rulers and States of India; loyalty and devotion to the Person and Throne of their beloved King-Emperor and faithful friendship and staunch attachment for the British Empire and the British Government, the very essence of their life. The proverbial loyalty of the Princely Houses and States of India, and the past traditions and achievements of my own House and State dating back to time beyond living memory-during the Moghul period, as well as from the day, some 114 years ago, when we had the honour of coming into political relations with the British Crown by means of Treaties of Perpetual Alliance and Friendship and unity of interests need no words from me to-night. Proof of that is to be found both in Peace and War; and many a Prince has even gone personally and risked his own life on the batle-fields of Europe, Asia and Africa; whilst our resources—infinitesimal as they are when compared with those of the King-Emperor's mighty Empire—and our loyal support in fulfilment of our Treaty obligations, have always been willingly and freely placed at the disposal of the Crown in dealing with any disloyal or subversive momements against the King-Emperor or which may threaten the peace and prosperity and the orderly advance of India on constitutional lines to her destined goal.

And, there are some extremely important problems, and serious griveances and disablities which very closely affect our States and our subjects, and their well-being and prosperity—the responsible task of dealing with which has been entrusted to the Committee of which you, Sir, are the Chairman. Let me assure you, from personal knowledge and experience, that—in spite of several sweeping charge which for a few years past it has become the fashion amongst a certain section of the Press, and on the platform, in British India to nurl indiscriminately, at those "terrible" and "tyrannical" autocrats, the Rulers of States, many of whom have devoted their entire lives and energies in the service of their States and their subjects -the Princes are very deeply and genuinely concerned, as part of their Sacred Duty, in the equitable handling of such problems and the removal of such grievances and disabilities. And I know that I am voicing the general feeling and earnest hope of the Princes and their States and Governments, when we ask, as a matter of justice and fairplay, that these grievances and past wrongs may now be finally and defrinitely put right.

Even though I may not say much that has not already been said in the past on some occasion or the other, this leads me to say a few words, it I may, in regard to the question of Federation which at the present moment is naturally engaging the attention of all sober-minded people, who have the interests of India and of the Empire at heart, and who ardently desire to see our two great Countries brought closer and closer together in indissoluble and lasting ties of friendship and love, and mutual help and co-operation, which must prove of incalculable benefit not only to Great Britain and India but, I venture to add, to Humanity and the World at large.

I must apologize, ladies and Gentlemen, for taking up your time. But at times important facts are apt—sometimes conveniently—to be lost sight of ; and I have recently seen it stated that the Princes and States generally are now going back on their word, and attempting to smash Federation and trying to impose new and impossible conditions, and so on. I venture to say that no such charges are fair, much less can they be justified. It has repeatedly and abundantly been made clear that no State can be forced or coerced against its free will to enter Federation, and that the final decision of the Princes on the subject must obviously and inevitably wait till the whole picture is complete, and all the necessary details have been filled in. There are still questions and details of the utmost importance to the States to be settled, of which the work, on which your Committee and other Committees are now engaged, is an important illustration in point. Then there are other no less, and in some cases, even more, important questions still under the consideration of the Consultative Committee, which is presided over by His Excellency the Viceroy; and for the honour and good name of the Princes I make bold to say, unequivocally and without fear of contradiction, that there is nothing inconsistent or unreasonable whatsoever—much less any change of attitude—on the part of the Princes and their Governments if they insist on the completion of the picture and on the previous satisfactory settlement of all essential details and safeguards.

I yield to no one in my love and patriotism for my Motherland, or in my sincere desire to see India taking her due and equal place amongst the Sister nations forming the British Commonwealth. And I am one of those who still believes that—taking everything into consideration—Federation is a good, and possibly the only, solution in the interess of India as a whole and of the Empire. But it is necessary briefly to recall certain facts. On the first day of the Plenary Session of the Round Table Conference on the 17th November, 1930, a cordial invitation was extended and an earnest appeal made to the Princes and States by British Indian leaders to join Federation, under which they were assured that the two Indias, though a single whole, in such Federation would each be autonomous and enjoy absolute independence within its borders; and in the course of such appeal by

British India the mutual advantages from the association of the Indian States with British India the mutual advantages from the association of the Indian States with British India were particularly welcomed for various reasons. I need not dilate upon the important considerations on which our response was based, namely, our Duty to the Crown and friendship for the Empire, even if some sacrifice were involved on our part; our desire in every reasonable manner to be of service to our Motherland, and the hope that in the long run such a Federation might also prove to be of some advantage, in certain directions, to the States and to their subjects.

There were questions involved of the most vital importance to the Rulers, Governments and subjects of the Indian States. Indeed some of them were such as might imperil the very existence of the States at some future date, In considering this appeal the Princes were not free agents, but trustees of their subjects whose rights they had to safeguard. The States and their subjects have, as already stated, for long had grievances also in regard to fiscal and financial matters, which the Princes and their Governments have so far striven in vain to get redressed. Anxious as the Princes were—and I am sure they still are—to serve the wider interests of their Motherland, and also of the Empire, they had to be sure that such rights and privileges were secured, and where infringed, repaired and restored. It was therefore a pround moment for me when I had the privilege, at the request and on behalf of he Princes and States, in responding to such appeal from British India to express our willingness to consider entering into such a Federation—subject to certain specific safeguards and conditions. And I made it clear beyond any doubt or dispute that any acceptance of the federal idea on the part of the Princes and States generally must be based on three fundamental conditions:

> first and foremost, on our unfaltering loyalty to the Throne and Person of His Imperial Majesty the King-Emperor, and our obligations of honour and plighted word;
> secondly, on the profound conviction that not only can each constituent part attain its full stature within the Empire under the aegis of the British Crown, but a higher development, politically and economically, than as an isolated unit; and thirdly, that our Treaty rights, and the rights of our States subjects, were scrupulously observed.

It has already been made clear on previous occasions that an equitable agreement must be reached between all the parties concerned to govern the relations of the two Indias, ensuring for the States their due position in the future constitution as co-equal partners with British India, Guaranteeing their Treaties and their Sovereignty and internal autonomy, and safeguarding their interests, including those of their subjects, on terms just and honourable alike to the States and to British India.

The position therefore can, I think, be fairly summed up in a nutshell, As has repeatedly been made clear by me and my Brother Princes, inside and outside the Round Table Conference and the Federal Structure Committee, the crux of the question as to whether the States will, or will not, enter Federation, is this. If the States feel safe and secure in entering Federation, and are guaranteed and receive adequate and essential safeguards by means of Treaties with the British Crown, buttressed and fortified by necessary conventions and other necessary provisions in the Federal Constitution as regards constitutional and political, and fiscal and financial, matters, as well as those relating to the Federal Court, ensuring and guaranteeing the continuance intact of the integral Sovereignty and the Treaty and other rights and privileges of the States and definitely providing against encroachment by the Federal Executive or Legislature on their internal autonomy beyond what my be voluntarily and specifically and clearly agreed to by the States, and if the final conclusions and scheme are just and equitable and ensure the future existence of thc States, the majority of the Princes will, I have no doubt, enter Federation and the rest will follow in due course. Otherwise—through I personally very much hope that Federation may come into being, and we have done our best to secure that very desirable end—no ruler or Government of any Indian States would obviously fmd it possible to enter Federation.

As for the future I must flfst and foremost give expression to my strong conviction, which I have all along consistently voiced and pressed, that for a satisfactory solution and generally for an acceptable agreement so far as the States as a body are concerned, a due place must be assigned to, and full and proper provision made for—what, for the sake of convenience, have come to be termed, comparatively speaking, as the Smaller States. For, I must again repeat to-night that I hold no less strongly that the interests of the Smaller States are the interests, generally speaking, of all the States; their welfare and continued existence is our most zealour care; their welfare and continued existence is our most zealous care; their Sovereign rights and privileges, it is also the duty of us, constituting the bigger States, equally faithfully to safeguard, as it is also our duty to further the legitimate aspirations of such Smaller States and sympathetically to consider and support their reasonable demands.

It follows therefore that, unless as I have also all along repeatedly and no less strongly urged and fought for—the Membership of the Upper Federal House is increased to permit of a total of 125 seats being assigned exclusively to the States, it will not, and cannot, satisfy the claims of the Sates as a body, or even the majority; and I have further consistently urged, too, the claims of the 109 States who are now Members, in their own right, of the Chamber of Princes, to equal and individual representation as Governments in the Upper House. This would still leave a margin for the inclusion of such other States as on examination might ultimately and fairly, by the existing tests and qualifications, be further proved to be eligible for such membership of the Chamber of Princes in their own right, as also for the group representation of the lesser units comprising Indian India.

Let there, I beg, not be the slightest misunderstanding on this point in the minds of anyone concerned. It is my honest belief, based on all I have been able to gather and judge, that the important question of the adequate and due representation of the States, big and small, is in itself alone one of the chief factors on which will to a large extent depend whether the States will enter, or not enter, accept or reject, Federation. I have frequently uttered a note of warming on this very question including in the Federal Structure Committee—for instance on the 24th September 1931—and I trust that I shall be excused if I repeat that warning to-day.

It is not only as regards the future, but also in view of past experience, that many States evince some anxiety as regards the implications and possible results of Federation. And it was also because of the alarm created in the minds of the Princs that, altogether independent of the question of Federation, and even many years before that question took a prominent shape, the Princes have had to take up with His Excellency the Viceroy some questions and details in regard to which certain claims were put forward in the name of the Paramount Power by some Departments of the Government of India which in the view of the States infringe on their Treaty rights. I trust that I shall not be considered out of order if I take this, the first public, oppotunity which has since offered itself, to give expression to the sense of the very deep gratitude which all Princes and States will feel for His Excellency Lord Willingdon for the great trouble and pains which he has been pleased to take in so throughly and patiently thrashing out this question with us in the last few months, and for the great sympathy and sense of justice and fairplay which he has displayed.

Let me conclude my observations by stating that being an optimist as I always happily have been, I venture to think that, in spite of some so-called internal differences amongst the States inter se, it will be found that the Princes, subject to such essential guarantees and safeguards, will be found only too ready to be of service to their King-Emperor and to their Motherland.

It only remains for me to wish this Committee, and the other Committees now engaged in their important tasks, all success. May they be the means of securing justice and rendering happier the people of both the Indian States and British India, and thus contributing to the lasting strength and stability of the Empire.

Ladies and Gentlemen, I now ask you to join me in drinking to the health of the Committee, and to couple with the toast the names of Lady Hastings and of Mr. Davidson.

# Annexure 8

**Speech delivered by Lieut.-General High Highness the Maharajah of Bikaner, G.C.S.I., G.C.I.E., G.C.V.O., G.B.E., K.C.N., A.D.C., LL.D., in the Chamber of Princes on the 25th March, 1933.**

*Your Excellency, Your Highnesses*

It is with the most unqualified pleasure that I rise to second this Resolution. It would be idle to conceal the fact that His Highness the Maharaj Jamsaheb and I have not always—though happily very rarely—seen eye to eye. But I am sure that His Highness is the first Prince to realise, and to appreciate, that they are healthy differences of opinion, and in no way personal to His Highness. I have now had the privilege of knowing His Highness for close upon 40 years; and he is one of the "Old Brigade", who has been associated with us, ever sinde 1916 at any rate, in fighting the battles of the States and in working for the States, And both out of the respect and regard which I entertain for His Highness and my personal friendship and esteem for him, I beg to second this Resolution.

# Annexure 9

**Speech delivered by Lieut.-General High Highness the Maharajah of Bikaner, G.C.S.I., G.C.I.E., G.C.V.O., G.B.E., K.C.B., A.D.C., LL.D., in the Chamber of Princes on the 25th March, 1933, on the subject of Allocation of Seats to the States inter-se in the Federal Legislature.**

*Your Excellency, Your Highnesses*

Time does not permit of any lengthy entry into details on this question which naturally concerns most vitally all the States from the biggest to the smallest. Nor would this be the proper occasion for dealing with such matters at length. But as one, who from time to time, even before the institution of the Chamber, has fully sympathised with all the legitimate aspirations of what are known, comparatively speaking, as the smaller States, and who has tried to render service to them and fought for them, I beg whole-heartedly to support this Resolution. History is in one way repeating itself; for, when the Chamber of Princes was started a little over a dozen years ago, there was the same question, when it was my good fortune to be of some service to some of the smaller States. It has been often declared—indeed if any such declaration was necessary—that two factors arising out of the Federation question will prove the determining factors in the entry of the Princes into Federation; there was first the question of safeguards which has been covered by the previous Resolution moved a little while ago, and the other was the question of the allocation of seats. It was because we knew that the very greatest difficulty would be experienced—even on the ideal, and the generally accepted, principle of most of the Federations, of equality of votes in the Upper Houses for States, as Sovereign States and Governments—and because we realised—as was made clear from the very commencement of the Round Table Conference by myself, His Highness the Nawab of Bhopal and other Princes, including, particularly, His Highness the Maharaja of Patiala—that nothing less than 125 seats would be possible on which to base any scheme which can afford us satisfaction. I quite realise some of the difficulties in raising the numbers to 125; and, if this is found impossible, I am at least grateful that the number has been raised from 80 to 100.

But, Sir, there is another complication. The ideal is one thing, and what may or may not be found possible may be another. But we were thinking at the time that, excepting for the special position of Hyderabad, there might be as far as possible one seat in the Upper House for each State of the Chamber. Now the difficulty has been rendered more acute by the proposal to give plural seats. And, without going into any anomalies and difficulties that will arise out of such a scheme, I wish to make two observations. The first point is this; if the Princes cannot come to a generally acceptable agreement—and the question cannot of course be left undecided—His Majesty" government will, in the circumstances, have no other alternative but to give their final proposals; and I see no other course. But I think they would do so with regret; and it is therefore very desirable that we should, if at all possible, make another determined effort to arrive at a reasonable compromise likely to be generally acceptable. For, whereas, the Communal Award had to be settled by a decision of His Majesty's Government to get on with the Scheme of Constitutional Reforms, and His Majesty's Government's decision has naturally to be accepted-unless it is altered by mutual consent of the parties concerned in British India—in this case, the decision of His Majesty's Government, if there is no other alternative, will be there; but it will again largely influence the States concerned in accpeting the allocation, or standing out of the Federation. That is a point which, I would impress, should be borne in mind by all concerned. And, secondly, I would urge that we should make a determined effort to try and arrive at some reasonable settlement and compromise.

I realise that all the Sovereign States cannot be satisfied—that would be impossible—because according to His Majesty's Government's Scheme, important States are to get larger representation, though how much, and whether it should be varied, and what anomalies there may be, is another matter. In supporting this Resolution, I would make a final appeal to all those who, like some of us here, are Rulers of important States, and who have had the good fortune for their States—or whatever we may put it as—of having secured plural representation, to try, by a self-denying ordinance, to accommodate, in a reasonable manner, the smaller States with due regard to the 'izzat' of our States, to a certain extent, at any rate, to make a larger number of seats available for the benefit of the smaller States and for the unity of the Indian States as a whole.

# Annexure 10

**Speech delivered by Lieut.-General High Highness the Maharajah of Bikaner, G.C.S.I., G.C.I.E., G.C.V.O., G.B.E., K.C.B., A.D.C., LL.D., in the Chamber of Princes on the 22nd January 1935 relating to Indian Constitutional Reforms.**

*Your Excellency; Your Highnesses;*

The resolution on this all important subject which has been moved by His Highness the Chancellor includes the suggestions of several Princes and Ministers who attended our Informal Meetings of the day before yesterday, and is in the form which, after prolonged consideration, was unanimously agreed upon and accepted by Their Highnesses without any dissentient voice having been raised by any of the Princes present.

I have also had the pleasure during the last few days of exchanging views on the subject with my friend and brother, His Highness the Chancellor; and, in order not to take up Your Highnesses' time unnecessarily, I intend to confine my remarks today only to some of the more important aspects of the question.

It is hardly necessary for me to add that my rising to speak on this resolution should not be taken as my necessarily identifying myself with everything that has been said in the course of this debate today.

It will, I trust, be asource of gratification to all friends and well-wishers of the Princes and States of India—and I am proud and happy to think that we call also claim many good friends in Great Britain—that the Chamber of Princes should, on this ocasion, re-afirm its previous declaration about the readiness of the States to accede to an all-India Federation, subject to the proviso that the essential conditions and guarantees, which have been pressed for on behalf of the States are adequately provided for. It would be superfluous on my part to explain the reasons why we desire that there should be a clear recognition of the Sovereignty and internal autonomy of our States and of our rights and prerogatives under our Treaties and Engagements.

Sir, I venture to submit at the outset that the attitude of the Princes in desiring to see first the completed picture, before they come to a final decision about acceding to Federation, is—as Your Excellency has just been pleased to say—a perfectly reasonable one and is wholly consistent with what they have all along said.

True, we have progressed some stages further since the first Round Table Conference. And, may I be permitted to say that, it affords me the greatest pleasure to acknowledge, on behalf of myself and of my many friends amongst the Ruling Princes of India, that so far as the Indian States are concerned the recommendations of the Joint Parliamentary Committee constitute a decided advance inseveral directions on the White Paper proposals.

To the Members of the Joint Parliamentary Committee—who have been so assiduous in their labours—and to His Mesesty's Government, as well as to my Right Hon. friend, Sir Samuel Hoare—who has so gallantly borne the heavy burdens involved and worked so nobly for the States as well as for British India—the grateful thanks of the States are due for having met to a considerable extent the demands of the States in matters so vitally necessary for safeguarding their rights and interests, and indeed their very existence in the future.

To you, Sir, as our Viceroy, are not less due our grateful and respectful thanks for once again giving practical proof of your deep and well-known sympathy and for the support that Your Excellency has given in regard to our legitimate demands.

Sir, I am aware that it is dangerous to prophesy. But I for one am rash enough once more to predict today that if the remaining essential conditions are forthcoming, and subject also to certain other necessary adjustments, it will be found that we, the Rulers of the bigger States, will all be only too glad to come into the Federation; and whether with us, or a little time afterwards, I have also no doubt in my own mind that—given such favourable conditions—the majority of the other States will equally gladly follow us.

It will, I am positive, be a source of the highest gratification to the Princes and States to note the recommendation of the Joint Committee that there must in future be a legal differentiation between the functions of the Viceroy and of the Governor-General, since, under the proposed Constitution, certain maters relating to the States, which are at present dealt with by the Governor-General-in-Council, cannot be exercised on behalf of the Crown by any Federal Authority, save in so far as they fall within the Federal sphere, and then only when they affect a State which has acceded to the Federation.

We thus welcome a much needed measure of reform, which we have so consistently pressed for several years past, and under which the rights and interests of the Princes and States will henceforth be entrusted to the keeping of the Viceroy as the representative of our beloved King—Emperor.

In the circumstances, it is, I submit, no less important in the interests of the States that they should be made aware also of what is proposed to be put in the Instrument of Instructions to the Viceroy.

We would therefore, beg Your Excellency to be pleased to impress upon His Majesty's Government the urgent necessity of making available to the States all such necessary particulars relating to the Treaties of Accession and the Instrument of Instructions to the Viceroy.

I would also express the hope that it will be possible at a very early date to have placed in Your Excellency's hands for your information and for transmission to His Majesty's Government certain outstanding details. And in this, as well as in other respects, I should like, if I may, to take this opportunity of gratefully acknowledging on behalf of myself and my friends the valuable work which has been done and is being continued by the Committee of Ministers—representing chiefly the bigger States—which was appointed some months ago in Bombay and which is so ably presided over by Sir Akbar Hydari.

Your Highnesses, I now come to the second, and what I deem to be the most important, part of my speech. The time is approaching when we the Princes of India will have to take a most momentous decision in regard to Federation which, for good or for evil, will profoundly affect the future destinies of our States as well as of our own Dynasties.

Your Highnesses therefore, need no word of caution from me to the effect that it behoves us to view the question as to whether we should federate or not with the utmost calmness and vigilence, and to beware lest we allow ourselves to be used as tools of my political or extreme parties in England or in India for their own selfish ends, or permit ourselves to be influenced by alarmists and mischief-makers and self-seekers.

We the Rulers of Indian States are not soldiers of fortune. And I take the liberty of stating that we, who, through centuries of heredity, can claim to have inherited the instincts of rule—and, I trust, a certain measure of statesmanship—should take the utmost care to safeguard against our being stampeded in a hurry to any hasty or ill-considered decision which not only we but also our successors may have bitter cause to regret in the years to come.

In the circumstances, may I be permitted respectfully to point out, and to express the hope, that Your Highnesses will share my views that, even before we have in our possession the full material on which to base our judgement, it is not only clearly premature, but greatly to be depreciated in the interests of the Princes and States, to talk of "an Act of Parliament based on the findings of the Joint Select Committee", which would "no doubt reduce the status of the Princes to that of political pensioners", or that it "would ultimately rob us of our present strength, prestige and status," or to subscribe to such wild statements as "what misery, what anarchy, what carnage may spring from this rach experiment"?

Ought we not, on the other hand, at least to bear seriously in mind the recent utterance of a great statesman, who is held by every one in Great Britain in the highest esteem as a man of honour ? I refer to Sir Austen Chamberlain, who, whilst still electing to remain a 'commoner', has been honoured by the Sovereign by the unique bestowal of the Order of the Garter. In this speech during the recent debate in the House of Commons Sir Austen said—"If I were an Indian Prince, I should join the Federation, because I should feel it is in the interests of my Dynasty and my State"—the very sentiments which—I would state in all modesty—influenced those of us in England in 1930 when we expressed our willingness to enter the Federation on certain essential terms.

I have also seen the fantastic statement in a London newspaper, holding extreme views on India, that "among the good, true, and loyal Princes" there is a growing disposition" "to resist the White Paper, because they genuinely feel that their loyalty is not so much to the servants of the Crown, however exalted they may be, or to the politicians in office at Whitehall, as to the King-Emperor and the Empire", and that therefore the Princes' "first, second and third consideration in anything" they "may be called upon to do shall be the preservation of "their" ties and genuine bonds with the House of Windsor, because in that way alone can the best interests of their States, India as a whole, and the Empire be served".

It would have been interesting if we had been told at the same time who in the world has ever demanded the Princes' loyalty to the "servants of the Crown, however exalted", or the "politicians in office at Whitehall" ! And am I wrong in claiming that no individual Prince, or group of Princes, has the sole monopoly of loyalty to their august King—Emperor, and further that at least some of us have given practical proof of our loyalty, not only in peace, but also in times of war, including the greatest war in modern history?

And may I ask who in the world also has ever contemplated, much less agreed to, anything that would in any way weaken the ties of loyalty and devotion which bind the Princes of India to His Imperial

Majesty the King—Emperor and his House of Empire?

I am tempted in this connection to quote the words of His Excellency the Viceroy in his recent speech in Rewa to the effect that "no change in the Constitution that may take place in the future shall be permitted to weaken or alter in any respect" "the link which indissolubly binds" the Princes to the Crown.

May I be permitted to remind Your Highnesses that long before the first Round Table Conference, the future position of the Indian States in the polity of India had been engaging the anxious and serious consideration of the Princes, and that, as the first Chancellor of the Chamber of Princes, I had the honour, at Your Highnesses' express wish, and under your authority, to request the Viceroy, Lord Reading, to have this question taken up urgently? Was it, therefore, really a rash plunge in the dark that the Princes, who had the honour of representing Your Highnesses in London, took when they expressed their willingness to consider entering the Federation on certain fundamental conditions, the most important of which were:

first, that India retains the British connection:

secondly, that an equitable agreement was reached between all the parties concerned of governing the relations of the two Indias, ensuring for the States their due position in the future Constitution as co-equal partners with British India, on terms just and honourable alike to the States and British India;

thirdly, that the Treaties and the Sovereignty and internal autonomy of the States, and their interests and those of their subjects, would be duly safeguarded and guaranteed.

Might I also refer Your Highnesses to the three important considerations which prompted the Princes at the First Round Table Conference in response to the invitation of British India, as conveyed by Sir Tej Bahadur Sapru, to express their willingness to consider entering a Federal Scheme, viz.:

first, our duty to the Crown and friendship for the Empire, even if some sacrifices were involved on our part in view of the grave situation prevailing in India;

Secondly, our natural desire in every reasonable manner to assist India in attaining Dominion Status as a co-equal and honoured member of the British Commonwealth of Nations and to help our brethren in British India to rise to their full stature under the aegis of the Crown, just as we of the States are desirous of ensuring the fullest freedom in our affairs and of retaining our Sovereignty and autonomy; and thirdly, because we felt that in the long run such a Federation was likely also to prove of some advantage in certain directions to the States and their subjects.

If I may transgress for a moment, I must confess to my disappointment at the hostility displayed towards the Princes and States from so many quarters in British India, and it really puzles me to see the various accusations hurled against us in regard to the Constitutional proposals now under review.

Before the Princes went to the Round Table Conference, a certain section of the politicians and Press in British India freely stated that the Princes would conbine with the British Government and the bureaucracy indenying to British India its just dues—a prophecy which the Princes and Ministers comprising the States Delegation happily proved to be incorrect.

And today, when, in the face of diffiiculties, many of us have still maintained our faith and attitude unshaken in regard to Federation, and in spite of our being prepared—subject to certain provisions—to make some sacrifices, all kinds of absurd and groundless motives are ascribed to the Princes, and they are unfairly accused for certain shortcomings in the recommendations of the Joint Committee's Report.

But to revert to the main point, it is true that the Princes have expressed their readiness to make some sacrifices and to delegate to the Crown, for the specific purpose of Federation—and for that alone—a part of their Dovereignty in regard to certain limited matters, which Sovereignty they would share with British India in the Federal Government and Legislature.

I have heard it said that neither the Crown nor the British Government have asked for such sacrifices that is perfectly true. But I would ask Your Highnesses and others concerned with the States whether, with the Sovereignty and future existence of the States safeguarded, such sacrifices are not worthy of the Princes and States of India, if thereby they were enabled at one and the same time to be of some service in these critical days to their beloved King-Emperor and to their Motherland and fellow-country-men in British India, as well as to their States and Dynasties and subjects-even though neither the Crown, not the British Government, not the present or past Viceroy has asked any such thing of us.

All this leads me to a subject on which I find it difficult to speak with restraint. I am prepared to pass over the astonishing allegations made in the House of Commons by the diehard group, some of which have again just been repeated in a certain London newspaper, to the effect that bribes on the one hand, and threats and intimidation on the other, had been held out by the British Government in England and in India to coax, cajole or coerce the Indian Princes to enter Federation.

They are indeed as sorry a compliment to the Ruling Princes of India, as they are unfair and unjust to His Excellency the Viceroy and His Majesty's Government and the Government of India. And such wild statements and charges can only result in completely exposing their authors, the lameness of their cause and the methods and tactics adopted by them.

I notice that one hon. Member said in the House of Commons that before he reached India certain Pricnes had been warned that it would be unwise to invcite him and his collegues to stay with them. it would have been interesting if the hon. gentleman in question had mentioned the names of the Princes whom he thus approached, and who refused to see him, and had nothing to do with him.

I for one can certainly say that at no time did I receive any such warning or suggestion from His Excellency the Viceroy, or from anyone else, in England or in India, in regard to the hon. member and his friends, or indeed in regard to anyone else. I would also add that the hon. gentleman in question and his friends never even intimated to me, directly or indirectly, their desire to see me or to visit my State. Otherwise I should have been glad to have seen them there and to have had a discussion with them. But may it no be that they did not visit me and several other Princes because they knew full well that our views were not likely to be swayed by all the horrors of Federation that were being depicted by them and their friends, or by their attempts to make our flesh creep by the various suggestions and efforts made to influence us into playing into their hands?

Sir, I am prepared so far as I and my friends are concerned to plead guilty to our being "so foolish" as to be prepared to give our consent to Federation—subject to certain adequate safeguards and guarantees being forthcoming. But, on the other hand, we may also be "so foolish" as to take such propaganda at its proper face value, and thereby to refuse to believe that, within 3 years or perhaps 3 months of the inauguration of the new Scheme, the Princes will be deprived of their position and privileges and thus hasten their own destruction and the doom of their States.

May I in all modesty say that the Princes have no intention of being allowed to be thus destroyed by anybody, and that should the time unfortunately come when the Crown is unable to afford the Indian States the necessary protection in fulfillment of its Treaty obligations, the Princes and States will die fighting to the bitter end?

But what we chiefly resent—and resent deeply—are the unworthy charges levelled against a Viceroy so universally respected, trusted and popular amongst the Princes and States as the Earl of Willingdon, who. has done his best to be fair to all concerned and just in all his dealings.

His Excellency, who is no less respected and trusted in his own country by his own countrymen, needs no defence by the Princes and States of India. But I should not be true to the traditions of the Princely Houses and States of India if, as a matter of honour, I did not take this opportunity, on behalf of myself and at any rate a large number of my friends from amongst the Ruling Princes, of giving the most emphatic contradiction to such base allegations.

Sir, Indian affairs have hitherto, or at least till recently, been held to be above party politics in England. May we not hope that this wholesome doctrine will once more be reverted to, and that, by a generous and statesmanlike response by His Majesty's Government and the British Parliament to the legitimate demands of the two Indias, Great Britain and India—which are so indispensable to each other—might be brought still closer together, and my Motherland enabled to contribute its fullest mite to the added prestige and glory of our beloved King-Emperor and his great Empire?

# Annexure 11

**Speech Delivered by His Highness the Maharaja at the State Banquet in Bikaner in Honour of their Excellencies the Viceroy and the Marchioness of Linlithgow on the 6th November, 1937**

*Your Excellencies, Ladies and Gentlemen;*

It is with the greatest pleasure that I extend to Your Excellencies a very warm welcome. All of us in Bikaner greatly appreciate the honour which Your Excellency, as the Representative of our beloved King-Emperor, has done us by paying your State Visit to Bikaner when my Golden Jubilee is being celebrated. I have already been privileged a year ago to welcome Your Excellency and Her Excellency Lady Linlithgow—who is devoting herself so assiduously to the welfare of the women and children of India- when you paid us a private visit; and we cherish the most pleasant memories of that occasion, when Your Excellencies, by your friendliness and infonnality, won the hearts of all Bikaneries.

When, fifty years ago, I became Maharajah of Bikaner, Lord Dufferin was Viceroy of lndia. In those days Bikaner was very difficult of access. I well remember that long and tedious journeys of some one hundred and forty miles which as a little boy I had to undertake. In great heat or cold we travelled in a camel carriage, with brief halts in little rest houses, to and from the nearest Railway Station.

It was only in December 1891 that the railway to Bikaner was oepned. On that occasion, as a boy of 11, I had to make my maiden speech of about two or three lines asking the then Agent to the Governor—General, the late Colonel Trevor, to drive in the last spike and to declare open the first 43 of the present 795 miles of the Bikaner State Railway.

Since that time my State has had the privilege of receiving visits from every Viceroy; and I was the first Ruler of Bikaner to welcome to my State in 1896 the Representative of the Crown in the person of Lord Elgin, during whose Viceroyalty two years later I came of age. Twenty five years ago, one of the greatest and most popular of Viceroys that India has ever had, Lord Hardinge, paid the first of his three visits to Bikaner on the occasion of my Silver Jubilee. Ten years ago another great Viceroy, also beloved by the people of India, Lord Irwin, now Lord Halifax, opened the Gang Canal at Ganganagar, on event which marked a turning point in the history of Bikaner.

Thus several Viceregal; visits have coincided with important stages of my career as a Ruler; and I rejoice that the present occasion of my Golden Jubilee has been equally signalised.

The last State Banquet which we had in Bikaner in honour of the Viceroy was during the visit, some three and a half years ago, of my old and valued friends, Lord and Lady Willingdon, who had so endeared themselves to the Princes and people of India. But, as my thoughts go back to that occasion, the saddest memories are evoked in my mind. For, one whose health we drank that night with such loyal fervour no longer presides over the destinies of the Empire. I refer, of course, to that great and beloved Sovereign, King George V, whose demise in January 1936 so engulfed a whole world in sorrow, and who, with our beloved Queen Mary, had gained in such a remarkable degree the affection and esteem of everyone in the Empire.

Sir, I am speaking from deep emotion, and not only because of many precious memories of personal association with His late Majesty for over a third of a century, but because, like other Indian States, we prize highly the bonds that unite us to the Imperial Throne. We recognise how, since 1818—when the Treaty of "perpetual friendship, alliance and unity of interests" was signed between the Representative of the British Crown and my Ancestor—the State of Bikaner has developed undisturbed under the protection of the Crown. This period of close upon 120 years has witnessed unparallelled changes in the world's history; but the alliance then contracted has stood firm, ensuring for us peace, progress and prosperity, and binding us with firm, ensuring forus peace, progress and prosperity, and binding us with ever closer ties to the Person and Throne of the King—Emperor.

I think I can justly claim that throughout that period Bikaner and its Rulers have been true to their obligations under the Treaty—not excluding, I venture to hope, the past fifty years in which I myself have consistently endeavoured to render what service lay in my power to no less than five successive British Sovereigns, from Queen Victoria to His present Majesty.

Your Excellency, I am aware that the contributions of the Indian States can bring only a modest reinforcement to the might of Great Britain. But I think it will also be agreed that the certainty of the Princes and States of India rallying round the British Flag in periods of crises is a moral asset of the Empire. We for our part, looking upon a world distraught with touble, are proud to be partners in an Empire which is a heaven of peace and freedom. Those of us who have personally experienced the horrors of war will be the first to pray that the present restlessness of the nations may not lead to a repetition of that calamity. I would, however, beg Your Excellency to convey to our gracious King—Emperor the loyal assurance that should the necessity arise, which God forbid, the swords of myself and of my Army, and of all my subjects of the fighting classes, as well as the entire resources of my State, will, without the slightest hesitation, be once more placed at the disposal of His Majesty.

I am sure that I am voicing the sentiments also of my brother Princes when I say how much I rejoice in the thought that His Majesty our present King—Emperor and his gracious Consort have, in their turn, secured such a warm place in the hearts of us all within so short a time and when I express the earnest hope that the condition of Europe will permit Their Majesties to honour India by their presence in our midst next year.

Of my own State I shall not say much. A Note has already been presented to Your Excellency reciting the more important facts and figures relating to the administration of my State since I came of age thirty-nine years ago. It is not for me to speak of these matters; but I trust I may without impropriety say that I have ungrudgingly devoted the best years of my life to the service of my State, and that my Government and I have striven, to the utmost of our capacity and resources, to contribute to the greater prosperity, happiness and contentment of my people. And I gratefully acknowledge that whatever success has been achieved during the past fifty years has been due in a large measure to the solicitude which the Crown and its Representatives in India have unfailingly shown towards the interests; of my State and to the loyal co-operation and valuable services of my Ministers and other Officers.

Sir, if I reflect upon the events of these five decades, I feel that no achievement has given me great satisfaction than the advent of the Gang Canal, which had been the most cherished ambition of my life ever since, as a youngman, I witnessed the ravages of the Great Famine of the year 1890. I am happy in the thought that at least in one part of my State that great venture has brought water to the desert and broad to the famished and created a thousand thriving villages out of the arid sand.

Human nature, however, is never content. It desires ever to reach forward to new ideals. I have hopes, through a still greater undertaking, of securing for my people in the other fertile parts of our State beyond the reach of the Gang Canal the benefits of irrigation. I referred to this subject at length in my speeches at the Banquets during the visits of Lord Irwin and Lord Willingdon; and Your Excellency, with your profound interest in agriculture, and your firsthand knowledge of rural conditions in India, acquired as Chairman of the Royal Commission on Agriculture, does not need to be reminded of what such irrigation would mean to the people of a country like mine, which, with its precarious rainfall, is so subject to failure of crops, to scarcity and famine.

Amongst the other schemes which we have under consideration, I need only mention the development of our mineral resources, as yet practically untapped, and the industrial utilisation of our raw products, especially in the area served by the Gang Canal. For the fruition of some of these schemes we shall be dependent in no small measure upon the active sympathy and support of Your Excellency and your Government; and I have every confidence that, when the time comes, the interests and claims of my State will receive the same generous consideration which they have always received at the hands of the Crown Representative.

This is hardly the proper place for a discussion of political problems; but I may be permitted to say a few words about a matter that is in all our minds; the question of the accession of the States to the proposed All India Federation. We in the Indian States have reason to be grateful to Your Excellency for the appreciation which you have shown from the beginning of your Viceroyalty of the problems confronting us. The special machinery which Your Excellency devised for ascertaining the views of the Princes and for helping to remove their doubts and difficulties clearly indicated the solicitude you felt for their interests. Your Excellency was good enough to tell us frankly during the session of the Chamber of Princes last February that one outcome of the discussions between the States and your special Representatives had been to present in a new light to your own mind more than one aspect of this manysided problem and to express the strong hope that means may be found in the not too distant future to reach conclusions satisfactory to all concerned, and to assure us that you would continue, as in the past, to do all in your power to afford us the necessary assistance in arriving at the momentous decision which we shall have to take ere long. All this has demonstrated to the Princes that they have in Your Excellency a statesman who will give to their views full wieght and, what is more, maintained and uphold their internal autonomy and their rights and privileges, based on Treaties and other engagements, against encroachment from any quarter.

insufficiently informed public opinion is apt to view with suspicion the inevitably long discussions and negotiations between the British Government and the Princes and to ascribe to the Governments of the States as a whole the intention to drive hard bargains at the expense of their brethren in British India.

I have for many years been a staunch believer in a Federal constitution for India, which would unite as equal partners the States of India already sovereign, and the British Indian Provinces recently made autonomous. To that faith I adhered to-day. But I may say that for such a federation to be successful, it is necessary that the States should have that freedom in their internal administration, that guarantee of their unhampered economic, political and social development, that opportunity to foster all that is great and noble in their traditions, which alone would enable them to make their fullest contribution to the common good of India.

It seems to be forgotten that seven years ago, when the Princes of India offered of their own accord to sacrifice some part of their sovereignty in order that the Foundation Stone should be laid of a United India, they were inspired by a genuine desire to facilitate the advance of India as a whole to Dominion States under the aegis of the British Crown. It is only natural that in the attempt to translate this glorious vision into constitutional reality the State had to face—to quote Your Excellency's words in your all complicated questions", which cannot be solved merely by a stroke of the pen. Nevertheless, should the States, as I greatly hope they will, find it possible to accede to the Federation, there need be no fear in anyone's mind that the activities of our representatives in the Federal sphere would, on account of our peculiar traditions and forms of government, be any the less inspired by the urge for the further progress and advancement of our cornmon Motherland than those of the other federating Units.

I will conclude my allusion to this subject by expressing the earnest hope, which I am sure is shared by all the States, that as a result of further negotiations the outstanding problems will be solved, and the safeguards essential to the preservation of the rights and interests of the States embodied in the revised draft of the Instrument of Accession. The fulfilment of this expectation will prove the way to that United India of which some of us of the Indian States had dreamt dreams long before the First Round Table Conference met in 1930.

Before I resume my seat, may I say how glad I am that so many friends, including those who have come out all the way from England, have been able to be present here in response to my invitation? Among them there is no one whom I, together with everyone in Bikaner, am more delighted to welcome than my old Tutor and Guardian and my dearest friend, Sir Brian Egerton, who, out of his love for me, has made a point of being with me on this occasion and to whom I and my subjects owe a debt of gratitude which we can never repay for all the care and affection which he bestowed upon me and the truly wonderful manner in which he tried to equip me for my great responsibilities.

I am also glad to see here several members of the Political Department, and especially Sir Bertrand Glancy, an old Rajputana friend. I welcome this opportunity of expressing once again the sense of indebtedness of the Princes and States to that great Department and its Officers for the invaluable help which they have so frequently given to the States.

I great miss today an old friend whom I saw aptly described the other day as the beau ideal of a Political Officer, Lieut—Colonel Sir George Ogilvie, by whose recent retirement Rajputana has suffered the loss of a most popular and sympathetic Political Officer. I am, however, glad to welcome, for the first time to Bikaner, his successor, Mr. Lothian, Whose intimate acquaintance with the problems of Federation will, we are confident, be of particular benefit to the States of Rajputana.

Ladies and gentlemen, I give you the toast of my illustrious friends, His Excellency the Viceroy and Her Excellency the Marchioness of Linlithgow, and I have the greatest pleasure in asking you to join me in wishing Their Excellencies every possible good fortune.

# Annexure 12

**Speech delivered by General His Highness the Maharajah of Bikaner, G.C.S.I., G.C.I.E., G.C.V.O., G.B.E., K.C.B., A.D.C. LL.D. at the Banquet given by His Highness Government on the 16th November 1937 in honour of the Golden Jubilee of His Highness the Maharaja's Accession to the Throne.**

*Prime Minister, Ladies and Gentlemen;*

To say to you—my Colleagues in the task of governing the State—that I thank you would be a mere formality. I want to express more fully what I feel at this moment; I feel that I am within the family circle of which I am regarded as the centre. it is this feeling, only intensified by the uniqueness of the occasion, which has sustanied me during the hard years behind me, and which will continue to sustain me, and I am sure you all, in treading the path of duty, steadfastly, in these days of rapid change.

Considering the temper of this age, I especially prize the tribute of my Officers, since they are in the best position to appreciate my aims. And I know that without the service-loyal and ungrudging—which I have received from my Officers—Bikaneries and others—during the last 39 years, we could not have achieved the measure of success which impartial judges may feel disposed to concede to us.

Impressed with the service so renderded, I have, in promoting the efficiency of the State's Services, tried to impart to them the greatest practicable measure of security, subject of course to the exigencies of administration. I think we may claim that we have banished corruption as far as that is an attainable dieal; but we need the co-operation of the people themselves in rooting out this evil. We have also, as far as conditions permitted, recruited our Services from indigenous talent. Since 1906 we have been training our young men with that object in view, and our ideal is to recruit every branch of the Services from all ranks of State subjects, who obviously have the prior right to be employed.

I am aware that some people believe that I have a weakness for employing European Officers: there has also been a complaint from time to time about the employment of persons from outside the State in offices of public responsibility. If it be a weakness to promote the interests of the State by selecting the best person available for a particular post, I have this weakness, and I am not ashamed of it. I have said it before publicly, and I say it again, that in my estimation the mere fact that a person is a European or a Pardeshi cannot be a bar to his employment in Bikaner so long as by qualification and experience he is found to be best suited for the position to which he is called. I would take this opportunity of expressing my indebtedness to the several European Officers in State employ who have rendered consicuous services—on no occasion more strikingly than on the occasion of the Jubliee—and also my sincere appreciation of the Pardeshi Officers whose work in their respective spheres has been no less valuable.

Of a piece with the criticism regarding the employment of Europeans and Pardeshi is the assertion that I am in the habit of doing everything myself, which is the same thing as saying that I do not decentralise the work and therefore do not give my Officers the opportunity of pulling their weight in the boat. Strangely enough, this impression is not confined to people outside the State; it also finds place in the minds of some State servants, though only such as are not brought into intimate touch with me. To discuss and to analyse this impression would be to set up a defence, which I have no need to do. However, I can honestly say that I am a firm believer in decentralization and that I have attempted to give it effect; indeed I have urged its necessity from time to time on those concerned. I only wish it were more commonly realised that not only on important occasions, but even generally, I long for relief from the strain which circumstances unavoidably impose upon me. Perhaps my great fault is my idealism. I do believe that if a thing is worth going, it is worth doing well; and I subscribe to the dictum that "the highest point of perfection is to do small things in a perfect manner". I do not think it can be denied that attention to detail is an essential prerequisite of success. If this principle were not translated into practice I doubt if His Excellency the Viceroy would have remarked in a letter which he wrote to me only a couple of days ago that the arrangements for his visit were "really perfect". It gives me very great pleasure to take this opportunity of conveying to all my Officers who were responsible for the elaborate arrangements to which His Excellency refers, the generous appreciation of the Viceroy. This recalls to my mind the Motto engraved on the ring of my famous Ancestor Balhara, of the Rathore Empire of the South, namely, "work commenced with resolute determination and carried on with perseverance must end in success".

There is one other relevant consideration which is often forgotten. It is the exigencies of service in any organised Government which necessitate superannuation and the replacement of old officers by new. The latter cannot always posses the requisite background or the ripe experience which their predecessors did. This lack of essential knowledge has to be made up by some one, and that some one has to be a person who, unlike the servants of the State, has got to carry, for all his living days, the responsibility for the State's work and its reputation. I mean the hereditary Ruler who cannot retire, but remains and goes on accumulating experience, while his tried co-adjutors, after serving their time out, can have a life of un-burdened serenity.

Prime Minister, you have touched upon many interesting points in your speech and I feel bound to refer to some of them.

As for my trust in my Ministers, the task of government has become so complex in these days that it is essential for every Ruler to consult his Ministers on every problem of administration. It is, therefore, nothing strange that I seek counsel with you whenever the occasion arises to take an important decision. You all know I do not merely do this, which I am bound to do, but that, in order to ensure that every aspect of any problem under consideration is thoroughly scrutinised, I also consult, whenever necessary, the leading non-officials of our States.

You have also referred to the unkind criticism which appeared in certain organs of the Press of measures which we had never adopted. Such criticism is to be expected in these days; partly because the means for verifying baseless reports spread by disaffected persons are not usually available to the Press and partly because a section of the reading public appreaciates stories which are sensational. While we may, as we do, correct misconceptions, we must not be put out by anything grotesque or utterly untrue. As for fair and well-intentioned criticism, why should anyone object to it? I certainly do no—indeed I welcome it—so long as the criticism is meant to be, and is in fact, helpful. At the same time, I wonder how many of the people who do criticise have any notion of the anxiety of the Rulers and their Ministers to confer upon their people all the benefits that the people really need, or realise the difficulties which prevent the Governments of the States from attaining their ideals in that respect. From the point of view alone, we should not be unduly sensitive of criticism. The shoulders of the Ruler and his Ministers should be broad enough to bear the brunt of the kind of criticism that is usually directed against them. And he must be a weak Ruler who seeks to defend himself by the assertion that if certain measures were not carried out it was not for want of foresight or initiative on his part. The criticism that one is accustomed to hear should make no difference to our honest purpose—service to the State by promoting the happiness of our people, according to our best lights. And while this purpose inspires the Ruler and his Ministers, they are entitled to the fullest support of one another.

I am very glad that the Council is examining with care and in detail the question of taxation with the view of aniving at balanced conclusions. We have no desire to overtax our people. not do we utilise the bulk of the revenue raised from taxation for any other purpose than the welfare of the body politic which requires an efficient administration, as much as it requires continuous additions to beneficent institutions. so long as we give back to the people what we take from them, give it back by the provision of amenities, of means to promote their health and to enlighten their minds, we need not feel conscience-stricken by the thought that we lay them under contribution. All governments tax their subjects: we too have to tax them. My policy, however, is that we must not unduly hamper their resources.

I am gratified by your allusion to the orders I passed sometime ago requiring that the problem of rural reconstruction must be seriously tackled to the end of reducing the indebtedness of our agricultural classes, of saving them from the expenses of litigation and of augmenting their assets by the improvement of their catle, their seeds and their implements.

I am keener than ever on the accomplishment of these objects and I am proud to think that His Excellency the Viceroy is with me in treating rural reconstruction as the fundamental problem of India's economic development. I want our Village Panchayats and our District Boards to become effective bodies and I want to see illiteracy banished from our State.

You have alluded to my personal loyalty to the King-Emperor. Our loyalty to the Person and Throne of the King-Emperor is a matter of the Rajput's word which cannot be broken. But the traditional loyalty of my House apart, I cannot forego this opportunity to say that the gracious courtesy, the solicitude for the happiness of myself and my family and for the prosperity of my State which the illustrious Occupants of that great Throne have been pleased to show shall remain with me ineffaceable memories—memories which make our devotion to His Majesty the King-Emperor deeper, if that were possible. I know that my people share my feelings in this matter and I also know that in any emergency that might arise they will prove by their deeds to be true the professions I have consistently made on my own behalf and theirs.

You have referred to our form of Government. That form has, I agree, been preserved in its essential elements as we inherited it from our forefathers; but efforts have, at the same time, been made in every direction possible to adapt it to the modern idea of state-craft.

That last twenty years have witnessed an upheaval in the social and political world, as sudden and violent as any upheaval of Nature. In the march of time, ambitions arise whihc transcend the settled principles of a certain social structure; new social theories engage people's attention and invite experiments; examples of distant lands prove infectious.

A great part of India is at this moment experiencing the impact of fresh ideas of Government upon its traditional social organisation. We in the Indian States are watching events with the greatest interest, anxious to bring to our people the benefits of any innovation that may prove advantageous, because we are aware that time does not stand still.

At the same time we must not hastily imitate what is being done elsewhere, because it may be that by such rasheness we would undermine our ancient forms of government without achieving what should be the real purpose of any political reform : an increase in the happiness of our people.

Similarly, seeing outside events in their correct perspective, it is legitimate to maintain that rivalry between communities forming parts of the same body politic should not only be discouraged but suppressed with a strong hand. I think the States have every justification for counteracting the insidious canker of communalism.

Autocracy seems to have come to mean something utterly evil, whereas the term stands simply for personal rule. A Ruler, it must be admitted, may be either despotic or benevolent; but can it not be claimed that a benevolent Ruler may be the true servant of his people, while popular government, which is now-a-days frequently regarded as the touchstone of progress, may well carry some elements of autocracy?

The Provinces of British India enjoy autonomy to-day. they have our best wishes for the realisation of all their hopes from that system of self-expression. If the measure of autonomy they have secured does not afford them complete satisfaction let them strive by all legitimate means to enlarge it. We shall have no reason to oppose such an effort. But, equally, we should be permitted to foster our heritage—our distinctive form of government. That form has been successful in the past. We want to make it even more successful in the future. We are, therefore, entitled to expect that we should be left to work out our salvation in our own way, so long as our people are content that their Rulers should guide their destinies. What we want to be spared is the inflaming of our people's minds, the weaning of them from their traditional loyalty. it was with this thought in mind that in the speech which I delivered on the 10thNovember 1913 when I inaugurated the Representative Assembly I advised it to "hasten slowly". I would repeat that advice now, with even greater insistence as I have recently given that body an elected majority.

I think we have every reason to feel grateful to a merciful Providence which has caused fortune to smile upon us. Our material resources have continued to expand and our people to benefit by the augmentation of our resources. We have escaped strife between different communities, and our people are happy in their traditional relations of trust with their Ruler. We have, inded, much to be thankful for.

The last thing I have to say to you, my Councillors, who are associated with me in the task of administering the State and who share my ideal of government, is that our courage must not flinch merely because some people obtrude their kind attentions upon us. We must go on labouring as heretofore for the well-being of our people.

Prime Minister, I thank you and all your colleagues for the very pleasant evening you have given me and my fellow guests, and I pray that the years that remain to me may be marked by the steady realisation of our common aims and objects.

# 11

# Conclusion

MAHARAJA GANGA SINGH was a visionary par excellence. Imbibed with western ideas and thought he tried to strike a fine balance between benevolent despotism and progressive outlook—a true "servant of the people'. It was Llyod George, the British Premier, who remarked about the Maharaja that "we soon found out that he was one of the Wise Men that came from the East. "In a similar vien the Viceroy, Lord Minto, had also noted that "the Maharaja, while recognizing what is good in Western ways of thought, has not allowed himself to become disassociated from the individuality of his own countrymen". Other insights into the personality of Maharaja Ganga Singh were provided by his biographer, Sardar Pannikar, who commented thus :

> "Essentially a soldier, statesman and administrator, the Maharaja is little moved by the appeal of the arts. . . His lack of humanistic interest gives the Maharaja a mainly utilitarian outlook on life . . . and consequently there is a rigidness and inelasticity in his ideas. It was therefore, not by versatility but by concentration on things of immediate interest that the Maharaja achieved greatness. In another place Ganga SinghJi was described as someone who occupied a great position in Indian politics and social life. A man of striking personal beauty, charm and great ambition. . . A very cosmopolitan, a very sophisticated man, but one who never forgot his Rajput past. He was a wonderful host and did not ignore old friends even if they were quite unimportant people. Neither did he ever fail to keep contact with friends old and new who were very important people. . . ."

Ganga Singh Ji, as mentioned above, had the rare gift of making friends with and influencing people from various walks of life. Royals, statesmen, political leaders—all viewed for his friendship. Among one of his very close friends was the King-Emperor of India, George V. The latter, even as Prince of Wales, was greatly impressed by the Maharaja with whom he formed an abiding friendship. The Prince also favoured Bikaner with a State visit in 1905 and went away with fond memories. President Chemencean of France was another friend of Ganga Singh Ji whom the latter greatly impressed during the Peace settlement. The friendship was cemented when the former French President visited Bikaner for a short in 1920.

It was however, with successive Viceroys that Maharaja Ganga Singh established personal rappart and most of his contemporary Viceroys honoured Bikaner with State visits. Beginning with the visit of Lord Elgin in 1896 to Bikaner, others continued the tradition over the years. Lord Curzon (1902) Lord Minto (1906 and 1908), Lord Hardinge (1912 and 1915), Lord Chelmsford (1920), Lord Reading (1922), Lord Irwin (1927), Lord Willington (1943), Marguis of Lintithgow (1937) were other Viceroys to visit Bikaner. In addition there were visits of British Army Commander -in-Chiefs in 1896 and 1913 respectively. The visits of these dignatories were occasions which were utilized by the Maharaja to outline the progress of the Bikaner State and put forward the State's perspective before the visiting dignatories.

The speeches also had an personal element injected in them by the Maharaja and thus spelled out his agenda forcefully. His relations with national leaders and freedom fighters were marked with an openness and frankness which was unusual for that age. His meeting with Gandhi in 1931 was significant as it was marked by rare acuteness and condidness. His letter to Sir Donald Field, the Prime Minister of Jodhpur, in 1937 with regard to the affairs of Jai Narain Vyas was an essay in political sagacity and the maturing of Maharaja Ganga Singh as the elder statesman of India. The Maharaja conceded that Jai Narayan Vyas was one of the bitterest critics of the Princely order and termed them as intolerent autocrats who perpetuated 'bad rule' or misrule in their States. But inspite of this Ganga Singh Ji held Vyas in very high esteem and deemed him as an honest politician committed to the welfare of the masses and Indian independence. Ganga Singh Ji also went on to state that the old order would inevitably change and in the changed circumstances it would be preferably if power was handed over to people like Vyas. If the Princes were to fall at the mercy of the elected governments, it was better if such governments were led by men like Vyas, so rare the argument of Maharaja Ganga

Singh. The Maharaja went on to add that when he was informed that that Vyas was facing financial problems, he had offered monetary aid through the Rao of Phalodi which Vyas has declined. Maharaja Ganga Singh requested Sir Donald Field to disuade Vyas from joining the cinema.

# *Appendices*

Appendix 1

## Select Speeches on Various Matters on Different Occasions

Speech at the State Banquet given to Their Excellencies the Viceroy and Lady Hardinge on Saturday, the 30th November, 1912.

**Your Excellencies, Your Honour, Ladies and Gentlemen,**

I beg to offer Your Excellencies the warmest of welcomes to my Capital. We much appreciate Your Excellency's honouring Bikaner with a visit and being present at the State festivities and I hope Your Excellency is already aware of the very genuine pleasure you have given me by accepting my invitation—pleasure which is considerably enhanced by the fact that Her Excellency Lady Hardinge has been able to accompany Your Excellency.

2. It was my good fortune to make Your Excellency's acquaintance from the very day of your assumption of the office of Viceroy and in return for the many kindnesses and much hospitality which I have invariably received at the hands of Lady Hardinge and yourself, I rejoice at this opportunity of showing my gratitude and offering what hospitality lies in your power.

3. The two years since Your Excellency's arrival out here have been very momentous ones for India. The close of Lord Minto's Viceroyalty was marked by a very considerable abatment in the political ferment which caused so much anxiety to all true lovers of India but it was ordained that during Your Excellency's regime the disquieting symptoms should practically disappear. This is due to no small extent to the unmistakeable sympathy which, as in the case of your predecessor, has characterized Your Excellency's Rule also and to your strict impartiality and the restoration of general confidence. A salient feature of Your Excellency's Viceroyalty is the ready access that you have accorded to all whether at Head Quarters or on tour, and there can be no doubt that this privilege, granted by Your Excellency at no small inconvenience to yourself and at the sacrifice of much valuable time, has been very widely and gratefully appreciated. It is the hope and conviction of Your Excellency's friends and well-wishers-amongst whom I hope I may be counted—that when

the time comes, you will be in a position to hand over India to your successor restored to its normal condition of peace and prosperity.

4. But the crowning event of this period is the ever memorable visit to India's shores of Their Imperial Majesties the King Emperor and the Queen Empress, whose progress might justly be described as one triumphant march. During this tour Their Majesties—who had already established themselves in the affections of the people during their previous visit to India in1905—by their gracious solicitude for the people of India and by the many prctical demonstrations of their well-known sympathy—of which our Kind Emperor has always been such an ardent advocate—captured the hearts of their millions of subjects wherever they went. The many brilliant and glorious scene enacted in Delhi and Calcutta will, by universal accord, produce a lusting and beneficial effect and will most materially strengthen the foundations of the empire and will be of inestimable advantages to India and its people. What Their Imperial Majestics have contributed towards allaying the unrest is not for me to describe. It will be writ large on the pages of history. Personal rule and the personal element count for a great deal in India. The wild outbursts of enthusiasm and deep devotion evinced at Delhi and Calcutta will never be effaced from the memories of those who, like myself, had the honour of being in attendance on His Imperial Majesty and of witnessing them. Happy the country and happy the Empire which can boast of such Sovereigns, and I am proud to think that it is only in a country like India where such scenes of reverential devotion to the King Emperor can be met with.

5. As an Indian I also rejoice to think that the Imperial visit, in addition to other lasting and substantial advantages, has been instrumental in dispelling the illusion, where it may have existed, in the minds of ill-informed or ignorant persons, as to the disloyalty of India and its people as a whole. And as one yielding to none in loyalty to the Sovereign, I rejoice no less to hink that the occasion has been not without a moral from another point of view. For it has been shown to the world in a manner which admits of no gainsaying that in this country, where the heart of India can be so stirred to its depths by the presence of the Sovereign, where the Person of the Emperor is held so sacred and where the Members of his Royal Family are so reverenced, republican and socialistic ideas cannot find a foothold or be acceptable to the people of India—for these ideas are clearly opposed to their natural instincts, traditions, and religious precepts.

6. Indeed, the Tour undertaken by Their Imperial Majesties on their own initiative in spite of the dismal forebodings and warnings

of self-styled prophets could not possibly have been more successful.

7. The gracious and generous boons and the sagacious and statesmanlike administrative measures sanctioned by His Imperial Majesty and announced at the Imperial Durbar at Delhi cannot but be productive of the most momentous results, and I venture to say that of the many beneficial steps then taken none will be more popular than the restoration of the old and Imperial City of Delhi as the Capital of India, which has given special gratification to the Ruling Princes.

8. Your Excellency, we, the Ruling Chiefs, and the Protected States, also have reason to be grateful that there is at the head of the Indian Government at the present moment a Viceroy like Your Excellency, who has already clearly demonstrated to us his solicitude for our welfare and prosperity and his wish to cultivate and maintain the most friendly and intimate relations with us. And the fact that a very large number of Ruling Chiefs since Your Excellency's arrival have spent so many days with Your Excellencies under your hospitable roofs in Calcutta and Simla is another proof of this, if proof were needed. Lord Minto and his then Foreign Secretary—Sir Harcourt Butler—were able in their time to do great deal in many ways for us and our States, and I know there is a general feeling of hope and belief that anything that may yet remain to be done will not be neglected or forgotten by Your Excellency and by my friend, Sir Henry McMahon.

9. The honourable part which the States have played in the past in co-operating with the Government of India in times of stress or anxiety, will always remain one of our most precious heritages and it is a matter of no less satisfaction to us that we can look back on those periods with pride and a clear conscience. For, it is not only because we are bound by ties of the deepest loyalty and devotion to the King Emperor and the British Throne—it is not only because we realise how very closely the interests of the British Government and those of the States are linked together—but because as Indians, and yielding, as we do, to none in our love for the mother country, we also realise that the future well-being of Indian as a whole and the prosperity and interests of the Indian people can only be best promoted and secured by the permance of British Rule, under which the territories of British India as well as those of the States enjoy such inestimable advantages.

10. Your Excellency is also entitled to our gratitude for the special interest you have evinced in the education of minor Chiefs and in the minority administration of our States. In this connection may I be permitted, as one who is closely associated by family ties and as

the senior in age of the Rulers of the Rathore States in Rajputana, to say how indebted we are for the arrangements which your Excellency was pleased to make for the administration of the Jodhpur State during the minority of His Highness the Maharajah. Time has shown that no better arrangements could have been made, and the nomination by Your Excellency of His Highness Sir Pratap Singh as Maharajah Regent of Jodhpur has shown us how wise the appointment was. The difficulties which Sir Pratap Singh has to contend with are great and his task is no easy one, but by his patience, coolness and unselfish devotion to duty His Highness has won the admiration of all of us who, as relations and neighbours, are acquainted with the internal affairs of the State.

11. As regards the administration of my State, I do not propose taking up time tonight with any lengthy review. I have had the pleasure of presenting Your Excellency with a Note regarding facts and figures of my fourteen years' actual administration. When Lord Minto paid his official visit here in 1906, I dwelt at some length in my speech on the urgent need for Irrigation in the State and the subject has been fully dealt with in my Note on this occasion also. Without going over the same ground tonight may I say that as the Sutlej Canal project has in the last six years advanced a step further, in that the surveys have been completed, we shall eagerly await the issue in due course of the final orders of the Government of India on this question of such vital importance to us. It has been a great pleasure to me that Your Excellency should have agreed to my suggestion to visit the Secretariat and the Public Offices at my Capital. Such a cursory inspection could not, I am aware, have enabled Your Excellency to judge of the standard of work turned out in the various branches of your administration, nor do we lay claim to have reached anywhere near the stage of perfection, but I hope it was sufficient to show Your Excellency that we are trying to do our best for the State and the people and that our aim is efficiency combined with decentralisation. Your Excellency's whole-hearted interest in Education in this country, of which so many indications are already tracelable in the educational policy of the Government of India, led me to hope that you would also honour the Dungar Memorial College and the Walter Nobles' School with a visit, to see for yourself our modest endeavours in this connection. I beg to thank Your Excellency most sincerely for visiting the Offices and these educational and other Institutions as also for honouring the Railway branch of our State Administration by opening the Bikaner—Ratangarh Chord Line—for the speedy completion of which great credit is due to Mr. La Touche, the able Manager of our

Railway, and to his Staff. All this will be source of great encouragement and stimulus to us in our many undertakings.

12. Ladies and gentlemen, I ask you to raise your glasses and to join me in drinking a bumper to the health of Their Excellencies the Viceroy and Lady Hardinge and in wishing them long life, success and every happiness.

## Speech Delivered by His Highness the Maharajah of Bikaner at the Farewell Dinner to Mr. Rudkin on 3-3-1920

*Your Highness, Ladies & Gentlemen,*

I hope not to detain you very long tonight for it is not by the length of a speech but by the sincerity of purpose inspiring the words used that one's feelings are gauged on the occasion like this.

I should in ordinary circumstances have preferred two separate functions instead of giving this banquet jointly in honour of Mr. LaTouche. But farewell dinners are always sad and dismal events of which I am sure nobody—much less the principal actors—desires to have too much. And unfortunately the time left between my return from Jamnagar and my going to Nepal also rendered that impossible. I think, however, that it will be agreed that there is something peculiarly appropriate in tonight's joint function in that both Mr. Rudkin and Mr. LaTouche are officers unusually popular and respected, both officially and socially, by everyone in the State and as such both entitled to our special gratitude.

I felt, however, that before available myself of a much-needed holiday in Nepal, I must take this opportunity of testifying once again to my high sense of appreciation of the really splendid services rendered to the Bikaner State by my friends Messrs Rudkin and LaTouche and of gratitude which all concerned in the State owe to them for their excell work, as also of giving expression our deep sense of genuine regret at their impending departure after so many years spent in our midst.

The 8 years of Mr. Rudkin's service in the State have been exceptionally busy ones. In the earlier period of his deputation here much heavy and important work devolved upon him as Revenue Commissioner in connection with the Land Revenue Settlement and the re-organization of the Revenue Department of the State and initiating and putting into effect the present policy of my Government as regards the grant of Occupancy Rights in the northern portion of my dominions. During this period not only did Mr. Rudkin gain special sucess but his marked ability and sympathy and sense of justice have won for him alike the administration and the confidence of both the State and its people. And I think it is noexaggeration to say that no official has ever been more popular in this State than Mr. Rudkin.

No more practical proof of his great popularity and of the high esteem in which he is held by everyone throughout the State can be given than that of his holding the office of a Member of the State Executive Council and of his being one of the three Ministers in the Cabinet, to both of which I had the pleasure of appointing him early in 1917 prior to my departure for England to take part in the Imperial War Conference and Cabinet Meetings of that year. For he is the first British Officer to receive such promotion or to have held the rank of a Cabinet Ministrer during the past 21 years and more, since I assumed the reins of government. Now let no one misunderstand me. My learnings towards Englishmen with whom I have been associated since my early childhood, are, I trust, well known; and at the Jubilee Banquet given by the British residents of the State on the 28th September, 1912, I had, in alluding to the policy persued by me and my Government, made it clear in my speech that where the interests of the State demanded it, and where we felt that the employment of British Officers of conspicuous ability eminently fitted for certain duties, would tend to usefulness and the enhanced efficiency of the State Administration, we would continue to avail ourselves of their services. But these remarks had special reference more to Departmental appointment and my not inconsiderable personal experience, confined not only to this State, and shown that all the desired results and expectations cannot always be achieved by the indiscriminate or peneral appointment of British Officers to a State Council. And this inspite of their high standard of integrity, ability, and conscientious devotion to duty. But the training, and the nature of their duties in British India, as also in the State Departments in which they may have already served, as so different from the special training, knowledge, experience and habit of mind required for carrying on the Government of an Indian State. Numerous other difficulties also come in the way and—although I am happy to feel that intrigue which was so ripe amongst certain State Officials when I came of a nearly a quarter of a century ago, is practically non-existent in our State—I have even known cases in other places of British Officials such appointments, finding themselves involved, quite unknown to themselves in a net-work of intrigue insiding and cleverly worked by designing experts of the game.

Although it is not improbable that in the future also we shall at times see a British Officer holding similar high appointment in the Government of the State, Mr. Rudkin's appointment to the Council and Cabinet was an exceptional measure taken by in exception circumstances and with exceptional hopes, and right well has Mr. Rudkin answered those expectations.

His Colleagues on the Cabinet and Council have often expressed to me their deep sense of obligation for the invaluable assistance which they have received from him and for the large share which he has had in the many important measures and reforms introduced during the past 3 years and no one is better aware than myself of this or of all the heavy duties which devolved on Mr. Rudkin as a Cabinet Minister and Member of Council. We shall all remain no less indebted to him for his equally meritorious work as President of the Bikaner State War Board. In fact I have no hesitation in saying that much of the success achieved in regard to the recruiting policy of the State and the War Loans is due to Mr. Rudkin's exceptional energies and able efforts. Amongst other matters it is also in no small measure due to Mr. Rudkin's labours that one of our greatest hopes—the Sutlej Canals project—is, we trust, now on the eve of realization.

Small wonder then, that we all should wish to pay this tribute of our gratitude and appreciation to Mr. Rudkin and that there should be universal desire to see back amongst us again, to help us in the many important schemes which we have before us, one, who by his whole-heartedly identifying himself with us in every way and through his courtesy tact any sympathy will always retain an abiding place in our hearts. At one time we greatly feared that Mr. Rudkin's proceeding on long leave might mean the end of his deputation to this State but I am indebted to my friend Sir Edward Maclagan for really a good turning in that His Honour, so thoughfully anticipating the great inconvenience which Mr. Rudkin's long leave would cause us has only given him leave for a year. Though I am truly sorry that his well-eamed rest is thus cut short. I am sure every one here will be really delighted to learn that there is now more than a reasonable prospect of Mr. Rudkin's coming back to us next summer—a happy consummation we all so earnestly desire.

Eight years is not an inconsiderable period in one's life time but three times that number of years and two more, is still greater and my old friend Mr. LaTouche has the record of having been longest in the service of the State amongst the British Officers, past and present. I have had the pleasure of referring on more occasions than one before this to his loyal and meritorious services and to the universal esteem and good will which he has won not only in Bikaner but also in Jodhpur through his unfailing courtesy, his intimate knowledge and understanding of the customs and ways of our people and his free and friendly intercourse with us all. What I said in my speech at the British Officers' Banquet in 1912 applies still more today, viz., that by his reciprocating in the same spirit the proverbial Rajput courtesy and by his genuine sympathy and love for the people of the country he has won our friendship regard and affection. Indeed I would go further and say today without fear of contradiction that Mr. La Touche has set a splendid example to the people of his race in all parts of the world of what the relations should be between Englishmen and Indians and of the manner in which a British Officer, serving under the Government of an Indian State, should associate himself with the State and the people with whom he is brought into official and social relations.

In passings, may I express the hope that depth of our cordiality of feeling for Mr. LaTouche equally clearly domonstrates the response which such efforts will invariably evoke from the Indian community!

We can also never forget that it is due largely to Mr. LaTouche, loyally supported by the British Officers serving under him, that the Railway Department of the State—by which term I here particularly allude to its personnel—is at present popular in the State and that everything connected with it is in such smooth working order now, I am reluctant to refer to past history of an unpalatable nature on this occasion, but a sense of grateful appreciation of Mr. LaTouche's laudable and successful efforts in this direction render a brief allusion to it unavoidable. When Mr. La Touche was appointed Manager in 1909, affairs connected with the State Railway were, through circumstances which I need not to detail here, in a particularly unsatisfactory condition and instead of the Railway being looked upon, as it essentially and undoubted is, a department of the State, a mistaken tendency was noticeable in certain quarters to regard it as something connected with the State Administration and beyond its authority and control. The tone set and the lead given by Mr. LaTouche has, I repeat, been the greatest advantage and I venture mutual benefit to all concerned and Mr. LaTouche, on his leaving us, has the satisfaction of feeling that at no time have the relations between State and its Railway been as cordial as they are at the present day.

I am sorry, in an after dinner speech to inflict upon you, Ladies and Gentlemen, some facts and figures, but I think they will be more eloquate in prasie of Mr. LaTouche than any words of mine can be.

When Mr. LaTouche took over chargew the total mileage the Jodhpur—Bikaner Railway system was 951; today the mileage of the open line alone amounts to 1,356 and this does not include the hundreds of miles of line actually under construction or about to be cobstrycted. Similarly in 1909 the receipts for the Jodhpur—Bikaner Railway, including the British Section, stood at 37-1/2 lakhs. At the close of the last year this figure stood at 108 lakhs. During this period the operation line mileage of the Bikaner Railway has been raised from 251 to 498 and with the schemes, which the Bikaner State alone has under consideration and with which we hope at last to be able to proceed, the mileage of the Bikaner Railway by itself will amount to 1114 or 163 miles more than the entire length of the joint system with which Mr. La Touche dealt when he first became Manager. What further testimony can we have than the above of Mr. La Touche's work and inestimable services? During the past 18 years we have, as is also the case with Jodhpur, had to consider vast Railway schemes of far reaching import in connection with which we had to lean a great deal for counsel and assistance on Mr. LaToucheas our expert adviser, and the soundness of his advice and the value and merit of his work is best amplified the fact that all the schemes—some of them more than interstatal importance—which he recommended to us. I am glad to say, on the ever of receiving the formal approval of the British Government.

I was naturally extremely anxious to have Mr. LaTouche at my side to help us in carrying these schemes through which but for the war would have been completed by now, I was without hope of inducing him to come back after a little well merited leave but after the inordinately long period that Mr. LaTouche has been here since he last took leave in England, I am reluctantly compelled to defer to his wishes.Another and even more important factor has been the state of the health of Mrs. LaTouche, with whom I am privileged to claim long friendship, and I regretfully realize that she cannot stand another hot weather in India.

It is thus with a heavy heart that I have to bid goodbye to an old and loyal friend and the State is the poorer by the loss of one of its most able and highly trusted officers. Mr. La Touche will cary with him the high esteem and lasting regard of myself and the Officers of the State and of his innumerable friends not only in Bikaner but I feel sure I can add, also in other parts of India where he has resided.

I hope, however, that we shall have the pleasure of seeing Mr. LaTouche here during some of the coming winters when we hope further to have the advantage of his advice on the numerous important

Railway matters which we shall have to tackle in the next few years.

Ladies and Gentlemen, I cannot conclude without saying how much we shall also miss Mrs. Rudkin and LaTouche who have graced so many our social functions in so many occasions in the past and who have so ably supported their husbands in many different ways both in official and social matters. They too, like their poorer halves, will always occupy a warm comer in our heart.

And now, Ladies and Gentle will ask you to join me in drink to the very best health of Mr. and Mrs. Rudkin and of Mr. and Mrs. LaTouche and in wishing them a safe voyage to England and all good fortune and prosperity.

## His Highness' speech at the Full Council Meeting held on the 18th March 1921 for fixing a programme of important matters to be taken in hand.

*Gentlemen,*

As we have a great deal of business to get through I do not propose to take up more time today than is necessary in dealing with the past history of such meeting which a perusal of the old files reveal to each and every one of you.

2. As, however, several of the Members of Council of the present day were either not on the council in the old days or not even in the State service, it would be as well if I were to attempt to bring out a few salient points before we proceed with the business of the day.

3. The few meetings of this nature that were held after the inauguration of the new system of administration in October, 1902 will make abundantly clear the very great importance which has in the past been rightly attached to such meetings and to such works.

4. The object of these meetings is to enable me and my Government to work on a settled policy and to take up in the order of importance or urgency, various far-reaching schemes and questions, which have no small a bearing on the efficiency of our administration or the well-being of the State and its people.

5. Whilst all Members of Council are individually expected to do the best they can in all such matters, on their own initiative, in regard to the various departments coming under their portfolios, it is indeed of immense help to them individually as well as to the Government as a whole, no less than to myself that we should discuss, at least once a year, such questions at a round-table Conference and then go ahead on a fixed programme. Of course, it does not mean that no the

questions except those settled at such periodical meetings would be taken up, but it means at least that such questions as are decided upon at such meetings should, as far as humanly possible, be proceeded with the utmost possible despatch so that each year we may have some substantial work done for the benefit of our people and something substantial to show to the credit of our Government.

6. As in the case of the Administrative conferences after the institution of the Legislative Assembly, so in regard to those meetings for framing annual programmes for important work to be taken in hand, no greater mistake was made by me and my ministers of that time than to discontinue the holding of these meetings subsequent to the Administrative Conference having been made an annual institution. Obviously the subjects coming up before the Administrative Conference were for the most part of a different nature to those we discussed at these meetings. And there was plenty of room and plenty of work for the two meetings to run side by side without clashing or our doing the same work at both the meetings. But, unfortunately, we not only abandoned these Council Meetings but also the Administrative conference and as you all know both are now being revived.

7. I will leave for another day what I have to say in connection with the work of the Administrative Conferences. But today I would like to say that I attach the utmost possible importance to these Council meetings and I am firmly convinced that there is no more important work than this which I and the Members of my Government, whether collectively or individually, could deal with in the whole year. I hope I shall not offend any of my members of council, past or present, when I say that, I fear, that the importance of such meetings and the value of the work done at or emanating from such meetings has not of late been fully realized. It me also to have to add that in addition to this, some work, which might very well have been done as a result of past Council meetings, has also not been done and what is even more sad is that no attention has been paid to the past proceedings and in dealing with and finishing work entrusted to various officers even 15 years ago or more.

8. However I am not here today to find fault but rather to ensure satisfactory and efficient work being done in the future and I know that I can rely on the loyal cooperation and good will of all the Members of Council of the present day or of the future in helping me to make these annual meetings worthy of the occasion and to enable them to fulfil and to lend to their fulfiling, the hopes which I entertained in regard to these meetings and to the work resulting

therefore. And if later on in the course of my suggestions for remedying present defects I have to give some instances, I trust that they will be taken in the spirit in which they are intended. .

9. On the 12th March 1918 I held a Council Meeting with a view to reviving these meetings and to restart the work which has been abandoned as explained. Unfortunately, at that time there was an unusual rush and pressure of work due to the war for all concerned and I specially had arrears of work subsequent to my frequent unavoidable absences on duty from my state. I could therefore only hold one hurried meeting which I was able to bring forward a lost of points and to discuss others at the meetings and to give instructions to the cabinet and to all concerned for the future.

10. I fully appreciate also that some of my ministers also were at the time kept extremely busy in dealing with affairs arising directly from the war, which did not leave them much time to attend properly to such additional heavy work. But I am constrained to add that making all these allowances for these Members who were unusually busy I do maintain that it was possible both for the Council or the Cabinet as a whole and particularly for some individual Members not so overworked at least to have proceeded with certain matters and to have shown some progress at any rate in the past three years if not in the very first year. But I doubt if a careful examination of the various points discussed was not to be made, whether the proportion of matters taken up much less dealt with and disposed of, would show anything like a reasonable or satisfactory percentage. In these remarks the Cabinet or the Council of the Members of Council are not alone included but also others such as the office of the Private Secretary of the time being etc.

11. So far as I can see the proceedings were submitted to me on the 29th March under the signature of the Vice President, and Mr. Rudkin and to avoid delay extracts from the proceedings were forwarded to different Members of Council in anticipation of my approval.

12. Incidentally I think that in a matter of such importance the full proceedings and not only the extracts should have been sent to each Member of Council, because he is not only in charge of his own particular portfolio but is also a member of the Government It would appear that after that, little, if anything was done in regard to the whole thing and apparently the council or Cabinet as a whole paid very little attention to the matter.

13. In July 1919, however, that is some 16 months after the first meeting, individual members were asked to note the action taken on

various items, in compliance with which request replies were received from 4 Departments whilst those of two others are still awaited in spite of frequent reminders. This was put up by the Secretary before the Cabinet on the 26th March last year and the Cabinet apprently filed the case with the single word 'seen'.

14. I am unable to speak of what has been done in the past three years in the various Departments or at least in those Departments which have replied to the Cabinet's enquiries because the statements received have not been submitted to me but after going through the proceedings and so far as my personal knowledge goes, I am prepared to take up the challenge and that very little has been done and certainly nothing commensurate with the importance of the work or the lapse of three years.

15.I am prepared unqualifiedly to take my full share of blame in the matter of delay but it would no doubt be recollected that, apart from an absence of 9 months from November 1918 to July 1919, the rush of other more important and pressing work connected with the war and the after math of the war as well as the State and owing to a large amount of my time having been taken up in dealing with important external affairs in which our State is also vitally concerned and lastly the break-down of my health in July 1920 have resulted in my not having been able to do anything further in the matter myself. But I do not think that this was particularly a matter where there might have been greater co-ordination between the Cabinet and the Private Secretary's office. For instance, in regard to various items such as those of the 'Extra orders and points' given or raised by me under heading II 14, 15, 16, of the Proceedings and some other points such as in regard to the collection of tools etc. purchased for the last famine, Palace and Fort Rules and Regulations, etc., etc., it was noted in the proceedings, 'His Highness would write further about it' but were any steps taken by anyone concerned even in matters so immediate or urgent to obtain my orders on them. For, however, busy I am it is well-known that where possible I at least do make a point of finding time for attending to and disposing of urgent matters and the responsibility of the various members as well as the Cabinet to bring such urgent matters pending to my notice and to obtain my orders has repeatedly been prominently brought out and emphasized.

16. None of the Members of Council responsible for the work were, I believe, really busy with extra war work which could have prevented their dealing with the reorganization of the Bada Karkhana and as the Cabinet was carrying on and responsible for the administration of the State, the issue of some orders on their part also, which could

not have occupied more than few minutes could at least have resulted in the work being started and proceeded at once. But nothing appears to have been done with the result that we had to face some scandal and unsatisfactory work in the Bada Karkhana which was suddenly brought to light about a year ago.

17. Another item I find "II (35): A list of places where there are no Dharamsalas or wells to be drawn up and to be taken up as a famine relief work" and below that is a significant note made by the Secretary to the Cabinet and passed by all concerned stating "not understood". This point is not even alluded to in the Cabinet's note when submitting the proceedings to me for approval. I suppose that it was intended that I should to through the whole file and find out what points the Cabinet wanted to be elucidated, and so on. But I am afraid I had no time to go through the proceedings and relied on the Cabinet, with whom I had had a full discussion and to whom I had given full instructions to go into and deal with this question. Now it is clear that all the points brought forward by me at the last meeting or even this meeting are not specially the points raised by me on my own behalf and greater coordination with the Private Secretary's office would have revealed to the Cabinet that many of them were the result of the examination by me of various proceedings of past Administrative Conferences and other items still undisposed which were raised at such conferences or in the Legislative Assembly Meetings etc. The points I allude to, as a matter of fact, is item 4 on the list of questions pending fmal settlement from past Administrative Conferences and I certainly maintain that it was not my business but that of the Council or Cabinet to try and understand the question from such lists or the proceedings of past Administrative Conferences or failing that to recommend to me the elimination of the point or to deal with it in some other way.

18. Similarly on such occasions I frequently asked about undisposed of questions which were accepted by my Government at former:

(i) Revenue or Administrative Conferences, and
(ii) Legislative Assembly Meetings.

and gave orders that they should be taken up and although the Home Member, according to the Proceedings was asked to submit the list, surely it was not, intended that the Cabinet should not do anything in the matter but shoot the list on to my head. [vide item 44(2)].

19. In 1918 at the last Council Meeting dealing with such matters I had significantly and pointedly asked the Cabinet to consider item

45 "Whether there is any advantage in writing to the Government of India in regard to our requirements after the War by way rail and railway materials, lorries etc. I find however that many railways did make known their indents to the Railway Board and are now already receiving rails and other material. Had the individual Member of the Council and the Cabinet taken any heed of my suggestions, we should not how be waiting for rails for constructing the Hanumangarh Rajgarh Chord line and the Bikaner—Kolayat Branch. But I suppose that with the rest of the work connected with this futile meeting no importance was attached by anyone to such work or details.

20. So much as regard past history, subsequent to the last meeting, but my intention of holding a meeting this year was, at any rate, known ever since my return from Abu last July. Have the Council or the Cabinet or individual Members of Cabinet taken the slightest trouble to show what is being done, to see to the requisite information being obtained from the various departments and at least to give me information of what has been done and what has not been done? Obviously in the absence of such information a certain portion of our time will be wasted now in looking into and ascertaining what has been done and finished and remains over from the old Agenda.

21. As I have said already I have not convened this meeting with a view to finding fault though I trust that the instances and detrails that I have given above will show the unsatisfactory State of affairs.

22. The first point, however, to make today is that and if any proof were needed the details, alluded to above bring home clearly and unmistakeably the truth of the allegation that whole Government from myself downwards and including the cabinet and Council collectively and individually—is too much pre-occupies with routine matters and with daily cabinet meetings where also much time is taken up and that they are, therefore unable to deal with or tackle or dispose of important matters or to formulate big schemes which are urgently required. It is for this reason that I recently appointed a Cabinet Committees to deal with this question and it is for this reason that I returned the papers to the Cabinet for further proposals with a view really to give enhanced powers all round and to effect greater decentralization. Unless and until that is done and the Daily Cabinet meetings over routine papers are things of the past we shall never proceed satisfactorily but we shall just carry on from hand to mouth from to day and year in and year out. I do trust, therefore, that serious efforts will be made at any rate to reduce the time occupied daily in the Cabinet meetings or the Council meetings, as the case may be, and that enhanced powers and further delegation of authority will

be seriously considered and delegated to the cabinet.

23. Whilst the cabinet was to its credit much useful work done and specially so in matters connected with the war and whilst I am further indebted to the Cabinet for carrying on the administration during my prolonged absence from the State is also bears out the point that what is now wanted is not merely to carry on but to show push and energy and put in vigour and initiative in achieving some substantial results.

24. Moreover, the cabinet is after all partly a substitute for the post of a Chief Minister or Dewan, and now that by the grade of God His Highness the Maharaj Kumar has been appointed Chief Minister it is for him also to see that such orders are borne in mind and carried out and I trust that he will not be flooded similarly with mere routine matters and thus prevented from seeing to such things but he will personally direct affairs which is one of the most important functions of a Chief Minister. And I do not want as was the case specially with Mr. Rudkin and that some one should have to bear the brunt of the cabinet work and thus perforce be large prevented from attending to the work of their own particular departments. This is another of the important matters in which the Vice President might very well assume greater responsibility and take special work on his shoulders and take interest in seeing that orders are transmitted and not forgotten and business expedited and facilitated.

25. As regards the work in front of us the situation which I have attempted to outline will further make it clear that we have a vast volume of arrears to deal with and therefore it is not likely that we shall be able to get clear in one year with any programme that we may fix now. Nor can we necessarily dispose of some matters in the very first year. It also follows that new items will arise and will have to be added to our programme as time goes on, perhaps, even during the course of the year. But the great thing is that we should now after effecting decentralization and giving more powers all round seriously set ourselves to work and to go ahead and to make as much progress as is humanly possible and as circumstances permit. The present state of affairs further clearly reveals the necessity of having Secretaries to assist the Ministers in carrying on the routine work and lengthening their labours to a certain extent even in regard to big questions and in bringing to their notice important work awaiting orders and tackling.

26. Although it may not be an added help in regard to the annual programme and work in this connection it seems very desirable also in connection with the question of appointing Secretaries that we

should also consider the point of enhancing the status and importance of the Secretary to the Cabinet. He has often to make messages and to issue reminders to ministers and other Departments in the Cabinet's name and though I am not in favour of the Council Cabinet as a body throwing all the unpleasant work and drudgery on the Secretary to the Cabinet the enhancing of his official position may be both beneficial and desirable in some ways.

27. Where necessary let us also in addition to the Secretaries appoint temporary special Officers to deal with various questions and accumulated arrears although of course, we must at the same time pay due regard to economy compatible with efficiency. But for Heaven's sake let us now get on and show some substantial results in 12 months' time. And above all I wish to impress upon the Cabinet and Council and the individual members whilst we may appoint wholetime Secretaries in various Departments and whilst we may find it necessary also to appoint additional officers on special duty the responsibility must rest in each case primarily and largely with the members in charge of the various departments concerned or with the Cabinet and Councilor with the Chief Minister as the case may be and that we must each and every one of us put our very best foot forward and make every effort that lies in our power without which nothing would avail. If any individual officer or officers, cannot cope with the question and deal with their work let him or them make way for some one else but the State work must go ahead and the interests of the State and its subjects cannot be subordinated to the convenience and comfort of an individual officials whether members of the Government or whether the Heads of Departments or anything else.

28. It must not be forgotten that the Council of the old days and the system of such meetings was originally instituted has been greatly strengthened not only by virtue of the experience gained since by Members who happened to be Ministers then, but also by the subsequent addition of further competent and highly trained officers and specially since the reforms inaugurated in 1917. Thus there is undoubtedly greater capacities and better machinery forthcoming in the Council of the present day for dealing with this question than there was 15 years ago and more and not less should therefore now be accomplished.

29. Much as I hate to be appearing to hasten the Council and the Cabinet it is really very important that not only the Chief Minister, but also myself should keep in touch with the important work that is being done and see for ourselves what progress is being made. I must therefore ask that four-monthly statements should be submitted to

me showing the progress made by the individual officers to whom such work is to be entrusted as well as by the Cabinet or Council collectively. The officers concerned of the Council and the Cabinet as the case may be, will therefore, be responsible to submit such statements to the Chief Minister each year by the 1st July, 1st November and 1st March at the latest who after going through and making necessary enquiries and taking further necessary action will in his turn submit the statement to me by the 15th July, 15th November and 15th March without fail together with his remarks and recommendations. Such statements might be somewhat on the lines the statements I prepared dated the 7th May 1904. In the statement new work of importance not in the programme should also be shown. Again I will repeat I can confidently rely on the best efforts and the loyal cooperation of my Ministers individually and collectively in helping me incarrying this matter through successfully.

30. 1 also think that it will be necessary for us now to frame some very simple rules in this connection while should be made to apply not only to our meetings but also to the work enturtsed to individual officer. It should not be necessary for me to have to approve the proceedings. That is a matter which surely the Chief Minister and the Council and Cabinet can deal with and only refer to me the points of difficulty or doubt. The main point is that if there are references necessary for a point while is not clear or if any change has to be made, then the case should come up to me but otherwise orders should issue at once. A Statement per body or the department should be made of work entrusted to the various Members of Council and Cabinet and they should be instructed forthwith to go ahead.

31. We must also see what officer or office is to be held responsible for the issue of such general instructions in the first instance after which they will be dealt with by individual members, also for the framing of rules etc. and dealing with the general question.

32.It is also a point for consideration whether we should not have a Chief Justice of our High Court in future also present at such meetings as also at other important Cabinet and Council meetings so that he could from his first hand knowledge bring up matters affecting the judicial branch of our administration. Perhaps in that case it would not be necessary to have the other two judges.

33. We have also to settle for the future whether we should not hold a second meeting say six months after words to revise the programme according to the new circumstances that may have since arising and to add new points that may since have been brought to the front.

34.1 further think myself that the annual meeting should be held before and not after the Administrative Conference and at such time as to enable us also to consider and discuss amongst ourselves beforehand the Agenda sent by other official or non-official members for the Administrative Conference.

35. Finally gentlemen let me once again urge upon you all the imperative necessity of each and every one of us pulling our full weight and upon our doing properly the work for which we alone individually or collectively are responsible. Mere blacking of papers or paper orders and instructions would not do. We complain and rightly so, of the standard of work falling off in the lower departments but we must put our own houses in order first, and let us ourselves set a really good example to all below us.

## Draft of His Highness' Speech at the Administrative Conference, 21st March, 1921

*Gentlemen,*

It is after a considerable lapse of time that we are having another meeting of the Administrative Conference, which used to be an annual fixture some years ago. First started in 1905 as Revenue Conference, which only official members attended, it was subsequently thought that the general efficiency of the administration and the happiness of the people would be better promoted if the Conference were strengthened by the addition of some non-official Members including re-presentatives of the Sardars as well as the Sahukars. In 1908 the scope and composition of the Conference were therefore, widened and many important changes and reforms were introduced.

2. It was when the present Legislative Assembly was inaugurated in 1913 that the view was held that there would hardly be any scope for such Conferences since elected representatives of the people had ample opportunities of expressing their views, and of submitting proposals in the Assembly for Administrative reforms. But experience has proved that the view held was not correect and there is not only ample scope for such work both at the Administrative Conference as well as in the Legislative Assembly but that there are several details in various directions which are better suited and easier to be dealt with only at the Administrative Conference. I, therefore, decided in 1916—only three years after the inauguration of the Assembly to revive the Administrative Conference and we are consequently met here today to resume the work interrupted for so many years. Had it not been

for the prolongation of the war and our many preoccupations of the past few years—mostly connected with the War—this meeting would have been convened much earlier then has unfortunately been found possible.

3. On the extreme importance of these Conference it is not necessary for me to dwell nor, if we set to work at such Meetings in the right way and with the right spirit, can the beneficial effects and results of such annual meetings be over-estimated. For it goes without saying that the help of each other and closer association and co-operation between all classes of Officers and the various Departments, whether in the Capital or in the Districts, are constantly needed. And all are being brought into close contact on all such occasions and are being enabled to exchange views freely and frankly and with considerable informality, which is undoubtedly a great advantage. These remarks apply not only to the officials but also to non-official members, such as the Sardars, Sahukars and other representatives of the general public. By the very nature of their work and the circumstances in which they are placed officers at Headquarters are accustomed to deal with the problems of administration from a more detached and broad point of view than is possible for the District Officers. They are also necessarily better acquainted with my views and the policy of my Government on the various questions with which they have to deal. The District Officers on the other hand are or at least ought to be in more intimate touch with the living needs of the locality in which they work and the requirements and difficulties of the people among whom they reside. They are or at least ought to be the mirrors of the thoughts and sentiments of my subjects and I look to them to put before me an accurate picture of the conditions under which they have to work, of the difficulties and anxieties of all classes and communities of my subjects and of the reforms and other measures that are needed for the enhanced efficiency of the Administration and the well-being and contentment of my people. It is therefore, necessary that we should be able to bring to a focus these verying points of view for the benefit of each other and all of us and this object can only be served by such Conferences where alone I and my Government can get to know first hand by a free and frank interchange of views what is needed and where and how such needs can be met.

4. It is also a comonly recognized principle of all good and civilized Governments that for the efficiency of the administration and the well-being of the State as a whole close intercourse between the officials and the general public and particularly their representatives

is essential. I was present in London when Mr. Lloyd George the Prime Minister, in the course of a remarkable speech at the Guildhall on the 27th April 1917, made some very significant remarks when touching upon the affairs of India; when he said:

> "Minds running in the same course for a long time are apt to get rutty, and the weightier the mind the deeper the ruts, and you require fresh minds to lift the cart out of these worn furrows."

The above striking passage applies with equal force to the Indian States and of course also to our own State as well. However able, hard-working and sympathetic the officials may be—of whatever grade- working in water-tight compartments and isolation undoubtedly lead, not only to loss of touch with the public, whose servant every State Officer must also regard himself to be, but to the narrowing down of the field of vision. And in addition to the dangers of getting into deep ruts from which it is difficult to get out, there are not the same opportunities open to them without such conferences and discussions for the infusion of new but wholesome ideas or of the tactics as they can only do by contact with non-official members whether at such conferences or on tours and that something more yet remains to be done, that all is not going as well with the outside non-official world in our State as they imagine and that they have at times in their seclusion unwittingly proved themselves to be the slaves of hidebound convention and red tape and followed on the old old lines whereas the rest of the world has been changing rapidly and that altered circumstances have demanded altered and improved methods and further measures—I have myself noticed that such annual gatherings and discussions also tend to making various Departments less thin-skinned and less sensitive to suggestions which they have gradually come to regard not in the light of criticisms but in the truer perspective of their being inspired by a desire to help each other in realizing the common goal, viz., the raising of the standard of our Administration and in ameliorating the condition of hundreds of thousands of my subjects.

5. Another advantage of such informal discussions is that instead of our being divided into water-tight compartments opportunities are open to the employees of other Departments—not necessarily the Head of the Department but other officers serving under them—also of making friendly suggestions in regard to other Departments not out of jeolousies or personal feelings but for the common weal. If such suggestions are made and received in the right spirit they also

cannot but be productive of the most satisfactory results.

6. There is, moreover, one ever-riding consideration which has exercised no small an influence in my deciding to renew these Conferences. I have noticed with great regret and concern the deterioration in the standard of efficiency in the administration for some years past, which is particularly noticeable in some branches, while of course there have been honourable exceptions as well which have to be acknowledged.

7. I should like in this connection to acknowledge the assistance loyally rendered to me as well as the work done by my dear cousin, Maharaj Shri Bhairon Singhji Bahadur, who in the reformed scheme of Administration will find a field for exercising considerable influence and for seeking to various important schemes being tackled and dealt with in time and in an efficient manner. No acknowledgements of this nature as regards the Council and Cabinet would be complete without the name of Rai Bahadur Babu Kamta Prasad, whose intimate experience of the State and knowledge of my views and policy has been of such help to the Government and from which His Highness the Maharaj Kumar is at present specially benefitting.

8. Although they do not hold any particular portfolios, it is a matter of congratulation to the State that the advice and experience of the Rajas ofMahajan and Reri are not lost to the State Council and that we will still have the benefit of their experience and advice.

9. The high regard I have for the loyalty and devotion to duty of Rao Bahadur Thakur Sadul Singh is well-known by the title of C.I.E. which I was happy to have secured for him as an Imperial honour and I have, in addition to other useful work rendered by him in the various Departments, particularly to acknowledge his meritorious services on the two occasions of my important mission to England in 1917 and 1919.

10. To the Military Member of my Council, Rao Bahadur Thakur Hari Singh, I and the State are indebted for the very special services rendered by him during the War which have contributed to maintaining the finetraditions of the State in the past in regard to such matters and it is a matter of congratulation also that in the reorganization scheme of the State Forces the Government will have an adviser and an Officer of his great experience.

11. I know that all in the State, Officials and non-officials, will rejoice at the fact that after one year's well-earned rest in England we are to have the further benefit of the services of Mr. Rudkin, who has been such a source of strength to the State, to the Administration as well as to the people during his long association with the State and in the

new Administrative reforms, which we hope to inaugurate at an early date, I am confident that we shall also receive the same help and advantages.

12. Since I last addressed any remarks on such a subject it has been a matter of gratification to me to acknowledge the loyal services of such an old and faithful servant of the State, Khan Bahadur Mr. Kaus Rustomji, by appointing him to be a Member of Council. In his portfolio are the most important departments of Education and Medicine—in regard to which I know you would all like to congratulate the State and its people on our securing such an exceptionally able officer and a good friend as Principal Medical Officer in the person of Major Moolgavkar—and particularly the new Department of Commerce and Industry which is being re-organized with a view to giving a much-needed stimulus to trade in the State and fostering present industries and establishing new ones.

13. Many of you present here, I know, had the privilege of serving under my old friend Sahibzada Hamiduzzafar Khan and like me are inspired by feelings of genuine respect and admiration for that most loyal friend and true gentleman. Some of us here were also acquainted in the good old days with our present Political Member of Council, Sahibzada Abdus-Samand Khan, C.I.E., and I feel sure that all will agree with me that his appointment to the Council is a very real and added source of strength to our Government and that his experience in another State will be of great help in tackling the various problems that await us.

14. Last but not least I desire to acknowledge the very valuable and devoted services of Mr. Wattal who, as my Private Secretary during the past three years, has had to bear an unusual burden of heavy but interesting work in unusual times and unusual circumstances and who as Finance Member of Council will, I am confident, be able to achieve a many much-needed reforms in that Department and also be an added source of strength to the Administration.

15. If with such a personnel on our Council and with the reforms that we are further considering, the Administration of the State does not gain in efficiency and if practical results are not forthcoming, the blame surely cannot be laid at my door, but will have to be laid elsewhere.

16. Dealing now with the deterioration of the administration I find that there is not the same interest in the work, there is not the same energy and push nor the same willingness to shoulder responsibility and to take initiative as there was say fifteen years ago. And this inspire of the pay and status of various grades of officers having been raised

and the Administration being strengthened by importing many more experienced and capable officers both in the Council and in the Departments. There is too much inkslinging in the departments without any attempt being made to get at the root of the matter or to shew substantial results and there is I think also a little too much of red tape and rigid departmentalism, regardless of the meaning and purpose which official methods and procedure are intended to serve. No need is paid to the calls for the prompt submission of accounts and the timely preparation of budgets which causes the utmost inconvenience to all concerned, from myself downwards. The accumulation of arrears of work is also a growing scandal in some offices, of which severe notice will have to be taken. Orders are issued by the various departments from myself downwards, but they are not enforced and are treated as dead letters by the officers receiving them. Time seems to be no consideration and work which has to be done by particular dates is allowed to lie unheeded long after those dates are past, sometimes long after the work itself has lost its usefulness. As between the departments themselves there is not the same co-operation and the same regard that all are working in the interests of the same master and for the well-being of the State and its people as I found in my younger days. And above all there is, I am constrained to add, not the same degree of sympathy with the people, not the same measure of attention shown to them in their difficulties and anxieties. There is instead an indifference and a frigid atmosphere noticeable in many quarters. Those who come to seek redress find themselves treated with such indifference and received with such coldness and even harshness that they lose confidence in the officers and get disgusted with the system of Administration. All this reflects both on the quality of the work turned out as well as on the mentality of the people. From their innate devotion to the Ruler and his Government there comes imperceptibly but surely over their minds a feeling of estrangement which is very deplorable and cannot be conductive of good to anyone. Particularly in these difficult times it must be the honest and whole-hearted aim and endeavour of all of us to set our shoulders to the wheel to pull each and everyone of us our full share and weight and to see that the machinery of the administration does not get clogged or rusty or to run backwards but that it is kept going smoothly and without friction.

17. All that I have said above is not intended with the object of finding fault but to an improvement effected. I have worked to the best of my ability and energy during the 22 years of my active rule. I cannot tolerate the idea of my life work crumbling to pieces and the

administration having to be reconstructed once again in the manner I had to do at the very beginning of my reign or that the Maharaj Kumar should have to face again all the difficulties which beset my administration 22 years ago. I have during the past 22 years not only dedicated the best years of my life to the service of the State and its people but at no time have I spared myself and have devoted far more than the usual number of office hours followed by some officers, in working ceaselessly to improve and strengthen the Administration and to give added strength the administration and to give added strength and happiness to my people. It has never been my habit to ask others to do any work which I was not myself prepared to do, whether it was in peace or war, whether it was in the office or in the districts or whether it was to face dangers on the field of battle. I have never spared myself but I have endeavoured to see all such labours and anxieties with my gallant troops and with my civil officers and I have endeavoured further to share in the haoppiness as well as in the sorows of my people. Is it therefore, asking too much of all my officers, high and low, at least to share with me in the labours which the responsibilities of office require and which our duties not only to the people but to God Almighty demand. The Maharaj Kumar has, by the grade of God, now grown up and has been enabled to share in such labours and whilst, he is, as we all know, inspired by the same lofty ideals in discharging his duty to the State and its people I am confident that he is equally anxious to share in the labours with the officers of the State, Civil and Military. Future years will bring their own problems and difficulties and it is a solemn duty that we owe to those who must in the course of time take our places that they are not, in addition to coping with their peculiar problems, handed legacies of arrears of work and an accumulation of schemes and problems overdue but not tackled in good time or in a full measure. Anxious as I am to show the utmost patience and good feeling towards all classes of officers in my service, both Bikaneries and outsiders, and desirous as I am of giving them the utmost support and encouragement that lies in my power in regard to all elgitimate matters, it is a matter for the consideration of each and every one of you as to how long such a state of things can be tolerated or allowed to continue. You must all realise now that the rush of the past 7 years or more is over and with the altered circumstances of the world, which is an additional factor apart from all points of obvious local considerations, I am determined not to tolerate such a state of affairs a moment longer than can be helped and although I have tried to put my views before you in a brief manner, I trust that the emphasis which I lay on the point, the importance which I attach and the strong line of action which I am compelled in the future to take in regard to any incapable, indifferent or otherwise unsuitable officers will be a sufficient warning to all concerned, nothing will please me more than if what I say today is traken to heart and is followed by an immediate improvement, in which case I am prepared to overlook the past but let me once more make it absolutely clear that such a state of affairs and the contingency of the State Administration deteriorating further cannot be tolerated by me any more.

18. It is possible, in fact, only too likely, that certain official acts and measures of the past, and indeed the policy of my Government have been to some extent responsible for the present state of affairs. But as I have said I am not here to find fauilt but to effect improvements forthwith and that I am prepared to let bygones be bygones and we must now set about and consider what measures are essential immediately to bring about the much desired reform.

19. I am, therefore, genuinely anxious that I should learn from you what you have got to say regarding this setback in the progress of our administration, what are the causes to which it can be ascribed and what are the ways and means which you can suggest for putting matters right. If you think the fault lies in the personnel of any particular Department or our past policy I shall give the matter my fullest and immediate attention. Considerations of individual hardship cannot be allowed to prevail against the sacred interests of the State and its people. We want the State Service filled by conscientious men of strong character, ability and enlightenment, men who are both willing and able to do their full shares of work, men who consider the work of the State as their own and above all other considerations, men whom the happiness and sorrow of the people within their charge is their own happiness and sorrow. In short, we want men possessing a strong sense of duty who will whole-heartedly identify and associate themselves with the State and its people who will consider no sacrifice too great that can be made in the common cause. Men who are not prepared to work under these conditions or are unable to discharge their responsibilities satisfactorily will have to go and make room for others more suited to the task. While giving this warning let me not be misunderstood. On the other hand those officers who do well can, as I said at the Durbar when the Maharaj Kumar came of age, rely on my fighting their battles for them and rest assured that their good and loyal services will on suitable occasions be justly and liberally rewarded without discrimination of deshies and pardeshies as has been done in the past 22 years. I shall invite you all tomorrow to have

a free and full discussion on this most important question and I hope you will give the subject added thought in the next 24 hours and come here prepared tomorrow with useful suggestions and notes.

19. Though I have not been able to attend as closely as I should have wished to the affairs of the administration for reasons which have been as pressing as they have been unavoidable, I have never for a moment lost sight of this crying need of the moment, namely, putting our house in order. Only last July when considerations of health obliged me to take a rest I appointed an Administration Committee—not a Royal Commission as some discontented or ill-informed correspondent put it in a Vernacular paper in British India—to examine the causes of the undoubbted deterioration in the administration in the last few years in all the departments, high and low, and to suggest remedies. This Committee—which was a purely administrative and Departmental Committee and which explains why no non-officials were appointed on it—has been taking the evidence of both official and non-official witnesses and I am in hopes that when their report is submitted, my Government will have at any rate some useful suggestions for their consideration. Reforms in the method of transacting business by the Members of the council and the Cabinet and by the Heads of Departments is also engaging my serious consideration and I hope, by delegating larger authority to the Members of Council and Heads of Departments and by enforcing responsibility for the proper exercise of those powers, to diminish the work that is now done several times over by the high officers of my Government. This I trust will leave them more leisure to deal with questions of policy and the higher problems of the administration and what is of even greater importance, I am looking forward to their devoting greater attention to matters connected with the happiness and contentment of my people, the pursuit of which is the main end of all systems of administration by whatever name they might be called.

20. The Finance Department is also being re-organized including the Treasury and the account and audit branches and I hope it may be found possible to settle various matters in that department that are open to grave objection. The question of departmental financial settlements is also being taken up and I invite your hearty and loyal co-operation in making the scheme the success that it deserves to be.

21. In one direction, I am happy to tell you, our efforts are about to bear fruit and I am in a position to announce one instalment of Judicial reforms which has been decided upon by me recently. It was in 1910 that I instituted a Chief Court, which at the time was a unique

institution in Rajputana. More than a decade has since gone by and the system now needs further development. I have accordingly decided to replace the Chief Court by a High Court presided over by a Chief Justice and composed of two judges. The Judges of the High Court will have an assured status and independent position as will be made clear by the proclamation which will be issued before long and the Chief Justice will take rank and precedence according to date of appointment with the Members of my Council and will be entitled to a voice in all matters of Judicial administration and even other questions which may have a bearing even indirect, on the administration of justice. Regarding the officers, selected to fill these high posts I do not wish to make, any announcement just yet but I am trying to secure the services of officers who I am confident will command the respect and good will of all with whom they will have to deal. I earnestly hope that this measure may lead to that restoration of confidence amongst my subjects which is the bed rock of all governments and administrations.

22. I must not omit to mention here the services rendered by the past and present judges of the Chief Court.

23. Babu Nihal Singh is an old and loyal servant of the State and I am glad to think that after his making over charge of the Revenue Portfolio to Mr. Rudkin, we will have the advantage of his ripe experience in another post of responsibility and trust.

24. To Sheikh Mohamed Ibrahim, the present Chief Judge, my thanks are due for the industrious manner in which he discharged his duties. He is now retiring from the service and I wish him every happiness and prosperity.

25. Mohta Abhey Singh the acting Second Judge belongs to our old and respected family in the State and I am sorry to feel that under the changed conditions he is retiring from the bench, and to him also I desire to convey my sincere thanks.

26. Regarding the subordinate Judiciary in the State I am also considering certain changes but I have not yet been enabled to pass final orders.

27. Finally, gentlemen, let me once again impress upon you the urgent necessity of a free and frank inter-change of views and discussion. Nothing is gained by silence. I shall not believe, even if you do not tell me, that, there are no defects in the Administration to remedy. Your silence will only lead me to think that you are either afraid to disclose your own shortcomings or that your heart is not in your work and that the well-being of the State and its people and the due discharge of your duties to me are not matters of the first concern

and interest to you. We are meeting here with the sincere desire to do all that we can to further the happiness of the people. I and my Government are giving our best thought to the question. It is for you gentlemen also to give us the benefit of your first hand experience and intimate knowledge of local facts and conditions. I hope you will so acquit yourselves that it will not be said that this meeting was convened to no useful purpose whatsoever but that the present Session may for ever be made memorable to every one in the State, high or low, as one which contributed to far-reaching reforms and for ushering in a new era of peace and prosperity and greater contentment and happiness to the people and the State.

## Speech delivered by His Highness The Maharajah of Bikaner of the 16th August 1926 at the Opening of The Ministers' Informal Meetings Held in Bikaner

*Gentlemen,*

Although I do not propose to address you in a formal manner, may I first of all take this opportunity of welcoming you all most warmly to Bikaner on this important occasion, and of expressing the great pleasure which I feel at seeing so many representatives from States including some of the best brains to be found in our Indian States.

2. Amongst those whom I see seated around my today are many old and honoured personal friends—Sir Manubhai Mehta, Qazi Azizuddin Ahmed, Colonel Haksar, Sir Sukhdeo Prasadji, Professor Rushbrook Williams and my old Private Secretary and Foreign and Political Minister, Mr. Wattal. And Sir Prabhashanker Pattani and Sirdar Kibe we hope to have amongst us very soon. It gives me special pleasure in also welcoming and seeing present here today the Dewan of Mysore, Mr. Mirza Mohamed Ismail, whom I first met when I visited Mysore ten years ago. I hope that after his visit on this occasion both he and I will be able to say that our acquintance has ripened into friendship also. I have pleasant recollections of the most unfailing care and courtesy which I received at his hands, specially during my shooting camp in Mysore, when he was Private Secretary to His Highness. Apart from the personal side, I also derive particular gratification at seeing him here today as the representative of a most distinguished and enlightened Ruler—my valued friend His Highness the Maharajah of Mysore—and as the Dewan of such an advanced and model Indian State.

3. On another important occasion—in December 1917—we had

the benefit of the advice and assistance of his predecessor Sir M. Visveswarayya; and I think, Genglemen, that the presence on this occasion of the Dewan of Mysore and of his collegue, Mr. Balasundaram Iyer—who has, I am glad to note, been nominated to represent the Mysore State on a Committee of the Chamber of Princes—testifies surely to the great interest His Highness of Mysore and his State and Government take in the common welfare of the Princes and States of India, and that it refutes the statement which is made in some quarters that His Highness of Mysore and his State will have nothing to do with the affairs of the Chamber.

4. It is true that the Chamber of Princes has not yet had the privilege of welcoming His Highness of My sore inside its walls; but I hope and believe that it is not due to any lack of friendly feeling for an institution which has already been instrumental in safeguarding the interests of, and securing substantial benefits to the Princes and States of India, and which, it is the hope of many, will in days to come play a very important part in the future destinies of the Princes and people of our Indian States. May I therefore, as one who had a not inconsiderable share in the establishment of the Chamber of Princes, express the hope that as the years go by, the Princes for the sake of the solidarity of their order will lend ever increasing sympathy and support to the Chamber. There are, as we know, many things which we would like to see improved in regard to the Chamber and its scope, and it is therefore all the more necessary that we should all join hands in our united interests with the object of making the Chamber of Princes what it ought to be both in name and effect.

5. I am glad also at the opportunity which has been afforded me on this occasion of making new friends, to all of whom also I extend a cordial welcome. I rejoice at the fact that His Highness the Nawab of Bhopal- who, by his Accession has, we feel, brought fresh accession of strength to the Order of Ruling Princes, and who we are confident will be a firm supporter of the Chamber—has been able to depute to this meeting Rai Bahadur Munshi Oudh Narayan, his Finance Minister and Qazi Ali Haider Abbasi, his Political Secretary.

6. I regret that this meetings should have been held at not the best of seasons considering our climatic conditions. But what Nature denies, we shall try and make up for by attempting to make your sojourn amongst us as little uncomfortable as possible and I trust that you will carry away with you not altogether unpleasant memories of your visit here.

7. Turning now to the detail of our meeting I should like it to be understood that I regard this meeting essentially as a meeting of

Ministers informally assembled here as expert advisers to advise His Highness the Chancellor and the other Princes in regard to the most important matters which confront us at this moment. I should have been guilty of a breach of the most elementary principles of courtesy had I not attended this inaugural sitting to offer you a personal welcome before you embarked upon your labours; but I do not desire to intrude in any way. As, however, the subjects to be discussed are of an all-absorbing interest and of the most vital importance, I should like very much to be present, whenever I find it possible, to benefit by listening to the interesting and instructive discussions which are to take place, but only if you are all certain that my presence is not likely to restrict frank discussion and a free and full exchange of views. I will try and sit as silently as possible and not interrupt you, though from force of habit formed at the Princes Standing Committees and our Informal Meetings I am unable to guarantee that I shall not ever break this, my best resolve! I hope, specially as the great majority of Ministers present here already know me well, that they will try and forget that I am a Prince or that I am a past Chancellor and that they will extend to me the privilege of counting me as one of themselves.

8. This meeting, as you are aware, is purely informal and commits none of you, who have been good enough to respond to my invitation, to anything. It has been convened for the express purpose of enabling us to hold prelimirany discussions and will, I trust, result in clearing the ground and our doing spade work before any formal Committee Meetings or discussions take place in regard to this and other equally important allied subjects. I have always held—and I trust that the Ministers present here will share my view—that before the Princes formally meet in Committees—whether of their own, or in concert with the representatives of the British Government—to discuss and deal with any such matters, and particularly before any formal consultations take place with the representatives of the British Government, and indeed before any such work is finally or formally tackled, or any proposals are formulated in Committee, it is very desirable—indeed essential—that we should hold a representative informal meeting of this nature in order to give careful consideration to much that demands it and to thrash out, and attempt to work out, the various necessary details on which future conditions and work will necessarily have to rest. And I feel particularly grateful to His Highness the Chancellor—whose unavoidable absence on this occasion we all regret—for the opportunity which he has given me of thus being of some further service to the Princes ans States.

9. As for procesure, time of meetins and adjourning and all such

details—these are matters which must of course entirely be settled by the Minister; though, if! may do so, i would like to suggest that a part of the time be spent at Gajner where meetings could be held with more convenience to all concerned as all of you could be accommodated there in one place. In any case, I should like that none of you leave Bikaner without visiting the one place worth seeing the our arid land.

10. Before I deal with the subjects which should form part of the Agenda, it is hardly necessary for me to deal with certain factors which of late have again caused us of the States no small anxiety. But I derive particular pleasure in touching on a subject which in itself is of no small import to the Princes and States. I have had the pleasure of meetins our new Viceroy, Lord Irwin, and from what I observed, and particularly from my conversations with His Excellency, I have come away, like othe Princes who have come in contact with His Excellency, with the impression firmly imprinted on my mind that in Lord Irwin we have happily now a Viceroy who is really interested in, and keen on doing his best for, the Princes and States. It will be the earnest prayer not only of those of us present here today but of all who belong to, or have at heart the best interests of, the Indian States that it may be vouchasafed to Lord Irwin to handle the affairs of the Indian States in such a mmmer as to remove our doubts and difficulties by effective and timely measures being taken—so far as it is possible for human agency to ensure it—to preserve the entity and to safeguard, and wherever possible even to strengthen, the position, rights and autonomy of our States and—instead of matters drifting and policies changing with altered circustances and the personal predilections of those who mould the destinies of the Princes and States—by inaugurating a carefully conceived and settled policy regarding the Princes and States on generous, liberal and sympathetic lines. Should it please the Almighty to ordain that His Excellency should be the instrument of achieving this great task, Lord Irwin will have succeeded not only in making us happier and in further strengthening the ties that bind us to our beloved King-Emperor but he will also have rendered truly valuable services to the Empire whose cause the Princes and States have unhesitatingly and consistently espoused through sunshine and storm in a manner befitting their proud position as Allies and Friends. it is, in the circumstances, all the more important that we should take the earliest opportunity of such favourable circumstances to get a move on at the very beginning of Lord Irwin's Viceroyalty, so as to derive a real and substantial benefit and to try and get some of the matters, which are capable of early solution

without any serious difficulty, satisfactorily disposed of, during His Excellency's term of office. This is all the more important in view of the fact that the Royal Commission will be coming out to India by 1929 at the latest in connection with British Indian Reforms. And if the future position of the Indian States and such matters are to be dealt with properly and without haste, it is all-important that we should have proposals and schemes, cut and dried, before such a Commission comes out to decide on what further stages India is to proceed on its march towards Self-Government.

11. Reverting to the subjects to be brought on the Agends paper, I need hardly say that this too is a matter which is entirely for you all to settle; and one of the first things you will no doubt proceed to do will be to draw up the Agenda. In case it may be of any help I have had a tentative Agenda paper drawn up indicating matters which appeared to me to be of the greatest importance at the present moment; other points will doubtless suggest themselves to you.

12. I do not propose to dwell at length on each of the questions placed on the tentative list. The most important subject of all is, obvisusly, that relating to the future position of the Indian States. Though I have naturally given much thought to a subject of such vital importance to us, I shall not enter into any further details here, not shall I touch on any possible solution and scheme in this connection. But, I am circulating for the personal use of the Ministers and Secretaries present here certain papers, some public and some of a strictly private and confidential nature, dealing with the subject, for which I was responsible during the time I was Chancellor. There are in addition some other important details with which it is essential you should be made acquainted by me before you proceed to take this question. I should also add that from what I could gather during my recent visit to Simla, it is more than probable that His Excellency the Viceroy will convene a meeting in November next immediately after the session of the Chamber of Princes for the purpose of an informal discussion on the subject with a certain number of Princes, whom he will invite for the purpose.

13. The next subject relates to Joint Deliberations in matters of common interest to the States and British India concerning which I addressed a letter to some Ministers while I was Chancellor last year and upon which I moved a resolution in the Chamber in January last.

14. A copy of my speech on that occasion is being placed in your hands. The subject is one which has doubtless received in the past much thought and attention from you. In the circumstances there are only two important points in this connection to which I feel called

upon specially to allude.

15. In the first place, there has for some time past existed, as you are aware, a marked difference of opinion in regard to one very important detail. Whilst some hold that the only satisfactory method by which the States can hope to secure an effective voice in matters of common interest, or those which directly or indirectly affect us in many ways, is for the States to be represented not only on all Royal Commissions and Committees and other enquiries but that we should expressly secure seats for the representatives of India States in the Upper Chamber of the Indian Legislature, viz, the Council of State.

16. Some on the other hand hold that it would be positively dangerous for the Princes and States to be thus directly represented in the Council of State or, indeed any other British Indian Legislature, since, as our States comprise only one-third of the area of India, we could not reasonably hope to secure a larger percentage of representation in any such Chamber than one-third, and that we should therefore not only be in a minority of one-third as against two-thirds representing the votes of British India, but that with such a minority we should be making our position worse in regard to various measures—fiscal, financial and so on—which may be dealt with and passed in the Central Indian Legislatures and that our being in such a Central Legislature might ultimately even lead to legislation being enacted of an all-India nature affecting the States, which at the present moment at any rate is not permissible to be enacted directly under the present moment at any rate is not permissible to be enacted directly under the Constitution. In short, it is feared by those holding this opinion that such a measure is fraught with grave possibilities and might some day very seriously prejudice the constitutional position, Sovereign rights and internal independence of the Indian States and their Rulers and people; and that we should therefore ponder very seriously before we voluntarily committee ourselves to any such measure. In support of these views they quote the case of the Self-Governing Dominions of the British Empire, who have gained as exceptionally strong and substantially altered status in the Empire as a result of the War, but who have declined to have anything to do with an Imperial Parliament and such other schemes which were at one time mooted, but who insist that all measures relating to, or affecting the Dominions can only be given effect to, or held as binding on them, when their own Parliaments have had an opportunity of discussing the subjects and of according approval to the same or of ratifying any proposals tentatively agreed to on their behalf by their own representatives at Imperial or inter-allied Conferences and other

occasions; and who in fact have preferred to leave their relations with Great Britain in a more or less fluid stage.

17. The second is the point on which I last year asked for the advice of the Ministers—viz., whether, taking a long view, it was really wise in the best interests of the Princes and States to have representatives appointed on all Royal Commissions and Committees and other enquiries in regard to matters of common interest or with which we are directly or indirectly concerned. At first sight the advantages appeared to be obvious; but I added that it has also to be considered whether the constitutional position of the Princes and States was likely to be impaired in the near or distant future by their having direct representation on such Commissions, Committees and enquiries by reason of the appointment of Ministers or other officers thereon.

18. In this connection I also pointed out that the view had been held that the Princes and States would be wise to avoid Parliamentary interference and enactments in regard to the relations of the Indian States with the British Crown and their affairs, which was likely to be one of the probable results of our participating in Royal Commissions, etc. And it will be observed that in the course of my speech when moving the resolution in the Chamber I briefly alluded to this point without expressing my personal opinion in the following words:

> "In certain quarters the view is held that the only adequate method of safeguarding the interests of the Indian States on occasions when an enquiry in undertaken into matters of common interest is that His Excellency the Viceroy should be pleased to provide for the representation of Indian States on the personnel of all Royal Commissions as well as on all Commissions and Committees of Enquiry appointed in India, to investigate matters in which the States are concerned. The advantages of such a procedure are obvious; and I think I have sufficiently spoken on this aspect of the question already. In some other quarters the apprehension is entertained that it might be unwise for the Indian States and dangerous as regards their Constitutional position and Sovereign rights, for them to take part in such Commissions and enquiries by direct representation. But I submit that the wording of my resolution is not only non-controversial but that it will serve the very object we have in view, viz., that the Committee which I moved should be appointed, consisting of Princes and Ministers, should consider in consultation with representatives of the British Government, what are the best means of safeguarding the interests of the Indian States when such enquiries are undertaken in matters

of common interest; and any dangers to the Princes and States will no doubt be duly taken note of by such a Committee in the course of their investigations and, we hope, also adequately provided for"

19. It is now for you, Gentlemen, to thrash out these points and, after taking into consideration the various points involved, to advise the Princes as to what will be in the best interests of themselves and their States.

20. I need not take up much of your time in dealing with the remaining points which have been placed on the tentative Agenda subject to your approval of the same.

21. The revision, where needed, of the Constitution, Regulations and Rules of Business relating to the Chamber of Princes and the Princes' Standing Committee have for some time past been placed by me as Chancellor on the Agenda of the Princes' Informal Meetings for Their Highnesses' consideration. In November 1924, it was finally proposed to appoint a committee to deal with this question consisting of:

1. Sir Manubhai Mehta.
2. Sir Prabhashanker Pattani.
3. Colonel Haksar.
4. Raja Sir Dayakishen Kaul.

and it was further proposed to secure the assistance of an eminent layer, like Sir Ali Imam or Sir Tej Bahadur Sapru, and failing that Their Highnesses decided that Sir Sukhdeo Prasad should be added to the Committee, but for various unavoidable reasons this important work has not yet been taken up.

22. I need only say that your work in this connection will possibly need to be divided under three main heads:

1. To compare them as they now stand with our original proposals as embodied finally in the Outlines of the Scheme or proposed by the Princes on at least two occasions when the Government of India were good enough to refer them to Their Highnesses' Committee for advice and suggestions and to suggest which, if any, of our original proposals we should again try and get embodied in the Constitution, Regulations and Rules of Business.
2. To see what further additions, alterations or modifications are essential and might properly be incorporated in them. For this purpose, altough we do not necessarly want to copy any such

procedure in its entirety, and examination of the provisions relating to the Imperial Central Legislatures and other Institutions may be found suggestive and helpful in framing your recommendations.

3. And What is most important, what further steps forward, or substantial changes, we should bear in mind and urge when the time comes, with a view to placing the Chamber and the Standing Committee on a more satisfactory and solid foundation and more effectively securing the objects aimed at when we formulated our original proposals and asked that the Chamber be brought into existence.

23. The Committee referred to in para 21 was also entrusted with the examination of the Government of India Resolution No.427-R., dated the 29th October 1920, regarding the appointment of Courts of Arbitration and to take similar action in regard to another Resolution of the Government of India relating to Commissions of Enquiry, both of which subjects had likewise for some time been placed by me for Their Highnesses' consideration on the Princes' Informal Meetings Agenda.

24. The Constitution, Regulations and Rules of Business relating to the Chamber of Princes and the Standing Committee will necessarily have to be considered in conjunction with the all-embracing subject of the future position of the Indian States. Also whether the Royal Commission to deal with the British Indian Reforms comes out in 1929 or earlier, it would not be unreasonable to presume that the time will have arrived, if it is not already overdue, for us to take stock of the position and to see how far the Chamber, as well as the other Reforms which formed the subject-matter of Chapter X in Montagu-Chelmsford Report, have answered our expectations. We could also reasonably expect that the Princes would be afforded an opportunity of placing their views and proposals before the Viceroy in regard to any fresh measures of reforms and for the further adjustment of the political machinery governing our relations with the British Government as well as any changes that might, in the light of past experience, or with due regard to the future, be found to be necessary. And this may be specially found necessary in regard to Commissions of Enquiry and Courts of Arbitration. There has been some amendment of the original Resolution of the Government of India relating to Courts of Arbitration. The subject of Commissions of Enquiry has been prominently brought to the front in view of some events of the past few months and it is more than probable that some

aspects connected therewith have been engaging your special attention. Hence their inclusion in the tentative Agenda.

25. The Government of India Memorandum on the ceremonies connected with Successions in Indian States, to which reference was made by the Viceroy at the Princes' Conference in November, 1917, and which is appended to the Proceedings, also raises issues, as will be readily appreciated, of a most far-reaching nature; and, when this subject first came up for consideration in the Princes' Conference of 1916, many of you will recall the excitement that was caused by the very first para of the Memorandum explanatory of Agendum No.1 where the following words were to be found:

> "Every succession requires the approval and sanction of the Government" and this was followed in the second para by the words: "It is essential that such approval and sanction should be announced in a formal Installation Durbar by a representative of the British Government."

This question, to quote Lord Chelmsford's words, was the subject furthermore of a "lively debate" on that occasion. In the Princes' reply to the Viceroy's Address, which I was elected to read on November 10th, 1917, we informed the Viceroy of our intention to address His Excellency "in due course" on the subject. This, it should be explained, was really to the fact that Mr. (now Sir John) Wood, the then Political Secretary, informally conveyed to us the special request of the Viceroy that—in spite of some of the obnoxious sentences in the original Memorandum having been altered—in view of the obvious controversial nature of some of the points involved, nothing further might be said on that occasion. In accordance with the Princes' decision intimated in their reply to the Viceroy's Address referred to above, this subject too had been placed by me on the Agenda of the Informal Meetings for Their Highnesses' consideration on more occasions than one and this question too, was referred to the Committee mentioned above. I have given instructions to my Political Department to place before you the various papers bearing on the subject.

26. To conclude my remarks on the subjects on the Agenda, it only remains for me to emphasize, as I have done both at Their Highnesses' Informal Meetings when discussing the future position of our Indian States as also in the course of my speech when moving the resolution regarding Joint Deliberations in the Chamber of Princes last January, that in taking up such questions we are actuated

by no unfriendliness whatever to our brethren in British India nor are we prompted by any desire to retard the progress of constitutional reforms therein. All that we desire is to safeguard the interests of our States and our subjects where they are directly or indirectly involved. Any hostility to the legitimate aspirations of British India would to my mind not only be unworthy of the Princes as sons of the Motherland but prove very seriously prejudicial to their own interests and future well-being. In these remarks I have little doubt that I shall have your unanimous agreement.

27. I shall not detain you much longer, my friends—and here I do not use the expression "friends" as a term of mere convention or empty compliment for to my mind who could be better fitted to be the friends of a Ruler than his responsible Ministers and advisers who are his colleagues in the task of ruling his State, who share the cares and anxieties, the joys and sorrows of their masters? In your noble mission and high resolve of devising the best ways and means of rendering the future secure and of safeguarding the honour, dignity, and prestige and the prerogatives, powers and privileges, and the rights and interest of the Princes and States, whose welfare you all have so much at heart, I would beg of you not to hesitate to put forward your ideas and proposals frankly with the one aim to advancing the best interests of the Princes and States as a body bearing I mind that unity is strength and that our proposals and schemes are so framed as to strengthen our solidarity.

28. On this and other occasions we can only delibrate and discuss and devise means for gaining the end in view. But no one who thinks seriously and earnestly can shut his eyes to the fact that our future really depends largely, if not almost exclusively, upon the Rulers of States themselves, upon the extent we the Princes realize our great responsibilities and the sacred duty God Almighty has committed to our care, upon the manner in which we direct the affairs of our States, upon the amount of care and thought which we bring to bear upon questions of vital importance to the well-being of our States and our subjects. Very difficult times unmistakably lie ahead of us. As against the many friends we have in British India there is no use blinking the fact that the trend of certain schools of political thought there is not in our favour. We have also some other disabilities to contend against. Times are changing, and the Princes and States too have to adapt themselves to modern environments. Some of our States have every reason to be proud of their splendid achievements and of the high goal towards which they are to assiduously working. In some States on the other hand the need for reform will no doubt be apparent. In

behaves us all-the Princes and their Ministers—to see to it that nothing which duty and prudence dictate is left unattended to. No doubt the future destiny of the Princes and States of India will be determined by the will of God; but if we discharge our duties properly and are not unmindful of our responsibilities, He in his infinite mercy will assuredly extend to us His protecting hand and guidance.

## Speech by Lieut.—General His Highness the Maharajah of Bikaner at the Federal Structure Committee Meeting on the 22nd September, 1931

*My Lord Chancellor,*

I trust that I shall first be permitted to express sincere gratitude, not only on behalf of myself but, I am sure I can add, on behalf of the Indian States Delegation, and indeed of the States of India, to so many of our distinguished British—Indian colleagues—several of whom I have the pleasure and privilege of hailing as my personal friends—for the ready willingness they have expressed to respect in every responsible manner the sovereignty and treaties of the States, and for the just recognition of the strength and validity of the claims and especial position of the Indian States, as well as our various difficulties.

We are particularly indebted to Sir Tej Bahadur Sapru, Sir Muhammad Shafi, Sardar Ujjal Singh, Sir Maneckji Dadabhoy, Sir Sultan Ahmed, Mr. Gavin Jones, Mahatma Gandhi, Sir P. C. Mitter and Diwan Bahadur Ramaswami Mudaliyar and Pandit Malaviya. I have kept till the end, as deserving of special mention, the name of the talented and charming representative of the fair and better six whom we are all so pleased to see amongst us, Mrs. Subbarayan.

It is very gratifying that such support and sympathy should have been forthcoming at this meeting from such a representative body of British—Indian leaders of different creeds and communities and political schools of thought. What they have stressed as regards the Indian States has made our task all the easier and rendered unnecessary certain observations which we would otherwise have had to make.

I should like, Sir, before proceeding to state the views of the Indian States Delegation generally on the various questions under Head I, to ask for your indulgence and that of my colleagues if I take a little time in making certain observations of importance to the States. I must apologise for taking up your time; but I hope and believe that our discussions on this and future occasions will be curtailed if the standpoint of the States is appreciated. It will also, I believe, help to shorten speeches on this side in the future. I seriously considered making such a statement earlier in our deliberations, but, apart from my reluctance to intrude unnecessarily, I had hoped that our close association of last time with our British—Indian friends had rendered such a course unnecessary. With however, some new colleagues—whom we are glad to see amongst us—it was perhaps inevitable that in regard to some points we should at some time or other have to traverse more or less over the same ground as we did last year.

May I say straight away also that any reasonable and feasible suggestions coming from any responsible British—Indian leaders will, of course, receive the fullest consideration of the States delegation and of the Princes and States, but I would ask some of the speakers we have heard lately to bear in mind that in view of certain vital considerations it is not fair to place anyone of us in the States delegation in the unpleasant position of having to say "No" to certain proposals such as those that have been made to us. I need say no more in my own words. No less eminent a leader than Mahatma Gandhi has stated as his opinion that no one has the right to dictate to the States what they should do or what they should not do, a point which I emphasised before expressing the States delegation's view on the questions under Head 2. As emphasised also by certain British—Indian leaders, including Mahatma Gandhi, there must in all matters between British India and the States be a spirit of reasonable give and take. Without it, to quote once more from the Mahatma's words: "We shall not be able to come to any definite scheme of federation, or if we do, we shall ultimately quarrel and break up". Above all, the co-operation of the States must be wholehearted, which can only be secured by their willing consent and not by dictation or coercion.

My Lord Chancellor, I cannot help thinking that some of the proposals and statements and demands would not have been put forward had there not been a certain lack of knowledge as regards the conditions, sovereign status, treaties and the rights of States, their relations with the Crown and their internal affairs. I take the liberty of stating that the ideas of some of our colleagues would undergo a considerable change if they came into closer touch with us and were able to acquaint themselves with facts at first hand by visits to our States. And I take this opportunity of cordially extending an invitation to such gentlemen to visit Bikaner as the guests of my State and of myself, and to travel over its length and breadth, preferably on our ships of the desert, the camel—(laughter). I make bold to predict that by such visits their eyes would be opened, and that they would then correctly realise that the relations happily existing between the rulers and the ruled, the vast majority of the Princes and their Governments on the one hand and the subjects of the States on the other, are totally different from what may be their present conception or as some papers are persons have tried to paint them. May I say also that it was particularly gratifying to us to hear from the lips of Mahatma Gandhi that he knows and feels that the Princes have the interests of their subjects zealously at heart.

In the words of some of those gentlemen who have attempted to prescribe to the States in regard to various matters, it was, I think, admitted that logic and politics do not always go together. Idealistic principles are not always reconcilable with what is attainable. Certain things are obviously not within the range of practical politics, nor in accordance with the sovereignty of the States and the conditions prevailing therein. And it is impossible for the states in all things to accept a uniform practice and procedure with British India, whether in the field of Federation or in other directions, if for no other reasons at least on the grounds of the diversified conditions amongst the States inter se. If impossible conditions are proposed it is obviously out of the question for the States or the Princes to accept them, and I venture to add that not only the vast majority of the States, but also the vast majority of the population and subjects of the entire Indian India, will share the same views. Even if we would, we could not possibly accept any impracticable propositions which would not be accepted by the States, and their rulers and governments, as a body. It therefore, follows that the decision in certain matters—and I emphasise the words certain matters—must, in the very nature of things, be left primarily, and essentially, and solely, to the individual government of the State concerned, or for the States to settle amongst themselves. My own personal views in regard to matters such as those of sending representatives from the Bikaner State to the Federal Legislature have already been made clear; and in view of the conditions happily prevailing in my State I and my govemment are in no way opposed to our Legislative Assembly having in some way or other a voice in the selection of our representatives. Indeed, I welcome that. His Highness of Bhopal has similarly made that point clear. For the rest, and in the natural solution of such problems, time, evoluation and the conditions prevailing, and above all public opinion in our States, will be important factors.

Reference has been made to the German and other federal

constitutions of States or Dominions, which will not be of much avail to us here. The States do not keep before them the old German or any other constitution. They have, as has been made clear repeatedly, from the beginning of our present deliberations and in the past, kept before them the position of the States, which is without its parallel in history. Need it once again be emphasised that we have to evolve a special federation to meet our unique conditions? In Germany I believe it is beyond dispute that all the federating German States were sovereign all along. This is not so in regard to India, where the States are already sovereign and autonomous, and British India and its provinces are at present not sovereign. It is upon the sovereignty of the States and their right to exist, as one of the two great entities in India that the States make their firm stand.

My Lord Chancellor, before we came here last year, it was at one time suggested that the Princes and States should come under the head of the most important of the "minorities" throughout the length and breadth of India. It is, however on much stronger grounds and claims, and on irrefutable and undisputed constitutional and historic facts, that the States base their claims. They stand on their sovereign status and powers, and on their treaty and other rights, as already stated. In these circumstances, as has been admitted by some of the critics of the scheme as evolved by us, no other Federal constitution can form any precedent or analogy.

We have in the past tried to meet British India as far as possible; indeed, some amongst us think that we went too far. We have met you as far as is practical and safe for the States. We shall continue to do so in every reasonable manner possible. But pray remember that all of us, at the best of times, are of conservative frame of mind, and that there is already a certain amount of alarm and suspicion which we have to overcome in our States, and that there is a limit beyond which it will be impossible for the States and the Princes to go.

It hardly needs repetition that the States cannot, therefore, be coerced or driven into Federation. The treaties of the States are with the Crown, and they can enter into a Federation only through another treaty with the Crown on receiving adequate and effective guarantees from the Crown ensuring to the States their existence as one of the two great entities of India, and ensuring the continuance of their sovereignty and their treaty and other rights except in so far as these may mutually and voluntarily, by agreement between us here, have been delegated to the Crown for the specific purposes of-Federation, and on the specific understanding that such delegated sovereignty will be shared by the States with British equally in the Federation, including—I do not emphasise the word "equally" here—including the legislature and the executive.

I have repeatedly been asked whether the States will come into the Federation. My faith in federation remains unaltered, and I consider that federation is the only alternative which will help India at this present juncture. But if I am asked at the present moment to say whether the States will come in, I can only say that I very much hope that that will be so, and that we are going to do our best to secure that very desirable end. So far as the States are concerned, the position can be summed up, as I have repeatedly said in the past, the these terms; The crux of the question to my mind is that when the Princes and States last year were invited to join a federation they generally and gladly expressed their willingness to consider the question on terms of equality with British India, and even to make some sacrifices on the conditions mentioned. Provided, therefore, that the remaining principles and details are dealth with as satisfactorily as have the various questions discussed so far-taking on the whole both the last Session and the present Session-and provided that the Princes, through essential provisions, feel that their future existence; and the sovereignty of their States-big and small-are not threatened. I am as sure to-day, as I was when we met the last time, that the great majority as a Trustee of his State and Subjects, and the custodian of their rights, will be a free agent to enter federation.

If we are asked, however, to agree to any proposition which is tantamount to the disruption of the States-big and small-either now or in the future, we can best reply in the words of Sir Austen Chamberlain. I would beg our friends who have criticised the past scheme to bear in mind the words which Sir Austen Chamberlain addressed to the League of Nations a not so very long ago when faced with proposals detrimental to the solidarity and well being of the British Empire. He said:

> "You do not know what you ask us. You are asking nothing less than the disruption of the British. I yield to no one in my devotion to this great League of Nations, but not even for this League of Nations will I destroy that smaller but older League of which my own country was the birth place and of which is remains the centre."

Great and sincere as is the devotion of the Princes to their Motherland, and ardently as they desire to co-operate with British Indian in assisting in India's progress towards Dominion Status as an independent, honoured, and equal member of the British

Commonwealth of nations, and willing as they are even to make reasonable sacrifices in this direction, it will I am sure be realised by many of our friends on the other side that it would be both unreasonable and impossible to expect the States to agree to any proposals which would in effect lead to the disappearance of the States, and the loss of their important sovereign rights or the individual entity of their people. Such would be a betrayal of the trust that they inherited and of the mandate that they have from their brother Princes.

One of the speakers spoke of the States coming in for selfish reasons, whilst it was also stated that the real gain to the Princes from federation was entry into the Federal Executive Government. Ideas differ. Rather it is considered a sacrifice on the part of the States. The two essential conditions precedent to entering federation are, as already stated, the safety and integrity of the States, and adequate safeguards or guarantees, but what of the gain to British India in unity, stability, experience, and especially in defence from the martial traditions and the fighting races of which the States can legitimately boast?

We were told that certain matters are not for the States to decide but for the Federal Committee. We have been incorrectly told that the Princes have agreed to join federation, and that they have agreed to accept interference by British India in certain domestic affairs, if I understood it rightly. To the second point our answer must definitely and inevitably be "No". To the first, it has been abundantly clear that, whilst the Princes and States have expressed their willingness to consider entering federation, this is not without qualification, but is based on certain essential conditions.

Similarly we made it clear in the past that the States are not agreeable that they must accept common criminal or other laws and legislation.

So far as the representatives of the States to the Federal Legislature are concerned and subject to what I have since stated, may I be permitted to quote the legal language used by your Lordship last year, namely, that the States' duty will be to deliver their representatives in good order and condition?

There has been a talk of divided mandates between the representatives of the States and of British India. There is no question whatsoever of States forming a solid bloc to oppose British India. Most of us on this side have not the slightest doubt that for the most part the representatives of the States and British India will vote almost entirely on regional lines. And may I also state that the Upper House need not necessarily be a Conservative body as in the India of today? It would represent the views of the various Govemments.

The only points of conflict that I can conceive between British India and the Indian States are these :

(i) if there is a proposal to break away from the Empire, which the scheme under consideration providing for India being placed on a footing of equality and partnership with other parts of the Commonwealth happily renders it unecessary to touch on;
(ii) if the very existence of the States were threatened, or there was any danger to the existence of the States or any desire to encroach upon the treaty and other sovereign rights of the States, except in so far as may be willingly and mutually agreed upon—on which point too I decline to believe that any serious proposition of that kind can be put forward on the part of the majority of our British Indian friends; and
(iii) there are fiscal and financial matters regarding which we hope that, by previous fiscal enquiry as well as the discussions which will take place here, all such matters will have been satisfactorily settled before the States enter into federation, and on which matters we demand in fairness to the States mutual satisfaction on all such points.

May I, in the interests of India, and of the federal scheme which I have so much at heart, express the earnest hope that we shall not hear any more from any gentleman of the States being permitted to exist only under certain conditions. I do not think I need say more on that point except that this would involve a violation of the sovereignty of the States by force, and that their treaties would be torn up, involving also a breach of faith on the part of Great Britain. I decline to believe that the doctrine of treaties being regarded as scraps of paper could ever be accepted by the great majority of the British—Indian leaders. I need only say that any such remarks are apt to lead to the forfeiting of the general sympathy of the States and Princes as a body in all matters in which we are desirous that we should work in close harmony and co-operation with our British—Indian brethren.

It will be recalled that when at the first Plenary Session of the Round—Table Conference on the 17th November last the Princes and States were invited by British India to join a federation and to visualize an India which will be one single whole, each part of which may be autonomous and may enjoy absolute independence within its borders, regulated by proper relations with the rest, our response was as sincere as it was spontaneous. It was my privilege on that occasion at the request and on behalf of my brother Princes to state that, whilst the final answer must obviously depend on the structure of the Government indicated and on other points involved, such, for instance, as certain necessary safeguards—constitutional and fiscal-which we regard as of vital importance to the protection of the rights and interests of our States and of our people, the Princes would only come into the federation of their own free-will and on terms which would secure the just rights of their States and subjects.

I mentioned two essential and broad conditions upon which the States were ready to consider entering the federation:

I. that India retains the British connection as an equal partner in the British Commonwealth of Nations; and
II. that an equitable agreement is reached between all the parties concerned to govern the relations of the two Indias, ensuring for the States their due position in the future constitution as co-equal partners with British India, guaranteeing their treaties and internal sovereignty, and safeguarding their interests, including those of their subjects, on terms just and honourable alike to the States and British India.

Amongst other important details in this connection I need only invite attention to what I said on that occasion about "Paramountcy", and I will deal later similarly with the important question of the federal Court.

It has thus been made abundantly clear on many occasions that, as the States demand freedom from interference in their own internal affairs, equally do they desire to refrain from interference in the purely domestic affairs of domestic concern to British India, and that the States can only come in on terms of absolute equality with British India, not in a position of subordination or inferiority, but as equal partners in the federation. I equally clearly stated that any idea of the States desiring to dominate over British India was totally foreign to our thoughts and our plans. On the other hand, it will be generally agreed that we are equally entitled to ask that the States should not be dominated by British India or anyone else, which would be totally opposed to the basic idea of any true federation. At the same time the States must take care to safeguard that the federal Executive does not encroach upon the sovereignty and treaty rights of the States, or interfere in matters, or have a voice in questions, other than those which may specifically and voluntarily and mutually be agreed upon and accepted by the States.

As regards the vote of censure, I made it clear, Sir, last year, on behalf of His Highness of Bhopal and myself, keeping in view the list of general subjects as drawn up at present, and subject to a fair and just and equitable settlement of the question of the number of State representatives in the two federal Houses, that the Indian States would, we thought, be perfectly content, as regards the percentage of the majority in throwing out the Federal Government, to leave this point to be settled by British India with the Crown. But in regard to the Executive, any votes of non-confidence likely to result in the overthrow of the Federal Government would obviously be a matter of great importance to the States; and if the States are invited to join the federation it would be out of the question for them to sit still and to have no voice at all in the overthrow of the Executive and in Governments changing hands repeatedly, as they do in some of the Continental constitutional countries, since they are directly concerned with a sound and stable Government, and in continuity of policy as far as possible with regard to matters of common concern to British India and the States.

At the same time, whilst therefore it is essential that the subjects, or representatives, of the States must also in no way be debarred from being members of the Federal Executive Cabinet, I submit that the right standpoint is for such members, while they are cabinet Ministers, to forget that they represent British India or the States, and not to attempt to look at any question coming before the Federal Government from the purely British—Indian or the Indian States' standpoint, but to view all matters coming within their purview from the standpoint of all India, its honour and its welfare, and with due regard to the legitimate rights and interests and claims of the two entities.

I would now invite the attention of my colleagues to the mandate which we on this side have received from the Chamber of Princes and the Rulers of the Indian States when the provisional decisions taken at the first session of this Conference were subjected to a close and prolonged examination by the body which speaks, so far as any corporate body can, for the Princes and States as a whole, namely the Chamber of Princes. The first resolution passed by the Chamber in March last was as follows:

"This Chamber places on record its high appreciation of the single-minded devotion and statesmanlike ability with which the representatives of the States, both rulers and ministers, represented the States at the Conference; and supports in principle the scheme outlined at the Round—Table Conference, which, while laying the foundations of a greater India, aims at securing to all parties in the country their legitimate cherished rights beyond risk of future encroachment."

The following is the second resolution adopted by the Chamber of Princes, on the motion of His Highness of Dholpur:

"This Chamber authorises its representatives further to carry on discussions and negotiations with due regard to the interests of the States and subject to the final confirmation and ratification by the Chamber and each individual State."

I will not touch at length upon certain resolutions passed by the Princes at a meeting of their own which preceded the formal session of the Chamber of Princes, where we desire to obviate and aim at obviating as far as possible ventilating in public any differences of opinion amongst ourselves. Even the resolutions passed in the Chamber of Princes are subjected to a thorough scrutiny, though of course all the Princes individually cannot be bound beforehand as to their views on such resolutions.

Amongst the resolutions passed by the Princes at their own meeting, a day or so before the Chamber of Princes met and passed the two resolutions I have just quoted, were resolutions which attached importance, naturally, to the sovereignty, internal autonomy and independence of the States being safeguarded and to an equitable adjustment of fiscal matters. The Princes were asked by the resolution to agree that the representatives of the Chamber of Princes at the Round Table Conference should negotiate with a view to securing individual representation in both the Federal Chambers for the States enjoying full or practically full powers.

Now, Sir, before coming to the question of qualifications I should like to say one word about another matter a reference has been made to there being something like 570 or some other number of States, and I think it has been said that some States with a revenue of Rs. 20 would also ask for individual representation in the future Federation. I can only say that this again represents a sad confusion of thought with regard to the position of the States possessing sovereign powers and that of the minor or lesser estates, talukdaris,jagirs, etc., in our

Indian States' territory. As was made clear in my speech in this Committee on December 5th last on behalf of our delegation, "the component elements of the Federation would be:

"(i) on the one side the States through their representatives, chosen by the Governments of their States; and
"(ii) on the other side British India."

One of the important details which no doubt will come up for discussion between the States, under the presidency of the Viceroy—whose friendly offices we feel we can always rely upon—will be to prescribe some test for the claims of States for individual entry into the Federation, and this leads me to deal with the question put to us.

Let me point out to you, Sir, that this is no new question. As anyone acquainted with the history of the States and the institution of the Chamber of Princes will know, this is a case of history repeating itself Alarms and jealousies were very naturally created some ten or twelve years ago when we were dealing with the constitution and membership of the Chamber of Princes. Similar alarms have been raised today, though from different causes and for different reasons, in regard to the individual entry of the States into the Federal legislature.

In regard to the membership of the Chamber of Princes, the essential qualifying tests prescribed, with the consent of the States and after mature consideration and approval by His Majesty's Government and the Viceroy, are:

a. Rulers of States who enjoy permanent dynastic salutes of 11 guns or over; and
b. Rulers of States who exercise full or practically full internal powers such as in the opinion of the Viceroy qualify them for admission to the Chamber of Princes.

This, I think, answers the queries put to us, and I would only add that no man in his senses has proposed, or could purpose, that small units of the Indian States' territory with revenues of Rs. 20 should enter the Federal constitution individually as sovereign States.

Sir, I am afraid it is a little late, but, if I am not out of order, before concluding my general remarks I should like to say that I did not deal with the question in the beginning because I wanted to hear the views of our British-Indian friends; but should any special seats be reserved for any important special interests in the constitution, it is my duty to urge the claims of the important Indian mercantile community, known popularly in India as the Marwari community, large numbers of whom come especially from Bikaner and ftom our next door friendly neighbour—the Jaipur State.

Now, Sir, befoi e giving you the views of the Indian States Delegation on Head-I, I should like to appeal strongly for greater—trust and confidence in the States. Trust, as we know, begets trust; and it is only by having confidence in one another that we can make real progress. I think we can fairly claim that the very fact that the Princes agreed to consider British India's invitation to enter into Federation, and that they are still proceeding with the matter, is a practical proof of their having confidence in all men of reason amongst our British—Indian brethren.

Before the last Conference assembled, and long before that, it was freely alleged in certain quarters that the Princes were entering into an unholy conspiracy with the British and Indian Governments in order to hinder the advance of British India towards her legitimate goal. When that libel was, happily, finally disproved last year at this Round-Table Conference, other motives were assigned to the willingness of the States to enter into federation. I appeal no less for acceptance of the idea that if the constitution is satisfactorily evolved, and if the States feel safe and confident of their security, in entering Federation, we shall, in the words of Pandit Madan Mohan Malaviya, have an India united even though divided in certain aspects; and the association of British India and the States leading to as great and abiding and mutually beneficial a co-partnership as was so eloquently pictured by Mahatma Gandhi when visualising a similar partnership between Great Britain and India. This idea I have for years thought of and worked for, and still confidently hope for.

## Appendix 2

**Dates of His Highness Maharaja Ganga Singhji's Visit Abroad to participate in Active Services during the First World War and for Signing of the Treaty of Versailles, League of Nations, Round Table Conference etc. etc. :**

| | | |
|---|---|---|
| 1. 1st World War | : | HH left Bikaner in early September 1914 for active services. |
| | : | HH reached at France in Oct., 1914<br>HH returned to Bikaner in April, 1915 |
| 2. War Conference | : | HH left Bikaner for England on 12th Feb., 1917.<br>HH arrived Bikaner on 20-6-1917 at 8.22 a.m. |
| 3. Treaty of Versailles | : | HH left Bikaner on 20-11-1918<br>Treaty signed on 28-6-1919. |
| 4. League of Nations | : | HH left Bikaner for Geneva on 13-08-1924, Sunday at 9.45 a.m.<br>HH arrived at Bikaner on 9-11-1924 - Sunday at 9.45 a.m. |
| 5. Round Table Conf.-I | : | HH left Bikaner on 14-8-1930 at 2.30 p.m.<br>HH reached London 31-8-1930 at 6.35 p.m.<br>HH came back-Bikaner on 7-2-1931 |
| 6. Round Table Conf.ll | : | HH left Bikaner for Round Table Conference - II on 9th August, 1931 at 2.10 P.M.<br>HH reached London on 2nd Sept., 1931 at 7.00 p.m.<br>HH returned Bikaner on 11th Nov. 1931 at 3.30 p.m. |
| 7. Europe visit to attend Conference | : | HH left Bikaner on 31-10-1932 Monday |

| | | |
|---|---|---|
| | | HH arrived London on 21-11-1932 |
| | | HH returned to Bikaner on 12-1-33 |
| 8. Europe visit to attend League of Nation & His Imperial Majesty's Silver Jubilee | : | HH left Bikaner on 25-3-35 at 12.50p.m. |
| | | HH arrived London on 1-5-1935 |
| | | HH left London on 4-6-1935 |
| | | HH returned to Bikaner on 1-7-35 |

## Appendix 3

**Honours and Titles Bestowed on His Highness Maharaja Sri Ganga Singhji Bahadur of Bikaner**

| | |
|---|---|
| Keshare Hind | : Keshare Hind Metal in 1899 |
| Major | : Gazetted Honorary Major in June 1900 |
| | : Young Major at the time of British Army) |
| KCIE | : Knight Commander of the Indian Empire-1901 (For China War services). |
| ADC | : Honorary Aide-de-Camp to the Prince of Wales in 1902<br>Coronation medal in 1902 |
| Hessian Order (Gennan) | : Order of Philip the magnaniuous conferred by his Royal Highness the Grand Duke of Hesse in 1903 |
| K.C.S.I. | : Knight Commander of the Star of India in 1904 |
| GCIE | : Knight Grand Commander of the Indian Empire in 1907 |
| Lt. Col. | : Hon.Lieutenant Colonel in 2nd Lancers in 1909 |
| Full Col. | : Hon. Colonel in British Army in 1910. |
| ADC | : Aide-de-Camp to King Emperor George V in 1910 |
| LL.D. | : Doctor of Law from Cambridge University, U.K. 1911 |
| GCSI | : Grand Commander of the Star of Indian in 1911 |
| Member | : Member of Imperial War Cabinet in 1917 |

| | |
|---|---|
| Member | : Member of Imperial War Conference 1917 |
| LL.D. | : Hon. Degree of Law from Edinburgh Univ. in 1917 |
| | : Major General in July 1917<br>Received Freedom of the "Cines of London" Edingurgh- Manchester, and Bristol |
| KCB | : Knight Commander of the Bath in 1918 (Military Division) |
| | : British War and Victory Medals in 1918. |
| | : General Service Medal in 1918 |
| | : Grand Cordon of the Order of the "NILE" by Sultan of Egypt in 1918 |
| DCL | : Doctor of Civil Law from Oxford Univ.1919 |
| Treaty | : Signed Treaty of Versailles in Paris in 1919 |
| GCVO | : Knight Grand Cross of the Royal Victorian Order in 1919<br>Chancellor of Chamber of Princes - 1921 |
| GBE | : Grand Cross of the British Empire in 1921 |
| LL.D. | : LL.D. from Benares Hindu University in 1927 |
| League of Nations | : Attended the Sessions of League of Nations in Geneva as representative of India—1930 |
| RTC | : Represented India in Round Table Conf. in 1930 and 1931 also. |
| General | : Hon. General in the Armed Forces in 1937 |
| ADC | : A.D.C. to H.I.M. the King Emperor GeorgeVI in 1938 |

*Posthumous Awards*

1914 War Star

Africa War Star

Indian Service Medal

1939 - 45 War Star

War medal.